THE BAKING BIBLE

The BAKING BIBLE

Rose Levy Beranbaum

PHOTOGRAPHY BY BEN FINK

Houghton Mifflin Harcourt

Boston New York

For information about permission to reproduce selections from this book, write to trade.permissions@hmhco.com
or to Permissions, Houghton Mifflin Harcourt Publishing Company, 3 Park Avenue,19ᵗʰFloor,
New York, New York 10016.

www.hmhco.com

Library of Congress Cataloging-in-Publication Data
Beranbaum, Rose Levy.
The Baking Bible / Rose Levy Beranbaum.
pages cm
ISBN 978-1-118-33861-2 (cloth); 978-0-544-18836-5 (ebook)
1. Baking. I. Title.
TX765.B466 2014
641.81'5—dc23
2014016319

Design by Vertigo Design NYC
Printed in China
C&C 10 9 8 7 6
4 5 0 0 6 5 3 5 4 0

This book is enhanced by my collaboration with Woody Wolston.
We dedicate it to our wonderful bloggers, who have formed
a baking community that brings us the world.

CONTENTS

CAKES 1

PIES, TARTS, AND OTHER PASTRIES 175

SCONES 179
Irish Cream Scones | Flaky Cream Cheese Scones |
Raspberry Butterscotch Lace Topping for Scones

FLAKY PASTRY BASIC RECIPE 187
Perfect Flaky and Tender Cream Cheese Pie Crust

FRUIT PIES AND TARTS 192
Luscious Apple Pie | Perfect Peach Galette | Sour Cherry Pie | Cherry Sweetie Pie |
Black and Blueberry Pie | ElderBlueberry Pie | BlueRhu Pie | Gooseberry Crisp |
Lemon and Cranberry Tart Tart | Lemon Curd and Raspberry Pielets |
The Araxi Lemon Cream Tart | Frozen Lime Meringue Pie |
French Orange Cream Tart | Pomegranate Winter Chiffon Meringue Pie

NUT AND CHOCOLATE PIES AND TARTS 259
Hungarian Raisin Walnut Tartlets | Pumpkin Pecan Pie | Mud Turtle Pie |
Frozen Pecan Tart | Fudgy Pudgy Brownie Tart | Chocolate Hazelnut Mousse Tart |
Posh Pie | Chocolate Ganache Tartlets

SAVORY PASTRIES 304
Perfect Savory Cream Puffs | Pizza Rustica

COOKIES AND CANDY 317

COOKIES DROPPED OR SHAPED BY HAND 321
Spritz Butter Cookies | Almond Coffee Crisps | Kourambiethes | Pepparkakors |
Luxury Oatmeal Cookies | Gingersnaps | Molasses Sugar Butter Cookies | Hazelnut
Praline Cookies | My Chocolate Chip Cookies | Double Chocolate Oriolos

ROLLED AND PASTRY TYPE COOKIES 353
The Dutch Pecan Sandies | The Ischler | Lemon Jammies | Coconut Crisps |
New Spin on Rollie Pollies | Giant Jam Cookie | Cookie Strudel |
Rugelach | Hamantaschen

CAKE TYPE COOKIES 388
Mini Gâteaux Bretons | Chocolate Sweetheart Madeleines |
Woody's Black and White Brownies

FOREWORD

I was browsing in a bookstore the first time I encountered Rose Levy Beranbaum's name on a big display of Christmas cookie books. Intrigued by the ecumenical cooking spirit of a Jewish woman writing about Christmas cookies, I picked it up. The very next weekend I had to bring three different kinds of cookies to a Christmas exchange. I picked Mahogany Buttercrunch Toffee, Cranberry-Chocolate Chippers, and Chocolate-Orange Paradise Bars. With all due modesty, I have to say that my cookies outshined the rest. When I tasted them, I knew I had just bought a book by a master, and every Rose recipe I've tried since then has confirmed this knowledge. There is simply nobody on earth who writes a better cookbook. There are at least four reasons why.

First, Rose's recipes are delicious. And they are delicious without fail. To my taste, her recipes are balanced (not too sweet, not too rich), nuanced (I've compared Rose's recipes with others of the same kind, and invariably I find her versions have a little something extra that makes them superior), and reliable. The only failure I've ever had with a Rose recipe was my fault; I didn't read the directions carefully. After e-mailing Rose a scathing review of the recipe, and receiving (to my amazement) a thoughtful reply within the hour, I eventually discovered my mistake and had to apologize to her. That recipe, the rosemary focaccia from *The Bread Bible*, has now become one of my favorites—and I now call it foolproof!

And that brings me to reason number two. Rose is a teacher. She doesn't just offer you great recipes; she also figuratively takes you by the hand and tells you how to be a better baker. Without Rose's recipes as the impetus, I would never have bought a scale and learned how to think of flour and sugar in grams, instead of in cups. Immediately after this one change, my baking became better and more consistent. I also started understanding how the amount of protein in flour affects the final product and why eggs should sometimes be at room temperature. Most cookbook authors don't tell you this (and you can make perfectly acceptable brownies without knowing). But once you know, you can move up to the next level, and closer to perfection.

Writing "closer to perfection" makes me realize that Rose, without your even being aware of it, lifts your standards. My cooking motto (and my motto in other things in life too, to be brutally honest) was "good enough is good enough." If one batch of cookies got a little burned, my husband could eat them. If a cake didn't rise enough, I could dump more frosting on it. That's no longer how I think, thanks to Rose. I check the recipe diligently to see where the oven racks go (something most recipes don't even bother to tell you). I use my instant-read thermometer to determine the temperature of caramel. For that matter, I make caramel.

And finally, Rose makes you believe that if you just follow her directions, there is nothing you can't do. Nothing. When I set out to make every recipe in *The Bread Bible*, I knew, but tried to put out of my mind, that there were some recipes that would be beyond me. Baguettes and croissants, for example. That's what bakeries exist for, so a normal person with a normal oven doesn't have to make a foolhardy attempt that's doomed to failure. But it turns out that a normal person can make baguettes and croissants, and can know that the joy of biting into a still-warm croissant that you've created yourself is even greater than the joy of eating a croissant, however delicious, that you brought home in a bag.

The knowledge that nothing is outside the realm of possibility became even clearer when I, along with other "Heavenly Cake Bakers," started working my way through *Rose's Heavenly Cakes*. I made perfect buttercreams! Using a pastry bag and tube for the first time in my life, I made ladyfingers! And I made spun sugar!

When I baked the last of the *Heavenly Cakes*, I'll admit that I couldn't see anything else that Rose could accomplish. She'd done three bibles, for heaven's sake, along with a masterful cookie book. *Heavenly Cakes* won the IACP Book of the Year award. What could she do to top that?

But I should have known that she had more tricks, and more recipes, up her sleeve. When I started to test some recipes for *The Baking Bible*, it became very clear that Rose was not resting on her baking laurels. Anyone leafing through this book has some wonderful treats in store. The Kouign Amann, for example: Sort of a combination of a sticky bun and a croissant, it just may be the most delicious thing you've ever eaten. And the Chocolate Pavarotti with Wicked Good Ganache. A ganache even better than Rose's standard ganache, with the surprising, but inspired, addition of cayenne. And the wafer-thin, absolutely addictive Pepparkakor cookies! (Start saving cardboard paper towel rolls now.) Although only a few savory recipes made the cut for this book, the ones that are included will become classics. My own personal favorite is the Pizza Rustica. If, like me, you look askance at the addition of sugar in a "pizza" crust, relax and trust. It's not too much; it doesn't taste weird; and it blends beautifully with the sage and thyme flavors in the crust. I can see this becoming part of a traditional holiday dinner, but it's too good to be relegated to a once-a-year category.

And, as they used to say on late-night TV, "There's more!" Cookies, cheesecakes, tarts, cupcakes—there are so many wonderful recipes here, any of which could become your own signature creation and all of which, with the help of Rose, you can make perfectly, on your first try.

—MARIE WOLF

Marie Wolf is a Minneapolis-based attorney whose friendship with Rose developed as she led a group of "Heavenly Cake Bakers" in baking, and blogging about, each and every recipe in *Rose's Heavenly Cakes*. Her new group, the "Beta Bakers," was indispensable in testing many of the recipes in *The Baking Bible*.

ACKNOWLEDGMENTS

This is my tenth cookbook, and never have I felt more supported, appreciated, and blessed than with this talented group of professionals and friends.

Thank you to the production crew:

Natalie Chapman, publisher of the cookbook division, Houghton Mifflin Harcourt, and true visionary, who gave the book its title and full support.

Stephanie Fletcher, editor, who left no stone unturned in the effort to produce ultimate excellence and accuracy, and who smoothly coordinated this large, complex book and diverse production team.

Pamela Chirls, acquiring editor, supportive and lifelong friend, who gave this book its early vision.

Marina Padakis Lowry, dedicated managing editor, and Jamie Selzer, production editor.

Alison Lew and Gary Philo at Vertigo Design NYC, inspired design, layout, and photography art direction. Alison Lew, cover design.

Deborah Weiss Geline, fastidious and dedicated copy editor and longtime friend; Matthew Boyer, brilliantly meticulous proofreader; and Justine Gardner, proofreader.

Ben Fink, photographer and dear friend, with an ever evolving artistic excellence in portraying my creations.

Caitlin Williams Freeman, head food stylist, artist, and best friend; Jason Schreiber, stylist's prep assistant; Erin McDowell, food stylist assistant, talented cook and baker; and Anna Molvic, inspired prop stylist.

Marilyn Flaig, indexer.

Brad Thomas Parsons, marketing, and Claire Holzman and Rebecca Liss, publicity.

Recipe testers Marie Wolf and the Beta Bakers: Vicki Bagatti, Nicola Blackler, Matthew Boyer, Lois Britton, Monica Caretto, Kate Coldrick, Hanaa El Azizi, Menachem Greenstein, Sharry Hickey, Jenn Jukur, Peggy Pegs, Katya Schapiro, Jennifer Steele, Kristina Taylor, Joan Wade, Bill Waldinger, Raymond Zitella.

Tasters: The Twin City T'ai Chi Chuan studio, who enthusiastically evaluated almost all of the recipes in the book.

SPECIAL MENTIONS

Chris Kimball, who, over 25 years ago, offered me the perfect platform for my scientific exploration and testing of recipes in articles for *Cook's* magazine.

Hector Wong, who is ever a great springboard for creative ideas.

My longtime friends Robert and Nicole Laub of Harold's Kitchen, who help me produce and market my Rose Levy Bakeware line of specialty baking equipment, especially Rose's Perfect Pie Plate, the pie plate of my dreams.

My friend and partner Gary Fallowes of NewMetro, who created my new "Rose Line" and works with me to produce great baking tools. His sister, chef Linda Fallowes, who so competently tested the babka recipe.

Travis Smith and Tee Jay Garcia of Hop studios, my beloved blog masters, who designed the blog and the forums and ensure that it all runs smoothly.

Rebecca Staffel, who created interactive charts for proofreading and checking all the numericals.

Diane Boate, my cherished friend, who organizes the best press events for my books in San Francisco.

Organic Valley, who supplied me with vast quantities of the best butter for all the recipe testing.

Gretchen Goehrend of India Tree, who unearthed and supplied the most delicious sugars.

Valrhona and Guittard, who supplied their amazing chocolates.

Mary Rodgers and Rachel Litner of Cuisinart and Beth Robinson of KitchenAid, whose mixers and food processors make us all better bakers.

Linus Kolmevic and Ashley McCord of Ankarsrum, whose bread machine is as beautiful as it is functional.

Mike Quinlan of Nordic Ware, whose excellent pans create beautifully shaped cakes.

Greg Skipper of Fat Daddio's, who produces great commercial quality bakeware.

Nancy Siler and my friends at Wilton, who are always so responsive to bakers' needs for specialty pans and cake decorating equipment.

Erin Kunesh and Noah Harber of Escali Scales, who conceptualized the "Rose Scale by Escali."

Randy Kaas of PourfectBowl, whose measuring spoons and cups are truly accurate.

Michael Taylor of Broad and Taylor, whose bread proofer is a great asset for bread baking.

The wonderful Giovannucci family of Fantes, the lovely Lisa Mansour of New York Cake and Baking Supply, and my friends at JB Prince and La Cuisine, all of whom make it possible for the home baker to have access to high-quality commercial equipment and imported specialty pans.

Retailers Match and dbO Home, who provided many of the props used during the photo shoot.

This book has been enriched by the inspiration of friends and colleagues.

Much valued is the major contribution by Kate Coldrick for bakers around the world in her work of transforming unbleached flour to improve the quality of cake baking in the United Kingdom and other countries where bleached flour is unavailable.

I am deeply grateful to my international community of bloggers, both professional and home bakers, for their continuous encouragement through their appreciation and feedback.

Much gratitude to the Menegus family of Hope, New Jersey, for their truly free-range eggs and true friendship.

Love to my parents, Lillian Wager Levy and Robert Maxwell Levy, who are always with me in spirit and from whom I derived my love of profession and work ethic.

Infinite appreciation always goes to my husband, Elliott, who gives me one hundred percent enablement and invaluable wisdom.

And profound thanks to Woody Wolston, who fully joined forces with me to create team "RoseWood"!

INTRODUCTION

When I was in the process of writing my first cookbook on cake baking, my best friend, the late renowned food writer Burt Greene, suggested that I call it "The Baking Bible." I didn't think that was the most accurate description of the book, because the book was all about cakes, and so the title became *The Cake Bible*.

After writing that book, I went on to write four more dessert cookbooks covering the entire baking spectrum: cookies, pies, tarts, pastry, bread, and revisiting cakes. But because I have the heart and soul of a baker, not to mention such a litany of perfected basic elements from which to draw, inspiration just keeps coming, from both my imagination and my travels. I thought I would stop after writing *Rose's Heavenly Cakes*, which included all of my new cakes post–*Cake Bible*. But one day I realized that not only had I created many new cakes, I had also kept revisiting the other subjects and now had many more new recipes I wanted to offer.

My plan was to call the book "Rose's Heavenly Baking," but Natalie Chapman, who was the publisher of *Rose's Heavenly Cakes* and now oversees the cookbook division at Houghton Mifflin Harcourt, dubbed it *The Baking Bible*. It was destiny fulfilled.

My collaborator, Woody Wolston, and I started retesting recipes, and in that process, even more recipes evolved. Because this was to be a "baking bible," we wanted to include basic types of cakes, doughs, pastries, cookies, and a sampling of yeast breads. The bread chapter also became the logical place for my favorite preserves, which I've been longing to share for many years.

Because I did not want to duplicate what I had already published in my previous books, I chose to share only new recipes that I developed over the past few years and, in a few cases, some old favorites that I've recently revisited and improved upon. Still, in the end, the book became so large we decided to reserve a wedding cake chapter for another book.

It was important, however, to include all the essential information on the hows and whys, which you'll find at the start of each chapter, to help you learn along the way and make you a better baker:

- **GOLDEN RULES,** which are mantras to internalize. Make them habits in your baking to ensure consistent success.

- **SPECIAL TIPS** that save time, make the process more streamlined, and lead to better results.

- And, in case things go wrong, **TROUBLESHOOTING** to help you correct the problem and avoid it next time.

Also, thanks to the power of the Internet, it is now possible to give still more information about ingredients on my blog (www.realbakingwithrose.com) for those who are fascinated by the science of baking and hunger for more details.

I feel really blessed to have this, my largest book in scope and the merging of all of my life's baking focus so far, in the hands of a publisher, editor, and production team that has made the most of my efforts and produced this amazingly stunning and useful tome. I couldn't have asked for more gifted and loving contributors than photographer Ben Fink and food stylist Caitlin Williams Freeman. It is my hope that you, my beloved readers and fellow bakers, will rejoice in the new ideas, concepts, and techniques; make these recipes part of your own repertoire; and send lots of feedback.

Rose's Golden Rules

Detailed instructions are given as part of each recipe in the book, but to ensure full success, I am highlighting the essentials here. See each chapter introduction for more highlights for success specific to the cakes, pies and pastry, cookies, and yeast breads and pastries in this book.

Designate equipment to use only for baking, especially items that are prone to retaining odors such as from garlic or onions from savory cooking. This equipment includes cutting boards, measuring spoons and cups, wooden spoons, and silicone or rubber spatulas. Many ingredients used in baking, such as butter and chocolate, also are highly prone to absorbing other aromas.

Before beginning to bake, **read the recipe through** and note the ingredients you will need, special equipment, and plan aheads.

Be sure to use the ingredients specified in the recipe. Different types of flour, sugar, butter, chocolate, and many other ingredients produce different results in baked goods. Also, if at all possible, make the recipe the way it is indicated. Don't substitute ingredients before making it at least once to see the way it's supposed to come out. When preparing ingredients ahead, cover them with plastic wrap so that they don't dry out or evaporate.

> **FLOUR** Be sure to use the flour specified in the recipe. If measuring flour rather than weighing it, avoid tapping or shaking the cup. This would pack in too much flour.

> **BUTTER** Use a high quality unsalted butter with standard fat content unless high butterfat is called for in the recipe, or when making clarified butter. Unsalted butter is preferable to make it easier to control the amount of salt added and for its fresher flavor. I recommend high quality butter such as Organic Valley cultured, Hotel Bar, or Land O'Lakes.

When a recipe calls for softened butter (65° to 75°F/19° to 23°C), it means the butter should still feel cool but be easy to press down. This usually takes about 30 minutes at room temperature, but slicing it into smaller pieces speeds up the process.

EGGS Use USDA grade AA or A large eggs and weigh or measure the volume. I recommend pasteurized eggs in the shell, such as Safest Choice, especially for buttercreams.

The correct amount of whole eggs, egg yolks, or egg whites is essential to the volume and texture of any baked good. The weight of the eggs and thickness of the shell can vary a great deal, even within a given weight class, as can the ratio of egg white to egg yolk. To achieve the ideal results, it is advisable to weigh or measure the whole eggs, egg yolks, and egg whites. Values for recipes in this book are given for weight and volume, so it's fine to use any size eggs if you weigh or measure them.

Bring eggs to room temperature by placing the eggs, still in their unbroken shells, in hot water for 5 minutes.

To break eggs the most evenly without shattering the shell, set a paper towel on the countertop to absorb any white that may spill out and rap the side of the egg sharply on top of the towel. The egg will break more neatly than if rapped against the edge of a bowl.

When separating eggs, especially for beating egg whites, pour each white into a smaller bowl before adding it to the larger amount of whites. If even a trace of yolk or grease gets into the white, it will be impossible to beat stiffly.

When beating egg whites, add ⅛ teaspoon of cream of tartar per egg white (¼ teaspoon for egg whites from eggs pasteurized in the shell). This magic formula stabilizes the egg whites so that you can achieve maximum volume without ever drying them out and deflating them by overbeating. Do not add more than this recommended amount; it will destabilize the egg whites. Use beaten egg whites as soon as possible after beating or they will start to stiffen and break down when folded into another mixture.

BAKING POWDER Use fresh baking powder. Check the expiration date, and if you are in a humid environment, replace the baking powder sooner. Both baking powder and baking soda are highly hygroscopic (readily absorb water) and are best measured rather than weighed, because the weight will vary.

SALT Use fine sea salt because it is easier to measure, dissolves quickly, and is not iodized. Iodized salt can give an unpleasant taste to baked goods.

CHOCOLATE Use the cacao content specified in the recipe. If the percentage is not indicated on the label, you can evaluate it by taste comparison. There is a vast range of the percentage of cacao versus sugar contained in what is usually labeled dark or bittersweet chocolate, which is why I've listed the percentages for each recipe.

When heating sugar syrups and caramel, **be sure that the burner heat is no higher than medium-low** as the mixture approaches the desired finished temperature. This helps to prevent the temperature of the syrup from rising after it is removed from the heat.

Weigh or measure ingredients carefully to achieve consistent flavor and texture. Weighing is faster and easier, but measuring will produce just as good a product, providing you measure carefully. Dry ingredients such as flour and sugar should be measured in solid measuring cups, that is, ones with unbroken rims. When measuring flour, spooning the flour into the cup before leveling off the excess with a metal spatula or knife will result in a greater weight of flour than sifting it into the cup. Both methods are used in this book; use the method indicated in the recipe. I chose the method that gives the volume that will coordinate closest with the weight.

When measuring liquids such as water, milk, sticky syrups, and juices, use a cup with a spout designed for measuring liquids and read the volume at eye level from the bottom of the meniscus (the curved upper surface of the liquid). Be sure to set the cup on a solid surface at eye level, not in your hand, which won't be as level a surface.

When mixing ingredients in a stand mixer, **start the mixer on low and then gradually increase the speed** to prevent the mixture from flying out of the bowl. You can also use the mixer's pouring shield or splash guard or cover the top of the mixer bowl with plastic wrap until the dry ingredients are moistened.

If you are using a handheld electric mixer, use a higher speed than specified for the stand mixer and a longer beating time. With both methods, it's important to scrape down the sides of the bowl several times during mixing to ensure that the batter on the sides gets mixed in evenly. Be sure to reach to the bottom of the bowl, especially when using the stand mixer (see BeaterBlade, page 531).

Always bake on the rack indicated in the recipe to ensure that the baked item will rise properly and for even baking and browning.

CAKES

The cakes in this chapter range from easy and informal, such as the Blueberry Buckle, to the more elaborate, such as The Polish Princess. The recipes encompass the primary categories of cakes: butter and oil cakes, cupcakes, sponge cakes, and cheesecakes.

The butter cakes are those that are made with butter in its solid form as opposed to cakes made with melted or clarified butter, such as a génoise, which is included with the sponge cakes. Most butter and oil cakes rely on chemical leavening (baking powder and/or baking soda) for their soft, velvety texture, whereas many sponge-type cakes, such as génoise and biscuit, are typically leavened with beaten whole eggs and/or egg whites. This chapter includes many exciting new cake creations—ones I discovered, such as the eggless molasses cakes, and others I imagined, such as The Renée Fleming Golden Chiffon. Flavorful, moist, and tender, yet substantial and satisfying, the happy surprise is that some of these cakes are simple to make. Several of them take their shape from the fluted designs of the pans, and are so moist and delicious they need no further adornment or frosting. Of course there are some fabulous new buttercreams and ganaches, such as the Caramel Buttercream, the Custom Rose Blend Milk Chocolate Ganache, and the Wicked Good Ganache. The frostings and many of the cakes can also be mixed and matched according to your personal preference.

I am also really thrilled to offer some amazing new cheesecakes. The Mango Bango has become the one I choose to make the most often. The Fourth of July Cheesecake is a delicious combination of red, white, and blue. And the diminutive, savory Stilton Baby Blue Cheesecakes are astonishingly luscious.

The Special Two-Stage Mixing Technique for Butter Cakes

I adapted this method of mixing butter cakes, long used in commercial kitchens, decades ago for *The Cake Bible* and have been using it ever since. I find it to be faster, easier, and better—the crumb finer and more velvety. In fact, many bakers have told me that they have converted to this method of mixing for all their butter layer cakes, even other people's recipes.

The one stipulation is that the butter needs to be no colder than 65°F/19°C and no warmer than 75°F/23°C. The eggs should also be at room temperature.

The main goal of mixing ingredients together to make a batter is to incorporate them evenly and smoothly so that they will work together to give the finished cake the correct texture. During the mixing process, the batter increases in volume, becoming airy and, because it is less dense, lighter in color. Most butter cake recipes begin by sifting or whisking the dry ingredients in one bowl, while creaming the butter and sugar in another. The dry ingredients are then added after all of the wet ingredients have been combined. I've reversed this process so that the butter and part of the liquid are added to the dry ingredients first, and then the rest of the wet ingredients are added subsequently.

The first advantage of this mixing method is that all of the dry ingredients (the flour, sugar, leavening, and salt) are added together at the beginning so it is possible to disperse them evenly with the beater instead of needing to sift them together. Sifting does not uniformly disperse dry ingredients unless repeated many times, so using the mixer instead is a great time and energy saver.

But the more important reason to use this method is that it produces cakes with a finer and more tender crumb. This is because, at the beginning of mixing, the butter is added to the flour together with a minimum amount of the cake's liquid (just enough to disperse the butter). The butter coats some of the gluten-forming proteins in the flour, preventing excessive gluten formation. This gives the batter a larger window of mixing without risk of becoming tough.

Storing Cakes

Room temperature means around 70°F/21°C. Times will vary depending on the temperature of the room or the refrigerator or freezer. Store unfrosted butter or oil cakes for 1 to 2 days at room temperature, 3 to 5 days refrigerated, or 3 months frozen. Butter cakes should be brought to room temperature before serving. Once a cake has been cut, place a piece of plastic wrap against each side of the open cuts to keep them from drying. Cakes stay freshest if also covered with a cake dome. Store unfrosted cupcakes for 1 day at room temperature, 3 days refrigerated, or 2 months frozen. Store butter or sponge cakes that have been brushed with syrup for 3 days at room temperature, 5 days to 1 week refrigerated, or 3 months frozen. Cheesecakes will keep, refrigerated, for 5 days to 1 week.

Store cakes frosted with buttercream for 1 day at room temperature, 1 week refrigerated, or 8 months frozen. You can also store the buttercream in an airtight container for the same length of time. Beat the buttercream before using. If it is cold, be sure to let it reach room temperature first to prevent its curdling.

Store cakes frosted with ganache for 3 days at room temperature, 2 weeks refrigerated, or 6 months frozen. You can also store the ganache in an airtight glass or plastic container for the same length of time. If frozen, remove it to the refrigerator overnight. Allow it to sit at room temperature for several hours to soften before using. (For more on ganache, see page 521.)

Some Special Tips

- Butter cakes in layer cake pans bake most evenly when encircled with cake strips (see page 537). The strips serve to slow down the baking at the perimeter of the pan so that the batter rises at the same rate as in the center, preventing a peaked surface. When preparing it for filling and baking, turn the pan upside down and gently stretch the silicone strip to fit around the sides.

- The bottom of layer cake pans should be lined with parchment to ensure the complete release of the cake, especially for chocolate cakes. (It is not necessary for non-chocolate cakes if using nonstick pans.) Coat the bottom of the pan with solid shortening to affix the parchment round. Coat the entire inside of the pan with baking spray with flour or with solid shortening and flour, tapping out any excess.

- I prefer the brand Baker's Joy (see page 523) for baking spray with flour because it is odorless, tasteless, and prevents sticking most effectively.

- When filling a fluted tube pan, spoon about one-third of the batter into the pan and press it back and forth with the back of a spoon. This will ensure that the batter goes into all of the crevices. Then pour in the rest of the batter.

- All mixtures that are beaten will vary in volume depending on how much air is beaten into them. Professional bakers assess this by color and by how much 1 cup of the mixture weighs. With cake batter made in the smaller quantities required by home bakers, the difference is not significant, but with buttercream, the volume will vary depending on the temperature and how long it is beaten. For this reason, the volume given for buttercream recipes is approximate.

- When frosting cake layers, it is best to place each layer bottom side up to avoid crumbs in the frosting. It is easiest to start with a very small amount of frosting to create a crumb coating before applying the rest.

TROUBLESHOOTING BUTTER AND OIL CAKES

PROBLEM: The cake has a cracked or peaked surface or large tunnels.
SOLUTION: The oven is too hot, or the batter is overmixed, or there is too much leavening, or a cake strip was not used. Bake at a lower temperature, do not overmix, use less leavening, or use a cake strip.

PROBLEM: The cake has a coarse grain and sunken center.
SOLUTION: The oven is too cold, or the batter is undermixed, or there is too much leavening. Increase the oven temperature, mix the batter until well combined, or use less leavening.

PROBLEM: The cake has poor volume, and compact structure.
SOLUTION: There is an inadequate amount of baking powder or baking soda, or the baking powder is old, or the butter and/or eggs are too cold. Increase the amount of leavener or replace old baking powder. Use room temperature butter and/or eggs.

PROBLEM: The cake is dry, and the crust is tough.
SOLUTION: The cake is overbaked, or the pan is too big. Decrease the baking time, or use the correct size pan.

PROBLEM: The bottom of the cake is burned and the batter is undercooked.
SOLUTION: There is inadequate air circulation in the oven. Place cake pans no closer than 1 inch from the walls of the oven and each other.

PROBLEM: There is a denser, darker, clearly demarcated layer of cake at the bottom.
SOLUTION: The butter is too cold or mixing is insufficient. Use room temperature butter; mix until thoroughly combined.

TROUBLESHOOTING SPONGE CAKES

PROBLEM: The cake doesn't rise enough.
SOLUTION: Beat for the amount of time specified in the recipe and work quickly but gently when incorporating the flour so that the batter does not deflate after aerating. When a meringue is used, be sure to beat it to stiff peaks as indicated in the recipe. Do not open the oven door until after the minimum baking time.

PROBLEM: The meringue does not beat to stiff peaks.
SOLUTION: Make sure the bowl and beater are totally grease free. Use the correct amount of cream of tartar in proportion to the volume or weight of the egg whites.

PROBLEM: The cake is not moist enough and the syrup is not evenly distributed.
SOLUTION: Use the amount of syrup indicated in the recipe, and apply the syrup to the cake a minimum of 1 day ahead of serving.

GOLDEN RULES OF CAKE BAKING

Weigh or measure ingredients carefully for consistent flavor and texture.

Use the ingredients specified in the recipe. For more details, see the Ingredients chapter (page 509).

FLOUR Be sure to use the flour specified in the recipe. Where both cake flour and all-purpose flour work, it is indicated in the recipe. If cake flour is specified and you have only bleached all-purpose flour, you will need to use the suggested amount of potato starch or cornstarch in place of some of the all-purpose flour (see Ingredient Equivalences and Substitutions, page 526).

In most layer cakes, unbleached flour will result in a sunken center. However, if you are using a tube pan, this is not a problem. Because unbleached flour is slightly higher in protein, the crust will be darker.

BUTTER Use a high-quality unsalted butter with standard fat content unless high butterfat is called for in the recipe or when making clarified butter. Most of the cakes in this book require standard AA grade unsalted butter. When butter is used in its solid form, it is essential for the butter to be cool room temperature (65° to 75°F/ 19° to 23°C).

EGGS Use USDA grade AA or A large eggs and weigh or measure the volume. I recommend pasteurized eggs in the shell, such as Safest Choice, especially for buttercreams.

The weight of the eggs and thickness of the shell can vary a great deal, even within a given weight class, as can the ratio of egg white to egg yolk. The correct amount of whole eggs, egg yolks, or egg whites is essential to the volume and texture of a cake. For this reason, it is advisable to weigh or measure the whole eggs, egg yolks, and egg whites.

When beating egg whites, use ⅛ teaspoon of cream of tartar per egg white (¼ teaspoon for egg whites from eggs pasteurized in the shell) to stabilize the meringue.

SUGAR Use superfine sugar for the finest texture. (You can make it by processing fine granulated sugar in the food processor for a few minutes.)

BAKING POWDER Use fresh baking powder— check the expiration date, and if you are in a humid environment, replace the baking powder sooner.

SALT Use fine sea salt (avoid iodized salt).

CHOCOLATE Use the cacao content specified in the recipe. If the percentage is not indicated on the label, you can evaluate it by taste comparison. If you use chocolate that is higher in chocolate components (cocoa solids and cocoa butter) and lower in sugar than what is called for, a cake will have a heavier texture and a bitter taste and a buttercream or ganache will have a stiffer texture, because in effect you are adding more chocolate and less sugar to the recipe.

Begin mixing on low speed to keep the ingredients from jumping out of the bowl, and then gradually increase the speed, as indicated in the recipe. You can also use the mixer's pouring shield or splash guard, or cover the top of the mixer bowl with plastic wrap, until the dry ingredients are moistened. If you are using a handheld electric mixer, use a deep bowl to avoid spattering (see MixerMate, page 538), and use a higher speed than specified for the stand mixer and a longer beating time. (Beat for 2 minutes after the dry ingredients are moistened and then 45 seconds after each addition of the egg mixture.) With both methods, it's important to stop the mixer and scrape down the sides of the bowl to ensure that the batter on the sides gets mixed in evenly. Be sure to reach to the bottom of the bowl, especially when using the stand mixer (see BeaterBlade, page 531).

Use the correct size pans. Choose round or square cake pans with straight, not sloped, sides because the sloped-sided pans have a smaller volume. If in doubt, never fill a pan more than two-thirds full unless indicated in the recipe. (Avoid adding more batter, because it could overflow and cause the cake to collapse.) The correct amount of batter for a specified pan size will affect the texture of the cake. An exception to this is a cake baked in a tube pan, which can come up to about 1 inch from the top of the pan.

Shiny, heavy aluminum pans conduct the heat best without overbrowning the crust. If using dark pans, lower the oven temperature by 25°F/15°C.

Prepare the pan before mixing the batter. Fluted tube pans should be sprayed with baking spray with flour (use a pastry brush if necessary to brush away any excess and to ensure that it goes into all of the grooves) or coated with solid vegetable shortening and flour, preferably Wondra (briskly tap the pan on the palm of your hand to distribute the flour evenly and then invert the pan and tap it lightly on the counter to get rid of any excess flour).

Transfer batter to the pan immediately after mixing. Batters, whether leavened with egg whites or chemicals such as baking powder or baking soda, will lose their leavening power if not transferred to pans soon after mixing. Batters leavened only with egg must be baked as soon as possible, but chemically leavened batters can be held in the pan, refrigerated, for up to an hour if oven space does not allow baking all of the batter at once. Chilling may increase the baking time by about 5 minutes.

Preheat the oven for 20 to 30 minutes before baking. If using a baking stone in the oven, preheat for 45 minutes. Use the correct oven temperature. If using a convection setting, lower the heat by 25°F/15°C. (This is not usually necessary for counter-top ovens.)

Bake as close to the center of the oven as possible, and allow for proper air circulation. Cake pans should be no closer than 1 inch from the walls of the oven and each other. If you have an oven with sufficient internal height, the racks can be set just below and just above the middle position and the pans staggered so that the one on the upper rack is not directly on top of the one on the rack below. To assure a level top and even front to back baking, unless the oven has a turntable, it is advisable to turn the cake halfway around, quickly and gently, after two-thirds of the estimated baking time. Sponge cakes, however, must be baked undisturbed, without opening the oven door, until toward the very end of baking.

Avoid underbaking or overbaking the cake. It may spring back before it is fully baked. Use a wire cake tester, toothpick, or wooden skewer, as indicated in the recipe. (An instant-read thermometer should read 190° to 205°F/88° to 96°C.) If a cake tester comes out with crumbs, the cake will sink a little on cooling.

Cool cakes completely on wire racks and store airtight. Choose cooling racks with fine wire mesh and spray them with nonstick cooking spray to prevent the cake layers from sticking to them.

Layer cakes usually should be cooled in the pan set on a rack for 10 minutes before unmolding. Invert the cake onto a wire rack that has been lightly coated with nonstick cooking spray and then reinvert it onto a second lightly coated wire rack. This prevents splitting if the top is slightly domed and ensures maintaining maximum height of the cake layer.

Sponge-type cakes baked in layer cake pans need to be unmolded immediately after baking. Sponge-type cakes baked in tube pans, such as chiffons and angel food cakes, need to be suspended upside down and away from drafts until completely cool.

Except when baking the cake in a fluted tube pan, always run a small metal spatula between the sides of the pan and the cake, pressing the spatula against the pan, to ensure complete release of the cake's sides with crumb intact.

Let cakes cool until they are no longer warm to the touch before storing or frosting. Any residual heat will make them soggy or melt the frosting.

BLUEBERRY BUCKLE

SERVES 8 TO 12

OVEN TEMPERATURE 375°F/190°C

BAKING TIME 30 to 40 minutes

A buckle is like a fruit crisp but with cake batter instead of crumb topping. It is a quick, easy, and delicious summer dessert—or even a breakfast—and can be made with any seasonal berries or fruit (see Variation, page 8). The light, soft cake and blueberry filling are easy to serve by simply spooning them into bowls.

SPECIAL EQUIPMENT One 9½ inch deep dish pie plate (preferably Pyrex), or a 7 to 9 cup casserole dish, or an 8 by 2 inch square cake pan, no preparation needed

BLUEBERRY FILLING

	VOLUME	WEIGHT	
lemon zest, finely grated	2 teaspoons, loosely packed	.	4 grams
lemon juice, freshly squeezed	2 tablespoons (30 ml)	1.1 ounces	32 grams
superfine sugar	½ cup	3.5 ounces	100 grams
cornstarch	4 teaspoons	.	12 grams
fine sea salt	a pinch	.	.
fresh blueberries	4 cups	20 ounces	567 grams

PREHEAT THE OVEN Thirty minutes or longer before baking, set oven racks at the middle and lowest levels. Preheat the oven to 375°F/190°C. Place a sheet of heavy-duty aluminum foil on the lower rack to catch any bubbling juices.

MAKE THE BLUEBERRY FILLING In the pie plate, stir together the lemon zest, lemon juice, sugar, cornstarch, and salt. Add the blueberries and toss to coat them.

Batter Topping

	VOLUME	WEIGHT	
2 large egg yolks, at room temperature	2 tablespoons plus 1 teaspoon (35 ml)	1.3 ounces	37 grams
sour cream	⅓ cup, *divided*	2.9 ounces	81 grams
pure vanilla extract	¾ teaspoon (3.7 ml)	.	.
bleached cake flour (or bleached all-purpose flour)	1 cup (or ¾ cup plus 2 tablespoons), sifted into the cup and leveled off	3.5 ounces	100 grams
superfine sugar	½ cup	3.5 ounces	100 grams
baking powder	¼ teaspoon	.	1.1 grams
baking soda	¼ teaspoon	.	1.4 grams
fine sea salt	¼ teaspoon	.	1.5 grams
unsalted butter (65° to 75°F/ 19° to 23°C)	6 tablespoons (¾ stick)	3 ounces	85 grams

MIX THE LIQUID INGREDIENTS In a medium bowl, whisk the egg yolks, 1 tablespoon of the sour cream, and the vanilla just until lightly combined.

MAKE THE BATTER TOPPING In the bowl of a stand mixer fitted with the flat beater, mix the flour, sugar, baking powder, baking soda, and salt on low speed for 30 seconds. Add the butter and remaining sour cream. Mix on low speed until the dry ingredients are moistened. Raise the speed to medium and beat for 1½ minutes. Scrape down the sides of the bowl. Starting on medium-low speed, gradually add the egg mixture in two parts, beating on medium speed for 30 seconds after each addition to incorporate the ingredients and strengthen the structure. Scrape down the sides of the bowl.

Using a silicone spatula, drop the batter onto the blueberries, leaving a 1 inch border between the batter and the sides of the pie plate and a 2 inch space in the middle.

BAKE THE CAKE Bake for 30 to 40 minutes, or until a wire cake tester inserted into the center (just into the cake) comes out clean and the cake springs back when pressed lightly in the center. After 30 minutes, if the top of the cake is browning too much, cover it loosely with aluminum foil that has been lightly coated with nonstick cooking spray.

COOL THE CAKE Let the cake cool in the pie plate on a wire rack until barely warm or room temperature. The flavors blend best when no longer hot.

STORE Airtight: room temperature, 2 days; refrigerated, 3 days; frozen, 3 months.

Variation: Black and Blueberry Spoon Cake

Replace half of the blueberries with an equal weight (10 ounces/283 grams) or 2½ cups of blackberries, plus an additional 1 tablespoon of sugar. Decrease the cornstarch to 1 teaspoon.

CRAN-RASPBERRY UPSIDE-DOWN CAKE

SERVES 8 TO 10

OVEN TEMPERATURE 350°F/175°C

BAKING TIME 35 to 45 minutes

I think of cranberries as the sour cherries of winter. The arpeggio of contrasting elements in this cake provides compelling flavor and texture. The sweet, tender butter cake and the tangy, tart crunch of the cranberries, mellowed by the raspberry preserves, are drawn into harmony by the billowy, creamy raspberry meringue. For a marvelous springtime version, make the rhubarb topping and strawberry meringue given in the Variation (page 14). Or, for a richer, more luxurious topping, make the strawberry whipped cream (page 122); if serving with the cran-raspberry cake, make a raspberry whipped cream by replacing the strawberry preserves in that recipe with seedless raspberry preserves.

SPECIAL EQUIPMENT One 9½ inch tarte tatin pan or 9 by 2 inch round cake pan, encircled with a cake strip | A baking stone or baking sheet

CRANBERRY TOPPING

	VOLUME	WEIGHT	
unsalted butter	4 tablespoons (½ stick), *divided*	2 ounces	57 grams
granulated sugar	½ cup	3.5 ounces	100 grams
lemon zest, finely grated	1 teaspoon, loosely packed	.	2 grams
lemon juice, freshly squeezed	2 teaspoons (10 ml)	.	10 grams
fine sea salt	a pinch	.	.
fresh or frozen cranberries (if frozen, unthawed)	2 cups	7 ounces	200 grams

PREHEAT THE OVEN Forty-five minutes or longer before baking, set an oven rack in the lower third of the oven and place the baking stone or baking sheet on it. Preheat the oven to 350°F/175°C.

MAKE THE CRANBERRY TOPPING In a small saucepan, over medium-low heat, melt the butter. Use about 1 tablespoon to prepare the pan: Brush a thin coat onto the bottom and sides of the pan, top with a parchment round, and brush the parchment with another coat of the melted butter.

Into the remaining butter, stir the sugar, lemon zest, lemon juice, and salt. Bring the mixture to a boil, stirring constantly with a light-colored silicone spatula. Stop stirring, but leave the spatula in place to judge the color, and simmer for about 3 minutes, or until bubbling thickly and light amber in color. (An instant-read thermometer should read 330° to 335°F/166° to 168°C.) Pour the mixture into the prepared pan, tilting to coat evenly. Strew the cranberries on top in an even layer.

Batter

	VOLUME	WEIGHT	
1 large egg, at room temperature	3 tablespoons plus ½ teaspoon (47 ml)	1.8 ounces	50 grams
1 large egg yolk, at room temperature	1 tablespoon plus ½ teaspoon (17 ml)	0.7 ounce	19 grams
sour cream	½ cup, *divided*	4.3 ounces	121 grams
pure vanilla extract	1¼ teaspoons (6 ml)	.	.
bleached all-purpose flour	1⅓ cups (sifted into the cup and leveled off)	5.3 ounces	150 grams
superfine sugar	¾ cup	5.3 ounces	150 grams
baking powder	¼ teaspoon	.	1.1 grams
baking soda	¼ teaspoon	.	1.4 grams
fine sea salt	¼ teaspoon	.	1.5 grams
unsalted butter (65° to 75°F/ 19° to 23°C)	9 tablespoons (1 stick plus 1 tablespoon)	4.5 ounces	128 grams

MIX THE LIQUID INGREDIENTS In a medium bowl, whisk the whole egg and egg yolk, 2 tablespoons/1.1 ounces/30 grams of the sour cream, and the vanilla just until lightly combined.

MAKE THE BATTER In the bowl of a stand mixer fitted with the flat beater, mix the flour, sugar, baking powder, baking soda, and salt on low speed for 30 seconds. Add the butter and the remaining sour cream. Mix on low speed until the dry ingredients are moistened. Raise the speed to medium and beat for 1½ minutes. Scrape down the sides of the bowl.

Starting on medium-low speed, gradually add the egg mixture to the batter in two parts, beating on medium speed for 30 seconds after each addition to incorporate the ingredients and strengthen the structure. Scrape down the sides of the bowl. Using a silicone spatula, scrape the batter on top of the cranberries. Smooth the surface evenly with a small offset spatula. It will fill the pan about three-quarters full.

BAKE THE CAKE Set the pan on the hot stone. Bake for 35 to 45 minutes, or until golden brown, a wooden toothpick inserted into the center comes out clean, and the cake springs back when pressed lightly in the center. (An instant-read thermometer inserted into the center should read 190°F/88°C.) During baking, the surface of the cake will form what appear to be many hillocks. They will flatten on unmolding.

After the first 30 minutes of baking, tent the top loosely with a dome of aluminum foil to keep the top from overbrowning.

UNMOLD AND COOL THE CAKE Set the pan on a wire rack. Run a small metal spatula between the sides of the pan and the cake, pressing firmly against the pan, and invert the cake at once onto a serving plate. Leave the pan in place for 1 to 2 minutes before lifting it off. If any cranberries have stuck to the pan, use a small metal spatula to place them back on the cake. Apply the glaze while the cake is still hot.

RASPBERRY GLAZE

	VOLUME	WEIGHT	
seedless raspberry preserves	3 tablespoons	2.1 ounces	60 grams

MAKE AND APPLY THE RASPBERRY GLAZE Heat the raspberry preserves in a small microwavable bowl, stirring with a whisk every 15 seconds (or in a small saucepan over medium-low heat, stirring with a whisk), until the preserves are smooth and fluid. Brush the preserves evenly onto the cranberries.

STORE Airtight: room temperature, 2 days; refrigerated, 5 days; frozen, 2 months.

RASPBERRY ITALIAN MERINGUE

MAKES 1 CUP PLUS 2 TABLESPOONS/3.5 OUNCES/100 GRAMS

	VOLUME	WEIGHT	
1 large egg white, at room temperature	2 tablespoons (30 ml)	1 ounce	30 grams
cream of tartar	⅛ teaspoon	.	.
superfine sugar	3 tablespoons plus 2 teaspoons, *divided*	1.6 ounces	45 grams
water	1 tablespoon (15 ml)	0.5 ounce	15 grams
seedless raspberry preserves (see Note, page 13)	1 tablespoon	0.7 ounce	20 grams

MAKE THE RASPBERRY ITALIAN MERINGUE Have ready a 1 cup or larger glass measure with a spout, and a handheld mixer.

Into a medium bowl, pour the egg white and add the cream of tartar.

In a small heavy saucepan, preferably nonstick, stir together the 3 tablespoons/ 1.3 ounces/38 grams of sugar and the water until all of the sugar is moistened. Heat on medium-high, stirring constantly, until the sugar dissolves and the syrup is bubbling. Stop stirring and reduce the heat to low. (On an electric range, remove the pan from the heat.)

Beat the egg white and cream of tartar on medium-low speed until foamy. Gradually raise the speed to medium-high and beat until soft peaks form when the beaters are raised. Gradually beat in the remaining 2 teaspoons of sugar until stiff peaks form when the beater is raised slowly.

Increase the heat under the sugar syrup to medium-high and continue to boil for a few minutes until an instant-read thermometer reads 248° to 250°F/120°C. Immediately transfer the syrup to the glass measure to stop the cooking.

With the handheld mixer on high speed, beat the syrup into the egg white in a steady stream. Do not let the syrup fall on the beaters or they will spin it onto the sides of the bowl.

Lower the speed to medium-high and continue beating for 2 minutes. Add the raspberry preserves and beat until evenly incorporated. Use a silicone spatula to finish folding to a uniform color. Cover with plastic wrap and set aside until the bowl is no longer warm to the touch, about 1 hour, or refrigerate for 5 to 10 minutes. Whisk after the first 5 minutes to test and equalize the temperature.

Store, covered, at room temperature for 2 hours or in the refrigerator for up to 2 days. Whisk lightly if necessary to restore its texture before spooning a dollop of raspberry meringue on the top or by the side of each serving.

NOTE If the seedless raspberry preserves are not smooth, heat the preserves in a small microwavable bowl, stirring with a whisk every 15 seconds (or in a small saucepan over medium-low heat, stirring with a whisk), until smooth and fluid.

Variation: RHUBARB UPSIDE-DOWN CAKE WITH STRAWBERRY MERINGUE
CARAMELIZED RHUBARB TOPPING

	VOLUME	WEIGHT	
fresh rhubarb, 1¼ pounds/ 567 grams	4 cups (cut into cubes)	1 pound	454 grams
light brown Muscovado sugar, or dark brown sugar	½ cup, firmly packed, *divided*	3.8 ounces	108 grams
fine sea salt	a pinch	.	.
cornstarch	1 tablespoon	.	9 grams
lemon zest, finely grated	1 teaspoon, loosely packed	.	2 grams
unsalted butter	4 tablespoons (½ stick), *divided*	2 ounces	57 grams

MAKE THE RHUBARB TOPPING Cut the rhubarb into ½ inch cubes. Weigh or measure out the correct amount and place it in a medium bowl. Mix in 2 tablespoons/1 ounce/ 27 grams of the brown sugar and the salt and let it sit for a minimum of 30 minutes or up to 2 hours. Transfer the rhubarb to a colander and strain and reserve the rhubarb syrup that forms. Return the rhubarb to the bowl and toss it with the cornstarch and lemon zest.

In a small saucepan, over medium-low heat, melt the butter. Use about 1 tablespoon to prepare the pan: Brush a thin coat onto the bottom and sides of the pan, top with a parchment round, and brush with another coat of the melted butter.

Into the remaining butter, stir the remaining brown sugar and the reserved liquid that has drained from the rhubarb. Bring the mixture to a boil, stirring constantly with a light-colored silicone spatula. Stop stirring, but leave the spatula in place to judge the color, and simmer for about 3 minutes until bubbling thickly and deep amber in color. (An instant-read thermometer should read 230° to 235°F/110° to 113°C.)

Pour the syrup into the prepared pan, tilting to coat evenly. Strew and press down the rhubarb on top in an even layer. For an appealing mosaic pattern you can arrange the rhubarb by placing it cut edges down.

Continue with the recipe as it appears on page 11.

MAKE THE STRAWBERRY MERINGUE Omit the raspberry preserves. In a small microwavable bowl, or in a saucepan over low heat, heat about 1½ tablespoons of strawberry jam and 1 teaspoon of water, stirring constantly. Press it through a strainer into a small bowl. You will need 1 tablespoon of the strained jam.

Make the meringue as it appears on page 12, adding the 1 tablespoon of strawberry jam in place of the raspberry preserves.

CREAM CHEESE BUTTER CAKE

OVEN TEMPERATURE 350°F/175°C

BAKING TIME 30 to 40 minutes

*T*his cake, which is similar in texture to a classic pound cake, received raves from the Beta Bakers who tested many of the recipes for this book. It evolved from my favorite pie crust, which employs cream cheese. I suspected that cream cheese would also make an excellent variation to my favorite sour cream cake. The result is a cake with a soft, fine crumb, moister than usual yet tender and light, with a flavorful tang from the cream cheese that is echoed in the lemon curd buttercream. This extraordinary buttercream is from Liz Pruitt of Tartine Bakery in San Francisco. The technique of adding the butter after cooking the curd is the secret to its glorious flavor and was adapted from that of the renowned pastry chef Pierre Hermé.

PLAN AHEAD Make the light lemon curd buttercream at least 3 hours ahead.

SPECIAL EQUIPMENT One 8 by 2 inch square baking pan, wrapped with a cake strip, bottom coated with shortening, topped with parchment, then coated with baking spray with flour

BATTER

	VOLUME	WEIGHT	
3 (to 4) large egg yolks, at room temperature	3½ tablespoons (52 ml)	2 ounces	56 grams
sour cream	½ cup, *divided*	4.3 ounces	121 grams
pure vanilla extract	1 teaspoon (5 ml)	.	.
bleached cake flour (see Note, page 16)	1½ cups (sifted into the cup and leveled off)	5.3 ounces	150 grams
superfine sugar	¾ cup	5.3 ounces	150 grams
baking powder	¼ teaspoon	.	1.1 grams
baking soda	⅜ teaspoon	.	2.1 grams
fine sea salt	¼ teaspoon	.	1.5 grams
unsalted butter (65° to 75°F/ 19° to 23°C)	6 tablespoons (¾ stick)	3 ounces	85 grams
cream cheese (65° to 75°F/ 19° to 23°C), cut into ½ inch cubes	2 tablespoons plus 2 teaspoons	1.5 ounces	42 grams

PREHEAT THE OVEN Twenty minutes or longer before baking, set an oven rack in the lower third of the oven and preheat the oven to 350°F/175°C.

MIX THE LIQUID INGREDIENTS In a medium bowl, whisk the egg yolks, 2 tablespoons/ 1 ounce/30 grams of the sour cream, and the vanilla just until lightly combined.

MAKE THE BATTER In the bowl of a stand mixer fitted with the flat beater, mix the flour, sugar, baking powder, baking soda, and salt on low speed for 30 seconds. Add the butter, cream cheese, and the remaining sour cream. Mix on low speed until the dry ingredients are moistened. Raise the speed to medium and beat for 1½ minutes. Scrape down the sides of the bowl.

Starting on medium-low speed, gradually add the egg mixture to the batter in two parts, beating on medium speed for 30 seconds after each addition to incorporate the ingredients and strengthen the structure. Scrape down the sides of the bowl. Using a large silicone spatula, scrape the batter into the prepared pan and smooth the surface evenly with a small offset spatula.

BAKE THE CAKE Bake for 30 to 40 minutes, or until golden brown, a wire cake tester inserted into the center comes out clean, and the cake springs back when pressed lightly in the center. The cake should start to shrink from the sides of the pan only after removal from the oven. The surface will be uneven but will flatten out on cooling.

COOL AND UNMOLD THE CAKE Let the cake cool in the pan on a wire rack for 10 minutes. Run a small metal spatula between the sides of the pan and the cake, pressing firmly against the pan, and invert the cake onto a wire rack that has been lightly coated with nonstick cooking spray. Cool completely upside down to flatten the surface. Reinvert the cake onto a serving plate.

NOTE It is best to use only bleached cake flour for the softest, lightest texture.

Light Lemon Curd Buttercream

MAKES 1¼ CUPS PLUS 2 TABLESPOONS/12 OUNCES/340 GRAMS

	VOLUME	WEIGHT	
2 large egg yolks	2 tablespoons plus 1 teaspoon (35 ml)	1.3 ounces	37 grams
1½ large egg whites	3 tablespoons (44 ml)	1.6 ounces	45 grams
granulated sugar	½ cup	3.5 ounces	100 grams
lemon juice, freshly squeezed and strained (about 2 large lemons)	¼ cup plus 1 tablespoon (74 ml)	2.8 ounces	79 grams
fine sea salt	a pinch	.	.
unsalted butter, cold	8 tablespoons (1 stick)	4 ounces	113 grams

SPECIAL EQUIPMENT A stand blender or immersion blender

MAKE THE LEMON CURD BUTTERCREAM Have ready a fine-mesh strainer suspended over a medium bowl.

In the top of a double boiler set over barely simmering water (do not let the bottom of the container touch the water), whisk the egg yolks and whites with the sugar until well blended. Whisk in the lemon juice and salt. Cook over medium-low heat, stirring constantly with a silicone spatula (be sure to scrape down the sides of the pan), until thickened and resembling hollandaise sauce, which thickly coats the spatula but is still liquid enough to pour. The mixture will change from translucent to opaque and begin to take on a yellow color on the spatula. Do not let it come to a boil or it will curdle. Whenever steam appears, remove the pan briefly from the heat, stirring constantly, to keep the mixture from boiling.

When the curd has thickened and pools thickly when a little is dropped on its surface and disappears (an instant-read thermometer should read 180° to 184°F/82° to 84°C), pour it at once into the strainer and press it through.

Scrape the curd into a blender (or leave it in the bowl if using the immersion blender) and let it cool just until less hot to the touch, about 20 minutes at room temperature. (An instant-read thermometer should read 130° to 135°F/55° to 57°C.) Cut the butter into 1 tablespoon slices. Blend on low speed, adding the butter 1 slice at a time, a few seconds apart, until all of it is incorporated.

Scrape the mixture into a medium bowl. Cover tightly and refrigerate until it has reached room temperature, 70° to 75°F/21° to 24°C, at least 2 hours. If refrigerating longer, let the buttercream reach room temperature before frosting.

The buttercream can be stored for 1 day at room temperature and up to 10 days in the refrigerator.

COMPOSE THE CAKE Spread ½ cup/4.3 ounces/123 grams of the lemon curd buttercream in a thin layer over the top of the cake. Refrigerate the remainder of the buttercream for another dessert (see Notes).

STORE Airtight: room temperature, 1 day; refrigerated, 3 days; frozen, 2 months (without the lemon curd buttercream).

NOTES The quantity for the buttercream is necessary for properly incorporating the butter using a standard blender. The recipe can be reduced if using an immersion blender.

The extra buttercream can be poured into a pie shell; whisked and poured into small ramekins, and refrigerated for 2 hours to serve as dessert; or blended into buttercreams or softly beaten whipped cream. (If using it as a buttercream, do not whisk it or it will not be firm enough for this use.)

BLUEBERRY CRUMB PARTY COFFEE CAKE

SERVES 12 TO 16

OVEN TEMPERATURE 350°F/175°C

BAKING TIME 55 to 65 minutes

*T*his is a blueberry version of my all-time best coffee cake, reconfigured to bake in a larger rectangular cake pan for easy serving to feed a crowd. It is an ideal summer holiday dessert.

SPECIAL EQUIPMENT One 13 by 9 by 2 inch high pan (16 cups), wrapped with cake strips (see Note, page 21), bottom coated with shortening, topped with parchment, then coated with baking spray with flour. (If the sides of the pan are sloped, coat them with shortening and line them with parchment extending about 1 inch up from the top to compensate for the smaller volume)

CRUMB FILLING AND TOPPING

	VOLUME	WEIGHT	
walnut halves	1½ cups	5.3 ounces	150 grams
light brown Muscovado sugar, or dark brown sugar	½ cup, firmly packed	3.8 ounces	108 grams
granulated sugar	3 tablespoons	1.3 ounces	37 grams
ground cinnamon	2 teaspoons	.	4.4 grams
bleached all-purpose flour	¾ cup (sifted into the cup and leveled off) plus 2 tablespoons	3.5 ounces	100 grams
unsalted butter, melted	5 tablespoons (½ stick plus 1 tablespoon)	2.5 ounces	71 grams
pure vanilla extract	¾ teaspoon (3.7 ml)	.	.

MAKE THE FILLING AND TOPPING In a food processor, pulse the walnuts, brown sugar, granulated sugar, and cinnamon until the walnuts are coarsely chopped. Remove and set aside 1¼ cups/6.3 ounces/178 grams to use for the filling.

To the remainder, add the flour, butter, and vanilla and pulse briefly to form a coarse, crumbly mixture for the topping. Scrape it into a medium bowl and refrigerate for about 20 minutes to firm up the butter to make it easier to crumble.

Batter

	VOLUME	WEIGHT	
3 large eggs, at room temperature	½ cup plus 1½ tablespoons (140 ml)	5.3 ounces	150 grams
sour cream	1 cup, *divided*	8.5 ounces	242 grams
pure vanilla extract	2¼ teaspoons (11 ml)	.	.
bleached all-purpose flour	2⅔ cups (sifted into the cup and leveled off)	10.6 ounces	300 grams
superfine sugar	1½ cups	10.6 ounces	300 grams
baking powder	½ teaspoon	.	2.2 grams
baking soda	¾ teaspoon	.	4.1 grams
fine sea salt	¼ teaspoon	.	1.5 grams
unsalted butter (65° to 75°F/ 19° to 23°C)	2¼ sticks	9 ounces	255 grams
blueberries, small fresh or frozen (if frozen, unthawed)	1¾ cups	7 ounces	200 grams

PREHEAT THE OVEN Twenty minutes or longer before baking, set an oven rack in the lower third of the oven and preheat the oven to 350°F/175°C.

MIX THE LIQUID INGREDIENTS In a medium bowl, whisk the eggs, ¼ cup/2.1 ounces/ 60 grams of the sour cream, and the vanilla just until lightly combined.

MIX THE BATTER In the bowl of a stand mixer fitted with the flat beater, mix the flour, sugar, baking powder, baking soda, and salt on low speed for 30 seconds. Add the butter and the remaining sour cream and mix on low speed until the dry ingredients are moistened. Raise the speed to medium and beat for 1½ minutes. Scrape down the sides of the bowl.

Starting on medium-low speed, gradually add the egg mixture in two parts, beating on medium speed for 30 seconds after each addition to incorporate the ingredients and strengthen the structure. Scrape down the sides of the bowl.

Using a silicone spatula, scrape about half of the batter (21 ounces/600 grams) into the prepared pan and smooth the surface evenly with a small offset spatula. Using your fingers, sprinkle lightly with the reserved 1¼ cups of crumb filling (do not press it into the batter). Drop the remaining batter in large blobs over the filling and carefully spread it evenly.

BAKE THE CAKE Bake for 40 minutes.

Meanwhile, use your fingertips to pinch together the crumb topping, breaking up the larger pieces so that about one-third of the mixture is formed into ¼ inch balls or clumps. (Do not make the balls larger because they will be hard to cut through when serving.) Let them fall onto a large piece of parchment and add the rest of the lightly pinched crumbs.

Remove the pan from the oven and gently place it on a wire rack. Scatter the blueberries onto the surface of the cake. Using the parchment as a funnel, quickly and evenly strew the crumb topping over the blueberries, which will sink slightly during baking. Continue baking for 15 to 25 minutes, or until a wooden toothpick inserted into the center comes out clean and the cake springs back when pressed lightly in the center. The crumb topping can make it difficult to test for doneness, so using an instant-read thermometer offers added assurance. The thermometer should read about 208°F/98°C.

COOL AND UNMOLD THE CAKE Let the cake cool in the pan on a wire rack for 30 minutes. Loosen the sides of the cake with a small metal spatula. Place a piece of plastic wrap that has been lightly coated with nonstick cooking spray on top of the cake and then a small folded dish towel. (The towel should come up to the rim of the pan to prevent the cake from splitting when inverting it.) Invert the cake onto a sheet pan. Reinvert it onto a cake board or baking sheet and cool completely, about 1½ hours.

STORE Airtight: room temperature, 3 days; refrigerated, 10 days; frozen, 2 months.

NOTE Cake strips (see page 537) help to keep the crust from browning too deeply during the long baking period.

ENGLISH DRIED FRUIT CAKE

SERVES 12 TO 14

OVEN TEMPERATURE
350°F/175°C

BAKING TIME
40 to 50 minutes

*T*his dried fruit cake is totally unlike the usual English fruitcake, which uses glacéed fruit. I adapted it from a recipe that my talented friend and fellow blogger Kate Coldrick gave me during my first visit to her in Devon, England. It is the one my dad requested that I send most often. One of its many virtues is that it ships well and has a long shelf life, especially if you pour as much rum onto it as my dad did!

PLAN AHEAD For best flavor, complete the cake 1 day ahead if using the rum.

SPECIAL EQUIPMENT One 13 by 9 by 2 inch high metal pan (or two 8 or 9 by 2 inch round cake pans), wrapped with cake strips, bottom coated with shortening, topped with parchment, then coated with baking spray with flour

BATTER

	VOLUME	WEIGHT	
pecan pieces	2 cups	8 ounces	227 grams
mixed dried fruit, coarsely chopped (see Note, page 25)	about 1 cup	5.3 ounces	150 grams
2 medium baking apples (12 ounces/343 grams)	2½ cups (chopped)	10 ounces (chopped)	284 grams (chopped)
lemon juice, freshly squeezed	1 tablespoon (15 ml)	0.6 ounce	16 grams
unsalted butter	8 tablespoons (1 stick)	4 ounces	113 grams
superfine sugar	1½ cups	10.6 ounces	300 grams
dark brown sugar, preferably Muscovado	¼ cup plus 3 tablespoons, firmly packed	3.5 ounces	100 grams
orange zest, finely grated	2 tablespoons, loosely packed	.	12 grams
pure vanilla extract	2 teaspoons (10 ml)	.	.

(ingredients continue)

	VOLUME	WEIGHT	
6 large eggs, at room temperature	1 cup plus 3 tablespoons (281 ml)	10.6 ounces	300 grams
bleached all-purpose flour	2⅔ cups (sifted into the cup and leveled off)	10.6 ounces	300 grams
baking powder	½ teaspoon	.	2.2 grams
baking soda	1 teaspoon	.	5.5 grams
fine sea salt	1 teaspoon	.	6 grams
ground cinnamon	1 teaspoon	.	2.2 grams
dark rum (optional)	¼ cup (59 ml)	1.9 ounces	55 grams

PREHEAT THE OVEN Twenty minutes or longer before baking, set an oven rack in the lower third of the oven and preheat the oven to 350°F/175°C.

TOAST THE PECANS Spread the pecans evenly on a baking sheet and bake for about 7 minutes to enhance their flavor. Stir once or twice to ensure even toasting and avoid overbrowning. Cool completely. With your hands, break the pecans into about ¼ inch pieces and place them in a small bowl.

SOAK THE FRUIT In a medium bowl, place the dried fruit and cover with boiling water. Let the fruit sit for 5 minutes and then drain well.

PREPARE THE APPLES Just before mixing the batter, peel and core the apples. Chop them into small pieces, about ¼ inch in size. Weigh or measure the apples, sprinkle them with lemon juice, and set aside.

MAKE THE BATTER In a medium saucepan, melt the butter and stir in the superfine sugar and brown sugar. Cook over low heat, stirring, for 1 minute. The mixture will look like wet sand. Remove the pan from the heat and stir in the chopped apples, orange zest, and vanilla. Add the eggs, 1 at a time, stirring after each addition until uniformly incorporated.

In a large bowl, whisk together the flour, baking powder, baking soda, salt, and cinnamon. Stir in the dried fruit and pecans until they are evenly coated with the flour mixture.

Add the apple mixture. Use a silicone spatula to stir and fold the batter until well mixed. Scrape the batter into the prepared cake pan (or divide it evenly between the round cake pans, about 31 ounces/880 grams in each). The pan(s) will be half full.

BAKE THE CAKE Bake for 40 to 50 minutes (30 to 40 minutes if using the two round pans), or until a wooden skewer inserted into the center comes out clean and the cake springs back when pressed lightly in the center.

COOL AND UNMOLD THE CAKE Let the cake cool in the pan on a wire rack for 10 minutes. Run a small metal spatula between the sides of the pan and the cake, pressing firmly against the pan, and invert the cake onto a wire rack that has been lightly coated with nonstick cooking spray. To prevent splitting, reinvert the cake so that the top side is up, and cool completely for about 2 hours.

APPLY THE OPTIONAL RUM If you enjoy a heightened rum flavor along with a little extra moistness, use the optional ¼ cup of rum. After initially inverting the cake, brush the bottom side with one-third of the rum. Set a serving plate (or a 13 by 9 inch cardboard rectangle wrapped in plastic wrap) on top and reinvert the cake. Poke the top all over with a thin skewer and brush the top and sides of the cake with the remaining rum.

Cool completely for about 2 hours and wrap airtight.

STORE Airtight: room temperature, 5 days; refrigerated, 3 weeks; frozen, 6 months. Add extra rum if the cake seems to be getting slightly drier.

SPECIAL UNMOLDING INSTRUCTIONS FOR LONG STORAGE If you are planning to store the cake for several weeks to 6 months, you will need to wrap the cake in a rum-soaked cheesecloth, followed by two layers of plastic wrap, and then heavy-duty aluminum foil.

Let the cake cool in the pan on a wire rack for 10 minutes. Cut a piece of cheesecloth large enough to wrap the entire cake, and sheets of plastic wrap to encase the cake airtight. Make a 13 by 9 inch cardboard rectangle, and one 40 by 18 inch sheet of heavy-duty aluminum foil. After inverting the cake onto a wire rack, sprinkle the cheesecloth with the optional rum and drape it over the cake. Then drape the pieces of plastic wrap over the cheesecloth. Place the cardboard rectangle on top. Invert the cake onto it and set it on the foil. Poke the top all over with a thin skewer. Bring up the sides of the cheesecloth and drape it over the top of the cake. Next, bring up the strips of plastic wrap to encase the entire cake, and finally bring up the sides of the foil, wrapping the cake tightly.

Store the cake in the refrigerator. Every 2 months, open the plastic wrap and sprinkle another 2 tablespoons of rum evenly over the cheesecloth before resealing.

NOTE Suggested dried fruits are apples, prunes, apricots, and pears.

Honey Cake for a Sweet New Year

OVEN TEMPERATURE 350°F/175°C, then 325°F/160°C

BAKING TIME 70 to 80 minutes

*M*y fellow writer, talented friend, and poet from Montreal, Marcy Goldman, is the authority on Jewish baking in Canada. She has developed the first honey cake I have ever loved, in good part because it is moist, flavorful, and not too sweet. The cake is *pareve* ("without dairy"), which means it can be served following a meal that includes meat, according to kosher practice; however, if you are not serving it after a meat meal (or if you do not keep kosher), crème fraîche is a perfect accompaniment.

SPECIAL EQUIPMENT One 9½ to 10 inch (12 to 16 cups) one-piece metal tube pan, preferably nonstick (for extra preparation for a two-piece metal tube pan, see Notes, page 28), encircled from the bottom with 2 cake strips, bottom coated with shortening and topped with a parchment ring, then lightly coated with nonstick cooking spray | Two stacked baking sheets

Batter

	VOLUME	WEIGHT	
4 large eggs, at room temperature	¾ cup plus 2 teaspoons (187 ml)	7 ounces	200 grams
canola or safflower oil, at room temperature	1 cup (237 ml)	7.6 ounces	215 grams
strong black coffee, at room temperature	1 cup (237 ml)	8.4 ounces	237 grams
orange juice, freshly squeezed and strained (about 2 large oranges)	½ cup (118 ml)	4.3 ounces	121 grams
whiskey or rye (see Notes, page 28)	¼ cup (59 ml)	1.9 ounces	55 grams
pure vanilla extract	1 tablespoon plus 1 teaspoon (20 ml)	.	.
superfine sugar	1¼ cups	8.8 ounces	250 grams
light brown Muscovado sugar, or dark brown sugar	½ cup, firmly packed	3.8 ounces	108 grams
all-purpose flour, preferably bleached	3½ cups (sifted into the cup and leveled off)	14.1 ounces	400 grams

	VOLUME	WEIGHT	
baking powder	1 tablespoon plus 1 teaspoon	0.6 ounce	18 grams
baking soda	¾ teaspoon	.	4.1 grams
fine sea salt	½ teaspoon	.	3 grams
unsweetened (alkalized) cocoa powder	1 tablespoon	.	5 grams
ground cinnamon	4 teaspoons	.	8.8 grams
ground ginger	½ teaspoon	.	.
ground cloves	⅛ teaspoon	.	.
honey	1 cup (237 ml)	11.8 ounces	336 grams

PREHEAT THE OVEN Twenty minutes or longer before baking, set an oven rack in the lower third of the oven and preheat the oven to 350°F/175°C.

COMBINE THE LIQUID INGREDIENTS AND SUGARS In a large bowl, whisk the eggs, oil, coffee, orange juice, whiskey, and vanilla until lightly combined. Add the superfine sugar and brown sugar and whisk until dissolved into the liquid mixture.

MAKE THE BATTER In the bowl of a stand mixer fitted with the whisk beater, mix the flour, baking powder, baking soda, salt, cocoa, cinnamon, ginger, and cloves on low speed for 30 seconds.

Remove the bowl and whisk beater. Add the liquid ingredients and sugars and stir with the whisk beater until the dry ingredients are moistened. Add the honey. Place the bowl back on the stand and reattach the whisk beater. Start on low speed, then gradually raise the speed to medium and beat for about 1½ minutes. The batter will have the consistency of a thick soup. Using a silicone spatula, scrape the batter into the prepared pan and set it on the stacked baking sheets.

BAKE THE CAKE Bake for 45 minutes. For even baking, rotate the pan halfway around. Lower the temperature to 325°F/160°C and bake for an additional 25 to 35 minutes, or until a wooden skewer inserted between the tube and the sides comes out clean and the cake springs back when pressed lightly in the center. The cake should start to shrink from the sides of the pan only after removal from the oven. During baking, if using the 12 cup pan, the center will rise to a little above the top of the pan, but on cooling it will be almost level with the pan.

COOL AND UNMOLD THE CAKE Let the cake cool in the pan on a wire rack for 20 minutes. To loosen the sides of the cake from the pan, use a rigid sharp knife or stiff metal spatula, preferably with a squared off end, scraping firmly against the pan's sides and slowly and carefully circling the pan. (If using a nonstick pan, use a plastic knife or spatula.) In order to ensure that you are scraping against the sides of the pan and removing the crust from the sides, leaving it on the cake, begin by angling the knife or spatula about 20 degrees away from the cake and toward the pan, pushing the cake inward a bit. It is best to use a knife blade that is at least 4 inches long and no wider than 1 inch. Dislodge the cake from the center tube with a wire tester or wooden skewer. Invert the cake onto a wire rack that has been lightly coated with nonstick cooking spray. Remove the bottom and center tube and peel off the parchment. Reinvert the cake onto a serving plate or cake carrier.

Let the cake cool for 2 to 3 hours, or until cool. (The cake can be served warm, but the pieces will be fragile. Slice with a sharp serrated knife and lean the cut-side piece against a pancake turner to move it for plating.)

STORE Airtight: room temperature, 3 days; refrigerated, 7 days; frozen, 2 months.

NOTES If using a two-piece tube pan, encircle from the bottom with 2 cake strips; coat the bottom of the pan with shortening and cut a 10 inch parchment round. Cut a circle from the center of the round to fit over the center tube. Slide the parchment ring down the center tube and press it onto the bottom. Press the outer part of the parchment against the sides of the pan, pleating as necessary to create a seal where the bottom part of the pan meets on the pan's sides. Lightly coat the inside of the pan with nonstick cooking spray. Place a sheet of aluminum foil on top of the stacked baking sheets to catch any leaking batter.

Orange juice, coffee, or water can be substituted for the whiskey or rye.

WHITE CHRISTMAS PEPPERMINT CAKE

OVEN TEMPERATURE 350°F/175°C

BAKING TIME 30 to 40 minutes

This cake is soft and tender with a velvety crumb, frosted with a silken white chocolate buttercream, filled and topped with a fine crunch of peppermint. My friend Joe Tully says it reminds him of Christmas morning. However, if you omit the peppermint extract and increase the vanilla extract to one tablespoon, you will have a lovely all-purpose white layer cake.

SPECIAL EQUIPMENT Two 9 by 2 inch round cake pans, encircled with cake strips, bottoms coated with shortening, topped with parchment rounds, then coated with baking spray with flour

BATTER

	VOLUME	WEIGHT	
6 large egg whites, at room temperature	¾ cup (177 ml)	6.3 ounces	180 grams
milk	1⅓ cups (315 ml), *divided*	11.3 ounces	322 grams
peppermint extract, preferably Flavorganics	2 teaspoons (10 ml)	.	.
pure vanilla extract	1 teaspoon (5 ml)	.	.
bleached cake flour (or bleached all-purpose flour)	4 cups (or 3½ cups), sifted into the cup and leveled off	14.1 ounces	400 grams
superfine sugar	2 cups	14.1 ounces	400 grams
baking powder	2 tablespoons plus ½ teaspoon	1 ounce	29 grams
fine sea salt	1 teaspoon	.	6 grams
unsalted butter (65° to 75°F/ 19° to 23°C)	16 tablespoons (2 sticks)	8 ounces	227 grams

PREHEAT THE OVEN Twenty minutes or longer before baking, set an oven rack in the lower third of the oven and preheat the oven to 350°F/175°C.

MIX THE LIQUID INGREDIENTS In a medium bowl, whisk the egg whites, ⅓ cup/79 ml/ 2.8 ounces/81 grams of the milk, the peppermint extract, and vanilla just until lightly combined.

MAKE THE BATTER In the bowl of a stand mixer fitted with the flat beater, mix the flour, sugar, baking powder, and salt on low speed for 30 seconds. Add the butter and the remaining milk. Mix on low speed until the dry ingredients are moistened. Raise the speed to medium and beat for 1½ minutes. Scrape down the sides of the bowl.

Starting on medium-low speed, gradually add the egg mixture to the batter in three parts, beating on medium speed for 20 seconds after each addition to incorporate the ingredients and strengthen the structure. Scrape down the sides of the bowl. Using a large silicone spatula, scrape the batter into the prepared pans and smooth the surfaces evenly with a small offset spatula. Each pan will be half full (27.2 ounces/770 grams in each).

BAKE THE CAKES Bake for 30 to 40 minutes, or until golden brown, a wire cake tester inserted into the centers comes out clean, and the cakes spring back when pressed lightly in the centers. The cakes should start to shrink from the sides of the pans only after removal from the oven.

COOL AND UNMOLD THE CAKES Let the cakes cool in the pans on a wire rack for 10 minutes. Run a small metal spatula between the sides of the pans and the cakes, pressing firmly against the pans, and invert the cakes onto wire racks that have been lightly coated with nonstick cooking spray. Cool completely upside down. This will help flatten the slight dome.

WHITE WHITE CHOCOLATE BUTTERCREAM

MAKES 6 CUPS/34 OUNCES/962 GRAMS

WHITE CHOCOLATE CUSTARD BASE

MAKES 3 CUPS/28 OUNCES/800 GRAMS

	VOLUME	WEIGHT	
white chocolate containing cocoa butter, preferably Valrhona Opalys, chopped	.	13.2 ounces	375 grams
unsalted butter (65° to 75°F/ 19° to 23°C)	13 tablespoons (1 stick plus 5 tablespoons)	6.6 ounces	188 grams
5 large eggs, at room temperature	1 cup (237 ml)	8.8 ounces	250 grams

MAKE THE WHITE CHOCOLATE CUSTARD BASE In the top of a double boiler set over barely simmering water (do not let the bottom of the container touch the water), melt together the chocolate and butter, stirring often until smooth and creamy.

Whisk the eggs lightly to break them up and then whisk them into the melted chocolate until incorporated. With a silicone spatula, continue stirring, being sure to scrape the mixture from the bottom of the container to prevent overcooking. Stir until an instant-read thermometer reads 160°F/71°C. The mixture will have thickened slightly. Remove it from the heat source. (If any lumps have formed, press them through a strainer.) Transfer the mixture to a bowl. Cover it tightly and refrigerate for about 1 hour, stirring every 15 minutes until cool to the touch. (An instant-read thermometer should read 65° to 70°F/19° to 21°C.) To speed cooling, place the bowl in an ice water bath (see page 538) and stir often.

COMPLETED WHITE WHITE CHOCOLATE BUTTERCREAM

	VOLUME	WEIGHT	
unsalted butter (65° to 75°F/ 19° to 23°C)	12½ tablespoons (1 stick plus 4½ tablespoons)	6.3 ounces	178 grams
White Chocolate Custard Base	3 cups	28 ounces	800 grams
pure vanilla extract	1¼ teaspoons (6 ml)	.	.

COMPLETE THE BUTTERCREAM In the bowl of a stand mixer fitted with the whisk beater, beat the butter on medium-low speed until creamy, about 30 seconds.

Gradually beat the custard base into the butter, scraping down the sides of the bowl as needed. Raise the speed to medium-high and beat for 2 minutes until stiff peaks form when the beater is raised.

Cover and set aside for 1½ to 2 hours, or until the mixture is slightly thickened and spongy. It should be no warmer than 70°F/21°C. If necessary, place the bowl in an ice water bath for a few minutes, stirring constantly. Beat on medium-high speed until smooth, light, and creamy. Beat in the vanilla.

Peppermint Topping

	VOLUME	WEIGHT	
peppermint sticks	.	3.5 ounces	100 grams

MAKE THE PEPPERMINT TOPPING Have ready a coarse-mesh strainer suspended over a medium bowl.

Place 1 or 2 peppermint sticks in a freezer-weight plastic bag. With a hammer or mallet, lightly break up the stick(s) into shards no larger than ¼ inch. Empty them into the strainer and stir to sift the powder-fine pieces into the bowl.

COMPOSE THE CAKE Cut each layer in half horizontally.

Spread a little buttercream on a cardboard round or serving plate and place one layer, rounded top side down. If using the serving plate, slide a few wide strips of parchment under the cake to keep the rim of the plate clean. Spread the cake with about ¾ cup/ 4 ounces/113 grams of the buttercream. Evenly sprinkle 1½ tablespoons of the peppermint pieces over the buttercream. Continue with the remaining layers, saving the bottom of one of them to use for the top of the cake so that it is perfectly level and crumb free. If the buttercream starts to become spongy, whisk it until smooth and creamy.

Frost the top and sides of the cake with the remaining buttercream. Refrigerate for about 30 minutes to set the buttercream. Sprinkle the powder-fine peppermint over the top of the cake and then sprinkle evenly with the remaining peppermint pieces. If using the parchment strips, slowly slide them out from under the cake.

Serve at room temperature.

STORE Airtight: room temperature, 1 day; refrigerated, 3 days; frozen, 2 months.

THE RED VELVET ROSE

OVEN TEMPERATURE 350°F/175°C

BAKING TIME 45 to 55 minutes

I couldn't resist the temptation to shape this bright red cake into a red red rose! Because frosting would hide the beautiful petal contours, I chose instead to enhance the color with a raspberry glaze, which keeps the cake moist as well. To complete the shape of a rose, this cake is formulated to dome so that the bottom is rounded and the sides are elevated slightly above the serving plate.

PLAN AHEAD Make the raspberry glaze several hours ahead.

SPECIAL EQUIPMENT One 10 cup metal rose (or other shape) fluted tube pan, coated with baking spray with flour

BATTER

	VOLUME	WEIGHT	
4 large egg whites, at room temperature	½ cup (118 ml)	4.2 ounces	120 grams
red liquid food coloring	2½ tablespoons (37 ml)	1.3 ounces	37 grams
pure vanilla extract	2 teaspoons (10 ml)	.	.
bleached cake flour (or bleached all-purpose flour)	2½ cups (or 2 cups plus 3 tablespoons), sifted into the cup and leveled off	8.8 ounces	250 grams
baking powder	1 tablespoon plus 2 teaspoons	0.8 ounce	22.5 grams
unsweetened cocoa powder	1¼ teaspoons	.	2.5 grams
fine sea salt	¾ teaspoon	.	4.5 grams
superfine sugar	1¼ cups	8.8 ounces	250 grams
unsalted butter (65° to 75°F/ 19° to 23°C)	5 tablespoons (½ stick plus 1 tablespoon)	2.5 ounces	71 grams
canola or safflower oil, at room temperature	⅓ cup (79 ml)	2.5 ounces	72 grams
low-fat buttermilk	¾ cup plus 1 tablespoon (192 ml)	6.9 ounces	197 grams

PREHEAT THE OVEN Twenty minutes or longer before baking, set an oven rack in the lower third of the oven and preheat the oven to 350°F/175°C.

MIX THE LIQUID INGREDIENTS In a medium bowl, whisk the egg whites, red food coloring, and vanilla just until lightly combined. (Caution: Be careful with the food coloring; it stains effectively, but also unmercifully.)

MIX THE DRY INGREDIENTS In a medium bowl, whisk together the flour, baking powder, cocoa, and salt.

MAKE THE BATTER In the bowl of a stand mixer fitted with the flat beater, mix the sugar, butter, and oil on medium speed for 2 minutes. The mixture will be smooth and creamy. Add the flour mixture and buttermilk. Mix on low speed until the dry ingredients are moistened. Raise the speed to medium-high and beat for 1½ minutes. Scrape down the sides of the bowl.

Starting on medium-low speed, gradually add the egg mixture to the batter in two parts, beating on medium speed for 30 seconds after each addition to incorporate the ingredients and strengthen the structure. Using a silicone spatula, scrape the batter into the prepared pan and smooth the surface evenly with a small spatula.

BAKE THE CAKE Bake for 45 to 55 minutes, or until a wire cake tester inserted between the tube and the sides comes out clean and the cake springs back when pressed lightly in the center. The cake will be domed above the rim of the pan and the sides should start to shrink from the sides of the pan only after removal from the oven.

COOL AND UNMOLD THE CAKE Let the cake cool in the pan on a wire rack for 10 minutes. Invert it onto a wire rack that has been lightly coated with nonstick cooking spray.

NOTES If you do not want to use red food coloring, you may substitute an equal amount of beet juice, although the color will not be as vibrant. Roast the well-washed, unpeeled beets, with an inch of root and stems intact, in an aluminum foil package at 350°F/175°C for about 45 minutes for medium beets or up to about 1 hour and 15 minutes for larger ones. Remove the beets and pour the juice from the foil into a small container.

For more chocolate flavor, you can use up to ¼ cup/0.7 ounce/21 grams cocoa, sifted before measuring, decreasing the flour by the same amount.

RASPBERRY SAUCE

MAKES ¾ CUP/177 ML/7.5 OUNCES/211 GRAMS

	VOLUME	WEIGHT	
frozen raspberries with no added sugar (one 12 ounce bag)	3 cups	12 ounces	340 grams
lemon juice, freshly squeezed	1 teaspoon (5 ml)	.	5 grams
granulated sugar	⅓ cup	2.3 ounces	67 grams

MAKE THE RASPBERRY SAUCE In a medium strainer suspended over a deep bowl, thaw the raspberries completely. This will take several hours. (To speed thawing, place the strainer and bowl in an oven with a pilot light or turn on the oven light.) Press the berries to force out all the juice. There should be about ½ cup/118 ml/4.5 ounces/128 grams of juice. Set aside the raspberries.

In a small saucepan (or in a 2 cup microwavable measure with a spout, lightly coated with nonstick cooking spray), boil the juice over medium-low heat until it is reduced to 2 tablespoons/30 ml/1 ounce/30 grams. If using the saucepan, pour the syrup into a glass measure with a spout, lightly coated with nonstick cooking spray, to stop the cooking and to cool.

Puree and strain the raspberries with a food mill fitted with the fine disk, or use a fine-mesh strainer suspended over a bowl to remove all of the seeds. (Raspberry seeds are tiny and can pass through most food mills. Only the finest strainer will remove all of the seeds.) There should be ½ cup/118 ml/4 ounces/113 grams of puree. Stir in the reduced raspberry syrup and lemon juice. There should be about ⅔ cup/158 ml/5 ounces/145 grams raspberry sauce. (If there is less, simply add proportionately less sugar. The correct amount of sugar is half the volume of the puree.) Stir the sugar into the sauce until it dissolves.

The sauce can be stored for 10 days refrigerated or for 1 year frozen. It can be thawed and refrozen at least three times without flavor loss.

GLAZE THE CAKE Using a removable tart pan bottom or two large pancake turners, transfer the cooled cake onto a serving plate. Slip a few pieces of parchment under the cake. Brush the entire cake with ½ cup/118 ml/4.7 ounces/135 grams of the sauce. Remove the strips.

Serve with lightly sweetened whipped cream (see page 516). If desired, use the remaining sauce to drizzle on the plates.

STORE Airtight: room temperature, 1 day; refrigerated, 3 days; frozen, 2 months.

HIGHLIGHTS FOR SUCCESS

Frozen berries must be used to make the sauce because freezing breaks down some of the cell structure, which releases some of the berries' liquid, making it possible to thicken this liquid while preserving the freshness of the uncooked pulp. Be sure to use frozen berries with no sugar added. The juices from berries in syrup cannot be reduced as much because the sugar starts to caramelize.

PINK PEARL LADY CAKE

OVEN TEMPERATURE
350°F/175°C

BAKING TIME
30 to 40 minutes for the cake; 15 to 20 minutes for the cupcake

*T*his special cake was created to honor my dearest friend and much esteemed colleague Lisa Yockelson. Lisa and I love heart shapes, her favorite color is pink (mine is rose), and because she is indeed a pearl of a person, these became my inspiration for the cake. A tiny touch of food coloring turns the cake batter a pale pink. White Chocolate Fondant, offered to me from cake baker Beth Anne Goldberg of Studio Cake in Menlo Park, California, is a delicious variation of my classic rolled fondant. The fondant pearls owe their exquisite luminosity to a light gilding of luster dust.

PLAN AHEAD Make the fondant a minimum of 6 hours ahead of composing the cake.

SPECIAL EQUIPMENT One 9 by 2 inch heart-shape or round cake pan (8 to 8⅔ cups), encircled with a cake strip, bottom coated with shortening, topped with parchment cut to shape, then coated with baking spray with flour | One cupcake liner set in a custard cup or ramekin, if using the heart-shape pan | Optional: one pearl bead mold (see Note, page 47)

BATTER

	VOLUME	WEIGHT	
4 (to 6) large egg yolks, at room temperature	¼ cup plus 2 teaspoons (69 ml)	2.6 ounces	74 grams
milk	⅔ cup (158 ml), *divided*	5.7 ounces	161 grams
pure vanilla extract	½ tablespoon (7.5 ml)	.	.
red liquid food coloring	⅛ teaspoon	.	.
bleached cake flour	2 cups (sifted into the cup and leveled off)	7 ounces	200 grams
superfine sugar	1 cup	7 ounces	200 grams
baking powder	2¾ teaspoons	.	12.4 grams
fine sea salt	⅜ teaspoon	.	2.2 grams
unsalted butter (65° to 75°F/ 19° to 23°C)	8 tablespoons (1 stick)	4 ounces	113 grams

PREHEAT THE OVEN Twenty minutes or longer before baking, set an oven rack in the lower third of the oven and preheat the oven to 350°F/175°C.

MIX THE LIQUID INGREDIENTS In a medium bowl, whisk the egg yolks, 3 tablespoons/ 44 ml/1.6 ounces/45 grams of the milk, the vanilla, and red food coloring just until lightly combined.

MAKE THE BATTER In the bowl of a stand mixer fitted with the flat beater, mix the flour, sugar, baking powder, and salt on low speed for 30 seconds. Add the butter and the remaining milk. Mix on low speed until the dry ingredients are moistened. Raise the speed to medium and beat for 1½ minutes. Scrape down the sides of the bowl.

Starting on medium-low speed, gradually add the egg mixture to the batter in two parts, beating on medium speed for 30 seconds after each addition to incorporate the ingredients and strengthen the structure. Scrape down the sides of the bowl. Spoon the batter into the cupcake liner, filling it two-thirds full (1.8 ounces/50 grams). Using a large silicone spatula, scrape the remaining batter into the prepared pan and smooth the surfaces evenly with a small offset spatula. (If using the round pan, scrape in all of the batter; you will not need to fill the cupcake liner.)

BAKE THE CAKES Bake for 30 to 40 minutes (15 to 20 minutes for the cupcake), or until golden brown, a wire cake tester inserted into the centers comes out clean, and the cakes spring back when pressed lightly in the centers. The cake should start to shrink from the sides of the pan only after removal from the oven.

COOL AND UNMOLD THE CAKE Let the cake cool in the pan on a wire rack for 10 minutes. Run a small metal spatula between the sides of the pan and the cake, pressing firmly against the pan, and invert the cake onto a wire rack that has been lightly coated with nonstick cooking spray. Cool completely upside down. This will slightly flatten the dome. Cool the cupcake in its liner. (You will not need the cupcake to complete the cake; eat it as a baker's treat.)

WHITE CHOCOLATE FONDANT

MAKES 1 POUND, 13.8 OUNCES/845 GRAMS

WHITE CHOCOLATE PLASTIQUE

MAKES 10 OUNCES/285 GRAMS

	VOLUME	WEIGHT	
white chocolate containing cocoa butter, chopped	.	7.7 ounces	218 grams
corn syrup	¼ cup (59 ml), cup lightly coated with nonstick cooking spray	2.9 ounces	82 grams

MAKE THE WHITE CHOCOLATE PLASTIQUE In a small microwavable bowl, stirring with a silicone spatula every 15 seconds (or in the top of a double boiler set over hot, not simmering, water, stirring often—do not let the bottom of the container touch the water), heat the white chocolate until almost completely melted.

Remove the chocolate from the heat source and continue stirring until it is completely melted.

Using a silicone spatula, stir in the corn syrup until uniform but not smooth in consistency. Cover the container tightly with plastic wrap. Cool for about 2 hours, until no warmer than 75°F/24°C (if warmer, the cocoa butter will leak out of the fondant while kneading it).

CLASSIC ROLLED FONDANT BASE

MAKES 20 OUNCES/567 GRAMS

	VOLUME	WEIGHT	
powdered sugar, preferably India Tree Fondant & Icing Powdered Sugar (see page 511)	4 cups (lightly spooned into the cup and leveled off)	1 pound	454 grams
water	2 tablespoons (30 ml)	1 ounce	30 grams
powdered gelatin	½ tablespoon	.	4.5 grams
glucose (see Notes, page 44)	¼ cup (59 ml), cup lightly coated with nonstick cooking spray	3 ounces	85 grams
glycerine (see Notes, page 44)	½ tablespoon (7.5 ml)	.	9 grams
solid white shortening, preferably Spectrum (see Notes, page 44)	1 tablespoon	.	12 grams

MAKE THE FONDANT BASE Into a large bowl, sift the powdered sugar.

Into a small bowl, pour in the water and sprinkle the gelatin over the top. Stir to moisten and soften the gelatin and let it sit for 5 minutes. Heat the gelatin in the microwave, stirring with a silicone spatula every several seconds (or set it over a pan of hot, not simmering, water, stirring constantly) until it has dissolved. Scrape the mixture into a small saucepan and stir in the glucose and glycerine. Add the shortening and heat the mixture over medium-low heat, stirring often, until the shortening has melted.

Pour the gelatin mixture over the powdered sugar. Using a wooden spatula or spoon, lightly coated with nonstick cooking spray, stir until the gelatin mixture is blended into the sugar. Lightly coat your hands with nonstick cooking spray. Mix and then knead until most of the sugar is incorporated.

Lightly coat a smooth work surface, such as Formica or marble, with nonstick cooking spray. Scrape the mixture onto the work surface and knead until smooth and satiny. If the fondant seems dry, spritz with water and knead well. If the fondant seems too sticky, knead in more powdered sugar. The fondant should resemble a smooth, well-shaped stone. When dropped, it should spread very slightly but retain its shape. It should be malleable like clay, but not sticky. Wrap the fondant tightly with plastic wrap and place it in an airtight container until ready to add the white chocolate plastique.

Completed White Chocolate Fondant

	VOLUME	WEIGHT	
White Chocolate Plastique	.	10 ounces	285 grams
Classic Rolled Fondant Base	.	20 ounces	567 grams
luster dust, preferably orchid color (see Note, page 47)	a small sprinkling	.	.

COMPLETE THE FONDANT Using a silicone spatula, stir and fold the white chocolate plastique until it is uniform in consistency and it begins to come together. Empty the mixture onto the counter and knead it to form a smooth ball that is uniform in color.

Lightly coat the counter and rolling pin with nonstick cooking spray. Roll the fondant base into an oval about ¼ inch thick. Roll the white chocolate plastique into an oval smaller than the fondant. Do not be concerned if the plastique tears or has holes because it will integrate smoothly into the fondant. Place the plastique on top of the fondant and fold the fondant over it in thirds, like a business letter. Turn it so that the closed end is to the left. Roll the fondant and plastique into a long rectangle. Fold the fondant into thirds, turn it to the left, and roll again. When the fondant begins to become uniform in color, knead it into a ball. Continue rolling and folding until the fondant is completely uniform with an ivory color. The fondant will be very elastic until the cocoa butter from the white chocolate has a chance to firm. If used sooner, it will stretch too thin and not look smooth on top of the cake.

Shape the fondant into a ball and flatten it into a disc. Wrap it tightly with plastic wrap and let it rest for several hours. The fondant will firm slightly on standing.

The fondant can be stored at room temperature for 1 month or frozen for 1 year.

NOTES The white chocolate plastique and fondant base can be combined in ratios for adjusting the white chocolate's flavor from 1:4 to 1:1 of white chocolate to fondant. More white chocolate will increase the yellow hue of the fondant and make it firmer.

One-quarter cup/59 ml/2.9 ounces/82 grams of corn syrup can be substituted for the glucose, but then use only 1½ tablespoons/22 ml/0.8 ounce/22 grams of water.

Use food grade glycerine, available in cake and baking supply stores (see Sources, page 527).

Spectrum brand shortening is interchangeable with the old style Crisco. The new Crisco without trans fat does not perform as well.

An excellent quality rolled fondant called Pettinice is produced by Bakels of New Zealand (see Sources, page 527).

Strawberry Mousseline

MAKES ABOUT 2¼ CUPS PLUS 2 TABLESPOONS/15.2 OUNCES/430 GRAMS

	VOLUME	WEIGHT	
unsalted butter, preferably high fat, slightly softened but cool (65°F to 68°F/19° to 20°C; see Notes, page 46)	13 tablespoons (1½ sticks plus 1 tablespoon)	6.5 ounces	184 grams
2 large egg whites, room temperature	¼ cup (59 ml)	2.1 ounces	60 grams
granulated sugar	¼ cup plus 3 tablespoons, *divided*	3 ounces	87 grams
water	2 tablespoons (30 ml)	1 ounce	30 grams
cream of tartar	¼ teaspoon	.	.
tart strawberry butter (see Notes, page 46)	½ cup plus 2 tablespoons, *divided*	6.2 ounces	177 grams
pure vanilla extract	½ teaspoon (2.5 ml)	.	.
red liquid food coloring (optional)	2 drops	.	.

BEAT THE BUTTER In the bowl of a stand mixer fitted with the flat beater, beat the butter on medium-high speed until creamy, about 1 minute. Set aside in a cool place (no warmer than 70°F/21°C).

PREPARE THE EGG WHITES Pour the egg whites into the bowl of a stand mixer, if you have a second mixer bowl, or into a medium bowl and have ready a handheld mixer.

HEAT THE SUGAR SYRUP Have ready a 1 cup or larger glass measure with a spout.

In a small heavy saucepan, preferably nonstick, stir together all but 2 tablespoons of the sugar and the water until all of the sugar is moistened. Heat on medium, stirring constantly, until the sugar dissolves and the mixture is bubbling. Stop stirring and reduce the heat to low. (On an electric range, remove the pan from the heat.)

BEAT THE EGG WHITES INTO A STIFF MERINGUE If using a stand mixer for the egg whites, attach the whisk beater. Beat the egg whites and cream of tartar on medium speed until foamy. Raise the speed to medium-high and beat until soft peaks form when the beater is raised. Gradually beat in the remaining 2 tablespoons of sugar, until stiff peaks form when the beater is raised slowly.

BRING THE SUGAR SYRUP UP TO THE PROPER TEMPERATURE Increase the heat under the sugar syrup and continue to boil the syrup for a few minutes until an instant-read thermometer reads 248° to 250°F/120°C. Immediately transfer the syrup to the glass measure to stop the cooking.

ADD THE SUGAR SYRUP TO THE EGG WHITES If using a stand mixer, with the mixer off to keep the syrup from spinning onto the sides of the bowl, add the syrup to the egg whites. Begin by pouring in a small amount of syrup. Immediately beat on high speed for 5 seconds. Add the remaining syrup the same way, in three parts. For the last addition, use a silicone spatula to remove the syrup clinging to the glass measure and scrape it off against the whisk beater. If the syrup has hardened before most of it has been poured, soften it to pouring consistency for a few seconds in the microwave.

If using a handheld mixer, beat the syrup into the egg whites in a steady stream. Do not let the syrup fall on the beaters or they will spin it onto the sides of the bowl.

Lower the speed to medium and continue beating for up to 2 minutes. Refrigerate the meringue for 5 to 10 minutes, or until an instant-read thermometer reads 70°F/21°C. Whisk after the first 5 minutes to test and equalize the temperature.

BEAT THE MERINGUE INTO THE BUTTER Set the mixer bowl containing the butter in the stand mixer and attach the whisk beater (no need to wash it). Beat on medium-high speed for about 3 minutes, or until the butter lightens in color and is no warmer than 70°F/21°C.

Scrape the meringue into the butter and beat on medium speed until smooth and creamy. Beat for about 2 minutes, scraping down the sides of the bowl as necessary. At first it will look slightly curdled. If it starts watering out, check the temperature. The mixture should feel cool and be no lower than 65°F/19°C, no higher than 70°F/21°C. If it is too warm, set the bowl in an ice water bath (see page 538) and stir gently to chill it down before continuing to whisk. If it is too cool, suspend the bowl over a pan of simmering water (do not let the bottom of the bowl touch the water) and heat very briefly, stirring vigorously when the mixture just starts to melt slightly at the edges. To stop the warming, dip the bottom of the bowl in an ice water bath for a few seconds to cool it. Remove the bowl from the ice water and beat the mousseline by hand until smooth.

Beat in ¼ cup plus 3 tablespoons/4.4 ounces/124 grams of the strawberry butter, the vanilla, and optional red food coloring until uniformly mixed. The mousseline becomes spongy and fluffy on standing. If you are not using it right away, whisk it lightly by hand to maintain a silky texture before applying it to the cake. If you have refrigerated it, let it come to room temperature (at least 70°F/21°C) before whisking; this prevents it from breaking down.

The mousseline makes a full cup extra and is great to freeze for cupcakes. Let it come to room temperature and then whisk it lightly before using.

NOTES High-fat (low-water) butter helps to ensure smooth emulsification. Temperature, however, is the key to the success of this buttercream, so you will need an instant-read thermometer. If the temperature of the meringue and butter is 65° to 70°F/19° to 21°C, it works easily and magnificently.

American Spoon (see page 527) makes a terrifically flavorful and tart strawberry butter. No red food coloring is necessary if you use this variety. You can use strawberry preserves; strain them and add a little lemon juice if they are too sweet.

COMPOSE THE CAKE When ready to compose the cake, invert it onto a flat serving plate or rigid cake board that is spread with a little mousseline, and set it onto a countertop. Slide a few wide strips of parchment under the cake to keep the rim of the plate clean.

BEVEL THE CAKE With a small serrated knife or Microplane, bevel the edges of the cake. This will make it easier to form smooth edges and to keep the fondant from cracking when it curves over the cake.

SPLIT AND FROST THE CAKE With a long serrated knife, split the cake into two layers, each about 1 inch high. Slide a transfer disc or the loose bottom of a tart pan between the layers and lift off the top layer. Spread the bottom layer with 1 cup/6.3 ounces/179 grams of the mousseline. Start by dropping large blobs of it onto the cake. Then, using a small offset spatula, spread it back and forth without lifting up the spatula in order to keep the crumbs from lifting away from the surface of the cake. Spread the remaining 3 tablespoons of strawberry butter evenly over the mousseline.

Slide the upper cake layer from the transfer disc on top of the frosted layer. Begin by lining up the edges as evenly as possible, and then pull the upper layer slightly toward you so that it aligns neatly with the opposite edge before setting it down. If it is not perfectly even, slip a small metal spatula between the layers and lift and stretch the upper layer slightly.

APPLY THE UNDERCOAT Brush off any crumbs from the cake and parchment strips. The mousseline undercoat needs to be a thin layer, as smooth and even as possible, because the fondant will reveal every imperfection beneath it. When applying the mousseline, first do a thin crumb coating on the sides and top layers. If necessary, fill any gaps between the layers with mousseline.

Refrigerate the cake layers for about 1 hour to firm the mousseline. Apply another thin coating of mousseline to form flat, smooth surfaces on the sides and top. Smooth the top edges of the cake so that they are slightly rounded. Refrigerate the cake for another hour, or until the mousseline is firm. Slowly slide the parchment strips out from under the cake.

APPLY THE FONDANT TO THE CAKE The fondant rolls most easily if it is 80°F/27°C. It can be softened if set in the microwave for about 5 seconds. Knead the fondant until it has softened enough to roll.

Lightly coat a smooth countertop and rolling pin with nonstick cooking spray. Roll the fondant into a ¼ inch thick 13 inch round disc.

Slip your hands, palm sides down, under the fondant and lift it above the cake. Drape the fondant evenly onto the cake. As the fondant is smoothed over the surface of the cake it will stretch slightly, but avoid pulling it because it will tear. Quickly smooth the fondant onto the cake, starting at the top center to prevent air bubbles, using the palm of your hand in a circular motion, and gradually easing it over the sides. (If an air bubble should form, it can be pierced with a sharp needle and smoothed out.) Use sharp scissors to cut away the triangular excess at the point of the heart and then smooth the seam with your fingertips.

Using a pizza cutter, sharp knife, or single-edge razor blade, trim the fondant flush with the serving plate. If using a pizza cutter, angle it away from the cake to avoid marking the side of the fondant and cut about ½ inch away from the cake to ensure that it will not be short. After it is smoothed into place, trim, if necessary. Knead together the fondant scraps and cover them with plastic wrap to keep them soft and pliable.

MAKE THE PEARLS Using the fondant scraps, make about 11 pearls. Pinch off small bits of the fondant and roll them with your finger, 1 at a time, in the palm of your hand into ⅓ to ½ inch balls. Wash and dry your hands thoroughly. Place a tiny amount of luster dust in your palm and, with the index finger of your other hand, roll the pearl in the luster dust to coat it. Set it on top of the fondant. Continue with the remaining balls. If the pearls are made shortly after the fondant is applied, they will stick to the fondant. Alternatively, dab the bottom of each pearl with a bit of melted white chocolate before setting it on top of the fondant.

If the fondant at the base of the cake is not perfectly even, you can make additional small ivory pearls to set around the base (see Note, below).

Let the cake sit, uncovered, for a minimum of 3 hours before serving or storing.

To serve, use a serrated knife to slice the cake.

STORE Lightly covered with plastic wrap or in a cake keeper: room temperature, 2 days; refrigerated, 5 days.

NOTE Cake and baking supply stores carry luster dust and silicone pearl bead molds ideal for making pearls that will be set around the base of the cake (see page 527).

MARBLE IN REVERSE WITH CUSTOM ROSE BLEND GANACHE GLAZE

OVEN TEMPERATURE 350°F/175°C

BAKING TIME 45 to 55 minutes

*M*ost marble cakes are yellow cake with swirls of chocolate. Woody and I envisioned the reverse—a chocolate cake with swirls of yellow cake. The most unusual feature is that there is no need to marble the batters, as the natural convection of the baking process creates attractive zebra-like swirls. The glaze could well be the most luscious of all ganache. It is my custom blend of white and dark chocolate, and the result is a milk chocolate that is perfectly balanced, rich, and creamy.

SPECIAL EQUIPMENT One 10 cup metal fluted tube pan (see Notes, page 51), coated with baking spray with flour

BATTER

	VOLUME	WEIGHT	
bittersweet chocolate, 60% to 62% cacao, chopped	.	4.6 ounces	130 grams
5 (to 8) large egg yolks, at room temperature	¼ cup plus 2 tablespoons (89 ml)	3.3 ounces	93 grams
sour cream	¾ cup, *divided*	6.4 ounces	181 grams
pure vanilla extract	2 teaspoons (10 ml)	.	.
bleached cake flour (or bleached all-purpose flour)	2¼ cups (or 2 cups), sifted into the cup and leveled off	7.9 ounces	225 grams
superfine sugar	1 cup plus 2 tablespoons	7.9 ounces	225 grams
baking powder, preferably Argo (see Notes, page 51)	1 teaspoon	.	4.5 grams
baking soda	½ teaspoon	.	2.7 grams
fine sea salt	⅜ teaspoon	.	2.2 grams
unsalted butter (65° to 75°F/ 19° to 23°C)	14 tablespoons (1¾ sticks)	7 ounces	200 grams

PREHEAT THE OVEN Twenty minutes or longer before baking, set an oven rack in the lower third of the oven and preheat the oven to 350°F/175°C (325°F/160°C if using a dark pan).

MELT THE CHOCOLATE In a small microwavable bowl, stirring with a silicone spatula every 15 seconds (or in the top of a double boiler set over hot, not simmering, water, stirring often—do not let the bottom of the container touch the water), heat the chocolate until almost completely melted. Remove the chocolate from the heat source and stir until fully melted. Let it cool until it is no longer warm to the touch but is still fluid.

MIX THE LIQUID INGREDIENTS In a medium bowl, whisk the egg yolks, ¼ cup/2.1 ounces/ 60 grams of the sour cream, and the vanilla just until lightly combined.

MAKE THE BATTER In the bowl of a stand mixer fitted with the flat beater, mix the flour, sugar, baking powder, baking soda, and salt on low speed for 30 seconds. Add the butter and the remaining sour cream. Mix on low speed until the dry ingredients are moistened. Raise the speed to medium and beat for 1½ minutes. Scrape down the sides of the bowl. Starting on medium-low speed, gradually add the egg mixture in two parts, beating on medium speed for 30 seconds after each addition to incorporate the ingredients and strengthen the structure. Scrape down the sides. Transfer just under one-third (2½ cups/10.6 ounces/300 grams) of the yellow batter to a bowl.

MAKE THE CHOCOLATE BATTER Scrape the melted chocolate into the remaining batter in the mixer bowl and mix on low speed just until uniform in color.

FILL THE CAKE PAN Spoon slightly more than one-third of the chocolate batter (9.3 ounces/265 grams) into the pan. Use a small offset spatula to smooth it evenly and then make a shallow trough in a ring around the middle of the batter.

In order to maintain distinct bands between the batters, spoon dollops of batter, pushing them off the spoon, letting them drop onto the batter beneath. Then use the offset spatula to press down the batter to form a ring. The layering of the bands has to be done in a timely manner to minimize the activation of the baking powder.

Spoon about one-quarter of the yellow batter (2.6 ounces/75 grams) into the center trough of the chocolate batter and smooth it in place.

Spoon a little less than one-third of the remaining chocolate batter (4.8 ounces/135 grams) over the yellow batter and spread it evenly to reach the sides and middle of the pan.

Spoon a little less than half of the remaining yellow batter (3.5 ounces/100 grams) in a ring over the chocolate batter.

Spoon a little less than half of the remaining chocolate batter (5.3 ounces/150 grams) over the yellow batter and spread it evenly to reach the sides and middle of the pan.

Spoon the remaining yellow batter in a ring over the chocolate batter.

Finish by spooning the remaining chocolate batter over the yellow batter and spread it evenly to reach the sides and middle of the pan.

BAKE THE CAKE Bake for 45 to 55 minutes, or until a wire cake tester inserted between the tube and the sides comes out clean and the cake springs back when pressed lightly in the center. The cake should start to shrink from the sides of the pan only after removal from the oven. During baking, the cake will rise above the center tube, but on cooling it will be almost level with the sides of the pan.

COOL AND UNMOLD THE CAKE Let the cake cool in the pan on a wire rack for 10 minutes. Loosen the cake by jiggling it up and down until it moves slightly. Invert it onto a wire rack that has been lightly coated with nonstick cooking spray. Cool completely before glazing or wrapping airtight.

NOTES The cake has the most attractive shape when baked in Nordic Ware's Bavaria or traditional Bundt pans.

Argo baking powder will result in less of a dome because it does not start to react until the cake is placed in the oven.

Custom Rose Blend Ganache Glaze

MAKES ⅔ CUP/6.6 OUNCES/188 GRAMS

	VOLUME	WEIGHT	
white chocolate containing cocoa butter, chopped	.	2.7 ounces	77 grams
bittersweet chocolate, 60% to 62% cacao, chopped	.	1.4 ounces	40 grams
heavy cream, hot	⅓ cup (79 ml)	2.7 ounces	77 grams

MAKE THE GANACHE GLAZE Have ready a fine-mesh strainer suspended over a 1 cup glass measure with a spout.

In a small microwavable bowl, stirring with a silicone spatula every 15 seconds (or in the top of a double boiler set over hot, not simmering, water, stirring often—do not let the bottom of the container touch the water), heat the white chocolate and bittersweet chocolate until almost completely melted.

Remove the chocolates from the heat source and stir until fully melted and combined.

Pour the hot cream on top of the chocolates and stir until smooth. Press the mixture through the strainer. Let the glaze cool, stirring very gently every 15 minutes to avoid creating air bubbles, until a small amount of the glaze dropped from the spatula mounds a bit before smoothly disappearing. (An instant-read thermometer should read about 75°F/24°C.) Use the glaze at once, or cover until ready to use and then reheat it in the microwave with 3 second bursts or in a hot water bath.

COMPOSE THE CAKE Set the cake on a serving plate. Pour the glaze evenly over the top of the cake, letting it drip down the sides and pool slightly on the serving plate.

STORE Airtight: room temperature, 2 days; refrigerated, 5 days; frozen, 2 months.

THE CHOCOLATE FLORO ELEGANCE WITH CARAMEL BUTTERCREAM

SERVES 12 TO 14

OVEN TEMPERATURE 350°F/175°C

BAKING TIME 30 to 40 minutes

*B*akers Dozen East and West—a group of dedicated bakers on both coasts—meet in this recipe. This is a special tribute to Flo Braker, long-time friend and much-respected colleague, and one of the founding members of Bakers Dozen West. I thought it would be fun to combine Flo's best chocolate cake, the Dark Chocolate Cake, with mine, the Chocolate Domingo. Flo's cake is more bittersweet, less dense, and moister, while the Domingo is more mellow and compact. The combination of the two turned out to be a very happy marriage, resulting in a bittersweet chocolate cake that is buttery, mellow, airy, and moist. The white chocolate caramel buttercream is a perfect foil for the bittersweet chocolate. For extra drama I like to add the optional lacquer glaze.

PLAN AHEAD Make the caramel buttercream at least 3 hours ahead.

SPECIAL EQUIPMENT Two 9 by 2 inch round cake pans, encircled with cake strips, bottoms coated with shortening, topped with parchment rounds, then coated with baking spray with flour

BATTER

	VOLUME	WEIGHT	
fine-quality unsweetened or 99% cacao chocolate, chopped	.	3 ounces	85 grams
unsweetened (alkalized) cocoa	2 tablespoons	.	9 grams
strong hot coffee (see Note, page 55)	¾ cup (177 ml)	6 ounces	174 grams
sour cream	1 cup	8.5 ounces	242 grams
pure vanilla extract	2 teaspoons (10 ml)	.	.
3 large eggs, at room temperature	½ cup plus 1½ tablespoons (140 ml)	5.3 ounces	150 grams
bleached cake flour	2¼ cups (sifted into the cup and leveled off)	8 ounces	228 grams
baking powder	2 teaspoons	.	9 grams
baking soda	¾ teaspoon	.	4.1 grams

	VOLUME		WEIGHT	
fine sea salt	¾ teaspoon	.		4.5 grams
unsalted butter (65° to 75°F/ 19° to 23°C)	12 tablespoons (1½ sticks)		6 ounces	170 grams
canola or safflower oil, at room temperature	1½ tablespoons (22 ml)		0.7 ounce	20 grams
superfine sugar	1¾ cups		12.3 ounces	350 grams

PREHEAT THE OVEN Twenty minutes or longer before baking, set an oven rack in the lower third of the oven and preheat the oven to 350°F/175°C.

MELT THE CHOCOLATE In a small microwavable bowl, stirring with a silicone spatula every 15 seconds (or in the top of a double boiler set over hot, not simmering, water, stirring often—do not let the bottom of the container touch the water), heat the chocolate until almost completely melted.

Remove the chocolate from the heat source and stir until fully melted. Set it in a warm spot to keep it warm.

DISSOLVE THE COCOA IN THE COFFEE In a small bowl, whisk together the cocoa and hot coffee until dissolved. Cover with plastic wrap to prevent evaporation and set the cocoa mixture in a warm spot to keep it warm.

MIX THE SOUR CREAM AND VANILLA In a small bowl, stir together the sour cream and vanilla.

WHISK THE EGGS In a 1 cup glass measure with a spout, lightly whisk the eggs.

MIX THE DRY INGREDIENTS In a medium bowl, whisk together the flour, baking powder, baking soda, and salt.

MIX THE BATTER In the bowl of a stand mixer fitted with the flat beater, beat the butter and oil on medium speed until creamy and lighter in color, about 45 seconds. Add the sugar in a steady stream, stopping the mixer occasionally to scrape down the sides of the bowl. Continue to beat on medium speed until the mixture is very light in color and fluffy, 3 to 4 minutes.

HIGHLIGHTS FOR SUCCESS

The addition of coffee heightens the chocolate flavor. Be sure to use freshly brewed coffee, or two shots of espresso diluted with hot water to equal the amount specified.

With the mixer on medium-low speed, gradually add the eggs, beating until incorporated. Scrape down the sides of the bowl and continue beating on medium-low speed until the mixture is well blended and lighter in color and texture, 3 to 4 minutes.

Stop the mixer and scrape in the melted chocolate. Immediately, to keep the chocolate from hardening, beat on low speed for about 45 seconds until incorporated.

With the mixer off between additions, add the flour mixture in three parts, alternating with the sour cream in two parts, beginning and ending with the flour mixture and mixing on low speed after each addition until incorporated, 10 to 15 seconds. Scrape down the sides of the bowl as needed. Detach the beater and bowl from the stand and scrape any batter clinging to the beater into the bowl. Add the warm coffee mixture in four parts, stirring gently with a silicone spatula until smooth.

Using a silicone spatula, scrape the batter into the prepared pans and smooth the surface evenly with a small offset spatula. They will be almost half full (24.7 ounces/700 grams in each).

BAKE THE CAKES Bake for 30 to 40 minutes, or until a wire tester inserted into the centers comes out clean and the cakes spring back when pressed lightly in the centers. The cakes should start to shrink from the sides of the pans only after removal from the oven.

COOL AND UNMOLD THE CAKES Let the cakes cool in the pans on a wire rack for 10 minutes. Run a small metal spatula between the sides of the pans and the cakes, pressing firmly against the pans, and invert the cakes onto wire racks that have been lightly coated with nonstick cooking spray. To prevent splitting, reinvert the cakes so that the tops are up. Cool completely.

NOTE The hot coffee can be replaced with equal volume or weight of hot water.

WHITE CHOCOLATE CARAMEL BUTTERCREAM
MAKES 5 CUPS/34.2 OUNCES/970 GRAMS

SOFT CARAMEL
MAKES 1 CUP/237 ML/10.6 OUNCES/300 GRAMS (SEE NOTE, PAGE 56)

	VOLUME	WEIGHT	
granulated sugar	1 cup	7 ounces	200 grams
corn syrup	1 tablespoon (15 ml)	0.7 ounce	20 grams
water	¼ cup (59 ml)	2 ounces	59 grams
heavy cream, hot	¼ cup plus 2 tablespoons (89 ml)	3.1 ounces	87 grams
unsalted butter (65° to 75°F/ 19° to 23°C)	2 tablespoons	1 ounce	28 grams
pure vanilla extract	2 teaspoons (10 ml)	.	.

MAKE THE SOFT CARAMEL Have ready a 2 cup glass measure with a spout, lightly coated with nonstick cooking spray.

In a medium heavy saucepan, preferably nonstick, stir together the sugar, corn syrup, and water until all the sugar is moistened. Heat, stirring constantly, until the sugar dissolves and the syrup is bubbling. Stop stirring completely and let the syrup boil undisturbed until it turns a dark amber (380°F/193°C). Remove it immediately from the heat because the temperature will continue to rise, or remove it slightly before it reaches temperature, and just as soon as it reaches temperature, slowly pour in the hot cream. It will bubble up furiously.

Use a silicone spatula or wooden spoon to stir the mixture gently, scraping the thicker part that settles on the bottom. Return it to very low heat, continuing to stir gently for 1 minute, until the mixture is uniform in color and the caramel fully dissolved.

Remove it from the heat and gently stir in the butter until incorporated. The mixture will be a little streaky but becomes uniform once cooled and stirred.

Pour the caramel into the prepared glass measure and let it cool for 3 minutes. Gently stir in the vanilla. Refrigerate for about 45 minutes, gently stirring every 15 minutes until cool to the touch. (An instant-read thermometer should read 70° to 75°F/21° to 24°C.)

NOTE There will be extra caramel to ensure that there is enough for the buttercream.

White Chocolate Custard Base

MAKES 2¼ CUPS PLUS 2 TABLESPOONS/22.6 OUNCES/640 GRAMS

	VOLUME	WEIGHT	
white chocolate containing cocoa butter, chopped	.	10.6 ounces	300 grams
unsalted butter (65° to 75°F/ 19° to 23°C)	10½ tablespoons (1 stick plus 2½ tablespoons)	5.3 ounces	150 grams
4 large eggs, at room temperature	¾ cup plus ½ tablespoon (185 ml)	7 ounces	200 grams

MAKE THE WHITE CHOCOLATE CUSTARD BASE In the top of a double boiler over barely simmering water (do not let the bottom of the container touch the water), melt the white chocolate and butter, stirring often, until smooth and creamy.

Whisk the eggs lightly to break them up and then whisk them into the melted chocolate until incorporated. With a silicone spatula, continue stirring, being sure to scrape the mixture from the bottom of the container to prevent overcooking. Stir until an instant-read thermometer reads 160°F/71°C. The mixture will have thickened slightly. Remove it from the heat source. (If any lumps have formed, press them through a strainer.) Transfer the mixture into a bowl. Cover it tightly, and refrigerate for about 1 hour, stirring every 15 minutes until cool to the touch. (An instant-read thermometer should read 65° to 70°F/19° to 21°C.) To speed cooling, place the bowl in an ice water bath (see page 538) and stir often.

COMPLETED WHITE CHOCOLATE
CARAMEL BUTTERCREAM

	VOLUME	WEIGHT	
unsalted butter (65° to 75°F/ 19° to 23°C)	10 tablespoons (1 stick plus 2 tablespoons)	5 ounces	142 grams
White Chocolate Custard Base	2¼ cups plus 2 tablespoons	22.6 ounces	640 grams
Soft Caramel (page 55)	⅔ cup (157 ml)	7 ounces	200 grams
Chocolate Lacquer Glaze (page 296, optional; see Note)	1 cup (237 ml)	10 ounces	285 grams

COMPLETE THE BUTTERCREAM In the bowl of a stand mixer fitted with the whisk beater, beat the butter on medium-low speed until creamy, about 30 seconds.

Gradually beat the white chocolate custard base into the butter, scraping down the sides of the bowl as needed. Raise the speed to medium-high and beat for 2 minutes, until stiff peaks form when the beater is raised.

Cover and set aside for 1½ to 2 hours, or until the mixture is slightly thickened and spongy. It should be no warmer than 70°F/21°C. If necessary, place the bowl in an ice water bath for a few minutes and stir constantly. Beat on medium-high speed for 30 seconds until smooth, light, and creamy.

Add the ⅔ cup/157 ml/7 ounces/200 grams of the soft caramel and beat just until incorporated. (The most accurate way to add the correct amount of caramel is to place the mixer bowl on a scale and weigh the addition of the sticky caramel.)

COMPOSE THE CAKE Spread a little of the buttercream on a 9 inch cardboard round or serving plate and set one layer on top. If using the plate, slide a few wide strips of parchment under the cake to keep the rim of the plate clean. Sandwich the layers with about 1 cup of the buttercream. Use the remainder of the buttercream to frost the top and sides. If using the parchment strips, slowly slide them out from under the cake before serving.

HIGHLIGHTS FOR SUCCESS

The white chocolate buttercream basic recipe without the caramel yields approximately 4 cups/27.2 ounces/770 grams. Once completed, the buttercream can accommodate a variety of extra flavorings such as this caramel, lemon or other curds, and fruit purees.

NOTE If using the lacquer glaze, chill the cake for 30 minutes to set the buttercream. While it is chilling, make 1½ times the lacquer glaze recipe on page 296 but let it cool to a finished temperature of 80°F/26°C. If making the glaze ahead, it will be thicker, so reheat it to 85°F/28°C. Pour the glaze onto the top of the cake, allowing it to cascade in irregular drips down the sides without coating them completely.

STORE Airtight: room temperature, 1 day; refrigerated, 3 days; frozen, 2 months.

Chocolate Pavarotti with Wicked Good Ganache

OVEN TEMPERATURE 350°F/175°C

BAKING TIME 30 to 40 minutes

*T*his cake is dedicated to Luciano Pavarotti, the only tenor I know of who was capable of reaching the E above high C to create a sound not of this earth. I've added white chocolate to both yellow and white cakes with the excellent results of higher rise and moister, melt-in-the-mouth texture, and it dawned on me that a dark chocolate cake might also benefit from this addition. For the frosting, I created the darkest and shiniest ganache ever. It is enriched with a mixture of unsweetened chocolate and corn syrup. The texture is incredibly smooth and the flavor is absolutely extraordinary. Keep a batch of the enrichment in your fridge to add to any basic ganache. It will keep for months. The touch of cayenne pepper doesn't alter the flavor, but instead heightens the taste sensation and gives the ganache a long finish. If you're a spice lover, go for the higher amount of cayenne. This is the cake I made for my Music and Art fiftieth high school reunion in New York. I overheard fellow classmates saying, "It sings in the mouth," which was just what I had intended.

PLAN AHEAD Make the ganache at least 4 hours ahead.

SPECIAL EQUIPMENT One 9 by 2 inch round cake pan, encircled with a cake strip, bottom coated with shortening, topped with a parchment round, then coated with baking spray with flour

Batter

	VOLUME	WEIGHT	
white chocolate containing cocoa butter, chopped	.	4 ounces	113 grams
unsweetened (alkalized) cocoa powder	½ cup plus 1 tablespoon (sifted before measuring)	1.5 ounces	42 grams
boiling water	½ cup (118 ml)	4.2 ounces	118 grams
2 large eggs, at room temperature	⅓ cup plus 1 tablespoon (94 ml)	3.5 ounces	100 grams
water	3 tablespoons (44 ml)	1.6 ounces	44 grams
pure vanilla extract	½ tablespoon (7.5 ml)	.	.
bleached cake flour	1½ cups (sifted into the cup and leveled off) plus 1 tablespoon	5.5 ounces	156 grams

	VOLUME	WEIGHT	
superfine sugar	¾ cup plus 1 tablespoon	5.7 ounces	162 grams
baking powder	1 tablespoon plus ¼ teaspoon	0.5 ounce	14.6 grams
fine sea salt	1 teaspoon	.	6 grams
unsalted butter (65° to 75°F/19° to 23°C)	8 tablespoons (1 stick)	4 ounces	113 grams
canola or safflower oil, at room temperature	2 tablespoons (30 ml)	1 ounce	27 grams

PREHEAT THE OVEN Twenty minutes or longer before baking, set an oven rack in the lower third of the oven and preheat the oven to 350°F/175°C.

MELT THE WHITE CHOCOLATE In a small microwavable bowl, stirring with a silicone spatula every 15 seconds (or in the top of a double boiler set over hot, not simmering, water, stirring often—do not let the bottom of the container touch the water), heat the white chocolate until almost completely melted. Remove the chocolate from the heat source and stir until fully melted. Let the chocolate cool until it is no longer warm to the touch but is still fluid.

MIX THE COCOA AND WATER In a medium bowl, whisk the cocoa and the ½ cup/118 ml of boiling water until smooth. Cover with plastic wrap to prevent evaporation and cool to room temperature, about 30 minutes. To speed cooling, place in the refrigerator. Bring the mixture to room temperature before proceeding.

MIX THE REMAINING LIQUID INGREDIENTS In another small bowl, whisk the eggs, the 3 tablespoons/44 ml of water, and the vanilla just until lightly combined.

MAKE THE BATTER In the bowl of a stand mixer fitted with the flat beater, mix the flour, sugar, baking powder, and salt on low speed for 30 seconds. Add the butter, oil, and cocoa mixture. Mix on low speed until the dry ingredients are moistened. Raise the speed to medium and beat for 1½ minutes. Scrape down the sides of the bowl.

Starting on medium-low speed, gradually add the egg mixture in two parts, beating on medium speed for 30 seconds after each addition to incorporate the ingredients and strengthen the structure. Scrape down the sides of the bowl. Add the melted chocolate and beat at medium speed for about 10 seconds until evenly incorporated. Scrape down the sides of the bowl. Using a silicone spatula, scrape the batter into the prepared pan and smooth the surface evenly with a small offset spatula.

BAKE THE CAKE Bake for 30 to 40 minutes, or until a cake tester inserted near the center comes out clean and the cake springs back when pressed lightly in the center. The cake should start to shrink from the sides of the pan only after removal from the oven. It will have a few cracks in the top.

COOL AND UNMOLD THE CAKE Let the cake cool in the pan on a wire rack for 10 minutes. Run a small metal spatula between the sides of the pan and the cake, pressing firmly against the pan, and invert it onto a wire rack that has been lightly coated with nonstick cooking spray. Immediately reinvert the cake so that the top side is up. Cool completely.

WICKED GOOD GANACHE

MAKES 1½ CUPS/13.8 OUNCES/390 GRAMS

	VOLUME	WEIGHT	
corn syrup	3 tablespoons (44 ml)	2.2 ounces	61 grams
unsweetened or 99% chocolate, chopped	.	0.8 ounce	24 grams
bittersweet chocolate, 60% to 62% cacao, chopped	.	6 ounces	170 grams
heavy cream	¾ cup minus 1 teaspoon (172 ml)	6 ounces	170 grams
cayenne pepper	¼ to ¾ teaspoon	.	.

MAKE THE WICKED GOOD GANACHE Have ready a fine-mesh strainer suspended over a medium glass bowl.

In a small microwavable bowl (or in a small saucepan over low heat, stirring often), heat the corn syrup just to a boil. Immediately remove it from the heat source and stir in the unsweetened chocolate until smoothly incorporated.

In a food processor, process the bittersweet chocolate until very fine.

In a 1 cup microwavable measure with a spout (or in a small saucepan over medium heat, stirring often), scald the cream (heat it to the boiling point; small bubbles will form around the periphery).

With the motor of the food processor running, pour the cream through the feed tube in a steady stream. Process for a few seconds until smooth, scraping down the sides of the bowl as needed. Pulse in the corn syrup and chocolate mixture. Pulse in the optional cayenne. (If you want just a whisper of heat, start with the ¼ teaspoon.) Be sure to pulse it in to distribute it evenly before tasting.

Press the ganache through the strainer and let it sit for 1 hour. Cover it with plastic wrap and let it cool for 3 to 4 hours, until the mixture reaches a soft frosting consistency (70° to 75°F/21° to 24°C).

The ganache keeps in an airtight container for 3 days at cool room temperature, 2 weeks refrigerated, or 6 months frozen. To restore to frosting consistency, defrost, if frozen, and reheat in a microwave with 3 second bursts, or in a double boiler set over hot, not simmering, water (do not let the bottom of the container touch the water), stirring gently to ensure that it does not overheat or incorporate any air.

COMPOSE THE CAKE When the cake is completely cool, set it on a serving plate. Frost the top and sides with swirls of the ganache.

STORE Airtight: room temperature, 3 days; refrigerated, 10 days; frozen, 2 months.

DOUBLE DAMAGE OBLIVION

SERVES 12 TO 16

OVEN TEMPERATURE
425°F/220°C for the Chocolate Oblivion;
350°F/175°C for the Deep Chocolate Passion

BAKING TIME
12 to 14 minutes for the Chocolate Oblivion;
25 to 35 minutes for the Deep Chocolate Passion

This incredible chocolate experience was Woody's inspiration and it doesn't get more chocolaty than this: my ultimate flourless chocolate cake sandwiched between layers of my ultimate deep chocolate passion layer cake. If you desire a small relief from all that chocolate, it's fine to substitute heated and strained preserves for the ganache "glue" that holds the two elements in place.

PLAN AHEAD Make the Chocolate Oblivion and the chocolate ganache at least 4 hours ahead of assembly.

SPECIAL EQUIPMENT FOR THE CHOCOLATE OBLIVION: One 9 by 2 inch or higher springform pan, bottom and the bottom third of the sides coated with butter, bottom topped with a parchment round, set in a slightly larger silicone pan or wrapped with a *double* layer of heavy-duty aluminum foil to prevent seepage | One 12 by 2 inch round cake pan or a roasting pan for the water bath | One 10 by 2 inch round cake pan or 10 to 11 inch diameter pot lid to cover the springform pan during baking

FOR THE DEEP CHOCOLATE PASSION: One 9 by 2 inch round cake pan, encircled with a cake strip, bottom coated with shortening, topped with a parchment round (leave the sides uncoated to prevent the top of the cake from shrinking inward)

CHOCOLATE OBLIVION

MAKES ONE 8¾ BY ½ INCH THICK CAKE

	VOLUME	WEIGHT	
bittersweet chocolate, 56% to 62% cacao, chopped	.	8 ounces	227 grams
unsalted butter (65° to 75°F/ 19° to 23°C)	8 tablespoons (1 stick)	4 ounces	113 grams
pure vanilla extract	½ tablespoon (7.5 ml)	.	.
3 large eggs, at room temperature	½ cup plus 1½ tablespoons (140 ml)	5.3 ounces	150 grams

PREHEAT THE OVEN Thirty minutes or longer before baking, set an oven rack in the lower third of the oven and preheat the oven to 425°F/220°C.

MELT THE CHOCOLATE AND BUTTER In a large heatproof bowl set over a pan of hot, not simmering, water (do not let the bottom of the bowl touch the water), place the chocolate and butter and let stand, stirring occasionally, until smooth and melted. Transfer the mixture to a large bowl. Stir in the vanilla. Set the chocolate mixture aside while beating the eggs.

BEAT THE EGGS In the bowl of a stand mixer, with a long-handled whisk, lightly whisk the eggs. Set the bowl over a pan of simmering water and heat just until lukewarm to the touch, stirring constantly with the whisk to prevent curdling.

Immediately transfer the bowl to the stand mixer and attach the whisk beater. Beat on high speed for about 5 minutes, until triple in volume and the eggs are billowy and almost ready to form soft peaks when the beater is raised. (If using a handheld mixer, beat the eggs over simmering water until they are hot. Then remove them from the heat and beat for a minimum of 5 minutes.)

Using a large balloon whisk, slotted skimmer, or silicone spatula, fold half of the eggs into the chocolate mixture until almost evenly incorporated. Fold in the remaining eggs until almost no streaks remain. Use a silicone spatula to finish folding, scraping up the mixture from the bottom to ensure that all the heavier chocolate mixture gets incorporated. Scrape the batter into the springform pan and smooth with an offset spatula.

BAKE THE CHOCOLATE OBLIVION Set the springform pan into the larger pan and surround it with 1 inch of very hot water. Bake for 5 minutes (7 minutes if using the silicone pan). Place the 10 inch cake pan on top of the springform pan and continue baking for another 7 minutes. The Chocolate Oblivion will appear set but will wobble slightly if the pan is moved. (An instant-read thermometer should read 170°F/77°C.)

CHILL THE CHOCOLATE OBLIVION Remove the pan from the water bath and set it on a wire rack to cool to room temperature or just until warm, about 1 hour. To absorb condensation, place a paper towel, curved side down, over the pan with the ends overhanging. Place an inverted plate, larger than the springform pan, on top of the paper towel. Refrigerate the Chocolate Oblivion for 4 hours to overnight.

DEEP CHOCOLATE PASSION
BATTER

	VOLUME	WEIGHT	
unsweetened (alkalized) cocoa powder	½ cup (sifted before measuring)	1.3 ounces	37 grams
boiling water	¼ cup (59 ml)	2.1 ounces	59 grams
bleached cake flour (see Note, page 65)	¼ cup (sifted into the cup and leveled off), plus 2 tablespoons	1.3 ounces	38 grams
bleached all-purpose flour	⅓ cup (sifted into the cup and leveled off)	1.3 ounces	38 grams
superfine sugar	¾ cup	5.3 ounces	150 grams
baking powder	1 teaspoon	.	4.5 grams
baking soda	½ teaspoon	.	2.7 grams
fine sea salt	⅛ teaspoon	.	0.7 gram
canola or safflower oil, at room temperature	¼ cup (59 ml)	1.9 ounces	54 grams
2 large eggs, separated, plus 1 white, at room temperature			
yolks	2 tablespoons plus 1 teaspoon (35 ml)	1.3 ounces	37 grams
whites	¼ cup plus 2 tablespoons (89 ml)	3.2 ounces	90 grams
pure vanilla extract	½ teaspoon (2.5 ml)	.	.

PREHEAT THE OVEN Twenty minutes or longer before baking, set an oven rack in the lower third of the oven and preheat the oven to 350°F/175°C.

MAKE THE COCOA MIXTURE In the bowl of a stand mixer, by hand, whisk the cocoa and boiling water until smooth. Cover with plastic wrap to prevent evaporation and cool to room temperature, about 1 hour. To speed cooling, place in the refrigerator. Bring the mixture to room temperature before proceeding.

MIX THE DRY INGREDIENTS In a medium bowl, whisk the cake flour, all-purpose flour, sugar, baking powder, baking soda, and salt. Sift the flour mixture onto a large piece of parchment.

MAKE THE BATTER Add the oil and egg yolks to the stand mixer bowl. Attach the whisk beater. Start on low speed, then gradually raise the speed to medium and beat for about 1 minute, or until smooth and shiny and resembling a buttercream. Scrape down the sides of the bowl. Beat in the vanilla for a few seconds.

Add half of the flour mixture to the chocolate mixture and beat on low speed until the dry ingredients are moistened. Scrape down the sides of the bowl. Repeat with the remaining flour mixture. Raise the speed to medium-high and beat for 1 minute. Scrape down the sides and bottom of the bowl. The mixture will be very thick. On low speed, add the egg whites. Gradually raise the speed to medium-high and beat for 2 minutes. The batter will now be like a thick soup. Using a silicone spatula, scrape the batter into the prepared pan.

BAKE THE DEEP CHOCOLATE PASSION Bake for 25 to 35 minutes, or until a wooden skewer inserted into the center comes out clean and the cake springs back when pressed lightly in the center. During baking, the batter will rise almost to the top of the pan and a little higher in the middle. It will start to lower just before the end of baking.

To prevent the collapse of the delicate foam structure while still hot, the cake must be unmolded as soon as it has baked. Have ready a small metal spatula and two wire racks that have been lightly coated with nonstick cooking spray.

UNMOLD AND COOL THE CAKE Immediately run a small metal spatula between the sides of the pan and the cake, pressing firmly against the pan, and invert the cake onto the prepared wire rack. Remove the parchment and immediately reinvert the cake onto the second rack so that the firm upper crust keeps it from sinking. Cool completely. (While still warm, invert again to loosen the cake from the rack and reinvert to finish cooling.)

NOTE Cake flour results in more tenderness, and all-purpose flour offers more moist fudginess, so I like to use a combination of the two. Alternatively, use ½ cup/2 ounces/57 grams bleached all-purpose flour and ¼ cup/1.3 ounces/36 grams cornstarch, and add $^{1}/_{16}$ teaspoon more baking powder.

CHOCOLATE GANACHE

MAKES ABOUT ⅔ CUP/6.5 OUNCES/185 GRAMS

	VOLUME		WEIGHT	
bittersweet chocolate, 60% to 62% cacao, chopped	.		3.5 ounces	100 grams
heavy cream	½ cup (118 ml)		4.1 ounces	116 grams
pure vanilla extract	½ teaspoon (2.5 ml)		.	.

MAKE THE GANACHE Have ready a fine-mesh strainer suspended over a small glass bowl.

In a food processor, process the chocolate until very fine.

In a 1 cup microwavable measure with a spout (or in a small saucepan over medium heat, stirring often), scald the cream (heat it to the boiling point; small bubbles will form around the periphery).

With the motor of the food processor running, pour the cream through the feed tube in a steady stream. Process for a few seconds until smooth, scraping down the sides of the bowl as needed. Pulse in the vanilla. Press the ganache through the strainer and let it sit for 1 hour. Cover it with plastic wrap and let it cool for 2 to 3 hours, or until the mixture reaches a soft frosting consistency (70° to 75°F/21° to 24°C).

The ganache keeps in an airtight container for 3 days at cool room temperature, 2 weeks refrigerated, and 6 months frozen. To restore to frosting consistency, defrost, if frozen, and reheat in a microwave with 3 second bursts, or in a double boiler set over hot, not simmering, water (do not let the bottom of the container touch the water), stirring gently to ensure that it does not overheat or incorporate any air.

COMPOSE THE CAKE Cut the Deep Chocolate Passion into two even layers.

Place the springform pan containing the Chocolate Oblivion on a wire rack. Remove the plate and paper towel. Use a small torch to heat the sides of the pan or wipe them with a dish towel run under hot water and wrung out. Release the sides of the springform pan.

Spread half of the ganache (⅓ cup/3.2 ounces/92 grams) evenly over the top of the Oblivion.

Place the bottom cake layer on top of the Oblivion, set a serving plate (or wire rack) on top of the cake, and invert the cake. Use a small torch to heat the bottom of the pan or wipe it with a dish towel run under hot water and wrung out. Carefully slide a small offset spatula between the parchment and the springform pan's bottom, and circle around the pan to release the bottom. Peel off the parchment. Spread the remaining ganache over the top of the Oblivion. Place the second cake layer, top side up, on top of the Oblivion.

Use a heated straight-edge knife to trim the Oblivion flush with the cake layers to create smooth sides. Reheat the knife and place the blade against the Oblivion to melt the edges slightly for a smooth and glossy finish.

If desired, dust the top of the cake lightly with unsweetened alkalized cocoa powder or powdered sugar. Use a straight-edge knife to slice the cake from top to bottom. Between slices, wipe off the knife to help minimize the Oblivion's spreading onto the cake.

STORE Airtight: refrigerated, 5 days. Do not freeze, because the texture will become less smooth.

White Chocolate Cupcakes with Raspberry Mousseline

MAKES 16 CUPCAKES

OVEN TEMPERATURE 375°F/190°C

BAKING TIME 17 to 22 minutes

*S*everal years ago, while giving a cooking demonstration in Montreal, I discovered this simple and beautiful technique for making a rose-shaped topper. Because the velvety White Chocolate Whisper Cake in *The Cake Bible* is many people's favorite white cake, I decided to create a cupcake version to pair with this piping technique.

PLAN AHEAD Make the raspberry glaze several hours ahead.

SPECIAL EQUIPMENT 16 cupcake liners set in muffin pans or custard cups | Optional: a 2 inch diameter ice cream scoop | A pastry bag fitted with a ½ inch open star pastry tube

Batter

	VOLUME	WEIGHT	
white chocolate containing cocoa butter, chopped	.	4 ounces	113 grams
3 large egg whites, at room temperature	¼ cup plus 2 tablespoons (89 ml)	3.2 ounces	90 grams
milk	⅔ cup (158 ml), *divided*	5.7 ounces	161 grams
pure vanilla extract	½ tablespoon (7.5 ml)	.	.
bleached cake flour (or bleached all-purpose flour)	2 cups (or 1¾ cups), sifted into the cup and leveled off	7 ounces	200 grams
superfine sugar	¾ cup	5.3 ounces	150 grams
baking powder	2¼ teaspoons	.	10.1 grams
fine sea salt	½ teaspoon	.	3 grams
unsalted butter (65° to 75°F/ 19° to 23°C)	6 tablespoons (¾ stick)	3 ounces	85 grams

PREHEAT THE OVEN Twenty minutes or longer before baking, set an oven rack in the lower third of the oven and preheat the oven to 375°F/190°C.

MELT THE WHITE CHOCOLATE In a small microwavable bowl, stirring with a silicone spatula every 15 seconds (or in the top of a double boiler set over hot, not simmering, water, stirring often—do not let the bottom of the container touch the water), heat the white chocolate until almost completely melted.

Remove the chocolate from the heat source and stir until fully melted. Let the chocolate cool until it is no longer warm to the touch but is still fluid.

MIX THE LIQUID INGREDIENTS In a small bowl, whisk the egg whites, about 3 tablespoons/ 44 ml/1.3 ounces/38 grams of the milk, and the vanilla just until lightly combined.

MAKE THE BATTER In the bowl of a stand mixer fitted with the flat beater, mix the flour, sugar, baking powder, and salt on low speed for 30 seconds. Add the butter and the remaining milk. Mix on low speed until the dry ingredients are moistened. Raise the speed to medium and beat for 1½ minutes. Scrape down the sides of the bowl.

Starting on medium-low speed, gradually add the egg mixture to the batter in two parts, beating on medium speed for 30 seconds after each addition to incorporate the ingredients and strengthen the structure. Scrape down the sides of the bowl. Add the melted chocolate and beat to incorporate it, about 10 seconds.

Use the optional ice cream scoop or a spoon to place the batter (1.8 ounces/50 grams) into each of the prepared cupcake liners, smoothing the surfaces evenly with a small metal spatula. The liners will be about three-quarters full.

Let the cupcakes sit for 20 minutes at room temperature before placing them in the oven. This resting period will ensure rounded tops.

BAKE THE CUPCAKES Bake for 17 to 22 minutes, or until golden brown, a wire cake tester inserted into the centers comes out clean, and the cupcakes spring back when pressed lightly in the centers.

COOL THE CUPCAKES Let the cupcakes cool in the pans on a wire rack for 10 minutes. Remove them from the pans and set them on a wire rack. Cool completely.

Raspberry Sauce

MAKES ¾ CUP/177 ML/7.5 OUNCES/211 GRAMS

	VOLUME	WEIGHT	
frozen raspberries with no sugar added (one 12 ounce bag)	3 cups	12 ounces	340 grams
lemon juice, freshly squeezed	1 teaspoon (5 ml)	.	5 grams
granulated sugar	⅓ cup	2.3 ounces	67 grams

MAKE THE RASPBERRY SAUCE In a medium strainer suspended over a deep bowl, thaw the raspberries completely. This will take several hours. (To speed thawing, place the strainer in an oven with a pilot light or turn on the oven light.) Press the berries to force out all the juice. There should be about ½ cup/118 ml/4.5 ounces/128 grams of juice.

In a small saucepan over medium-low heat (or in a 2 cup microwavable measure with a spout, lightly coated with nonstick cooking spray), boil the juice until it is reduced to 2 tablespoons/30 ml/1 ounce/30 grams. If using a saucepan, pour the syrup into a glass measure with a spout, lightly coated with nonstick cooking spray, to stop the cooking and to cool.

Puree and strain the raspberries with a food mill fitted with the fine disc, or use a fine-mesh strainer suspended over a bowl to remove all of the seeds. (Raspberry seeds are tiny and can pass through most food mills. Only the finest strainer will remove all of the seeds.) There should be about ½ cup/118 ml/4 ounces/113 grams of puree. Stir in the reduced raspberry syrup and lemon juice. There should be about ⅔ cup/158 ml/5.1 ounces/145 grams of raspberry puree. (If you have less, add proportionately less sugar. The correct amount of sugar is half the volume of the puree.)

Stir the sugar into the sauce until it dissolves. You will need ⅓ cup/79 ml/3.3 ounces/95 grams of sauce to make the raspberry mousseline.

The sauce can be stored for 10 days refrigerated or for 1 year frozen. It can be thawed and refrozen at least three times without flavor loss.

Highlights for Success

Frozen berries must be used to make the sauce because freezing breaks down some of the cell structure, which releases some of the berries' liquid, making it possible to thicken this liquid while preserving the freshness of the uncooked pulp. Be sure to use frozen berries with no sugar added. The juices from berries in syrup cannot be reduced as much because the sugar starts to caramelize.

RASPBERRY MOUSSELINE

MAKES ABOUT 2¾ CUPS/18 OUNCES/510 GRAMS

	VOLUME	WEIGHT	
unsalted butter, preferably high fat, slightly softened but cool (65° to 68°F/19° to 20°C; see Note, page 72)	16 tablespoons (2 sticks)	8 ounces	227 grams
2½ large egg whites, at room temperature	¼ cup plus 2 tablespoons (89 ml)	2.6 ounces	75 grams
cream of tartar	¼ plus ¹⁄₁₆ teaspoon	.	1 gram
granulated sugar	½ cup plus 2 teaspoons, *divided*	3.8 ounces	109 grams
water	2½ tablespoons (37 ml)	1.3 ounces	37 grams
Raspberry Sauce	⅓ cup (79 ml)	3.3 ounces	95 grams

BEAT THE BUTTER In the bowl of a stand mixer fitted with the flat beater, beat the butter on medium-high speed until creamy, about 1 minute. Set aside in a cool place (no warmer than 70°F/21°C).

PREPARE THE EGG WHITES Pour the egg whites into the bowl of a stand mixer, if you have a second mixer bowl, or into a medium bowl and have ready a handheld mixer. Add the cream of tartar.

HEAT THE SUGAR SYRUP Have ready a 1 cup or larger glass measure with a spout.

In a small heavy saucepan, preferably nonstick, stir together all but 3 tablespoons/ 1.3 ounces/37 grams of the sugar and the water until all of the sugar is moistened. Heat on medium, stirring constantly, until the sugar dissolves and the mixture is bubbling. Stop stirring and reduce the heat to low. (On an electric range, remove the pan from the heat.)

BEAT THE EGG WHITES INTO A STIFF MERINGUE If using the stand mixer for the egg whites, attach the whisk beater. Beat the egg whites and cream of tartar on medium speed until foamy. Raise the speed to medium-high and beat until soft peaks form when the beater is raised. Gradually beat in the remaining 3 tablespoons of sugar until stiff peaks form when the beater is raised slowly.

BRING THE SUGAR SYRUP UP TO THE PROPER TEMPERATURE Increase the heat under the sugar syrup and continue to boil the syrup for a few minutes until an instant-read thermometer reads 248° to 250°F/120°C. Immediately transfer the syrup to the glass measure to stop the cooking.

ADD THE SUGAR SYRUP TO THE EGG WHITES If using a stand mixer, with the mixer off to keep the syrup from spinning onto the sides of the bowl, add it to the egg whites. Begin by pouring in a small amount of syrup. Immediately beat on high speed for 5 seconds. Add the remaining syrup the same way in three parts. For the last addition, use a silicone spatula to remove the syrup clinging to the glass measure and scrape it off against the whisk beater. If the syrup has hardened before most of it has been poured, soften it to pouring consistency for a few seconds in the microwave.

If using a handheld mixer, beat the syrup into the egg whites in a steady stream. Do not let the syrup fall on the beaters or they will spin it onto the sides of the bowl.

Lower the speed to medium and continue beating for up to 2 minutes. Refrigerate the meringue for 5 to 10 minutes, or until an instant-read thermometer reads 70°F/21°C. Whisk after the first 5 minutes to test and equalize the temperature.

BEAT THE MERINGUE INTO THE BUTTER Set the mixer bowl containing the butter in the stand mixer and attach the whisk beater (no need to wash it). Beat on medium-high speed for about 3 minutes, or until the butter lightens in color and is no warmer than 70°F/21°C.

Scrape the meringue into the butter and beat on medium speed until smooth and creamy. Beat for about 2 minutes, scraping down the sides of the bowl as necessary. At first it will look slightly curdled. If it starts watering out, check the temperature. The mixture should feel cool and be no lower than 65°F/19°C, no higher than 70°F/21°C. If it is too warm, place the bowl in an ice water bath (see page 538) and stir gently to chill it down before continuing to whisk. If it is too cool, suspend the bowl over a pan of simmering water (do not let the bottom of the bowl touch the water) and heat very briefly, stirring vigorously when the mixture just starts to melt slightly at the edges. To stop the warming, dip the bottom of the bowl in an ice water bath for a few seconds to cool it. Remove the bowl from the ice water and beat the mousseline by hand until smooth.

Beat in the raspberry sauce until uniformly mixed. The mousseline becomes spongy and fluffy on standing. If it was not used right away, whisk it lightly by hand to maintain a silky texture before applying it to the cupcakes. If it was refrigerated let it come to room temperature (at least 70°F/21°C) before whisking; this prevents it from breaking down.

NOTE High-fat (low water) butter helps to ensure smooth emulsification. Temperature, however, is the key to the success of this buttercream, so you will need an instant-read thermometer. If the temperature of the meringue and butter is between 65° to 70°F/19° to 21°C, it works easily and magnificently.

FROST THE CUPCAKES Fill the pastry bag with the mousseline buttercream. Hold the bag at a 45 to 90 degree angle with the tube slightly above the center of the cupcake. Squeeze firmly, allowing the buttercream to begin fanning out. Then move the tube in a circular motion, piping spiral coils of frosting that slightly overlap each other until reaching the edges of the cupcake. Gradually relax the pressure so that the buttercream will meld into the last coil. The piped buttercream should resemble a rose.

Alternatively, use a small metal spatula to swirl the top of each cupcake with about 2 tablespoons of the buttercream.

If desired, garnish each plate with a tiny crystallized rose (see Coco Savvy, page 527).

STORE Airtight: room temperature, 1 day; refrigerated, 3 days; frozen, 2 months.

Coconut Cupcakes with Milk Chocolate Ganache

MAKES 16 CUPCAKES

OVEN TEMPERATURE 350°F/175°C

BAKING TIME 20 to 25 minutes

At the request of his t'ai chi instructor, *Sifu* Paul, Woody reconfigured the recipe for The Southern (Manhattan) Coconut Cake from *Rose's Heavenly Cakes* in miniature. Instead of topping them with coconut buttercream, they are coated in delicious milk chocolate ganache, but I have also included the buttercream recipe as a variation.

PLAN AHEAD Make the ganache at least 4 hours ahead.

SPECIAL EQUIPMENT 16 cupcake liners set in muffin pans or custard cups | Optional: a 2 inch diameter ice cream scoop

Batter

	VOLUME	WEIGHT	
3 large egg whites, at room temperature (reserve yolks if making the Silk Meringue Buttercream variation, page 77)	¼ cup plus 2 tablespoons (89 ml)	3.2 ounces	90 grams
canned coconut milk (see Note, page 74)	⅔ cup (158 ml), *divided*	5.7 ounces	161 grams
pure vanilla extract	¾ teaspoon (3.7 ml)	.	.
coconut extract, preferably Flavorganics	¾ teaspoon (3.7 ml)	.	.
bleached cake flour (or bleached all-purpose flour)	2 cups (or 1¾ cups), sifted into the cup and leveled off	7 ounces	200 grams
superfine sugar	1 cup	7 ounces	200 grams
baking powder	2¼ teaspoons	.	10.1 grams
fine sea salt	½ teaspoon	.	3 grams
unsalted butter (65° to 75°F/ 19° to 23°C)	8 tablespoons (1 stick)	4 ounces	113 grams
Décor: toasted sweetened coconut flakes	1 cup	3 ounces	85 grams

PREHEAT THE OVEN Twenty minutes or longer before baking, set an oven rack in the lower third of the oven and preheat the oven to 350°F/175°C.

MIX THE LIQUID INGREDIENTS In a small bowl, whisk the egg whites, 2½ tablespoons/ 37 ml/1.3 ounces/38 grams of the coconut milk, the vanilla, and coconut extract just until lightly combined. (Spray the reserved yolks lightly with nonstick cooking spray, cover with plastic wrap, and refrigerate until ready to make the buttercream, if using.)

MAKE THE BATTER In the bowl of a stand mixer fitted with the flat beater, mix the flour, sugar, baking powder, and salt on low speed for 30 seconds. Add the butter and the remaining coconut milk. Mix on low speed until the dry ingredients are moistened. Raise the speed to medium and beat for 1½ minutes. Scrape down the sides of the bowl.

Starting on medium-low speed, gradually add the egg mixture to the batter in two parts, beating on medium speed for 30 seconds after each addition to incorporate the ingredients and strengthen the structure. Scrape down the sides of the bowl.

Use the optional ice cream scoop or a spoon to place the batter (1.7 ounces/48 grams) into each of the prepared cupcake liners, smoothing the surfaces evenly with a small metal spatula. The liners will be about three-quarters full.

Let the cupcakes sit for 20 minutes at room temperature before being placed in the oven. This resting period will ensure rounded tops.

BAKE THE CUPCAKES Bake for 20 to 25 minutes, or until golden brown, a wire cake tester inserted into the centers comes out clean, and the cupcakes spring back when pressed lightly in the centers.

COOL THE CUPCAKES Let the cupcakes cool in the pans on a wire rack for 10 minutes. Remove them from the pans and set them on a wire rack. Cool completely.

TOAST THE COCONUT While the oven is still on, it is convenient to toast the coconut for the décor.

Spread the coconut evenly in a single layer on a quarter sheet pan or baking sheet and bake for 7 to 10 minutes, or until the coconut just begins to turn a light brown. Stir once or twice to ensure even toasting. Watch carefully to prevent overbrowning. Set the pan on a wire rack until the coconut cools completely. Leave the coconut on the pan and crumble it slightly to separate the pieces.

NOTE Before measuring the coconut milk, scrape it into a bowl and whisk to a uniform consistency. (The solid coconut oil tends to separate from the liquid on standing.)

Custom Rose Blend
Milk Chocolate Ganache

MAKES 1⅞ CUPS/17 OUNCES/482 GRAMS

Chocolate, especially milk chocolate, is a lovely complement to coconut. I created this custom blend of milk chocolate and it could well be the most luscious of all ganaches. It is perfectly balanced, rich, and creamy.

	VOLUME	WEIGHT	
white chocolate containing cocoa butter, chopped	.	4.7 ounces	133 grams
bittersweet chocolate, 60% to 62% cacao, chopped	.	4.7 ounces	133 grams
heavy cream	1 cup (237 ml)	8.2 ounces	232 grams

MAKE THE MILK CHOCOLATE GANACHE Have ready a fine-mesh strainer suspended over a medium glass bowl.

In a food processor, process the white chocolate and bittersweet chocolate until very fine.

In a 2 cup or larger microwavable measure with a spout (or in a small saucepan over medium heat, stirring often), scald the cream (heat it to the boiling point; small bubbles will form around the periphery).

With the motor of the food processor running, pour the cream through the feed tube in a steady stream. Process for a few seconds until smooth, scraping down the sides of the bowl as needed. Press the ganache through the strainer and let it sit for 1 hour. Cover it with plastic wrap and let it cool for 2 to 3 hours, or until the mixture reaches soft frosting consistency (70° to 75°F/21° to 24°C).

The ganache keeps in an airtight container for 3 days at cool room temperature, 2 weeks refrigerated, or 6 months frozen. To restore to frosting consistency, defrost, if frozen, and reheat in a microwave with 3 second bursts, or in a double boiler set over hot, not simmering, water (do not let the bottom of the container touch the water), stirring gently to ensure that it does not overheat or incorporate any air.

COMPOSE THE CUPCAKES With a small metal spatula, spread 1 to 2 tablespoons of the ganache on the top of each cupcake. Hold the cupcakes over the pan and sprinkle with the toasted coconut.

STORE Airtight: room temperature, 1 day; refrigerated, 3 days; frozen, 2 months.

Variation: COCONUT SILK MERINGUE BUTTERCREAM

MAKES ABOUT 2¼ CUPS/18.5 OUNCES/525 GRAMS

CRÈME ANGLAISE

	VOLUME	WEIGHT	
granulated sugar	¼ cup	1.8 ounces	50 grams
3 large egg yolks, at room temperature	3½ tablespoons (52 ml)	1.7 ounces	47 grams
coconut milk (see Note, page 74)	¼ cup (59 ml)	2.1 ounces	60 grams
pure vanilla extract	½ teaspoon (2.5 ml)	.	.
coconut extract, preferably Flavorganics	½ teaspoon (2.5 ml)	.	.

MAKE THE CRÈME ANGLAISE Have ready a fine-mesh strainer suspended over a medium bowl.

In a medium heavy saucepan, combine the sugar and egg yolks.

In a small saucepan, bring the coconut milk to a boil. Add 1 tablespoon of the coconut milk to the egg yolk mixture, stirring constantly. Gradually stir in the remaining coconut milk and cook over medium-low heat, continuing to stir constantly, just until below the boiling point. The mixture will start to steam slightly and an instant-read thermometer should read 170°F/77°C. Immediately pour the mixture through the strainer, scraping up any clinging to the bottom of the pan. Press it through the strainer.

Cool, stirring occasionally. Stir in the vanilla and coconut extract. To speed cooling, place the bowl in an ice water bath (see page 538).

Set a piece of plastic wrap, lightly coated with nonstick cooking spray, directly onto the surface of the crème anglaise to keep a skin from forming. Refrigerate for up to 5 days, or until ready to complete the buttercream.

ITALIAN MERINGUE

	VOLUME	WEIGHT	
1 large egg white, at room temperature	2 tablespoons (30 ml)	1 ounce	30 grams
cream of tartar	⅛ teaspoon	.	.
superfine sugar	¼ cup, *divided*	1.8 ounces	50 grams
water	1 tablespoon (15 ml)	0.5 ounce	15 grams

MAKE THE ITALIAN MERINGUE Have ready a 1 cup or larger glass measure with a spout and a handheld mixer.

Into a medium bowl, pour the egg white and add the cream of tartar.

In a small heavy saucepan, preferably nonstick, stir together 3 tablespoons/1.3 ounces/37 grams of the sugar and the water until the sugar is completely moistened. Heat on medium-high, stirring constantly, until the sugar dissolves and the syrup is bubbling. Stop stirring and reduce the heat to low. (If using an electric range, remove the pan from the heat.)

With the handheld mixer, beat the egg white and cream of tartar on medium-low speed until foamy. Gradually raise the speed to medium-high and beat until soft peaks form when the beater is raised. Gradually beat in the remaining sugar until stiff peaks form when the beater is raised slowly.

Increase the heat under the sugar syrup to medium-high and continue to boil for a few minutes until an instant-read thermometer reads 248° to 250°F/120°C. Immediately transfer the syrup to the glass measure to stop the cooking.

Beat the syrup into the egg white on high speed in a steady stream. Do not let the syrup fall on the beaters or they will spin it onto the sides of the bowl.

Lower the speed to medium and beat for 2 minutes. Decrease the speed to low and continue beating until no longer warm to the touch, about 5 minutes.

COMPLETED SILK MERINGUE BUTTERCREAM

	VOLUME	WEIGHT	
unsalted butter (65° to 75°F/ 19° to 23°C)	16 tablespoons (2 sticks)	8 ounces	227 grams
Crème Anglaise (70° to 75°F/ 21° to 24°C), page 77	.	.	.
Italian Meringue (70° to 75°F/ 21° to 24°C)	.	.	.
coconut rum, preferably Cocoribe (optional)	1 tablespoon (15 ml)	0.5 ounce	16 grams

COMPLETE THE BUTTERCREAM In the bowl of a stand mixer fitted with the whisk beater, beat the butter on medium speed for 30 seconds, or until creamy. Gradually beat in the crème anglaise until smooth. Add the Italian meringue and beat just until incorporated. If the mixture looks curdled instead of smooth, it is too cold. Let it sit at room temperature to warm to 70°F/21°C before continuing to beat, or suspend the bowl over a pan of simmering water (do not let the bottom of the bowl touch the water) and heat very briefly, stirring vigorously when the mixture just starts to melt slightly at the edges. To stop the warming, dip the bottom of the bowl into an ice water bath (see page 538) for a few seconds to cool it.

Remove the bowl from the ice water and beat the buttercream by hand until smooth. (Having the crème anglaise and the Italian meringue within a few degrees temperature of each other will guarantee a smooth, noncurdled buttercream.) Beat in the coconut rum, if using.

Use at once to frost the cupcakes or transfer the buttercream to an airtight container. The buttercream keeps for 1 week refrigerated or for 6 months frozen.

COMPOSE THE CUPCAKES With a small metal spatula, spread 1 to 2 tablespoons of the buttercream on the top of each cupcake. Hold the cupcakes over the pan and sprinkle with the toasted coconut.

COFFEE CRUMB CAKE MUFFINS

OVEN TEMPERATURE
350°F/175°C

BAKING TIME
25 to 35 minutes

*T*his is my all time most loved coffee cake baked in a muffin pan for individual size servings. I love the way the batter rises up and over part of the apple slices, resembling a wee chef's toque.

SPECIAL EQUIPMENT Six large cupcake liners set in a Texas size muffin pan or large custard cups (1 cup capacity)

CRUMB TOPPING

	VOLUME	WEIGHT	
walnut halves	½ cup	1.8 ounces	50 grams
light brown Muscovado sugar, or dark brown sugar	2 tablespoons plus 2 teaspoons, firmly packed	1.3 ounces	36 grams
granulated sugar	1 tablespoon	0.5 ounce	13 grams
ground cinnamon	¾ teaspoon	.	1.6 grams
bleached all-purpose flour	¼ cup (lightly spooned into the cup and leveled off)	1 ounce	30 grams
unsalted butter, melted	2 tablespoons	1 ounce	28 grams
pure vanilla extract	½ teaspoon (2.5 ml)	.	.

MAKE THE CRUMB TOPPING In a food processor, pulse the walnuts, brown sugar, granulated sugar, and cinnamon until the walnuts are coarsely chopped. Remove ¼ cup/ 1 ounce/30 grams to use for the filling.

To the remainder, add the flour, butter, and vanilla and pulse briefly to form a coarse, crumbly mixture for the topping. Scrape it into a medium bowl and refrigerate for about 10 minutes to firm up the butter to make it easier to crumble for the topping.

Use your fingers to pinch together the refrigerated crumb topping, breaking up the larger pieces so that about one-third of the mixture is formed into small clumps and the rest is in small particles.

BATTER

	VOLUME	WEIGHT	
1 small tart apple, such as Rhode Island Greening or Granny Smith	.	5.5 ounces	155 grams
lemon juice, freshly squeezed	1 teaspoon (5 ml)	.	5 grams
2 large egg yolks, at room temperature	2 tablespoons plus 1 teaspoon (35 ml)	1.3 ounces	37 grams
sour cream	⅓ cup, *divided*	2.9 ounces	81 grams
pure vanilla extract	¾ teaspoon (3.7 ml)	.	.
bleached cake flour (or bleached all-purpose flour)	1 cup (or ¾ cup plus 2 tablespoons), sifted into the cup and leveled off	3.5 ounces	100 grams
superfine sugar	½ cup	3.5 ounces	100 grams
baking powder	¼ teaspoon	.	1.1 grams
baking soda	¼ teaspoon	.	1.4 grams
fine sea salt	⅛ teaspoon	.	0.7 gram
unsalted butter (65° to 75°F/ 19° to 23°C)	6 tablespoons (¾ stick)	3 ounces	85 grams

PREHEAT THE OVEN Twenty minutes or longer before baking, set an oven rack in the middle of the oven and preheat the oven to 350°F/175°C.

PREPARE THE APPLE SLICES Just before mixing the batter, peel, core, and slice the apple into rings ⅛ inch thick (6 slices/2.7 ounces/77 grams). Do not be concerned if they break in half. Use a fingertip to dab the slices with the lemon juice.

MIX THE LIQUID INGREDIENTS In a medium bowl, whisk the egg yolks, 1½ tablespoons of the sour cream, and the vanilla, just until lightly combined.

MAKE THE BATTER In the bowl of a stand mixer fitted with the flat beater, mix the flour, sugar, baking powder, baking soda, and salt on low speed for 30 seconds. Add the butter and the remaining sour cream and mix on low speed until the dry ingredients are moistened. Raise the speed to medium and beat for 1½ minutes. Scrape down the sides of the bowl.

Starting on medium-low speed, gradually add the egg mixture in two parts, beating on medium speed for 30 seconds after each addition to incorporate the ingredients and strengthen the structure. Scrape down the sides of the bowl.

Highlights for Success

Spoon the batter (2.3 ounces/64 grams) into each of the prepared liners. The liners will be about half full. Sprinkle each with 2 teaspoons of the crumb filling. With a small metal spatula or spoon, fold the crumb filling into the batter with three or four strokes. Set an apple slice on top of each and press it down so that some of the batter rises up a little above the slice. Smear it across the top of the slice. Spoon about 2 tablespoons of the crumb topping evenly over the top of each muffin and use your fingers to press it down gently.

BAKE THE MUFFINS Bake for 25 to 35 minutes, or until a wooden toothpick inserted into the centers comes out clean and the muffins spring back when pressed lightly in the centers. (An instant-read thermometer should read about 208°F/98°C.)

COOL THE MUFFINS Cool the muffins in the pans on a wire rack for 10 minutes. Remove them from the pans and set them on a wire rack. Cool completely.

STORE Room temperature, 3 days; refrigerated, 5 days; frozen, 2 months.

MOLASSES CRUMB CAKELETS

OVEN TEMPERATURE 350°F/175°C

BAKING TIME 8 to 10 minutes

I discovered these incredibly moist and flavorful little cakes when invited to dinner by Elliott's and my close friends the Meneguses at the Hampton Winds restaurant at Northampton Community College in Bethlehem, Pennsylvania. I was thrilled to discover that they contain no eggs, making them the only cakes in my repertoire suitable for vegans (however, they are especially flavorful reheated and spread with a little butter). This recipe is the creation of chef Meghan Singer, who is a teacher in the well respected culinary arts program at the college.

SPECIAL EQUIPMENT Four 12 cup mini muffin pans (1½ inches at the base), coated with baking spray with flour

CRUMB TOPPING AND MOLASSES BATTER

	VOLUME	WEIGHT	
bleached all-purpose flour	2¼ cups (sifted into the cup and leveled off) plus ½ tablespoon	9.2 ounces	260 grams
sugar	1 cup	7 ounces	200 grams
fine sea salt	½ teaspoon	.	3 grams
canola or safflower oil, at room temperature	½ cup (118 ml)	3.8 ounces	108 grams
molasses, preferably Grandma's light	½ cup (118 ml), cup lightly coated with cooking spray	5.7 ounces	161 grams
boiling water	1 cup (237 ml)	8.4 ounces	237 grams
baking soda	½ teaspoon	.	2.7 grams

PREHEAT THE OVEN Twenty minutes or longer before baking, set an oven rack in the middle of the oven and preheat the oven to 350°F/175°C.

MAKE THE CRUMB TOPPING In the bowl of a stand mixer fitted with the flat beater, mix the flour, sugar, salt, and oil on low speed until crumbly, about 15 seconds. Lightly spoon ½ cup/2.8 ounces/80 grams of the mixture into a medium bowl to reserve for the crumb topping. With your fingertips, crumble the mixture into small particles.

MAKE THE BATTER Add the molasses, water, and baking soda to the remaining crumb mixture and mix on low speed for 1 minute. Scrape the batter into a 4 cup glass measure.

Pour or spoon the batter (0.6 ounce/17 grams) into each of the prepared muffin cups. The cups will be about three-quarters full. Sprinkle a few pinches of the reserved crumbs on top of each cakelet.

BAKE THE CAKELETS Bake for 8 to 10 minutes, or until the cakelets spring back when pressed lightly in their centers with a fingertip.

COOL AND UNMOLD THE CAKELETS Let the cakelets cool in the pans on wire racks for 10 minutes. Run a small metal spatula between the sides of the cups and the cakelets, pressing the blade against the cups, and invert the cakelets onto wire racks that have been lightly coated with nonstick cooking spray. To prevent splitting, reinvert the cakelets so that their tops are up. Cool completely.

STORE Airtight: room temperature, 7 days; refrigerated, 14 days; frozen, 2 months.

THE RENÉE FLEMING GOLDEN CHIFFON

SERVES 10 TO 12

OVEN TEMPERATURE 350°F/175°C

BAKING TIME 35 to 40 minutes

This lemony cake soars above all others in my repertoire, making it the soprano of golden lemon cakes. (It is the counterpart to the Chocolate Domingo from *The Cake Bible*, which I call the tenor of chocolate cakes.) It is extraordinarily light, tender, moist, and lemony—in a word: divine. It required seventeen tests between Woody and me to perfect the texture. The breakthrough came with the discovery of beating the whites beyond the stiff peak stage, which gave higher volume, and raising the oven temperature slightly to set the structure more quickly. This cake is dedicated to my favorite soprano of the golden voice: the incomparable Renée Fleming. The special garnish is a stardust trail of powdered golden lemon zest.

SPECIAL EQUIPMENT One 9 by 3 inch springform pan, encircled with 2 cake strips overlapped to cover the entire sides | A flat bottom rose nail (used for cake decorating), 2½ inches long (minimum) | A wire rack, lightly coated with nonstick cooking spray, elevated about 4 inches or higher above the work surface by setting it on top of 3 or 4 cans, coffee mugs, or glasses of equal height

BATTER

	VOLUME	WEIGHT	
4 large eggs, separated, plus about 1 additional white, at room temperature			
yolks	¼ cup plus 2 teaspoons (69 ml)	2.6 ounces	74 grams
whites	½ cup plus 2 tablespoons (148 ml)	5.3 ounces	150 grams
canola or safflower oil, at room temperature	¼ cup (59 ml)	1.9 ounces	54 grams
water	¼ cup plus 2 tablespoons (89 ml)	3.1 ounces	89 grams
lemon zest, finely grated	1 tablespoon, loosely packed	.	6 grams
pure lemon oil, preferably Boyajian	¼ teaspoon (1.2 ml)	.	.
pure vanilla extract	½ teaspoon (2.5 ml)	.	.
unbleached all-purpose flour (see Note, page 88)	1 cup (sifted into a cup and leveled off)	4 ounces	114 grams
superfine sugar	¾ cup, *divided*	5.3 ounces	150 grams
baking powder	1¼ teaspoons	.	5.6 grams
fine sea salt	¼ teaspoon	.	1.5 grams
cream of tartar	½ plus ⅛ teaspoon	.	1.9 grams

PREHEAT THE OVEN Twenty minutes or longer before baking, set an oven rack in the lower third of the oven and preheat the oven to 350°F/175°C (325°F/160°C if using a dark pan).

MIX THE LIQUID INGREDIENTS In a 2 cup or larger glass measure with a spout, combine the egg yolks, oil, water, lemon zest, lemon oil, and vanilla.

MAKE THE BATTER In the bowl of a stand mixer fitted with the whisk beater, mix the flour, all but 1 tablespoon of the sugar, the baking powder, and salt on low speed for 30 seconds. Make a well in the center. Add the egg mixture to the well and beat on low speed until the dry ingredients are moistened, scraping down the sides of the bowl as necessary. Raise the speed to medium-high and beat until very thick, about 1½ minutes.

If you don't have a second mixer bowl, scrape this mixture into a large bowl and thoroughly wash, rinse, and dry the mixer bowl and whisk beater to remove any trace of oil.

BEAT THE EGG WHITES INTO A STIFF MERINGUE In the bowl of a stand mixer fitted with the whisk beater, beat the egg whites and cream of tartar on medium-low speed until foamy. Gradually raise the speed to medium-high and beat until soft peaks form when the beater is raised. Beat in the remaining 1 tablespoon sugar and continue beating until very stiff clumps form when the beater is raised, about 2 minutes.

ADD THE MERINGUE TO THE BATTER Using a large balloon wire whisk, slotted skimmer, or large silicone spatula, gently fold the meringue into the batter in three parts, folding until partially blended between additions and then folding until completely incorporated after the last addition. If using the whisk, you will need to gently shake out the meringue that gathers in the center as you fold.

Using a silicone spatula, scrape the batter into the pan. Run a small offset spatula in circles through the batter to prevent air pockets and smooth the surface. Insert the rose nail, base side down, into the center of the batter so that it sits on the bottom of the pan. (The batter should fill a 3 inch high pan just under half full.)

BAKE THE CAKE Bake for 35 to 40 minutes. The cake will dome above the top of the pan. Avoid opening the oven door before the minimum baking time or the fragile cake could fall. Watch carefully. When the cake lowers slightly, and a wooden skewer inserted between the sides and the center comes out clean, remove the cake from the oven.

COOL AND UNMOLD THE CAKE Let the cake sit for about 1 minute, just until it is no longer higher than the rim of the pan. Immediately invert the cake, still in the pan, onto the prepared wire rack and let it cool for about 1½ hours, or until the outside of the pan is cool to the touch.

Invert the pan again. Run a small metal spatula between the sides of the pan and the cake, pressing it firmly against the pan and moving it in a sideways manner. Remove the cake strips and the sides of the springform and release the bottom of the cake from the bottom of the pan, pressing the spatula against the bottom of the pan. Invert the cake and lift off the pan bottom. Remove the rose nail and reinvert the cake onto a serving plate.

NOTE Unbleached all-purpose flour prevents the cake from deflating significantly.

LEMON CURD WHIPPED CREAM

	VOLUME	WEIGHT	
lemon zest, finely grated	1 teaspoon, loosely packed	.	2 grams
2 large egg yolks	2 tablespoons plus 1 teaspoon (35 ml)	1.3 ounces	37 grams
granulated sugar	¼ cup plus 2 tablespoons	2.8 ounces	79 grams
unsalted butter (65° to 75°F/ 19° to 23°C)	2 tablespoons	1 ounce	28 grams
lemon juice, freshly squeezed and strained (about 1 large lemon)	3 tablespoons (44 ml)	1.7 ounces	47 grams
fine sea salt	a small pinch	.	.
heavy cream, cold	1 cup (237 ml)	8.2 ounces	232 grams

MAKE THE LEMON CURD Have ready a fine-mesh strainer suspended over a medium bowl containing the lemon zest.

In a medium heavy saucepan, whisk the egg yolks, sugar, and butter until well blended. Whisk in the lemon juice and salt. Cook over medium-low heat, stirring constantly with a silicone spatula and scraping down the sides of the pan as needed, until thickened and resembling hollandaise sauce, which thickly coats the spatula but is still liquid enough to pour. The mixture will change from translucent to opaque and begin to take on a yellow color on the spatula. Do not let it come to a boil or it will curdle. Whenever steam appears, remove the pan briefly from the heat, stirring constantly, to keep the mixture from boiling.

When the curd has thickened and will pool thickly when a little is dropped on its surface (an instant-read thermometer should read no higher than 196°F/91°C), pour it at once into the strainer and press it through into the bowl. Stir gently to mix in the zest and let the curd cool for 30 minutes. There will be ½ cup/4.6 ounces/132 grams.

Cover tightly and refrigerate, whisking occasionally to prevent the curd from setting, until cooled to room temperature, 20 to 30 minutes.

MAKE THE LEMON CURD WHIPPED CREAM Into a mixing bowl, pour the cream. Refrigerate for at least 15 minutes. (Chill a handheld mixer's beaters alongside the bowl.)

Starting on low speed and gradually raising the speed to medium-high as it thickens, whip the cream just until beater marks begin to show distinctly. Add the lemon curd and whip just until the mixture mounds softly when dropped from a spoon.

The lemon curd will act as a stabilizer, keeping the cream from watering out. It will keep for 6 hours at room temperature, after which it becomes slightly spongy. It will keep for 48 hours refrigerated.

POWDERED LEMON ZEST

MAKES 2 TEASPOONS/5 GRAMS

	VOLUME	WEIGHT	
lemon zest, finely grated (from 3 to 5 medium lemons)	2 tablespoons, loosely packed	.	12 grams
superfine sugar	1 teaspoon	.	.

SPECIAL EQUIPMENT A mortar and a pestle | Optional: bread proofer (see page 539) or oven with a pilot light or viewing light

MAKE THE POWDERED LEMON ZEST In a small bowl, combine the lemon zest and sugar and rub the sugar into the zest. Spread the sugared zest in a thin layer on a plate. Place the plate in the bread proofer with the temperature set at 110°F/43°C (or in the oven with the light turned on). Let the zest dry to the touch, about 4 hours, scraping the plate every hour to dislodge any zest stuck to the plate. (The zest can be dried at room temperature, which can take 12 to 16 hours.)

Have ready a medium-mesh strainer suspended over a medium bowl.

Place the dried zest in the mortar and grind it as much as possible to a powder. Sift it into the bowl. Grind and sift the zest remaining in the strainer 2 more times. Pour the powdered zest into a small airtight container. Save any larger flakes of zest in a separate container for sprinkling on ice cream or enlivening a savory dish.

The powdered lemon zest keeps in an airtight container for 2 days at room temperature, 5 days refrigerated, or 2 months frozen.

ASSEMBLE AND SERVE THE CAKE Shortly before serving, swirl the cream into the depression on top of the cake or scrape it into a bowl to pass on the side. Dust each plate with a little of the powdered lemon zest.

STORE (Without the whipped cream) airtight: room temperature, 2 weeks; frozen, 6 months.

BANANA SPLIT CHIFFON CAKE

OVEN TEMPERATURE 325°F/160°C

BAKING TIME 50 to 60 minutes

*T*he chocolate and caramel drizzle glazes, topping an intense but ethereal banana chiffon cake, make for a glorious combination. It is sublime served with strawberry ice cream, whipped cream, and chopped toasted walnuts.

SPECIAL EQUIPMENT One uncoated 10 inch (16 cups) two-piece metal tube pan, encircled with 2 cake strips (see Notes, page 95) | A wire rack elevated about 4 inches or higher above the work surface by setting it on top of 3 or 4 cans, coffee mugs, or glasses of equal height OR a long-neck glass bottle (weighted with sugar or marbles to keep it from tipping) OR a large inverted metal funnel that will fit into the opening at the top of the pan

BATTER

	VOLUME	WEIGHT	
2 large very ripe bananas, peeled and lightly mashed	1 cup	8 ounces	226 grams
walnut oil, at room temperature (see Notes, page 95)	¼ cup plus 2 tablespoons (89 ml)	2.9 ounces	81 grams
canola or safflower oil, at room temperature	2 tablespoons (30 ml)	1 ounce	27 grams
lemon juice, freshly squeezed	2 tablespoons (30 ml)	1.1 ounces	32 grams
7 large eggs, separated, plus about 3 additional whites, at room temperature			
yolks	½ cup (118 ml)	4.6 ounces	130 grams
whites	1¼ cups (296 ml)	10.6 ounces	300 grams
pure vanilla extract	1 teaspoon (5 ml)	.	.
bleached cake flour	2¼ cups (sifted into the cup and leveled off)	8 ounces	225 grams
superfine sugar	1¼ cups, *divided*	8.8 ounces	250 grams
baking powder	2 teaspoons	.	9 grams
fine sea salt	½ teaspoon	.	3 grams
cream of tartar	1¼ teaspoons	.	3.9 grams

PREHEAT THE OVEN Twenty minutes or longer before baking, set an oven rack in the lower third of the oven and preheat the oven to 325°F/160°C.

MIX THE BANANAS AND THE LIQUID INGREDIENTS In a food processor, process the bananas, walnut oil, canola oil, and lemon juice until smooth, stopping the processor and scraping down the sides of the bowl as needed. Add the egg yolks and vanilla and process until combined, about 10 seconds.

MAKE THE BATTER In the bowl of a stand mixer fitted with the whisk beater, mix the flour, all but 2 tablespoons of the sugar, the baking powder, and salt on low speed for 30 seconds. Make a well in the center. Add the banana mixture to the well and beat on low speed until the dry ingredients are moistened, scraping down the sides of the bowl as necessary. Raise the speed to medium-high and beat until very thick, about 1½ minutes.

If you don't have a second mixer bowl, scrape this mixture into a large bowl and thoroughly wash, rinse, and dry the mixer bowl and whisk beater to remove any trace of oil.

BEAT THE EGG WHITES INTO A STIFF MERINGUE In the mixer bowl fitted with the whisk beater, beat the egg whites and cream of tartar on medium-low speed until foamy. Gradually raise the speed to medium-high and beat until soft peaks form when the beater is raised. Beat in the remaining 2 tablespoons of sugar and continue beating until stiff peaks form when the beater is raised slowly.

ADD THE MERINGUE TO THE BATTER Using a large balloon wire whisk, slotted skimmer, or large silicone spatula, gently fold the meringue into the batter just until blended. If using the whisk, you will need to shake out the meringue that gathers in the center as you fold.

Scrape the batter into the pan. Run a small spatula in circles through the batter to prevent air pockets. There is no need to smooth the surface. The batter will come to about 1¼ inches from the top of the rim.

BAKE THE CAKE Bake for 50 to 60 minutes, or until a wooden skewer inserted between the tube and the sides comes out clean and the cake springs back when pressed lightly in the center. During baking, the cake will dome above the top of the pan and cracks will form. Avoid opening the oven door before the minimum baking time or the fragile cake could fall.

COOL AND UNMOLD THE CAKE Immediately invert the pan onto the prepared wire rack or invert the center tube opening of the pan onto the neck of the bottle to suspend it well above the countertop. Cool completely in the pan, about 1½ hours.

To loosen the sides of the cake from the pan, use a rigid sharp knife or stiff metal spatula, preferably with a squared off end, scraping firmly against the pan's sides and slowly and carefully circling the pan. In order to ensure that you are scraping against the sides of the pan and removing the crust from the sides, leaving it on the cake, begin by angling the knife or spatula about 20 degrees away from the cake and toward the pan, pushing the cake inward a bit. It is best to use a knife blade that is at least 4 inches long and no wider than 1 inch.

Grasp the center core and lift out the cake. Run a wire cake tester or wooden skewer around the center core. Dislodge the cake from the bottom with a metal spatula or thin sharp knife. Invert the cake onto a flat plate covered with plastic wrap that has been lightly coated with nonstick cooking spray and reinvert it onto a serving plate. Let the cake sit for 1 hour, or until the top is no longer tacky. Then cover it with a cake dome or wrap it airtight.

To cut the cake, for the fluffiest texture, use two forks instead of a knife to tear apart the slices. Insert the forks back to back, pushing them downwards to the bottom of the cake as you pull them apart, thus splitting the cake into slices. Alternatively, use a serrated knife but hold the cake gently without compressing it as you cut.

To plate, pipe or spoon lightly sweetened whipped cream (see page 516) on the side of each slice and pipe or drizzle chocolate glaze and caramel (see page 55) on top.

STORE Airtight: room temperature, 2 days; refrigerated, 5 days; frozen, 2 months.

NOTES Cake strips (see page 537) will result in a less brown crust, but it's fine to omit them.

Walnut oil enhances the banana flavor, but the cake is still delicious using all vegetable oil.

CHOCOLATE DRIZZLE GLAZE

MAKES A FULL ¾ CUP/7.5 OUNCES/212 GRAMS

	VOLUME	WEIGHT	
bittersweet chocolate, 60% to 62% cacao, chopped	.	4 ounces	113 grams
heavy cream, hot	½ cup minus ¾ teaspoon (115 ml)	4 ounces	113 grams

MAKE THE CHOCOLATE DRIZZLE GLAZE In a small microwavable bowl, stirring with a silicone spatula every 15 seconds (or in the top of a double boiler set over hot, not simmering, water, stirring often—do not let the bottom of the container touch the water), heat the chocolate until almost completely melted.

Remove the chocolate from the heat source and stir until fully melted. Pour the cream on top of the chocolate and stir until smooth. The mixture should drop thickly from a spoon. If it is too thin, let it cool for a few minutes. Use it at once to pipe or drizzle over the cake. To pipe, pour the glaze into a disposable pastry bag or a quart-size reclosable freezer bag with a very small semicircle cut from the tip or one corner, and close it securely.

LEMON ICEBOX CAKE

OVEN TEMPERATURE
350°F/175°C

BAKING TIME
30 to 40 minutes

Fine Cooking magazine once asked me to create a recipe for a classic old-time lemon icebox cake. I had already perfected the two components, the angel food cake and the lemon mousse, as separate desserts, so the challenge was to transform them into one spectacular pièce de resistance. The angel food cake is cut into two rings for the top and bottom of the cake. The rest of the cake is cut into cubes and folded into the lemon mousse. The cake rings and filling are then arranged in the tube pan in which the cake was baked and allowed to set before unmolding. This is a perfect cake for Mother's Day or for any special summertime occasion. The lemon angel food cake is also wonderful on its own if you're in the mood for something simpler.

PLAN AHEAD Complete the filled cake 12 hours before serving.

SPECIAL EQUIPMENT One uncoated 10 inch (16 cups) two-piece metal tube pan | A wire rack elevated about 4 inches or higher above the work surface by setting it on top of 3 or 4 cans, coffee mugs, or glasses of equal height OR a long-neck glass bottle (weighted with sugar or marbles to keep it from tipping) OR a large inverted metal funnel that will fit into the opening at the top of the pan

ANGEL FOOD CAKE BATTER

	VOLUME	WEIGHT	
superfine sugar	1½ cups, *divided*	10.6 ounces	300 grams
bleached cake flour	1 cup (sifted into the cup and leveled off)	3.5 ounces	100 grams
fine sea salt	¼ teaspoon	.	1.5 grams
16 large egg whites, at room temperature	2 cups (473 ml)	16.9 ounces	480 grams
cream of tartar	2 teaspoons	.	6.2 grams
lemon juice, freshly squeezed	1 tablespoon (15 ml)	0.6 ounce	16 grams
pure vanilla extract	1 tablespoon plus 1 teaspoon (20 ml)	.	.

PREHEAT THE OVEN Twenty minutes or longer before baking, set an oven rack in the lower third of the oven and preheat the oven to 350°F/175°C.

COMBINE HALF THE SUGAR, THE FLOUR, AND SALT In a small bowl, whisk together ¾ cup/5.3 ounces/150 grams of the sugar, the flour, and salt until evenly combined. Sift the remaining sugar onto a piece of parchment.

BEAT THE EGG WHITES INTO A STIFF MERINGUE In the bowl of a stand mixer fitted with the whisk beater, beat the egg whites and cream of tartar on medium-low speed until foamy. Gradually raise the speed to medium-high and beat until soft peaks form when the beater is raised. Gradually beat in the remaining sugar and continue beating on medium-high speed until very stiff peaks form when the beater is raised slowly. Beat in the lemon juice and vanilla until combined.

MAKE THE BATTER Sift the flour mixture over the meringue, ¼ cup at a time. With a large balloon whisk, slotted skimmer, or large silicone spatula, fold in the flour mixture quickly but gently. It is not necessary to incorporate every speck until the last addition.

Using a long narrow spatula or silicone spatula, spread a thin layer of batter onto the sides of the pan to ensure smooth sides. Gently scoop the rest of the batter, distributing it evenly into the pan. In a 16 cup pan, it will be ½ inch from the top of the rim. Run a small metal spatula or knife through the batter to prevent air pockets and smooth the surface evenly.

BAKE THE CAKE Bake for 30 to 40 minutes, or until golden brown, a wire cake tester inserted between the tube and the side comes out clean, and the cake springs back when pressed lightly in the center. (A wooden skewer will still have a few moist crumbs clinging to it.) During baking, the center will rise about 2 inches above the pan, but will sink almost to level with the pan when done. The surface will have deep cracks like a soufflé.

COOL AND UNMOLD THE CAKE Immediately invert the pan onto the prepared wire rack or invert the center tube opening of the pan onto the neck of the bottle to suspend it well above the countertop. Cool completely in the pan, about 1½ hours.

To loosen the sides of the cake from the pan, use a rigid sharp knife or stiff metal spatula, preferably with a squared off end. Scrape firmly against the pan's sides and slowly and carefully circle the pan. In order to ensure that you are scraping against the sides of the pan and removing the crust from the pan, leaving it on the cake, begin by angling the knife or spatula about 20 degrees away from the cake and toward the pan, pushing the cake inward a bit. It is best to use a knife blade that is at least 4 inches long and no wider than 1 inch.

Grasp the center core and lift out the cake. Run a wire cake tester or wooden skewer around the center core. Dislodge the cake from the bottom with a metal spatula or thin sharp knife. Invert the cake onto a flat plate covered with plastic wrap that has been lightly coated with nonstick cooking spray and then reinvert it onto a serving plate. Let the cake sit for 1 hour, or until the top is no longer tacky. Then cover it with a cake dome or wrap it airtight. Wash and dry the tube pan to use for assembling the cake.

LEMON MOUSSE FILLING

MAKES 10⅔ CUPS/45 OUNCES/1270 GRAMS

LEMON CURD

MAKES 1½ CUPS/14 OUNCES/400 GRAMS (MINUS THE CREAM)

	VOLUME	WEIGHT	
lemon zest, finely grated	1½ tablespoons, loosely packed	.	9 grams
6 (to 8) large eggs, separated, at room temperature			
yolks	¼ cup plus 3 tablespoons (103 ml)	4 ounces	112 grams
whites (to be reserved for the Light Italian Meringue)	¾ cup (177 ml)	6.3 ounces	180 grams
sugar	¼ cup plus 2 tablespoons	2.6 ounces	75 grams
unsalted butter (65° to 75°F/ 19° to 23°C)	6 tablespoons (¾ stick)	3 ounces	85 grams
lemon juice, freshly squeezed and strained (about 3 large lemons)	½ cup plus 1 tablespoon (133 ml)	5 ounces	142 grams
fine sea salt	a pinch	.	.
heavy cream, cold	1½ cups (355 ml)	12.3 ounces	348 grams

MAKE THE LEMON CURD Have ready a fine-mesh strainer suspended over a medium bowl containing the lemon zest.

In a medium heavy saucepan, whisk the egg yolks, sugar, and butter until well blended. Whisk in the lemon juice and salt. Cook over medium-low heat, stirring constantly with a silicone spatula and scraping down the sides of the pan as needed until thickened and resembling hollandaise sauce, which thickly coats the spatula but is still liquid enough to pour. The mixture will change from translucent to opaque and begin to take on a yellow color on the spatula. Do not let it come to a boil or it will curdle. Whenever steam appears, remove the pan briefly from the heat, stirring constantly, to keep the mixture from boiling.

When the curd has thickened and will pool thickly when a little is dropped on its surface (an instant-read thermometer should read no higher than 196°F/91°C), pour it at once into the strainer and press it through into the bowl. Stir gently to mix in the zest and let the curd cool for 30 minutes.

Cover tightly and refrigerate, whisking occasionally to prevent it from setting, until cooled to room temperature, about 1 hour.

WHIP THE CREAM Into a large mixing bowl, pour the cream and refrigerate for at least 15 minutes. (Chill a handheld mixer's beaters alongside the bowl.)

When the lemon curd has cooled, whip the cream, starting on low speed and gradually raising the speed to medium-high as it thickens, until the cream mounds softly when dropped from a spoon. With a whisk or silicone spatula, fold in the lemon curd until completely incorporated. Cover the bowl tightly with plastic wrap and refrigerate.

LIGHT ITALIAN MERINGUE
MAKES 7½ CUPS/17 OUNCES/480 GRAMS

	VOLUME	WEIGHT	
cold water	3 tablespoons (44 ml)	1.6 ounces	44 grams
powdered gelatin	2 teaspoons	.	6 grams
reserved egg whites (from page 99)	¾ cup (177 ml)	6.3 ounces	180 grams
cream of tartar	¾ teaspoon	.	2.3 grams
granulated sugar	1⅓ cups, *divided*	9.4 ounces	267 grams
water	¼ cup plus 2 tablespoons (89 ml)	3.1 ounces	89 grams

MAKE THE ITALIAN MERINGUE Have ready a 2 cup or larger glass measure with a spout.

Into a 1 cup glass measure with a spout, pour the 3 tablespoons/44 ml of cold water and sprinkle the gelatin over the top. Stir to moisten the gelatin and let it sit for a minimum of 5 minutes. If it will sit longer, cover with plastic wrap to prevent evaporation.

Set the cup in a pan of simmering water for a few minutes, stirring occasionally, until the gelatin is dissolved. It will thicken slightly. Remove the pan from the heat. (This can also be done in a microwave, with 3 second bursts, stirring once or twice until dissolved.)

Pour the egg whites into the bowl of a stand mixer fitted with the whisk beater, or into a large bowl and have ready the handheld mixer. Add the cream of tartar.

In a small heavy saucepan, preferably nonstick, stir together 1 cup/7 ounces/200 grams of the sugar and the ¼ cup plus 2 tablespoons/89 ml of water until the sugar is completely moistened. Heat on medium-high, stirring constantly, until the sugar dissolves and the syrup is bubbling. Stop stirring and reduce the heat to low. (If using an electric range, remove the pan from the heat.)

Beat the egg whites and cream of tartar on medium-low speed until foamy. Raise the speed to medium-high and beat until soft peaks form when the beater is raised. Gradually beat in the remaining ⅓ cup of sugar until stiff peaks form when the beater is raised slowly.

Increase the heat under the sugar syrup to medium-high and continue to boil for a few minutes until an instant-read thermometer reads 248° to 250°F/120°C. Immediately transfer the syrup to the glass measure to stop the cooking.

If using a stand mixer, with the mixer off to keep the syrup from spinning onto the sides of the bowl, add the syrup to the egg whites. Begin by pouring in a small amount. Immediately beat on high speed for 5 seconds. Add the remaining syrup the same way in three parts. For the last addition, use a silicone spatula to remove the syrup clinging to the glass measure and scrape it against the beater. If the syrup has hardened before most of it has been poured, soften it to pouring consistency for a few seconds in the microwave.

If using a handheld mixer, beat the syrup into the egg whites on high speed in a steady stream. Do not let the syrup fall on the beaters or they will spin it onto the sides of the bowl.

Lower the speed to medium, add the gelatin mixture, and beat for 2 minutes. Decrease the speed to low and continue beating until no longer warm to the touch, about 10 minutes, longer if using a handheld mixer.

COMPLETE THE LEMON MOUSSE FILLING Use a large balloon whisk or silicone spatula to fold the Italian meringue into the lemon cream mixture in three parts.

PREPARE THE CAKE Place two 3 foot long sheets of parchment on a flat surface. Slice off the crusty top of the cake to make a semiflat surface. Measure down ¾ inch and score the cake with a serrated knife. Using the scored line as a guide, cut through the cake. With two spatulas, lift the cut cake ring off the cake and place it on the parchment.

Invert the cake. Measure down ½ inch and score the cake with a serrated knife. Using the scored line as a guide, cut through the cake. With two spatulas, lift the cut cake ring off the cake and place it on the parchment.

Cut the remaining cake into ¾ inch cubes or tear it into roughly ¾ inch pieces and place them on the second piece of parchment.

Cover the two rings and cubed or torn pieces with plastic wrap. Leave the cubed or torn pieces uncovered if the cake is very moist.

ASSEMBLE THE CAKE Lightly coat the sides and bottom of the tube pan with nonstick cooking spray. Place the smaller cake layer into the pan. Spoon a little less than one-third/14.1 ounces/400 grams of the lemon filling on top. Strew half of the cubed cake pieces evenly over the filling, making sure some of the pieces are up against the sides of the pan. Spoon on a little less than half/14.8 ounces/420 grams of the remaining lemon filling over the cubes. Strew the remaining cake cubes over the filling. Spoon on the remaining lemon filling and smooth with an offset spatula. Top with the remaining larger cake layer, trimmed side up, and lightly press it down. Cover tightly with plastic wrap and refrigerate for at least 12 hours before unmolding.

Highlights for Success

UNMOLD THE CAKE Chill the serving plate. Lightly moisten the plate with water to make it easy to reposition and center the cake.

Run a wire cake tester or wooden skewer around the center core. Heat a dish towel by running it under very hot water and wringing out the excess. Wipe the sides and bottom of the cake pan with the hot towel to help release the cake.

Set the cake pan on top of a canister with a diameter smaller than the removable portion of the pan's bottom and taller than the pan's sides, and gently press down on the sides of the pan. If the sides do not slide down easily, apply more heat.

Run a long metal spatula between the bottom of the cake and the pan. Set the serving plate on top and invert the cake onto it.

Serve with raspberry sauce (see page 38) or lightly sweetened whipped cream (see page 516), if desired.

STORE Airtight: refrigerated, 5 days.

Light Sponge Cake (Biscuit)

OVEN TEMPERATURE 450°F/230°C

BAKING TIME 7 to 10 minutes

$\mathcal{T}$his versatile cake, which is used in varying ways for several recipes throughout the book, takes about 10 minutes to mix and 10 minutes or less to bake. It is a slender, airy, yet velvety cake layer containing no fat other than that from the egg yolks, making it sturdy enough to absorb moisture from other components without falling apart. The following recipe gives instructions for baking the cake in a half sheet pan. The cake can also be made in two 10 inch round cake or 9½ inch round tart pans, which are ideal for making two round cake bases. One base can be used for the recipe, while the other can be frozen for future use. Individual recipes will specify modifications to this recipe.

THIS RECIPE IS A COMPONENT OF:
Prune Preserves and Caramel Cream Cake Roll (page 105)
Heavenly Chocolate Mousse Cake (page 131)
Mango Bango Cheesecake (page 148)

SPECIAL EQUIPMENT One 17¼ by 12¼ by 1 inch half sheet pan, bottom coated with shortening, then lined with parchment (cut the parchment to extend 1 inch past one of the long sides of the pan) coated with baking spray with flour | One large uncoated wire rack | One baking sheet or extra half sheet pan (inverted), lightly coated with nonstick cooking spray

Batter

	VOLUME	WEIGHT	
bleached cake flour (or bleached all-purpose flour)	⅓ cup (or ¼ cup plus 2 teaspoons), sifted into the cup and leveled off	1.2 ounces	33 grams
cornstarch	2½ tablespoons	.	22 grams
5 (to 8) large eggs, separated, at room temperature			
yolks	¼ cup plus 2 tablespoons (89 ml)	3.3 ounces	93 grams
whites (about 4)	½ cup (118 ml), *divided*	4.2 ounces	120 grams
superfine sugar	½ cup plus 1 tablespoon, *divided*	4 ounces	113 grams
pure vanilla extract	¾ teaspoon (3.7 ml)	.	.
cream of tartar	¼ teaspoon	.	0.8 gram

PREHEAT THE OVEN Thirty minutes or longer before baking, set an oven rack in the middle of the oven and preheat the oven to 450°F/230°C.

MIX THE DRY INGREDIENTS In a small bowl, whisk together the flour and cornstarch until well combined.

MIX THE EGG MIXTURE In the bowl of a stand mixer fitted with the whisk beater, place the egg yolks, half of the egg whites (¼ cup/59 ml/2.1 ounces/60 grams), and ½ cup/3.5 ounces/100 grams of the sugar. Beat on high speed until thick, fluffy, and tripled in volume, about 5 minutes. Lower the speed and beat in the vanilla. If you don't have a second mixer bowl, scrape this mixture into a large bowl and thoroughly wash, rinse, and dry the mixer bowl and whisk beater to remove any trace of oil.

MAKE THE BATTER Sift half of the flour mixture over the egg mixture and, using a large balloon whisk, slotted skimmer, or silicone spatula, fold it in gently but rapidly until almost all of the flour has disappeared. Repeat with the remaining flour mixture until all traces of the flour have disappeared.

BEAT THE EGG WHITES INTO A STIFF MERINGUE In the bowl of a stand mixer fitted with the whisk beater, beat the remaining egg whites and the cream of tartar on medium-low speed until foamy. Gradually raise the speed to medium-high and beat until soft peaks form when the beater is raised. Gradually beat in the remaining 1 tablespoon of sugar and continue beating until stiff peaks form when the beater is raised slowly.

ADD THE MERINGUE TO THE BATTER Using a large balloon whisk, slotted skimmer, or large silicone spatula, gently fold the meringue into the batter. Scrape the batter into the prepared pan and, using an offset spatula, smooth it as evenly as possible.

BAKE THE CAKE Bake for 7 to 10 minutes, or until golden brown and the cake springs back when pressed lightly in the center. Have ready a small sharp knife.

UNMOLD AND COOL THE CAKE If necessary, loosen the sides with the tip of the sharp knife. Unmold the cake at once. Slip a small offset spatula under the narrow edge of the parchment to loosen it. Grasp the parchment and gently slide the cake onto the large uncoated wire rack. Let the cake cool completely, about 20 minutes. Invert the cake onto the baking sheet or inverted half sheet pan and peel off the parchment.

STORE Airtight: in a single layer, room temperature, 3 days; refrigerated, 5 days; frozen, 2 months. Once frozen, multiple layers (if baking in two round cake or tart pans) can be stacked and placed in freezer bags.

Variation: LIGHT ALMOND SPONGE CAKE

THIS RECIPE IS A COMPONENT OF: Lemon Almond Cheesecake (page 160)

Reduce the flour to 3 tablespoons/0.7 ounce/21 grams. Replace the cornstarch with ⅓ cup/1.2 ounces/33 grams blanched sliced almonds, toasted and ground.

TOAST AND GRIND THE ALMONDS Spread the almonds evenly on a baking sheet and bake for about 4 minutes, or until pale gold. Stir once or twice to ensure even toasting and avoid overbrowning. Cool completely. In a small food processor, process until fairly fine.

PRUNE PRESERVES AND CARAMEL CREAM CAKE ROLL

OVEN TEMPERATURE
450°F/230°C

BAKING TIME
7 to 10 minutes

I adore this exquisitely light cake roll, filmed with a layer of prune lekvar and filled with caramel whipped cream. The flavor combination of dusky, velvety prune and the deeply caramelized sugar in the whipped cream is astonishingly good. A tiny bit of the caramel is added to the dark chocolate piping ganache to give the ganache extra shine. Don't make me change the name to Dried Plum Preserves to get you to give this recipe a try!

SPECIAL EQUIPMENT FOR THE CAKE: See Light Sponge Cake (Biscuit), page 103

FOR THE GANACHE PIPING GLAZE: A disposable pastry bag fitted with a ⅛ inch round decorating tip (number 4)

LIGHT SPONGE CAKE (BISCUIT)

	VOLUME	WEIGHT	
Light Sponge Cake (Biscuit), page 103	.	.	.

MAKE THE CAKE Make the light sponge cake (biscuit).

UNMOLD AND COOL THE CAKE ROLL Run the tip of a sharp knife around the sides to dislodge any cake that may have attached itself to the sides of the pan and unmold the cake at once.

Grasp the parchment and gently slide the cake from the pan onto a flat work surface. Invert the pan. Cover the back of the pan with plastic wrap. Dust the surface of the cake lightly with powdered sugar and invert it onto the back of the pan. Carefully remove the parchment. Set a clean dish towel on top of the cake and set a large baking sheet or wire rack on top. Reinvert the cake and, while it is still hot, roll it and the towel up from the short end.

Set the roll on a wire rack and cool until it is no longer warm to the touch, about 40 minutes.

Prune Lekvar

MAKES ½ CUP/5.5 OUNCES/156 GRAMS

	VOLUME	WEIGHT	
pitted prunes	1 cup, tightly packed	4 ounces	113 grams
water	½ cup (118 ml)	4.2 ounces	118 grams
granulated sugar	1 tablespoon	0.5 ounce	13 grams
lemon zest, finely grated	½ teaspoon, loosely packed	.	.

MAKE THE PRUNE LEKVAR In a medium saucepan with a tight-fitting lid, combine the prunes and water and let them sit for 2 hours to soften. (If the prunes are cut in half, it will take only 1 hour.) Bring the water to a boil, cover the pan tightly, and simmer for 20 to 30 minutes on the lowest possible heat until the prunes are very soft when pierced with a skewer. If the water evaporates, add a little extra.

In a food processor, place the prunes and any remaining liquid, the sugar, and lemon zest and process until smooth.

Scrape the prune mixture back into the saucepan and simmer, stirring constantly with a wooden spatula or spoon to prevent scorching, for 10 to 15 minutes, or until it is a deep rich brown and very thick. A tablespoon of the mixture when lifted should take about 3 seconds to fall from the spoon. Transfer the lekvar to a small bowl and let it cool completely.

Syrup

MAKES ⅓ CUP/79 ML/3.5 OUNCES/100 GRAMS

	VOLUME	WEIGHT	
granulated sugar	2 tablespoons plus a pinch	1 ounce	28 grams
water	¼ cup (59 ml)	2.1 ounces	59 grams
vanilla cognac (or pure vanilla extract)	1 tablespoon (15 ml) (or 1 teaspoon)	0.5 ounce	14 grams

MAKE THE SYRUP In a small saucepan with a tight-fitting lid, bring the sugar and water to a rolling boil, stirring constantly. Cover immediately, remove it from the heat, and cool completely. Transfer the syrup to a glass measure with a spout and stir in the cognac. If the syrup has evaporated slightly, add enough water to equal ⅓ cup/79 ml of syrup.

Caramel Whipped Cream
Caramel

MAKES ¾ CUP/177 ML/8 OUNCES/227 GRAMS (SEE NOTE)

	VOLUME	WEIGHT	
granulated sugar	¾ cup	5.3 ounces	150 grams
golden syrup or corn syrup	2 teaspoons (10 ml)	0.5 ounce	14 grams
water	3 tablespoons (44 ml)	1.6 ounces	44 grams
heavy cream, hot	¼ cup plus 2 tablespoons (89 ml)	3.1 ounces	87 grams
unsalted butter, softened	1½ tablespoons	0.7 ounce	21 grams
pure vanilla extract	½ tablespoon (7.5 ml)	.	.

MAKE THE CARAMEL Have ready a 1 cup glass measure with a spout, lightly coated with nonstick cooking spray.

In a medium heavy saucepan, preferably nonstick, stir together the sugar, golden syrup, and water until all the sugar is moistened. Heat, stirring constantly, until the sugar dissolves and the syrup is bubbling. Stop stirring completely and let it boil undisturbed until it turns a dark amber (370°F/188°C on an instant-read thermometer if using golden syrup, or 380°F/193°C if using corn syrup). Remove it immediately from the heat because the temperature will continue to rise, or remove it slightly before it reaches temperature and, just as soon as it does, slowly pour in the hot cream. It will bubble up furiously.

Use a silicone spatula or wooden spoon to stir the mixture gently, scraping the thicker part that settles on the bottom. Return it to very low heat, continuing to stir gently for 1 minute, until the mixture is uniform in color and the caramel is fully dissolved.

Remove it from the heat and gently stir in the butter until incorporated. The mixture will be a little streaky, but will become uniform once cooled and stirred.

Pour the caramel into the prepared glass measure and let it cool for 3 minutes. Gently stir in the vanilla. Refrigerate for about 45 minutes, gently stirring every 15 minutes until completely cool. (An instant-read thermometer should read 65° to 70°F/18° to 21°C.) Cover and let it sit at room temperature.

NOTE There will be extra caramel to ensure that there is enough for the piping glaze.

Completed Caramel Whipped Cream

MAKES 2⅓ CUPS/13.2 OUNCES/375 GRAMS

	VOLUME	WEIGHT	
heavy cream, cold	1 cup (237 ml)	8.2 ounces	232 grams
Caramel	½ cup (118 ml)	5.3 ounces	150 grams

COMPLETE THE CARAMEL WHIPPED CREAM Into the bowl of a stand mixer, pour the cream and refrigerate for at least 15 minutes. (Chill the whisk beater alongside the bowl.)

In the chilled bowl, whip the cream until very soft peaks form when the beater is raised. On low speed, continue beating while adding the room temperature caramel sauce. Raise the speed to medium and whip just until soft peaks form when the beater is raised.

COMPOSE THE CAKE ROLL Gently unroll the cake. Brush the syrup evenly over the surface. Using a small offset spatula, spread the lekvar in a thin, even layer to cover the cake completely.

Spread the caramel whipped cream evenly on the cake up to 2 inches from the top short edge and about ¼ inch from each long edge. Starting at the bottom short edge, roll the cake. It helps to support the cake with an 18 inch long ruler behind the towel to get it started. To make an even roll, cup your hands over the cake and press gently along the roll after each turn. When the cake is rolled completely, roll it, seam side down, onto a serving plate or cutting board. The seam needs to be on the underside of the cake, so, if necessary, roll it first onto a piece of parchment and then use the parchment to flip it over, seam side down. Set it aside at cool room temperature or refrigerate, lightly covered.

Caramel Ganache Piping Glaze

	VOLUME	WEIGHT	
dark chocolate, 85% cacao, chopped	.	1 ounce	28 grams
heavy cream	2 tablespoons (30 ml)	1 ounce	29 grams
Caramel	1 tablespoon	0.6 ounce	18 grams

MAKE THE PIPING GLAZE Have ready a fine-mesh strainer suspended over a 1 cup glass measure with a spout.

In a small food processor, or by hand, process or chop the chocolate until very fine. Transfer it to a small heatproof glass bowl.

In a small saucepan, combine the cream and caramel. Stirring constantly with a silicone spatula, over medium heat, scald the caramel cream (heat it to the boiling point: small bubbles will form around the periphery) and then pour it over the chocolate. Cover the bowl for 5 minutes to let the chocolate melt. Using a silicone spatula, gently stir together the chocolate and the caramel cream until smooth.

Press the mixture through the strainer and use at once to pipe.

PIPE THE GLAZE Scrape the glaze into the pastry bag. Alternatively, you can use a pint- or quart-size reclosable freezer bag with a very small semicircle cut from one corner. Pipe zigzags or swirls to decorate the top of the cake. If the glaze stops flowing while piping, gently squeeze the bag over the measuring cup until the glaze flows again at the proper consistency.

STORE Cool room temperature, 6 hours; refrigerated, lightly covered, 2 days. Do not freeze, because the whipped cream will deflate on thawing.

LEMON POSSET SHORTCAKES

SERVES 6

OVEN TEMPERATURE
350°F/175°C

BAKING TIME
15 to 22 minutes

$\mathscr{T}$he recipe and word "posset" date from medieval times and refer to the small pot in which the dessert was presented. This recipe was inspired by a trip to Minneapolis, where Woody and I had an exquisite version created by pastry chef Ann Bridges at Restaurant Alma. The lemon posset, which was prepared with Meyer lemon juice and presented in ramekins, had the purest, cleanest flavor I've ever experienced. It is a soft lemon cream that, unlike lemon curd, contains neither butter nor eggs; nor unlike panna cotta, gelatin. It relies entirely on the acidity of the lemons to set the cream. The pairing of the lemon posset with my favorite individual sponge cakes makes this the most ethereal of cakes, but I always make extra lemon posset without the cake as a special treat to be eaten by the spoonful during the day.

PLAN AHEAD The lemon posset can be made after the cakes have been brushed with syrup.

SPECIAL EQUIPMENT One Marianne or shortcake pan with 6 cavities, or six 10 ounce (4 by 2 inches) Pyrex dessert dishes, coated with baking spray with flour (if using the dessert dishes, set them on a baking sheet) | A quarter sheet pan or baking sheet lined with plastic wrap

BATTER

	VOLUME	WEIGHT	
unsalted butter	5 tablespoons (½ stick plus 1 tablespoon)	2.5 ounces	71 grams
pure vanilla extract	¾ teaspoon (3.7 ml)	.	.
2 large eggs	⅓ cup plus 1 tablespoon (94 ml)	3.5 ounces	100 grams
1 large egg yolk	1 tablespoon plus ½ teaspoon (17 ml)	0.7 ounce	19 grams
superfine sugar	⅓ cup	2.3 ounces	67 grams
Wondra flour (see Note, page 114)	½ cup (lightly spooned into the cup and leveled off) minus ½ tablespoon	2.3 ounces	66 grams

PREHEAT THE OVEN Twenty minutes or longer before baking, set an oven rack in the middle of the oven and preheat the oven to 350°F/175°C.

CLARIFY AND BROWN THE BUTTER (BEURRE NOISETTE) Have ready a fine-mesh or cheesecloth-lined strainer suspended over a 1 cup glass measure with a spout.

In a small heavy saucepan over very low heat, melt the butter. Raise the heat to low and cook, uncovered, watching carefully to prevent burning. Move away any foam on the surface to check the progress. As soon as the milk solids become a deep brown, immediately pour the butter through the strainer, scraping the solids into the strainer.

Measure or weigh 3½ tablespoons/52 ml/1.5 ounces/43 grams of the browned butter. Let it cool slightly to 110° to 120°F/40° to 50°C. Stir in the vanilla, cover, and keep warm. Refrigerate or freeze the milk solids for a future use (see page 514).

BEAT THE EGGS AND SUGAR In the bowl of a stand mixer, using a long-handled wire whisk, lightly combine the eggs, egg yolk, and sugar. Set the bowl over a pan of simmering water (do not let the bottom of the bowl touch the water) and heat just until lukewarm to the touch, stirring constantly with the whisk to prevent curdling.

Set the bowl on the stand mixer and attach the whisk beater. Beat the mixture on high speed for a minimum of 5 minutes. The mixture will more than quadruple in volume and be very thick and airy. (A handheld mixer will take at least 10 minutes.)

MAKE THE BATTER Remove almost ½ cup/1 ounce/26 grams of the beaten egg foam and whisk it thoroughly into the melted butter.

Dust about half of the flour (sift it if substituting the flour mixture described in the Note, page 114) over the remaining egg mixture and fold it in gently but rapidly with a large balloon whisk, slotted skimmer, or silicone spatula until almost all the flour has disappeared. Repeat with the remaining flour until all traces of flour have disappeared.

Fold in the butter mixture just until incorporated. With a silicone spatula, reach to the bottom of the pan to be sure to moisten all the flour.

FILL THE PANS Using a tablespoon, spoon the batter into the prepared Marianne cavities, filling each three-quarters full (1.5 ounces/43 grams). If using the Pyrex dishes, they will be one-third full.

BAKE THE CAKES Bake for 15 to 20 minutes, or until golden brown and the cakes start to shrink slightly from the sides of the pan cavities. In the Pyrex dessert dishes, the cakes will puff slightly, but will not pull away from the sides. They will rise in the center to a little above the sides of the pans and then sink slightly when baked fully. Avoid opening the oven door before the minimum baking time because the fragile cakes could fall. Test toward the end of baking by opening the door a crack and if the cakes do not appear done, continue baking for another 2 minutes.

HIGHLIGHTS FOR SUCCESS

Evenly spoon the batter into the cavities by spooning tablespoons from both the bottom and the top of the batter.

COOL AND UNMOLD THE CAKES To prevent the collapse of their delicate foam structure while still hot, the cakes must be unmolded as soon as they are baked. Have ready a small metal spatula and a wire rack lightly coated with nonstick cooking spray. Immediately loosen the sides of the cakes with the small metal spatula. Place the wire rack on top of the pan and invert it. The Pyrex dishes need to be inverted individually. Cool completely.

NOTE Wondra flour is easiest to integrate into the batter and results in the most tender texture. Instead of Wondra flour, you can sift together a combination of flour and cornstarch: ⅓ cup/1.2 ounces/33 grams bleached cake flour (sifted into the cup and leveled off) and ¼ cup (lightly spooned into the cup and leveled off) plus 1 teaspoon/1.2 ounces/33 grams cornstarch.

(You can substitute ¼ cup plus 2 teaspoons bleached all-purpose flour, sifted into the cup and leveled off, for the cake flour.)

LEMON SYRUP

MAKES ¼ CUP PLUS 2 TABLESPOONS/89ML/3.4 OUNCES/96 GRAMS

	VOLUME	WEIGHT	
water	⅓ cup (79 ml)	2.8 ounces	79 grams
granulated sugar	2 tablespoons	0.9 ounce	25 grams
lemon juice, freshly squeezed	1 teaspoon (5 ml)	.	5 grams

MAKE THE SYRUP In a small saucepan with a tight-fitting lid, stir together the water and sugar until all of the sugar is moistened. Bring the mixture to a rolling boil, stirring constantly. Cover it at once and remove it from the heat. Cool completely. Transfer the syrup to a glass measure with a spout and stir in the lemon juice. If the syrup has evaporated slightly, add water to equal ¼ cup plus 2 tablespoons/89 ml.

APPLY THE SYRUP When the cakes are cool, place them on the prepared sheet pan. Brush the cakes all over with the syrup, especially on the sides and on top of the sides around the indentation. There will be 1 tablespoon/15 ml of syrup for each little cake.

If the cakes were baked in custard cups, leave them inverted and use a small sharp knife to cut a ¼ to ⅜ inch deep circle out of the center of the cake, leaving a ¼ inch wide rim around the outer edge. Brush with syrup as above.

Allow the syrup 3 hours to distribute into the cakes before applying the apple glaze.

APPLE GLAZE

MAKES ¼ CUP/2.4 OUNCES/69 GRAMS

	VOLUME	WEIGHT	
apple jelly	¼ cup	3 ounces	85 grams
water	1 or 2 teaspoons	.	.

MAKE THE APPLE GLAZE Have ready a fine-mesh strainer suspended over a small bowl.

In a small saucepan over medium-low heat (or in a microwavable glass measure with a spout), heat the apple jelly until bubbling. Pass it through the strainer and add enough of the water to achieve a thick consistency that is just barely pourable.

APPLY THE GLAZE With a small, clean artist's paintbrush or pastry brush, brush the glaze onto the cakes, covering the sides and top border well to keep them from drying. Let the glaze set for 30 minutes before filling the cakes.

LEMON POSSET

MAKES ABOUT 1 CUP/237 ML/10 OUNCES/283 GRAMS

	VOLUME	WEIGHT	
heavy cream	¾ cup plus 2 tablespoons (207 ml)	7.2 ounces	203 grams
granulated sugar	¼ cup	1.8 ounces	50 grams
Meyer lemon juice, freshly squeezed and strained (about 1½ lemons), see Notes, page 116	2 tablespoons plus 2 teaspoons (39 ml)	1.5 ounces	43 grams

MAKE THE POSSET Have ready a fine-mesh strainer suspended over a 2 cup glass measure with a spout and a second 2 cup glass measure with a spout alongside (or use one glass or porcelain container with a 5 to 6 inch flat base).

In a 1 cup microwavable measure with a spout (or in a small saucepan [see Notes, page 116] over medium heat), scald the cream (heat it to the boiling point; small bubbles will form around the periphery). Remove it from the heat and keep it warm.

In a small saucepan, with a silicone spatula, stir together the sugar and lemon juice until all of the sugar is moistened. Heat over medium heat, stirring constantly, until near the boiling point.

Remove the pan from the heat. Stir in the heated cream until the mixture is uniform in consistency. Pour it at once into the strainer and press it through into the glass measure. Pour half of the posset mixture into the second 2 cup glass measure (or all of the mixture into the glass container). The depth of the lemon posset should be no more than ¾ inch, which is necessary for the posset to firm up to the right consistency.

Refrigerate, uncovered, for 3 to 4 hours before filling the shortcakes. The posset will have a smooth sheen across its surface and form a custardlike layer to about halfway down from its surface. Do not stir the custard because it will not thicken properly and the thicker top layer is needed to seal the cake and keep most of the creamier posset from soaking into it.

COMPOSE THE SHORTCAKES Using a tablespoon, spoon equal amounts of the posset's custardlike top layer into each cake's depression. Refrigerate the partially filled shortcakes for 1 hour and then spoon the remaining creamier posset to fill each shortcake nearly to the top. Avoid spooning any watery posset at the bottom of the measuring cups. If necessary, smooth the surfaces with the spoon. If properly set, the layer of posset in the cakes should be about ½ inch thick.

Refrigerate the shortcakes, uncovered, for at least 2 hours to set. When set, the lemon posset will have a smooth sheen. If not serving at once, set the shortcakes in an airtight container and refrigerate.

To serve, let the shortcakes sit for 10 minutes at room temperature. The tops of the possets and the plates can be sprinkled with powdered lemon zest (see page 91). If desired, garnish with curled strips of lemon zest.

STORE Airtight: room temperature, 1 hour; refrigerated, 2 days. Do not freeze, because the texture will become less smooth.

NOTES If using standard variety lemon juice, increase the sugar to ¼ cup plus 2 teaspoons/2 ounces/58 grams. (Alternatively, use half lemon juice and half orange juice.)

Avoid using copper or Teflon-lined pans for heating the cream and lemon syrup, or plastic measuring cups or containers for refrigerating the posset, because they will taint the flavor or prevent the posset from setting properly.

Variation: LEMON POSSET ALMA

If serving the lemon posset without the cake, prepare a double recipe to make five ½ cup servings. After combining the cream and the lemon syrup and straining it into the 2 cup glass measure, pour equal amounts into five small ramekins or Pyrex custard cups. Refrigerate, uncovered, for 4 hours. Once the mixture is set, cover each ramekin tightly with plastic wrap. Let the possets sit for 10 minutes at room temperature before serving.

Strawberry Shortcake Génoise

OVEN TEMPERATURE
350°F/175°C

BAKING TIME
15 to 30 minutes

*S*trawberry shortcake is one of America's favorite desserts. In my version, strawberry is added to every component. The rhubarb compote, however, is a fabulously synergistic accompaniment. The Nordic Ware Fancy Marianne woven basket weave pan provides a spectacular presentation and can be used with any fruit you desire.

PLAN AHEAD Defrost the frozen strawberries and extract their syrup at least 8 hours before making the cake. As with all cakes with syrup, you should make the cake a day before you plan to serve it. Serve at room temperature or lightly chilled.

SPECIAL EQUIPMENT One 10 cup Marianne fluted tart pan with a recess, well coated with baking spray with flour, or one 9 by 2½ inch or higher springform pan, bottom coated with shortening, topped with a parchment round, then coated with baking spray with flour (see Notes, page 120)

Frozen Strawberries for the Strawberry Syrup and Puree

MAKES ABOUT ⅔ CUP/148 ML/5 OUNCES/142 GRAMS OF STRAWBERRY SYRUP

	VOLUME		WEIGHT	
frozen strawberries with no sugar added	.		10 ounces	287 grams
granulated sugar	2 tablespoons		0.9 ounce	25 grams
lemon juice, freshly squeezed	1 teaspoon (5 ml)		.	5 grams

MACERATE THE FROZEN STRAWBERRIES In a medium bowl, place the frozen strawberries and sprinkle them with the sugar and lemon juice. Holding on to either side of the bowl, toss gently to coat the berries. Let them sit until the sugar dissolves.

Place the strawberries and sugar syrup in a strainer suspended over a bowl. Cover with plastic wrap and let the syrup drain into the bowl for about 8 hours. Alternatively, refrigerate for about 12 hours. Gently press on the strawberries to extract more syrup until you have about ⅔ cup/148 ml/5 ounces/142 grams.

Place the strawberries, which will measure about ¾ cup, in a small bowl, cover, and refrigerate until ready to compose the cake and make the puree. Transfer the strawberry syrup to an airtight container or a small saucepan. Cover and refrigerate until ready to make the Strawberry Grand Marnier Syrup.

BATTER

	VOLUME	WEIGHT	
unsalted butter	6 tablespoons (¾ stick)	3 ounces	85 grams
pure vanilla extract	1 teaspoon (5 ml)	.	.
5 large eggs	1 cup (237 ml)	8.8 ounces	250 grams
1 large egg yolk	1 tablespoon plus ½ teaspoon (17 ml)	0.7 ounce	19 grams
superfine sugar	½ cup plus 2 tablespoons	4.4 ounces	125 grams
bleached cake flour	⅔ cup, sifted into the cup and leveled off	2.3 ounces	66 grams
cornstarch, preferably Rumford (see Notes, page 120)	½ cup	2 ounces	60 grams

PREHEAT THE OVEN Twenty minutes or longer before baking, set an oven rack in the lower third of the oven and preheat the oven to 350°F/175°C.

CLARIFY AND BROWN THE BUTTER (BEURRE NOISETTE) Have ready a fine-mesh or cheesecloth-lined strainer suspended over a 1 cup glass measure with a spout.

In a small heavy saucepan over very low heat, melt the butter. Raise the heat to low and cook, uncovered, watching carefully to prevent burning. Move away any foam on the surface to check the progress. As soon as the milk solids become a deep brown, immediately pour the butter through the strainer, scraping the solids into the strainer.

Measure or weigh ¼ cup/59 ml/1.8 ounces/50 grams of the browned butter. Let it cool slightly to 110° to 120°F/40° to 50°C. Stir in the vanilla, cover, and keep warm. Refrigerate or freeze the milk solids for a future use (see page 514).

BEAT THE EGGS AND SUGAR In the bowl of a stand mixer, using a long-handled wire whisk, lightly combine the eggs, egg yolk, and sugar. Set the bowl over a pan of simmering water and heat just until lukewarm to the touch, stirring constantly with the whisk to prevent curdling.

Set the bowl on the stand mixer and attach the whisk beater. Beat the mixture on high speed for a minimum of 5 minutes. The mixture will more than quadruple in volume and be very thick and airy. (A handheld mixer will take at least 10 minutes.)

MIX THE FLOUR AND CORNSTARCH While the eggs are beating, sift together the flour and cornstarch.

MAKE THE BATTER Remove 1 cup/2.1 ounces/60 grams of the egg foam and whisk it thoroughly into the melted butter.

Sift about half of the flour mixture over the remaining egg mixture and, with a large balloon whisk, slotted skimmer, or silicone spatula, fold it in gently but rapidly until almost all of the flour has disappeared. Repeat with the remaining flour mixture until all traces of flour have disappeared.

Fold in the butter mixture just until incorporated. With a silicone spatula, reach to the bottom of the pan to be sure to moisten all of the flour.

Scrape the batter into the prepared pan and smooth the surface evenly with a small metal spatula. If you have beaten it long enough, the batter will fill the pan about half full.

BAKE THE CAKE Bake for 15 to 25 minutes, or until a deep golden brown and the cake springs back when pressed lightly in the center. It will lower slightly and pull away slightly from the sides. Avoid opening the oven door before the minimum time or the fragile cake could fall. Test toward the end of baking by opening the oven door a crack, and if the cake does not appear done, continue baking for another 5 minutes.

To prevent the collapse of its delicate foam structure while still hot, the cake must be unmolded as soon as it is baked. Have ready a small metal spatula and two wire racks that have been lightly coated with nonstick cooking spray. If using the Marianne pan, also have a 10 inch parchment round.

UNMOLD AND COOL THE CAKE If using the Marianne pan, immediately loosen the top edges of the cake with the small metal spatula. Place the parchment round and then the prepared wire rack on top of the cake and invert the cake. Remove the pan and cool completely.

If using the springform pan, run the small metal spatula between the sides of the pan and the cake, pressing firmly against the pan. Remove the sides of the pan and invert the cake onto one of the prepared wire racks. Remove the bottom of the pan. Leaving the parchment in place, immediately reinvert the cake onto the second prepared wire rack so that the firm upper crust keeps it from sinking. Cool completely.

NOTES If your pan is slightly smaller, the cake will rise a little above the pan during baking, but this is not a problem.

I prefer Rumford cornstarch for this recipe. Other brands may result in a coarser texture. The cornstarch can be replaced by using all cake flour (increase the cake flour to 1¼ cups/4.4 ounces/126 grams), but the cake will not be quite as high or as soft and fine in texture.

STRAWBERRY GRAND MARNIER SYRUP

MAKES 1 CUP/237 ML/9.6 OUNCES/272 GRAMS

	VOLUME	WEIGHT	
Strawberry Syrup (page 117)	about ⅔ cup (148 ml)	5.4 ounces	142 grams
granulated sugar	⅓ cup	2.3 ounces	67 grams
Grand Marnier (see Notes)	¼ cup (59 ml)	2.2 ounces	61 grams

MAKE THE GRAND MARNIER SYRUP In a small saucepan with a tight-fitting lid, stir the strawberry syrup and sugar until all of the sugar is moistened. Bring the mixture to a simmer, stirring constantly. Cover at once and remove it from the heat. Cool completely. Transfer the syrup to a glass measure with a spout and stir in the Grand Marnier. If the syrup has evaporated slightly, add water to equal 1 cup/237 ml. (If making the springform cake, discard 2 tablespoons of the syrup [see Notes]). Cover the syrup and set it aside until ready to syrup the cake.

APPLY THE SYRUP For the cake baked in the Marianne pan, place a folded paper towel in the center depression of the cake and then a prepared wire rack on top of the cake. Invert the cake and rack.

For the springform cake, with a sharp serrated knife, cut a circle about ½ inch from the sides and ¼ inch deep. Carefully cut the top off the cake within the inscribed circle to form a depression on the top of the cake. Place a folded paper towel in the center of the cake and then a prepared wire rack on top of the cake. Invert the cake and slowly peel off the parchment round, which should also remove most of the bottom crust.

For either cake, carefully slice off any remaining crust from the bottom of the cake. (For the cake baked in the springform pan a serrated knife works best to scrape off the thin layer of crust.) Brush a third of the syrup evenly on the bottom of the cake. Reinvert the cake onto a serving plate. Brush the remaining syrup on the top of the cake and, if desired, on the sides as well. Cover the cake and let it sit at room temperature or refrigerated for 8 to 12 hours.

NOTES If you prefer a syrup with no alcohol content, you can substitute ¼ cup of water/ 59 ml/2 ounces/59 grams plus 1 teaspoon of orange extract.

Less syrup is needed for the cake baked in the springform pan because you lose some of the cake when creating the depression to hold the strawberries.

Fresh Strawberries

	VOLUME	WEIGHT	
fresh strawberries, hulled and halved	2 pints	1 pound	454 grams
granulated sugar	2 tablespoons	0.9 ounce	25 grams
lemon juice, freshly squeezed	1 teaspoon (5 ml)	.	5 grams

MACERATE THE FRESH STRAWBERRIES In a medium bowl, sprinkle the strawberries with the sugar and lemon juice. (Quarter the strawberries if they are very large.) Holding on to either side of the bowl, toss gently to coat the berries. Place the strawberries in a strainer suspended over a bowl and let the syrup drain into the bowl for 2 hours at room temperature or up to 8 hours refrigerated.

There will be about ¼ cup/59 ml of syrup, which can be reduced to about 1 tablespoon in a microwave, and then, if desired, brushed on the berries after they are set on the cake (or used for another purpose, such as pouring over fresh berries).

Strawberry Jam Whipped Cream

MAKES 2½ CUPS/11 OUNCES/312 GRAMS

	VOLUME	WEIGHT	
heavy cream, cold	1 cup (237 ml)	8.2 ounces	232 grams
seedless strawberry jam	¼ cup	3 ounces	83 grams

MAKE THE STRAWBERRY JAM WHIPPED CREAM Into the bowl of a stand mixer, pour the cream and refrigerate for at least 15 minutes. (Chill the whisk beater alongside of the bowl.)

Starting on low speed and gradually raising the speed to medium-high as it thickens, whip the cream just until beater marks begin to show distinctly. Add the jam and beat just until stiff peaks form when the beater is raised. Use at once.

COMPOSE THE CAKE In a food processor, puree the reserved ¾ cup strawberries until smooth. Spread this puree to cover the depression on top of the cake. Make a ring of the fresh strawberries, with their uncut sides facing up, around the perimeter of the depression on top of the pureed strawberries. Spoon the remaining strawberries to cover the pureed strawberries. Spoon the whipped cream onto the center of the strawberries and swirl with a silicone spatula to within about 1 inch of the edge of the strawberries.

STORE Airtight: room temperature, 4 hours; refrigerated, 2 days.

Optional: RHUBARB COMPOTE

MAKES 2 CUPS/16.2 OUNCES/460 GRAMS

	VOLUME	WEIGHT	
fresh rhubarb, 1¼ pounds	4 cups (cut)	1 pound	454 grams
granulated sugar	½ cup	3.5 ounces	100 grams
fine sea salt	a pinch	.	.
lemon zest, finely grated	1 teaspoon, loosely packed	.	2 grams

MAKE THE RHUBARB COMPOTE Rinse, dry, and cut the rhubarb into ½ inch cubes. Weigh or measure out the correct amount and place it in a medium heavy saucepan. Mix in the sugar, salt, and lemon zest. Let the mixture stand at room temperature for at least 15 minutes, or until the rhubarb exudes some juice. Bring the mixture to a boil over moderately high heat, stirring constantly. Reduce the heat to low, partially cover, and simmer, stirring occasionally, until the rhubarb is tender and the liquid thickened, about 7 to 10 minutes. Remove the lid when almost tender—for the last 4 minutes of cooking—so extra liquid can evaporate. Remove the pan from the heat and let the mixture cool without stirring. (If you find that there is too much liquid after cooling, simply drain it, reduce it in the microwave or on the cooktop, and add it back to the rhubarb.)

Variation: MINI STRAWBERRY SHORTCAKES

Individual shortcakes also make a lovely presentation. Both Chicago Metallic and Nordic Ware make charming 6 cavity pans or you can use six 10 ounce (4 by 2 inches) Pyrex dessert dishes set on a baking sheet. Prepare the pans as for the large cake. Make a half recipe of all of the components except the cake. For the cake, you will need a 2 egg recipe, so multiply everything by 0.4. Use about 1 ounce/33 grams of batter in each depression, and bake for 14 to 15 minutes. Don't be concerned if the batter rises above the tops of the pans because it will go down quite a bit when fully baked and flatten on unmolding. The syrup will yield 6½ tablespoons.

THE POLISH PRINCESS

OVEN TEMPERATURE 350°F/175°C

BAKING TIME 20 to 30 minutes

*T*his extraordinary cake is named for Ava Wilder-Zhan, the incomparable production editor of *Rose's Heavenly Cakes*. Its original name in Polish was The Ambassador, and it is a contemporary, not a traditional cake. The cake came into popularity in the early 1990s, after the fall of communism when there was an influx of quality chocolate, alkalized cocoa, and raisins from abroad. When Ava described it to me and offered to help me re-create it, I was sufficiently intrigued to give it a try. As she described it, the cake has one simple baked layer, a sponge cake. It is then topped with two layers of vanilla pudding, one enhanced with cocoa and walnuts, and the other studded with chopped chocolate and raisins. After finally perfecting the cake, I made it as a wedding present for Ava and her husband, Luke.

PLAN AHEAD The cake component can be made 1 day before assembling with the pastry buttercreams. Assemble the cake at least 8 hours before serving.

SPECIAL EQUIPMENT One 9 by 3 inch springform pan, encircled with a cake strip, coated with baking spray with flour, then topped with a parchment round (see Notes, page 127)

BATTER

	VOLUME	WEIGHT	
bleached all-purpose flour	1¼ cups (sifted into the cup and leveled off) plus 1 tablespoon	5.3 ounces	150 grams
baking powder	1 teaspoon	.	4.4 grams
4 (to 6) large eggs, separated			
yolks	¼ cup plus 2 teaspoons (69 ml)	2.6 ounces	74 grams
whites (about 3)	6 tablespoons (89 ml)	3.2 ounces	90 grams
superfine sugar	¾ cup	5.3 ounces	150 grams
warm water	3 tablespoons (44 ml)	1.6 ounces	44 grams

PREHEAT THE OVEN Twenty minutes or longer before baking, set an oven rack in the lower third of the oven and preheat the oven to 350°F/175°C.

MIX THE DRY INGREDIENTS In a small bowl, whisk together the flour and baking powder.

BEAT THE EGG WHITES INTO A STIFF MERINGUE In the bowl of a stand mixer fitted with the whisk beater, beat the egg whites on medium speed until soft peaks form when the beater is raised. Raise the speed to medium-high. Gradually add the sugar and beat until the mixture is very glossy and stiff peaks form when the beater is raised slowly.

MAKE THE BATTER Continuing on medium-high speed, add the egg yolks, 1 at a time, beating for about 20 seconds between each addition. Scrape down the sides of the bowl as needed.

Sift the flour mixture over the egg mixture, and with a slotted skimmer or silicone spatula, fold gently until all traces of flour have disappeared. With a silicone spatula, reach to the bottom of the bowl to be sure to moisten all of the flour. Gently fold in the water until incorporated. This will deflate the batter slightly.

Scrape the batter into the prepared pan. Use a small offset spatula to smooth the surface evenly. The pan will be only about one-third full.

BAKE THE CAKE Bake for 20 to 30 minutes, or until the cake springs back when pressed lightly in the center and a wooden skewer inserted into the center comes out clean. (An instant-read thermometer inserted into the center should read 193°F/90°C.) The cake should not start to come away from the sides of the pan. The cake's sides will have risen to a little more than halfway up the sides of the pan.

COOL AND UNMOLD THE CAKE Set the pan on a wire rack to cool for 10 minutes. Run a small metal spatula between the sides of the pan and the cake, pressing firmly against the pan, and remove the sides of the pan. Let the cake cool completely. Invert the cake onto a wire rack that has been lightly coated with nonstick cooking spray and remove the bottom of the pan and parchment.

TEA VODKA SYRUP

MAKES 1 CUP MINUS 1 TABLESPOON/222 ML/7.8 OUNCES/222 GRAMS

	VOLUME	WEIGHT	
water	¾ cup (177 ml)	6.2 ounces	177 grams
black tea	1 tea bag	.	.
granulated sugar	1 tablespoon	0.5 ounce	13 grams
lemon juice, freshly squeezed	½ tablespoon (7.5 ml)	.	8 grams
vodka, preferably Ultimat Polish vodka	¼ cup (59 ml)	2 ounces	57 grams

MAKE THE TEA VODKA SYRUP In a small saucepan with a tight-fitting lid over medium-high heat, bring the water to a rolling boil. Remove the pan from the heat. Add the tea bag, cover, and let it steep for 2 minutes. Discard the tea bag. Pour the tea into a glass measure and stir in the sugar, lemon juice, and vodka until the sugar is dissolved. Cover it tightly and let it cool just until warm or room temperature.

SYRUP THE CAKE Poke the cake all over with a thin skewer. Brush one-third of the syrup onto the bottom of the cake. Set the bottom of the springform pan on top of the cake and reinvert the cake (see Notes). Poke the cake's top all over with the skewer. Brush the top of the cake evenly with the remaining syrup. Attach the sides of the springform pan to the bottom. If composing the cake the next day, cover the pan tightly with plastic wrap.

NOTES A 9 by 2¾ inch springform pan can be used for baking the cake. However, for composing the cake, a collar made from heavy-duty aluminum foil will need to be attached with shortening to the inside of the springform pan's sides to give a total height of 3 inches to accommodate the top layer of pastry buttercream.

It is best to set the cake on the base of the springform pan before syruping, and then reattach the sides as described in the recipe, because the cake is more fragile after syruping and would break when lowering it into the pan.

If you prefer to compose the cake directly on a serving plate, carefully reinvert the cake onto the serving plate. Slide the springform pan's sides around the cake and lock them in position.

Pastry Buttercream Base for the Two Buttercream Layers

MAKES 5½ CUPS/37.4 OUNCES/1060 GRAMS

	VOLUME	WEIGHT	
milk	2⅓ cups (551 ml), *divided*	19.9 ounces	564 grams
cornstarch	3 tablespoons	1 ounce	28 grams
4 large egg yolks	¼ cup plus 2 teaspoons (69 ml)	2.6 ounces	74 grams
1 vanilla bean (½ bean if Tahitian)	.	.	.
granulated sugar	1 cup	7 ounces	200 grams
unsalted butter, preferably high fat (65° to 70°F/18° to 21°C)	3 sticks	12 ounces	340 grams

PREPARE THE EGG MIXTURE Have ready a fine-mesh strainer suspended over the bowl of a stand mixer.

In a medium bowl, whisk together ½ cup/118 ml/4.3 ounces/121 grams of the milk and the cornstarch until smooth. Whisk in the egg yolks until completely blended.

MIX THE VANILLA BEAN WITH THE SUGAR With a small sharp knife, split the vanilla bean pod lengthwise in half.

In a medium heavy saucepan, add the sugar. Scrape the vanilla bean seeds into the sugar and rub them in with your fingers. Add the vanilla pod.

COMPLETE THE PASTRY CREAM Add the remaining milk to the sugar and vanilla mixture, and scald it over medium heat, stirring often (heat it to the boiling point; small bubbles will form around the periphery). Whisk vigorously while adding ¼ cup of the hot milk mixture to the egg mixture. Quickly add all of the egg mixture into the remaining hot milk mixture, whisking rapidly. Continue whisking rapidly over medium heat for about 30 seconds, or until the mixture is very thick and beginning to bubble.

Remove the mixture from the heat and strain it into the bowl. Use the back of a spoon or a silicone spatula to scrape any thickened cream from the bottom of the pan and press it through the strainer. Whisk it slightly. Coat a piece of plastic wrap with nonstick cooking spray and set it directly on the surface of the pastry cream to prevent a skin from forming. Set the cream aside to cool for 1 hour.

Refrigerate the pastry cream until cooled to 65° to 70°F/19° to 21°C, very gently folding it every 15 minutes. Between foldings, place plastic wrap coated with nonstick cooking spray directly on the surface of the pastry cream to prevent a skin from forming. This will take about 2 hours. For faster cooling (under 1 hour), you can set the bowl in an ice water bath (see page 538) immediately after straining the pastry cream, folding every several minutes.

ADD THE PASTRY CREAM TO THE BUTTER In the bowl of a stand mixer fitted with the whisk beater, beat the butter on medium speed until light and creamy.

Add the cooled pastry cream to the butter, a large spoonful at a time, beating at medium-high speed for several seconds after each addition until smoothly incorporated. Scrape down the sides of the bowl as necessary.

Remove 2¾ cups/18.7 ounces/530 grams of the pastry buttercream base to a medium bowl. Cover both bowls with plastic wrap until ready to complete the pastry buttercreams.

Cocoa and Walnut Pastry Buttercream Layer

	VOLUME	WEIGHT	
walnut halves	1 cup	3.5 ounces	100 grams
Pastry Buttercream Base	2¾ cups	18.7 ounces	530 grams
unsweetened (alkalized) cocoa powder	3 tablespoons (sifted before measuring)	0.5 ounce	14 grams

PREHEAT THE OVEN Twenty minutes or longer before baking, set an oven rack in the middle of the oven and preheat the oven to 350°F/175°C.

TOAST THE WALNUTS Spread the walnuts evenly on a baking sheet and bake for about 7 minutes to enhance their flavor. Stir once or twice to ensure even toasting and avoid overbrowning. Turn them out onto a clean dish towel. With a small sharp knife and your fingers, scrape off and discard as much skin as possible. Cool completely.

Cut each walnut into thin slices.

COMPLETE THE COCOA AND WALNUT PASTRY BUTTERCREAM Set the mixer bowl containing the pastry buttercream in the stand mixer fitted with the whisk beater. Add the cocoa and beat on low speed until smoothly incorporated. With a silicone spatula, fold in the walnuts.

CHOCOLATE AND RAISIN PASTRY BUTTERCREAM LAYER

	VOLUME	WEIGHT	
raisins	½ cup	2.5 ounces	72 grams
bittersweet chocolate, preferably 70% cacao, coarsely chopped	.	2 ounces	56 grams
Pastry Buttercream Base (page 128)	2¾ cups	18.7 ounces	530 grams
Décor: bittersweet chocolate for grating, 60% to 63% cacao	a small thick block	1 ounce	28 grams

SOFTEN THE RAISINS In a small bowl, place the raisins and add hot water just to cover. Let them sit for 10 minutes. Drain the raisins and dry them well on paper towels.

COMPLETE THE CHOCOLATE AND RAISIN BUTTERCREAM With a silicone spatula, fold the coarsely chopped chocolate and the raisins into the pastry buttercream base. Cover the bowl with plastic wrap.

COMPOSE THE CAKE Scrape the cocoa and walnut buttercream onto the cake in the springform pan and, with a small offset spatula, spread it evenly, taking care not to get any of the buttercream on the sides of the pan above the layer of the buttercream. Cover the top of the pan with plastic wrap and refrigerate for about 1 hour, or until firm. Then spread the chocolate and raisin buttercream layer evenly on top.

Set the pan on a sheet of parchment to catch any falling grated chocolate. Using a coarse shredder, grate the chocolate on top of the cake to cover the buttercream completely. Lift the pan from the parchment and use the parchment to transfer any of the fallen grated chocolate onto the cake. Cover the cake with a large bowl or cake carrier dome. To meld the flavors of the components, chill the composed cake overnight in the refrigerator.

UNMOLD THE CAKE Use a small torch or a dish towel run under hot water and wrung dry of excess water to heat the sides of the pan. Release the sides of the pan. Place a heated straight-edge knife flush with the buttercream and the cake. Circle the knife around the cake to create a smooth and glossy finish on the sides of the buttercreams.

Let the cake sit for about 20 minutes to soften before serving. To cut cleanly through the cake, run the knife blade under hot water and wipe it off between each slice.

STORE Airtight: refrigerated, 3 days. Do not freeze, because the texture of the buttercreams will become less smooth.

Heavenly Chocolate Mousse Cake

OVEN TEMPERATURE 450°F/230°C

BAKING TIME 7 to 10 minutes

$\mathcal{M}$any years ago, when my parents moved from New York City upstate to Grafton, New York, my mother reported with great excitement that they had discovered an amazing bakery in Saratoga Springs called Mrs. London's. After I had visited the bakery and was treated to an array of just about every fabulous dessert on the menu, this simple mousse cake is the one that I was most moved to re-create. A gossamer soft and delicate sponge cake (biscuit) is cut to fit and line a loaf pan that is then filled with an equally ethereal and deliciously mellow and velvety chocolate mousse.

PLAN AHEAD The sponge cake (biscuit) can be baked, cooled, and placed in the pan while the chocolate custard is cooling before you complete the mousse. Alternatively, the cake can be made a day ahead.

SPECIAL EQUIPMENT FOR THE CAKE: See Light Sponge Cake (Biscuit), page 103

FOR ASSEMBLING THE CAKE: One 8½ by 4½ inch (6 cups) loaf pan | One baking sheet or extra half sheet pan (inverted), lightly coated with nonstick cooking spray

Light Sponge Cake (Biscuit)

	VOLUME	WEIGHT	
Light Sponge Cake (Biscuit), page 103	.	.	.

MAKE THE CAKE Make the light sponge cake (biscuit).

UNMOLD AND COOL THE CAKE Run the tip of a sharp knife around the sides to dislodge any cake that may have attached itself to the sides of the pan and unmold the cake at once. Slip a small offset spatula under the narrow edge of the parchment to loosen it. Grasp the parchment and gently slide the cake from the pan onto a baking sheet or inverted sheet pan. Cover with plastic wrap lightly coated with nonstick cooking spray. Cool until it is no longer warm to the touch, about 20 minutes.

MAKE THE TEMPLATES Make the templates for cutting the cake into 4 pieces: 1 continuous piece for the bottom and sides, 2 ends, and 1 top. Measure the outside of the pan and transfer the measurements to sheets of paper or card stock. The templates should be slightly oversized to allow for trimming to fit. Cut out the templates.

CHOCOLATE MOUSSE FILLING

MAKES 4 CUPS/29.6 OUNCES/840 GRAMS

	VOLUME	WEIGHT	
bittersweet chocolate, 60% to 62% cacao, chopped	.	9.5 ounces	270 grams
heavy cream	2 cups (473 ml)	16.4 ounces	464 grams
10 (to 14) egg yolks, at room temperature	¾ cup (177 ml)	6.5 ounces	186 grams
pure vanilla extract	1 tablespoon (15 ml)	.	.
1 egg white, at room temperature	2 tablespoons (30 ml)	1 ounce	30 grams
cream of tartar	⅛ teaspoon	.	.
superfine sugar	3 tablespoons	1.3 ounces	37 grams

MAKE THE CHOCOLATE CUSTARD Have ready a fine-mesh strainer suspended over a stand mixer bowl and a handheld mixer.

In the top of a double boiler set over hot, not simmering, water (do not let the bottom of the container touch the water), heat the chocolate and cream. Stir often with a silicone spatula until the chocolate is completely melted. Remove it from the heat.

In a medium bowl, lightly whisk the egg yolks. Stir several tablespoons of the hot chocolate mixture into the yolk mixture. Gradually pour the yolk mixture into the remaining chocolate mixture, stirring constantly.

Continue stirring, occasionally scraping the bottom of the container to ensure uniform consistency. Heat the mixture to just before the boiling point (170° to 180°F/77° to 82°C). Steam will begin to appear and the mixture will be slightly thicker than cream. It will leave a well-defined track when a finger is run across the spatula. Immediately remove the container from the heat and pour the mixture through the strainer into the mixer bowl, scraping up the thickened cream that settles on the bottom of the container. Press it through the strainer and stir in the vanilla.

Press a piece of plastic wrap onto the surface of the chocolate custard to prevent a skin from forming. Refrigerate for 2½ to 3 hours, stirring every 20 minutes, until cool to the touch. If you are ready to fill the cake-lined pan sooner, you can speed cooling by setting the bowl in an ice water bath (see page 538) and stirring frequently. Do not let the mixture get too cold or it will be too stiff to incorporate air from the meringue. The ideal temperature is 65° to 68°F/19° to 20°C.

BEAT THE EGG WHITE INTO A STIFF MERINGUE In a medium bowl, beat the egg white and cream of tartar on medium-low speed until foamy. Gradually raise the speed to medium-high and beat until soft peaks form when the beater is raised. Gradually beat in the sugar until stiff peaks form when the beater is raised.

The chocolate mixture will continue to thicken after a few minutes at room temperature. The safest way to prevent overbeating is to use the stand mixer until the mixture starts to thicken and then continue by hand with a whisk when folding in the meringue.

COMPLETE THE CHOCOLATE MOUSSE FILLING With the whisk beater, on low speed, beat the chocolate mixture for about 30 seconds, or just until very soft, floppy peaks form when the beater is raised. Gently fold the meringue into the mousse until uniform in color.

CUT THE CAKE PIECES Invert the cake onto a wire rack and carefully remove the parchment. Reinvert the cake onto the baking sheet or inverted sheet pan and remove the plastic wrap. Place the templates on top of the cake so that they all fit. Use kitchen scissors to cut out the 4 cake pieces.

LINE THE PAN WITH THE CAKE PIECES Line the loaf pan with a sheet of plastic wrap cut 2 feet long, with the excess extending past one end of the pan. Lightly coat the plastic wrap with nonstick cooking spray. Carefully insert the bottom and sides piece of cake into the pan, crust side against the pan. Trim the 2 end pieces to fit tightly against the bottom and sides of the cake.

COMPOSE THE CAKE Spoon half of the chocolate mousse into the cake-lined pan. With a small metal offset spatula, lightly press the mousse into the pan to ensure that the mousse fills the corners of the cake. Repeat with the rest of the chocolate mousse. If necessary, trim the tops of the cake pieces to be flush with the top of the pan. Place the top cake piece, crust side up, over the mousse filling and trim its edges to fit inside the cake's side and end pieces.

Fold over the extended plastic wrap to cover the top of the pan. Lightly press down on the cake's top. Wrap any excess plastic wrap tightly around the sides of the pan. Set a small cutting board or heavy pan large enough to cover the entire top of the loaf pan on top.

Let the cake sit for 3 hours at room temperature for the chocolate mousse to set. The cake cuts best and has the best texture at room temperature.

UNMOLD THE CAKE Remove the cutting board and fold back the plastic wrap to uncover the top of the cake. Place a serving plate or the cutting board on top of the pan and invert the cake. Remove the pan. Gently peel off the plastic wrap.

Use a straight-edge knife to slice the cake from top to bottom. Between slices, wipe off the knife to minimize the likelihood of the chocolate mousse spreading onto the cake.

STORE Airtight: room temperature, 6 hours; refrigerated, 3 days. Do not freeze, because the texture will become less smooth.

CHOCOLATE CUDDLE CAKE

OVEN TEMPERATURE
350°F/175°C

BAKING TIME
40 to 50 minutes

*T*his is a chocolate chiffon cake with an amazingly delicate texture. It evolved from one of my favorite cakes, The Renée Fleming Golden Chiffon (page 86). Inspired to make a chocolate version one day when walking along the Hudson River, I rushed home to try it at once. The fabulous caramel whipped cream, which has just a hint of chocolate, holds at room temperature for up to six hours.

PLAN AHEAD The cake can be made 1 day ahead before composing. Make the ganache at least 3 hours ahead.

SPECIAL EQUIPMENT One 9 by 3 inch springform pan (the pan must not be less than 2¾ inches high), only the sides coated with shortening, encircled with 2 cake strips overlapped to cover the sides completely. Cut a 33 by 3 inch band of parchment. Wrap and press it against the inside wall of the pan. Use some extra shortening to coat the overlapping end to hold it in place (if the bottom of the springform pan has a lip, the parchment may extend about ¼ inch above the pan, which is fine) | A flat bottom rose nail (used for cake decorating) 2½ inches long (minimum) | A wire rack, lightly coated with nonstick cooking spray, elevated about 4 inches or higher above the work surface by setting it on top of 3 or 4 cans, coffee mugs, or glasses of equal height | Optional: a small pastry bag fitted with a ½ inch open star pastry tube

Batter

	VOLUME	WEIGHT	
unsweetened (alkalized) cocoa powder	⅔ cup (sifted before measuring)	1.8 ounces	50 grams
boiling water	½ cup (118 ml)	4.2 ounces	118 grams
canola or safflower oil, at room temperature	¼ cup (59 ml)	1.9 ounces	54 grams
4 (to 6) large eggs, separated, plus about 1 white, at room temperature			
yolks	¼ cup plus 2 teaspoons (69 ml)	2.6 ounces	74 grams
whites	½ cup plus 2 tablespoons (148 ml)	5.3 ounces	150 grams
pure vanilla extract	1 teaspoon (5 ml)	.	.
unbleached all-purpose flour (see Note, page 138)	1 cup (sifted into the cup and leveled off)	4 ounces	114 grams
superfine sugar	1¼ cups, *divided*	8.8 ounces	250 grams
baking powder	1¼ teaspoons	.	5.6 grams
fine sea salt	¼ teaspoon	.	1.5 grams
cream of tartar	½ plus ⅛ teaspoon	.	1.9 grams

PREHEAT THE OVEN Twenty minutes or longer before baking, set an oven rack in the lower third of the oven and preheat the oven to 350°F/175°C (325°F/160°C if using a dark pan).

MIX THE COCOA AND LIQUID INGREDIENTS In a 2 cup or larger glass measure with a spout, whisk together the cocoa and boiling water. Whisk in the oil and let the mixture cool until no longer warm to the touch. Whisk in the egg yolks and vanilla.

MAKE THE BATTER In the bowl of a stand mixer fitted with the whisk beater, mix the flour, ¾ cup/5.3 ounces/150 grams of the sugar, the baking powder, and salt on low speed for 30 seconds. Make a well in the center. Add the chocolate mixture to the well and beat on low speed until the dry ingredients are moistened, scraping down the sides of the bowl as necessary. Raise the speed to medium-high and beat until very thick, about 1½ minutes, scraping down the sides of the bowl as necessary.

If you don't have a second mixer bowl, scrape this mixture into a large bowl and thoroughly wash, rinse, and dry the mixer bowl and whisk beater to remove any trace of oil.

BEAT THE EGG WHITES INTO A STIFF MERINGUE Sift the remaining sugar (½ cup/ 3.5 ounces/100 grams) onto a piece of parchment.

Lining the pan's sides with parchment results in the most even surface of the cake and also prevents the slight shrinking in toward the top of the cake. It also makes unmolding the cake easier. The sides will be smoother but slightly puckered. For the best results, choose a pan that is 3 inches high measured from the inside (see page 535). If the pan is only 2¾ inches high, before inverting the baked cake, let it sink to the level of the sides of the pan.

In the bowl of a stand mixer fitted with the whisk beater, beat the egg whites and cream of tartar on medium-low speed until foamy. Gradually raise the speed to medium-high and beat until soft peaks form when the beater is raised. Use the parchment to pour the remaining sugar in a steady stream into the meringue. Continue beating until glossy and stiff peaks form when the beater is raised, about 1 minute.

ADD THE MERINGUE TO THE BATTER Using a large balloon wire whisk, slotted skimmer, or large silicone spatula, gently fold the meringue into the batter in three parts, folding until partially blended in between and then folding until completely incorporated after the last addition. If using the whisk, you will need to shake out the meringue that gathers in the center as you fold.

Using a silicone spatula, scrape the batter into the pan. Run a small offset spatula in circles through the batter to prevent air pockets and smooth the surface. Insert the rose nail, base side down, into the center of the batter so that it sits on the bottom of the pan. (The batter should fill a 3 inch high pan half full.)

BAKE THE CAKE Bake for 40 to 50 minutes. The cake will dome about 1 inch above the top of the pan and split in the center and a little at the sides. Avoid opening the oven door before the minimum baking time because the fragile cake could fall. Watch carefully. When the cake lowers slightly and a wooden skewer inserted near the center into the moist split comes out clean, remove the cake from the oven.

COOL AND UNMOLD THE CAKE Let the cake sit on a heatproof counter or an uncoated wire rack for about 1 minute, just until the center is no longer domed. Immediately set the coated wire rack on top of the cake and invert the cake and rack onto the prepared supports. Let it cool for about 1½ hours, or until the outside of the pan is cool to the touch.

Remove the cake strips and the sides of the springform pan. The parchment will be wrinkled. Slide a thin bladed knife or long metal spatula between the cake and the bottom of the pan, pressing firmly against the bottom of the pan to release the bottom of the cake. If the bottom of the pan has a lip, first use a small offset spatula to go under the edges. Invert the cake and lift off the pan bottom. Remove the rose nail and reinvert the cake onto a serving plate. Use a damp sponge or dish towel to moisten the parchment. Wait for 1 minute and then carefully peel off the parchment strip.

NOTE Unbleached all-purpose flour strengthens the structure of the cake just enough to prevent it from deflating significantly.

Chocolate Ganache

MAKES ALMOST 1½ CUPS/12.3 OUNCES/350 GRAMS

	VOLUME	WEIGHT	
bittersweet chocolate, 60% to 62% cacao, chopped	.	6 ounces	170 grams
heavy cream	¾ cup (177 ml)	6.1 ounces	174 grams
Kahlúa or additional heavy cream	1½ tablespoons (22 ml)	0.9 ounce	25 grams
pure vanilla extract	½ teaspoon (2.5 ml)	.	.

MAKE THE GANACHE Have ready a fine-mesh strainer suspended over a small glass bowl.

In a food processor, process the chocolate until very fine.

In a 1 cup microwavable measure with a spout (or in a small saucepan over medium heat, stirring often), scald the cream (heat it to the boiling point; small bubbles will form around the periphery).

With the motor of the food processor running, pour the cream through the feed tube in a steady stream. Process for a few seconds until smooth, scraping down the sides of the bowl as needed. Pulse in the Kahlúa and vanilla. Press the ganache through the strainer and let it sit for 1 hour. Cover it with plastic wrap and let it cool for about 2 to 3 hours, or until the mixture reaches a soft frosting consistency (70° to 75°F/21° to 24°C).

The ganache keeps in an airtight container for 3 days at cool room temperature, 2 weeks refrigerated, or 6 months frozen. To restore to frosting consistency, defrost, if frozen, and reheat in a microwave with 3 second bursts, or in a double boiler set over hot, not simmering, water (do not let the bottom of the container touch the water), stirring gently to ensure that it does not overheat or incorporate any air.

CARAMEL WHIPPED CREAM

MAKES 3 CUPS/10 OUNCES/284 GRAMS

CARAMEL

	VOLUME	WEIGHT	
granulated sugar	½ cup	3.5 ounces	100 grams
golden syrup or corn syrup	½ tablespoon (7.5 ml)	.	10 grams
water	2 tablespoons (30 ml)	1 ounce	30 grams
heavy cream, hot	¼ cup plus 2 tablespoons, *divided* (89 ml)	3.1 ounces	87 grams
unsalted butter, softened	1 tablespoon	0.5 ounce	14 grams
unsweetened cocoa powder	2 teaspoons	.	4 grams

MAKE THE CARAMEL Have ready a 1 cup heatproof glass measure with a spout, lightly coated with nonstick cooking spray.

In a medium heavy saucepan, preferably nonstick, stir together the sugar, golden syrup, and water until the sugar is completely moistened. Heat, stirring constantly, until the sugar dissolves and the syrup is bubbling. Stop stirring completely and let the syrup boil undisturbed until it turns a deep amber (370°F/188°C on an instant-read thermometer if using golden syrup, or 380°F/193°C if using corn syrup). Remove it immediately from the heat because the temperature will continue to rise, or remove it slightly before it reaches temperature and, just as soon as it does, slowly pour in ¼ cup/59 ml of the hot cream. It will bubble up furiously.

Use a silicone spatula or wooden spoon to stir the mixture gently, scraping the thicker part that settles on the bottom. Return it to very low heat, continuing to stir gently for 1 minute, until the mixture is uniform in color and the caramel fully dissolved.

Remove it from the heat and gently stir in the butter until incorporated. The mixture will be a little streaky, but becomes uniform once cooled and stirred.

Pour ½ cup/118 ml/5.3 ounces/150 grams of the caramel into the glass measure. Store any remaining caramel for future use.

In a 1 cup microwavable measure with a spout (or in a custard cup set in a saucepan surrounded by simmering water, stirring often), scald the remaining cream (heat it to the boiling point; small bubbles will form around the periphery). Remove it from the heat and whisk in the cocoa. Stir this cocoa mixture into the hot caramel until uniform in color. Cover with plastic wrap and let it cool until 65° to 70°F/19° to 21°C, about 40 minutes.

COMPLETED CARAMEL WHIPPED CREAM

	VOLUME	WEIGHT	
heavy cream	1 cup (237 ml), *divided*	8.2 ounces	232 grams
powdered gelatin	½ teaspoon	.	1.5 grams
pure vanilla extract	2 teaspoons (10 ml)	.	.
Caramel	½ cup (118 ml)	5.3 ounces	150 grams

COMPLETE THE CARAMEL WHIPPED CREAM Into a medium bowl, pour ¾ cup plus 2 tablespoons/207 ml/7.2 ounces/203 grams of the cream and refrigerate for at least 15 minutes. (Chill a handheld mixer's beaters and a medium whisk alongside the bowl.)

In a 1 cup glass measure with a spout, stir together the remaining 2 tablespoons of cream and the gelatin and let it soften for at least 3 minutes. If it will sit longer, cover with plastic wrap to prevent evaporation.

Place the cup in a pan of simmering water for a few minutes, stirring occasionally, until the gelatin is dissolved. (This can also be done in a microwave, with 3 second bursts, stirring once or twice until dissolved.) The gelatin will thicken slightly. Remove it from the heat, cover, and let it cool for about 20 minutes until it is 85° to 90°F/29° to 32°C. (If cooler, the gelatin will set and will need to be reheated.) Stir in the vanilla.

In the chilled bowl, whip the cream with the handheld mixer just until traces of the beater marks begin to show. Scrape in the caramel mixture and use the chilled whisk to whip the cream by hand, just until soft peaks form when the whisk is lifted. While whisking, add the gelatin mixture and continue whisking just until stiff peaks form when the whisk is lifted. Cover and refrigerate until ready to use.

COMPOSE THE CAKE Slide a few wide strips of parchment under the cake to keep the rim of the plate clean. Frost the sides with the ganache, bringing it up a little higher than the top to create a border to contain the caramel whipped cream. Alternatively, bring the ganache just to the top, scrape the remaining ganache into the pastry bag, and then pipe half shells (see page 254) around the edges to create a border.

Lightly whisk the caramel whipped cream to restore the smooth texture, and spoon dollops of it on top of the cake. Use a small metal spatula to create opulent swirls. The whipped cream will keep at cool room temperature for up to 6 hours. If desired, decorate with chocolate curls (see page 520). Slowly slide the parchment strips out from under the cake before serving.

STORE (Without the whipped cream) airtight: room temperature, 2 days; refrigerated, 5 days; frozen, 2 months.

ChocolaTea Cake

SERVES 14 TO 18

OVEN TEMPERATURE 350°F/175°C

BAKING TIME 25 to 35 minutes

*T*he moist chocolate génoise from *The Cake Bible* was a favorite for its intense chocolate flavor and velvety, light texture. The tricky part of the recipe was always trying to integrate the flour into the chocolate mixture, and preventing the formation of hard little pellets. Matthew Boyer, one of the star participants on my blog, came up with the great technique of combining the chocolate and flour before folding it into the meringue, which makes this process much easier.

Many years ago, my mentor Cecily Brownstone of the Associated Press started a column called Copy Cat Recipes. She asked me to re-create the tea liqueur called Tiffin, which I have employed here as the syrup for the cake. I would never have thought that tea and chocolate would make such a good combination until I tasted Maurice Bernachon's tea chocolate bar years ago in Lyon, France, when I was translating his and his son Jean-Jacques's book *La Passion du Chocolat*. You don't actually taste the tea in this cake, but it does wonders to make the chocolate surprisingly intense.

PLAN AHEAD For best flavor, compose the cake 1 day ahead. Make the ganache at least 4 hours ahead.

SPECIAL EQUIPMENT Two 9 by 2 inch round cake pans, coated with baking spray with flour, then topped with parchment rounds

Batter

	VOLUME	WEIGHT	
bittersweet chocolate, 60% to 62% cacao, chopped	.	8 ounces	227 grams
boiling water	1 cup (237 ml)	8.4 ounces	237 grams
8 large eggs	1½ cups plus 4 teaspoons (375 ml)	14.1 ounces	400 grams
superfine sugar	1 cup	7 ounces	200 grams
bleached cake flour (or bleached all-purpose flour)	1½ cups (or 1⅓ cups), sifted into the cup and leveled off	5.3 ounces	150 grams

PREHEAT THE OVEN Twenty minutes or longer before baking, set an oven rack in the lower third of the oven and preheat the oven to 350°F/175°C.

COOK THE CHOCOLATE Into a heavy saucepan, place the chocolate and pour the boiling water on top. Bring the mixture to a boil over low heat, stirring constantly with a silicone spatula. Simmer, stirring constantly, until the chocolate thickens to a puddinglike consistency, about 5 minutes. It should fall from the spatula and pool thickly when a little is dropped on its surface. If the chocolate separates, whisking will bring it together into a smooth, shiny mass.

Transfer the chocolate to a medium bowl. Cover it with plastic wrap to prevent evaporation, and cool it until it is warm to the touch (about 100°F/38°C), about 1 hour. To speed cooling, place the bowl in an ice water bath (see page 538) or, uncovered, in the refrigerator and whisk often. Reheat in a hot water bath if necessary.

BEAT THE EGGS AND SUGAR In the bowl of a stand mixer, with a long-handled wire whisk, lightly combine the eggs and sugar. Set the bowl over a pan of simmering water (do not let the bottom of the bowl touch the water) and heat just until lukewarm to the touch, stirring constantly with the whisk to prevent curdling. If the eggs are already at warm room temperature (80°F/27°C), there is no need to heat the eggs for this type of génoise.

Set the bowl in the stand mixer and attach the whisk beater. Beat the mixture on high speed for a minimum of 5 minutes. It will quadruple in volume and be very thick and airy. (A handheld electric mixer will take at least 10 minutes.)

COMBINE THE FLOUR AND CHOCOLATE Sift the flour onto a large sheet of parchment and then add it to the chocolate. Whisk the flour into the chocolate until it is incorporated. Use a silicone spatula to stir the mixture and check to see that the flour has integrated completely. The finished mixture will have the consistency of thick pudding.

FOLD IN THE CHOCOLATE AND FLOUR MIXTURE Remove 1 cup/2 ounces/60 grams of egg foam and fold it into the chocolate and flour mixture to lighten it. With the silicone spatula, gently slide half of the chocolate and flour mixture down the side of the mixer bowl. Fold it in gently but rapidly with a large wire whisk until the mixture has been mostly incorporated. Repeat with the second half of the chocolate and flour mixture until incorporated, being sure to reach to the bottom of the bowl. Use the silicone spatula to scrape down the sides and bottom of the mixer bowl and gently fold to a uniform color. Scrape the batter into the prepared pans, which will be a little more than half full.

BAKE THE CAKES Bake for 25 to 35 minutes, or until a cake tester inserted into the centers enters as easily as it does when inserted closer to the side. The cakes rise almost to the top of the pans during baking and will lower slightly when done, pulling slightly away from the sides. Avoid opening the oven door before the minimum baking time because the fragile cakes could fall. Test toward the end of baking by opening the door a crack, and if the cakes do not appear done, continue baking for another 5 minutes.

To prevent the collapse of the delicate foam structure while still hot, the cakes must be unmolded as soon as they are baked. Have ready a small metal spatula and three wire racks that have been lightly coated with nonstick cooking spray.

COOL AND UNMOLD THE CAKES Set the cake pans on wire racks. Run the small metal spatula between the sides of the pans and the cakes, pressing firmly against the pans, and invert the cakes onto the prepared wire racks. Leaving the parchment in place, immediately reinvert the cakes onto the prepared racks so that the firm upper crust keeps them from sinking. Cool completely before wrapping airtight.

Tea Cognac Syrup

MAKES 1½ CUPS/354 ML/14 OUNCES/400 GRAMS

	VOLUME	WEIGHT	
granulated sugar	½ cup plus 1 tablespoon	4 ounces	113 grams
water	1 cup (237 ml)	8.4 ounces	237 grams
black tea	1 tea bag	.	.
cognac	¼ cup (59 ml)	2 ounces	56 grams

MAKE THE TEA COGNAC SYRUP In a small saucepan with a tight-fitting lid, stir together the sugar and the water until all of the sugar is moistened. Over medium-high heat, bring the mixture to a rolling boil, stirring constantly. Remove the pan from the heat and wait for 1 minute. Add the tea bag, cover, and let it steep for 2 minutes. Discard the tea bag. Cool completely. Transfer the syrup to a glass measure and stir in the cognac. If the syrup has evaporated slightly, add water to equal 1½ cups/354 ml/14 ounces/400 grams.

Tea Ganache

MAKES 3½ CUPS/31.7 OUNCES/900 GRAMS

	VOLUME	WEIGHT	
bittersweet chocolate, 60% to 62% cacao, chopped	.	1 pound	454 grams
instant powdered lemon tea	2 tablespoons plus 2 teaspoons	0.3 ounces	8.4 grams
crème fraîche	2 cups	16.4 ounces	464 grams
heavy cream	¼ cup plus 2 tablespoons (88 ml)	3 ounces	87 grams
cognac	2 tablespoons (30 ml)	1 ounce	28 grams

MAKE THE TEA GANACHE Have ready a fine-mesh strainer suspended over a medium glass bowl.

In a food processor, process the chocolate until very fine. Pulse in the instant powdered tea.

In a 4 cup microwavable measure with a spout (or in a small saucepan over medium heat, stirring often), scald the crème fraîche and heavy cream (heat them to the boiling point; small bubbles will form around the periphery).

With the motor of the food processor running, pour the cream mixture through the feed tube in a steady stream. Process for a few seconds until smooth, scraping down the sides of the bowl as needed. Pulse in the cognac. Press the ganache through the strainer and let it sit for 1 hour. Cover it with plastic wrap and let it cool for 3 to 4 hours, or until the mixture reaches a soft frosting consistency (70° to 75°F/21° to 24°C).

The ganache keeps in an airtight container for 3 days at cool room temperature, 2 weeks refrigerated, or 6 months frozen. To restore to frosting consistency, defrost, if frozen, and reheat in a microwave with 3 second bursts, or in a double boiler set over hot, not simmering, water (do not let the bottom of the container touch the water), stirring gently to ensure that it does not overheat or incorporate any air.

COMPOSE THE CAKE Use a long serrated knife and your fingertips to remove the top crusts. Remove the parchment and scrape off any remaining bottom crust.

Brush the tea syrup evenly on the top and bottom of the cakes. The cakes are now tender and fragile and need to be supported by a removable tart pan bottom or cardboard round when moved.

Spread a small amount of ganache on a 9 inch cardboard round wrapped in plastic wrap or a serving plate and set one cake on top. If using the plate, slide a few strips of parchment under the cake to keep the plate clean. Sandwich the layers with about 1 cup of the ganache. Frost the top and sides of the cake with the remaining ganache. If using the parchment strips, slowly slide them out from under the cake.

Serve at room temperature or lightly chilled. To cut cleanly through the ganache without its cracking or pulling away from the cake, run the knife blade under hot water and wipe it off between each slice.

STORE Airtight: génoise with or without syrup: room temperature, 2 days; refrigerated, 5 days; frozen, 2 months.

Some Special Tips for Cheesecakes

DO NOT USE THE MORE EXPENSIVE "NATURAL" SPECIALTY CREAM CHEESE. Philadelphia brand, available almost all over the world, or other regional commercial brands such as Organic Valley, offer the best and most consistent flavor and texture for these cakes. Cream cheese without gums will aerate more, yielding more volume and less creaminess.

BAKE A CHEESECAKE IN A WATER BATH to keep the sides as creamy as the center. Placing the springform pan in a silicone pan before placing it in the water bath works wonderfully to keep the water from leaking into the springform pan. Silicone, however, is very slow to conduct heat. If using a silicone pan for this purpose, bake the cake an additional 5 to 7 minutes to compensate. To help prevent staining the aluminum cake pan if used as the water bath, add about 1 teaspoon of cream of tartar to the water.

IF PLANNING TO TRANSPORT A CHEESECAKE, or to give it as a gift, place a gold or silver foil cardboard round in the bottom of the pan, trimmed to fit if necessary.

IF YOUR OVEN HAS A WINDOW, when you look in, the edges of the cheesecake should show some browning and/or the top will look set when it is done. Bake longer than the given baking time if necessary. If you prefer a less creamy and more firm cheesecake, instead of letting the cheesecake cool in the turned off oven, bake it for a total of 1 hour plus 10 minutes, or until an instant-read thermometer inserted into the center reads 147° to 160°F/64° to 70°C and the center bounces back when pressed lightly (the higher temperature will be more firm). With this method, the edges of the cake will have little cracks and be browned. The sides will rise a little but will sink level with the center on cooling.

TO STORE A CHEESECAKE, remove the pan from the water bath and set it on a wire rack to cool to room temperature or just until warm, about 1 to 2 hours. To absorb condensation, place a paper towel, curved side down, over the pan with the ends overhanging. Place an inverted plate, larger than the springform pan, on top of the paper towel. Refrigerate the cheesecake for 4 hours or overnight.

KEEP IN MIND THAT CHEESECAKES NEED MANY HOURS OF REFRIGERATION to firm before unmolding. Baking them the day ahead of serving is ideal. If adding a hot topping, the filling needs to be very firm before pouring it on. Once the topping has been added, let the cheesecake sit for 15 minutes to allow the steam to escape from the topping. Then unmold the cake or refrigerate it, covered with a large bowl, until ready to unmold.

TO UNMOLD THE CHEESECAKE, remove the plate and paper towel. Use a small butane or propane torch to warm the sides of the pan or wipe them with a dish towel that has been run under hot water and wrung out. Release the sides of the springform pan. If the cheesecake is uneven, run a small metal spatula under hot water, dry it, and use it to smooth the sides.

Mango Bango Cheesecake

SERVES 10 TO 12

OVEN TEMPERATURE
350°F/175°C

BAKING TIME
50 minutes (55 minutes if using a silicone pan with the water bath), plus 1 hour with the oven off

I created this spectacular cheesecake at the request of the charming and renowned cookbook author and screen actress Madhur Jaffrey. She was hoping that the cake would be similar to a mango fool, with streaks of the mango pulp throughout. This turned out to be a challenge because the mango wanted to integrate into the cheese filling. The solution was to concentrate the mango pulp before streaking it through the filling, which then formed lovely stratalike little pools of intense mango flavor.

PLAN AHEAD Make at least 1 day ahead.

SPECIAL EQUIPMENT FOR THE CAKE BASE: Two 9½ by 1 inch tart pans, or two 10 by 2 inch round cake pans, bottoms coated with shortening, topped with parchment rounds, then coated with baking spray with flour | Two wire racks | Two wire racks, lightly coated with nonstick cooking spray

FOR THE CHEESECAKE: One 9 by 3 inch or 2¾ inch high springform pan, lightly coated with nonstick cooking spray, set in a slightly larger silicone pan or wrapped with a *double* layer of heavy-duty aluminum foil to prevent seepage | One 12 inch round cake pan or a roasting pan to serve as a water bath

Cake Base

MAKES TWO 9 X ½ OR 9 X ⅜ INCH THICK LAYERS

(only one is needed for the recipe; the second layer can be frozen for future use)

	VOLUME	WEIGHT	
Light Sponge Cake (Biscuit), page 103, or ladyfingers (one 2 ounce package)	24 fingers	2 ounces	56 grams

MAKE THE CAKE BASE Make the light sponge cake (biscuit), baking it in the two 9½ inch tart pans or 10 inch cake pans. The cake also can be baked in the half sheet pan as described in the recipe on page 103. (If using the sheet pan, you will cut one 9 inch round for the cheesecake base. From the remainder, cut a rectangle to use as a small cake roll or to freeze for future use.)

UNMOLD AND COOL THE CAKE BASE If necessary, loosen the sides with the tip of a sharp knife. Unmold the cakes at once. Invert the pans onto the coated wire racks and lift off the pans. Leaving the parchment in place, reinvert onto the uncoated wire racks. Let the cakes cool completely. Reinvert the cakes onto the coated wire racks and peel off the parchment.

TRIM THE CAKE BASE Set the base of the springform pan or a 9 inch cardboard round on top of one of the cake base layers. Use scissors to trim the base to fit snugly within the springform pan. (Wrap the extra cake base tightly in plastic wrap and reserve for another use.)

LINE THE CAKE PAN Set the cake base on the bottom of the pan, or cut off the rounded edges of the ladyfingers and arrange the ladyfingers on the bottom of the pan, placing them crust sides down, and cutting or tearing smaller pieces to fit into any gaps. Cover the pan with plastic wrap while making the filling.

Optional: THINNER CAKE BASE The biscuit layer will be a little more than ½ inch high. The biscuit as a base will compress to about ¼ inch by the weight of the cheesecake filling. If you prefer a thinner layer, split it in half, using a long serrated knife held horizontally to make a shallow cut halfway down the sides of the layer all the way around. Using this cut as a track for the knife, with a sawing motion, slice from one side all the way through to the other. As you proceed, be sure to check that the far end of the blade has stayed in the groove.

MANGO FILLING

	VOLUME	WEIGHT	
mango pulp, preferably Alphonso (Ratna brand; see Notes, page 152)	1¼ cups (296 ml), *divided*	11.7 ounces	333 grams
cardamom seeds (optional)	1 teaspoon	.	2.5 grams
granulated sugar	1 cup	7 ounces	200 grams
cream cheese (65° to 70°F/ 19° to 21°C)	1¾ cups	1 pound	454 grams
8 (to 12) large egg yolks, at room temperature	½ cup plus 4 teaspoons (138 ml)	5.2 ounces	149 grams
lime juice, freshly squeezed	1 tablespoon (15 ml)	0.6 ounce	16 grams
pure vanilla extract	1 teaspoon (5 ml)	.	.
fine sea salt	¼ teaspoon	.	1.5 grams
full fat yogurt, Greek style thickened, such as Fage Total (see Notes, page 152)	2 cups	15.2 ounces	432 grams

PREHEAT THE OVEN Twenty minutes or longer before baking, set the oven rack in the lower third of the oven and preheat the oven to 350°F/175°C.

MAKE THE MANGO CONCENTRATE Set a fine-mesh strainer over a medium bowl and use a silicone spatula or the back of a large spoon to press the mango pulp through it.

Pour ¾ cup/177 ml/7 ounces/200 grams of the mango pulp into a 4 cup microwavable glass measure, lightly coated with nonstick cooking spray. Reduce it in the microwave to ½ cup/118 ml/4.6 ounces/130 grams. It will take about 7 minutes. (Alternatively, use a small heavy saucepan over low heat.) With either method, watch closely to prevent scorching. On the cooktop, stir constantly. Cover and set it aside to cool to room temperature.

MAKE THE FILLING If using the cardamom seeds, in a small spice grinder or in a mortar with a pestle, grind the cardamom seeds together with about ¼ cup of the sugar until the cardamom is powder fine. Whisk it into the remaining sugar.

In the bowl of a stand mixer fitted with the whisk beater, beat the sugar and cream cheese on medium-high speed until very smooth, scraping down the sides of the bowl once or twice, about 3 minutes. Gradually beat in the egg yolks, beating until smooth and scraping down the sides of the bowl once or twice. On medium-low speed, add the lime juice, vanilla, and salt and beat until incorporated. Add the yogurt and the remaining ½ cup of mango and continue beating just until fully blended, about 20 to 30 seconds. Detach the whisk beater and use it to reach down and whisk in any mixture that has settled to the bottom of the bowl.

Using a silicone spatula, scrape half of the filling into the prepared pan. Dot with half of the concentrated mango pulp, using a teaspoon to make about 14 dollops, each one about 1 inch wide. Use a small whisk to swirl the mango into the filling. Top with the remaining filling and swirl the remaining concentrated mango pulp into this layer of filling. Be sure to break up the mango pulp on the surface into thin streaks so that they do not separate from the filling on baking.

BAKE THE CAKE Set the springform pan into the larger pan and surround it with 1 inch of very hot water. Bake for 25 minutes. For even baking, rotate the pan halfway around. Continue baking for 25 minutes (30 minutes if using the silicone pan). Turn off the oven without opening the door and let the cake cool for 1 hour. When the pan is moved, the center will jiggle slightly.

CHILL THE CAKE Remove the pan from the water bath but leave the silicone pan or foil in place to catch any liquid that may seep from the cake. Set it on a wire rack to cool to room temperature or just until warm, about 1 to 2 hours. To absorb condensation, place a paper towel, curved side down, over the pan with the ends overhanging. Place an inverted plate, larger than the springform pan, on top of the paper towel.

Refrigerate the cheesecake for 4 hours or overnight. (The filling needs to be very firm before you pour on the topping.) Remove the cake from the refrigerator. Remove the plate, paper towel, and silicone pan or foil before making the mango topping.

MANGO TOPPING

	VOLUME	WEIGHT	
mango pulp, preferably Alphonso (Ratna brand; see Notes)	¾ cup (177 ml)	7 ounces	200 grams
cornstarch	2 teaspoons	.	6 grams
water	3 tablespoons (44 ml)	1.6 ounces	44 grams

MAKE THE MANGO TOPPING Set a fine-mesh strainer over a medium bowl and use a silicone spatula or the back of a large spoon to press the mango pulp through it.

In a small saucepan, using the silicone spatula, stir together the cornstarch and water until the cornstarch is dissolved. Stir in the mango pulp. Over low heat, bring the mixture to a boil, stirring constantly. Let it simmer, stirring very gently, for about 30 seconds, or until thickened. It will pool for a moment on the surface when a little is dropped from the spatula.

Immediately pour the topping evenly onto the chilled cheesecake. Tilt the pan to bring it to the edges and smooth it with a small offset spatula. If desired, make concentric rings, finishing in the middle. Let the cheesecake sit for 15 minutes to allow the steam to escape from the topping. Unmold the cake or refrigerate it, covered with a large bowl, until ready to unmold.

UNMOLD THE CAKE Use a small torch or wipe the sides of the pan with a dish towel that has been run under hot water and wrung out. Release the sides of the springform pan. If the sides of the cheesecake are uneven, run a small metal spatula under hot water, dry it, and use it to smooth them.

STORE Airtight: refrigerated, 5 days. Do not freeze, because the texture will become less smooth.

NOTES Use the recommended brand and variety of mango, Ratna Alphonso, available from Indian supply stores or specialty food stores such as Kalustyan's (see page 527). Avoid brands that contain sugar syrup, because they will be less bright in color and flavor.

Greek style yogurt is essential for this recipe because most of the whey is removed, making it much thicker and creamier. It is usually made with whole milk and cream, giving it a richer and sweeter flavor.

FOURTH OF JULY
CHEESECAKE

SERVES 12

OVEN TEMPERATURE
350°F/175°C

BAKING TIME
18 to 25 minutes for the red velvet cake base; 45 minutes
(50 minutes if using a silicone pan with the water bath),
plus 1 hour with the oven off, for the cheesecake

*W*hat could be a more perfect celebration cake than a layer of red velvet cake topped with tangy, creamy cheesecake, encased in a complementary white chocolate cream cheese frosting and gilded with juicy fresh blueberries? The filling is a basic cheesecake recipe that can also be used interchangeably with different crusts and toppings.

PLAN AHEAD Make the cheesecake at least 1 day ahead of serving.

SPECIAL EQUIPMENT FOR THE RED VELVET CAKE AND COMPOSING: One 10 by 2 inch round cake pan, encircled with a cake strip, bottom coated with shortening, topped with a parchment round, then coated with baking spray with flour | One 9 by 2 inch round cake pan for composing the cake | A small pastry bag fitted with a ¼ inch open star decorating tip (number 22) | A single-edge razor blade or thin sharp knife

FOR THE CHEESECAKE: One 9 by 2½ inch or higher springform pan, bottom coated with shortening, topped with a parchment round, then coated with nonstick cooking spray, set in a slightly larger silicone pan or wrapped with a *double* layer of heavy-duty aluminum foil to prevent seepage | One 12 inch round cake pan or a roasting pan to serve as a water bath

RED VELVET CAKE BASE

MAKES ONE 9 BY ¾ INCH HIGH CAKE

	VOLUME	WEIGHT	
2 large egg whites, room temperature	¼ cup (59 ml)	2.1 ounces	60 grams
red liquid food coloring	1 tablespoon plus 1 teaspoon (20 ml)	0.7 ounce	20 grams
pure vanilla extract	1 teaspoon (5 ml)	.	.
bleached cake flour (or bleached all-purpose flour)	1⅓ cups (or 1 cup plus 2½ tablespoons), sifted into the cup and leveled off	4.7 ounces	133 grams
superfine sugar	⅔ cup	4.7 ounces	133 grams
baking powder	2 teaspoons	.	9 grams
unsweetened cocoa powder	¾ teaspoon (sifted before measuring)	.	1.1 grams
fine sea salt	⅜ teaspoon	.	2.2 grams
unsalted butter (65° to 75°F/ 19° to 23°C)	2 tablespoons plus 2 teaspoons	1.3 ounces	38 grams
canola or safflower oil, at room temperature	2 tablespoons plus 2 teaspoons (39 ml)	1.3 ounces	36 grams
low-fat buttermilk	⅓ cup (79 ml)	2.9 ounces	81 grams

PREHEAT THE OVEN Twenty minutes or longer before baking, set an oven rack in the lower third of the oven and preheat the oven to 350°F/175°C.

MIX THE LIQUID INGREDIENTS In a medium bowl, whisk the egg whites, red food coloring, and vanilla just until lightly combined. (Caution: Be careful with the food coloring; it stains effectively, but also unmercifully.)

MIX THE DRY INGREDIENTS In a medium bowl, whisk together the flour, sugar, baking powder, cocoa, and salt.

MIX THE BATTER In the bowl of a stand mixer fitted with the flat beater, mix the butter and oil on medium speed for 1 minute. The mixture will not be completely smooth. Add the flour mixture and the buttermilk. Mix on low speed until the dry ingredients are moistened. Raise the speed to medium and beat for 1½ minutes. Scrape down the sides of the bowl.

Starting on medium-low speed, gradually add the egg mixture to the batter in two parts, beating on medium speed for 30 seconds after each addition to incorporate the ingredients and strengthen the structure. Using a silicone spatula, scrape the batter into the prepared pan and smooth the surface with a small offset spatula. The pan will be just one-quarter full.

BAKE THE CAKE Bake for 18 to 25 minutes, or until a wire cake tester inserted into the center comes out clean and the cake springs back when pressed lightly in the center. The cake should start to shrink from the sides of the pan only after removal from the oven.

COOL AND UNMOLD THE CAKE Let the cake cool in the pan on a wire rack for 10 minutes. Run a small metal spatula between the sides of the pan and the cake, pressing firmly against the pan, and then invert the cake onto a wire rack that has been lightly coated with nonstick cooking spray. Reinvert so that the top side is up. Cool completely.

CHEESECAKE FILLING

	VOLUME	WEIGHT	
cream cheese (65° to 70°F/ 19° to 21°C)	1¾ cups	1 pound	454 grams
granulated sugar	1 cup	7 ounces	200 grams
8 (to 12) large egg yolks, at room temperature	½ cup plus 4 teaspoons (138 ml)	5.2 ounces	149 grams
lemon juice, freshly squeezed	3 tablespoons (44 ml)	1.7 ounces	47 grams
pure vanilla extract	½ tablespoon (7.5 ml)	.	.
fine sea salt	¼ teaspoon	.	1.5 grams
sour cream	3 cups	25.6 ounces	726 grams

PREHEAT THE OVEN Twenty minutes or longer before baking, set an oven rack in the lower third of the oven and preheat the oven to 350°F/175°C.

MAKE THE FILLING In the bowl of a stand mixer fitted with the whisk beater, beat the cream cheese and sugar on medium-high speed until very smooth, scraping down the sides of the bowl once or twice, about 3 minutes. Gradually beat in the egg yolks, beating until smooth and scraping down the sides of the bowl once or twice. On medium-low speed, add the lemon juice, vanilla, and salt and beat until incorporated. Add the sour cream. Continue beating just until fully blended, about 20 to 30 seconds. Detach the whisk beater and use it to reach down and whisk in any mixture that has settled to the bottom of the bowl.

Using a silicone spatula, scrape the filling into the prepared springform pan and smooth the surface evenly with an offset spatula.

BAKE THE CAKE Set the springform pan into the larger pan and surround it with 1 inch of very hot water. Bake for 25 minutes. For even baking, rotate the pan halfway around. Continue baking for 20 minutes (25 minutes if using the silicone pan). Turn off the oven without opening the door and let the cake cool for 1 hour. When the pan is moved, the center will jiggle slightly.

CHILL THE CAKE Remove the pan from the water bath, but leave the silicone pan or foil in place to catch any liquid that may seep from the cake. Set it on a wire rack to cool to room temperature or just until warm, about 1 to 2 hours. To absorb condensation, place a paper towel, curved side down, over the pan with the ends overhanging. Place an inverted plate, larger than the springform pan, on top of the paper towel.

Refrigerate the cheesecake for 6 hours or overnight. (The filling needs to be very firm before you complete the assembly of the cake.)

DREAMY CREAMY WHITE CHOCOLATE FROSTING

MAKES 3½ CUPS/29 OUNCES/822 GRAMS

(make a half recipe if not frosting the sides of the cake)

	VOLUME	WEIGHT	
white chocolate containing cocoa butter, chopped	.	10.6 ounces	300 grams
cream cheese, softened but still cool (65° to 70°F/19° to 21°C)	1½ cups plus 1 tablespoon	14.1 ounces	400 grams
unsalted butter, softened but still cool (65° to 70°F/19° to 21°C)	8 tablespoons (1 stick)	4 ounces	113 grams
crème fraîche or sour cream	5 teaspoons	0.9 ounce	25 grams
pure vanilla extract	½ teaspoon (2.5 ml)	.	.

MELT THE WHITE CHOCOLATE In a medium microwavable bowl, stirring with a silicone spatula every 15 seconds (or in the top of a double boiler set over hot, not simmering, water, stirring often—do not let the bottom of the container touch the water), heat the white chocolate until almost completely melted.

Remove the chocolate from the heat source and stir until fully melted. Let the chocolate cool until it is no longer warm to the touch but is still fluid (75° to 80°F/24° to 27°C).

MAKE THE FROSTING In a food processor, process the cream cheese, butter, and crème fraîche for a few seconds until smooth and creamy. Scrape down the sides of the bowl. Add the cooled melted chocolate and pulse several times until it is smoothly incorporated. Add the vanilla and pulse it in.

RASPBERRY PRESERVES COATING

	VOLUME	WEIGHT	
seedless raspberry preserves	¼ cup plus 2 tablespoons	4.2 ounces	118 grams

MAKE THE RASPBERRY PRESERVES COATING Heat the raspberry preserves in a small micro-wavable bowl, stirring with a whisk every 15 seconds (or in a small saucepan over medium-low heat, stirring constantly), until the preserves are smooth and fluid. Using a spoon or silicone spatula, press them through a strainer into a small bowl. If necessary, whisk in a tiny bit of water so that they are fluid.

UNMOLD THE CHEESECAKE Remove the plate, paper towel, and silicone pan or foil. Use a small torch or wipe the sides of the pan with a dish towel that has been run under hot water and wrung out. Release the sides of the springform pan.

COMPOSE THE CAKE If serving the cake the same day, you can leave the sides unfrosted to reveal the beautiful layers. Alternatively, frosting the sides of the cake will keep it moist for longer storage.

Place a piece of plastic wrap, lightly coated with nonstick cooking spray, on top of the cheesecake. Set the 9 inch cake pan, bottom side down, on top of the cake. Invert the cake together with the pan and set the pan on a counter. Remove the springform pan bottom and the parchment and blot any moisture from the cake with a paper towel. Wash and dry the pan bottom.

Using a small offset spatula, spread about 3 tablespoons of the raspberry preserves onto the bottom of the cheesecake.

Transfer the red velvet cake, top side up, to a cutting board. If the cake is not perfectly flat, use a long serrated knife to level it to ¾ inch high. Place the springform pan bottom on top as a guide. Using the single-edge razor blade, trim the cake to a 9 inch disc. Begin by lightly scoring the top of the cake and then score the cake a little deeper each time, keeping the blade straight up and down, not angled, until you cut completely through the cake.

Reinvert the cake and, using the removable bottom of a tart pan lightly coated with non-stick cooking spray, or two large pancake turners, set the red velvet cake on top of the cheesecake. Position the cake so that its sides are flush with the cheesecake's sides. Place a serving plate on top of the cake. Slip the palm of your hand under the 9 inch cake pan and, holding the bottom of the serving plate with your other hand, quickly reinvert the cake.

Slide a few wide strips of parchment under the cake to keep the rim of the plate clean. Carefully spread as much of the remaining raspberry preserves as necessary onto the sides of the red velvet cake to seal in the crumbs. Slide out the parchment strips and use a paper towel to wipe any preserves from the serving plate. Slide a clean set of parchment strips under the cake and carefully apply a thin layer of the buttercream to the red velvet cake as an undercoat. Wipe off any red-tinted frosting from the spatula before frosting the rest of the cake.

Refrigerate the cake for 10 minutes to firm up the undercoat. Reserve ¾ cup/5.7 ounces/ 162 grams of the buttercream for piping, if desired. Use the remainder of the buttercream to frost the top and sides of the cake. (You will have about 1 cup left over, which can be refrigerated or frozen for future use.) Work quickly because the cold cheesecake will cause the buttercream to set. Slowly slide the parchment strips out from under the cake.

If desired, pipe a border of stars or shells (see page 254) around the top edge of the cake.

Refrigerate the cake for a minimum of 20 minutes to firm up the buttercream. Up to 6 hours before serving, make the blueberry topping.

FRESH BLUEBERRY TOPPING

	VOLUME	WEIGHT	
fresh blueberries	2¾ cups	12 ounces	340 grams
arrowroot or cornstarch	1 tablespoon	.	9 grams
granulated sugar	¼ cup	1.8 ounces	50 grams
water	½ cup (118 ml)	4.2 ounces	118 grams
lemon juice, freshly squeezed	½ tablespoon (7.5 ml)	.	8 grams

MAKE THE BLUEBERRY TOPPING Have ready a strainer or colander large enough to hold the berries suspended over a medium bowl.

Rinse the berries and dry well with paper towels. Place them in a bowl.

In a small saucepan, mix the arrowroot and sugar. Stir in the water and lemon juice and heat over medium heat, stirring constantly, until clear and thickened. Remove the pan from the heat and add the blueberries, tossing until coated.

Transfer the coated berries to the strainer, drain, and discard any glaze not clinging to the berries. Let the berries cool until no longer warm to the touch, about 20 minutes. Carefully spoon them onto the top of the cake and arrange them in a single layer.

Refrigerate the cake until about 40 minutes before serving time. Run a knife blade under hot water and wipe it dry between each cut. This makes it possible to cut through the firm buttercream and keeps the red from the red velvet cake from staining the ivory color of the cheesecake. Let the slices soften for 20 to 30 minutes at room temperature before serving.

STORE Airtight: refrigerated, 5 days without the blueberry topping (3 days with the blueberry topping). Do not freeze, because the texture of the cheesecake will become less smooth.

LEMON ALMOND CHEESECAKE

SERVES 10 TO 12

OVEN TEMPERATURE
350°F/175°C

BAKING TIME
50 minutes (55 minutes if using a silicone pan with the water bath), plus 1 hour with the oven off

*T*he Golden Lemon Almond Cake from *Rose's Heavenly Cakes* is my favorite non-chocolate cake in the book, and I can never resist licking the beater, because the creamy batter is so luscious. This gave me the idea to make a cheesecake version that would maintain a creamy texture after baking. Adding ground almonds contributes an appealingly fluffy texture to the cake; here, toasted almonds are also added to the sponge cake base.

PLAN AHEAD Make the cheesecake at least 1 day ahead.

SPECIAL EQUIPMENT FOR THE CAKE BASE: Two 9½ by 1 inch tart pans, or two 10 by 2 inch round cake pans, bottoms coated with shortening, topped with parchment rounds, then coated with baking spray with flour | Two wire racks | Two wire racks, lightly coated with nonstick cooking spray

FOR THE CHEESECAKE: One 9 by 3 inch or 2¾ inch high springform pan, lightly coated with nonstick cooking spray, set in a slightly larger silicone pan or wrapped with a *double* layer of heavy-duty aluminum foil to prevent seepage | One 12 inch round cake pan or a roasting pan to serve as a water bath

CAKE BASE

MAKES TWO 9 X ½ OR 9 X ⅜ INCH THICK LAYERS

(only one is needed for the recipe; the second layer can be frozen for future use)

	VOLUME	WEIGHT	
Light Almond Sponge Cake (Biscuit), page 104, or ladyfingers (one 2 ounce package)	24 fingers	2 ounces	56 grams

MAKE THE CAKE BASE Make the light sponge cake (biscuit), baking it in the two 9½ inch tart pans or 10 inch cake pans. The cake also can be baked in the half sheet pan as described in the recipe on page 103. (If using the sheet pan, you will cut one 9 inch round for the cheesecake base. From the remainder, cut a rectangle to use separately as a small cake roll or to line the sides of the cake, following the instructions given on page 167 for the Marble White and Dark Chocolate Cheesecake.)

UNMOLD AND COOL THE CAKE BASES If necessary, loosen the sides with the tip of a sharp knife. Unmold the cakes at once. Invert the pans onto the coated wire racks and lift off the pans. Leaving the parchment in place, reinvert onto the uncoated wire racks. Let the cakes cool completely. Reinvert the cakes onto the coated wire racks and peel off the parchment.

TRIM THE CAKE BASE Set the base of the springform pan or a 9 inch cardboard round on top of one of the cake base layers. Use scissors to trim the base to fit snugly within the springform pan. (Wrap the extra cake base tightly in plastic wrap and reserve for another use.)

LINE THE CAKE PAN Set the cake base on the bottom of the pan, or cut off the rounded edges of the ladyfingers and arrange them on the bottom of the pan, placing them, crust sides down, and cutting or tearing smaller pieces to fit into any gaps. Cover the pan with plastic wrap while making the filling.

Optional: THINNER CAKE BASE The biscuit layer will be a little more than ½ inch high. The biscuit as a base will compress to about ¼ inch by the weight of the cheesecake filling. If you prefer a thinner layer, split it in half, using a long serrated knife held horizontally to make a shallow cut halfway down the sides all the way around. Using this cut as a track for the knife, with a sawing motion, slice from one side all the way through to the other. As you proceed, be sure to check that the far end of the blade has stayed in the groove.

ALMOND LEMON FILLING

	VOLUME	WEIGHT	
blanched sliced almonds	.	2.3 ounces	66 grams
turbinado sugar, preferably Sugar in the Raw	1 cup, *divided*	7 ounces	200 grams
cream cheese (65° to 70°F/ 19° to 21°C)	1¾ cups	1 pound	454 grams
fine sea salt	¼ teaspoon	.	1.5 grams
8 (to 12) large egg yolks, at room temperature	½ cup plus 4 teaspoons (138 ml)	5.2 ounces	149 grams
lemon zest, finely grated (from 3 to 5 lemons)	2 tablespoons, loosely packed	.	12 grams
lemon juice, freshly squeezed	2 tablespoons (30 ml)	1.1 ounces	32 grams
pure almond extract	2 teaspoons (10 ml)	.	.
pure vanilla extract	1 teaspoon (5 ml)	.	.
pure lemon oil, preferably Boyajian	⅜ teaspoon (1.5 ml)	.	.
sour cream	3 cups	25.6 ounces	726 grams

PREHEAT THE OVEN Twenty minutes or longer before baking, set an oven rack in the lower third of the oven and preheat the oven to 350°F/175°C.

TOAST AND GRIND THE ALMONDS Spread the almonds evenly on a baking sheet and bake for about 7 minutes, or until pale gold. Stir once or twice to ensure even toasting and avoid overbrowning. Cool completely, and then process until fairly fine. Add ¼ cup/1.8 ounces/50 grams of the sugar and process until very fine.

MAKE THE FILLING In the bowl of a stand mixer fitted with the whisk beater, beat the cream cheese, the remaining ¾ cup of sugar, and the salt on medium-high speed until very smooth, scraping down the sides of the bowl once or twice, about 3 minutes. Gradually beat in the egg yolks, beating until smooth and scraping down the sides of the bowl once or twice. On medium-low speed, add the lemon zest, lemon juice, almond extract, vanilla, and lemon oil and beat until incorporated. Add the sour cream and the almond mixture, and continue beating just until fully blended, about 20 to 30 seconds. Detach the whisk beater and use it to reach down and whisk in any mixture that has settled to the bottom of the bowl.

Using a silicone spatula, scrape the filling into the prepared pan and smooth the surface evenly with an offset spatula.

BAKE THE CAKE Set the pan into the larger pan and surround it with 1 inch of very hot water. Bake for 25 minutes. For even baking, rotate the pan halfway around. Continue baking for 25 minutes (30 minutes if using the silicone pan). Turn off the oven without opening the door and let the cake cool for 1 hour. When the pan is moved, the center will jiggle slightly.

CHILL THE CAKE Remove the pan from the water bath, but leave the silicone pan or foil in place to catch any liquid that may seep from the cake. Set the cake on a wire rack to cool to room temperature or just until warm, about 1 to 2 hours. To absorb condensation, place a paper towel, curved side down, over the pan with the ends overhanging. Place an inverted plate, larger than the springform pan, on top of the paper towel.

Refrigerate the cheesecake for 4 hours or overnight. (The filling needs to be very firm before you pour on the topping.) Remove the cake from the refrigerator and remove the plate, paper towel, and silicone pan or foil before making the lemon curd topping.

LEMON CURD GLAZE

MAKES ¾ CUP/7 OUNCES/200 GRAMS

	VOLUME	WEIGHT	
3 (to 4) large egg yolks, at room temperature	3½ tablespoons (52 ml)	2 ounces	56 grams
granulated sugar	½ cup minus ½ tablespoon	3.3 ounces	94 grams
unsalted butter (65° to 75°F/ 19° to 23°C)	3 tablespoons	1.5 ounces	42 grams
lemon juice, freshly squeezed and strained (about 3 large lemons)	¼ cup plus ½ tablespoon (66 ml)	2.5 ounces	71 grams
fine sea salt	a pinch	.	.

MAKE THE LEMON CURD GLAZE Have ready a fine-mesh strainer suspended over a 2 cup glass measure with a spout.

In a medium heavy saucepan, whisk the egg yolks, sugar, and butter until well blended. Whisk in the lemon juice and salt. Cook over medium-low heat, stirring constantly with a silicone spatula and scraping down the sides of the pan as needed, until thickened and resembling hollandaise sauce, which thickly coats the spatula but is still liquid enough to pour. The mixture will change from translucent to opaque and begin to take on a yellow color on the spatula. Do not let it come to a boil or it will curdle. Whenever steam appears, remove the pan briefly from the heat, stirring constantly, to keep the mixture from boiling.

When the curd has thickened and will pool when a little is dropped onto its surface (an instant-read thermometer should read no higher than 186°F/86°C), pour it at once into the strainer and press it through. Avoid scraping the saucepan because the residue is thicker and will mar the surface of the cheesecake.

APPLY THE GLAZE For the smoothest topping, use the glaze immediately by pouring it quickly onto the chilled cheesecake. Shake the pan from side to side to even the topping. If necessary, smooth the topping with a small offset spatula. Let it sit for 15 minutes to allow the steam to escape from the topping.

Refrigerate the cheesecake, covered again with a paper towel, curved side down, and plate, for at least 2 hours before unmolding.

UNMOLD THE CAKE Remove the plate and paper towel. Use a small torch or wipe the sides of the pan with a dish towel that has been run under hot water and wrung out. Release the sides of the springform pan. If the sides of the cheesecake are uneven, run a small metal spatula under hot water, dry it, and use it to smooth them.

STORE Airtight: refrigerated, 5 days. Do not freeze, because the texture will become less smooth.

Marble White and Dark Chocolate Cheesecake

OVEN TEMPERATURE

450°F/230°C for the chocolate biscuit; 350°F/175°C for the cheesecake

BAKING TIME

7 to 10 minutes for the chocolate biscuit; 45 minutes (50 minutes if using a silicone pan for the water bath),
plus 1 hour with the oven off, for the cheesecake

*T*raditionally, marble cake recipes call for making a single batter and using part of it to create the darker chocolate batter. In this version, Woody made two separate batters, one with white chocolate and the other with bittersweet chocolate, so that each batter had a perfect flavor and consistency.

PLAN AHEAD Make the cheesecake at least 1 day before serving.

SPECIAL EQUIPMENT FOR THE CHOCOLATE BISCUIT: One 17¼ by 12¼ by 1 inch half sheet pan, coated with shortening or nonstick cooking spray, bottom lined with parchment and then coated with baking spray with flour (cut the parchment to extend 1 inch past one of the long sides of the pan) | One large wire rack | One baking sheet or inverted extra half sheet pan, lightly coated with nonstick cooking spray

FOR THE CHEESECAKE FILLING: One 9 by 2½ inch or higher springform pan, the sides coated with shortening, set in a slightly larger silicone pan or wrapped with a *double* layer of heavy-duty aluminum foil to prevent seepage. For the sides, cut a 30 by 2 inch wide band of parchment. Wrap and press it against the inside walls of the pan. Use shortening to coat the overlapping ends to hold them in place. Lightly coat the parchment with nonstick cooking spray | An expandable flan ring, 8¾ inch pot lid, or 8¾ inch cardboard template | One 12 inch round cake pan or a roasting pan to serve as a water bath

Light Chocolate Sponge Cake (Biscuit)

Batter

	VOLUME	WEIGHT	
unsweetened (alkalized) cocoa powder	⅓ cup (sifted before measuring)	0.9 ounce	25 grams
boiling water	¼ cup (59 ml)	2.1 ounces	59 grams
pure vanilla extract	¾ teaspoon (3.7 ml)	.	.
bleached cake flour (or bleached all-purpose flour)	⅓ cup (or ¼ cup plus 2 teaspoons), sifted into the cup and leveled off	1.2 ounces	33 grams
5 (to 7) large eggs, separated, at room temperature			
yolks	¼ cup plus 2 tablespoons (89 ml)	3.3 ounces	93 grams
whites (about 4)	½ cup (118 ml), *divided*	4.2 ounces	120 grams
superfine sugar	⅔ cup plus 1 tablespoon, *divided*	5.1 ounces	146 grams
cream of tartar	¼ teaspoon	.	.

PREHEAT THE OVEN Twenty minutes or longer before baking, set an oven rack in the middle of the oven and preheat the oven to 450°F/230°C.

MIX THE COCOA AND WATER In a small bowl, with a silicone spatula, stir together the cocoa and boiling water until smooth. Stir in the vanilla, cover tightly with plastic wrap to prevent evaporation, and cool to room temperature, about 20 minutes. To speed cooling, place the bowl in the refrigerator. Bring the mixture to room temperature before proceeding.

SIFT THE FLOUR Sift the flour onto a large piece of parchment or into another small bowl.

MIX THE EGG MIXTURE In the bowl of a stand mixer fitted with the whisk beater, place the egg yolks, half of the egg whites (¼ cup/59 ml/2.1 ounces/60 grams), and ⅔ cup/4.7 ounces/ 133 grams of the sugar. Beat on high speed until thick, fluffy, and tripled in volume, about 5 minutes. Lower the speed to medium and add the cocoa mixture, beating a few seconds until incorporated.

If you don't have a second mixer bowl, scrape this mixture into a large bowl and thoroughly wash, rinse, and dry the mixer bowl and whisk beater to remove any trace of oil.

MAKE THE BATTER Sift half of the flour over the egg mixture and, using a large balloon whisk, slotted skimmer, or silicone spatula, fold it in gently but rapidly until almost all of the flour has disappeared. Repeat with the remaining flour until all traces of the flour have disappeared.

BEAT THE EGG WHITES INTO A STIFF MERINGUE In the bowl of a stand mixer fitted with the whisk beater, beat the remaining egg whites and the cream of tartar on medium-low speed until foamy. Gradually raise the speed to medium-high and beat until soft peaks form when the beater is raised. Gradually beat in the remaining 1 tablespoon of sugar and continue beating until stiff peaks form when the beater is raised slowly.

ADD THE MERINGUE TO THE BATTER Using the large balloon whisk, slotted skimmer, or large silicone spatula, gently fold the meringue into the batter. Scrape the batter into the prepared pan and, using a small offset spatula, smooth the surface as evenly as possible.

BAKE THE CAKE Bake for 7 to 10 minutes, or until the cake springs back when pressed lightly in the center. Have ready a small sharp knife.

UNMOLD AND COOL THE CAKE Run the tip of a sharp knife around the sides to dislodge any cake that may have attached itself to the sides of the pan and unmold the cake at once. Slip a small offset spatula under the edge of the parchment to loosen it. Grasp the parchment and gently slide the cake onto the wire rack. Let the cake cool completely, about 20 minutes. Invert the cake onto the baking sheet or inverted half sheet pan and peel off the parchment. If not using the cake right away, cover with plastic wrap.

CUT THE CAKE PIECES Begin by cutting the cake widthwise into 2 unequal rectangles: 1 needs to be 8¾ inches wide for the round cake base.

To make the round cake base, set the expandable flan ring on the cake and mark around it with the tip of a sharp knife. Use kitchen scissors to cut out the disc.

To make the side pieces, use a long serrated knife and a ruler to cut a 10 by 5¼ inch rectangle from the remaining cake rectangle. With the knife, cut the rectangle the long way into 3 strips, each 1¾ inches wide. Alternatively, with the tip of a sharp knife, mark where the cuts should be and then use scissors to cut out the strips.

Wrap each cake piece in plastic wrap to keep it soft and fresh, and refrigerate them until ready to line the pan and add the filling.

LINE THE SPRINGFORM PAN WITH THE CAKE Press the 3 side strips, with the top crust sides facing the sides of the pan, against the parchment. Trim 1 of the pieces to make a seamless fit. Set the cake disc, with the top crust side facing down, on the bottom of the pan, wedged against the side strips.

CHOCOLATE FILLING

	VOLUME	WEIGHT	
white chocolate containing cocoa butter, chopped	.	5.3 ounces	150 grams
bittersweet chocolate, 60% to 62% cacao, chopped	.	3.2 ounces	92 grams
cream cheese (65° to 70°F/ 19° to 21°C)	3½ cups	2 pounds	908 grams
granulated sugar	1 cup	7 ounces	200 grams
4 (to 6) large eggs, at room temperature	¾ cup plus 2 teaspoons (187 ml)	7 ounces	200 grams
heavy cream	½ cup (118 ml)	4.1 ounces	116 grams
pure vanilla extract	1 tablespoon (15 ml)	.	.
cornstarch	1 tablespoon	.	9 grams
fine sea salt	¼ teaspoon	.	1.5 grams

PREHEAT THE OVEN Twenty minutes or longer before baking, set an oven rack in the lower third of the oven and preheat the oven to 350°F/175°C.

MELT THE CHOCOLATES In a small microwavable bowl, stirring with a silicone spatula every 15 seconds (or in the top of a double boiler set over hot, not simmering, water, stirring often—do not let the bottom of the container touch the water), heat the white chocolate until almost completely melted.

Remove the white chocolate from the heat source and stir until fully melted. Let it cool until it is no longer warm to the touch but is still fluid.

Repeat the same process to melt the dark chocolate.

MAKE THE BATTER In the bowl of a stand mixer fitted with the whisk beater, beat the cream cheese and sugar on medium-high speed until very smooth, scraping down the sides of the bowl once or twice, about 3 minutes. Beat in the eggs, 1 at a time, beating until smooth and scraping down the sides of the bowl once or twice. Add the cream, vanilla, cornstarch, and salt, and beat on medium-low speed until incorporated. Detach the whisk beater and use it to whisk in any mixture that has settled to the bottom of the bowl.

Pour 2½ cups (20.8 ounces/590 grams) of the batter into a medium bowl. Scrape the melted dark chocolate into it and, with a large whisk, whisk until the batter is a uniform color.

Scrape the melted white chocolate into the stand mixer bowl. Return the bowl to the mixer and mix on medium-low speed for about 30 seconds, or until the white chocolate is incorporated.

Pour about half (17.6 ounces/500 grams) of the white chocolate batter into the springform pan and spread it evenly with a small offset spatula. Spoon the dark chocolate batter on top of the white chocolate batter and spread it evenly. Scrape the remaining white chocolate batter over the dark chocolate batter and spread it evenly. Use a whisk or large spoon to swirl the two batters lightly, in an over and under motion, to create a marbled effect.

BAKE THE CAKE Set the springform pan into the larger pan and surround it with 1 inch of very hot water. Bake for 20 minutes. For even baking, rotate the pan halfway around. Continue baking for 25 minutes (30 minutes if using the silicone pan). Turn off the oven without opening the door and let the cake cool for 1 hour. When the pan is moved, the center will barely move.

CHILL THE CAKE Remove the pan from the water bath, but leave the silicone pan or foil in place to catch any liquid that may seep from the cake. Set it on a wire rack to cool to room temperature or just until warm, about 1 to 2 hours. To absorb condensation, place a paper towel, curved side down, over the pan with the ends overhanging. Place an inverted plate, larger than the springform pan, on top of the paper towel. Refrigerate the cheesecake for 4 hours or overnight.

UNMOLD THE CAKE Remove the plate, paper towel, and silicone pan or foil. Run a spatula between the sides of the springform pan and the parchment and release the sides of the springform pan. Carefully peel off the parchment by rolling it as it releases from the cake.

If the cheesecake's sides above the biscuit are uneven, run a small metal spatula under hot water, dry it, and use it to smooth the sides even with the biscuit.

STORE Airtight: refrigerated, 5 days. Do not freeze, because the texture will become less smooth.

STILTON BABY BLUE CHEESECAKES

OVEN TEMPERATURE
350°F/175°C for the walnuts; 225°F/107°C for the cheesecakes

BAKING TIME
7 to 9 minutes for the walnuts; 30 to 35 minutes for the cheesecakes

I first met and greatly admired chef Thomas Haas when he was pastry chef at Daniel restaurant in New York City. He is now owner of Thomas Haas Chocolates and Patisserie in Vancouver, British Columbia. Chef Haas generously shared one of his most popular recipes from the bakery. These fabulously delicious, creamy cheesecakes double as either an appetizer accompanied by a salad, or a dessert accompanied by fresh ripe pear slices and a glass of Sauternes.

PLAN AHEAD Make the cheesecakes at least 4 hours ahead.

SPECIAL EQUIPMENT Two 6 cup silicone muffin pans, lightly coated with nonstick cooking spray, set on a wire rack and then on a baking sheet, or one 12 cup muffin pan, bottoms coated with shortening, topped with parchment rounds, then lightly coated with nonstick cooking spray | Optional: a disposable pastry bag

WALNUT BASE AND BATTER

	VOLUME	WEIGHT	
walnut halves	¾ cup plus 1½ tablespoons	3 ounces	84 grams
sugar	¼ cup plus 2 tablespoons	2.6 ounces	75 grams
cornstarch	1 tablespoon	.	9 grams
fine sea salt	a pinch	.	.
cream cheese (65° to 70°F/ 19° to 21°C), cut into pieces	1⅓ cups	12 ounces	340 grams
sour cream	¼ cup	2.1 ounces	60 grams
Stilton or other strong flavored blue cheese	2 tablespoons	1.2 ounces	35 grams
2 large eggs, lightly beaten	⅓ cup plus 1 tablespoon (94 ml)	3.5 ounces	100 grams

PREHEAT THE OVEN Twenty minutes or longer before baking, set an oven rack in the middle of the oven and preheat the oven to 350°F/175°C.

TOAST THE WALNUTS Spread the walnuts evenly on a baking sheet and bake for about 7 minutes to enhance their flavor. Stir once or twice to ensure even toasting and avoid overbrowning. Turn the walnuts onto a clean dish towel and roll and rub them around to loosen the skins. Discard the skins and cool completely.

Lower the oven temperature to 225°F/107°C.

MAKE THE WALNUT BASE In a food processor, pulse the walnuts until they are finely chopped but not powder fine. Spoon 1 tablespoon/0.2 ounce/7 grams into each cup and press the nuts evenly onto the bottom.

MAKE THE FILLING In the bowl of a stand mixer fitted with the flat beater, mix the sugar, cornstarch, and salt on low speed for 30 seconds. Add the cream cheese and beat on low speed until the mixture begins to come together. Raise the speed to medium and beat for 1 minute, or until very smooth. Scrape down the sides of the bowl.

In a small bowl, using a fork, mash together the sour cream and Stilton cheese until well combined. Scrape this mixture into the mixer bowl and beat on low speed for 15 seconds, or just until incorporated.

Add the eggs and beat on low speed for 15 seconds, or just until incorporated. The batter should be thick like sour cream.

FILL THE CUPS The easiest way to fill the cups is to scrape the batter into a disposable pastry bag, or quart-size reclosable freezer bag with a ½ inch semicircle cut from one corner, and pipe the batter into the cups, filling them almost to the top (1.8 ounces/50 grams each). Alternatively, scrape the batter into a large measuring cup or pitcher with a spout and pour it in. Smooth the surfaces evenly with a small offset spatula.

BAKE THE CHEESECAKES Bake for 15 minutes. For even baking, rotate the pans halfway around. Continue baking for 15 to 20 minutes, or until an instant-read thermometer reads 160°F/71°C. When the pans are moved, the batter will jiggle like jelly, and the tops will be set and will bounce back when pressed lightly.

COOL THE CHEESECAKES Set the baking sheet on a wire rack. Lift the hot rack with the muffin pans onto another wire rack or heatproof surface to cool for 30 minutes, or just until warm. Cover the surface of the cheesecakes with plastic wrap that has been lightly coated with nonstick cooking spray and refrigerate for a minimum of 4 hours before unmolding.

UNMOLD THE CHEESECAKES If using metal muffin pans, run a small spatula that has been heated under hot water and wiped off between the sides of the muffin cups and the cakes. (This is not necessary if using silicone pans.)

Highlights for Success

If the batter is beaten too long, it will thin and the centers of the cheesecakes will dip about ¼ inch. The cheesecakes bake at a very low temperature, which results in a perfectly creamy consistency throughout.

Place a baking sheet on top of the plastic wrap–covered muffin pan and invert it. Wet a dish towel with very hot water. Wring out the excess and set it over the muffin pan, draping it into the depressions. Let it to sit for about 2 minutes. Remove the towel and lift off the muffin pan. If the cheesecakes do not release readily, reapply the hot towel and let it sit for another minute. Place a second sheet pan on top of the cheesecakes and reinvert them.

If the cakes were baked in the metal muffin pan, use a small spatula that has been heated in boiling water and wiped off to smooth the sides of the cakes.

Use a pancake turner to lift each cheesecake onto a serving plate.

STORE Refrigerated, 5 days.

Variation: Savory Stilton Cheesecakes

For bolder, more pungent tasting cheesecakes that can be served as an appetizer, increase the Stilton cheese to 3 tablespoons/1.8 ounces/52 grams. Serve with wheat crackers.

For larger servings, the cheesecake batter can also be baked in six (6 to 8 ounce capacity) ramekins and filled with 3.5 ounces/100 grams per ramekin. Reduce the walnut halves to ½ cup/1.8 ounces/50 grams. Bake for 40 to 50 minutes.

PIES, TARTS, AND OTHER PASTRIES

This chapter includes all kinds of pastry, from simple scones to galettes, pies, tarts, and even savory cream puffs. Some recipes, such as the Luscious Apple Pie, are riffs on classics and others, such as the Pomegranate Winter Chiffon Meringue Pie, are entirely new concepts.

I have included only two basic types of crust: my favorite Perfect Flaky and Tender Cream Cheese Pie Crust, and the Sweet Cookie Tart Crust (Pâte Sucrée), several variations of which appear throughout this chapter. This is not so much for simplicity's sake or in consideration of book real estate as the fact that despite all of the delicious pie crusts in my repertoire, the cream cheese crust is the one I always choose. I find no other pie crust to be its equal in flavor and ease of use. It rolls like a dream and keeps its shape the best. The sweet cookie crust is ideal for tarts that will be unmolded from the pan and pies that will be chilled or frozen because it is more tender and stays crisper than the flaky pie crust.

Some Special Tips

- It is easiest to roll flaky pie dough when it has been refrigerated for 45 minutes, at which point it will be chilled sufficiently but still malleable. Dough rolls best at 60°F/16°C. If there is an area in your house that is close to this temperature, such as a wine cellar or pantry, it is fine to leave it there for several hours before rolling.

- Brush off any excess flour on top of the dough after shaping it because it will taste bitter after baking.

- To cut a round disc of dough, use an expandable flan ring, which functions like a large cookie cutter, or make a cardboard template the size of the disc you need and use a small sharp knife to cut the dough. You can also use a cake pan of the appropriate size: Cover the dough with plastic wrap to keep the cake pan from sticking and then set the pan on top of the plastic wrap. Lift up the plastic wrap and cut around the edge of the pan with a small sharp knife. Press down lightly on the pan when cutting to keep it from moving.

- I have developed a unique and effective way of fitting tart dough perfectly into the pan (see photos, page 225). For a 9 inch tart pan, invert an 8 inch cake pan onto a work surface. After removing the top sheet of plastic wrap and cutting the disc of dough, use the bottom sheet of plastic wrap to lift the dough and set it, plastic side down, over the 8 inch cake pan. Smooth down the sides so they will fit into the tart pan. Place the removable bottom of the tart pan on top. Then carefully place the fluted ring, upside down, on top. Place a flat plate or cardboard round over the tart pan to keep it from separating and invert the pans. Remove the cake pan and carefully peel off the plastic wrap. Gently ease the dough down to reach the bottom and sides of the pan.

- Rolling sweet cookie tart dough is the fastest and most even way to line the tart pan; however, it is also fine to press the dough into the pan with your fingers. Once the dough is distributed in the pan, line it with plastic wrap and use your fingers or a flat-bottom measure or custard cup to smooth the dough over the bottom of the pan. To make a beautiful border, be sure to press the dough ⅛ to ¼ inch higher than the sides of the pan.

- If time allows, after lining the pan and crimping or fluting the edges, cover the dough with two layers of plastic wrap and freeze overnight before baking. This will ensure that the border will have the best possible shape.

Storing Pies and Pastry

Flaky pastry dough can be refrigerated for up to 2 days and frozen for up to 3 months. If making a single crust pie, after lining the pie plate or tart pan, it is fine to refrigerate it for up to 24 hours, or freeze it for up to 6 months if it is well wrapped to avoid loss of moisture. Use a gallon-size reclosable freezer bag if freezing or two layers of plastic wrap if refrigerating. Sweet cookie tart dough can be refrigerated for up to 1 week and frozen for up to about 1 year.

Store baked fruit pies and tarts for 2 days at room temperature or 4 days refrigerated. Pies, tarts, and pastries with cream fillings will keep for about 3 hours at room temperature or 5 days refrigerated. Soft meringue should be refrigerated and will keep for 1 to 2 days.

TROUBLESHOOTING FLAKY PIE CRUST AND PIES

PROBLEM: The dough sticks when rolling and the baked pie crust is not flaky.
SOLUTION: The dough is too warm and needs to be chilled until firm.

PROBLEM: The pie crust shrinks during baking.
SOLUTION: Lift the dough and allow it to shrink in while rolling and avoid stretching it when placing it in the pie plate. Let it rest, refrigerated, for a minimum of 1 hour before baking.

PROBLEM: The pie crust is too tender.
SOLUTION: Avoid mixing the cream cheese and/or butter too finely into the flour. Knead the dough until slightly stretchy when tugged so that it will hold together.

PROBLEM: The pie crust is too tough.
SOLUTION: Use a lower protein flour such as pastry flour or, if making your own, increase the proportion of cake flour to bleached all-purpose flour.

PROBLEM: When setting parchment in the dough-lined pan, it pleats and doesn't conform to the shape of the pan.
SOLUTION: Crumple the parchment lightly before setting it in the pan.

PROBLEM: The pie crust develops holes during baking.
SOLUTION: Seal the hole or holes with a little egg white, and return the pan to the oven for 30 seconds for the egg white to set and become opaque. Alternatively, seal the hole or holes with a little melted white chocolate and chill or let it set at room temperature before adding the filling.

PROBLEM: The border becomes too dark during baking.
SOLUTION: Protect the border with a foil ring right from the beginning of baking.

PROBLEM: The bottom of the pie or tart is soggy.
SOLUTION: Preheat a baking stone for a minimum of 45 minutes and bake the pie or tart by placing the pan directly on the hot stone. Alternatively, set the pie or tart on the floor of the oven for the first 20 minutes of baking, then raise it to a rack. For very juicy pies, such as the Luscious Apple Pie, baking it from frozen gives the bottom crust a chance to start baking before the filling thaws.

PROBLEM: The filling does not set.
SOLUTION: Bake until the filling is bubbling or the cornstarch will not be activated fully. Let it cool completely before slicing.

TROUBLESHOOTING SWEET COOKIE TART CRUST (PÂTE SUCRÉE)

PROBLEM: The dough cracks when rolling it.
SOLUTION: Gather it up and knead it until smooth. If absolutely necessary, spritz with a little water.

PROBLEM: The crust is too thick where the bottom meets the sides.
SOLUTION: Use the bottom of a glass tumbler or your fingers to press it well to thin it in this area before chilling and baking.

PROBLEM: During blind baking in a tart pan, the dough slips down.
SOLUTION: The dough will always slip down about ¼ inch, but to prevent it from slipping further or becoming uneven, make sure to chill the dough-lined tart pan thoroughly (freeze it for best results) before baking and push the rice, beans, or pie weights well up against the sides of the pan.

GOLDEN RULES OF PIE AND PASTRY BAKING

Weigh or measure ingredients carefully for consistent flavor and texture.

Use the ingredients specified in the recipe. For more details, see the Ingredients chapter (page 509).

FLOUR Be sure to use the flour specified in the recipe. Pastry flour is ideal for the flaky pie crust. Making your own by combining a national brand of bleached all-purpose flour and cake flour comes close, but pastry flour is best (see page 511).

BUTTER Use a high quality unsalted butter with standard fat content unless high fat butter is called for in the recipe or if making clarified butter.

EGGS Use USDA grade AA or A large eggs for most recipes and weigh or measure the volume. I recommend pasteurized eggs in the shell, such as Safest Choice.

The weight of the eggs and thickness of the shell can vary a great deal, even within a given weight class, as can the ratio of egg white to egg yolk. For this reason, it is advisable to weigh or measure the whole eggs, egg yolks, and egg whites. Values for recipes in this book are given for weight and volume, so it's fine to use any size eggs if you weigh or measure them. Bring eggs to room temperature by placing the eggs, still in their unbroken shells, in hot water for 5 minutes.

When beating egg whites, use ⅛ teaspoon of cream of tartar per egg white (¼ teaspoon for egg whites from eggs pasteurized in the shell) to stabilize the meringue.

BAKING POWDER Use fresh baking powder— check the expiration date and if you are in a humid environment, replace the baking powder sooner. Use only a nonaluminum, all-phosphate product containing calcium acid phosphate, such as Rumford, for the flaky pie crust to avoid an unpleasant taste (see page 518).

CHOCOLATE Use the cacao content percentage specified in the recipe.

Make an aluminum foil ring to protect the border of the crust during baking (see page 537).

Preheat the oven for 20 to 30 minutes before baking. If using a baking stone in the oven, preheat for 45 minutes. Use the correct oven temperature and set the pie or pastry on the rack specified in the recipe. If a pie or pastry is browning too much on the bottom, raise the pie plate to a higher rack or "double pan" it (set one baking sheet on top of another and set the pie plate on top). If a pie or pastry is browning too much on the top, move it to a lower rack or tent it loosely with aluminum foil.

Cool baked pastry completely on wire racks and store as indicated in the recipe.

IRISH CREAM SCONES

OVEN TEMPERATURE
400°F/200°C

BAKING TIME
15 to 20 minutes

*S*cones are like a cross between a pie crust with more liquid and a cake without eggs. My cherished friend and colleague Nancy Weber (writer, caterer, and Irish at heart) gave me this exceptional recipe from Paul Kelly, the award-winning executive pastry chef at The Merrion Hotel in Dublin. I had never before heard of making scones with all cream and no butter, but I loved the idea because cream has a floral quality that is lost when churned into butter. Of course the quality of the cream plays a big part in the flavor. Scones are delicious eaten still warm from the oven, but the moisture distributes most evenly if the scones are stored a minimum of four hours or overnight and then reheated.

SPECIAL EQUIPMENT One 8 inch round cake pan | A baking sheet lined with parchment or lightly coated with baking spray with flour

DOUGH

	VOLUME	WEIGHT	
Gold Medal bread flour (or half other brand bread flour/half unbleached all-purpose flour)	2⅓ cups (lightly spooned into the cup and leveled off)	10.6 ounces	300 grams
raisins	½ cup	2.5 ounces	72 grams
sugar	3 tablespoons	1.3 ounces	37 grams
baking powder (use only an aluminum free variety; see page 518)	1 tablespoon	0.5 ounce	13.5 grams
fine sea salt	⅜ teaspoon	.	2.2 grams
lemon zest, finely grated	1 tablespoon, loosely packed	.	6 grams
honey	1 tablespoon plus 1 teaspoon (20 ml)	1 ounce	28 grams
heavy cream, cold	1⅓ cups plus ½ tablespoon (323 ml), *divided*	11.1 ounces	316 grams

Highlights for Success

I prefer to shape the scones into wedges because cutting rounds always necessitates reworking the remaining dough, which toughens it slightly.

To reheat frozen scones, bake them in a preheated 300°F/150°C oven for 20 minutes. The outside will be crunchy and a cake tester inserted into the center will feel warm. To reheat room temperature scones, place them in a preheated 350°F/175°C oven for about 10 minutes.

If it's warm in your kitchen, place the flour, sugar, baking powder, and salt in a container or gallon-size reclosable freezer bag and freeze for at least 15 minutes.

It is essential to knead the dough very lightly and only as long as necessary for it to hold together in order to achieve light and tender scones.

The unbaked scones can be cut, individually wrapped in plastic wrap, and frozen for up to 3 months. To bake, place 1 or more on a prepared baking sheet. Add 5 to 7 minutes to the baking time. (The scones have a more even shape when baked frozen.)

PREHEAT THE OVEN Thirty minutes or longer before baking, set an oven rack in the lower third of the oven and preheat the oven to 400°F/200°C.

MAKE THE DOUGH In a medium bowl, whisk together the flour, raisins, sugar, baking powder, salt, and lemon zest. Make a well in the center and pour in the honey and 1⅓ cups of the cream. Using a silicone spatula, starting from the center, gradually stir the flour mixture into the cream until all of the flour is moistened. If dry particles still remain and, when pinched, the dough does not hold together, add the remaining cream.

Scrape the mixture onto a lightly floured surface. Gather it up and gently knead it into a soft dough.

Line the cake pan with plastic wrap and press the dough evenly into it or shape the dough into an 8 by ¾ inch thick disc. Press in any loose raisins. Cover with plastic wrap and refrigerate for 10 minutes.

SHAPE THE SCONES Lift out the scone disc using the plastic wrap. Use a sharp knife to cut the dough into 8 even wedges. Place the wedges, 2 inches apart, on the prepared baking sheet. For the highest rise, but slightly less flakiness, press lightly against the sides of the dough with your finger to seal them slightly, which causes the scones to puff a bit more. (I know this is counterintuitive, but it really works!)

BAKE THE SCONES Bake for 8 minutes. For even baking, rotate the sheet halfway around. Continue baking for 7 to 12 minutes, or until lightly browned. (An instant-read thermometer should read 205° to 212°F/96° to 100°C.)

COOL THE SCONES Place a linen or loose-weave towel on a large wire rack. Set the baking sheet on another wire rack. Use a pancake turner to transfer the scones to the towel. Fold the towel over loosely and let the scones cool until warm or room temperature.

STORE Airtight: room temperature, 2 days; frozen, 3 months.

Irish Cream Scones, Flaky Cream Cheese Scones (page 182),
Rose's Scone Toppers (page 184), and Raspberry
Butterscotch Lace Topping for Scones (page 185)

FLAKY CREAM CHEESE SCONES

OVEN TEMPERATURE
400°F/200°C

BAKING TIME
20 to 25 minutes

*B*ecause cream cheese pie crust is my number one pie crust, I thought it would also make a great scone. The result of my experiments is a scone that is softer, moister, and mellower than the classic scone. Be sure to try the scone topper variation that follows: I find the best part of the scone to be the top, so I created a variation to be bottomless!

SPECIAL EQUIPMENT One 9 inch round cake pan | A baking sheet lined with parchment or lightly coated with baking spray with flour

	VOLUME	WEIGHT	
unsalted butter, cold	8 tablespoons (1 stick)	4 ounces	113 grams
cream cheese, cold	½ cup	4.5 ounces	128 grams
heavy cream, cold	¾ cup (177 ml)	6.1 ounces	174 grams
Gold Medal bread flour (or half other brand bread flour/half unbleached all-purpose flour)	2⅓ cups (lightly spooned into the cup and leveled off)	10.6 ounces	300 grams
sugar	3 tablespoons	1.3 ounces	37 grams
baking powder (use only an aluminum free variety; see page 518)	1 tablespoon	0.5 ounce	13.5 grams
fine sea salt	⅜ teaspoon	.	2.2 grams
lemon zest, finely grated	1 tablespoon, loosely packed	.	6 grams
dried blueberries, or dried cranberries (cut in half)	½ cup	2.6 ounces	74 grams
honey	1 tablespoon plus 1 teaspoon (20 ml)	1 ounce	28 grams

PREHEAT THE OVEN Thirty minutes or longer before baking, set an oven rack in the lower third of the oven and preheat the oven to 400°F/200°C.

Highlights for Success

See Irish Cream Scones (page 180).

MAKE THE DOUGH Cut the butter into ½ to ¾ inch cubes and the cream cheese into ¾ inch cubes. Cover each separately with plastic wrap and return them to the refrigerator to chill for a minimum of 30 minutes.

Into a mixing bowl, pour the cream and refrigerate for at least 15 minutes. (Chill a hand-held mixer's beaters alongside the bowl.)

Whip the cream just until soft peaks form when the beater is lifted. Place it in the refrigerator.

In a large bowl, whisk together the flour, sugar, baking powder, salt, and lemon zest. Add the cream cheese and cut it into the flour mixture, using a pastry blender or two knives, until the cream cheese is no larger than small peas. Add the butter and, with a fork, toss to coat with the flour. Press the butter cubes between your fingers to form very thin flakes. Stir in the blueberries or cranberries. Make a well in the center. Place the whipped cream and the honey in the well and, with a silicone spatula, stir the flour mixture into the cream until all of it is moistened.

Lightly knead the dough in the bowl just until it holds together. Turn it out onto a lightly floured counter. Gently knead it a few times until it is a little stretchy and can be shaped into a smooth disc.

Line the cake pan with plastic wrap and press the dough evenly into it or shape the dough into a 9 by ¾ inch thick disc. Press in any loose blueberries. Cover with plastic wrap and refrigerate for 10 minutes.

SHAPE THE SCONES Lift out the scone disc using the plastic wrap. Use a sharp knife to cut the disc into 8 even wedges. Place the wedges, 2 inches apart, on the prepared baking sheet. For the highest rise, but slightly less flakiness, press lightly against the sides of the dough with your finger to seal them slightly, which causes the scones to puff a bit more.

BAKE THE SCONES Bake for 10 minutes. For even baking, rotate the sheet halfway around. Continue baking for 10 to 15 minutes, or until lightly browned. (An instant-read thermometer should read 205° to 212°F/96° to 100°C.)

COOL THE SCONES Place a linen or loose-weave towel on a large wire rack. Set the baking sheet on another wire rack. Use a pancake turner to transfer the scones to the towel. Fold the towel over loosely and let the scones cool until warm or room temperature.

STORE Airtight: room temperature, 2 days; frozen, 3 months.

Variation: ROSE'S SCONE TOPPERS

MAKES TWENTY-FOUR 3 BY 2 INCH TOPPERS

BAKING TIME
12 to 15 minutes for each of two batches

MAKE THE DOUGH Make the dough as it appears on page 182. After lightly kneading the finished dough, divide the dough in half, about 14.8 ounces/420 grams each. Shape each half into a 5 by 4 by ½ inch high rectangle.

Press in any loose berries. Wrap each piece of dough in plastic wrap and set it on a baking sheet. Refrigerate for 10 minutes.

SHAPE THE SCONE TOPPERS Set 1 piece of dough on a lightly floured counter. Lightly flour the dough and cover it with plastic wrap. Roll the dough into a 12 by 6 by ¼ inch high rectangle, using a bench scraper butted up against the sides to make the rectangle even.

With a sharp knife, cut the dough into twelve 3 by 2 inch rectangles. Place them, 1 inch apart, on the prepared baking sheet. For the highest rise, but slightly less flakiness, press lightly against the sides of the dough to seal them slightly.

BAKE THE SCONE TOPPERS Bake for 6 minutes. For even baking, rotate the sheet halfway around. Continue baking for 6 to 9 minutes, or until lightly browned. (An instant-read thermometer should read 205° to 212°F/96° to 100°C.) For crispier scones, allow the toppers to bake until they are a deeper brown.

While the scones are baking, shape the dough for the next batch.

COOL THE SCONE TOPPERS Let the scone toppers cool on the sheet on a wire rack for 10 minutes to firm. Use a pancake turner to transfer them to wire racks. Cool, uncovered to maintain crispness, until warm or room temperature.

RASPBERRY BUTTERSCOTCH LACE TOPPING FOR SCONES

MAKES ABOUT ½ CUP/125 ML/5.4 OUNCES/154 GRAMS

*T*his rose tinged, lilting raspberry butterscotch sauce was inspired by raspberry caramels—the creation of pastry chef Marc Aumont of The Modern in New York City. I use Muscovado sugar to give it extra flavor dimension, but any brown sugar is also delicious. It is lovely laced on scones, fruit tarts, or chocolate or other cake, and hard to resist eating by the spoonful. It is also perfect for stabilizing and flavoring whipped cream.

RASPBERRY PUREE

MAKES ¼ CUP MINUS 1 TEASPOON/54 ML/2 OUNCES/56 GRAMS

	VOLUME	WEIGHT	
frozen raspberries with no sugar added	1 cup	4 ounces	114 grams
pure vanilla extract	½ teaspoon (2.5 ml)	.	.
fine sea salt	a pinch	.	.
lemon juice, freshly squeezed	1 teaspoon (5 ml)	.	5 grams

MAKE THE RASPBERRY PUREE In a strainer suspended over a bowl, thaw the raspberries completely. This will take several hours. (To speed thawing, place the strainer and bowl in an oven with a pilot light or turn on the oven light.) Press the berries to force out all the juice. There should be about 2½ tablespoons/37 ml of juice. Cover and set aside.

In a food processor, puree the raspberries. To remove the seeds, pass them through a food mill with a fine disc, or a fine-mesh strainer suspended over a medium bowl. There should be 2 tablespoons plus 2 teaspoons/39 ml of puree. Stir in the vanilla and salt and set aside.

Pour the raspberry juice into a small saucepan over medium heat (or into a 1 cup microwavable measure with a spout, lightly coated with nonstick cooking spray), and bring it to a boil, stirring constantly. Lower the heat and simmer, stirring constantly, until it becomes very syrupy and is reduced to 2 teaspoons/10 ml. Stir in the lemon juice and then stir the mixture into the puree. Into a 1 cup glass measure with a spout, pour 2 tablespoons plus 2 teaspoons/39 ml/1.3 ounces/36 grams of the raspberry puree. (Reserve any remaining puree to add to taste to the butterscotch.)

RASPBERRY BUTTERSCOTCH

MAKES ABOUT ⅓ CUP/81 ML/4.1 OUNCES/116 GRAMS

	VOLUME	WEIGHT	
unsalted butter (65° to 75°F/ 19° to 23°C)	2 tablespoons	1 ounce	28 grams
light brown Muscovado sugar, or dark brown sugar	¼ cup, firmly packed	1.9 ounces	54 grams
corn syrup	½ tablespoon (7 ml)	.	10 grams
heavy cream	2 tablespoons (30 ml)	1 ounce	29 grams
Raspberry Puree (reserved from page 185)	2 tablespoons plus 2 teaspoons (39 ml)	1.3 ounces	36 grams

MAKE THE RASPBERRY BUTTERSCOTCH In a small saucepan, using a silicone spatula, stir together the butter, brown sugar, corn syrup, and cream until the sugar dissolves. Bring the mixture to a boil over medium-low heat, stirring constantly. Simmer for about 4 minutes, stirring gently, until thickly bubbling. (An instant-read thermometer should read 244°F/118°C.) Remove the pan from the heat and pour the butterscotch into the raspberry puree, stirring to combine.

Allow the raspberry butterscotch to cool to room temperature, about 45 minutes. If desired, add more of the reserved raspberry puree to taste. Pour the raspberry butterscotch into a disposable pastry bag or quart-size reclosable freezer bag and cut a very small semicircle from one corner. Lace the raspberry butterscotch onto the scones.

STORE Airtight, room temperature, 1 day; refrigerated, 1 week.

Variation: RASPBERRY BUTTERSCOTCH WHIPPED CREAM

For a flavorful whipped cream, whisk ¼ cup/59 ml/2.6 ounces/73 grams of the raspberry butterscotch into ½ cup/118 ml/4.1 ounces/116 grams cold heavy cream that has been whipped just until the beater marks begin to appear distinctly. Whisk just until soft peaks form when the beater is raised. It can be refrigerated for up to 24 hours.

HIGHLIGHTS FOR SUCCESS

Frozen berries must be used to make the sauce because freezing breaks down some of the cell structure, which releases some of the berries' liquid, making it possible to thicken this liquid while preserving the freshness of the uncooked pulp. Be sure to use frozen berries with no sugar added. The juices from berries in syrup cannot be reduced as much because the sugar starts to caramelize.

Do not substitute commercial raspberry puree because it will not result in a smooth consistency.

PERFECT FLAKY AND TENDER CREAM CHEESE PIE CRUST

*I*n my book *The Pie and Pastry Bible* I have many pie crusts, but in recent years, when I bake a pie, the pie crust I always turn to is this one. I am offering it here for all the different sizes of pies in this book. If you want to use this pie crust for a savory pie, use one and a quarter times the salt.

I always use pastry flour because it produces the perfect ratio of tenderness to flakiness. Bleached all-purpose flour, with its higher protein content, will not be as tender, and unbleached all-purpose flour will be less tender still. There are two solutions if you are unable to find pastry flour. The first is to cut the all-purpose flour with cake flour. Use two parts bleached all-purpose flour to one part cake flour by weight or almost two to one by volume. The second solution is to use bleached all-purpose flour and work the dough as little as possible to create a minimum of elasticity. The food processor method is the easiest way to mix the dough because it's faster and the dough gets handled less and stays more chilled, but if you work quickly, the hand method will produce a crust that will be slightly flakier. With either method, be sure to keep the ingredients very cold to maintain flakiness.

DOUGH FOR A 9 INCH STANDARD PIE SHELL

MAKES 11 OUNCES/312 GRAMS

	VOLUME	WEIGHT	
unsalted butter, cold	6 tablespoons (¾ stick)	3 ounces	85 grams
pastry flour (or bleached all-purpose flour)	1¼ cups plus 1 tablespoon (or 1 cup plus 3 tablespoons), lightly spooned into the cup and leveled off	5.1 ounces	145 grams
fine sea salt	¼ teaspoon	.	1.5 grams
baking powder (use only an aluminum free variety; see page 518)	⅛ teaspoon	.	0.6 gram
cream cheese, cold	¼ cup	2.3 ounces	64 grams
heavy cream	1½ tablespoons (22 ml)	0.7 ounce	21 grams
cider vinegar	½ tablespoon (7.5 ml)	.	.

DOUGH FOR A DEEP DISH 9½ INCH PIE SHELL, OR A 12 TO 14 INCH GALETTE (FREE-FORM TART)

MAKES 14.6 OUNCES/414 GRAMS

	VOLUME	WEIGHT	
unsalted butter, cold	8 tablespoons (1 stick)	4 ounces	113 grams
pastry flour (or bleached all-purpose flour)	1½ cups plus 2 tablespoons (or 1½ cups), lightly spooned into the cup and leveled off	6.5 ounces	184 grams
fine sea salt	¼ plus ¹⁄₁₆ teaspoon	.	1.9 grams
baking powder (use only an aluminum free variety; see page 518)	⅛ plus ¹⁄₃₂ teaspoon (a dash)	.	0.7 gram
cream cheese, cold	⅓ cup	3 ounces	85 grams
heavy cream	2 tablespoons (30 ml)	1 ounce	29 grams
cider vinegar	2 teaspoons (10 ml)	.	.

DOUGH FOR A 9 INCH STANDARD 10 STRIP LATTICE PIE

MAKES 17 OUNCES/480 GRAMS

	VOLUME	WEIGHT	
unsalted butter, cold	9 tablespoons (1 stick plus 1 tablespoon)	4.6 ounces	131 grams
pastry flour (or bleached all-purpose flour)	1¾ cups plus 2 tablespoons (or 1¾ cups), lightly spooned into the cup and leveled off	7.5 ounces	213 grams
fine sea salt	¼ plus ⅛ teaspoon	.	2.2 grams
baking powder (use only an aluminum free variety; see page 518)	⅛ plus ¹⁄₁₆ teaspoon	.	0.8 gram
cream cheese, cold	⅓ cup plus 1 tablespoon	3.5 ounces	100 grams
heavy cream	2 tablespoons plus 1 teaspoon (34 ml)	1.2 ounces	34 grams
cider vinegar	2⅓ teaspoons (11.5 ml)	.	.

DOUGH FOR A STANDARD DOUBLE CRUST OR 14 STRIP LATTICE 9 INCH PIE

MAKES 22 OUNCES/624 GRAMS

	VOLUME	WEIGHT	
unsalted butter, cold	12 tablespoons (1½ sticks)	6 ounces	170 grams
pastry flour (or bleached all-purpose flour)	2½ cups plus 1 tablespoon (or 2⅓ cups plus 1 tablespoon), lightly spooned into the cup and leveled off	10.2 ounces	290 grams
fine sea salt	½ teaspoon	.	3 grams
baking powder (use only an aluminum free variety; see page 518)	¼ teaspoon	.	1.1 grams
cream cheese, cold	½ cup	4.5 ounces	128 grams
heavy cream	3 tablespoons (44 ml)	1.5 ounces	43 grams
cider vinegar	1 tablespoon (15 ml)	.	.

MAKE THE DOUGH FOR THE PIE CRUSTS

FOOD PROCESSOR METHOD Cut the butter into small (about ½ inch) cubes. Wrap it in plastic wrap and freeze it until frozen solid, at least 30 minutes.

In a gallon-size reclosable freezer bag, place the flour, salt, and baking powder and freeze for at least 30 minutes. In the food processor, place the flour mixture. Cut the cream cheese into 3 or 4 pieces and add it to the flour. Process for about 20 seconds, or until the mixture resembles coarse meal. Add the frozen butter cubes and pulse until none of the cubes is larger than the size of peas. (Toss with a fork to see the size better.) Remove the cover and add the cream and vinegar. Pulse until most of the butter is reduced to the size of small peas. The mixture will be in particles and will not hold together. Spoon it into the plastic bag or, wearing latex gloves (which help to prevent sticking), empty it onto the counter. (For a double crust pie, it is easiest to divide the mixture in half. Spoon one-half into the bag, knead as described below, and then repeat with the second half.)

Hold either side of the bag opening and alternate using the heel of your hand and your knuckles to knead and press the mixture, from the outside of the bag, until most of the mixture holds together in one piece. Cut open the bag and empty the dough onto a large sheet of plastic wrap. Use the plastic wrap to finish kneading together the dough just until it feels slightly stretchy when pulled. (If using latex gloves, use the heel of your hand to push and flatten the dough against the counter.)

DIVIDE THE DOUGH For a pie shell and standard 10 strip lattice, divide the dough into two-thirds and one-third. Use about 9.5 ounces/269 grams for the shell and the rest for the lattice, flattening the smaller part into a rectangle. Wrap each piece and refrigerate for 45 minutes or up to 2 days.

For a double crust or 14 strip lattice pie, divide the dough into 2 equal pieces, about 11 ounces/312 grams each. Wrap each piece and refrigerate for 45 minutes or up to 2 days.

For an extra flaky pie crust approaching puff pastry but more tender, roll the dough into a rectangle and give it a business letter fold (fold it into thirds). Roll it again to flatten it and make it a fairly even square. Wrap the dough, flatten it into a disc (or 2 discs for a double crust or lattice pie), and refrigerate for 45 minutes or up to 2 days.

HAND METHOD Place a medium mixing bowl in the freezer to chill. Cut the butter into small (about ½ inch) cubes. Wrap it in plastic wrap and refrigerate for at least 30 minutes.

Place the flour, salt, and baking powder in a medium bowl and whisk to combine. Add the cream cheese and rub the mixture between your fingers to blend the cream cheese into the flour until it resembles coarse meal. Spoon the mixture, together with the cold butter, into a gallon-size reclosable freezer bag. Express any air from the bag and close it. Use a rolling pin to flatten the butter into thin flakes. Place the bag in the freezer for at least 10 minutes, or until the butter is very firm. Transfer the mixture to the chilled bowl, scraping the sides of the bag. Set the bag aside. Sprinkle the mixture with the cream and vinegar, tossing lightly with a silicone spatula. Spoon the mixture back into the plastic bag. (For a double crust pie, it is easiest to divide the mixture in half. Spoon one-half into the bag, knead as described below, and then repeat with the second half.)

Hold either side of the bag opening and alternate using the heel of your hand and your knuckles to knead and press the mixture, from the outside of the bag, until it holds together in one piece and feels slightly stretchy when pulled.

DIVIDE THE DOUGH For a pie shell and 10 strip lattice, divide the dough into two-thirds and one-third. Use about 9.5 ounces/269 grams for the shell and the rest for the lattice, flattening the smaller part into a rectangle. Wrap each piece and refrigerate for 45 minutes or up to 2 days.

For a double crust or 14 strip lattice pie, divide the dough into 2 equal pieces. Wrap each piece and refrigerate for 45 minutes or up to 2 days.

STORE Refrigerated, up to 2 days; frozen, 3 months.

ROLL THE DOUGH The ideal temperature for rolling dough is 60°F/16°C, which is the temperature of most wine cellars. At this temperature, the dough is malleable enough to roll without cracking, but cool enough to keep the butter from softening.

My favorite surface on which to roll the dough is the Magic Dough pastry mat (see page 541). Alternatively, roll the dough on top of two large sheets of overlapping plastic wrap, preferably Freeze-Tite (see page 541), or a pastry cloth rubbed with flour. (If using plastic wrap, two or three times during rolling, flip the dough over, lift off the plastic wrap to prevent it from creasing into the dough, and dust the dough lightly with flour, if needed.) For the top of the dough, a pastry sleeve, slipped onto the rolling pin and rubbed with flour, is also a great aid in keeping the dough from sticking. Alternatively, set two overlapping sheets of plastic wrap on top of the dough. If the dough softens while rolling and becomes sticky, slip a large baking sheet under the mat, cover the dough with plastic wrap, and refrigerate for about 10 minutes before continuing to roll it.

Specially designed rubber bands that fit over the ends of a rolling pin and serve as spacers between the counter and rolling pin are great for ensuring an evenly rolled crust. (Note that if stretching them to fit larger rolling pins, the bands will thin, resulting in less space between the pin and the rolling surface.) My preference is to roll the dough ⅛ inch thick or slightly less. Roll the dough from the center outward, using a firm, steady pressure. Avoid pressing down on the edges, which would make them too thin. Lift the dough from time to time as you are rolling and add flour as necessary to keep it from sticking. Before measuring the dough, make sure to lift it from the surface to allow it to shrink in so that it doesn't retract when set in the pie plate.

CUT THE DOUGH AND LINE THE PIE PLATE It's easier to shape the dough evenly and to the right size for the pie plate before you transfer the dough to the pie plate. To determine the ideal size, measure your pie plate. Use a flexible tape measure and start at one inside edge, not including the rim. Go down the side, across the bottom, and up the other side. Then measure the rim. Enough dough is needed to make a decorative crimped border, but if it is too thick, it will droop and/or not bake through.

For a single crust pie, a double thickness border is desirable, so multiply the size of the rim by 4. For a lattice pie, multiply the size of the rim by 3. For a double crust pie, multiply the size of the rim by 2. To cut a round disc of dough, use an expandable flan ring or make a cardboard template. Cut out the dough for the bottom crust. To fit it into the pie plate, fold the dough gently into fourths, position the point in the center of the pan, and gently unfold it. Ease the dough into place, but do not stretch it or it will shrink during baking.

If making a lattice, after cutting the dough for the bottom crust, add any scraps to the dough reserved for the lattice by layering the strips on top of it. When cutting lattice strips, remember that they should extend ½ inch over the edge of the pie plate so that they can be tucked under the bottom crust, which has a thinner border than a single crust pie in order to accommodate the extra layers of dough from the lattice strips.

For a double crust pie, when lining the pie plate, the bottom crust should come to the outer edge of the pie plate. When draping the top crust over the filling, the crust will extend far enough so that it can be tucked under the bottom crust, pressed down, and fluted decoratively, if desired.

MAKE A BORDER For a rustic style, simply press the dough down with your fingers. Alternatively, use the tines of a fork or crimp the dough with your fingers. If the dough softens, either refrigerate it until firm or dip your fingers in flour.

Crimping pie crust edges.

LUSCIOUS APPLE PIE

SERVES 8

OVEN TEMPERATURE 425°F/220°C

BAKING TIME 45 to 55 minutes

*A*commenter on my blog came up with the idea to add thickened apple cider to the apples in an apple pie to make more sauce in the filling—a request from her husband. I tried the idea and love the luscious texture and added flavor the apple cider gives to the apples. I still like to concentrate the apples' juices to keep the bottom of the crust from getting soggy and to add a wonderful caramel undertone to the filling.

SPECIAL EQUIPMENT One 9 inch pie plate | An expandable flan ring or 12 inch round cardboard template | A baking stone or baking sheet | A foil ring to protect the edges of the crust

PERFECT FLAKY AND TENDER
CREAM CHEESE PIE CRUST

	VOLUME	WEIGHT	
dough for a standard double crust 9 inch pie (page 189)	.	22 ounces	624 grams

ROLL THE DOUGH FOR THE BOTTOM CRUST Remove the dough for the bottom crust from the refrigerator. If necessary, let it sit for about 10 minutes, or until it is malleable enough to roll.

On a floured pastry cloth, pastry mat, or between two sheets of lightly floured plastic wrap, roll the dough into a ⅛ inch thick disc, 12 inches in diameter or large enough to line the bottom of the pie plate and extend slightly past the edge of the rim. Lift the dough from time to time and add flour as necessary to keep it from sticking. Before measuring the dough, make sure to lift it from the surface to allow it to shrink in so that it doesn't retract when set in the pie plate. Use the expandable flan ring, or a small sharp knife with the cardboard template as a guide, to cut a 12 inch disc of dough.

LINE THE PIE PLATE Transfer the dough to the pie plate, easing it into place. If necessary, trim the edge almost even with the edge of the plate. Cover with plastic wrap and refrigerate for a minimum of 30 minutes or up to 3 hours.

FILLING

	VOLUME	WEIGHT	
about 6 medium baking apples (2½ pounds/1,134 grams), see Notes, page 195	8 cups (sliced, see below)	2 pounds (sliced)	907 grams (sliced)
lemon juice, freshly squeezed	1 tablespoon (15 ml)	0.6 ounce	16 grams
light brown Muscovado sugar, or dark brown sugar	¼ cup, firmly packed	1.9 ounces	54 grams
granulated sugar (see Notes, page 195)	¼ cup	1.8 ounces	50 grams
ground cinnamon (see Notes, page 195)	½ to 1½ teaspoons	.	1.1 to 3.3 grams
nutmeg, freshly grated	¼ teaspoon	.	.
fine sea salt	¼ teaspoon	.	1.5 grams
unpasteurized apple cider, unsweetened	½ cup (118 ml)	4.3 ounces	122 grams
cornstarch (for the apple cider)	½ tablespoon	.	5 grams
unsalted butter	2 tablespoons	1 ounce	28 grams
cornstarch (for the apples)	1 tablespoon plus 1 teaspoon	.	12 grams

PREPARE THE APPLES Peel the apples and slice them in half. Use a melon baller to remove the cores and a small sharp knife to cut away any remaining peel. Slice the apples ¼ inch thick. Weigh or measure the apple slices and toss them with the lemon juice.

In a large bowl, mix together the brown sugar, granulated sugar, cinnamon, nutmeg, and salt. Add the apples and toss to coat them with the sugar mixture. Let the apples macerate at room temperature for a minimum of 30 minutes or up to 3 hours.

THICKEN THE APPLE CIDER In a small saucepan, stir together the apple cider and the ½ tablespoon of cornstarch. Bring the mixture to a boil, stirring constantly. It will become very thick. Scrape it into a small bowl, cover tightly, and set it aside.

DRAIN AND CONCENTRATE THE APPLE JUICES Transfer the apples and their juices to a colander suspended over a bowl to capture the liquid. The mixture will release at least ½ cup/118 ml/5 ounces/142 grams of liquid.

Transfer this liquid to a 4 cup microwavable measure with a spout that has been lightly coated with nonstick cooking spray. Add the butter and microwave for about 6 to 7 minutes until reduced to about ⅓ cup/79 ml/3.1 ounces/88 grams—or a little more if you started with more than ½ cup of liquid. It will be syrupy and lightly caramelized. Watch carefully to prevent burning. Alternatively, reduce the liquid in a saucepan, preferably non-stick, over medium-high heat. Swirl but do not stir it.

COMPLETE THE FILLING Transfer the apples to a large bowl and toss them with the 1 tablespoon plus 1 teaspoon of cornstarch until all traces of it have disappeared. Pour the reduced syrup over the apples, tossing gently. (Do not be concerned if the syrup hardens on contact with the apples; it will dissolve during baking.) Scrape in the thickened apple cider and again toss gently to mix it in. Spoon the apples into the dough-lined pie plate. Moisten the border of the bottom crust by brushing it lightly with water.

ROLL THE DOUGH FOR THE TOP CRUST AND CRIMP Roll out the dough for the top crust large enough to cut a 12 inch disc. Use the expandable flan ring, or a sharp knife with the cardboard template as a guide, to cut the disc of dough.

Place the top crust over the apple filling. Tuck the overhang under the bottom crust border and press down all around the top to seal it. Crimp the border using your forefinger and thumb or a fork, and use a small sharp knife to make 5 evenly spaced 2 inch slashes in the top crust, starting about 1 inch from the center and radiating toward the edge. Cover the pie loosely with plastic wrap and refrigerate it for 1 hour before baking to chill and relax the dough. This will maintain flakiness and help to keep the crust from shrinking.

PREHEAT THE OVEN Forty-five minutes or longer before baking, set an oven rack at the lowest level and place the baking stone or baking sheet on it. Place a large sheet of non-stick aluminum foil or foil lightly coated with nonstick cooking spray on top of the stone to catch any juices. Preheat the oven to 425°F/220°C.

BAKE THE PIE Place the foil ring on top of the pie to protect the edges from overbrowning and set the pie on the foil-topped baking stone. Bake for 20 minutes. For even baking, rotate the pie halfway around. Continue baking for 25 to 35 minutes, or until the juices bubble through the slashes and the apples feel tender but not mushy when a cake tester or small sharp knife is inserted through a slash.

COOL THE PIE Cool on a wire rack for at least 4 hours before cutting. Serve warm or at room temperature.

STORE Room temperature, 2 days; refrigerated, 4 days.

NOTES It's fine to combine three or four kinds of apples, but be sure to choose apples with a low water content. Some of my favorites are Macoun, Cortland, Jonathan, Stayman Winesap, Rhode Island Greening, Golden Delicious, York Imperial, Northern Spy, Newtown Pippin, Idared, Pink Lady, and Granny Smith.

If the apples are very tart, add up to ¼ cup/1.8 ounces/50 grams more sugar.

If using a very strong specialty cinnamon, use ¼ to ¾ teaspoons, depending on how much of a cinnamon flavor you want to give to the apples.

PERFECT PEACH GALETTE

OVEN TEMPERATURE
400°F/200°C

BAKING TIME
40 to 45 minutes

*T*his is my favorite peach pie transformed into a galette. A galette is made with pie dough, but instead of making two discs of dough, the dough is rolled large enough so that it can be draped over the filling to become either a narrow border or an entire top crust. It is designed to work with a less deep filling than a pie and it is my preference because the balance of fruit to thin crisp pastry is perfectly pleasing to me. A galette works for most fruit, but especially well for peaches, which, compared with nectarines and apples, are a little softer and don't hold up as well in a thicker layer. The combination of buttery crust and luscious peach slices is truly a slice of heaven. For a larger crowd, make two or, if you're a seasoned pie baker, double the recipe and roll the dough to 24 inches to make one very large galette.

SPECIAL EQUIPMENT One 10 to 12 inch pizza pan, preferably dark metal, or a baking sheet | A baking stone or baking sheet

PERFECT FLAKY AND TENDER CREAM CHEESE PIE CRUST

	VOLUME	WEIGHT	
dough for a 12 to 14 inch galette (page 188), see Notes, page 199	.	14.6 ounces	414 grams

PEACH FILLING

	VOLUME	WEIGHT	
1½ pounds ripe peaches (4 to 5 medium), see Notes, page 199	3¼ cups (sliced, see below)	20 ounces (sliced)	567 grams (sliced)
sugar	⅓ cup	2.3 ounces	67 grams
fine sea salt	a pinch	.	.
lemon juice, freshly squeezed	½ tablespoon (7.5 ml)	.	8 grams
unsalted butter	1 tablespoon	0.5 ounce	14 grams
cornstarch	2 teaspoons	.	6 grams
pure almond extract	¼ teaspoon (1.2 ml)	.	.

PREPARE THE PEACHES Bring a large pot of water to a boil. Remove it from the heat and add the peaches. Allow them to blanch for 1 minute. Empty the peaches into a colander and run cold water over them. If the peaches are ripe, the skins will slip off.

In a large bowl, place the sugar and salt. Cut each peach in half. Remove the pits and slice the peaches ¼ inch thick. As you cut the slices, place them into the bowl, sprinkle with some of the lemon juice, and toss to coat them.

Let the peaches macerate for a minimum of 30 minutes or up to 1½ hours.

DRAIN AND CONCENTRATE THE PEACH JUICES Transfer the peaches and their juices to a colander suspended over a bowl to capture the liquid. The mixture will release at least ½ cup/118 ml/4.3 ounces/121 grams and up to ⅔ cup/157 ml/5.7 ounces/161 grams of juice. Transfer this liquid to a 2 cup microwavable measure with a spout that has been lightly coated with nonstick cooking spray. Add the butter and microwave for 6 to 9 minutes, until reduced to about ⅓ cup/79 ml/3.8 ounces/108 grams—or a little more if you started with more than ½ cup/118 ml of liquid. It will be syrupy and lightly caramelized. Watch carefully toward the end to avoid burning. Alternatively, reduce the liquid in a saucepan, preferably nonstick, over medium-high heat. Swirl but do not stir it.

Empty the peaches into a large bowl, pour the syrup over them, and toss gently. (Do not be concerned if the liquid hardens on contact with the peaches; it will dissolve during baking.) Add the cornstarch and almond extract and toss gently until all traces of the cornstarch have disappeared.

ROLL THE DOUGH Remove the dough from the refrigerator. If necessary, let it sit for about 10 minutes, or until it is malleable enough to roll.

The dough needs to be rolled very thin, so if the room is at all warm (above 72°F/22°C), chill the counter with ice packs and dry it well before rolling. If the dough softens while rolling, slip it onto a flat baking sheet, cover, and refrigerate it until firm.

On a well-floured pastry cloth or between overlapping sheets of lightly floured plastic wrap (preferably freezer weight), roll the dough into a disc. Make it as thin as possible—a minimum of 16 to 17 inches. Lift the dough from time to time, if using the pastry cloth, or use the plastic wrap to flip it over, adding flour as necessary to keep it from sticking. If necessary, trim to 17 inches. Gently fold it in half and transfer it to the pizza pan. Carefully unfold the dough. The border of the dough will overlap the pan.

Scrape the peach mixture onto the dough and spread it in a single layer about 9 inches in diameter. Carefully drape the border over the peaches, allowing it to pleat as evenly as possible. It will leave a small area in the center exposed.

CHILL THE GALETTE Cover the galette loosely with plastic wrap and put it in the refrigerator for 1 hour or up to 3 hours before baking. This will maintain flakiness.

PREHEAT THE OVEN Forty-five minutes or longer before baking, set an oven rack at the lowest level and place the baking stone or baking sheet on it. Preheat the oven to 400°F/200°C.

BAKE THE GALETTE For a delightfully crunchy crust, spritz or brush the pastry all over with water and sprinkle with about 1 teaspoon of superfine sugar. Brush away any sugar that may fall on the pan.

Set the pan directly on the baking stone and bake for 20 minutes. For even baking, rotate the pan halfway around. Continue baking for 20 to 25 minutes, or until the juices bubble thickly in the center opening and the peaches feel tender with just a little resistance when a cake tester or small sharp knife is inserted. If the crust starts to overbrown, cover loosely with aluminum foil with a slash cut in the middle to allow steam to escape.

COOL THE GALETTE Cool on a wire rack for about 3 hours until warm or room temperature before serving.

NOTES If you are experienced in rolling out pie dough, you can use less dough, which will result in a thinner crust. Make the recipe for the 9 inch standard pie shell/11 ounces/ 312 grams (page 187).

Frozen peach slices can be substituted for the fresh peach slices. Allow them to defrost in the refrigerator for several hours or up to overnight. Use 1 tablespoon of cornstarch.

STORE Room temperature, 2 days; refrigerated, 4 days.

SOUR CHERRY PIE

OVEN TEMPERATURE 425°F/220°C

BAKING TIME 40 to 50 minutes

*S*our cherry pie is my husband's and my favorite pie, and it was also my father's. I made it for his July birthday every year until he was ninety-seven, always tweaking it a little more toward perfection. This is my ultimate rendition. The filling is now thickened before baking the pie to make it easier to apply the lattice. The number of strips is increased to fourteen so that they are spaced just widely enough apart for everyone to see the beautiful bright red cherries but closely enough to maintain the juiciness of the filling. I also include the optional addition of cherry concentrate from Michigan. Because sour cherries have a lamentably short season, I give instructions for freezing. Here, too, are two variations, including one made with a wonderful preserved product in a jar. This pie is just too good to miss. I once met a little boy of eight who confided in me that his dream was to have a home-made cherry pie. My heart went out to him—so I baked him one!

SPECIAL EQUIPMENT One 9 inch pie plate | An expandable flan ring or 12 inch round cardboard template | A pastry jagger or pizza wheel for cutting the lattice strips | A baking stone or baking sheet | A foil ring to protect the edges of the crust

PERFECT FLAKY AND TENDER
CREAM CHEESE PIE CRUST

	VOLUME	WEIGHT	
dough for a 14 strip lattice 9 inch pie (page 189)	.	22 ounces	624 grams

ROLL THE DOUGH FOR THE BOTTOM PIE CRUST Remove the dough for the bottom crust from the refrigerator. If necessary, let it sit for about 10 minutes, or until it is malleable enough to roll.

On a floured pastry cloth, pastry mat, or between two sheets of lightly floured plastic wrap, roll the bottom crust into a ⅛ inch thick disc, 12 inches in diameter or large enough to line the pie plate and extend enough to turn about halfway under the border. Lift the dough from time to time and add flour as necessary to keep it from sticking.

Before measuring the dough, make sure to lift it from the surface to allow it to shrink in so that it doesn't retract when set in the pie plate. Use the expandable flan ring, or a sharp knife with the cardboard template as a guide, to cut a 12 inch disc of dough. Layer the scraps on top of the refrigerated dough for the lattice crust.

LINE THE PIE PLATE Transfer the dough to the pie plate, easing it into place. If necessary, trim the edge to make it even. Turn under the crust so that it is even with the edge of the pie plate. Cover with plastic wrap and refrigerate for a minimum of 30 minutes or up to 3 hours.

FILLING

	VOLUME	WEIGHT	
fresh sour cherries	about 3¾ cups (3½ cups pitted)	24 ounces (20 ounces pitted)	680 grams (567 grams pitted)
sugar (see Notes, page 204)	¾ cup plus 2 tablespoons	6.2 ounces	175 grams
cornstarch	2½ tablespoons	0.8 ounce	22 grams
fine sea salt	a pinch	.	.
pure almond extract	¼ teaspoon (1.2 ml)	.	.
cherry concentrate (see Notes, page 204; optional)	2 tablespoons (30 ml)	1.4 ounces	40 grams

MAKE THE FILLING Pit the cherries (see Notes, page 204), placing them in a medium bowl along with any juices that form. There should be 3½ cups/20 ounces/567 grams.

In a medium saucepan, stir together the sugar, cornstarch, and salt. Gently stir in the cherries along with any juices. Let the mixture sit for at least 10 minutes to liquefy the sugar mixture. Over medium heat, stirring constantly, bring it to a boil and simmer for about 1 minute until thickened. Scrape the cherry mixture into a wide bowl or pie plate and let it cool completely. Stir in the almond extract and optional cherry concentrate, and scrape the mixture into the dough-lined pie plate.

ROLL THE DOUGH AND MAKE THE LATTICE Roll the second disc of dough into a 12 by 11 inch oval (⅛ inch thick) and cut fourteen 12 inch long, ¾ inch wide strips, using a ruler and the pastry jagger or pizza cutter. (If you are right-handed, start from the left side.)

To create a woven lattice, arrange half of the strips evenly over the filling, starting in the center. Gently curve back every other strip, a little past the center, so that the next strip can be placed perpendicular to the first strips, right at the center. Uncurve the strips so that they lie flat on top of the perpendicular strip. Working in the same direction, curve back the strips that were not curved back the first time. Lay a second perpendicular strip on top and uncurve the strips. Repeat with 2 more strips.

Apply the remaining 3 strips to the other side of the pie. Start toward the center and work in the opposite direction toward the edge. Remember always to alternate the strips that are curved back so that the strips weave in and out.

Use sharp kitchen scissors to trim the strips to a ½ inch overhang. Moisten under the ends of each strip with water and tuck the overhang under the bottom crust border, pressing down to make it adhere and to keep the border from being too thick. If desired, crimp the border using your forefinger and thumb.

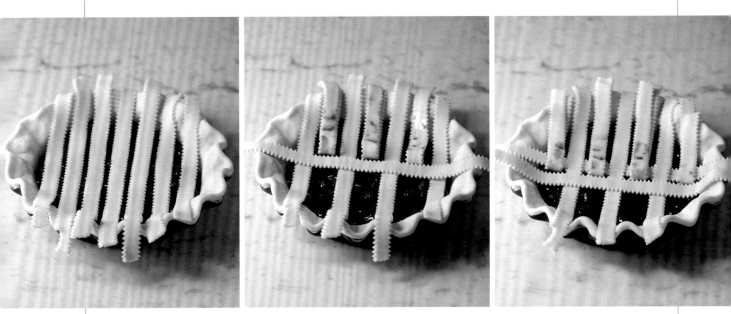

LEFT TO RIGHT: Arranging the first lattice strips. Curving back every other strip and placing the perpendicular strip on top. Curving back the alternate strips and placing the second perpendicular strip.

LEFT TO RIGHT: Uncurving the strips; the beginning of the lattice pattern. The complete lattice pattern with the ends ready to be trimmed. Trimmed edges tucked under the bottom crust and pressed down.

Refrigerate the pie for at least 45 minutes, loosely covered with plastic wrap. Just before baking, if a crunchy and sparkling effect is desired, spritz or brush the lattice with a little milk or water (avoid the border because it will get too dark on baking) and dust it lightly with sugar.

PREHEAT THE OVEN Forty-five minutes or longer before baking, set an oven rack at the lowest level and place the baking stone or baking sheet on it. Place a large sheet of non-stick aluminum foil or foil lightly coated with nonstick cooking spray on top of the stone to catch any juices. Preheat the oven to 425°F/220°C.

BAKE THE PIE Place the foil ring on top of the pie to protect the edges from overbrowning and set the pie on the foil-topped baking stone. Bake for 20 minutes. For even baking, rotate the pie halfway around. Continue baking for 20 to 30 minutes, or until thickly bubbling all over and the center is slightly puffed.

COOL THE PIE Cool on a wire rack for at least 3 hours before cutting. When set, the filling will remain juicy with just a little flow. Serve warm or at room temperature.

STORE Room temperature, 2 days; refrigerated, 4 days.

NOTES A large heavy hairpin is the ideal sour cherry pitter. It works well to insert the prongs into a cork, especially a champagne cork that has a rounded end. Insert the looped end of the hairpin into the stem end of the cherry, hook it around the pit, and pull it out.

To freeze the cherries, after pitting, add ¼ cup/1.8 ounces/50 grams of the sugar. Place the cherry mixture in a quart-size canning jar and mark on the cap the amount of sugar added so that you will remember to subtract it from the total amount of sugar when making the pie. In a freezer that maintains a temperature below 0°F/-18°C, the cherries will last for 3 years or even longer. Defrost them either overnight in the refrigerator or for a few hours at room temperature before adding the rest of the ingredients.

The amount of sugar listed in the chart is the amount that I usually use, but some years and some varieties of sour cherries are more tart and I may use as much as 1 cup/ 7 ounces/200 grams.

Cherry concentrate is a secret given to me by Justin Rachid of American Spoon. He recommended a brand called Michelle's Miracle (available from www.michellesmiracle.com), an intensely concentrated sour cherry syrup made from Montmorency sour cherries. It adds an astonishing depth of flavor. Creator Michelle White advises that refrigerated or frozen it keeps just about indefinitely.

Variation: "Churrant" Pie

Currants, tart and tiny bright red globes, come into season in early July, at the same time as sour cherries, and make an exciting addition to cherry pie. Stuffed into the cherries, they keep the cherries full and plump and seem to give more cherry taste without imparting a flavor of their own. No one will ever guess what the mysterious enhancer is or why this cherry pie has so much delicious extra flavor and texture.

Choose ¼ cup/2 ounces/58 grams of the smallest currants available. Stuff each one into the center of a pitted cherry. Use a total of 1 cup/7 ounces/200 grams of sugar and 2 tablespoons plus 2½ teaspoons/1 ounce/28 grams cornstarch. Be very gentle when stirring so that the currants don't pop out. Alternatively, the currants can simply be added to the cherry mixture, but the presentation is much more dramatic to stuff them inside the cherries!

Variation: FRUIT PERFECT CHERRY PIE

	VOLUME	WEIGHT	
2 jars (14 ounces each) Fruit Perfect Cherries (see page 525)	.	27.5 ounces	780 grams
cornstarch	1 tablespoon	.	10 grams
water	1 tablespoon (15 ml)	0.5 ounce	15 grams
sugar	¼ cup	1.8 ounces	50 grams

Empty the jarred cherries, with their thickened juices, into a medium bowl. In one of the Fruit Perfect jars, stir together the cornstarch and water to dissolve the cornstarch. Gently and evenly stir this mixture into the cherries with the sugar. Bake as for Sour Cherry Pie (page 204), but at 400°F/200°C for 30 to 40 minutes.

CHERRY SWEETIE PIE

SERVES 6 TO 8

OVEN TEMPERATURE
425°F/220°C

BAKING TIME
35 to 45 minutes

*D*ark sweet cherries make a luscious cherry pie, especially when combined with red plums, which provide a flavorful tartness. This idea was inspired by an article in *Cook's Illustrated* magazine. The moment I read it, I knew it was the missing element for sweet cherry pie perfection.

SPECIAL EQUIPMENT One 9 inch pie plate | An expandable flan ring or 12 inch round cardboard template | A pastry jagger or pizza wheel for cutting the lattice strips | A baking stone or baking sheet | A foil ring to protect the edges of the crust

PERFECT FLAKY AND TENDER CREAM CHEESE PIE CRUST

	VOLUME	WEIGHT	
dough for a 14 strip lattice 9 inch pie (page 189)	.	22 ounces	624 grams

ROLL THE DOUGH FOR THE BOTTOM PIE CRUST Remove the dough for the bottom crust from the refrigerator. If necessary, let it sit for about 10 minutes, or until it is malleable enough to roll.

On a floured pastry cloth, pastry mat, or between two sheets of lightly floured plastic wrap, roll the bottom crust into a ⅛ inch thick disc, 12 inches in diameter or large enough to line the pie plate and extend enough to turn about halfway under the border. Lift the dough from time to time and add flour as necessary to keep it from sticking. Before measuring the dough, make sure to lift it from the surface to allow it to shrink in so that it doesn't retract when set in the pie plate. Use the expandable flan ring, or a sharp knife with the cardboard template as a guide, to cut a 12 inch disc of dough. Layer the scraps on top of the refrigerated dough for the lattice crust.

LINE THE PIE PLATE Transfer the dough to the pie plate, easing it into place. If necessary, trim the edge to make it even. Turn under the crust so that it is even with the edge of the pie plate. Cover with plastic wrap and refrigerate for a minimum of 30 minutes or up to 3 hours.

FILLING

	VOLUME	WEIGHT	
fresh or frozen Bing cherries	about 3¾ cups (3½ cups pitted)	24 ounces (20 ounces pitted)	680 grams (567 grams pitted)
2 ripe red plums	.	5.9 ounces	166 grams
sugar	¾ cup minus 1 tablespoon	4.8 ounces	137 grams
cornstarch	2 tablespoons plus 2 teaspoons	0.8 ounce	24 grams
fine sea salt	a pinch	.	.
lemon zest, finely grated	1 teaspoon, loosely packed	.	2 grams
pure vanilla extract	¼ teaspoon (1.2 ml)	.	.

MAKE THE FILLING Pit the cherries (see Notes, page 208), placing the cherries in a medium bowl along with any juices that form. If the cherries are very large (1 inch), use kitchen scissors to cut them in half.

Pit the plums and remove and discard the peel. (If necessary, use a potato peeler.) Use a small food processor or immersion blender to puree the pulp. There should be ½ cup/ 118 ml/4 ounces/113 grams.

In a medium saucepan, stir together the sugar, cornstarch, and salt. Gently stir in the cherries, any juices, and the pureed plums. Let the mixture sit for at least 10 minutes to liquefy the sugar mixture. Over medium heat, stirring constantly, bring it to a boil and simmer for about 1 minute until thickened. Scrape the cherry mixture into a wide bowl or pie plate and let it cool completely. Stir in the lemon zest and vanilla, and then scrape the mixture into the dough-lined pie plate.

ROLL THE DOUGH AND MAKE THE LATTICE Roll the second disc of dough into a 12 by 11 inch oval (⅛ inch thick) and cut fourteen 12 inch long, ¾ inch wide strips, using a ruler and the pastry jagger or pizza cutter. (If you are right-handed, start from the left side.)

To create a woven lattice, arrange half of the strips evenly over the filling, starting in the center (see Sour Cherry Pie, page 203). Gently curve back every other strip a little past the center so that the next strip can be placed perpendicular to the first strips, right at the center. Uncurve the strips so that they lie flat on top of the perpendicular strip. Working in the same direction, curve back the strips that were not curved back the first time. Lay a second perpendicular strip on top and uncurve the strips. Repeat with 2 more strips.

Apply the remaining 3 strips to the other side of the pie. Start toward the center and work in the opposite direction toward the edge. Remember always to alternate the strips that are curved back so that the strips weave in and out.

Use sharp kitchen scissors to trim the strips to a ½ inch overhang. Moisten under the ends of each strip with water and tuck the overhang under the bottom crust border, pressing down to make it adhere and to keep the border from being too thick. If desired, crimp the border using your forefinger and thumb.

Refrigerate the pie for at least 45 minutes, loosely covered with plastic wrap.

PREHEAT THE OVEN Forty-five minutes or longer before baking, set an oven rack at the lowest level and place the baking stone or baking sheet on it. Place a large sheet of non-stick aluminum foil or foil lightly coated with nonstick cooking spray on top of the stone to catch any juices. Preheat the oven to 425°F/220°C.

BAKE THE PIE Place the foil ring on top of the pie to protect the edges from overbrowning and set the pie on the foil-topped baking stone. Bake for 20 minutes. For even baking, rotate the pie halfway around. Continue baking for 15 to 25 minutes, or until golden brown, the center is slightly puffed, and the juices just start to bubble.

COOL THE PIE Cool on a wire rack for at least 3 hours before cutting. When set, the filling will remain juicy with just a little flow. Serve warm or at room temperature.

STORE Room temperature, 2 days; refrigerated, 4 days.

NOTES The best and easiest way to pit sweet cherries is a tip I picked up on the terrific blog Food52. Set a cherry on the neck of an empty glass bottle with a small neck, such as a beer bottle. Gently hold the cherry and use a chopstick or the back of a wooden skewer set into the stem end to push the pit through the bottom of the cherry, letting the pit fall into the bottle.

To freeze the cherries, after pitting, add ¼ cup/1.8 ounces/50 grams of the sugar. Place the cherry mixture in a quart-size canning jar and mark on the cap the amount of sugar added so that you will remember to subtract it from the total amount of sugar when making the pie. Defrost the cherries either overnight in the refrigerator or for a few hours at room temperature before adding the rest of the ingredients.

BLACK AND BLUEBERRY PIE

SERVES 8 TO 10

OVEN TEMPERATURE
425°F/220°C

BAKING TIME
45 to 55 minutes

*O*ddly, a little everyday black-and-blue mark triggered what turned out to be a terrific combination of ingredients—and a delicious berry pie.

SPECIAL EQUIPMENT One 9 inch pie plate | An expandable flan ring or 12 inch round cardboard template | A ½ inch round pastry tube | A baking stone or baking sheet | A foil ring to protect the edges of the crust

PERFECT FLAKY AND TENDER CREAM CHEESE PIE CRUST

	VOLUME	WEIGHT	
dough for a standard double crust 9 inch pie (page 189)	.	22 ounces	624 grams

ROLL THE DOUGH FOR THE BOTTOM CRUST Remove the dough for the bottom crust from the refrigerator. If necessary, let it sit for about 10 minutes, or until it is malleable enough to roll.

On a floured pastry cloth, pastry mat, or between two sheets of lightly floured plastic wrap, roll the dough into a ⅛ inch thick disc, 12 inches in diameter or large enough to line the bottom of the pie plate and extend slightly past the edge. Lift the dough from time to time and add flour as necessary to keep it from sticking. Before measuring the dough, make sure to lift it from the surface to allow it to shrink in so that it doesn't retract when set in the pie plate. Use the expandable flan ring, or a sharp knife with the cardboard template as a guide, to cut a 12 inch disc of dough.

LINE THE PIE PLATE Transfer the dough to the pie plate, easing it into place. If necessary, trim the edge almost even with the edge of the plate. Cover with plastic wrap and refrigerate for a minimum of 30 minutes or up to 3 hours.

FILLING

	VOLUME	WEIGHT	
sugar	¾ cup	5.3 ounces	150 grams
cornstarch	4½ tablespoons	1.4 ounces	40 grams
fine sea salt	a pinch	.	.
lemon zest, finely grated	1 tablespoon, loosely packed	.	6 grams
lemon juice, freshly squeezed and strained (about 1 large lemon)	3 tablespoons (44 ml)	1.7 ounces	47 grams
blackberries	4½ cups	18 ounces	510 grams
blueberries	1½ cups	9 ounces	255 grams

MAKE THE FILLING In a medium bowl, stir together the sugar, cornstarch, salt, lemon zest, and lemon juice. Add the blackberries and blueberries and toss to coat them. Transfer the berry mixture to the dough-lined pie plate. Moisten the border of the bottom crust by brushing it lightly with water.

ROLL THE DOUGH FOR THE TOP CRUST AND CRIMP Roll out the dough for the top crust large enough to cut a 12 inch disc. Use the expandable flan ring, or a sharp knife with the cardboard template as a guide, to cut the disc of dough.

To create a berry motif, use the ½ inch round pastry tube to cut little circles from the crust in three little clusters. (Stay within an 8½ inch diameter circle because the rest of the dough will become the raised border.) To maintain the design with no distortion, slip the dough onto a flat baking sheet, cover it with plastic wrap, and refrigerate it for about 10 minutes until firm.

Place the top crust over the berry filling. Tuck the overhang under the bottom crust border and press down all around the top to seal it. Crimp the border using your forefinger and thumb, or a fork. (If you did not make the berry motif, use a small sharp knife to make 5 evenly spaced 2 inch slashes in the top crust, starting about 1 inch from the center and radiating toward the edges.) Cover the pie loosely with plastic wrap and refrigerate it for 1 hour before baking to chill and relax the dough. This will maintain flakiness and help to keep the crust from shrinking.

PREHEAT THE OVEN Forty-five minutes or longer before baking, set an oven rack at the lowest level and place the baking stone or baking sheet on it. Place a large sheet of non-stick aluminum foil or foil lightly coated with nonstick cooking spray on top of the stone to catch any juices. Preheat the oven to 425°F/220°C.

BAKE THE PIE Place the foil ring on top of the pie to protect the edges from overbrowning and set the pie on the foil-topped baking stone. Bake for 20 minutes. For even baking, rotate the pie halfway around. Continue baking for 25 to 35 minutes, or until the juices bubble thickly through the holes or slashes.

COOL THE PIE Cool on a wire rack for at least 2 hours before cutting. When set, the filling will remain juicy with just a little flow. Serve warm or at room temperature.

STORE Room temperature, 2 days; refrigerated, 4 days.

ElderBlueberry Pie

SERVES 6 TO 8

OVEN TEMPERATURE
425°F/220°C

BAKING TIME
40 to 50 minutes

*S*everal years ago, my green-thumbed friend and neighbor Maria Menegus, who has an enormous elderberry bush, gave me a generous supply of the berries with which to experiment. Maria had assumed that as a food writer I knew that it is necessary to cook the berries to render them edible and flavorful, but this was my first encounter with elderberries, so after tasting a berry or two, and even sugaring a few more, I found them to be so bitter I threw out the rest. The following summer I started to create a recipe for elderberry pie and this time found the berries so seedy I almost gave up, but for their hauntingly unique flavor. Then inspiration struck. I replaced some of the elderberries with blueberries to interrupt the seedy quality. No one would ever guess there were blueberries in this pie and the smaller amount of seeds provides a delightful crunch. Now, every August I look forward to the appearance of elderberries—although Maria and I have fierce competition from the birds, who also adore them.

SPECIAL EQUIPMENT One 9 inch pie plate | An expandable flan ring or 12 inch round cardboard template | A ½ inch round pastry tube | A baking stone or baking sheet | A foil ring to protect the edges of the crust

Perfect Flaky and Tender Cream Cheese Pie Crust

	VOLUME	WEIGHT	
dough for a standard double crust 9 inch pie (page 189)	.	22 ounces	624 grams

ROLL THE DOUGH FOR THE BOTTOM CRUST Remove the dough for the bottom crust from the refrigerator. If necessary, let it sit for about 10 minutes, or until it is malleable enough to roll.

On a floured pastry cloth, pastry mat, or between two sheets of lightly floured plastic wrap, roll the dough into a ⅛ inch thick disc, 12 inches in diameter or large enough to line the bottom of the pie plate and extend slightly past the edge of the rim. Lift the dough from time to time and add flour as necessary to keep it from sticking. Before measuring the dough, make sure to lift it from the surface to allow it to shrink in so that it doesn't retract when set in the pie plate. Use the expandable flan ring, or a small sharp knife with the cardboard template as a guide, to cut a 12 inch disc of dough.

LINE THE PIE PLATE Transfer the dough to the pie plate, easing it into place. If necessary, trim the edge almost even with the edge of the plate. Cover with plastic wrap and refrigerate for a minimum of 30 minutes or up to 3 hours.

FILLING

	VOLUME	WEIGHT	
elderberries	2 cups	10 ounces	284 grams
blueberries	2 cups	10 ounces	284 grams
cornstarch	3 tablespoons plus 1 teaspoon	1 ounce	30 grams
water	¼ cup plus 2 tablespoons (89 ml)	3.1 ounces	89 grams
sugar	¾ cup	5.3 ounces	150 grams
fine sea salt	a pinch	.	.
lemon juice, freshly squeezed	2 teaspoons (10 ml)	.	10 grams

MAKE THE FILLING Wash the berries and dry them thoroughly on paper towels.

In a medium saucepan, stir together the cornstarch and water until the cornstarch is dissolved. Add the sugar, salt, and berries. Over medium heat, bring them to a boil, stirring and crushing the blueberries (most of the elderberries will remain whole). Reduce the heat to low and simmer for about 1 minute until thickened. Stir in the lemon juice and scrape the mixture into a bowl to cool to room temperature.

Transfer the berry mixture to the dough-lined pie plate. Moisten the border of the bottom crust by brushing it lightly with water.

ROLL THE DOUGH FOR THE TOP CRUST AND CRIMP Roll out the dough for the top crust large enough to cut a 12 inch disc. Use the expandable flan ring, or a small sharp knife with the cardboard template as a guide, to cut the disc of dough.

To create a berry motif, use the ½ inch round pastry tube to cut little circles from the dough in three little clusters. (Stay within an 8½ inch diameter circle because the rest of the dough will become the raised border.) To maintain the design with no distortion, slip the dough onto a flat baking sheet, cover it with plastic wrap, and refrigerate it for about 10 minutes until firm.

It is essential that the elderberries are completely ripe or they will be very bitter. They should be dark purple to black with no sign of red.

A great tip from my friend Justin Rashid of American Spoon, who sells delicious elderberry preserves: If you have an elderberry bush, you can freeze the berries, on their humbles (fine branches), in large plastic bags. This makes it easier to remove the berries when you are ready to use them.

Place the top crust over the berry filling. Tuck the overhang under the bottom crust border and press down all around the top to seal it. Crimp the border using your forefinger and thumb or a fork. (If you did not make the berry motif, use a small sharp knife to make 5 evenly spaced 2 inch slashes in the top crust, starting about 1 inch from the center and radiating toward the edges.) Cover the pie loosely with plastic wrap and refrigerate it for 1 hour before baking to chill and relax the dough. This will maintain flakiness and help to keep the crust from shrinking.

PREHEAT THE OVEN Forty-five minutes or longer before baking, set an oven rack at the lowest level and place the baking stone or baking sheet on it. Place a large sheet of nonstick aluminum foil or foil lightly coated with nonstick cooking spray on top of the stone to catch any juices. Preheat the oven to 425°F/220°C.

BAKE THE PIE Place the foil ring on top of the pie to protect the edges from overbrowning and set the pie on the foil-topped baking stone. Bake for 20 minutes. For even baking, rotate the pie halfway around. Continue baking for 20 to 30 minutes, or until the juices bubble thickly through the holes or slashes.

COOL THE PIE Cool on a wire rack for at least 2 hours before cutting. When set, the filling will remain juicy with just a little flow. Serve warm or at room temperature.

STORE Room temperature, 2 days; refrigerated, 4 days.

Variation: LATTICE CRUST VERSION

After pouring the fruit into the pie shell, freeze it for about 1 hour, or until firm, before applying the lattice (see Sour Cherry Pie, page 203). You will need to add a few minutes more to the baking time if the fruit is still frozen.

BlueRhu Pie

OVEN TEMPERATURE 425°F/220°C

BAKING TIME 30 to 40 minutes

I discovered this terrific combination of blueberries and rhubarb long ago while I was doing a radio show to publicize *The Pie and Pastry Bible* and a listener called in to ask if I had a recipe for this Amish pie her mother used to make. I have to admit that I never would have come up with such an unusual mélange on my own. I was so curious, however, that I wasted no time before trying it. Fabulous! Because the filling is so beautiful and juicy, I use fewer strips than usual for the lattice.

SPECIAL EQUIPMENT One 9 inch pie plate | An expandable flan ring or 12 inch round cardboard template | A pastry jagger or pizza wheel for cutting the lattice strips | A baking stone or baking sheet | A foil ring to protect the edges of the crust

PERFECT FLAKY AND TENDER CREAM CHEESE PIE CRUST

	VOLUME	WEIGHT	
dough for a 9 inch standard 10 strip lattice pie (page 188)	.	17 ounces	480 grams

ROLL THE DOUGH FOR THE BOTTOM CRUST Remove the dough for the bottom crust from the refrigerator. If necessary, let it sit for about 10 minutes, or until it is malleable enough to roll.

On a floured pastry cloth, pastry mat, or between two sheets of lightly floured plastic wrap, roll the bottom dough into a ⅛ inch thick disc, 12 inches in diameter or large enough to line the bottom of the pie plate and enough to turn about halfway under the border. Lift the dough from time to time and add flour as necessary to keep it from sticking. Before measuring the dough, make sure to lift it from the surface to allow it to shrink in so that it doesn't retract when set in the pie plate. Use the expandable flan ring, or a small sharp knife with the cardboard template as a guide, to cut a 12 inch disc of dough. Layer the scraps on top of the refrigerated dough for the lattice crust.

LINE THE PIE PLATE Transfer the dough to the pie plate, easing it into place. If necessary, trim the edge to make it even. Turn under the dough so that it is even with the edge of the pie plate. Cover with plastic wrap and refrigerate for a minimum of 30 minutes or up to 3 hours.

FILLING

	VOLUME	WEIGHT	
sugar	½ cup plus 1 tablespoon	4 ounces	113 grams
cornstarch	1 tablespoon plus 2¼ teaspoons	0.6 ounce	16 grams
lemon zest, finely grated	1 teaspoon, loosely packed	.	2 grams
fine sea salt	a pinch	.	.
water	¼ cup (59 ml)	2.1 ounces	59 grams
blueberries, fresh or frozen	1¼ cups	6.2 ounces	177 grams
fresh rhubarb, cut into ½ inch pieces	2¼ cups	9 ounces	255 grams

MAKE THE FILLING In a medium saucepan, stir together the sugar, cornstarch, lemon zest, and salt. Stir in the water, then the blueberries and rhubarb. Let the mixture macerate for at least 15 minutes. Over medium heat, stirring constantly, bring the mixture to a boil. Simmer for 1 minute, stirring gently.

Scrape the mixture into a bowl and let it cool completely at room temperature or refrigerated. (It is best not to stir the mixture after cooking to maintain the firm texture of the rhubarb.)

Transfer the mixture to the dough-lined pie plate, making sure to distribute the blueberries and rhubarb evenly.

ROLL THE DOUGH AND MAKE THE LATTICE Roll the second disc of dough into a 10½ by 8 inch oval (about ⅛ thick) and cut ten ¾ inch strips, using a ruler and the pastry jagger or pizza cutter. (If you are right-handed, start from the left side.)

To create a woven lattice, arrange half of the strips evenly over the filling, starting in the center (see Sour Cherry Pie, page 203). Gently curve back every other strip, a little past the center, so that the next strip can be placed perpendicular to the first strips, right at the center. Uncurve the strips so that they lie flat on top of the perpendicular strip. Working in the same direction, curve back the strips that were not curved back the first time. Lay a second perpendicular strip on top and uncurve the strips. Repeat with 1 more strip.

Apply the remaining 2 strips to the other side of the pie. Start toward the center and work in the opposite direction toward the edge. Remember always to alternate the strips that are curved back so that the strips weave in and out.

Use sharp kitchen scissors to trim the strips to a ½ inch overhang. Moisten under the ends of each strip with water and tuck the overhang under the bottom crust border, pressing down to make it adhere and to keep the border from being too thick. If desired, crimp the border using your forefinger and thumb.

Refrigerate the pie for at least 30 minutes, loosely covered with plastic wrap. Just before baking, if a crunchy and sparkling effect is desired, spritz or brush the lattice with a little milk or water (avoid the border because it will get too dark on baking) and dust it lightly with granulated sugar.

PREHEAT THE OVEN Forty-five minutes or longer before baking, set an oven rack at the lowest level and place the baking stone or baking sheet on it. Place a large sheet of non-stick aluminum foil or foil lightly coated with nonstick cooking spray on top of the stone to catch any juices. Preheat the oven to 425°F/220°C.

BAKE THE PIE Place the foil ring on top of the pie to protect the edges from overbrowning and set the pie on the foil-topped baking stone. Bake for 15 minutes. For even baking, rotate the pie halfway around. Continue baking for 15 to 25 minutes, or until thickly bubbling all over and the center is slightly puffed.

COOL THE PIE Cool on a wire rack for at least 3 hours before cutting. When set, the filling will remain juicy with just a little flow. Serve warm or at room temperature.

STORE Room temperature, 2 days; refrigerated, 4 days.

Gooseberry Crisp

OVEN TEMPERATURE
375°F/190°C (400°F/200°C if not using a glass baking dish)

BAKING TIME
20 to 25 minutes

*G*ooseberries are related to currants. They are a pale celadon green, turning burgundy as they continue to ripen, and have a globelike shape and papery thin skin. Their uniquely tart flavor is an excellent complement to the sweet and crunchy crumb topping in this crisp.

I've adopted my friend Kate Coldrick's marvelous technique for thickening these juicy berries, a technique she uses to make gooseberry pie with gooseberries from her own bush in Devon, England. By slightly precooking the berries in the sugar, the berries soften and release their juices, making it possible to concentrate the syrup that forms. This intensifies the flavor and offers a beautiful rosy color and luscious texture to the filling, which can also be used for a pie. Conversely, other berry or fruit fillings can be used with this crisp topping (see Notes, page 221).

Gooseberries are wild berries available from June through August, depending on the region, at some farmers' markets and are well worth the search. Once you've tasted them, you will look forward to their appearance every summer. Lemon, buttermilk, or vanilla ice cream is a lovely accompaniment.

SPECIAL EQUIPMENT One 8 inch square baking dish, preferably Pyrex, no preparation needed

Gooseberry Filling

	VOLUME	WEIGHT	
sugar	1¼ cups	8.8 ounces	250 grams
fine sea salt	a pinch	.	.
lemon zest, finely grated	1 tablespoon, loosely packed	.	6 grams
lemon juice, freshly squeezed and strained (about 2 large lemons)	¼ cup (59 ml)	2.2 ounces	63 grams
gooseberries, stemmed (see Notes, page 221)	4 cups	21.2 ounces	600 grams
cornstarch	1 to 2 tablespoons	0.3 to 0.7 ounce	10 to 19 grams
unsalted butter	6 tablespoons (¾ stick)	3 ounces	85 grams

MAKE THE GOOSEBERRY FILLING Have ready a fine-mesh strainer suspended over a medium bowl.

In a large saucepan, stir together the sugar, salt, lemon zest, and lemon juice. Add the gooseberries and bring the mixture to a boil over medium-low heat, stirring often with a silicone spatula. Continue cooking for 3 to 4 minutes, or until the gooseberries soften.

Pour the mixture into the strainer and drain the gooseberries well, using the silicone spatula to fold them gently in the strainer. Scrape the juices back into the saucepan and empty the gooseberries into the bowl. (There will be about 1½ cups of gooseberries.) Add 1 tablespoon of the cornstarch to the gooseberries and mix until fully incorporated.

Add the butter to the juices and bring them to a boil over medium heat. Boil, stirring often, until the juices begin to thicken. Lower the heat and continue cooking until they darken to a rosy color and reach a thick, syrupy consistency (1⅓ cups/315 ml/13 ounces/368 grams). Do not let the mixture reach a temperature higher than 260°F/127°C, or reduce to less than the volume given, or the juices will caramelize and brown. If the juices do not become thick enough, remove them from the heat and pour them into a heatproof cup to stop the cooking, and stir the remaining cornstarch into the gooseberries. (Riper berries tend to thicken less than green ones.) Scrape the thickened juices into the gooseberry mixture and gently fold them together until evenly combined. Scrape the mixture into the pan.

PREHEAT THE OVEN Thirty minutes or longer before baking, set an oven rack in the lower third of the oven. Preheat the oven to 375°F/190°C (400°F/200°C if not using a Pyrex dish).

CRUMB TOPPING

MAKES ALMOST 1 CUP/4.4 OUNCES/123 GRAMS

	VOLUME	WEIGHT	
light brown Muscovado sugar, or dark brown sugar	2 tablespoons, firmly packed	1 ounce	27 grams
granulated sugar	½ tablespoon	.	6 grams
old-fashioned rolled oats	⅓ cup	0.9 ounce	25 grams
fine sea salt	a pinch	.	.
bleached all-purpose flour	¼ cup plus 2 teaspoons (lightly spooned into the cup and leveled off)	1.3 ounces	36 grams
unsalted butter (65° to 75°F/ 19° to 23°C)	2 tablespoons	1 ounce	28 grams
pure vanilla extract	¼ teaspoon (1.2 ml)	.	.

MAKE THE CRUMB TOPPING FOOD PROCESSOR METHOD In a food processor, pulse together the brown sugar, granulated sugar, oats, and salt until well combined. Add the flour, butter, and vanilla and pulse until the mixture is coarse and crumbly. Empty the mixture into a small bowl and, with your fingertips, lightly pinch it together to form little clumps.

ELECTRIC MIXER METHOD In the bowl of a stand mixer fitted with the flat beater, on medium speed, mix the butter, brown sugar, granulated sugar, and vanilla until smooth and creamy.

In a medium bowl, whisk together the flour, oats, and salt. Add this mixture to the butter mixture and mix on low speed just until incorporated. Remove the bowl from the stand and, with your fingers, lightly pinch together the mixture to form little clumps.

APPLY THE TOPPING Sprinkle the topping evenly over the gooseberry filling.

BAKE THE CRISP Bake for 20 to 25 minutes, or until the topping is crisp and golden brown and the juices beneath are bubbling thickly around the edges.

COOL THE CRISP Cool on a wire rack for 20 minutes. Serve the crisp warm or at room temperature, preferably with a scoop of ice cream slowly melting on top.

STORE Room temperature, lightly covered, 2 days; refrigerated, lightly covered, 3 days; frozen, 6 months.

NOTES Do not confuse gooseberries with cape gooseberries, which have husks.

If using frozen gooseberries, allow them to defrost.

Other fruit fillings may be used in place of the gooseberries. Use about 4 cups of any fruit filling, such as those used for the Perfect Peach Galette (page 197), Sour Cherry Pie (page 200), or Black and Blueberry Pie (page 209). Decrease the cornstarch by 1 teaspoon per 4 cups filling.

LEMON AND CRANBERRY TART TART

OVEN TEMPERATURE
425°F/220°C for the tart shell; 300°F/150°C for the lemon curd and cranberry tart

BAKING TIME
30 to 40 minutes for the tart shell; 12 to 18 minutes for the lemon curd and cranberry tart

*T*his gorgeous tart is perfect for the holidays. Lemon and cranberry is a synergistic combination. If you have a major sweet tooth, you can modify the tartness by adding up to another two tablespoons of sugar to the lemon curd, but the tartness tempers the creamy richness.

PLAN AHEAD The finished tart needs to sit for a minimum of 6 hours before serving.

SPECIAL EQUIPMENT One 9½ by 1 inch high fluted tart pan with a removable bottom, sprayed with baking spray with flour if not a nonstick pan | An expandable flan ring or 12 inch round cardboard template | One 8 inch round cake pan | A baking sheet lined with nonstick or lightly sprayed aluminum foil | A large coffee urn filter, several smaller cup-style filters, or pleated parchment to be filled with beans or rice as weights (spray the bottom(s) lightly with nonstick cooking spray) | A foil ring to protect the edges of the crust

SWEET ALMOND COOKIE TART CRUST (PÂTE SUCRÉE)

MAKES 1 FULL CUP/11.5 OUNCES/326 GRAMS

	VOLUME	WEIGHT	
unsalted butter, cold	6 tablespoons (¾ stick)	3 ounces	85 grams
bleached all-purpose flour	¾ cup (lightly spooned into the cup and leveled off) plus 2 tablespoons	3.7 ounces	106 grams
fine sea salt	⅛ teaspoon	.	0.7 gram
sliced almonds, preferably unblanched	½ cup	1.8 ounces	50 grams
superfine sugar	3 tablespoons	1.3 ounces	37 grams
1 large egg yolk	1 tablespoon plus ½ teaspoon (17 ml)	0.7 ounce	19 grams
heavy cream, cold	2 tablespoons (30 ml)	1 ounce	29 grams

MAKE THE COOKIE TART DOUGH FOOD PROCESSOR METHOD Cut the butter into ½ inch cubes and refrigerate until ready to use.

In a medium bowl, whisk together the flour and salt.

In a food processor, pulse together the almonds and sugar until the almonds are finely ground. Add the cold butter cubes and pulse until the almond mixture coats the butter. Add the flour mixture and pulse until the butter is no larger than small peas.

In a small bowl, stir together the egg yolk and cream. Add it to the mixture and pulse just until incorporated, about 8 times. The dough will be in crumbly pieces.

Empty the dough into a plastic bag and press it from the outside just until it holds together. Remove the dough from the plastic bag and place it on a very large sheet of plastic wrap. Using the plastic wrap, knead the dough only a few times until the dough becomes one smooth piece. There should be no visible pieces of butter. (Visible pieces of butter in the dough will melt and form holes during baking. If there are visible pieces of butter, continue kneading the dough or use the heel of your hand to press them in a forward motion to spread them into the dough.)

HAND METHOD Use a nut grater to grate the almonds. If necessary, pass them through the grater several times until finely grated. In a medium bowl, stir together the almonds, flour, sugar, and salt. With a pastry cutter or two knives, cut in the cold butter until the mixture resembles coarse meal.

In a small bowl, stir together the egg yolk and cream. Mix it into the flour mixture until the dough comes together and can be formed into a large ball.

CHILL THE DOUGH Flatten the dough into a 6 inch disc. Wrap it well and refrigerate it for 30 minutes, or until firm enough to roll or pat into the pan. It can be refrigerated for up to 3 days or frozen for up to 6 months. If chilled for more than 30 minutes, it can take as long as 40 minutes at room temperature to become malleable enough to roll.

ROLL THE DOUGH Set the dough between two lightly floured large sheets of plastic wrap. Roll it evenly into a ⅛ inch thick disc larger than 12 inches in diameter. While rolling the dough, sprinkle it with a little more flour on each side as needed and if the dough softens significantly, slip it onto a baking sheet and refrigerate it until firm (see Notes, page 226). From time to time, flip the dough with the plastic wrap, and lift off and flatten out the plastic wrap as necessary to make sure it does not wrinkle into the dough.

LINE THE TART PAN Remove the top sheet of plastic wrap and use the expandable flan ring, or a pizza wheel or small sharp knife with the cardboard template as a guide, to cut a 12 inch disc. If using a pizza wheel or knife, take care not to cut through the bottom plastic wrap. (Excess dough can be frozen for several months.) If the dough softens after cutting, refrigerate it until firm. It will not drape over the pan unless it is flexible, so if it becomes too rigid in the refrigerator, let it sit and soften for a few minutes.

Invert the 8 inch cake pan onto a work surface. Use the bottom sheet of plastic wrap to lift the dough and set it, plastic side down, over the 8 inch cake pan. Smooth down the sides

LEFT TO RIGHT: Cutting the dough disc with a flan ring. Setting the dough on the inverted cake pan.
Smoothing the dough over the cake pan.

LEFT TO RIGHT: Setting the tart ring on top. Folding down the edges. Marking the edges with a knife.

so they will fit into the tart pan and place the removable bottom of the tart pan on top. Then carefully place the fluted ring, upside down, on top. Place a flat plate, cardboard round, or wire rack over the tart pan to keep it from separating. Invert the pans and remove the cake pan. Carefully peel off the plastic wrap. Gently ease the dough down to reach the bottom and sides of the pan. If the dough breaks when transferring it into the pan, patch and press it into the pan with your fingers.

Fold in the excess dough to halfway down the sides of the tart pan. Press it against the sides so that it extends ⅛ to ¼ inch above the top of the pan. If the dough is thicker in places, press it so that it becomes thinner (it will rise higher). Use small sharp kitchen scissors to trim it to ⅛ to ¼ inch above the top of the pan. If pressing in the dough with your fingers, press it at the juncture where the bottom meets the sides, which often tends to be thicker. For a decorative border, use the back of a knife to make diagonal marks all around, using each flute as a guide.

CHILL THE TART SHELL Cover with plastic wrap and refrigerate it or freeze it for a minimum of 1 hour.

PREHEAT THE OVEN Thirty minutes or longer before baking, set oven racks at the middle and lowest levels and preheat the oven to 425°F/220°C.

BAKE THE TART SHELL Run a finger along the outside fluted edge of the pan to make sure that no dough is attached. The dough must not extend onto the outside of the pan, or as the sides slip down a bit on baking, it will make a hole when the baked crust is removed.

Line the pan with the coffee filter or parchment and fill it three-quarters full with beans or rice to weight it, pushing the weights up against the sides. Carefully transfer the tart pan to the foil-lined baking sheet and set the sheet on the lower rack.

Bake for 5 minutes, lower the heat to 375°F/190°C, and bake for 15 to 20 minutes, or until set. If not set, the dough will stick more to the filter. Lift out the filter with the weights. Place the foil ring on top of the tart shell to protect the edges from overbrowning, and continue baking for 5 to 10 minutes more. If the dough starts to puff in places, press it down quickly with your fingertips or the back of a spoon. Bake until pale gold (the edges will be a deeper brown) and the tart shell feels set but still soft to the touch. (It will continue firming while cooling, just the way cookies do.)

COOL THE TART SHELL Remove the tart pan, still on the baking sheet, to a wire rack. Remove the foil ring and set it aside. If any holes have formed, seal them with a little egg white and return the pan to the oven for 30 seconds for the egg white to set and become opaque. Alternatively, seal the hole or holes with a little melted white chocolate.

Lower the oven temperature to 300°F/150°C.

The unbaked tart shell can be refrigerated for 1 week or frozen for about 1 year. The baked tart shell will keep at room temperature in an airtight container for 2 days.

NOTES When letting it rest, always keep the dough covered to prevent drying or crusting.

It is best only to press down, not pierce, the dough as it puffs. If it is pierced with a fork, there is the risk of accidentally piercing all the way through the bottom, which would cause the filling to leak through on further baking and stick to the bottom of the pan.

CRANBERRY SAUCE

MAKES ⅓ CUP/79 ML/3.5 OUNCES/100 GRAMS

	VOLUME	WEIGHT	
water	1½ tablespoons (22 ml)	0.8 ounce	22 grams
sugar	3 tablespoons	1.3 ounces	37 grams
fine sea salt	a pinch	.	.
cranberries, fresh or frozen (defrosted)	½ cup	1.8 ounces	50 grams
lemon juice, freshly squeezed	½ teaspoon (2.5 ml)	.	.

MAKE THE CRANBERRY SAUCE In a medium saucepan over medium-low heat, stir together the water, sugar, and salt and bring it to a boil, stirring constantly. Add the cranberries, reduce the heat to low, and simmer for 5 minutes, stirring occasionally. Remove from the heat and stir in the lemon juice. Let the mixture cool for 5 minutes.

With an immersion blender or stand blender, puree the cranberries. The puree will not be completely smooth. Cover tightly with plastic wrap.

The cranberry sauce can be stored for 1 month or more refrigerated, and for several months frozen. Bring it to room temperature before using.

LEMON CURD FILLING

MAKES 2½ CUPS/23.3 OUNCES/660 GRAMS

	VOLUME	WEIGHT	
8 (to 12) large egg yolks, at room temperature	½ cup plus 4 teaspoons (138 ml)	5.2 ounces	149 grams
sugar	1½ cups	10.6 ounces	300 grams
unsalted butter (65° to 75°F/ 19° to 23°C)	8 tablespoons (1 stick)	4 ounces	113 grams
lemon juice, freshly squeezed and strained (about 4 large lemons)	¾ cup (177 ml)	6.7 ounces	189 grams
powdered gelatin (see Note, page 228)	½ teaspoon	.	1.5 grams
fine sea salt	¼ teaspoon	.	1.5 grams

MAKE THE LEMON CURD FILLING Have ready a fine-mesh strainer suspended over a 4 cup glass measure with a spout and a 1 cup or larger glass measure with a spout.

In a medium heavy saucepan, whisk the egg yolks, sugar, and butter until well blended. Whisk in the lemon juice, gelatin, and salt. Cook over medium-low heat, stirring constantly with a silicone spatula and scraping down the sides of the pan as needed, until thickened and resembling hollandaise sauce, which thickly coats the spatula but is still liquid enough to pour. The mixture will change from translucent to opaque and begin to take on a yellow color on the spatula. Do not let it come to a boil or it will curdle. Whenever steam appears, remove the pan briefly from the heat, stirring constantly, to keep the mixture from boiling.

When the curd has thickened and will pool thickly when a little is dropped on its surface (an instant-read thermometer should read no higher than 196°F/91°C), pour it at once into the strainer and press it through.

NOTE The gelatin is used to ensure that the thick layer of lemon curd will be firm enough to slice well, but it can be omitted; the curd will be slightly softer.

COMPOSE THE TART If it is not already there, carefully place the tart pan on the baking sheet. It is now necessary to work quickly to integrate the cranberry sauce into the lemon curd before the gelatin in the lemon curd causes it to set. Scrape ½ cup/4.7 ounces/ 132 grams of the lemon curd into the 1 cup glass measure for topping the cranberries and cover tightly with plastic wrap.

Immediately pour the remaining lemon curd onto the tart shell. If necessary, with an offset spatula, quickly smooth the surface. With a small spoon, spread the cranberry sauce in thin bands onto the lemon curd in back and forth loops. With a small offset spatula, press the cranberry sauce lightly into the lemon curd.

Briefly whisk the reserved lemon curd. Carefully pour the curd in thin bands over the cranberry sauce bands. With the offset spatula, quickly smooth the surface to cover the cranberry sauce bands.

BAKE THE TART Place the foil ring on top of the tart to protect the edges from overbrowning and set the baking sheet with the tart on the middle rack. Bake for 12 to 18 minutes, or until an instant-read thermometer inserted near the center reads 160° to 165°F/71° to 74°C.

COOL THE TART Use a cake lifter or 10 inch or longer grill spatula to slide the tart pan onto a wire rack to cool completely, about 1½ hours. Refrigerate the tart, uncovered, for 4 hours or overnight. (If storing longer than 1 day, cover with plastic wrap that has been lightly coated with nonstick cooking spray.)

UNMOLD THE TART Place the tart pan on top of a canister that is smaller than the bottom opening of the tart pan's outer rim. Press down on both sides of the tart ring. The outer rim should slip away easily. Slip a long metal spatula between the crust and the bottom of the pan, loosening it all around if necessary, and slide the tart onto a serving plate. If desired, spoon lightly sweetened whipped cream (see page 516) on the side of each slice.

STORE Refrigerated, 5 days. Do not freeze, because the flavor will be less vibrant.

LEMON CURD AND RASPBERRY PIELETS

OVEN TEMPERATURE
425°F/220°C

BAKING TIME
15 to 18 minutes

I adore these little pies. A layer of intense lemon curd filling is enhanced by a luxurious topping of lemon curd whipped cream. This is a great company dish, since the lemon curd stabilizes the whipped cream for as long as six hours at room temperature; the pielets can also be made the day ahead and refrigerated.

SPECIAL EQUIPMENT Twelve 4¼ by 1 inch pie plates | A 7 inch diameter bowl or round cardboard template | A baking sheet | Twelve small cup-style coffee filters or pieces of pleated parchment to be filled with beans or rice as weights (spray the bottoms lightly with nonstick cooking spray) | Twelve foil rings to protect the edges of the crusts

SWEET COOKIE TART CRUST (PÂTE SUCRÉE)

MAKES 2½ CUPS/28.2 OUNCES/800 GRAMS

	VOLUME	WEIGHT	
unsalted butter, cold	15 tablespoons (1 stick plus 7 tablespoons)	7.5 ounces	213 grams
bleached all-purpose flour	3 cups (lightly spooned into the cup and leveled off) plus 2 tablespoons	13.2 ounces	375 grams
fine sea salt	¼ teaspoon plus ¹⁄₁₆ teaspoon	.	1.7 grams
superfine sugar	½ cup minus ½ tablespoon	3.2 ounces	92 grams
lemon zest, finely grated	1 tablespoon, loosely packed	.	6 grams
3 (to 4) large egg yolks (reserve the whites for sealing the baked crusts)	3 tablespoons (44 ml)	1.6 ounces	46 grams
heavy cream, cold	⅓ cup (79 ml)	2.7 ounces	77 grams

MAKE THE COOKIE TART DOUGH FOOD PROCESSOR METHOD Cut the butter into ½ inch cubes and refrigerate until ready to use.

In a medium bowl, whisk together the flour and salt.

In a food processor, pulse together the sugar and lemon zest until the zest is finely grated. Add the cold butter cubes and pulse until the sugar mixture coats the butter. Add the flour mixture and pulse until the butter is no larger than small peas.

In a small bowl, stir together the egg yolks and cream. Add to the mixture and pulse just until incorporated, about 8 times. The dough will be in crumbly pieces.

Empty the dough into a plastic bag and press it from the outside of the bag just until it holds together. Remove the dough from the plastic bag and place it on a very large sheet of plastic wrap. Using the plastic wrap, knead the dough only a few times until it becomes one smooth piece. There should be no visible pieces of butter. (Visible pieces of butter in the dough will melt and form holes during baking. If there are visible pieces of butter, continue kneading the dough or use the heel of your hand to press them in a forward motion to spread them into the dough.)

HAND METHOD Finely chop the lemon zest. In a medium bowl, stir together the lemon zest, flour, sugar, and salt. With a pastry cutter or two knives, cut in the cold butter until the mixture resembles coarse meal.

In a small bowl, stir together the egg yolks and cream. Mix it into the flour mixture until the dough comes together and can be formed into a large ball.

Divide the dough into two-thirds and one-third (18.6 ounces/528 grams and 9.6 ounces/ 272 grams). Sprinkle each piece of dough on both sides with a little flour, wrap the dough with plastic wrap, and flatten it into discs. Refrigerate the dough for at least 45 minutes, or preferably overnight.

ROLL THE DOUGH Remove the larger disc of dough from the refrigerator. If necessary, let it sit for about 10 minutes, or until it is malleable enough to roll.

On a floured pastry cloth, pastry mat, or between two sheets of lightly floured plastic wrap, roll the dough into a ⅛ inch thick disc or oval. Lift the dough from time to time as you are rolling and add flour as necessary to keep it from sticking. Before measuring and cutting the dough, make sure to lift it from the surface to allow it to shrink in so that it doesn't retract when set in the pie plates. Use the inverted 7 inch bowl or template and a sharp knife to cut several 7 inch discs of dough. Stack the remaining dough scraps and reroll the dough to cut a total of 6 discs. Add the scraps to the remaining dough for the second batch.

LINE THE PIE PLATES Transfer each disc of dough to a pie plate, easing it into place. Use a small sharp knife to trim the excess dough flush to the edge of the pie plate. If the dough softens, refrigerate it for a few minutes before making the border. Use a fork to crimp the border.

CHILL THE PIE SHELLS Cover the pie plates with plastic wrap and refrigerate them for a minimum of 30 minutes or up to 3 days. Repeat rolling, cutting, and lining the pie plates with the second batch of dough.

PREHEAT THE OVEN Thirty minutes or longer before baking, set an oven rack at the lowest level. Preheat the oven to 425°F/220°C.

BAKE THE PIE SHELLS Place six of the pie plates on the baking sheet.

Line the plates with the coffee filters or parchment and fill them three-quarters full with beans or rice to weight them, pushing the weights up against the sides.

Set the baking sheet with the pie plates in the oven. Bake for 10 minutes. Lift out the filters with the weights. Place the foil rings on top of the pie shells to protect the edges from overbrowning and continue baking for 5 to 8 minutes more. If the dough starts to puff in places, press it down quickly with your fingertips or the back of a spoon. Bake until pale gold.

COOL THE PIE SHELLS Remove the pie plates, still on the baking sheet, to a wire rack. If any holes have formed, seal them with a little egg white and return the pan to the oven for 30 seconds for the egg white to set and become opaque. Alternatively, seal the hole or holes with a little melted white chocolate and chill or let it set at room temperature before adding the filling. Bake the remaining 6 pie shells.

The unbaked pie shells can be stored refrigerated for up to 3 days or frozen for 3 months. The baked pie shells will keep at room temperature in an airtight container for 2 days.

LEMON CURD FILLING

MAKES 4 CUPS/38.8 OUNCES/1,100 GRAMS

	VOLUME	WEIGHT	
14 (to 18) large egg yolks, at room temperature	1 cup (237 ml)	9.2 ounces	260 grams
sugar	2½ cups	17.6 ounces	500 grams
unsalted butter (65° to 75°F/ 19° to 23°C)	13 tablespoons (1 stick plus 5 tablespoons)	6.5 ounces	184 grams
lemon juice, freshly squeezed and strained (about 7 large lemons)	1¼ cups (296 ml)	11.1 ounces	315 grams
fine sea salt	⅜ teaspoon	.	2.5 grams

MAKE THE LEMON CURD FILLING Have ready a fine-mesh strainer suspended over a medium bowl and a 4 cup glass measure with a spout.

In a medium heavy saucepan, whisk the egg yolks, sugar, and butter until well blended. Whisk in the lemon juice and salt. Cook over medium-low heat, stirring constantly with a silicone spatula and scraping the sides of the pan as needed, until thickened and resembling hollandaise sauce, which thickly coats the spatula but is still liquid enough to pour. The mixture will change from translucent to opaque and begin to take on a yellow color on the spatula. Do not let it come to a boil or it will curdle. Whenever steam appears, remove the pan briefly from the heat, stirring constantly, to keep the mixture from boiling.

When the curd has thickened and will pool lightly when a little is dropped on its surface (an instant-read thermometer should read no higher than 196°F/91°C), pour it at once into the strainer and press it through.

Remove ⅔ cup/6.5 ounces/183 grams to a small bowl for the whipped cream and set it aside, covered, to cool, about 45 minutes. Scrape the remaining lemon curd into the 4 cup glass measure. You will need almost 3⅓ cups/31.7 ounces/900 grams to fill the pie shells.

FILL THE PIE SHELLS Pour about ¼ cup/2.6 ounces/75 grams of the hot lemon curd into each pie shell, filling it about ¼ inch thick. Set the pielets on the baking sheets and refrigerate for 45 minutes to 1 hour, until set. Remove them to room temperature.

LEMON CURD WHIPPED CREAM

MAKES ABOUT 3⅓ CUPS/17 OUNCES/480 GRAMS

	VOLUME	WEIGHT	
heavy cream, cold	1⅓ cups (316 ml)	10.9 ounces	309 grams
lemon curd (reserved from page 233)	⅔ cup	6.5 ounces	183 grams

MAKE THE LEMON CURD WHIPPED CREAM Into a mixing bowl, pour the cream and refrigerate for at least 15 minutes. (Chill the handheld mixer's beaters alongside the bowl.)

Starting on low speed and gradually raising the speed to medium-high as it thickens, whip the cream just until beater marks begin to show distinctly. Add the lemon curd and whip just until the mixture mounds softly when dropped from a spoon.

The lemon curd will act as a stabilizer, keeping the cream from watering out. It will keep for 6 hours at room temperature, after which it becomes slightly spongy. It will keep for 48 hours refrigerated.

COMPOSE THE PIELETS Up to 6 hours before serving, spoon about ¼ cup/1.4 ounces/40 grams of the whipped cream onto the lemon curd in each pielet. Use a small offset spatula to smooth the surface, ending with a small dollop in the center.

FRESH RASPBERRY TOPPING

	VOLUME	WEIGHT	
fresh raspberries	3 cups	12 ounces	340 grams

GARNISH THE PIELETS Choose the most attractive raspberries and place them side by side against the edge of the crust to form a ring.

STORE Refrigerated, 2 days. Do not freeze, because the flavor will be less vibrant.

THE ARAXI LEMON
CREAM TART

SERVES 10 TO 12

OVEN TEMPERATURE
425°F/220°C for the tart shell; 350°F/175°C for the lemon cream filling

BAKING TIME
30 to 40 minutes for the tart shell; 40 to 50 minutes for the lemon cream filling

*S*ummer of 2012, after finishing the testing for all of the recipes for this book, I visited the Araxi restaurant in Whistler, British Columbia, where I encountered this amazing lemon tart. I was beyond delighted when the restaurant sent the recipe, but I decided to modify it to work in a tart pan that the average person would be likely to have rather than in the 10 by 1½ inch flan ring of the original. The texture is just as good in the 1 inch high tart pan, but should you want to make the higher version, see the Note on page 239.

The silky-smooth lemon filling contains only eggs, lemon juice, lemon zest, sugar, and cream. I had never seen a recipe like this before and was intrigued. To my amazement, when I compared it with my Lemon Pucker Pie in *The Pie and Pastry Bible*, I discovered that coincidentally, the ratio of ingredients was virtually identical, except instead of the butter contained in my lemon curd, the Araxi tart contains cream. Also, the egg whites in this recipe are not whipped. This results in a very thin, spongy foam at the top, and a fabulously creamy—rather than light and puffy—texture within. The contrast of the crispy crust and tart, creamy filling is nothing short of thrilling.

SPECIAL EQUIPMENT One 9½ by 1 inch high fluted tart pan with a removable bottom, sprayed with baking spray with flour if not a nonstick pan | An expandable flan ring or 12 inch round cardboard template | One 8 inch round cake pan | A baking sheet lined with nonstick or lightly sprayed aluminum foil | A large coffee urn filter, several smaller cup-style filters, or pleated parchment to be filled with beans or rice as weights (spray the bottom(s) lightly with nonstick cooking spray)

SWEET COOKIE TART CRUST (PÂTE SUCRÉE)

MAKES 1 CUP/11.3 OUNCES/321 GRAMS

	VOLUME	WEIGHT	
unsalted butter, cold	6 tablespoons (¾ stick)	3 ounces	85 grams
bleached all-purpose flour	1¼ cups (lightly spooned into the cup and leveled off)	5.3 ounces	150 grams
fine sea salt	⅛ teaspoon	.	0.7 gram
superfine sugar	3 tablespoons	1.3 ounces	37 grams
lemon zest, finely grated	½ tablespoon, loosely packed	.	3 grams
1 large egg yolk (reserve the white for sealing the baked crust)	1 tablespoon plus ½ teaspoon (17 ml)	0.7 ounce	19 grams
heavy cream, cold	2 tablespoons (30 ml)	1 ounce	29 grams

MAKE THE COOKIE TART DOUGH FOOD PROCESSOR METHOD Cut the butter into ½ inch cubes and refrigerate until ready to use.

In a medium bowl, whisk together the flour and salt.

In a food processor, pulse together the sugar and lemon zest until the zest is finely grated. Add the cold butter cubes and pulse until the sugar mixture coats the butter. Add the flour mixture and pulse until the butter is no larger than small peas.

In a small bowl, stir together the egg yolk and cream. Add it to the mixture and pulse just until incorporated, about 8 times. The dough will be in crumbly pieces.

Empty the dough into a plastic bag and press it from the outside of the bag just until it holds together. Remove the dough from the plastic bag and place it on a very large sheet of plastic wrap. Using the plastic wrap, knead the dough only a few times until it becomes one smooth piece. There should be no visible pieces of butter. (Visible pieces of butter in the dough will melt and form holes during baking. If there are visible pieces of butter continue kneading the dough or use the heel of your hand to press them in a forward motion to spread them into the dough.)

HAND METHOD Finely chop the lemon zest. In a medium bowl, stir together the lemon zest, flour, sugar, and salt. With a pastry cutter or two knives, cut in the cold butter until the mixture resembles coarse meal.

In a small bowl, stir together the egg yolk and cream. Mix it into the flour mixture until the dough comes together and can be formed into a large ball.

CHILL THE DOUGH Flatten the dough into a 6 inch disc. Wrap it well and refrigerate it for 30 minutes, or until firm enough to roll or pat into the pan. It can be refrigerated for up to

3 days or frozen for up to 6 months. If chilled for more than 30 minutes, it can take as long as 40 minutes at room temperature to become malleable enough to roll.

ROLL THE DOUGH Set the dough between lightly floured large sheets of plastic wrap. Roll it evenly into a ⅛ inch thick disc larger than 12 inches in diameter. While rolling the dough, sprinkle it with a little more flour on each side as needed and if the dough softens significantly, slip it onto a baking sheet and refrigerate it until firm (see Notes, page 238). From time to time, flip the dough with the plastic wrap and lift off and flatten out the plastic wrap as necessary to make sure it does not wrinkle into the dough.

LINE THE TART PAN Remove the top sheet of plastic wrap and use the expandable flan ring, or a pizza wheel or small sharp knife with the cardboard template as a guide, to cut a 12 inch disc. If using the pizza wheel or knife, take care not to cut through the bottom plastic wrap. (Excess dough can be frozen for several months.) If the dough softens after cutting, refrigerate it until firm. It will not drape over the pan unless it is flexible, so if it becomes too rigid in the refrigerator, let it sit and soften for a few minutes.

Invert the 8 inch cake pan onto a work surface. Use the bottom sheet of plastic wrap to lift the dough and set it, plastic side down, over the 8 inch cake pan (see Lemon and Cranberry Tart Tart, page 225). Smooth down the sides so they will fit into the tart pan and place the removable bottom of the tart pan on top. Then carefully place the fluted ring, upside down, on top. Place a flat plate, cardboard round, or wire rack over the tart pan to keep it from separating. Invert the pans and remove the cake pan. Carefully peel off the plastic wrap. Gently ease the dough down to reach the bottom and sides of the pan. If the dough breaks when transferring it into the pan, patch and press it into the pan with your fingers.

Fold in the excess dough to halfway down the sides of the tart pan. Press it against the sides so that it extends ⅛ to ¼ inch above the top of the pan. If the dough is thicker in places, press it so that it becomes thinner (it will rise higher). Use small sharp kitchen scissors to trim it to ⅛ to ¼ inch above the top of the pan. If pressing in the dough with your fingers, press it at the juncture where the bottom meets the sides, which often tends to be thicker. For a decorative border, use the back of a knife to make diagonal marks all around, using each flute as a guide.

CHILL THE TART SHELL Cover with plastic wrap and refrigerate it or freeze it for a minimum of 1 hour.

PREHEAT THE OVEN Thirty minutes or longer before baking, set oven racks at the middle and lowest levels and preheat the oven to 425°F/220°C.

BAKE THE TART SHELL Run a finger along the outside fluted edge of the pan to make sure that no dough is attached. The dough must not extend onto the outside of the pan or as the sides slip down a bit on baking, it will make a hole when the baked crust is removed.

Line the pan with the coffee filter or parchment and fill it three-quarters full with beans or rice to weight it, pushing the weights up against the sides. Carefully transfer the tart pan to the foil-lined baking sheet and set the tart on the lower rack.

Bake for 5 minutes, lower the heat to 375°F/190°C, and bake for 15 to 20 minutes, or until set. If not set, the dough will stick more to the filter. Lift out the filter with the weights, and continue baking for 5 to 10 minutes more. If the dough starts to puff in places, press it down quickly with your fingertips or the back of a spoon (see Notes). Bake until pale gold (the edges will be a deeper brown) and the tart shell feels set but still soft to the touch. (It will continue firming while cooling, just the way cookies do.)

COOL THE TART SHELL Remove the tart pan, still on the baking sheet, to a wire rack. If any holes have formed, seal them with a little egg white and return the pan to the oven for 30 seconds for the egg white to set and become opaque. Alternatively, seal the hole or holes with a little melted white chocolate.

Let the tart shell cool for 3 minutes and then brush the bottom and sides to coat well with some of the reserved egg white, lightly beaten, to moisture-proof the crust. Cool completely.

Lower the oven temperature to 350°F/175°C.

The unbaked tart shell can be refrigerated for 1 week or frozen for about 1 year. The baked tart shell without the brushed egg white will keep at room temperature in an airtight container for 2 days.

NOTES When letting it rest, always keep the dough covered to prevent drying or crusting.

It is best only to press down, not pierce, the dough as it puffs. If it is pierced with a fork, there is the risk of accidentally piercing all the way through the bottom, which would cause the filling to leak through on further baking and stick to the bottom of the pan.

LEMON CREAM FILLING

MAKES 3½ CUPS/23 OUNCES/650 GRAMS

	VOLUME	WEIGHT	
heavy cream, cold	½ cup (118 ml)	4.1 ounces	116 grams
5 large eggs, cold	1 cup (237 ml)	8.8 ounces	250 grams
sugar	¾ cup plus 2 tablespoons	6.2 ounces	175 grams
lemon juice, freshly squeezed and strained (about 3 large lemons)	½ cup (118 ml)	4.4 ounces	126 grams
lemon zest, finely grated	2 teaspoons, loosely packed	.	4 grams

MAKE THE LEMON CREAM FILLING Into a medium bowl, pour the cream and refrigerate for at least 15 minutes. (Chill a handheld mixer's beaters alongside the bowl.)

In a medium bowl, whisk together the eggs and sugar until well combined. Gradually whisk in the lemon juice. Strain the mixture into a large bowl. Stir in the lemon zest.

Starting on low speed and gradually raising the speed to high as it thickens, whip the cream until it mounds softly when dropped from a spoon.

Use a large whisk to fold the whipped cream into the lemon mixture. It will not be totally uniform. Refrigerate the lemon cream filling for 30 minutes. The filling will separate with a frothy cream covering the lemon-color mixture. After 30 minutes, use the large whisk to fold the filling with a few strokes to make it more even. Pour the filling into a 4 cup glass measure with a spout.

BAKE THE TART Set the tart shell, still on the foil-lined baking sheet, on the middle rack of the oven and carefully pour in the filling. It will fill the tart shell to the top. If your tart crust has shrunk or lowered in the pan, there will be some extra filling. Lower the heat to 325°F/160°C and bake for 20 minutes. Carefully turn the tart halfway around, lower the heat to 300°F/150°C, and continue baking for 15 minutes. Turn off the oven and let the tart sit for 5 to 15 minutes. When moved, the center should jiggle very slightly. (An instant-read thermometer should read about 170°F/77°C.)

COOL THE TART Avoid touching the filling's surface because it will tear and stick to your finger. Use a cake lifter or 10 inch or longer grill spatula to slide the tart onto a wire rack to cool completely, about 45 minutes.

UNMOLD THE TART Place the tart pan on top of a canister that is smaller than the bottom opening of the tart pan's outer rim. Press down on both sides of the tart ring. The outer rim should slip away easily. Slip a long metal spatula between the crust and the bottom of the pan, loosening it all around if necessary, and slide the tart onto a serving plate. The tart cuts easily, even into slim servings.

If desired, sprinkle powdered sugar on top of each slice shortly before serving the tart and accompany it with raspberry sauce (see page 38).

STORE Refrigerated, 5 days. Do not freeze, because the flavor will be less vibrant.

NOTE To make a larger tart in a 10 by 1½ inch flan ring as described on page 235, you will need to multiply all the tart crust ingredients by 1.5 and multiply all the filling ingredients by 2.5. The baking time will be about 5 minutes longer.

FROZEN LIME MERINGUE PIE

SERVES 8 TO 10

OVEN TEMPERATURE
350°F/175°C for the almonds; broiler for the meringue

BAKING TIME
7 to 9 minutes for the almonds; less than 1 minute for the meringue

*T*his pie for lime lovers was adapted from one of my most spectacular cake recipes: The Lemon Canadian Crown in *Rose's Heavenly Cakes*, which features a semi-frozen citrus custard filling.

PLAN AHEAD Freeze the pie filling for at least 5 hours or up to 5 days ahead.

SPECIAL EQUIPMENT One baking sheet | One 9 inch pie plate

VANILLA ALMOND CRUMB CRUST

	VOLUME	WEIGHT	
sliced almonds, preferably unblanched	½ cup	1.8 ounces	50 grams
vanilla wafers	1 cup crumbs (after grinding), lightly packed	4.2 ounces	120 grams
sugar	1 tablespoon	0.5 ounce	13 grams
fine sea salt	2 pinches	.	.
unsalted butter, melted	4 tablespoons (½ stick)	2 ounces	57 grams

PREHEAT THE OVEN Twenty minutes or longer before baking, set an oven rack in the middle of the oven and preheat the oven to 350°F/175°C.

TOAST THE ALMONDS Spread the almonds evenly on a baking sheet and bake for about 7 minutes, or until pale gold. Stir once or twice to ensure even toasting and avoid over-browning. Cool completely.

MAKE THE CRUMB CRUST FOOD PROCESSOR METHOD Process the wafers with the almonds, sugar, and salt until the cookies become fine crumbs, about 20 seconds. Add the melted butter and pulse about 10 times, just until incorporated.

HAND METHOD Place the wafers in a freezer bag and use a rolling pin to crush them into fine crumbs. Use a nut grater to grind the almonds fine but not powder-fine. In a medium bowl, combine the wafers, almonds, sugar, and salt and toss with a fork to blend. Stir in the melted butter and toss to incorporate it.

FORM AND CHILL THE PIE SHELL Scrape the mixture into the pie plate and, using your fingers, begin by pressing the mixture evenly into the bottom and partway up the sides. To help make the bottom even, use a flat-bottom measuring or custard cup to smooth the crumbs over the bottom. To create an attractive top edge, as you press the crumbs against the sides and up above the rim, use your forefinger to press against them from the other direction, forming a little ridge or peak. (Chilling the crust for a few minutes firms the butter and makes this task easier.) Refrigerate the completed pie shell while making the filling.

The pie shell can be refrigerated for 1 week or frozen for about 6 months.

LIME FILLING

	VOLUME	WEIGHT	
lime zest, finely grated	2 teaspoons, loosely packed	.	4 grams
3 (to 4) large eggs, separated, at room temperature			
yolks	3½ tablespoons (52 ml)	2 ounces	56 grams
whites	¼ cup plus 2 tablespoons (89 ml), *divided*	3.2 ounces	90 grams
sugar	¾ cup, *divided*	5.3 ounces	150 grams
lime juice, freshly squeezed	½ cup (118 ml)	4.4 ounces	126 grams
fine sea salt	a pinch	.	.
heavy cream, cold	1¼ cups (296 ml)	10.2 ounces	290 grams

MAKE THE LIME FILLING Have ready a fine-mesh strainer suspended over a large bowl containing the lime zest.

In the top of a double boiler, whisk together the egg yolks, 2½ tablespoons/37 ml/1.3 ounces/36 grams of the egg whites, all but 2 tablespoons/0.9 ounce/25 grams of the sugar, the lime juice, and salt. (Refrigerate the remaining whites for the meringue.) Set the double boiler over simmering water (do not let the bottom of the container touch the water). Cook, stirring and scraping the bottom and sides with a silicone spatula, until the mixture has thickened and will pool lightly when a little is dropped on its surface, about 7 minutes. (An instant-read thermometer should read no higher than 180° to 182°F/82° to 83°C.)

Immediately scrape the mixture into the strainer and press all of it through. Stir to incorporate the lime zest evenly. Let the mixture cool completely to the touch, gently stirring every 15 minutes, about 1 hour at room temperature, or place in an ice water bath (see page 538), gently stirring often, for about 15 minutes.

WHIP THE CREAM Into the bowl of a stand mixer, pour the cream. Add the remaining 2 tablespoons of sugar and refrigerate for at least 15 minutes. (Chill the whisk beater alongside the bowl.)

Starting on low speed and gradually raising the speed to medium-high as it thickens, whip the cream just until thickened and it mounds very softly when dropped from a spoon. Do not overwhip, because the whipped cream will continue to thicken after it is mixed with the lime mixture. Using a large balloon whisk, slotted skimmer, or large spatula, stir about ½ cup of the whipped cream into the lime mixture to lighten it. Scrape in the remaining whipped cream and gently but thoroughly fold it into the mixture until only a few streaks remain. Switch to a silicone spatula and continue folding, reaching to the bottom, until the mixture is uniform in color.

FREEZE THE FILLING Scrape the filling into the pie shell and smooth the surface evenly with a small offset spatula. The filling will fill the pie shell to just below its rim. Cover it tightly with plastic wrap and freeze it for a minimum of 5 hours or up to 5 days.

MERINGUE TOPPING

	VOLUME	WEIGHT	
4 large egg whites, at room temperature	½ cup (118 ml)	4.2 ounces	120 grams
cream of tartar	½ teaspoon	.	0.8 gram
powdered sugar	⅓ cup (lightly spooned into the cup and leveled off)	1.3 ounces	38 grams

PREHEAT THE OVEN Position an oven rack so that the rim of the pie crust will be about 4 inches below the broiler. Preheat the broiler. If using an electric broiler, preheat for a minimum of 10 minutes.

MAKE THE MERINGUE TOPPING In the bowl of a stand mixer fitted with the whisk beater, beat the egg whites and cream of tartar on medium-low speed until foamy. Gradually raise the speed to medium-high and beat until soft peaks form when the beater is raised. Sift the powdered sugar evenly over the surface and continue beating until stiff peaks form when the beater is raised slowly.

COMPOSE THE PIE Scrape the meringue on top of the lime filling. Using a small metal spatula, spread it evenly into a dome. Bring the meringue right up against the pie crust so that it attaches to the pie crust. (This will keep the meringue from shrinking and separating from the pie crust.) Make swirls and peaks in the meringue.

Place the pie on a baking sheet, set it under the broiler, and allow the meringue to turn golden brown. It will take less than 1 minute. Start checking at about 10 seconds and watch carefully to prevent burning. Remove it from the broiler. Alternatively, use a torch to brown the meringue.

CHILL THE PIE Immediately return the pie to the freezer for a minimum of 1 hour or up to 3 weeks. If freezing longer than 1 hour, after the first hour, cover the top with plastic wrap.

SERVE THE PIE The ideal temperature to serve the pie is when an instant-read thermometer inserted into the center reads 28° to 32°F/-2° to 0°C. The filling is most delicious when very cold but creamy. Depending on the freezer temperature and room temperature, it will require anywhere from 1 to 1½ hours at room temperature to reach the ideal consistency.

To release the pie from the pan, either wipe the bottom and sides of the pan with a dish towel that has been run under very hot water and wrung out (it will be necessary to repeat this several times) or lower the pie plate carefully into a bowl of hot water for a few seconds. Use a thin sharp blade to cut the pie. There is no need to wet it between slices if the pie has been allowed to soften. (The unsoftened pie can be sliced with a hot wet knife and the slices allowed to sit for 30 minutes or more before serving.)

STORE Airtight: freezer, 3 weeks.

FRENCH ORANGE CREAM TART

SERVES 6 TO 8

OVEN TEMPERATURE
425°F/220°C for the tart shell; 300°F/150°C for the orange cream tart

BAKING TIME
30 to 40 minutes for the tart shell; 30 to 40 minutes for the orange cream tart

This exquisite recipe was inspired by one I enjoyed at a dinner at L'École, the restaurant at The International Culinary Center in New York City. Chef Tina Casaceli, the owner of Milk & Cookies Bakery in New York City and a chef instructor at L'École at the time, shared the special filling and caramelizing technique with me: The tart is filled with the creamiest of true orange fillings and topped with the finest possible crunch of caramel.

SPECIAL EQUIPMENT One 9½ by 1 inch high fluted tart pan with a removable bottom, sprayed with baking spray with flour if not a nonstick pan | An expandable flan ring or 12 inch round cardboard template | One 8 inch round cake pan | A baking sheet lined with nonstick or lightly sprayed aluminum foil | A large coffee urn filter, several smaller cup-style filters, or pleated parchment to be filled with beans or rice as weights (spray the bottom(s) lightly with nonstick cooking spray) | A foil ring to protect the edges of the crust | A splashguard or plastic wrap for the stand mixer

SWEET COOKIE TART CRUST (PÂTE SUCRÉE)

MAKES 1 CUP/11.3 OUNCES/321 GRAMS

	VOLUME	WEIGHT	
unsalted butter, cold	6 tablespoons (¾ stick)	3 ounces	85 grams
bleached all-purpose flour	1¼ cups (lightly spooned into the cup and leveled off)	5.3 ounces	150 grams
fine sea salt	⅛ teaspoon	.	0.7 gram
turbinado sugar, preferably Sugar in the Raw, or superfine sugar	3 tablespoons	1.3 ounces	37 grams
1 large egg yolk	1 tablespoon plus ½ teaspoon (17 ml)	0.7 ounce	19 grams
heavy cream, cold	2 tablespoons (30 ml)	1 ounce	29 grams

MAKE THE COOKIE TART DOUGH FOOD PROCESSOR METHOD Cut the butter into ½ inch cubes and refrigerate until ready to use.

In a medium bowl, whisk together the flour and salt.

In a food processor, process the sugar until fine. Add the cold butter cubes and pulse until the sugar disappears. Add the flour mixture and pulse until the butter is no larger than small peas.

In a small bowl, stir together the egg yolk and cream. Add it to the mixture and pulse just until incorporated, about 8 times. The dough will be in crumbly pieces.

Empty the dough into a plastic bag and press it from the outside of the bag just until it holds together. Remove the dough from the plastic bag and place it on a very large sheet of plastic wrap. Using the plastic wrap, knead the dough only a few times until it becomes one smooth piece. There should be no visible pieces of butter. (Visible pieces of butter in the dough will melt and form holes during baking. If there are visible pieces of butter continue kneading the dough or use the heel of your hand to press them in a forward motion to spread them into the dough.)

HAND METHOD In a medium bowl, stir together the flour, sugar (use superfine or fine granulated), and salt. With a pastry cutter or two knives, cut in the cold butter until the mixture resembles coarse meal.

In a small bowl, stir together the egg yolk and cream. Mix it into the flour mixture until the dough comes together and can be formed into a large ball.

CHILL THE DOUGH Flatten the dough into a 6 inch disc. Wrap it well and refrigerate it for 30 minutes, or until firm enough to roll or pat into the pan. It can be refrigerated for up to 3 days or frozen for up to 6 months. If chilled for more than 30 minutes, it can take as long as 40 minutes at room temperature to become malleable enough to roll.

ROLL THE DOUGH Set the dough between lightly floured large sheets of plastic wrap. Roll it evenly into a ⅛ inch thick disc larger than 12 inches in diameter. While rolling the dough, sprinkle it with a little more flour on each side as needed and if the dough softens significantly, slip it onto a baking sheet and refrigerate it until firm (see Notes, page 249). From time to time, flip the dough with the plastic wrap, and lift off and flatten out the plastic wrap as necessary to make sure it does not wrinkle into the dough.

LINE THE TART PAN Remove the top sheet of plastic wrap and use the expandable flan ring, or a pizza wheel or small sharp knife with the cardboard template as a guide, to cut a 12 inch disc. If using the pizza wheel or knife, take care not to cut through the bottom plastic wrap. (Excess dough can be frozen for several months.) If the dough softens after cutting, refrigerate it until firm. It will not drape over the pan unless it is flexible, so if it becomes too rigid in the refrigerator, let it sit and soften for a few minutes.

Invert the 8 inch cake pan onto a work surface. Use the bottom sheet of plastic wrap to lift the dough and set it, plastic side down, over the 8 inch cake pan (see Lemon and Cranberry Tart Tart, page 225). Smooth down the sides so they will fit into the tart pan and place the removable bottom of the tart pan on top. Then carefully place the fluted ring, upside down, on top. Place a flat plate or cardboard round over the tart pan to keep it from separating. Invert the pans and remove the cake pan. Carefully peel off the plastic wrap. Gently ease the dough down to reach the bottom and sides of the pan. If the dough breaks when transferring it into the pan, patch and press it into the pan with your fingers.

Fold in the excess dough to halfway down the sides of the tart pan. Press it against the sides so that it extends ⅛ to ¼ inch above the top of the pan. If the dough is thicker in places, press it so that it becomes thinner (it will rise higher). Use small sharp kitchen scissors to trim it to ⅛ to ¼ inch above the top of the pan. If pressing in the dough with your fingers, press it at the juncture where the bottom meets the sides, which often tends to be thicker. For a decorative border, use the back of a knife to make diagonal marks all around, using each flute as a guide.

CHILL THE TART SHELL Cover with plastic wrap and refrigerate it or freeze it for a minimum of 1 hour.

PREHEAT THE OVEN Thirty minutes or longer before baking, set oven racks at the middle and lowest levels and preheat the oven to 425°F/220°C.

BAKE THE TART SHELL Run a finger along the outside fluted edge of the pan to make sure that no dough is attached. The dough must not extend onto the outside of the pan because as the sides slip down a bit on baking, it will make a hole when the baked crust is removed.

Line the pan with the coffee filter or parchment and fill it three-quarters full with beans or rice to weight it, pushing the weights up against the sides. Carefully transfer the tart pan to the foil-lined baking sheet and set it on the lower rack.

Bake for 5 minutes, lower the heat to 375°F/190°C, and bake for 15 to 20 minutes, or until set. If not set, the dough will stick more to the filter. Lift out the filter with the weights. Place the foil ring on top of the tart to protect the edges from overbrowning and continue baking for 5 to 10 minutes more. If the dough starts to puff in places, press it down quickly with your fingertips or the back of a spoon (see Notes, page 249). Bake until pale gold (the edges will be a deeper brown) and the tart shell feels set but still soft to the touch. (It will continue firming while cooling, just the way cookies do.)

COOL THE TART SHELL Remove the tart pan, still on the baking sheet, to a wire rack. If any holes have formed, seal them with a little egg white and return the pan to the oven for 30 seconds for the egg white to set and become opaque. Alternatively, seal the hole or holes with a little melted white chocolate.

Lower the oven temperature to 300°F/150°C.

The unbaked tart shell can be refrigerated for 1 week or frozen for about 1 year. The baked tart shell will keep at room temperature in an airtight container for 2 days.

NOTES When letting it rest, always keep the dough covered to prevent drying or crusting.

You will have enough tart crust left over to make about six Hamantaschen (page 384).

It is best only to press down, not pierce, the dough as it puffs. If it is pierced with a fork, there is the risk of accidentally piercing all the way through the bottom, which would cause the filling to leak through on further baking and stick to the bottom of the pan.

ORANGE CREAM FILLING

	VOLUME	WEIGHT	
orange zest, finely grated (from 1 orange)	2 tablespoons, loosely packed	.	12 grams
lemon zest, finely grated	1 teaspoon, loosely packed	.	2 grams
granulated sugar	½ cup plus 1 tablespoon plus 1 teaspoon	4.1 ounces	115 grams
orange juice, freshly squeezed and strained (about 2 large oranges)	½ cup plus 1½ tablespoons (140 ml)	5 ounces	143 grams
lemon juice, freshly squeezed and strained	2½ tablespoons (40 ml)	1.4 ounces	40 grams
Grand Marnier (optional)	1 teaspoon (5 ml)	.	.
6 (to 9) large egg yolks	¼ cup plus 3 tablespoons (103 ml)	4 ounces	112 grams
heavy cream	1 cup (237 ml)	8.2 ounces	232 grams
powdered sugar (for dusting)	1 tablespoon	.	9 grams

MAKE THE ORANGE CREAM FILLING In a food processor, place the orange zest, lemon zest, and granulated sugar and process until the zest is very fine. Alternatively, chop the zest with a sharp chef's knife.

Into a 4 cup glass measure with a spout, lightly coated with nonstick cooking spray, or a medium saucepan, pour the orange juice and lemon juice. Reduce the juices in the microwave or on the cooktop to 6 tablespoons/89 ml/3 ounces/86 grams. Let the mixture cool to room temperature and stir in the Grand Marnier, if using.

In the bowl of a stand mixer fitted with the flat beater and splash guard, on low speed, beat the zest-sugar mixture and egg yolks for about 2 minutes, or until well combined. Gradually beat in the cream and then the cooled juice mixture.

Pour and scrape the filling into the prepared tart shell still on the foil-lined baking sheet. The filling will be close to the top of the crust.

BAKE THE TART Place the foil ring on top of the tart to protect the edges from overbrowning and set the baking sheet with the completed tart on the middle rack. Bake for 30 to 40 minutes, or until set, removing the foil ring after 15 minutes. When the baking sheet is moved, the filling should jiggle only very slightly. The orange cream will balloon about ¼ inch above the rim of the crust and will have a thin skin on it, but look slightly moist toward the center. (An instant-read thermometer should read about 185°F/85°C.)

COOL THE TART Remove the tart pan, still on the baking sheet, to a wire rack to cool to room temperature, about 1 hour. Cover it with an inverted plate or large bowl and place it in the refrigerator for a minimum of 1 hour.

CARAMELIZE THE POWDERED SUGAR When ready to serve the tart, sift half of the powdered sugar evenly over the surface of the tart and use a torch to caramelize it until it is a deep amber color. Return the tart to the refrigerator for about 10 minutes to cool the surface and then repeat with the remaining sugar. Alternatively, simply dust the top of the tart with the powdered sugar.

UNMOLD THE TART Place the tart pan on top of a canister that is smaller than the bottom opening of the tart pan's outer rim. Press down on both sides of the tart ring. The outer rim should slip away easily. Slip a long metal spatula between the crust and the bottom of the pan, loosening it all around if necessary, and slide the tart onto a serving plate. Serve the tart immediately while the thin coating of caramelized sugar is still crisp.

STORE Refrigerated, 1 day (the caramelized topping will soften completely on storage).

POMEGRANATE WINTER CHIFFON MERINGUE PIE

OVEN TEMPERATURE 200°F/90°C

BAKING TIME
2 hours 20 minutes to 2 hours 50 minutes for the meringue shell

*W*hen I was eleven, I had the enchanting experience of performing as a toy soldier in George Balanchine's staging of the famous Christmastime ballet *The Nutcracker*. Every night, while waiting backstage for our curtain call, I watched another young ballerina snack on a fruit I had never seen before. This charming girl was eating a pomegranate (which her mother called a Chinese apple), one seed at a time, with delicate fingers that looked as if they were dancing a ballet of their own. It seemed so magical to me that ever since, I've enjoyed picking out the seeds and eating them one at a time the way she did. Still, I imagined that there must be a way to experience a pomegranate in a grander way. So at last I created a dessert worthy of the fruit's beauty and compelling flavor. The pomegranate chiffon filling can also be poured into a glass and served as a mousse. The pomegranate glaze is most beautiful when piped, but it can also be drizzled on top of the filling. The arils, which are the individual pieces of the fruit coating the seeds, provide a lovely garnish.

PLAN AHEAD Let the crisp meringue pie shell or lemon cookie crust (see Variation, page 257) cool for 2 hours before adding the pomegranate chiffon mixture.

SPECIAL EQUIPMENT One 9½ inch deep dish pie plate, bottom, sides, and rim coated with shortening and then coated with flour, preferably Wondra | A large pastry bag fitted with a ½ inch star pastry tube or quart-size reclosable freezer bag with a ½ inch semicircle cut from one corner for the star tube

CRISP MERINGUE PIE SHELL

	VOLUME	WEIGHT	
4 large egg whites, at room temperature	½ cup (118 ml)	4.2 ounces	120 grams
cream of tartar	½ teaspoon	.	1.6 grams
superfine sugar	½ cup plus 1 tablespoon	4 ounces	113 grams
powdered sugar	1 cup (lightly spooned into the cup and leveled off)	4 ounces	113 grams

PREHEAT THE OVEN Twenty minutes or longer before baking, set an oven rack in the middle of the oven and preheat the oven to 200°F/90°C.

BEAT THE EGG WHITES INTO A STIFF MERINGUE In the bowl of a stand mixer fitted with the whisk beater, beat the egg whites and cream of tartar on medium-low speed until foamy. Gradually raise the speed to medium-high and beat until soft peaks form when the beater is raised. Gradually beat in the superfine sugar until glossy and stiff peaks form when the beater is raised slowly.

Remove the mixer bowl from the stand and sift the powdered sugar over the meringue. Using a silicone spatula, gently fold the powdered sugar into the meringue, scraping the bottom of the bowl, until incorporated.

PIPE THE MERINGUE SHELL Insert the star tube into the pastry or freezer bag and fill it with half of the meringue. Hold the bag in a vertical position (straight up and down) with the tube at least 1½ inches above the pan. To achieve the full height, the batter must be allowed to fall from the tube (not pressed against the pan).

Starting at the center of the pie plate, pipe a spiral coil to cover the bottom of the plate. To prevent gaps, let the spirals of meringue fall against the side, almost on top of the previous spirals. The weight of the meringue will cause them to fall perfectly into place. Continue piping until the coil has reached the sides of the plate.

Refill the bag with the remaining meringue. For the sides, pipe three single rings of meringue; the last ring should come just above the rim. Smooth the top edge of the meringue to form a level, ½ inch wide top edge. To reinforce where the sides and bottom coils meet and to prevent cracking, pipe a coil of meringue against the bottom side coil

LEFT TO RIGHT: Piping the meringue shell. Smoothing the top edge. Piping the shell border.

and smooth it with a spoon. Fill in any gaps in the meringue coils and smooth the surface with a spoon or small offset spatula. Alternatively, use a large spoon to spread a ½ inch thick layer of meringue over the bottom and sides of the plate. Smooth the top edge of the meringue to form a level top edge ½ inch wide.

PIPE THE SHELL BORDER Pipe the shells so that they are directly above the top of the meringue, resting slightly on the rim of the pan for support.

Hold the bag at a 45 to 90 degree angle with the end of the bag pointed toward you and the tube slightly above the top edge. Squeeze firmly, allowing the meringue to fan out. Then move the tube to the left, up and around, in a question-mark shape. Gradually relax the pressure as you pull the tube down to the right, forming a straight tail.

Continue the next shell as above, overlapping the tail of the previous shell. Continue piping shells around the edge of the meringue. Form the last shell's tail to curve under the first shell.

BAKE THE MERINGUE SHELL Bake for 2 hours without opening the oven door to prevent cracking. The meringue should not be brown. To check for doneness, without removing the meringue from the oven, use the tip of a small sharp knife to dig out a little from the center. It can still be slightly sticky because it will continue to dry while cooling. If it is more than slightly sticky, continue to bake it, checking every 10 minutes, until it is done.

To prevent cracking, turn off the oven and prop open the oven door slightly with a wooden spoon handle. Let the meringue sit for 10 minutes. Then open the oven door completely and let the meringue sit for another 10 minutes. Remove it from the oven and place it on a countertop. Place a cake carrier dome or large bowl over the pie plate and cool the meringue for another 30 minutes.

If the meringue has severe cracks or any cracks that go through to the plate, use the white chocolate glaze to fill them. (Minor cracks are not a problem because the pomegranate chiffon mixture will not soften the meringue's outer crust.)

WHITE CHOCOLATE GLAZE

	VOLUME	WEIGHT	
white chocolate containing cocoa butter, chopped	.	8.2 ounces	232 grams
heavy cream	½ cup (118 ml)	4.1 ounces	116 grams

MAKE THE WHITE CHOCOLATE GLAZE Have ready a fine-mesh strainer suspended over a small glass bowl. Place the chopped white chocolate in another small bowl.

In a medium saucepan, heat the cream until it starts to simmer (or place it in a 4 cup microwavable measure with a spout and microwave for 1½ to 2 minutes). Remove it from the heat source and pour the cream over the white chocolate. Whisk the mixture until smooth and then press it through the strainer. Cool until warm to the touch.

APPLY THE WHITE CHOCOLATE GLAZE With a silicone pastry brush, brush the glaze onto the meringue shell to fill and cover any cracks that have developed. Let the glaze harden to room temperature before filling the meringue shell, about 30 minutes.

RELEASE THE MERINGUE SHELL'S SIDES Once the meringue has cooled and any cracks have been filled, slip a small sharp knife underneath the shell border where it meets the rim of the pie plate. Then slip the knife between the meringue and the sides of the pan and, with an up and down motion while holding the knife firmly against the pan's sides, carefully circle the pan to release the sides of the meringue shell.

POMEGRANATE CHIFFON FILLING

MAKES 3½ CUPS/23.4 OUNCES/664 GRAMS

	VOLUME	WEIGHT	
heavy cream, cold	½ cup (118 ml)	4.1 ounces	116 grams
100% pure pomegranate juice, preferably POM Wonderful (see Note, page 257)	1½ cups (355 ml)	13.5 ounces	382 grams
powdered gelatin	2½ teaspoons	.	7.5 grams
sugar	¾ cup plus 2 tablespoons, *divided*	6.2 ounces	175 grams
lemon juice, freshly squeezed	1 teaspoon (5 ml)	.	5 grams
2 egg whites	¼ cup (59 ml)	2 ounces	60 grams
cream of tartar	¼ teaspoon	.	.

MAKE THE POMEGRANATE AND GELATIN MIXTURE Into a medium bowl, pour the cream and refrigerate it for at least 15 minutes. (Chill a handheld mixer's beaters alongside the bowl.)

In a medium saucepan, pour the pomegranate juice and sprinkle the gelatin on top. Swirl the mixture gently to moisten the gelatin and let it sit for 5 minutes. (If it will sit longer, cover it to prevent evaporation.) Add ½ cup plus 2 tablespoons/4.4 ounces/125 grams of the sugar and stir until moistened. Heat the mixture over medium heat, stirring constantly, until it reaches the boiling point (190°F/88°C). Bubbles will begin to appear on the surface. Remove it from the heat and pour it into a large bowl. Stir in the lemon juice.

Let it cool until no longer hot, about 20 minutes, and then set it in the refrigerator. Stir every 15 minutes just until it begins to thicken, about 45 minutes. (The thickened mixture will jiggle slightly when stirred gently with a spatula. If it becomes solid, briefly set it over a bowl of hot water, stirring gently, to soften it slightly.)

MAKE THE MERINGUE NO MORE THAN 20 MINUTES BEFORE USING IT In a medium bowl, with the handheld mixer, beat the egg whites and cream of tartar on medium speed until foamy. Raise the speed to medium-high and beat until soft peaks form when the beaters are raised. Beat in the remaining ¼ cup/1.8 ounces/50 grams of sugar and continue beating until stiff peaks form when the beaters are raised slowly.

Scrape the meringue into the pomegranate mixture and, using a balloon whisk, gently fold it in just until most of the meringue is incorporated.

WHIP THE CREAM With the hand-held mixer, starting on low speed and gradually raising the speed to medium-high as it thickens, whip the cream just until it mounds softly when dropped from a spoon. Scrape the whipped cream into the pomegranate mixture and, continuing with the whisk, gently fold it in until only a few streaks remain. Finish folding with a silicone spatula, reaching to the bottom to incorporate all of the pomegranate mixture. If the completed pomegranate mixture is not pink in color, add red food coloring and gently whisk to incorporate until you have achieved a uniform pink color (see Note, page 257).

COMPLETE THE PIE Pour the filling into the prepared meringue shell or cookie crust (see Variation, page 257) and refrigerate it, uncovered, for a minimum of 1 hour, until the surface is set, before decorating with the optional pomegranate arils. (Covering it would soften the meringue shell.)

STORE If using the meringue shell, refrigerated, 1 day; if using the cookie crust variation, refrigerated, 3 days; frozen, up to 3 weeks.

POMEGRANATE GLAZE

MAKES ⅓ CUP/2.5 OUNCES/71 GRAMS

	VOLUME	WEIGHT	
100% pure pomegranate juice, preferably POM Wonderful (see Note, page 257)	¼ cup (59 ml)	2.3 ounces	64 grams
sugar	1 tablespoon	0.5 ounce	13 grams
cassava or cornstarch	1 teaspoon	.	.
pomegranate arils (optional)	.	.	.

MAKE THE POMEGRANATE GLAZE In a small saucepan, stir together the pomegranate juice, sugar, and cassava until dissolved. Cook over medium heat, stirring constantly, until clear and thickened. If using cassava, this will happen just after boiling; if using cornstarch, the liquid needs to be simmered for about 30 seconds after reaching a boil.

Remove the pomegranate mixture from the heat and pour it into a glass measure with a spout. Let it cool until no longer hot, about 20 minutes. Scrape it into a squeeze bottle or a quart-size reclosable freezer bag with a small semicircle cut from one corner. Pipe a simple design onto each plate. If the glaze stops flowing while piping, gently squeeze the bottle over the cup until the glaze flows again at the proper consistency.

NOTE Before using the pomegranate juice, pour a small amount into a clear glass to see if the juice's color is a deep reddish pink. If it is a darker red wine color, the pomegranate chiffon mixture and glaze will become a mauve color, requiring the addition of red food coloring. A suggested level is ½ to ¾ teaspoon for the chiffon and ⅛ teaspoon for the glaze. (POM Wonderful pomegranate juice results in a lovely color.)

Variation: LEMON COOKIE CRUST

MAKES ABOUT 1½ CUPS/15.5 OUNCES/440 GRAMS

OVEN TEMPERATURE 425°F/220°C

BAKING TIME 30 to 40 minutes

SPECIAL EQUIPMENT One 9 inch pie plate coated with baking spray with flour | An expandable flan ring or 12 inch round cardboard template | One 8 inch round cake pan | A large coffee urn filter, several smaller cup-style filters, or pleated parchment to be filled with beans or rice as weights (spray the bottom(s) lightly with nonstick cooking spray) | A foil ring to protect the edges of the crust

	VOLUME	WEIGHT	
lemon zest, finely grated	1 tablespoon, loosely packed	.	6 grams
sugar	¼ cup plus 2 tablespoons	2.6 ounces	75 grams
fine sea salt	¼ teaspoon	.	1.5 grams
unsalted butter, cold	8 tablespoons (1 stick)	4 ounces	113 grams
1 large egg, lightly beaten, refrigerated	3 tablespoons plus ½ teaspoon (47 ml)	1.8 ounces	50 grams
pure vanilla extract	¾ teaspoon (3.7 ml)	.	.
bleached all-purpose flour	2 cups (lightly spooned into the cup and leveled off)	8.5 ounces	242 grams

MAKE THE COOKIE CRUST DOUGH In a food processor, process the lemon zest with the sugar and salt until the zest is very fine.

Cut the butter into several pieces and add it with the motor running. Process until smooth and creamy. Add the egg and vanilla and process until incorporated, scraping down the sides of the bowl as needed. Add the flour and pulse in just until incorporated. The mixture should hold together if pinched.

CHILL THE DOUGH Scrape the mixture onto a large sheet of plastic wrap and use the wrap to press down on the dough, kneading it until it is smooth. Press to form a flat 7 to 8 inch disc. Refrigerate in a reclosable bag for 2 hours or up to 2 days to firm and give the dough a chance to absorb the moisture evenly to make rolling easier. Remove the dough from the refrigerator and let the dough soften for about 10 minutes, or until malleable enough to roll.

ROLL THE DOUGH Set the dough between lightly floured large sheets of plastic wrap. Roll it evenly into a ⅛ inch thick disc larger than 12 inches in diameter. While rolling the dough, sprinkle it with a little more flour on each side as needed and if the dough softens significantly, slip it onto a baking sheet and refrigerate it until firm. From time to time, flip the dough with the plastic wrap, and lift off and flatten out the plastic wrap as necessary to make sure it does not wrinkle into the dough.

LINE THE PIE PLATE Remove the top sheet of plastic wrap and use the expandable flan ring, or a pizza wheel or small sharp knife with the cardboard template as a guide, to cut a 12 inch disc. If using the pizza wheel or knife, take care not to cut through the bottom plastic wrap. (Excess dough can be frozen for several months.) If the dough softens after cutting the disc, refrigerate it until firm. It will not drape over the pan unless it is flexible, so if it becomes too rigid in the refrigerator, let it sit and soften for a few minutes.

Invert the 8 inch cake pan onto a work surface. Use the bottom sheet of plastic wrap to lift the dough and set it, plastic side down, over the 8 inch cake pan (see Lemon and Cranberry Tart Tart, page 225). Smooth down the sides so they will fit into the pie plate. Place the pie plate on top and invert it. Remove the cake pan and carefully peel off the plastic wrap. If the dough breaks when transferring it into the pan, patch and press it into the pan with your fingers.

Turn under the edges of the dough. Do not allow it to extend past the sides of the plate, or it will droop and fall off during baking. Press down the dough or create a simple decorative border. If your fingers are warm, dip them occasionally into a bowl of ice water and dry them well. If the dough softens slightly, dip you fingers into flour as you work (a little extra flour will help the decorative border hold its shape during baking, but if the dough becomes very soft, it is best to cover and chill it briefly before continuing).

Cover the cookie crust shell with a double layer of plastic wrap and refrigerate for 6 to 24 hours before baking.

PREHEAT THE OVEN Thirty minutes or longer before baking, set an oven rack in the middle of the oven and preheat the oven to 425°F/220°C.

BAKE THE COOKIE CRUST SHELL Line the pie shell with the coffee filter or parchment and fill it three-quarters full with beans or rice to weight it, pushing the weights up against the sides of the crust.

Bake for 5 minutes, lower the heat to 375°F/190°C, and bake for 15 to 20 minutes, or until set. If not set, the dough will stick more to the filter. Lift out the filter with the weights and prick the crust lightly with a fork. Set the foil ring on top and continue baking for 5 to 10 minutes more. Lift up the foil ring to check for doneness. The cookie crust is done when the edges begin to brown lightly. The sides will be soft but will spring back when touched gently with a finger.

COOL THE COOKIE CRUST SHELL Set the pie plate on a wire rack and let the baked cookie crust shell cool for 2 hours before completing the pie.

Hungarian Raisin Walnut Tartlets

MAKES 24 TO 26 TARTLETS

OVEN TEMPERATURE 350°F/175°C

BAKING TIME 18 to 22 minutes

My lovely friend Sally Longo, who, like me, had a Hungarian grandmother, gave me this family heirloom, along with this note: "My Hungarian grandmother Matilda made these tarts from a recipe that dates back to the mid-1800s. The oldest woman in our family makes them every year at Christmastime and divides the spoils among her children and grandchildren. That used to be my grandmother, then my mother, and is now me. It's not Christmas in our family without these! My mother started freezing the crust in November and then made hundreds of the tarts the third week of December." I adore this recipe, and Sally and I now carry on the tradition.

SPECIAL EQUIPMENT Two 12 cup muffin pans, lightly coated with baking spray with flour | Two foil-lined baking sheets | A 4½ inch round cutter, lightweight bowl, or cardboard template | One 6 cup muffin pan (in reserve for making more tarts with any remaining filling)

Perfect Flaky and Tender Cream Cheese Pie Crust

	VOLUME	WEIGHT	
a triple recipe of dough for a 9 inch standard pie shell (page 187)	.	33 ounces	936 grams

PREHEAT THE OVEN Twenty minutes or longer before baking, set an oven rack in the lower third of the oven and preheat the oven to 350°F/175°C.

ROLL THE DOUGH Remove the dough from the refrigerator. If necessary, let it sit for about 10 minutes, or until it is malleable enough to roll.

Divide the dough in half, about 16.5 ounces/468 grams each. Flatten each piece into a 6 inch disc. Wrap 1 disc in plastic wrap and return it to the refrigerator.

Fitting the 4½ inch dough disc into the muffin cup.

On a floured pastry cloth, pastry mat, or between two sheets of lightly floured plastic wrap, roll the dough into a ⅛ inch thick oval. Lift the dough from time to time, as necessary, to keep it from sticking. Before cutting the dough, make sure to lift it from the surface to allow it to shrink in so that it doesn't retract when set in the muffin cups. Use the round cutter, or a small sharp knife and the small bowl or the template as a guide, to cut 4½ inch discs of dough, about 1.2 ounces/35 grams each. Stack the remaining dough scraps and reroll the dough to cut more discs. Add any remaining scraps to the second large disc of dough.

With your fingers, fold one 4½ inch dough disc in four places towards its center and upwards to form a letter X. Gently ease it into one of the muffin cups. Open up the folds of the dough. First press it down gently to form the bottom lining of the cup. The edge of the dough should rise slightly above the muffin cup. Pleat and press the dough against the sides of the cup. Repeat with 11 more discs to fill the muffin pan.

Cover the muffin pan with plastic wrap and refrigerate it. Repeat with the second large disc of dough, cutting it into 12 smaller discs and filling the second muffin pan. If enough dough remains, layer, roll it together, wrap, and refrigerate it in case there is extra filling.

Raisin Walnut Filling

	VOLUME	WEIGHT	
walnut halves	2½ cups, *divided*	8.8 ounces	250 grams
raisins	2 cups	10.2 ounces	288 grams
5 large eggs	1 cup (237 ml)	8.8 ounces	250 grams
sugar	2⅓ cups	16.5 ounces	467 grams
unsalted butter (65° to 75°F/ 19° to 23°C)	14 tablespoons (1 stick plus 6 tablespoons)	7 ounces	200 grams
milk	⅔ cup (158 ml)	5.7 ounces	161 grams
pure vanilla extract	1¼ teaspoons (6 ml)	.	.
fine sea salt	a pinch	.	.

TOAST AND BREAK THE WALNUTS Spread the walnuts evenly on a baking sheet and bake for about 7 minutes to enhance their flavor. Stir once or twice to ensure even toasting and avoid overbrowning. Turn the walnuts onto a clean dish towel. Reserve 26 of the best looking walnuts for decorating the tarts. Roll and rub the remaining nuts around in the towel to loosen the skins. Coarsely break the skinned nuts into a bowl, scraping off and discarding as much of the skins as possible. Cool the walnuts completely and then chop them into small pieces (¼ inch).

COMBINE THE WALNUTS AND RAISINS Place the walnuts in a coarse-mesh strainer and sift out any small particles. Put the walnuts and raisins in a medium bowl. With your fingers, mix the walnuts and raisins to combine them evenly and to separate any clumps of raisins.

MAKE THE RAISIN WALNUT FILLING FOOD PROCESSOR METHOD In a food processor, process the eggs, sugar, butter, milk, vanilla, and salt for 1 minute. Pour the mixture into a 4 cup measure with a spout. The mixture will look slightly curdled from flecks of butter, which will rise to the surface.

ELECTRIC MIXER METHOD In the bowl of a stand mixer fitted with the flat beater, place the eggs, sugar, butter, milk, vanilla, and salt. Mix on medium speed for 1 minute. Pour the mixture into a 4 cup measure with a spout. The mixture will look slightly curdled due to flecks of butter.

COMPLETE THE FILLING Pour ½ cup/5 ounces/140 grams of the mixture over the walnuts and raisins. With a silicone spatula, stir the mixture to coat the walnuts and raisins.

FILL THE TART SHELLS IN THE MUFFIN PANS Remove the dough-lined muffin pans from the refrigerator and set them on the prepared baking sheets. Spoon about 2 tablespoons/ 0.8 ounce/23 grams of the walnut and raisin mixture into each tart shell. Then carefully spoon 1½ tablespoons/1.2 ounces/34 grams of the liquid mixture into each tart shell. The filling will be two-thirds to three-quarters full with both mixtures, depending on the thickness of the crust. There will be enough extra filling either to make additional tarts or to make a deeper filling. The tarts can be filled as much as nearly to the top, as they will lower to slightly below the crust's edge on cooling. Occasionally stir the liquid mixture to distribute the butter evenly. Do not allow any of the liquid to slip between the sides of the pans and the dough because it will make unmolding difficult.

BAKE THE TARTS Bake for 10 minutes. For even baking, rotate the baking sheets halfway around. Continue baking for 8 to 12 minutes, or until the filling is puffed and golden and the tart crusts are light golden brown. (An instant-read thermometer inserted near the center should read 190° to 195°F/88° to 90°C.)

While the tarts are baking, if there is any of the remaining mixtures left over, roll out and cut the remaining dough into the appropriate number of discs that then can be filled to make more tarts. Lightly coat the number of cups needed to be filled in the 6 cup muffin pan with baking spray with flour. Insert and form the tart shells and spoon in the two mixtures. Place the muffin pan in the refrigerator until ready to bake the tarts.

COOL AND UNMOLD THE TARTS Place the muffin pans on wire racks and cool for 30 minutes. Use a wooden skewer to dislodge the tarts or, if necessary, run a small metal spatula between the sides of the muffin cups and the tarts until each is dislodged. Place a sheet of plastic wrap over the top of one of the muffin pans and then place a folded cloth towel and a wire rack on top. Invert the muffin pan and lift it off. Reinvert the tarts onto wire racks. Repeat with the other muffin pan. Cool the tarts completely. Place a reserved walnut half on top of each tart.

STORE Airtight: room temperature, 10 days.

PUMPKIN PECAN PIE

SERVES 10 TO 12

OVEN TEMPERATURE
350°F/175°C

BAKING TIME
16 to 22 minutes for the pecan filling; 45 to 55 minutes for the pumpkin filling

*P*umpkin and pecan is a natural flavor combination, but what makes this pie extra exciting is the interplay of textures. The silky pumpkin pie filling sits atop the happy surprise of a sticky, chewy pecan filling.

SPECIAL EQUIPMENT One 9½ inch (7 cups) deep dish pie pan with a rim (see Note, page 265) | A 15 inch round cardboard template | A baking stone or baking sheet | A foil ring to protect the edges of the crust

PERFECT FLAKY AND TENDER CREAM CHEESE PIE CRUST

	VOLUME	WEIGHT	
dough for a deep dish 9½ inch pie shell (page 188)	·	14.6 ounces	414 grams

ROLL THE DOUGH Remove the dough from the refrigerator. If necessary, let it sit for about 10 minutes, or until it is soft enough to roll.

On a floured pastry cloth, pastry mat, or between two sheets of lightly floured plastic wrap, roll the dough into a ⅛ inch thick disc 15 inches in diameter, or large enough to line the bottom of the pie plate and extend ¾ inch past the edge of the rim. Lift the dough from time to time as you are rolling and add flour as necessary to keep it from sticking. Before measuring the dough, make sure to lift it from the surface to allow it to shrink in so that it doesn't retract when set in the pie plate. Use a sharp knife and the template as a guide to cut a 15 inch disc of dough.

LINE THE PIE PLATE Transfer the dough to the pie plate, easing it into place. If necessary, trim the edge to extend ¾ to 1 inch from the edge of the plate. Fold this dough under so that it is flush with the outer edge of the pie plate. If desired, crimp the border using your forefinger and thumb or a fork.

NOTE It is essential to use a deep dish pie plate with a rim to keep the crust from sinking when baking the pecan layer because the sides of the crust will not be supported until the pumpkin layer is added.

CHILL THE PIE SHELL Cover the pie shell with plastic wrap and refrigerate it for a minimum of 30 minutes or up to 3 hours.

PREHEAT THE OVEN Forty-five minutes or longer before baking, set an oven rack at the lowest level and place the baking stone or baking sheet on it. Preheat the oven to 350°F/175°C.

PECAN FILLING

	VOLUME	WEIGHT	
golden syrup or corn syrup	⅓ cup (79 ml)	4 ounces	113 grams
light brown Muscovado sugar, or dark brown sugar	½ cup, firmly packed	3.8 ounces	108 grams
4 (to 6) large yolks, at room temperature	¼ cup plus 2 teaspoons (69 ml)	2.6 ounces	74 grams
heavy cream	¼ cup (59 ml)	2 ounces	58 grams
unsalted butter (65° to 75°F/ 19° to 23°C)	4 tablespoons (½ stick)	2 ounces	57 grams
fine sea salt	a pinch	.	.
pure vanilla extract	1 teaspoon (5 ml)	.	.
pecans, coarsely chopped	1½ cups	6 ounces	170 grams

MAKE THE PECAN FILLING Have ready a fine-mesh strainer suspended over a 2 cup glass measure with a spout.

In a medium heavy saucepan, combine the golden syrup, brown sugar, egg yolks, cream, butter, and salt. Cook over medium-low heat, stirring constantly with a silicone spatula, until the mixture is uniform in color and just begins to thicken slightly, without letting it boil, 7 to 10 minutes. (An instant-read thermometer should read 160°F/71°C. It will continue to thicken when baked; the initial cooking is just to cause the part of the yolk that is less smooth to set so it can be strained out.) Pour the mixture at once into the strainer and press it through. Stir in the vanilla.

FILL THE PIE Spread the pecans evenly over the bottom of the crust. Starting at the center, with the measuring cup's spout just above the pecans, slowly pour in the filling, lightly coating the nuts and moving from the center to the edge. Once the filling is completely poured, the pecans will float. Gently shake the pie plate to distribute the pecans more evenly.

BAKE THE PECAN FILLING Place the pie on the baking stone and bake for 16 to 22 minutes, or until the filling is puffed and just beginning to bubble around the edges. The filling will shimmy slightly when moved and an instant-read thermometer inserted near the center should read 185° to 190°F/85° to 88°C. Check early to prevent overbaking, which would result in a dry fillling.

COOL THE PECAN FILLING Cool on a wire rack for at least 30 minutes. Make the pumpkin filling while the pecan filling is cooling and move the baking stone to the middle rack.

PUMPKIN FILLING

	VOLUME	WEIGHT	
unsweetened pumpkin, preferably Libby's	1 cup plus 2 tablespoons	10 ounces	283 grams
light brown Muscovado sugar, or dark brown sugar	½ cup, firmly packed	3.8 ounces	108 grams
ground ginger	1¼ teaspoons	.	1.3 grams
ground cinnamon	1 teaspoon	.	2.2 grams
fine sea salt	¼ teaspoon	.	1.5 grams
heavy cream	½ cup (118 ml)	4.1 ounces	116 grams
milk	⅓ cup (79 ml)	2.9 ounces	81 grams
2 large eggs, at room temperature	⅓ cup plus 1 tablespoon (94 ml)	3.5 ounces	100 grams
pure vanilla extract	½ teaspoon (2.5 ml)	.	.

MAKE THE PUMPKIN FILLING In a small heavy saucepan, stir together the pumpkin, brown sugar, ginger, cinnamon, and salt and bring the mixture to a sputtering simmer over medium heat, stirring constantly. Reduce the heat to low and cook, stirring constantly, for 3 to 5 minutes, until thick and shiny. (The mixture may have some small lumps, which will disappear when processed.)

Using a silicone spatula, scrape the mixture into a small food processor (or use an immersion blender) and process for 1 minute with the feed tube open. Scrape down the sides. With the motor running, add the cream and then the milk and process for several seconds, or until smoothly incorporated. Scrape down the sides. Add the eggs and vanilla, and process for 5 seconds, or just until incorporated. Scrape the filling into a medium bowl.

Gently ladle the pumpkin filling over the pecan filling, with the ladle held just above the surface, so that it does not break through the pecan layer. If necessary, smooth the surface evenly with an offset spatula.

BAKE THE PUMPKIN FILLING Place the foil ring on top of the pie to protect the edges from overbrowning and set the pie on the baking stone. Bake for 45 to 55 minutes, or until a knife inserted ½ inch between the center and the sides comes out clean. The pumpkin filling will have puffed and the surface dulled, except for the center. (The filling will shake like jelly when moved. This will happen before it has finished baking, so it cannot be used as a firm indicator of doneness; conversely, if it does not have this jellylike consistency, it is not baked adequately. An instant-read thermometer, when inserted near the center just into the pumpkin filling, should read 190° to 195°F/88° to 91°C.)

COOL THE PIE Cool on a wire rack for at least 2 hours, or until cool to the touch, before topping with the pecan décor and serving.

PECAN DÉCOR

	VOLUME	WEIGHT	
12 pecan halves	·	·	·
golden syrup or corn syrup	·	·	·

MAKE THE PECAN DÉCOR Turn each pecan rounded side up. Brush the tops with the golden syrup and then dab a little on the bottom of each one before arranging them around the outside edge of the pie.

STORE Room temperature, 2 days; refrigerated, 4 days.

MUD TURTLE PIE

OVEN TEMPERATURE
425°F/220°C for the pie shell; 350°F/175°C for the turtle pie

BAKING TIME
23 to 27 minutes for the pie shell; 16 to 25 minutes for the turtle pie

I think of a turtle pie as being thick and muddy with chocolate. The rich, tangy stickiness of pecan pie filling blends perfectly with this new milk chocolate ganache "mud" topping. Both deserve a decorative little turtle perched on top.

PLAN AHEAD Make the ganache 1 to 2 hours before spreading it on the cooled pie.

SPECIAL EQUIPMENT One 9 inch pie plate | An expandable flan ring or 13 inch round cardboard template | A large coffee urn filter, several smaller cup-style filters, or pleated parchment to be filled with beans or rice as weights (spray the bottom(s) lightly with nonstick cooking spray) | A baking stone or baking sheet | A foil ring to protect the edges of the crust

PERFECT FLAKY AND TENDER CREAM CHEESE PIE CRUST

	VOLUME	WEIGHT	
dough for a 9 inch standard pie shell (page 187)	.	11 ounces	312 grams

ROLL THE DOUGH Remove the dough from the refrigerator. If necessary, let it sit for about 10 minutes, or until it is malleable enough to roll.

On a floured pastry cloth, pastry mat, or between two sheets of lightly floured plastic wrap, roll the dough into a ⅛ inch thick disc 13 inches in diameter, or large enough to line the bottom of the pie plate and extend ¾ inch past the edge of the rim. Lift the dough from time to time and add flour as necessary to keep it from sticking. Before measuring the dough, make sure to lift it from the surface to allow it to shrink in so that it doesn't retract when set in the pie plate. Use the expandable flan ring, or a small sharp knife with the cardboard template as a guide, to cut a 13 inch disc of dough.

LINE THE PIE PLATE Transfer the dough to the pie plate, easing it into place. If necessary, trim the edge to extend about ¾ inch from the edge of the plate. Fold this dough under so that it is flush with the outer edge of the pie plate. If desired, use your forefinger and thumb or a fork to crimp the border. Cover it with a double layer of plastic wrap and refrigerate for a minimum of 30 minutes or up to 24 hours, or set it in a gallon-size reclosable freezer bag and freeze for up to 6 months.

PREHEAT THE OVEN Forty-five minutes or longer before baking, set an oven rack at the lowest level and place the baking stone or baking sheet on it. Preheat the oven to 425°F/220°C.

BAKE THE PIE SHELL Line the pie shell with the coffee filter or parchment and fill it three-quarters full with beans or rice to weight it, pushing the weights up against the sides.

Set the pie plate on the baking stone. Bake for 20 minutes. Lift out the filter with the weights. Place the foil ring on top of the pie shell to protect the edges from overbrowning and continue baking for 3 to 7 minutes, until pale gold. If the dough starts to puff in places, press it down quickly with your fingertips or the back of a spoon.

COOL THE PIE SHELL Remove the foil ring and set the pie plate on a wire rack. If any holes have formed, seal them with a little egg white and return the pan to the oven for 30 seconds for the egg white to set and become opaque. Alternatively, seal the hole or holes with a little melted white chocolate.

Lower the oven temperature to 350°F/175°C.

The baked pie shell will keep at room temperature in an airtight container for 2 days.

PECAN FILLING

	VOLUME	WEIGHT	
golden syrup or corn syrup	⅓ cup (79 ml), cup lightly coated with nonstick cooking spray	4 ounces	113 grams
light brown Muscovado sugar, or dark brown sugar	½ cup, firmly packed	3.8 ounces	108 grams
4 (to 6) large egg yolks, at room temperature	¼ cup plus 2 teaspoons (69 ml)	2.6 ounces	74 grams
heavy cream	¼ cup (59 ml)	2 ounces	58 grams
unsalted butter (65° to 75°F/ 19° to 23°C)	4 tablespoons (½ stick)	2 ounces	57 grams
fine sea salt	a pinch	.	.
pure vanilla extract	1 teaspoon (5 ml)	.	.
pecans, coarsely chopped	1¾ cups	7 ounces	200 grams

HIGHLIGHTS FOR SUCCESS

Golden syrup and unrefined light brown sugar, such as Muscovado, make a real difference in quality of flavor.

MAKE THE PECAN FILLING Have ready a strainer suspended over a 2 cup glass measure with a spout or medium measuring bowl, preferably with a lip.

In a medium heavy saucepan, combine the golden syrup, brown sugar, egg yolks, cream, butter, and salt. Cook over medium-low heat, stirring constantly with a silicone spatula, until it is uniform in color and just begins to thicken slightly, without letting the mixture boil, 7 to 10 minutes. (An instant-read thermometer should read 160°F/71°C.) Pour it at once into the strainer and press it through. Stir in the vanilla.

FILL THE PIE Spread the pecans on the bottom of the crust. Starting at the center, with the glass measure's spout just above the pecans, slowly pour in the filling, lightly coating the nuts and working from the center to the edge. Once the filling is completely poured, the pecans will float. Gently shake the pie plate to distribute the pecans more evenly.

BAKE THE PIE Re-place the foil ring on top of the pie to protect the edges from overbrowning. Bake for 16 to 25 minutes, or until the filling is puffed and golden and just beginning to bubble around the edge. The filling will shimmy slightly when moved and an instant-read thermometer inserted near the center should read 190° to 200°F/88° to 93°C. Check early to prevent overbaking, which would result in a dry filling.

COOL AND UNMOLD THE PIE Cool on a wire rack for at least 1 hour, or until the filling feels very firm to the touch, before topping with the chocolate ganache.

CUSTOM ROSE BLEND MILK CHOCOLATE GANACHE

MAKES ABOUT ¾ CUP PLUS 1½ TABLESPOONS/7.7 OUNCES/218 GRAMS

	VOLUME		WEIGHT	
white chocolate containing cocoa butter, chopped	.		2.4 ounces	68 grams
bittersweet chocolate, 60% to 62% cacao, chopped	.		2.4 ounces	68 grams
heavy cream	¼ cup plus 2 tablespoons (89 ml)		3.1 ounces	87 grams

MAKE THE MILK CHOCOLATE GANACHE Have ready a fine-mesh strainer suspended over a small glass bowl.

In a food processor, process the white chocolate and bittersweet chocolate until very fine.

In a 1 cup or larger microwavable measure with a spout (or in a small saucepan over medium heat, stirring often), scald the cream (heat it to the boiling point; small bubbles will form around the periphery).

With the motor of the food processor running, pour the cream through the feed tube in a steady stream. Process for a few seconds until smooth, scraping down the sides of the bowl as needed. Press the mixture through the strainer and let it sit for 1 hour. Cover it with plastic wrap and let it cool for 2 to 3 hours, or until the mixture is thick enough to hold a well defined impression (68° to 72°F/20° to 22°C). Remove 1 tablespoon, which will be used to make a turtle for the décor, and let it set or chill until firm enough to mold.

The ganache keeps in an airtight container for 3 days at cool room temperature, 2 weeks refrigerated, and 6 months frozen. To restore to spreading consistency, defrost, if frozen, and reheat in a microwave with 3 second bursts, or in a double boiler set over hot, not simmering, water (do not let the bottom of the container touch the water), stirring gently to ensure that it does not overheat or incorporate any air.

APPLY THE GANACHE LAYER Scrape the ganache onto the pie and, with a small offset spatula, spread the ganache evenly over the entire surface. Use the spatula to make a "water wave" design in the ganache by rippling across the top of the ganache in rows.

Let the pie sit for 1 hour, uncovered, and then cover it with a cake carrier dome or large bowl for several hours to set the ganache.

PECAN TURTLE DÉCOR

	VOLUME	WEIGHT	
Milk Chocolate Ganache (reserved from above)	1 tablespoon	.	.
5 pecan halves	.	.	.
corn syrup (optional)	.	.	.
several Valrhona dark chocolate pearls (optional)	.	.	.

MAKE THE PECAN TURTLE DÉCOR With your fingers or a small metal spatula, form the ganache into an oval shape, about 1 inch wide and 1¼ inches long. Place the turtle's "shell" on the pie. Use the tip of a knife to draw lines in each direction to make a crosshatch pattern on the shell.

Cut 1 of the pecan halves in half the short way to become the turtle's head. If making the eyes, set the turtle's head, rounded side up, on a counter. Dab a small dot of corn syrup on either side, about halfway down. Place a chocolate pearl on each of the dots of corn syrup. To keep the pearls from sliding, set a stack of four pennies on either side up against the pearls to support them until they set. Allow them to sit for about 10 minutes. Position the cut edge against one end of the turtle's shell and set the pecan at a 45 degree angle up from the pie's surface.

Position the remaining 4 pecan halves, rounded side up, on the sides of the turtle's shell to make the turtle's legs. If desired, place a few chocolate pearls, starting at the end of the shell, to make the turtle's tail.

Cut the pie with a sharp, thin blade, dipped in hot water and wiped dry between each slice.

STORE Room temperature, 5 days; refrigerated, 1 week.

Variation: DARK CHOCOLATE GANACHE
MAKES ¾ CUP/6.2 OUNCES/176 GRAMS

	VOLUME	WEIGHT	
bittersweet chocolate, 60% to 62% cacao, chopped	.	3.5 ounces	100 grams
heavy cream	⅓ cup (79 ml)	2.7 ounces	77 grams
pure vanilla extract	2 teaspoons (10 ml)	.	.

MAKE THE GANACHE In a food processor, process the chocolate until very fine.

In a 1 cup or larger microwavable measure with a spout (or in a small saucepan over medium heat, stirring often), scald the cream (heat it to the boiling point; small bubbles will form around the periphery).

With the motor of the food processor running, pour the cream through the feed tube in a steady stream. Process for a few seconds until smooth, scraping down the sides of the bowl as needed. Pulse in the vanilla. Press the mixture through the strainer and let it sit for 1 hour. Cover it with plastic wrap and let it cool for about 2 to 3 hours, or until the mixture is thick enough to hold a well defined impression (an instant-read thermometer should read 68° to 72°F/20° to 22°C). Remove 1 tablespoon to make a turtle for the décor and let it set or chill until firm enough to mold.

FROZEN PECAN TART

OVEN TEMPERATURE
425°F/220°C for the tart shell; 350°F/175°C for the pecan tart

BAKING TIME
30 to 40 minutes for the tart shell; 15 to 20 minutes for the pecan tart

*T*his is a truly magical riff on my best pecan pie. Not only does it have the same mellow butterscotch flavor imparted by the golden syrup and Muscovado sugar, it is less sweet and more chewy because it is designed to be eaten frozen. In fact, it stays just soft enough when frozen to make cutting slices easy. It is one of my most beloved holiday pies and has the additional advantage of being able to be frozen well ahead of serving.

SPECIAL EQUIPMENT One 9½ by 1 inch high fluted tart pan with a removable bottom, sprayed with baking spray with flour if not a nonstick pan | An expandable flan ring or 12 inch round cardboard template | One 8 inch round cake pan | A baking sheet lined with nonstick or lightly sprayed aluminum foil | A large coffee urn filter, several smaller cup-style filters, or pleated parchment to be filled with beans or rice as weights (spray the bottom(s) lightly with nonstick cooking spray) | A foil ring to protect the edges of the crust

SWEET COOKIE TART CRUST (PÂTE SUCRÉE)

	VOLUME	WEIGHT	
Sweet Cookie Tart Crust (Pâte Sucrée), page 245	1 cup	11.3 ounces	321 grams

ROLL THE DOUGH Set the dough between lightly floured large sheets of plastic wrap. Roll it evenly into a ⅛ inch thick disc larger than 12 inches in diameter. While rolling the dough, sprinkle it with a little more flour on each side as needed and if the dough softens significantly, slip it onto a baking sheet and refrigerate it until firm (see Notes, page 277). From time to time, flip the dough with the plastic wrap, and lift off and flatten out the plastic wrap as necessary to make sure it does not wrinkle into the dough.

LINE THE TART PAN Remove the top sheet of plastic wrap and use the expandable flan ring, or a pizza wheel or small sharp knife with the cardboard template as a guide, to cut a 12 inch disc. If using the pizza wheel or knife, take care not to cut through the bottom plastic wrap. (Excess dough can be frozen for several months.) If the dough softens after cutting the disc, refrigerate it until firm. It will not drape over the pan unless it is flexible, so if it becomes too rigid in the refrigerator, let it sit and soften for a few minutes.

Golden syrup and unrefined light brown sugar, such as Muscovado, make a real difference in quality of flavor.

The photograph shows the pecans arranged in a random pattern. Alternatively, the pecans can be arranged in symmetrical rows: Start by placing larger pecans around the edge of the tart shell and continue with consecutive rows of the smaller pecans, arranging the pecans so that they point toward the center.

Invert the 8 inch cake pan onto a work surface. Use the bottom sheet of plastic wrap to lift the dough and set it, plastic side down, over the 8 inch cake pan (see Lemon and Cranberry Tart Tart, page 225). Smooth down the sides so they will fit into the tart pan and place the removable bottom of the tart pan on top. Then carefully place the fluted ring, upside down, on top. Place a flat plate, cardboard round, or wire rack over the tart pan to keep it from separating. Invert the pans and remove the cake pan. Carefully peel off the plastic wrap. Gently ease the dough down to reach the bottom and sides of the pan. If the dough breaks when transferring it into the pan, patch and press it into the pan with your fingers.

Fold in the excess dough to halfway down the sides of the tart pan. Press it against the sides so that it extends ⅛ to ¼ inch above the top of the pan. If the dough is thicker in places, press it so that it becomes thinner (it will rise higher). Use small sharp kitchen scissors to trim it to ⅛ to ¼ inch above the top of the pan. If pressing in the dough with your fingers, press it at the juncture where the bottom meets the sides, which often tends to be thicker. For a decorative border, use the back of a knife to make diagonal marks all around, using each flute as a guide.

CHILL THE TART SHELL Cover with plastic wrap and refrigerate it or freeze it for a minimum of 1 hour.

PREHEAT THE OVEN Thirty minutes or longer before baking, set oven racks at the middle and lowest levels and preheat the oven to 425°F/220°C.

BAKE THE TART SHELL Run a finger along the outside fluted edge of the pan to make sure that no dough is attached. The dough must not extend onto the outside of the pan because as the sides slip down a bit on baking, it will make a hole when the baked crust is removed.

Line the pan with the coffee filter or parchment and fill it about three-quarters full with beans or rice to weight it, pushing the weights up against the sides. Carefully transfer the tart pan to the foil-lined baking sheet and set it on the lower rack.

Bake for 5 minutes, lower the heat to 375°F/190°C, and bake for 15 to 20 minutes, or until set. If not set, the dough will stick more to the filter. Lift out the filter with the weights. Place the foil ring on top of the tart shell to protect the edges from overbrowning, and continue baking for 5 to 10 minutes more. If the dough starts to puff in places, press it down quickly with your fingertips or the back of a spoon (see Notes, page 277). Bake until pale gold (the edges will be a deeper brown) and the tart shell feels set but still soft to the touch. (It will continue firming while cooling, just the way cookies do.)

COOL THE TART SHELL Remove the tart pan, still on the baking sheet, to a wire rack. Remove the foil ring and set it aside. If any holes have formed, seal them with a little egg white and return the pan to the oven for 30 seconds for the egg white to set and become opaque. Alternatively, seal the hole or holes with a little melted white chocolate.

Lower the oven temperature to 350°F/175°C.

The unbaked tart shell can be refrigerated for 1 week or frozen for about 1 year. The baked tart shell will keep at room temperature in an airtight container for 2 days.

NOTES When letting it rest, always keep the dough covered to prevent drying or crusting.

It is best only to press down, not pierce, the dough as it puffs. If it is pierced with a fork, there is the risk of accidentally piercing all the way through the bottom, which would cause the filling to leak through on further baking and stick to the bottom of the pan.

FILLING

	VOLUME	WEIGHT	
golden syrup or corn syrup	⅓ cup (79 ml), cup lightly coated with nonstick cooking spray	4 ounces	113 grams
light brown Muscovado sugar, or dark brown sugar	½ cup, firmly packed	3.8 ounces	108 grams
4 (to 6) large egg yolks, at room temperature	¼ cup plus 2 teaspoons (69 ml)	2.6 ounces	74 grams
heavy cream	¼ cup (59 ml)	2 ounces	58 grams
unsalted butter (65° to 75°F/ 19° to 23°C)	4 tablespoons (½ stick)	2 ounces	57 grams
fine sea salt	a pinch	.	.
pure vanilla extract	1 teaspoon (5 ml)	.	.
pecan halves (see Note, page 278)	1¾ cups	6 ounces	170 grams

MAKE THE FILLING Have ready a strainer suspended over a 2 cup glass measure with a spout.

In a medium heavy saucepan, combine the golden syrup, brown sugar, egg yolks, cream, butter, and salt. Cook over medium-low heat, stirring constantly with a silicone spatula, until it is uniform in color and just begins to thicken slightly, without letting the mixture boil, 7 to 10 minutes. (An instant-read thermometer should read 160°F/71°C.) Pour it at once into the strainer and press it through. Stir in the vanilla.

ASSEMBLE THE TART Arrange the pecans, top sides up, on the bottom of the baked tart shell. Starting at the center, with the cup's spout just above the pecans, slowly pour the filling, lightly coating the nuts and working from the center to the edge of the tart. Once the filling is completely poured, the pecans will float. Gently shake the tart pan to shift the pecans. This will create a little more space; add more pecans to form a tight blanket of nuts.

BAKE THE TART Place the foil ring on top to protect the edges from overbrowning and set the baking sheet with the assembled tart on the middle rack. Bake for 15 to 20 minutes, or until the filling is puffed and golden and just beginning to bubble around the edges. The filling will shimmy slightly when moved and an instant-read thermometer inserted near the center will read 190° to 200°F/88° to 93°C. Check early to prevent overbaking, which would result in a dry filling.

COOL THE TART Remove the tart, still on the baking sheet, and set it on a wire rack. Remove the foil ring. Immediately use a metal cake lifter or 10 inch or longer grill spatula to slide the tart pan onto a wire rack to cool completely, about 45 minutes.

UNMOLD THE TART Place the tart pan on top of a canister that is smaller than the bottom opening of the tart pan's outer rim. Wet a dish towel with hot water and wring it out well. Apply it to the bottom and sides of the tart pan. Press down on both sides of the tart ring. The outer rim should slip away easily. If not, apply more heat. Slip a long metal spatula between the crust and the bottom of the pan, loosening it all around if necessary, and slide the tart onto a serving plate. If desired, decorate with the chocolate lace topping.

NOTE Start with 2 cups/7 ounces/200 grams of pecans or more so that you can choose the right size of unbroken and most attractive pecans.

Optional: CHOCOLATE LACE TOPPING

MAKES 3½ TABLESPOONS/1.9 OUNCES/53 GRAMS

	VOLUME	WEIGHT	
dark chocolate, 60% to 62% cacao, chopped	.	1 ounce	28 grams
heavy cream, hot	2 tablespoons (30 ml)	1 ounce	28 grams

MAKE THE CHOCOLATE LACE TOPPING In a small microwavable bowl, stirring with a silicone spatula every 15 seconds (or in the top of a double boiler set over hot, not simmering, water, stirring often—do not let the bottom of the container touch the water), heat the chocolate until almost completely melted.

Remove the chocolate from the heat source and stir until completely melted.

Pour the cream on top of the chocolate and stir until smooth. The mixture should drop thickly from the spatula. If too thin, let it cool for a few minutes. If too thick, add more cream or a little bourbon.

DECORATE THE TART Pour the chocolate topping into a small disposable pastry bag, or a pint- or quart-size reclosable freezer bag, with a very small semicircle cut from the tip or one corner. Close the bag securely. Drizzle lines of chocolate back and forth over the top of the pecans, first in one direction (front to back) and then the other (side to side), to form a lacy design of chocolate webbing. Let the chocolate set before freezing the tart.

FREEZE THE TART Slide the completed pecan tart into a gallon-size reclosable freezer bag and freeze it for a minimum of 2 hours. The tart cuts perfectly well frozen. Serve it frozen or let it sit for 3 minutes to soften slightly.

STORE Frozen, up to 3 months.

Variation: FROZEN CHOCOLATE PECAN TART

Unsweetened (alkalized) cocoa powder added to the filling gives the perfect balance of chocolate without overwhelming the pecans. Add ⅓ cup (sifted into the cup and leveled off)/1 ounce/28 grams to the egg yolk mixture before cooking the filling. Because the filling will be slightly deeper, be sure to coat the underside of the foil ring lightly with nonstick cooking spray to keep it from sticking to the surface of the filling. You can also use the Sweet Chocolate Cookie Tart Crust (page 280) in place of the Sweet Cookie Tart Crust for either version.

Fudgy Pudgy Brownie Tart

OVEN TEMPERATURE
325°F/160°C

BAKING TIME
35 to 45 minutes

*T*he ultimate of all my many brownie recipes deserves a container as delicious as itself. This crisp chocolate cookie crust also serves to keep the outside of the brownie moist and chewy. Unbelievable!

SPECIAL EQUIPMENT One 9½ by 1 inch high fluted tart pan with a removable bottom, sprayed with baking spray with flour if not a nonstick pan | An expandable flan ring or 12 inch round cardboard template | One 8 inch round cake pan | A baking sheet lined with nonstick or lightly sprayed aluminum foil

Sweet Chocolate Cookie Tart Crust (Pâte Sucrée)

MAKES ABOUT 1½ CUPS/16 OUNCES/455 GRAMS

	VOLUME	WEIGHT	
unsalted butter, cold	8 tablespoons (1 stick)	4 ounces	113 grams
bleached all-purpose flour	1½ cups (lightly spooned into the cup and leveled off), plus ½ tablespoon	6.5 ounces	185 grams
unsweetened (alkalized) cocoa powder	¼ cup plus 1 tablespoon (sifted before measuring)	0.8 ounce	23 grams
fine sea salt	a pinch	.	.
powdered sugar	¾ cup (lightly spooned into the cup and leveled off)	3 ounces	86 grams
1 large egg, lightly beaten	3 tablespoons plus ½ teaspoon (47 ml)	1.8 ounces	50 grams

MAKE THE COOKIE TART DOUGH FOOD PROCESSOR METHOD Cut the butter into ½ inch cubes and refrigerate until ready to use.

In a medium bowl, sift together the flour, cocoa, and salt.

In a food processor, pulse the cold butter cubes and powdered sugar until the sugar disappears. Add the flour mixture and pulse until the butter is no larger than small peas.

Add the egg to the mixture and pulse just until incorporated, about 8 times. The dough will be in crumbly pieces.

Empty the dough into a plastic bag and press it from the outside just until it holds together. Remove the dough from the plastic bag and place it on a very large sheet of plastic wrap. Using the plastic wrap, knead the dough only a few times until it becomes one smooth piece. There should be no visible pieces of butter. (Visible pieces of butter in the dough will melt and form holes during baking. If there are visible pieces of butter, continue kneading the dough or use the heel of your hand to press them in a forward motion to spread them into the dough.)

HAND METHOD In a medium bowl, stir together the flour, cocoa, salt, and powdered sugar. With a pastry cutter or two knives, cut in the cold butter until the mixture resembles coarse meal.

Add the egg and mix it into the flour mixture until the dough comes together and can be formed into a large ball.

CHILL THE DOUGH Flatten the dough into a 6 inch disc. Wrap it well and refrigerate it for 30 minutes, or until firm enough to roll or pat into the pan. It can be refrigerated for up to 3 days or frozen for up to 6 months. If chilled for more than 30 minutes, it can take as long as 40 minutes at room temperature to become malleable enough to roll.

ROLL THE DOUGH Set the dough between lightly floured large sheets of plastic wrap. Roll it evenly into a ⅛ inch thick disc larger than 12 inches in diameter. While rolling the dough, sprinkle it with a little more flour on each side as needed and if the dough softens significantly, slip it onto a baking sheet and refrigerate it until firm (see Note, page 283). From time to time, flip the dough with the plastic wrap, and lift off and flatten out the plastic wrap as necessary to make sure it doesn't wrinkle into the dough.

LINE THE TART PAN Remove the top sheet of plastic wrap and use the expandable flan ring, or a pizza wheel or small sharp knife with the cardboard template as a guide, to cut a 12 inch disc. If using the pizza wheel or knife, take care not to cut through the bottom plastic wrap. (Excess dough can be frozen for several months.) If the dough softens after cutting the disc, refrigerate it until firm. It will not drape over the pan unless it is flexible, so if it becomes too rigid in the refrigerator, let it sit and soften for a few minutes.

Invert the 8 inch cake pan onto a work surface. Use the bottom sheet of plastic wrap to lift the dough and set it, plastic side down, over the 8 inch cake pan (see Lemon and Cranberry Tart Tart, page 225). Smooth down the sides so they will fit into the tart pan and place the removable bottom of the tart pan on top. Then carefully place the fluted ring, upside down, on top. Place a flat plate, cardboard round, or wire rack over the tart pan to keep it from separating. Invert the pans and remove the cake pan. Carefully peel off the plastic wrap. Gently ease the dough down to reach the bottom and sides of the pan. If the dough breaks when transferring it into the pan, patch and press it into the pan with your fingers.

Fold in the excess dough to halfway down the sides of the tart pan. Press it against the sides so that it extends ⅛ to ¼ inch above the top of the pan. If the dough is thicker in places, press it so that it becomes thinner (it will rise higher). Use small sharp kitchen scissors to trim it to ⅛ to ¼ inch above the top of the pan. If pressing in the dough with your fingers, press it at the juncture where the bottom meets the sides, which often tends to be thicker. For a decorative border, use the back of a knife to make diagonal marks all around, using each flute as a guide.

CHILL THE TART SHELL Cover with plastic wrap and refrigerate or freeze it for a minimum of 1 hour.

NOTE When letting it rest, always keep the dough covered to prevent drying or crusting.

FUDGY PUDGY BROWNIE

	VOLUME	WEIGHT	
walnut or pecan halves	1 cup plus 2 tablespoons	4 ounces	113 grams
unsalted butter (65° to 75°F/ 19° to 23°C)	12 tablespoons (1½ sticks)	6 ounces	170 grams
fine-quality unsweetened or 99% cacao chocolate, chopped	.	5 ounces	142 grams
white chocolate containing cocoa butter, chopped	.	3 ounces	85 grams
unsweetened (alkalized) cocoa powder	3½ tablespoons (sifted before measuring)	0.6 ounce	16 grams
sugar	1⅓ cups	9.4 ounces	266 grams
3 large eggs, at room temperature	½ cup plus ½ tablespoon (140 ml)	5.3 ounces	150 grams
pure vanilla extract	½ tablespoon (7.5 ml)	.	.
bleached all-purpose flour	¾ cup (spooned into the cup and leveled off)	3.2 ounces	91 grams
fine sea salt	a pinch	.	.

PREHEAT THE OVEN Twenty minutes or longer before baking, set an oven rack in the middle of the oven and preheat the oven to 325°F/160°C.

TOAST AND CHOP THE WALNUTS Spread the walnuts evenly on a baking sheet and bake for about 10 minutes to enhance their flavor. Stir once or twice to ensure even toasting and avoid overbrowning. If using walnuts, turn them out onto a clean dish towel and rub them in the towel to remove as much skin as possible. Using a chef's knife, chop the walnuts in four batches so that they are no larger than ¼ inch. Discard any skin. (Do not use the food processor, because it will create excess nut dust, also referred to as nut flour.)

MELT THE BUTTER AND CHOCOLATES In a double boiler over hot, not simmering, water (do not let the bottom of the container touch the water), melt the butter, unsweetened chocolate, white chocolate, and cocoa, stirring often. Scrape the melted chocolate mixture into a large mixing bowl.

MAKE THE BATTER Whisk the sugar into the melted chocolate mixture until incorporated. Whisk in the eggs and vanilla until the mixture becomes thick and glossy. Add the flour and salt and stir just until the flour is fully moistened. Stir in the walnuts.

Carefully place the chilled dough-lined pan on the baking sheet. Scrape the batter into the pan. It will reach the top of the pan and be just under the top of the crust. Smooth the surface evenly with an offset spatula.

BAKE THE BROWNIE TART Place the tart, on the baking sheet, in the oven. Bake for 35 to 45 minutes, or until the batter has puffed slightly and set only up to 1 inch from the edge. (An instant-read thermometer inserted into the center will read about 190°F/88°C.)

COOL THE TART Remove the tart, still on the baking sheet, to a wire rack and let it cool until no longer warm to the touch.

UNMOLD THE TART Place the tart pan on top of a canister that is smaller than the bottom at the opening of the tart pan's outer rim. Wet a dish towel with hot water and wring it out well. Apply it to the bottom and sides of the tart pan. Press down on both sides of the tart ring. The outer rim should slip away easily. If not, apply more heat. Slip a long metal spatula between the crust and the bottom of the pan, loosening it all around if necessary, and slide the tart onto a serving plate.

Refrigerate the tart for a minimum of 1 hour before serving. It is at its most deliciously fudgy when chilled or frozen.

STORE Airtight: room temperature, 3 days; refrigerated, 2 weeks; frozen, 6 months.

Chocolate Hazelnut Mousse Tart

OVEN TEMPERATURE
375°F/190°C

BAKING TIME
12 to 14 minutes

*T*he Chocolate Peanut Butter Mousse Tart is one of the most loved tarts in *The Pie and Pastry Bible*. It was even chosen by *Food & Wine* for the magazine's book called *Best of the Best*. Because my charming friend Marko Gnann doesn't like peanuts but adores hazelnuts, I created this version, which I dedicate to him. The hazelnut cookie crust is unlike any other. Along with a delicious hazelnut flavor, it is both soft and chewy. It also makes fabulous cookies (see page 344). The idea for the optional caramelized hazelnuts for the décor was contributed by Beta Baker Matthew Boyer.

SPECIAL EQUIPMENT One 9½ by 1 inch high heart-shape or round tart pan with a removable bottom, lightly coated with baking spray with flour, set on a baking sheet

Hazelnut Cookie Crust

MAKES 1¼ CUPS/11.3 OUNCES/320 GRAMS

	VOLUME	WEIGHT	
unsalted butter, cold	4 tablespoons (½ stick)	2 ounces	57 grams
bleached all-purpose flour	⅔ cup (lightly spooned into the cup and leveled off)	2.9 ounces	81 grams
baking soda	½ teaspoon	.	2.7 grams
fine sea salt	¹⁄₁₆ teaspoon	.	0.4 gram
superfine sugar	3 tablespoons	1.3 ounces	37 grams
hazelnut praline paste (see Notes, page 289)	¼ cup plus 2 tablespoons	4 ounces	114 grams
½ large egg	1½ tablespoons (23 ml)	0.9 ounce	25 grams
pure vanilla extract	¼ teaspoon (1.2 ml)	.	.

MAKE THE TART DOUGH Cut the butter into 1 inch cubes and refrigerate until ready to use.

In a small bowl, whisk together the flour, baking soda, and salt.

FOOD PROCESSOR METHOD In a small food processor, place the sugar. (Granulated sugar can be used if processed for several minutes until very fine.)

With the motor running, add the butter cubes. Add the praline paste and process until smooth and creamy, about 10 seconds. With the motor running, add the egg and vanilla and process until incorporated. Scrape down the sides and bottom of the bowl. Add the flour mixture and pulse just until incorporated.

STAND MIXER METHOD Soften the butter to 65° to 75°F/19° to 23°C.

In the bowl of a stand mixer fitted with the flat beater, beat together the sugar, butter, and praline paste on medium speed for several minutes, or until very smooth and creamy. Add the egg and vanilla and beat until incorporated. Scrape down the sides of the bowl. On low speed, gradually beat in the flour mixture just until incorporated.

LINE THE TART PAN Using a small offset spatula, spread the dough into the tart pan and slightly up the sides. Lightly dust the dough with flour. Lay a sheet of plastic wrap directly on top of the dough. Use a flat-bottom measure or custard cup, or your hand, to press the dough evenly into the tart pan. Press the dough at the juncture where the bottom meets the sides, which often tends to be thicker. Push up the sides a little past the top of the rim. Leave the plastic wrap in place and refrigerate for at least 1 hour.

PREHEAT THE OVEN Thirty minutes or longer before baking, set an oven rack in the middle of the oven and preheat the oven to 375°F/190°C.

BAKE THE TART SHELL Bake for 12 to 14 minutes, or until golden. The bottom will puff up and the sides will be soft but spring back when touched gently with a fingertip.

COOL THE TART SHELL Remove the tart pan, still on the baking sheet, to a wire rack and let it cool for a few minutes. Lightly press the sides and the bottom of the tart shell with your fingers to form straight sides and a flat bottom. Cool it completely on a wire rack. The crust will be soft to the touch.

HAZELNUT PRALINE MOUSSE FILLING

MAKES 2½ CUPS/14.6 OUNCES/415 GRAMS

	VOLUME	WEIGHT	
heavy cream, cold	¾ cup (177 ml)	6.1 ounces	174 grams
cream cheese, softened	½ cup minus 1 tablespoon	4 ounces	112 grams
hazelnut praline paste (see Notes, page 289)	¼ cup plus 2 tablespoons	4 ounces	114 grams
light brown Muscovado sugar, or dark brown sugar	1 tablespoon, firmly packed	0.5 ounce	14 grams
pure vanilla extract	1 teaspoon (5 ml)	.	.

WHIP THE CREAM Into a mixing bowl, pour the cream and refrigerate for 15 minutes. (Chill a handheld mixer's beaters alongside the bowl.) Starting on low speed and gradually raising the speed to medium-high as it thickens, whip the cream just until it mounds softly when dropped from a spoon. Be careful not to overwhip because it will be mixed a lot more when combined with the praline paste.

MAKE THE MOUSSE FILLING In the bowl of a stand mixer fitted with the whisk beater, beat the cream cheese, praline paste, and brown sugar on medium speed until uniform in color, about 3 minutes. On low speed, beat in the vanilla. Scrape down the sides of the bowl. Continuing on low speed, beat in ¼ cup of the whipped cream just until incorporated. Scrape down the sides of the bowl as necessary. With a balloon whisk or silicone spatula, fold in the rest of the whipped cream just until blended.

FILL THE TART Scrape the mousse filling into the prepared crust and, using a small offset spatula, smooth the surface so that it is level. Set a large bowl over the tart to cover, and refrigerate the tart for a minimum of 1 hour before applying the ganache glaze.

FRANGELICO GANACHE GLAZE

MAKES ABOUT ¾ CUP/177 ML/7 OUNCES/200 GRAMS

	VOLUME	WEIGHT	
bittersweet chocolate, 60% to 62% cacao, chopped	.	4 ounces	113 grams
heavy cream	¼ cup plus 2 tablespoons (89 ml)	3.1 ounces	87 grams
Frangelico (hazelnut liqueur)	2 teaspoons (10 ml)	.	.

MAKE THE GANACHE GLAZE Have ready a fine-mesh strainer suspended over a glass bowl.

In a food processor, process the chocolate until very fine.

In a 1 cup microwavable measure with a spout (or in a small saucepan over medium heat, stirring often), scald the cream (heat it to the boiling point; small bubbles will form around the periphery).

With the motor of the food processor running, pour the cream through the feed tube in a steady stream. Process for a few seconds until smooth, scraping down the sides of the bowl as needed. Pulse in the Frangelico. Press the ganache through the strainer. Cover it with plastic wrap and cool just until cool to the touch (under 90°F/32°C) but still fluid. If necessary, reheat in the microwave with 3 second bursts or in a hot water bath.

GLAZE THE TART Pour the ganache glaze in a circular motion over the mousse filling so that it does not land too heavily in any one spot and cause a depression. With a small offset spatula, start by spreading the ganache to the edge of the pastry. Then spread it evenly to cover the entire surface. Make a spiral pattern by lightly pressing the spatula against the surface and running it in spirals from the outside to the center.

Refrigerate the tart, uncovered, for at least 2 hours to set the filling and glaze. The crust will remain slightly soft.

UNMOLD THE TART Place the tart pan on top of a canister that is smaller than the bottom opening of the tart pan's outer rim. Press down on both sides of the tart ring. The outer rim should slip away easily. If the crust sticks to the pan when unmolding, insert a thin needle to loosen any parts that may have stuck. Slip a long metal spatula between the crust and the bottom of the pan, loosening it all around if necessary, and slide the tart onto a serving plate. Cut with a sharp, thin blade dipped in hot water and dried between each slice.

STORE Room temperature, 6 hours; refrigerated, 5 days; frozen, 3 months.

NOTES Different brands of commercial praline paste vary widely between 20 to 50 percent sugar. Also, some contain almonds as well as hazelnuts, some roast the nuts, and some use caramelized sugar, all of which have a great impact on flavor. I recommend American Almond Praline Paste (see page 527) because the nuts are 100 percent hazelnut and are roasted. It contains 33 percent sugar. I also recommend Maison Glass praline paste (see page 527), which contains 100 percent hazelnuts and 35.3 percent caramelized sugar.

Praline paste needs to be stirred before measuring because the oil tends to separate and rise to the top. Once open, the praline paste keeps refrigerated for about 6 months.

You can make your own praline paste but it will not be quite as smooth as the commercial variety. Make the praline powder on page 344. Add 2½ teaspoons/12.5 ml of hazelnut or canola oil and process until smooth. It will make about 1¼ cups of praline paste.

Amazingly, the ganache stays shiny even after freezing as long as it is wrapped in plastic wrap after it is frozen so that the plastic wrap does not mar the surface.

Optional: CARAMELIZED HAZELNUTS DÉCOR

	VOLUME	WEIGHT	
16 blanched hazelnuts	.	.	.
sugar	2 cups	14.1 ounces	400 grams
water	½ cup (118 ml)	4.2 ounces	118 grams
cream of tartar	⅟₁₆ teaspoon	.	.

SPECIAL EQUIPMENT 16 wooden toothpicks | Two large apples

PREPARE THE HAZELNUTS Stick a toothpick into each hazelnut.

MAKE THE CARAMELIZED SUGAR In a small saucepan, preferably nonstick, stir together the sugar, water, and cream of tartar. Heat, stirring constantly, until the sugar is dissolved and comes to a boil. Continue boiling, without stirring, until the syrup caramelizes to deep amber (about 360°F/182°C or a few degrees lower because the temperature will continue to rise). Immediately remove the pan from the heat and set the bottom of the pan briefly in ice water to stop the cooking. Alternatively, to make reheating easier, immediately pour the caramel into a 2 cup microwavable measure with a spout that has been lightly coated with nonstick cooking spray.

If it is in the saucepan, it helps to maintain the temperature by setting it in a bowl of hot water or on a warming tray.

DIP THE HAZELNUTS INTO THE CARAMEL Dip each hazelnut into the caramel, holding it by the toothpick, and lift it out. Rotate the toothpick to coat the hazelnut evenly. For a deeper color, give it a second coat. Stick the other end of the toothpick into the side of the apple. Twist out the toothpicks from the hazelnuts as soon as the caramel hardens.

If the caramel becomes too thick, it will form thick tails dripping from the nuts. Reheat it over low heat or in a microwave in 5 second bursts until more fluid.

Set 3 of the caramelized hazelnuts on the tart shortly before serving, and 1 or 2 on each plate.

Posh Pie

OVEN TEMPERATURE 350°F/175°C

BAKING TIME
16 to 20 minutes for each of two batches of wafers for the cookie crust

*T*his is an instance where the name came to me before the actual dessert! I had to think long and hard to decide what pie would be worthy of such a grand and elegant title. Once I had the concept—a deeply chocolate cookie crust; a creamy, mellow chocolate filling; and a stunning glaze adorned with gold leaf—it took a few tries to get all the textures and flavors just right. It was well worth the effort. What's more, the chocolate wafers for the crust also double as first class cookies.

PLAN AHEAD For best flavor, complete the pie 1 day ahead. The chocolate dough, Bavarian cream, and lacquer glaze must each be refrigerated for at least 4 hours in between steps.

SPECIAL EQUIPMENT Two 15 by 12 inch cookie sheets lined with parchment | One 9½ inch (7 cups) deep dish pie pan, preferably Pyrex

Chocolate Wafers for the Cookie Crust

MAKES TWENTY-SIX 2 BY 2 INCH SQUARE WAFERS/11.3 OUNCES/320 GRAMS

	VOLUME	WEIGHT	
bleached all-purpose flour	⅔ cup (lightly spooned into the cup and leveled off), plus ½ tablespoon	3 ounces	86 grams
unsweetened (alkalized) cocoa powder	½ cup plus 1 tablespoon (sifted before measuring)	1.5 ounces	42 grams
fine sea salt	⅛ teaspoon	.	.
light brown Muscovado sugar, or dark brown sugar	¼ cup plus 2 tablespoons, firmly packed	2.9 ounces	81 grams
granulated sugar	¼ cup plus 2 tablespoons	2.6 ounces	75 grams
unsalted butter (65° to 75°F/ 19° to 23°C)	3 tablespoons	1.5 ounces	42 grams
pure vanilla extract	¾ teaspoon (3.7 ml)	.	.
1½ large egg whites	3 tablespoons (44 ml)	1.6 ounces	45 grams

PREHEAT THE OVEN Twenty minutes or longer before baking, set an oven rack in the middle of the oven and preheat the oven to 350°F/175°C.

MAKE THE WAFER DOUGH In a medium bowl, whisk together the flour, cocoa, and salt.

In the bowl of a stand mixer fitted with the flat beater, beat the brown sugar, granulated sugar, butter, and vanilla on medium speed until light, about 5 minutes, scraping down the sides of the bowl occasionally. Add the egg whites and beat until smoothly incorporated, about 30 seconds. Scrape down the sides of the bowl and add the flour mixture. Mix on low speed for 30 seconds until incorporated.

Scrape the dough onto a sheet of plastic wrap and loosely overlap both ends to cover the dough, then use the plastic wrap to press the dough into a rectangle. Divide the dough in half, 5.6 ounces/160 grams each. Wrap each in plastic wrap and set both pieces on a small flat baking sheet. Refrigerate the dough until it is firm, about 4 hours or overnight. The dough will be firm enough to roll but still pliant.

ROLL THE DOUGH Set 1 piece of dough on a lightly floured pastry mat or piece of parchment. Lightly flour the dough and cover it with plastic wrap. Roll the dough into a ¼ inch thick rectangle, using a bench scraper butted up against the sides to make it even. To make cutting easier, slide the shaped dough, still on the pastry mat, onto a flat cookie sheet and set it in the freezer for about 5 minutes.

With a pizza wheel or chef's knife, cut the dough into roughly 2 inch squares. There will be some remaining irregular shapes, which can bake alongside the squares. Set the dough squares a minimum of 1 inch apart on the cookie sheet. With a fork, pierce each cookie several times to prevent puffing.

BAKE THE WAFERS Bake for 8 minutes. For even baking, rotate the cookie sheet halfway around. Continue baking for 8 to 12 minutes, or until slightly puffed and firm but still slightly soft.

COOL THE WAFERS Set the cookie sheet on a wire rack and let the wafers cool completely.

While the first batch of wafers is baking, shape the dough for the next batch. The wafers can be stored airtight at room temperature for 7 days, refrigerated for 2 weeks, or frozen for 3 months.

COOKIE PIE CRUST

MAKES A ⅛ INCH THICK CRUST (see Note, page 294)

	VOLUME	WEIGHT	
Chocolate Wafers	.	9 ounces	255 grams
unsalted butter, melted	7 tablespoons (¾ stick plus 1 tablespoon)	3.5 ounces	100 grams

MAKE THE COOKIE CRUST DOUGH In a food processor, break the wafers into smaller pieces and process into fine crumbs. Check by lifting with a fork to make sure there are no larger pieces. (If measuring instead of weighing, there should be 2 cups of crumbs, lightly packed.) Add the melted butter and pulse about 10 times just until incorporated.

FORM AND CHILL THE PIE SHELL Scrape the mixture into the pie plate and, using your fingers, begin by pressing the mixture evenly into the bottom and partway up the sides. Press the crumbs up to the top. To help make the bottom even, use a flat-bottom measure or custard cup to smooth the crumbs over the bottom. Press the dough at the juncture where the bottom meets the sides, which often tends to be thicker. Refrigerate the pie shell while making the filling.

NOTE For a thicker crust, use 2½ cups/11.3 ounces/320 grams of chocolate wafers and 9 tablespoons/4.5 ounces/127 grams of butter.

CHOCOLATE BAVARIAN CREAM FILLING

MAKES 4½ CUPS/22.9 OUNCES/650 GRAMS

	VOLUME	WEIGHT	
dark chocolate, 60% to 62% cacao, chopped	.	4.5 ounces	128 grams
heavy cream, cold	⅔ cup (158 ml)	5.5 ounces	155 grams
3 (to 4) large eggs, separated, at room temperature			
yolks	3½ tablespoons (52 ml)	2 ounces	56 grams
whites	¼ cup (59 ml)	2.1 ounces	60 grams
sugar	5 tablespoons, *divided*	2.2 ounces	62 grams
½ Tahitian vanilla bean, split lengthwise (see Note, page 295)	.	.	.
powdered gelatin	½ tablespoon	.	4.5 grams
fine sea salt	a pinch	.	.
milk	1 cup (237 ml)	8.5 ounces	242 grams
cognac (or pure vanilla extract)	1 tablespoon (1 teaspoon)	0.5 ounce	14 grams
cream of tartar	¼ teaspoon	.	.

MAKE THE CUSTARD In a food processor, process the chocolate until very fine. Scrape the chocolate into a medium bowl and set a fine-mesh strainer suspended over it.

Into a mixing bowl, pour the cream and refrigerate it for at least 15 minutes. (Chill a hand-held mixer's beaters alongside the bowl.)

Into the bowl of a stand mixer, pour the egg whites and cover the bowl tightly with plastic wrap. Place the egg yolks in a small bowl.

In a small heavy saucepan, place 3 tablespoons/1.3 ounces/38 grams of the sugar. Scrape the vanilla bean seeds into the sugar and rub them in with your fingers. Add the vanilla bean pod. Add the egg yolks, gelatin, and salt. Using a silicone spatula, stir until well blended.

In another small saucepan (or in a 2 cup microwavable measure with a spout), scald the milk (heat it to the boiling point; small bubbles will form around the periphery). Whisk a few tablespoons into the egg yolk mixture and then gradually add the remaining milk, stirring constantly. Over medium-low heat, bring the mixture to just below the boiling point (170° to 180°F/77° to 82°C), stirring constantly. Steam will begin to appear and the mixture will be slightly thicker than cream. A finger will leave a well-defined track when it is run through the custard on the back of the spoon.

Immediately remove the custard from the heat and pour it through the strainer onto the chocolate in the bowl, scraping up the thickened cream that has settled to the bottom of the pan and pushing it through with the back of a spoon or silicone spatula. Stir until the chocolate is melted and the mixture is uniform in color. Remove the vanilla pod from the strainer (rinse, dry, and reserve the pod for another use).

Refrigerate the chocolate custard, uncovered, folding gently every 15 minutes for about 45 minutes to keep the custard against the bowl from setting. Continue folding until ribbons form and a small amount dropped from a spoon mounds heavily. (An instant-read thermometer should read 60° to 63°F/16° to 17°C.) Whisk in the cognac.

WHIP THE CREAM With the handheld mixer, whip the cream to soft peaks. (Avoid overbeating because the cream will continue to stiffen once folded into the custard.) Refrigerate while you make the meringue.

BEAT THE EGG WHITES INTO A STIFF MERINGUE In the bowl of a stand mixer fitted with the whisk beater, beat the egg whites and cream of tartar on medium-low speed until foamy. Gradually raise the speed to medium-high and beat until soft peaks form when the beater is raised. Gradually beat in the remaining 2 tablespoons of sugar and continue beating until stiff peaks form when the beater is raised slowly.

COMPLETE THE CHOCOLATE BAVARIAN CREAM FILLING Using a balloon whisk, fold the egg whites and then the cream into the chocolate custard until uniform in color. Pour the mixture into the prepared shell and smooth the surface evenly with a small offset spatula.

SET THE FILLING Place the pie in the refrigerator and cover it with a large bowl or inverted cake pan. Refrigerate for a minimum of 4 hours, or preferably overnight.

NOTE If using a Madagascar or Mexican vanilla bean, use ¾ of a bean. Vanilla beans offer the fullest, most aromatic flavor, but you may substitute ¾ teaspoon/3.7 ml pure vanilla extract, adding it after the custard mixture has cooled to room temperature.

CHOCOLATE LACQUER GLAZE

MAKES ⅔ CUP/158 ML/6.7 OUNCES/190 GRAMS

	VOLUME	WEIGHT	
sugar	⅓ cup	2.3 ounces	67 grams
water	2 tablespoons plus 2 teaspoons (40 ml)	1.4 ounces	40 grams
corn syrup	2 teaspoons (10 ml)	0.5 ounce	14 grams
unsweetened (alkalized) cocoa powder	½ cup minus 1 tablespoon (sifted before measuring)	1.2 ounces	33 grams
heavy cream	2 tablespoons plus 2 teaspoons (40 ml)	1.3 ounces	38 grams
cold water	2 tablespoons (30 ml)	1 ounce	30 grams
powdered gelatin	1 teaspoon	.	3 grams

MAKE THE LACQUER GLAZE Have ready a fine-mesh strainer suspended over a small metal bowl, as well as a 1 cup glass measure with a spout.

In a small heavy saucepan over medium heat, whisk together the sugar and the 2 table-spoons plus 2 teaspoons/40 ml of water. Stir constantly with the whisk until the sugar dissolves.

Remove the pan from the heat and, with the whisk, gently stir in the corn syrup and then the cocoa until smooth, making sure to reach into the corners of the pan. The mixture will be glossy. Using a silicone spatula, stir in the cream.

Return the pan to medium heat and, stirring constantly, bring the mixture to the boiling point (190°F/88°C). Bubbles will just start to form around the edges. Remove the pan from the heat and strain the mixture into the metal bowl. Cool until an instant-read thermometer reads 122° to 140°F/50° to 60°C, about 30 minutes.

While the mixture is cooling, in a custard cup, pour in the 2 tablespoons/30 ml of cold water and sprinkle the gelatin over the top. Stir to moisten the gelatin and let it sit for a minimum of 5 minutes. If it will sit longer, cover tightly with plastic wrap to prevent evaporation.

With the silicone spatula, stir the softened gelatin into the glaze until it dissolves completely and the mixture is no longer streaky.

Strain the glaze into the 1 cup glass measure with a spout. (Metal will impart an undesirable flavor if the glaze is stored in it.) Cool for a few minutes, stirring very gently so as not to incorporate any air. If using the same day, let it cool to 85°F/29°C before coating the filling.

The glaze also can be made ahead and reheated. After about 1 hour, the cooled glaze can be covered and refrigerated for up to 1 week or frozen for 6 months. Reheat it very carefully in a microwave with 3 second bursts, or in a double boiler set over hot, not simmering, water (do not let the bottom of the container touch the water), stirring gently to ensure that it does not overheat or incorporate air. The reheated glaze will be thicker and should be heated to 90°F/32°C. Alternatively, you can add a very small amount of water, a few drops at a time, as you reheat it to thin the glaze to the desired consistency and help restore maximum shine.

GLAZE THE PIE Remove 1 tablespoon/15 ml of the glaze for the chocolate whipped cream and let it cool to a cool room temperature (70°F/21°C).

With the measuring cup's spout just above the center of the pie, slowly pour the glaze until the surface of the filling is nearly covered. There is enough glaze to cover the filling without scraping the measuring cup, which might mar the surface with solid particles (see Note). Gently tilt the pie plate from side to side to coat evenly. Should they appear, any tiny bubbles can be pierced with a sharp needle.

SET THE GLAZE Refrigerate, uncovered, for 4 hours or longer until set.

CHOCOLATE WHIPPED CREAM

MAKES ¾ CUP PLUS 1 TABLESPOON/3.5 OUNCES/100 GRAMS

	VOLUME	WEIGHT	
heavy cream, cold	¼ cup plus 2 tablespoons (89 ml)	3.1 ounces	87 grams
Chocolate Lacquer Glaze (reserved from page 296)	1 tablespoon (15 ml)	0.6 ounce	17 grams

MAKE THE WHIPPED CREAM Into a mixing bowl, pour the cream and refrigerate for at least 15 minutes. (Chill the handheld mixer's beaters alongside the bowl.)

If the chocolate lacquer glaze is no longer fluid, place it in a custard cup and set it in a bowl filled with a little hot water. Gently stir the glaze until it becomes fluid, then let it cool until no longer warm to the touch.

Starting at low speed and gradually raising the speed to medium-high as it thickens, whip the cream just until beater marks begin to show distinctly. Add the glaze and beat just until stiff peaks form when the beater is raised slowly.

COMPLETE THE PIE If desired, place a few flecks of gold leaf on the glazed surface of the pie.

Just before serving, use a dish towel run under very hot water to wipe the bottom and sides of the pie plate two or three times to loosen the crust. Alternatively, dip the pie plate in a pan of very hot water for several seconds, being careful to go just up to below the rim.

To serve, spoon a dollop of the chocolate whipped cream onto the side of the plate alongside each slice.

STORE Refrigerate, 5 days. Do not freeze, because the texture will become less smooth.

NOTE If any solid particles of glaze fall onto the surface of the glaze, they can mar it. Use a sharp needle or tiny measuring spoon to remove them and tilt the pie plate to smooth the surface.

CHOCOLATE GANACHE TARTLETS

OVEN TEMPERATURE 350°F/175°C

BAKING TIME 8 to 12 minutes for each of two batches

I first met François Payard in 1990, when he had just come to America from France and was working as a pastry chef at Daniel restaurant in New York City. He went on to open his own very popular pastry shops and has authored several cookbooks. This exceptionally light, smooth, and creamy ganache, which uses milk instead of the usual cream, is from his first book, *Simply Sensational Desserts*.

    I've paired it with a delicious butter cookie crust. With a few adjustments, these tarts also work for the lactose intolerant: Replace the cream in the crust with extra egg and use the almond milk ganache variation (see page 303), which adds a lovely almond flavor.

SPECIAL EQUIPMENT 46 mini brioche pans, 1 inch at the bottom, 1¾ inches at the top (1 tablespoon capacity), preferably nonstick, lightly coated with baking spray with flour | Two 17¼ by 12¼ by 1 inch half sheet pans | A disposable pastry bag or quart-size freezer bag fitted with a coupler and a ¼ inch open star decorating tip (number 22) | A long, thin sewing needle for unmolding

SWEET COOKIE TART CRUST WITH CLARIFIED BUTTER (PÂTE SUCRÉE)

MAKES ABOUT 1⅓ CUPS/14.1 OUNCES/400 GRAMS

	VOLUME	WEIGHT	
unsalted butter	11 tablespoons (1 stick plus 3 tablespoons)	5.5 ounces	156 grams
turbinado sugar, preferably Sugar in the Raw, or superfine sugar	¼ cup	1.8 ounces	50 grams
bleached all-purpose flour	1⅔ cups (lightly spooned into the cup and leveled off)	7 ounces	200 grams
fine sea salt	⅛ teaspoon	.	0.7 gram
1 large egg yolk, at room temperature	1 tablespoon plus ½ teaspoon (17 ml)	0.7 ounce	19 grams
heavy cream, cold	3 tablespoons (44 ml)	1.5 ounces	43 grams

CLARIFY THE BUTTER Have ready a fine-mesh strainer, or a strainer lined with cheesecloth, suspended over a 2 cup glass measure with a spout.

In a medium heavy saucepan over low heat, heat the butter until melted. Continue cooking, stirring constantly and watching carefully to prevent browning, until the milk solids just begin to turn golden. Immediately pour the clarified butter through the strainer into the glass measure.

Measure ½ cup/118 ml/3.5 ounces/100 grams into another glass measure and let the butter cool to room temperature. Store any remaining clarified butter in the refrigerator for up to a year. Refrigerate or freeze the milk solids for a future use (see page 514).

MAKE THE COOKIE TART DOUGH FOOD PROCESSOR METHOD In a food processor, process the sugar until fine. Add the clarified butter and pulse it in just until the sugar disappears. Add the flour and salt and pulse again until the butter is no larger than small peas.

In a small bowl, stir together the egg yolk and cream. Add it to the processor and pulse just until incorporated, about 8 times. The dough will still be in crumbly pieces.

Empty the dough into a plastic bag and press it from the outside just until it holds together. Remove the dough from the plastic bag and place it on a very large sheet of plastic wrap. Using the plastic wrap, knead the dough only a few times until it becomes one smooth piece. There should be no visible pieces of butter. (Visible pieces of butter in the dough will melt and form holes during baking. If there are visible pieces of butter, continue kneading the dough or use the heel of your hand to press them in a forward motion to spread them into the dough.)

HAND METHOD In a medium bowl, stir together the flour, sugar (preferably superfine), and salt. With a fork, mix in the clarified butter until the mixture resembles coarse meal.

In a small bowl, stir together the egg yolk and cream. Mix it into the flour mixture until the dough comes together and can be formed into a large ball.

CHILL THE DOUGH Divide the dough in half, about 7 ounces/200 grams each. Wrap each piece loosely with plastic wrap, and press to flatten into discs. Rewrap them tightly and refrigerate for 30 minutes or freeze for 10 minutes until firm enough to shape into balls. The dough can be refrigerated for up to 3 days or frozen for up to 6 months. If chilled for more than 30 minutes, it can take as long as 40 minutes at room temperature to become malleable enough to shape into balls.

PREHEAT THE OVEN Twenty minutes or longer before baking, set an oven rack in the middle of the oven and preheat the oven to 350°F/175°C.

LINE THE BRIOCHE PANS Remove 1 dough disc from the refrigerator. With floured hands, roll rounded teaspoons (0.3 ounce/8.5 grams) of dough into 1 inch balls. Press them into the pans, starting by making a depression in the center with your knuckle. With a floured finger, press and shape the dough to form the tartlet shell. Use a small tool, such as the handle of a small artist's brush, a round chopstick, or a cuticle pusher, to press the dough into the fluted edges and slightly above the sides of the pan.

Set the dough-lined brioche pans at least ½ inch apart on one of the sheet pans and refrigerate them, covered with plastic wrap, for a minimum of 30 minutes, or freeze for a minimum of 15 minutes. While the first batch of dough is chilling, shape the dough for the second batch.

BAKE THE TARTLETS Set the first sheet pan in the oven and bake for 8 to 12 minutes, or until pale gold (the edges will be a deeper brown).

COOL AND UNMOLD THE TARTLETS Remove the sheet pan to a wire rack. If the dough has puffed up in the middle, gently use the handle end of a wooden spoon to tamp down the centers. Cool completely. Use the needle to slip between one of the edges of the pan and the pastry to loosen it. The tartlets should pop out easily from the pans. Set them on another wire rack to cool completely.

Repeat with the second batch.

The unbaked tartlet shells can be stored refrigerated for 1 week or frozen for about 1 year. The baked tartlet shells will keep at room temperature in an airtight container for 2 days.

GANACHE FILLING

MAKES 1 CUP MINUS 1 TABLESPOON/9 OUNCES/253 GRAMS

	VOLUME	WEIGHT	
bittersweet chocolate, 60% to 62% cacao, chopped	.	4.7 ounces	133 grams
unsalted butter (65° to 75°F/ 19° to 23°C)	3 tablespoons	1.5 ounces	42 grams
milk	⅓ cup (79 ml)	2.9 ounces	81 grams

MAKE THE GANACHE FILLING Have ready a fine-mesh strainer suspended over a medium glass bowl.

In the bowl of a food processor, process the chocolate until very fine. Add the butter and process just until incorporated.

In a 1 cup microwavable measure with a spout (or in a small saucepan over medium heat, stirring often), scald the milk (heat it to the boiling point; small bubbles will form around the periphery).

With the motor of the food processor running, pour the milk through the feed tube in a steady stream. Process for a few seconds until smooth, scraping down the sides of the bowl as needed. Press the ganache through the strainer and let it sit for 1 hour. Cover it with plastic wrap and cool for about 2 to 3 hours, until the mixture reaches a soft piping consistency (70° to 75°F/21° to 24°C).

FILL THE TARTLETS Fill the pastry bag with the ganache. Pipe a rosette of ganache into each tart shell, 0.2 ounce/5 grams in each. Alternatively, use a small spoon to add the ganache to the tart shells.

STORE Airtight: room temperature, 2 days; refrigerated, 5 days.

Variation: DAIRY-FREE GANACHE TARTLETS

This variation is for those who are lactose intolerant. For the Sweet Cookie Tart Crust, replace the egg yolk and cream with 1 whole egg (1.8 ounces/50 grams) plus 1 extra tablespoon of egg white (0.5 ounce/15 grams). The Sweet Cookie Tart Crust on page 299 is not firm enough to roll. This variation, however, results in a firmer dough that can be rolled instead of pressed into the pan for larger tarts. It also bakes to a crisper texture.

WOODY'S ALMOND MILK GANACHE

MAKES ABOUT 1 CUP/9.7 OUNCES/276 GRAMS

	VOLUME	WEIGHT	
bittersweet chocolate, 60% to 62% cacao, chopped	.	4.7 ounces	132 grams
almond milk (original)	⅔ cup (158 ml)	5.5 ounces	157 grams
pure vanilla extract	1 teaspoon (5 ml)	.	.

MAKE THE ALMOND MILK GANACHE Have ready a fine-mesh strainer suspended over a medium glass bowl.

In a food processor, process the chocolate until very fine.

In a 1 cup microwavable measure with a spout (or in a small saucepan over medium heat, stirring often), scald the almond milk (heat it to the boiling point; small bubbles will form around the periphery).

With the motor of the food processor running, pour the almond milk through the feed tube in a steady stream. Process for a few seconds until smooth. Pulse in the vanilla. Press the ganache through the strainer and let it sit for 1 hour. Cover it with plastic wrap and cool for 2 to 3 hours, or until the mixture reaches a soft piping consistency (70° to 75°F/ 21° to 24°C).

This almond milk ganache keeps in an airtight container for 5 days at cool room temperature, 2 weeks refrigerated, and 6 months frozen. To restore to frosting consistency, defrost, if frozen, and reheat in a microwave with 3 second bursts, or in a double boiler set over hot, not simmering, water (do not let the bottom of the container touch the water), stirring gently to ensure that it does not overheat or incorporate any air.

PERFECT SAVORY CREAM PUFFS

OVEN TEMPERATURE 425°F/220°C; then 350°F/175°C for the cream puffs; 300°F/150°C for the faux gras

BAKING TIME 25 to 30 minutes for the cream puffs; 30 to 35 minutes for the faux gras

*T*hese cream puffs can be filled with any manner of things from whipped cream or ice cream to savory fillings such as pâté or foie gras. As foie gras traditionally is accompanied by dessert wine, whose sweet acidity complements the richness of the foie gras, I have topped these cream puffs, which make elegant hors d'oeuvres, with ruby port caramel. The port lends the caramel a stunning mahogany hue and multidimensional flavor. The homemade "faux gras" is adapted from *Happy in the Kitchen* by Michel Richard.

PLAN AHEAD If filling with the faux gras, make the faux gras at least 4 hours ahead.

SPECIAL EQUIPMENT FOR THE PUFFS: One inverted 17¼ by 12¼ by 1 inch half sheet pan, lined with parchment or coated with shortening and then floured | A pastry bag fitted with a ½ inch plain round pastry tube | A wire rack set on a baking sheet

FOR THE FAUX GRAS FILLING: Two 8 ounce/237 ml terrines or two 8 ounce/237 ml to 10 ounce/296 ml ramekins | A baking pan large enough to hold the two terrines to serve as a water bath

CREAM PUFF PASTRY

MAKES 1⅓ CUPS/11.4 OUNCES/324 GRAMS

	VOLUME	WEIGHT	
bleached all-purpose flour	½ cup (lightly spooned into the cup and leveled off) plus 1½ tablespoons	2.5 ounces	71 grams
water	½ cup (118 ml)	4.2 ounces	118 grams
unsalted butter	4 tablespoons (½ stick)	2 ounces	57 grams
sugar	½ teaspoon	.	.
fine sea salt	a pinch	.	.
2½ large eggs, lightly beaten	½ cup (118 ml)	4.4 ounces	125 grams

PREHEAT THE OVEN Thirty minutes or longer before baking, set an oven rack in the middle of the oven and preheat the oven to 425°F/220°C.

MAKE THE CREAM PUFF PASTRY Sift the flour onto a large piece of parchment.

In a medium saucepan, combine the water, butter, sugar, and salt and bring it to a full rolling boil. Immediately remove the saucepan from the heat and add the flour all at once. Stir with a wooden spoon until the mixture forms a ball, leaves the sides of the pan, and clings slightly to the spoon. Return the pan to low heat and cook, stirring and mashing continuously, for about 3 minutes to cook the flour.

FOOD PROCESSOR METHOD Without scraping the pan, transfer the mixture to a food processor. With the feed tube open to allow steam to escape, process for 15 seconds. With the motor running, pour in the eggs all at once and continue processing for 30 seconds. If necessary, remove the blades and, using a silicone spatula, mix the pastry to a uniform consistency.

HAND METHOD Without scraping the pan, empty the mixture into a bowl. Add the eggs, 1 at a time, beating vigorously with a wooden spoon after each addition.

SHAPE THE PUFFS The mixture will be smooth and shiny and it should be too soft to hold peaks when lifted with a spoon. If it is too stiff, add a little extra water. (The dough can be stored in an airtight container and refrigerated overnight or up to 2 days.) Beat the mixture lightly with a wooden spoon before piping.

Dab a small dot of the dough in each corner of the inverted half sheet pan under the floured parchment and press the parchment lightly to affix it.

Scrape the cream puff mixture into the pastry bag. For the savory puffs, pipe puffs about 1 inch in diameter and ½ to ¾ inch high (about 0.3 ounce/9 grams each), about 1 inch apart onto the half sheet pan. For larger dessert puffs, pipe them about 1½ inches in diameter (about 0.6 ounce/18 grams each). Alternatively, use a teaspoon lightly coated with nonstick cooking spray to scoop out the dough. With a fingertip, push the dough off the spoon and onto the half sheet pan.

Dip a fingertip into water and smooth the tops of the puffs. Spritz or brush the puffs lightly with water.

BAKE THE PUFFS Bake for 10 minutes. To prevent the puffs from collapsing, do not open the oven door. Lower the heat to 350°F/175°C and continue baking for 15 to 20 minutes, or until golden brown. Turn off the oven.

Set the pan on a wire rack for 1 minute. Using your fingers or tongs, transfer the puffs to the wire rack set on the baking sheet. Return the puffs to the oven. Use a wooden spoon to prop open the oven door and let the puffs dry for 10 minutes. Close the oven door and leave the puffs in the oven for 1½ hours to dry out completely (or continue baking at

200°F/90°C for 45 minutes). Test a puff by cutting it in half horizontally. The dough inside should not be soft to the touch. If it is still soft, let it dry for a little longer.

COOL THE PUFFS Remove the puffs from the oven and let them cool completely on the wire rack. Store them in a gallon-size reclosable freezer bag or airtight container until ready to fill.

STORE Airtight: Room temperature, 1 day; refrigerated, 1 week; frozen, 6 months.

FILL THE PUFFS Use a serrated knife to cut each puff horizontally in half.

For a savory appetizer, fill each puff with a rounded teaspoon/0.5 ounce/14 grams of foie gras, "faux gras" (page 308), or the filling of your choice.

For a dessert version, fill each puff with 2 teaspoons of lightly sweetened whipped cream (see page 516) or 1 tablespoon of softened ice cream.

For crispy puffs, fill only the puffs that are to be served. Refrigerate and store extra faux gras in its own container.

Variation: DELUXE PUFFS

For extra light and airy puffs, substitute an equal weight of bread flour or unbleached all-purpose flour. (Because bread flour is heavier than all-purpose, the volume measurement if using bread flour will be ½ cup, lightly spooned, plus ½ tablespoon.) In place of the whole eggs, use 1½ egg yolks (1½ tablespoons/22 ml/1 ounce/28 grams) and 3 egg whites (6 tablespoons/89 ml/3.2 ounces/90 grams).

Instead of lining the pan with parchment, coat it with shortening and flour. (Do not use baking spray with flour; it will make piping the puffs too slippery.)

Michel Richard's Chicken Faux Gras

MAKES 2 CUPS/14.1 OUNCES/400 GRAMS

	VOLUME	WEIGHT	
unsalted butter	8 tablespoons (1 stick), *divided*	4 ounces	113 grams
onion, finely chopped	½ cup	2.5 ounces	70 grams
heavy cream	¼ cup (59 ml)	2 ounces	58 grams
garlic, minced	1 small clove	.	.
chicken livers, trimmed	.	8 ounces	227 grams
fine sea salt	½ teaspoon	.	3 grams
black pepper, freshly ground	¼ teaspoon	.	.

PREHEAT THE OVEN Twenty minutes or longer before baking, set an oven rack in the middle of the oven and preheat the oven to 300°F/150°C.

MAKE THE LIVER PUREE In a small heavy saucepan over low heat, melt 2 tablespoons/ 1 ounce/28 grams of the butter. Add the onion and cook, covered, for 5 minutes until translucent. Stir in the cream and garlic and simmer, covered, for another 5 minutes.

Add the remaining butter and heat, stirring, just until it is melted and the mixture is well combined. Scrape the mixture into a medium bowl. Add the livers, salt, and pepper and, with an immersion blender, puree the mixture until smooth. Alternatively, use a blender or food processor, scraping down the sides of the bowl as needed.

Set a fine-mesh strainer over a medium bowl and press the liver mixture through with the back of a spoon. Scrape the mixture into the terrines. Cover them tightly with aluminum foil and set them in the baking pan. Fill the pan with boiling water to come halfway up the sides of the terrines.

BAKE THE FAUX GRAS Bake for 30 minutes, or just until set. (An instant-read thermometer should read 148°F/64°C.)

CHILL THE FAUX GRAS Cover tightly and chill for at least 3 hours or up to 3 days.

RUBY PORT CARAMEL

MAKES A FULL ½ CUP/118 ML/6 OUNCES/170 GRAMS

	VOLUME	WEIGHT	
ruby port	3 tablespoons (44 ml)	1.6 ounces	45 grams
heavy cream	1 tablespoon (15 ml)	0.5 ounce	14 grams
sugar	½ cup	3.5 ounces	100 grams
corn syrup	½ tablespoon (7.5 ml)	.	10 grams
water	2 tablespoons (30 ml)	1 ounce	30 grams
unsalted butter (65° to 75°F/ 19° to 23°C)	1 tablespoon	0.5 ounce	14 grams
pure vanilla extract	1 teaspoon (5 ml)	.	.

MAKE THE RUBY PORT CARAMEL Have ready a 1 cup glass measure with a spout, lightly coated with nonstick cooking spray.

In a small microwavable measure with a spout, stir together the port and cream. Heat for about 20 seconds, or until hot. Cover it to prevent evaporation and to keep warm.

In a medium heavy saucepan, preferably nonstick, stir together the sugar, corn syrup, and water until all of the sugar is moistened. Heat, stirring constantly, until the sugar dissolves and the syrup is bubbling. Stop stirring completely and let the syrup boil undisturbed until it turns a deep amber (360°F/180°C or a few degrees below because the temperature will continue to rise). Remove the syrup from the heat as soon as it reaches temperature. Slowly and carefully pour the warm port syrup into the caramel. It will bubble up furiously.

Use a silicone spatula or wooden spoon to stir the mixture gently, scraping the thicker part that settles on the bottom. Return it to very low heat, continuing to stir gently for 1 minute, until the mixture is uniform in color and the caramel fully dissolved. The caramel will be like a thin sauce, but will thicken after the butter is added and it has cooled.

Remove the caramel from the heat and gently stir in the butter until incorporated. The mixture will be a little streaky but will become uniform once cooled and stirred.

Pour the caramel into the prepared glass measure and let it cool for 3 minutes. Gently stir in the vanilla and let it cool to room temperature, stirring it gently once or twice.

APPLY THE CARAMEL Shortly before serving, scrape the caramel into a small bowl. Dip the tops of the filled puffs into the caramel and then set them, bottom side down, on serving plates. Do not cover the puffs once the caramel has been applied because the caramel will soften and liquefy.

PIZZA RUSTICA

OVEN TEMPERATURE 350°F/175°C

BAKING TIME 40 to 50 minutes

I enjoyed this delectable Italian sausage and cheese pie many years ago at my fellow cookbook author and longtime friend Nick Malgieri's Christmas dinner. I had never before tasted pasta frolla and immediately adored the unusual interplay of this slightly sweet crust and the savory sausage and ricotta filling. Nick told me he makes this every Christmas—a great tradition. I like to add a little sage and thyme to the dough for extra flavor that complements the filling.

This is an exciting party recipe because it is so decorative and slices beautifully. It is very convenient because it can be made and baked a day ahead and it is best eaten warm or at room temperature. It also has an excellent texture and intensified flavor when reheated.

SPECIAL EQUIPMENT One 9 by 2 inch round cake pan (preferably with a removable bottom), lightly coated with nonstick cooking spray | A baking stone or baking sheet (see Note, page 315) | A foil ring to protect the edges of the crust

PASTA FROLLA

MAKES 2½ CUPS/25.3 OUNCES/718 GRAMS

	VOLUME	WEIGHT	
unsalted butter, cold	10 tablespoons (1 stick plus 2 tablespoons)	5 ounces	142 grams
milk	¼ cup (59 ml)	2.1 ounces	60 grams
1 large egg	3 tablespoons plus ½ teaspoon (47 ml)	1.8 ounces	50 grams
bleached all-purpose flour	3 cups (lightly spooned into the cup and leveled off), *divided*	12.8 ounces	363 grams
dried thyme	½ tablespoon	.	.
powdered sage	½ teaspoon	.	.
sugar	½ cup	3.5 ounces	100 grams
baking powder (use only an aluminum free variety; see Note, page 312)	½ teaspoon	.	2.2 grams
fine sea salt	½ teaspoon	.	3 grams

MAKE THE PASTA FROLLA Cut the butter into ½ inch cubes and refrigerate until ready to use.

In a small bowl, lightly beat together the milk and egg.

FOOD PROCESSOR METHOD In a food processor, place ½ cup/2.1 ounces/60 grams of the flour, the thyme, and sage, and process until the herbs are well dispersed. Add the remaining flour, the sugar, baking powder, and salt, and process for 30 seconds. Add the butter and pulse until the mixture resembles fine meal. Remove the cover and add the egg mixture. Pulse just until the mixture starts to clump together.

HAND METHOD With a sharp knife, chop together the thyme and sage with ½ cup/ 2.1 ounces/60 grams of the flour until the herbs are very fine. Place the mixture in a medium bowl. Whisk in the remaining flour, the sugar, baking powder, and salt.

With your fingers, rub the butter into the flour mixture until the mixture is in fine crumbs. It should remain cool and powdery. If the mixture starts becoming pasty, refrigerate or freeze it for a few minutes.

With a fork, stir the egg mixture into the flour mixture just until the dough holds together.

CHILL THE DOUGH Empty the dough onto a large sheet of plastic wrap. Holding each end of the plastic wrap, use your knuckles to knead the dough just until the dough becomes one smooth piece.

Cut off one-third of the dough (8.4 ounces/240 grams). Shape and flatten it into a 4 by 4 by ½ inch thick square and wrap it well in plastic wrap. Flatten the remaining dough into a 6 by ¾ inch thick disc and wrap it well. Refrigerate the dough for 45 minutes, or until firm enough to roll.

The dough can be refrigerated for up to 3 days or frozen for up to 3 months.

NOTE The reason to use only baking powder that is calcium (not aluminum) based is that aluminum will produce a bitter flavor, whereas calcium will add a pleasant one.

FILLING

	VOLUME	WEIGHT	
whole-milk ricotta cheese, preferably fresh	1 cup plus 1 tablespoon	16 ounces	454 grams
3 large eggs	½ cup plus 1½ tablespoons (140 ml)	5.3 ounces	150 grams
fine sea salt	¼ teaspoon	.	1.5 grams
black pepper, freshly ground	½ teaspoon	.	.
pecorino Romano cheese, grated	½ cup	1.5 ounces	42 grams
whole-milk mozzarella cheese, preferably a firmer variety	.	8 ounces	227 grams
dried sausage, such as cacciatorino or sopressata (see Note)	.	8 ounces	227 grams

MAKE THE FILLING Place a fine-mesh strainer over a medium bowl and press the ricotta through it. Add the eggs, salt, and pepper and whisk until blended. Whisk in the grated pecorino.

Slice the mozzarella thinly and peel and cut the sausage into ¼ inch cubes.

NOTE Choose a sopressata that is slightly moist, not dry or hard.

PREHEAT THE OVEN Forty-five minutes or longer before baking, set an oven rack at the lowest level and place a baking stone or baking sheet on it. Preheat the oven to 350°F/175°C.

EGG GLAZE

	VOLUME	WEIGHT	
1 large egg yolk	1 tablespoon plus ½ teaspoon (17 ml)	0.7 ounce	19 grams
milk	1 teaspoon (5 ml)	.	.

MAKE THE EGG GLAZE In a small bowl, whisk together the egg yolk and milk. Cover tightly with plastic wrap to prevent evaporation.

ROLL THE DOUGH FOR THE BOTTOM CRUST Remove the larger piece of dough from the refrigerator. If necessary, let it sit for about 10 minutes, or until it is malleable enough to roll.

On a floured pastry cloth, pastry mat, or between two sheets of lightly floured plastic wrap, roll and trim the bottom crust into a ¼ inch thick disc roughly 14 inches in diameter. Fold it gently into fourths and transfer it to the cake pan. Unfold the dough, easing it into the pan without stretching it. Allow the dough to hang over the edge of the pan. Layer the scraps on top of the refrigerated dough for the lattice crust.

FILL THE PIZZA RUSTICA Spread 1 cup/8.1 ounces/230 grams of the ricotta mixture into the dough-lined pan. Arrange half of the mozzarella evenly on top to cover the ricotta completely. Strew half of the sausage evenly over the mozzarella. Top with another 1 cup of the ricotta mixture. Arrange the remaining mozzarella on top and strew the remaining sausage evenly over the mozzarella. Using a small offset spatula, spread the remaining ricotta mixture evenly over the sausage.

ROLL THE DOUGH AND MAKE THE LATTICE Roll the remaining dough into a 10 inch square. Cut it into ten 1 inch wide strips.

Moisten the top of the dough resting on the rim of the pan with the egg glaze. To create a woven lattice decoration, arrange half of the strips evenly over the filling, starting in the center. Gently curve back every other strip a little past the center so that the next strip can be placed at a 45 degree angle to the first strips, right at the center. Uncurve the strips so that they lie flat on top of the angled strip. Working in the same direction, curve back the strips that were not curved back the first time. Lay a second angled strip on top and uncurve the strips. Repeat with 1 more strip.

Apply the remaining 2 strips to the other side of the pie. Start toward the center and work in the opposite direction toward the edge. Remember always to alternate the strips that are curved back so that the strips weave in and out.

If desired, for an easier method of applying the strips, instead of weaving them, simply place 5 strips, ½ inch apart, in each direction (at a 45 degree angle).

Press the tops of the strips firmly into the dough where they rest against the rim. With scissors, trim the overhanging dough so that it is even with the rim of the pan and push the dough away from the rim so that it rests completely within the pan. (This makes unmolding easier.) Brush the strips well with the egg glaze.

BAKE THE PIZZA RUSTICA Set the pan directly on the baking stone. Bake for 20 minutes. Place the foil ring on top of the pie to protect the edges from overbrowning. Bake for another 20 to 30 minutes, or until the pastry is pale gold and the filling is set and slightly puffed. (An instant-read thermometer should read 165°F/74°C.)

COOL AND UNMOLD THE PIZZA RUSTICA Cool the pizza rustica on a wire rack for about 2 hours, or until barely warm, before unmolding it.

To unmold, place one or more folded paper towels on top of the lattice crust to be even with the rim of the pan. Cover the top of the pan with a dish towel to protect the crust's edges. Invert the pan onto a flat plate and lift off the pan. Reinvert the pie onto a serving plate and remove the towels. (If using a pan with a removable bottom, place the pan on top of a container that is smaller than the opening of the pan's outer rim. Slide down the sides of the pan. Slide a pancake turner between the bottom of the pizza rustica and the pan's bottom and slide it onto a serving plate.) Serve warm or at room temperature.

STORE Room temperature, 4 hours. Airtight: refrigerated, 3 days.

NOTE A baking stone is best to ensure that the bottom crust bakes sufficiently.

COOKIES and CANDY

There is no end to the creation of new and wonderful cookies. As a cookie lover, I have unearthed some real treasures since writing *Rose's Christmas Cookies* many years ago. For example, people have been asking me for years for my version of the classic chocolate chip cookie and I have finally included it here. Woody's Black and White Brownies are three flavors of chocolate at their creamiest best. One of my new top favorite cookies of all time is the fragrant with almonds, dissolving in the mouth Greek Kourambiethes. Most unusual and cherished are chef Vinnie Scotto's Praline Pecan Meringue Ice Cream Sandwiches. Most addictive are Pepparkakors, followed closely by the Rugelach. And if I had just one cookie to represent me, it would be the exquisite chocolate and apricot Ischler.

Cookie is a word that derives from the Dutch *koekje*, the diminutive of the Dutch word for cake, *koek*. Most cookies, however, are a cross between cake and pastry. And because cookies and candy are similar in size, I have also included some of my special candies, such as toffee and pralines.

The typical cookie is easier to make than a cake or pastry because cookie dough, due to its higher sugar content, is much more forgiving of overmixing and overhandling. Scraps of dough can be reshaped several times without changing a cookie's texture.

MIXING COOKIE DOUGH

There are three basic methods for mixing most cookie doughs, and all three methods produce essentially the same results.

The food processor is my first choice because it is the fastest, and it also makes it possible to use fine granulated sugar in place of superfine (because it will be processed into superfine during mixing). This method is given where applicable. If you are making a small batch of dough and your food processor is too large, you will need to scrape the sides of the bowl often or use an immersion blender.

The method for using an electric mixer (stand mixer or handheld) is also given where applicable.

Finally, most cookie doughs can be mixed by hand using a large bowl (at least 4 quart capacity) and a wooden spoon (that has not been used for spicy or savory ingredients). In making the recipes, follow the same basic instructions as for the electric mixer, with the following modifications: Instead of beating the butter and sugar together, start by beating the butter until it is creamy. Then add the sugar and beat the two together for a few minutes, or until the mixture becomes very light in color. If eggs are used, beat them lightly before adding them.

BAKING COOKIES

Because cookies bake quickly and most evenly on the middle rack of the oven, most cookie recipes in this book bake in separate batches. The standard 15 by 12 inch cookie sheet was used to determine the batch size. For cookies that require no pan preparation, lining with parchment is optional for ease in cleanup. It also works well to set a piece of parchment on the countertop and arrange the shaped cookies on top. When one batch is baked and removed from the cookie sheet, the parchment with the unbaked cookie dough can be slipped onto the hot sheet quickly and baked immediately, so that the dough doesn't start spreading prematurely.

SOME SPECIAL TIPS

- The type of flour and sugar used to make a cookie dough will have a great effect on the baked cookies.

- Flour contributes a major part of the structure. I recommend bleached all-purpose flour in most of my recipes because it possesses just the right protein content needed to create the ideal texture and flavor. Unbleached all-purpose flour and bread flour contain higher amounts of protein and produce cookies that are browner, flatter, and more chewy. Higher protein absorbs more liquid, forming gluten, which is tough and leaves less available liquid in the dough to turn to steam and aerate the cookies. Cake flour contains less protein, so because less water is tied up by the flour, the water turns to steam and makes the cookies puffier. Less gluten forms as well, which makes the cookies more fragile. The cookies brown less because protein is largely responsible for browning.

- A great tip from my generous friend Maria Menegus, who got it from her friend Jean Seaver, discovered by her grandmother Nanny, is to roll cookie dough in buckwheat flour. The flour is very fine so it rolls beautifully and gives a lovely, crisp texture to the outside of the cookie. It also darkens and adds an interesting effect and subtle, pleasant flavor.

- Sugar raises the setting point of the dough while it bakes, so cookie dough with a higher amount of sugar can spread more before setting, resulting in a thinner, crunchier cookie.

- The finer the granulation of the sugar, the less cracking in the surface of the dough during baking. Fine granulation results in a finer crumb and lighter texture because, with its smaller crystals, more surface area is available to trap air. In the mixing or creaming process, the sharp or angular surfaces of the sugar crystals catch air. If the surfaces of the grains of sugar were smooth, as they are in powdered sugar, the grains would clump together and not allow air in between them. The more crystals there are, the more air will be incorporated. Finer sugar also dissolves more easily and makes lighter, more delicate meringues. Powdered sugar, however, does result in a delightfully fragile cookie, such as the Kourambiethes.

Storing Cookie Dough and Cookies

Most cookie doughs can be refrigerated for at least 3 days or frozen for several weeks and then thawed overnight in the refrigerator. It is easiest to shape cookie dough, however, if it has not been refrigerated for more than 3 hours. If the dough cracks on rolling or shaping, the dough is either too dry or too cold. If too dry, spritz with a little water and knead it in. If too cold, divide the chilled dough into quarters and let it sit at room temperature for about 15 minutes, or until it is malleable and soft enough to roll but is still chilled.

Most baked cookies keep for weeks after baking if they are stored carefully. If they are stored in a cool room, they will keep for months. There is, however, something extra special about certain cookies that are freshly baked, especially those containing pieces of chocolate. Within four to six hours after baking, the chocolate is still slightly soft and adds an extra dimension to both texture and taste. If you prefer soft cookies, storing them in airtight containers in the refrigerator will keep them softer for longer. Be sure to store them airtight so that they do not pick up conflicting aromas from other foods. For the best flavor and texture, let them warm to room temperature before serving.

Freezing cookies keeps them almost as fresh as the day they were baked. If you want to freeze cookies, use reclosable freezer bags, expelling as much air as possible, or airtight containers, filling any airspace at the top with crumpled plastic wrap or wax paper. Fragile cookies can be flash frozen in single layers on cookie sheets and, once frozen solid, packed in airtight containers. Bar cookies can be frozen whole, before cutting, wrapped in plastic wrap and then heavy-duty aluminum foil.

Individual cookies will defrost at room temperature in about 20 minutes if they are taken out of their containers.

When storing cookies, always be sure to cool them completely first and to store crisp cookies and soft ones in different containers. It is also best to store each variety of cookie separately to prevent transfer of flavors. Place sheets of parchment or wax paper between the layers of cookies to keep the cookies crisp and to separate those that are sticky.

To recrisp cookies, place them on cookie sheets in a preheated 300°F/150°C oven for about 5 minutes. Cool them on wire racks.

Troubleshooting Cookies

PROBLEM: The cookie dough cracks when rolling it.
SOLUTION: Try covering the dough with plastic wrap before rolling. If it still doesn't come together smoothly, spritz with a little water and knead it together until smooth. Or, if the dough is too cold, allow it to sit at room temperature until softened.

PROBLEM: The cookies spread too much while baking and are too flat.
SOLUTION: Use a lower protein flour and/or less sugar. Flour your hands before shaping to make a more rounded cookie. It also helps to chill the shaped cookie dough before baking. Avoid placing the cookie dough on hot or warm baking sheets.

PROBLEM: Cookie dough rolled into a log flattens on one side.
SOLUTION: Place the plastic wrapped dough log in PVC plastic tubing or a cardboard tube from a roll of paper towels. If necessary, cut the cardboard tube along the length so that it can be opened up to accommodate the size of the dough log. Secure it at both ends with rubber bands and stand it on end in the freezer. If the tube is too long, cut it into sections and divide the dough log accordingly.

PROBLEM: The cookies brown too much on the bottoms.
SOLUTION: Bake them on a higher rack, or use insulated or double cookie sheets.

PROBLEM: The cookies are not soft enough.
SOLUTION: Remove them from the oven while they are still a little soft. Remove them from the cookie sheet as soon as they are firm enough to lift without bending.

Golden Rules of Cookie Baking

Weigh or measure ingredients carefully for consistent flavor and texture.

Use the ingredients specified in the recipe. For more details, see the Ingredients chapter (page 509).

FLOUR Bleached all-purpose flour is usually the best choice for cookies because its protein content results in the ideal texture and flavor.

BUTTER Use a high quality unsalted butter with standard fat content unless high butterfat is called for in the recipe or if making clarified butter.

NUTS Use unsalted nuts.

Make cookies the same size, shape, and thickness in each batch so that they bake evenly, and arrange them at regular intervals on the baking sheet. (Do not leave large, empty spaces.)

Cookies require flat baking sheets without sides for even heating and air circulation, but an inverted 17¼ by 12¼ by 1 inch half sheet pan will work equally well. Use shiny heavy-gauge aluminum cookie sheets, not darkened ones, so the cookies will brown evenly and not excessively.

Preheat the oven for 20 to 30 minutes before baking the cookies.

Bake cookies in the center of the oven, if possible. If the rack is too high, the tops will overbrown; if too low, the bottoms will overbrown. It is, therefore, ideal to bake one sheet of cookies at a time. Because most cookies bake quickly, while one sheet is baking, the next batch of cookie dough can be shaped.

If you prefer to bake more sheets at a time, allow a minimum of 2 inches between the sides of the cookie sheets and all of the sides of the oven. If your oven is not large enough to bake two cookie sheets side by side, place the oven racks so that they divide the oven in thirds. Rearrange and rotate the cookie sheets in the oven from side to side and front to back halfway through baking for even baking. If baking cookie sheets on two different levels, exchange the positions on the racks.

Do not overbake the cookies. Cookies continue baking after they are removed from the oven. If they require further baking, they can be returned to the oven. For softer rather than crisper cookies, underbake them slightly.

Cool cookie sheets between batches so that the cookies do not start to melt and thin at the edges before the heat of the oven can set them. Alternatively, arrange cookies on sheets of parchment, slip them quickly onto the hot baking sheets, and place them immediately in the oven.

Remove the cookies from the cookie sheets with a pancake turner as soon as they are rigid enough to transfer. Cool them on wire racks so that they remain crisp and do not continue cooking from the heat of the cookie sheets.

Cool the cookies completely before storing them airtight to maintain the best possible texture.

Spritz Butter Cookies

MAKES TWENTY-EIGHT ROSETTE OR FIFTY-SIX STAR SHAPED 2 INCH ROUND COOKIES

OVEN TEMPERATURE 375°F/190°C

BAKING TIME 10 to 12 minutes for each of four batches

*T*his traditional Christmas cookie is one that I enjoy year round, so when my delightful friend and fellow cookbook writer Sally Longo suggested replacing some of the flour with cornstarch, I was eager to try it. The result: a more delicate cookie that is also easier to pipe or push through a cookie press.

SPECIAL EQUIPMENT Two 15 by 12 inch cookie sheets, no preparation needed or lined with parchment | A large pastry bag fitted with a ½ inch star pastry tube or a cookie press

Cookie Dough

MAKES 26.7 OUNCES/750 GRAMS

	VOLUME	WEIGHT	
blanched sliced almonds	½ cup minus 1 tablespoon	1.5 ounces	44 grams
bleached all-purpose flour	2 cups (lightly spooned into the cup and leveled off) plus 2 tablespoons	9.1 ounces	257 grams
cornstarch	¼ cup (lightly spooned into the cup and leveled off)	1 ounce	30 grams
fine sea salt	a pinch	.	.
superfine sugar	¾ cup	5.3 ounces	150 grams
unsalted butter (65° to 75°F/ 19° to 23°C)	16 tablespoons (2 sticks)	8 ounces	227 grams
1 large egg, at room temperature	3 tablespoons plus ½ teaspoon (47 ml)	1.8 ounces	50 grams
pure vanilla extract	1 teaspoon (5 ml)	.	.
pure almond extract	1 teaspoon (5 ml)	.	.
glacéed cherries, sugar sprinkles, or dragées, for decorating	.	.	.

PREHEAT THE OVEN Thirty minutes or longer before baking, set an oven rack in the middle of the oven and preheat the oven to 375°F/190°C.

TOAST THE ALMONDS Spread the almonds evenly on a baking sheet and bake for about 5 minutes, or until pale gold. Stir once or twice to ensure even toasting and avoid over-browning. Cool completely.

MIX THE DRY INGREDIENTS In a medium bowl, whisk together the flour, cornstarch, and salt.

MAKE THE DOUGH FOOD PROCESSOR METHOD In a food processor, process the almonds and sugar until fairly fine. Cut the butter into several pieces and add it with the motor running. Process until smooth and creamy. Add the egg, vanilla, and almond extract and process until incorporated. Scrape down the sides of the bowl. Add the flour mixture and pulse in just until blended.

STAND MIXER METHOD Use a nut grater to grate the almonds powder fine and then whisk them into the flour mixture.

In the bowl of a stand mixer fitted with the flat beater, on medium speed, beat the sugar and butter until fluffy. Scrape down the sides of the bowl. Add the egg, vanilla, and almond extract and beat for 30 seconds, or until incorporated. Scrape down the sides of the bowl. On low speed, gradually add the flour mixture and mix until incorporated.

Scrape the mixture onto a sheet of plastic wrap and use the outside of the plastic wrap to knead together the dough until it is completely even and soft enough to pipe smoothly.

SHAPE THE COOKIES Scoop the dough into the pastry bag (or spoon some of the dough into the cookie press and cover the remaining dough). Pipe 7 rosettes or 14 stars about 1¾ inches in diameter onto the cookie sheet, no less than 1 inch apart.

To get the best possible shape for the rosettes, use your fingers to smooth the ends of the rosettes after piping. For the stars, hold the bag in a vertical position (straight up and down) with the toothed edge of the tube just slightly above the cookie sheet. Squeeze the bag firmly without moving it until the shape is as wide as desired, just at the point when the lines in the dough are on the verge of curving. Stop squeezing the tube and push the tube down slightly. Lift the tube straight up and away. Decorate with the glacéed cherries set in the centers, and/or top with sugar sprinkles or dragées.

BAKE THE COOKIES Bake for 5 minutes. For even baking, rotate the cookie sheet halfway around. Continue baking for 5 to 7 minutes, or until pale gold.

COOL THE COOKIES Set the cookie sheet on a wire rack and use a pancake turner to lift the cookies onto another wire rack. Cool completely.

While each batch of cookies is baking, shape the dough for the next batch.

STORE Airtight: room temperature, 1 month; refrigerated or frozen, 6 months.

Spritz Butter Cookies, The Dutch Pecan Sandies (page 353),
and Coconut Crisps (page 366)

ALMOND COFFEE CRISPS

OVEN TEMPERATURE 350°F/175°C

BAKING TIME 10 to 15 minutes for each of three batches

*I*n 1994, I had the honor of working with ten other chefs to prepare a dinner for charity at the famed Charlie Trotter's restaurant in Chicago. My husband, Elliott, even joined in as maître d'. Celebrated chef Jean-Louis Palladin was still alive and at least as colorfully temperamental as Gordon Ramsay is today. We spent the entire day in the state-of-the-art kitchen prepping, and in the evening we were invited to a glorious dinner at the home of noted Chicago gastronome Robert "Tubby" Bacon and his wife, Julie, who gave me this exquisite recipe. She said it was her favorite cookie recipe and now, twenty years later, I am sharing it with you! The only change I've made is to use baking powder instead of asking you to make your own by combining cream of tartar and baking soda, which would result in a slightly puffier cookie. If you love coffee, you will adore this crisp, fragile, ethereal cookie, which is like eating coffee-imbued air.

SPECIAL EQUIPMENT Two 15 by 12 inch cookie sheets, no preparation needed or lined with parchment | Optional: a makeup brush designed to apply blush, used only for dusting the cookies

COOKIE DOUGH
MAKES 13.3 OUNCES/378 GRAMS

	VOLUME	WEIGHT	
blanched or unblanched sliced almonds	½ cup	1.8 ounces	50 grams
unbleached all-purpose flour	⅔ cup (lightly spooned into the cup and leveled off)	2.8 ounces	81 grams
instant espresso powder, preferably Medaglia D'Oro	1 tablespoon, *divided*	.	3.6 grams
baking powder	½ tablespoon	.	6.8 grams
fine sea salt	⅛ teaspoon	.	0.7 gram
superfine sugar	⅔ cup	4.7 ounces	133 grams
unsalted butter (65° to 75°F/ 19° to 23°C)	8 tablespoons (1 stick)	4 ounces	113 grams
pure vanilla extract	½ tablespoon (7.5 ml)	.	.

PREHEAT THE OVEN Twenty minutes or longer before baking, set an oven rack in the middle of the oven and preheat the oven to 350°F/175°C.

TOAST THE ALMONDS Spread the almonds evenly on a baking sheet and bake for about 7 minutes, or until pale gold. Stir once or twice to ensure even toasting and avoid overbrowning. Cool completely.

PROCESS THE ALMONDS In a food processor, combine the almonds, flour, 2 teaspoons of the instant espresso powder, the baking powder, and salt. Process until the almonds are powder fine, about 2 minutes. Empty the mixture onto a piece of parchment or into a bowl.

MAKE THE DOUGH Place the sugar into the food processor and, with the motor running, add the butter, about 1 tablespoon at a time. Process for a few seconds until smooth. Add the vanilla and pulse just to incorporate it. Scrape down the sides of the bowl. Add the flour mixture and pulse just until combined. Scrape the mixture onto a large sheet of plastic wrap and use the outside of the plastic wrap to knead together the dough until completely even and there are no visible streaks of butter. (Visible pieces of butter in the dough will melt and form holes during baking. If there are visible pieces of butter, continue kneading the dough or use the heel of your hand to press them in a forward motion to spread them into the dough.)

Divide the dough into thirds, about 4.4 ounces/126 grams each. Wrap 2 of the pieces in plastic wrap and refrigerate them while rolling the first piece.

ROLL THE DOUGH INTO BALLS Scoop out 12 rounded teaspoons of dough (0.4 ounce/10 grams). Roll each piece of dough between the palms of your hands into a 1 inch ball. Set the dough balls a minimum of 2½ inches apart on a baking sheet and press them down to 1¾ inches wide by ¼ inch high. (Do this 1 at a time, flattening each ball right after you roll it, or roll each ball a second time before pressing it to soften it, which will result in smooth edges.)

BAKE THE COOKIES Bake for 5 minutes. For even baking, rotate the cookie sheet halfway around. Continue baking for 5 to 10 minutes. The cookies should just begin to brown and still feel slightly soft when pressed very lightly with a fingertip but not keep the impression.

COOL THE COOKIES Set the cookie sheet on a wire rack. Lay a sheet of parchment on the counter and place another wire rack on top. Use a pancake turner to lift the cookies onto the wire rack.

Place ⅓ teaspoon of the remaining espresso powder in a small bowl and use your thumb and index finger to sprinkle it over the surface of the cookies. Alternatively, use the brush, dipping it into the espresso powder and then lightly tapping it over the cookies.

While the first batch of cookies is baking, roll out the dough balls for the second batch. Repeat baking, cooling, and applying the espresso powder with the second and then third batches.

STORE Airtight: room temperature, 3 weeks; frozen, 6 months.

Kourambiethes

OVEN TEMPERATURE 350°F/175°C

BAKING TIME 15 to 20 minutes for each of three batches

I am a fool for explosively light, crunchy with nuts, and powdery with sugar coating cookies with a lingering taste of butter. Many nationalities have a variation on this theme, such as Mexican or Portuguese wedding cakes, both made with finely ground pecans, but it is the Greek version (pronounced koo-rahm-BYEH-thes) that pleases me the most, especially this one. After I thought I had perfected the recipe, my protégé and closest friend David Shamah suggested using clarified butter, because many Middle Eastern cookies made with clarified butter have an exceptional melt-in-the-mouth quality. He mentioned that cookbook author and friend Paula Wolfert beats the chilled clarified butter, which lightens the texture of the cookies.

SPECIAL EQUIPMENT Two 15 by 12 inch cookie sheets, no preparation needed or lined with parchment

Cookie Dough

MAKES 40 OUNCES/1,134 GRAMS

	VOLUME	WEIGHT	
unsalted butter (65° to 75°F/ 19° to 23°C)	4 sticks	1 pound	454 grams
slivered almonds	1 cup	4.2 ounces	120 grams
powdered sugar	1 cup (lightly spooned into the cup and leveled off)	4.1 ounces	115 grams
2 large egg yolks	2 tablespoons plus 1 teaspoon (35 ml)	1.3 ounces	37 grams
pure vanilla extract	1 teaspoon (5 ml)	.	.
brandy, or orange juice, freshly squeezed and strained	3 tablespoons (44 ml)	1.5 ounces	42 grams
bleached all-purpose flour	3½ cups (lightly spooned into the cup and leveled off)	15 ounces	424 grams
baking powder, preferably aluminum free (see Notes, page 329)	1 tablespoon plus 1 teaspoon	0.6 ounce	18 grams
powdered sugar, for dusting	1 cup (lightly spooned into the cup and leveled off)	4.1 ounces	115 grams

CLARIFY THE BUTTER Have ready a fine-mesh or cheesecloth-lined strainer suspended over a medium bowl, preferably silicone (see Notes, page 329).

In a medium heavy saucepan over medium-low heat, melt the butter. When the butter looks clear, cook, watching carefully, without stirring. Move aside any foam that forms in order to check the progress of the solids. (If necessary, skim off some of the foam and discard it.) As soon as the milk solids at the bottom barely begin to color (the bubbling will diminish), immediately pour the butter through the strainer into the bowl.

Chill the clarified butter until solid, about 2 hours. Refrigerate or freeze the milk solids for a future use (see page 514).

PREHEAT THE OVEN Twenty minutes or longer before baking, set an oven rack in the middle of the oven and preheat the oven to 350°F/175°C.

TOAST THE ALMONDS Spread the almonds evenly on a baking sheet and bake for about 7 minutes, or until pale gold. Stir once or twice to ensure even toasting and avoid over-browning. Cool completely and chop medium-fine.

MAKE THE DOUGH Unmold the clarified butter onto a cutting board. (If not using a silicone container, dip the container into a bowl of very hot water for a few seconds, or until it can be unmolded.) Cut the butter into ½ inch cubes and set the cubes in the bowl of a stand mixer fitted with the flat beater. Add the 1 cup of powdered sugar and, starting on low speed, beat until the sugar mixes into the butter. Raise the speed to medium and beat for 10 minutes. The mixture will lighten in color and be very creamy. Scrape down the sides of the bowl. Add the egg yolks, vanilla, and brandy, and beat for 1 minute. Add the almonds and beat on low speed for a few seconds to combine thoroughly. In a small bowl, whisk together the flour and baking powder and, on the lowest speed, add it to the mixture and beat just until incorporated, about 20 seconds. The dough will be soft and slightly tacky.

Cover the bowl with plastic wrap and refrigerate for 20 to 30 minutes to firm slightly.

SHAPE THE DOUGH Remove one-third (about 13.3 ounces/378 grams) of the dough from the mixer bowl to a small bowl. Cover the mixer bowl and return it to the refrigerator. Pinch off 12 walnut size pieces of dough, 1.1 ounces/31.5 grams each. Roll each piece of dough gently between the palms of your hands into a 1½ inch ball. Do not be concerned if there are small cracks around the edges. Set the dough balls on a cookie sheet a minimum of 1½ inches apart and flatten them to 2 inches wide by ½ inch high.

BAKE THE COOKIES Bake for 8 minutes. For even baking, rotate the cookie sheet halfway around. Continue baking for 7 to 12 minutes, or just until they begin to brown very lightly.

COOL THE COOKIES Set the cookie sheet on a wire rack. Lay a sheet of parchment on the counter and place another wire rack on top. Use a pancake turner to lift the cookies onto the other wire rack.

While each batch of cookies is baking, shape the dough for the next batch.

DUST THE COOKIES WITH POWDERED SUGAR Spoon the powdered sugar for dusting into a sifter or fine-mesh strainer and coat the cookies. After giving the cookies a first coat, repeat, dusting them with a second coat so that they are heavily coated with the sugar. Let them cool completely. Lift away the rack and sift any remaining powdered sugar onto the parchment. Set the cookies on top of the sugar to coat the bottoms of the cookies.

STORE THE COOKIES Set the cookies in a container, dusting with powdered sugar between each layer of cookies. To keep moisture from softening the sugar and making it sticky, leave the container uncovered for 8 hours before covering it tightly. This will maintain the powdery sugar coating.

STORE Airtight: room temperature, 1 month; frozen, 6 months (redust with powdered sugar).

NOTES The baking powder will not cause the dough to puff. Its function is to add tenderness. Aluminum-based baking powder will produce a bitter taste, so be sure to use a nonaluminum based one, such as Rumford or Argo.

A silicone container is ideal for the clarified butter because its flexibility makes unmolding so easy.

Pepparkakors

OVEN TEMPERATURE 350°F/175°C

BAKING TIME 8 to 9 minutes for each of four batches

*W*oody's t'ai chi *Sifu* ("master"), Paul Abdella, gave Woody his treasured family recipe for this unusual Norwegian cookie. The black pepper gives the cookie a subtle underlying sensation of heat on the palate that brings the spicy flavors into harmony. These are perfect as they are, but when spread with a soft goat cheese, they also serve as a delicious and unusual savory hors d'oeuvre.

PLAN AHEAD Freeze the dough at least 8 hours ahead of baking the cookies.

SPECIAL EQUIPMENT Two 15 by 12 inch cookie sheets, lightly coated with nonstick cooking spray and then wiped to give a thin coating | One 12 by 1⅝ (measured from the inside) cardboard tube from a paper towel roll, cut into quarters (or four 3 inch lengths of PVC plastic piping) | A heavy sharp knife with a 1½ to 2 inch wide blade, preferably a cleaver

Cookie Dough

MAKES 16.2 OUNCES/460 GRAMS

	VOLUME	WEIGHT	
bleached all-purpose flour	1¼ cups (lightly spooned into the cup and leveled off) plus 2 tablespoons	5.9 ounces	167 grams
baking soda	½ teaspoon	.	2.7 grams
fine sea salt	¼ teaspoon	.	1.5 grams
ground ginger	½ tablespoon	.	1.5 grams
ground cinnamon	1 teaspoon	.	2.2 grams
ground cloves	1 teaspoon	.	2.5 grams
freshly ground black pepper	¾ teaspoon	.	1.9 grams
unsalted butter (65° to 75°F/ 19° to 23°C)	8 tablespoons (1 stick)	4 ounces	113 grams
granulated sugar	½ cup	3.5 ounces	100 grams
molasses, preferably Grandma's light	¼ cup (59 ml), cup lightly coated with cooking spray	2.8 ounces	80 grams
Demerara or pearl sugar	¼ cup	1.8 ounces	50 grams

MIX THE DRY INGREDIENTS In a medium bowl, whisk together the flour, baking soda, salt, ginger, cinnamon, cloves, and pepper.

MAKE THE DOUGH In the bowl of a stand mixer fitted with the flat beater, beat the butter and granulated sugar on medium speed until light and creamy, about 1 minute. Scrape down the sides of the bowl. Scrape in the molasses and beat until incorporated. Scrape down the sides of the bowl. Detach the flat beater and use it to stir in the flour mixture until moistened. Reattach the flat beater and beat on low speed until evenly incorporated, about 15 seconds. The dough will resemble a thick, fluffy buttercream.

Scrape the dough onto a large sheet of plastic wrap. Use the plastic wrap to knead the dough a few times until it becomes one smooth piece. Wrap the dough loosely with the plastic wrap and flatten it into a 5 by 4 inch rectangle. Refrigerate the dough for at least 1 hour, or until firm enough to shape. (An instant-read thermometer should read below 63°F/17°C.)

SHAPE THE DOUGH INTO LOGS Divide the dough into quarters, about 4.1 ounces/ 115 grams each. Work with 1 piece at a time. Wrap the remaining pieces in plastic wrap and refrigerate.

Roll 1 piece of dough between the palms of your hands into a log just under 1⅝ inches in diameter, about 3 inches long. Lightly tamp each end on the work surface to flatten it. Wrap the dough log in plastic wrap and slide it into one of the cardboard tubes. Stand the tube on the work surface. With your fingers, press the dough down until it reaches the bottom and fits snugly into the tube. Repeat with the other 3 pieces of dough. Stand the tubes on end in the freezer.

If not using the cardboard tube, roll the dough logs to about 1⅝ inches in diameter. Wrap with plastic wrap and freeze the dough logs for 1 hour. Remove them from the freezer and quickly roll them again to minimize flattening. Then stand them on end. The dough logs need to freeze for at least 8 hours, or until an instant-read thermometer reads below 32°F/0°C, to firm them for even cutting. The dough cuts most easily when slightly thawed.

The unbaked dough can be frozen for up to 3 months.

PREHEAT THE OVEN Twenty minutes or longer before baking, set an oven rack in the middle of the oven and preheat the oven to 350°F/175°C.

CUT THE DOUGH INTO COOKIES In a small bowl, place the Demerara sugar.

Remove 1 of the frozen dough logs from the freezer and let it soften slightly. Cut 15 to 17 slices, each ⅛ inch thick. While you are cutting the dough, the log will start to flatten. Simply roll it lightly to maintain the round shape. Set the dough rounds ½ inch apart on the cookie sheet. Smooth any rough edges with a small metal spatula. Sprinkle each cookie with a little of the Demerara sugar and bake at once.

BAKE THE COOKIES Bake for 4 minutes. For even baking, rotate the cookie sheet halfway around. Continue baking for 4 to 5 minutes, or until set to the touch. Pressing lightly on the cookie with a fingertip should leave only a slight impression.

COOL THE COOKIES Set the cookie sheet on a wire rack and let the cookies cool for about 1 minute, or just until they can be lifted without distorting their shapes. Use a pancake turner to lift the cookies onto another wire rack. (Do not leave them on the cookie sheet because they will continue to bake and become too brittle.)

While each batch of cookies is baking, remove the next dough log to soften and slice the dough for the next batch.

STORE Airtight: room temperature, 1 month; refrigerated, 3 months; frozen, 6 months.

Variation: HOT NICK PEPPARKAKORS

Fellow t'ai chi student and chef Nick Cronin suggested upping the ante by replacing some of the black pepper with cayenne pepper. This not only increases the fire but also intensifies the peppery flavor. Replace ¼ teaspoon of the black pepper with ⅛ teaspoon cayenne pepper.

LUXURY OATMEAL COOKIES

MAKES THIRTY-SIX 3 INCH COOKIES

OVEN TEMPERATURE
225°F/107°C for the granola; 375°F/190°C for the cookies

BAKING TIME
20 to 22 minutes for the granola; 12 to 15 minutes for the cookies for each of three batches

*W*hat makes this cookie really special is that instead of adding rolled oats and nuts to the dough, I make my own granola. The oats and nuts get tossed with just enough brown sugar and maple syrup to sweeten them lightly and then they are baked at a very low temperature to crisp and infuse them with the sweetener and fully bring out their flavor. The granola recipe, a gift from my multi-talented friend and fellow cookbook author Caitlin Williams Freeman of San Francisco MOMA and Blue Bottle Coffee, also contains cinnamon and vanilla, and any left over is excellent sprinkled over yogurt. These cookies are crisp and chewy and soften slightly on storage.

SPECIAL EQUIPMENT One 17¼ by 12¼ by 1 inch half sheet pan | Two 15 by 12 inch cookie sheets, no preparation needed or lined with parchment

GRANOLA

MAKES ABOUT 5 CUPS/18.3 OUNCES/520 GRAMS

	VOLUME	WEIGHT	
old-fashioned rolled oats	3 cups	7.8 ounces	222 grams
walnut halves, coarsely chopped	1 cup	3.5 ounces	100 grams
light brown Muscovado sugar, or dark brown sugar	¼ cup, firmly packed	1.9 ounces	54 grams
ground cinnamon	1 teaspoon	.	2.2 grams
fine sea salt	½ teaspoon	.	3 grams
pure maple syrup	6 tablespoons (89 ml)	4.5 ounces	127 grams
canola or safflower oil, at room temperature	3 tablespoons (44 ml)	1.4 ounces	40 grams
pure vanilla extract	½ tablespoon (7.5 ml)	.	.

PREHEAT THE OVEN Twenty minutes or longer before baking, set an oven rack in the middle of the oven and preheat the oven to 225°F/107°C.

Molasses Sugar Butter Cookies (page 341) and Luxury Oatmeal Cookies

MAKE THE GRANOLA In a large bowl, toss together the oats, walnuts, brown sugar, cinnamon, and salt. Pour on the maple syrup, oil, and vanilla and toss to coat the oat mixture thoroughly. Spread the mixture evenly on the half sheet pan and bake for 20 minutes. Turn the pan halfway around after the first 10 minutes. Remove the pan to a wire rack to cool to room temperature. You will need 4 cups/14.8 ounces/420 grams of granola for the cookie dough.

Raise the oven temperature to 375°F/190°C.

COOKIE DOUGH

MAKES 53.3 OUNCES/1,512 GRAMS

	VOLUME	WEIGHT	
Granola	4 cups	14.8 ounces	420 grams
raisins	1½ cups	7.6 ounces	216 grams
bittersweet chocolate chips, 55% to 63% cacao (see Note, page 337)	1 cup	6 ounces	170 grams
bleached all-purpose flour	1¾ cups (lightly spooned into the cup and leveled off) plus 2 tablespoons	8 ounces	227 grams
baking powder	1 teaspoon	.	4.5 grams
baking soda	1 teaspoon	.	5.5 grams
fine sea salt	½ teaspoon	.	3 grams
2 large eggs	⅓ cup plus 1 tablespoon (94 ml)	3.5 ounces	100 grams
pure vanilla extract	1 teaspoon (5 ml)	.	.
light brown Muscovado sugar, or dark brown sugar	⅔ cup, firmly packed	5 ounces	145 grams
granulated sugar	2 tablespoons	0.9 ounce	25 grams
unsalted butter (65° to 75°F/ 19° to 23°C)	16 tablespoons (2 sticks)	8 ounces	227 grams

MAKE THE COOKIE DOUGH In a large bowl, toss together the granola, raisins, and chocolate chips. Store any extra granola, in an airtight container, refrigerated for up to 3 months.

In a small bowl, whisk together the flour, baking powder, baking soda, and salt.

In another small bowl, lightly whisk together the eggs and vanilla.

FOOD PROCESSOR METHOD In a food processor, process the brown sugar and granulated sugar until blended. Cut the butter into a few pieces and add it with the motor running. Process until smooth and creamy, scraping down the sides of the bowl if necessary.

HIGHLIGHTS FOR SUCCESS

The dough must rest for a minimum of 30 minutes after mixing for the oats to soften and the moisture to distribute evenly. Without this resting period, the oats would be harder and the moisture in the dough would cause it to spread more.

With the motor off, add the egg mixture. Process just until incorporated. Scrape down the sides of the bowl and add the flour mixture. Pulse just until all of the flour disappears.

STAND MIXER METHOD In the bowl of a stand mixer fitted with the flat beater, on low speed, beat the brown sugar and granulated sugar until blended. Add the butter and beat on medium speed until smooth and creamy, about 1 minute. Scrape down the sides of the bowl. With the mixer on, add the egg mixture and beat on medium speed for 30 seconds, or until incorporated. Scrape down the sides of the bowl and add the flour mixture. Beat on low speed just until all of the flour disappears.

COMBINE THE COOKIE DOUGH AND GRANOLA AND CHILL With a wooden spatula or your hands, mix the dough into the granola until evenly incorporated. The dough will be sticky. Wrap the dough in plastic wrap and refrigerate it for a minimum of 30 minutes or up to 24 hours. Divide the dough into thirds, about 17.8 ounces/504 grams each. Wrap 2 of the pieces in plastic wrap and refrigerate them while rolling the first piece.

ROLL THE DOUGH INTO BALLS Scoop out 12 pieces of dough (2 level tablespoons/ 1.5 ounces/42 grams each). Roll each piece of dough between the palms of your floured hands into a 1¾ inch ball. Set the dough balls a minimum of 2 inches apart on a cookie sheet and press them down to about 2 inches wide by ¾ inch high.

BAKE THE COOKIES Bake the cookies for 6 minutes. For even baking, rotate the cookie sheet halfway around. Continue baking for 6 to 9 minutes. The cookies should be brown around the edges, just begin to brown on the tops, and still feel slightly soft when pressed lightly with a fingertip.

COOL THE COOKIES Set the cookie sheet on a wire rack and let the cookies cool for 1 minute so that they will be firm enough to transfer to a wire rack to finish cooling. Use a pancake turner to lift the cookies onto another wire rack. They will firm up as they cool and are most delicious when eaten slightly warm.

While each batch of cookies is baking, shape the dough for the next batch.

STORE Airtight: room temperature, 2 weeks; refrigerated, 1 month; frozen, 3 months.

NOTE Use your favorite chocolate. Recommendations are Ghirardelli bittersweet chips 60%, Scharffen Berger bittersweet chunks 61%, or Valrhona dark chocolate baking pearls 55%.

Gingersnaps

MAKES THIRTY-TWO 3 INCH COOKIES

OVEN TEMPERATURE
350°F/175°C

BAKING TIME
10 to 12 minutes for each of three batches

*T*hese cookies were adapted from the ones I loved so much on my first visit to my brilliant friend Kate Coldrick in Devon, England. Because flour available in the United States is different from that in the United Kingdom, I chose to add one extra egg white to my recipe. The result is equally crisp and chewy, but slightly puffier. If you live in the UK, see the Notes on page 340 for the original recipe ingredients. The golden syrup and golden superfine (caster) sugar (available from India Tree; see page 527) both contribute to the best tasting gingersnaps ever.

SPECIAL EQUIPMENT Two 15 by 12 inch cookie sheets, nonstick or lined with parchment

Cookie Dough

MAKES 30 OUNCES/850 GRAMS

	VOLUME	WEIGHT	
unsalted butter	8 tablespoons (1 stick)	4 ounces	113 grams
golden syrup or corn syrup	⅓ cup (79 ml)	4 ounces	113 grams
bleached all-purpose flour	2¾ cups (lightly spooned into the cup and leveled off) plus 2 tablespoons	12.3 ounces	348 grams
golden baker's sugar or caster sugar (see Notes, page 340)	1 cup	7 ounces	200 grams
baking powder	1 tablespoon plus 1 teaspoon	0.6 ounce	18 grams
baking soda	2 teaspoons	.	11 grams
fine sea salt	½ teaspoon	.	3 grams
ground ginger	3 teaspoons	.	3 grams
1 large egg, at room temperature	3 tablespoons plus ½ teaspoon (47 ml)	1.8 ounces	50 grams
1 large egg white, at room temperature	2 tablespoons (30 ml)	1 ounce	30 grams

PREHEAT THE OVEN Twenty minutes or longer before baking, set an oven rack in the middle of the oven and preheat the oven to 350°F/175°C.

MELT THE BUTTER WITH THE GOLDEN SYRUP In a medium heavy saucepan over low heat, stirring constantly with a silicone spatula, heat the butter and golden syrup until the butter is almost fully melted. Remove the pan from the heat and stir until the butter is fully melted. Let the mixture cool for about 10 minutes, or until cool to the touch, while measuring the rest of the ingredients.

MIX THE DRY INGREDIENTS Into the bowl of a stand mixer fitted with the flat beater, sift together the flour, sugar, baking powder, baking soda, salt, and ginger. Mix on low speed for 30 seconds to blend well.

MIX THE EGG AND EGG WHITE In a small bowl, lightly whisk the egg and the egg white.

MAKE THE DOUGH Add the butter mixture to the flour mixture and beat on low speed for 1 minute until evenly combined. The mixture will be crumbly. Add the egg mixture and mix for about 30 seconds until well combined. Scrape down the sides of the bowl.

Divide the dough into thirds, about 10 ounces/283 grams each. Wrap each third in plastic wrap and refrigerate for a minimum of 30 minutes or up to 24 hours.

ROLL THE DOUGH INTO BALLS If the dough has been chilled for more than 30 minutes, remove each batch about 10 minutes before rolling to make it malleable. Pinch off 10 heaping tablespoons of dough (0.9 ounce/27 grams each). Roll each piece of dough between the palms of your hands into a 1¼ inch ball. Add any small amount of dough remaining to the third batch of dough. Set the dough balls a minimum of 2 inches apart on a cookie sheet.

BAKE THE COOKIES Bake the cookies for 5 minutes. For even baking, rotate the cookie sheet halfway around. Continue baking for 5 to 7 minutes. Cracks will appear on the surface and the cookies should be golden brown. The cookies will still feel slightly soft when pressed very lightly with a fingertip but not keep an impression. (An instant-read thermometer inserted into the center of a cookie should read 200° to 212°F/93° to 100°C.)

COOL THE COOKIES Set the cookie sheet on a wire rack and let the cookies cool for 5 minutes so that they will be firm enough to transfer to a wire rack to finish cooling. Use a pancake turner to lift the cookies onto another wire rack. They will firm up as they cool, resulting in a crispy surface and soft, chewy interior. (Baking longer will result in a darker cookie that is crisper throughout.)

While the first batch of cookies is baking, roll out the 10 dough balls for the second batch and again add any remaining dough to the third batch, which will make 12 cookies.

STORE Airtight: room temperature, 1 week; refrigerated, 2 weeks; frozen, 3 months.

Highlights for Success

Heating the butter until just melted and then allowing the butter mixture to stand until cool to the touch will give the cookies the nicest shape. If the mixture is warmer, it will cause the cookies to spread more and puff less.

Keeping the dough cool in between batches prevents the baking soda from activating, ensuring cookies that are uniform in size and shape. The time it takes to roll the 10 dough balls is about the same as it takes to bake the first batch.

NOTES A combination of ¾ cup fine or superfine granulated sugar (5.3 ounces/150 grams) and ¼ cup light brown sugar (1.9 ounces/54 grams) can be substituted for the golden sugar. (If using superfine sugar, the surface of the cookies will not have cracks.)

For UK bakers, use 12 ounces/340 grams self-raising flour, eliminate the baking powder and salt, and use only 1 egg. If the dough is too crumbly, mix in more egg.

MOLASSES SUGAR BUTTER COOKIES

MAKES THIRTY-TWO 2¾ INCH COOKIES

OVEN TEMPERATURE 375°F/190°C

BAKING TIME 8 to 10 minutes for each of three batches

When Woody and I appeared on Sally Longo's television show, *Dinner at 8*, Sally brought her favorite molasses cookies. We loved the chewy middle and crisp crust and immediately asked for the recipe. The original came from Sally's aunt Evelyn, who made the cookies with shortening, which was responsible for the special texture. Because I prefer the taste of butter, especially beurre noisette ("browned butter"), we tried substituting it for the shortening. Clarifying the butter removes the milk solids and water, making it comparable in moisture to shortening and producing the same terrific texture.

SPECIAL EQUIPMENT Two 15 by 12 inch cookie sheets, no preparation needed or lined with parchment | Optional: a 1½ inch diameter cookie scoop

COOKIE DOUGH

MAKES 26.5 OUNCES/750 GRAMS

	VOLUME	WEIGHT	
unsalted butter	16 tablespoons (2 sticks)	8 ounces	227 grams
bleached all-purpose flour	2¼ cups (lightly spooned into the cup and leveled off)	9.6 ounces	272 grams
baking soda	2 teaspoons	.	11 grams
fine sea salt	¼ plus ⅛ teaspoon	.	2.3 grams
ground cinnamon	1 teaspoon	.	2.2 grams
ground cloves	½ teaspoon	.	1.3 grams
ground ginger	½ teaspoon	.	0.5 gram
superfine sugar	¾ cup plus 1½ tablespoons	6 ounces	170 grams
molasses, preferably Grandma's light	¼ cup (59 ml), cup lightly coated with cooking spray	2.8 ounces	80 grams
1 large egg, at room temperature	3 tablespoons plus ½ teaspoon (47 ml)	1.8 ounces	50 grams
superfine sugar, for rolling the dough balls (see Notes, page 343)	⅓ cup	2.3 ounces	67 grams

CLARIFY AND BROWN THE BUTTER (BEURRE NOISETTE) Have ready a fine-mesh or cheese-cloth-lined strainer suspended over a 1 cup glass measure with a spout.

In a medium heavy saucepan over very low heat, melt the butter. Raise the heat to low and cook, uncovered, watching carefully to prevent burning. Move away any foam on the surface to check the progress. As soon as the milk solids become a deep brown, immediately pour the butter through the strainer into the measure, scraping the solids into the strainer.

Measure or weigh ¾ cup/177 ml/5.1 ounces/146 grams of the butter and add the browned solids to it. Let it cool to below 80°F/27°C (see Notes, page 343).

MIX THE DRY INGREDIENTS In a medium bowl, whisk together the flour, baking soda, salt, cinnamon, cloves, and ginger.

MAKE THE DOUGH In the bowl of a stand mixer fitted with the flat beater, mix the clarified butter, sugar, molasses, and egg on low speed for 1 minute. Add the flour mixture. Start on the lowest speed to moisten the flour. Raise the speed to low and beat for 30 seconds.

Scrape the dough onto a piece of plastic wrap and divide it into thirds, about 8.8 ounces/ 250 grams each. Wrap each piece in plastic wrap and refrigerate for 1 hour, or until firm enough to handle.

PREHEAT THE OVEN Thirty minutes or longer before baking, set an oven rack in the middle of the oven and preheat the oven to 375°F/190°C.

ROLL THE DOUGH INTO BALLS In a small bowl or large custard cup, place the sugar for rolling the dough balls. Remove one piece of dough from the refrigerator.

Measure the dough into the cookie scoop and level it off with a small metal spatula, or scoop out a heaping tablespoon (0.8 ounce/23 grams). There will be 11 pieces of dough. Roll each piece between the palms of your hands into a 1¼ inch ball.

After making each dough ball, roll it around in the bowl of sugar to coat it well. Set the dough balls a minimum of 1½ inches apart on a cookie sheet.

BAKE THE COOKIES Bake for 4 minutes. For even baking, rotate the cookie sheet halfway around. They will still be ball shaped. Continue baking for 4 to 6 minutes. The cookies will flatten, and cracks will appear on the surface, but the inside will look slightly underbaked.

COOL THE COOKIES Set the cookie sheet on a wire rack and let the cookies cool for 5 minutes so that they will be firm enough to transfer to a wire rack to finish cooling. Use a pancake turner to lift the cookies onto another wire rack to finish cooling. The cookies will firm up as they cool, resulting in a crispy surface and soft, chewy interior. (Baking longer will result in a darker cookie that is crisper throughout.)

While each batch of cookies is baking, shape the dough for the next batch.

Highlights for Success

Keeping the dough cool in between batches prevents the baking soda from activating, ensuring cookies that are uniform in size and shape. The time it takes to roll the 11 dough balls is about the same as it takes to bake the first batch.

The raw dough freezes nicely. However, if the dough is not baked on the same day it is mixed, the cookies will be slightly larger, flatter, and darker in color.

STORE Airtight: room temperature, 1 week; refrigerated, 2 weeks; frozen, 3 months.

NOTES Superfine sugar will give the finest, most even crunch to the surface of the cookies, but if desired, turbinado sugar can be used instead and will offer more sparkle.

It is essential to clarify the butter, because just melting it would result in a thinner cookie that doesn't bake through.

If the brown butter is used at a temperature higher than 80°F/27°C, the cookies will not expand to 2¾ inches and will not form cracks. They will also require another 2 minutes of baking.

Variation: MOLASSES SUGAR COOKIES MADE WITH SHORTENING

To make the cookies using shortening instead of butter, substitute an equal weight or volume of solid shortening (preferably Spectrum), melted and cooled for about 1 hour, or until no longer warm to the touch. (Melted, it will measure ⅔ cup/158 ml.) Decrease the flour to 2 cups/8.5 ounces/242 grams.

Hazelnut Praline Cookies

OVEN TEMPERATURE

350°F/175°C for the hazelnuts; 375°F/190°C for the hazelnut cookies

BAKING TIME

20 minutes for the hazelnuts; 12 to 14 minutes for the cookies for each of two batches

*T*hese crisp and chewy cookies are for the hazelnut lover. They evolved from the hazelnut cookie tart crust on page 285, but using homemade caramelized praline powder instead of praline paste gives a crunchier texture.

SPECIAL EQUIPMENT FOR THE HAZELNUT POWDER: One baking sheet, no preparation needed or topped with a nonstick liner such as a Silpat | If not using the nonstick liner, a second baking sheet topped with aluminum foil and lightly coated with nonstick cooking spray

FOR THE HAZELNUT COOKIES: Two 15 by 12 inch cookie sheets, no preparation needed or lined with parchment

Hazelnut Praline Powder

MAKES 2⅓ CUPS/9.3 OUNCES/265 GRAMS

	VOLUME	WEIGHT	
water	3 cups (710 ml)	25 ounces	710 grams
baking soda	¼ cup	2.1 ounces	60 grams
hazelnuts	1½ cups	7.5 ounces	213 grams
granulated sugar	⅓ cup	2.3 ounces	67 grams
water	⅓ cup (79 ml)	2.8 ounces	79 grams

PREHEAT THE OVEN Twenty minutes or longer before baking, set an oven rack in the middle of the oven and preheat the oven to 350°F/175°C.

REMOVE THE HAZELNUT SKINS In a 3 quart or larger saucepan, bring the 3 cups/710 ml water to a boil. Remove from the heat and stir in the baking soda. The water will bubble furiously. Add the hazelnuts and return the pan to the heat. Boil the nuts for 3 minutes. The water will turn a deep maroon from the color of the skins. Test a nut by running it under cold water. The skin should slip off easily. If it does not, boil for a couple of minutes longer. Pour the nuts into a colander and rinse them under cold running water. Place several nuts in a bowl of cold water. Slide off the skins and place the nuts on a clean dish towel to dry. As necessary, empty the bowl, refill with cold water, and add more nuts.

TOAST THE HAZELNUTS Set the hazelnuts on the baking sheet and bake for about 20 minutes, or until lightly browned. Stir once or twice to ensure even toasting and avoid overbrowning. Set the baking sheet on a wire rack. If not using the Silpat, transfer the hazelnuts to the second baking sheet.

MAKE THE PRALINE POWDER In a small saucepan, preferably nonstick, stir together the granulated sugar and the ⅓ cup/79 ml water and heat, stirring constantly, until the sugar dissolves and comes to a boil. Continue boiling, without stirring, until the syrup caramelizes to deep amber (an instant-read thermometer should read about 370°F/188°C or a few degrees lower because the temperature will continue to rise).

Immediately remove the pan from the heat and pour the caramel over the hazelnuts. Let it harden completely, about 15 to 30 minutes.

Remove the praline from the sheet and break it into several pieces. In a food processor, pulse the praline until it is powder fine.

COOKIE DOUGH

MAKES 11.2 OUNCES/318 GRAMS

	VOLUME	WEIGHT	
unsalted butter, cold	4 tablespoons (½ stick)	2 ounces	57 grams
bleached all-purpose flour	⅔ cup (lightly spooned into the cup and leveled off)	2.8 ounces	80 grams
baking soda	½ teaspoon	.	2.7 grams
fine sea salt	1/16 teaspoon	.	0.4 gram
superfine sugar	3 tablespoons	1.3 ounces	37 grams
Hazelnut Praline Powder (see Notes, page 346)	1 cup	4 ounces	113 grams
canola or safflower oil, at room temperature	1 teaspoon (5 ml)	.	4 grams
½ large egg	1½ tablespoons (23 ml)	0.9 ounce	25 grams
pure vanilla extract	¼ teaspoon (1.2 ml)	.	.

MAKE THE DOUGH Cut the butter into 1 inch cubes and refrigerate until ready to use.

Into a small bowl, sift together the flour, baking soda, and salt. Whisk to combine well.

FOOD PROCESSOR METHOD In a food processor, place the superfine sugar. (Granulated sugar can also be used, processed for several minutes or until very fine.) With the motor running, add the butter cubes. Add the praline powder and oil and process until smooth and creamy, about 20 seconds. With the motor running, add the egg and vanilla and process until incorporated. Scrape down the sides of the bowl. Add the flour mixture and pulse just until incorporated.

STAND MIXER METHOD Soften the butter to 65° to 75°F/19° to 23°C.

In the bowl of a stand mixer fitted with the flat beater, on medium speed, beat together the superfine sugar, butter, praline powder, and oil for several minutes, or until very smooth and creamy. Add the egg and vanilla and beat until incorporated, scraping down the sides of the bowl. On low speed, gradually beat in the flour mixture just until incorporated.

CHILL THE DOUGH Scrape the dough onto a piece of plastic wrap and divide it in half, about 5.6 ounces/159 grams each. Wrap each piece in plastic wrap and refrigerate for a minimum of 1 hour before shaping.

PREHEAT THE OVEN Thirty minutes or longer before baking, set an oven rack in the middle of the oven and preheat the oven to 375°F/190°C.

ROLL THE DOUGH INTO BALLS Scoop out 15 rounded teaspoons of dough (0.4 ounce/10 grams each). Roll each piece of dough between the palms of your hands into a 1 inch ball. Set the dough balls a minimum of 1½ inches apart on a cookie sheet and press them down to 1½ inches wide by ½ inch high.

BAKE THE COOKIES Bake for 7 minutes. For even baking, rotate the cookie sheet halfway around. Continue baking for 5 to 7 minutes, or until lightly browned and set. A fingertip pressed lightly onto the top of a cookie will yield slightly to the pressure.

COOL THE COOKIES Set the cookie sheet on a wire rack and let the cookies cool for 1 minute so that they will be firm enough to transfer to a wire rack to finish cooling. Use a pancake turner to lift the cookies onto another wire rack.

While the cookies are baking, shape the dough for the next batch.

STORE Airtight: room temperature, 3 weeks; frozen, 6 months.

NOTES The remaining hazelnut praline powder can be stored in an airtight container, refrigerated for 2 months or frozen for 6 months.

Hazelnut praline paste can be substituted for the hazelnut praline powder and canola oil; however, the cookies will be sweeter and less nutty in flavor. Use ¼ cup plus 2 tablespoons/4 ounces/114 grams. Different brands of commercial praline paste vary widely between 20 and 50 percent sugar. Also, some contain almonds as well as hazelnuts, some roast the nuts, and some use caramelized sugar, all of which will have an impact on the flavor. I recommend American Almond Praline Paste (see page 527) because the nuts are 100 percent hazelnut and are roasted, and because it contains 33 percent sugar. Maison Glass's (see page 527) also contains 100 percent hazelnuts and is 35.3 percent caramelized sugar.

Praline paste needs to be stirred before measuring because the oil tends to separate and rise to the top. Once open, the praline paste keeps refrigerated for about 6 weeks.

My Chocolate Chip Cookies

OVEN TEMPERATURE
325°F/160°C for the walnuts; 375°F/190°C for the cookies

BAKING TIME
7 minutes for the walnuts; 7 to 10 minutes for the cookies for each of two batches

*R*eaders have long been asking me for my version of the chocolate chip cookie, but I always wondered how I could possibly improve on this classic. After much thought, finally I did indeed find a way.

In France, the *financier*, or ingot, is the fingerprint of the pastry chef. In the United States, however, the cookie that can make a pastry chef's reputation is indisputably the chocolate chip cookie. Chocolate chip cookies vary from baker to baker in the proportion of ingredients chosen, the quality of these ingredients, and how the cookies are shaped and baked. My new version is crisp, chewy, and also lactose free if you do not add the browned milk solids. The two most important factors that contribute to its flavor and texture are decreasing the usual amount of sugar and browning the butter—an extra step that offers an amazingly delicious taste and evaporates the water contained in the butter for a firmer cookie. I toast the walnuts lightly to enhance their flavor and remove as much of the bitter peel as possible. I have also reduced the salt for a better balance. Although great with conventional light brown sugar, to make this cookie extra special I use Muscovado light brown sugar from India Tree (see page 511).

PLAN AHEAD For the best flavor and texture, make the cookie dough 12 to 24 hours ahead of baking.

SPECIAL EQUIPMENT Two 15 by 12 inch cookie sheets, no preparation needed or lined with parchment

COOKIE DOUGH

MAKES 22.9 OUNCES/648 GRAMS

	VOLUME	WEIGHT	
unsalted butter	9 tablespoons (1 stick plus 1 tablespoon)	4.5 ounces	127 grams
walnut halves	¾ cup	2.6 ounces	75 grams
bleached all-purpose flour	1⅓ cups (lightly spooned into the cup and leveled off)	5.7 ounces	161 grams
baking soda	½ teaspoon	.	2.7 grams
fine sea salt	¼ teaspoon	.	1.5 grams
light brown Muscovado sugar, or dark brown sugar	¼ cup plus 2 tablespoons, firmly packed	2.9 ounces	81 grams
granulated sugar	2 tablespoons	0.9 ounce	25 grams
1 large egg	3 tablespoons plus ½ teaspoon (47 ml)	1.8 ounces	50 grams
pure vanilla extract	1 teaspoon (5 ml)	.	.
bittersweet chocolate chips, 55% to 63% cacao (see Note, page 350)	1 cup	6 ounces	170 grams

PREHEAT THE OVEN Twenty minutes or longer before baking, set an oven rack in the middle of the oven and preheat the oven to 325°F/160°C.

CLARIFY AND BROWN THE BUTTER (BEURRE NOISETTE) Have ready a fine-mesh or cheesecloth-lined strainer suspended over a 1 cup glass measure with a spout.

In a small heavy saucepan over very low heat, melt the butter. Raise the heat to low and cook, uncovered, watching carefully to prevent burning. Move away any foam on the surface to check the progress. As soon as the milk solids become a deep brown, immediately pour the butter through the strainer into the glass measure, scraping the solids into the strainer.

Measure or weigh 7 tablespoons/104 ml/3 ounces/84 grams of the butter and add the browned solids to it. Let it cool to below 80°F/27°C.

TOAST AND CHOP THE WALNUTS Spread the walnuts evenly on a baking sheet and bake for about 7 minutes to enhance their flavor. Stir once or twice to ensure even toasting and avoid overbrowning. Turn the walnuts onto a clean dish towel and roll and rub them around to loosen the skins. Coarsely break the walnuts, scraping off and discarding as much of the skins as possible. Cool completely and coarsely chop the walnuts.

If baking the cookies shortly after making the dough, raise the oven temperature to 375°F/190°C.

MIX THE DRY INGREDIENTS In a medium bowl, whisk together the flour, baking soda, and salt.

MAKE THE DOUGH In the bowl of a stand mixer fitted with the flat beater, mix the clarified butter, brown sugar, granulated sugar, egg, and vanilla on low speed for 1 minute.

Add the flour mixture. Start on the lowest speed to moisten the flour. Raise the speed to low and beat for 30 seconds. Add the chocolate chips and walnuts and beat on low speed just until evenly incorporated.

Divide the dough in half, about 11.4 ounces/324 grams each. Wrap each piece in plastic wrap and refrigerate. The cookies can be shaped and baked after 30 minutes of chilling, but the baked cookies will be slightly smaller, softer, and more rounded. For flatter, crisper 3 inch cookies, chill the dough for a minimum of 12 hours or up to 24 hours. Remove the dough for each batch about 10 minutes before rolling to make it malleable.

ROLL THE DOUGH INTO BALLS Scoop out 10 heaping tablespoons of dough (1.1 ounces/31 grams each). Roll each piece of dough between the palms of your hands into a 1½ inch ball. Set the dough balls a minimum of 2 inches apart on a cookie sheet and press them down to about 2 inches wide by ½ inch high.

BAKE THE COOKIES Bake for 4 minutes. For even baking, rotate the cookie sheet halfway around. Continue baking for 3 to 6 minutes. The cookies should be brown around the edges, just beginning to brown on the tops, and still feel slightly soft when pressed lightly with a fingertip.

COOL THE COOKIES Set the cookie sheet on a wire rack and let the cookies cool for 1 minute so that they will be firm enough to transfer to a wire rack to finish cooling. Use a pancake turner to lift the cookies onto another wire rack. They will firm up as they cool and are most delicious when eaten slightly warm.

While the first batch of cookies is baking, shape the dough for the second batch.

STORE Airtight: room temperature, 2 weeks; refrigerated, 1 month; frozen, 3 months.

NOTE Use your favorite chocolate. Recommendations are Ghirardelli bittersweet chips 60%, Scharffen Berger bittersweet chunks 61%, or Valrhona dark chocolate baking pearls 55%.

Variation: MELT-IN-THE-MOUTH CHOCOLATE CHIP COOKIES

My friend Maria Menegus adds grated chocolate to her favorite chocolate chip cookies. The grated chocolate dissolves immediately on eating, contributing to a melt-in-the-mouth quality. Simply add 2 ounces/56 grams of grated milk, semisweet, or bittersweet chocolate together with the chocolate chips and walnuts.

Bake the cookies for 12 to 14 minutes. They will form cracks across their tops, but these will diminish slightly while cooling.

DOUBLE CHOCOLATE ORIOLOS

OVEN TEMPERATURE
325°F/160°C

BAKING TIME
20 to 25 minutes for each of three batches

*N*amed to honor Richard Oriolo, who was the art director of many of my cookbooks, these cookies are intensely chocolaty and buttery but light in texture. The cookies are terrific as they are, but the recipe is also a fine addition to Bourbon Pecan Butter Balls (page 406).

SPECIAL EQUIPMENT Two 15 by 12 inch cookie sheets, no preparation needed or lined with parchment

COOKIE DOUGH

MAKES 15.1 OUNCES/429 GRAMS

	VOLUME	WEIGHT	
walnut halves	½ cup	1.8 ounces	50 grams
unsalted butter, cold	10 tablespoons (1¼ sticks)	5 ounces	142 grams
granulated sugar	⅓ cup	2.3 ounces	67 grams
powdered sugar	⅓ cup (lightly spooned into the cup and leveled off)	1.3 ounces	38 grams
unsweetened (alkalized) cocoa powder	¼ cup plus 1 tablespoon (sifted before measuring)	0.8 ounce	23 grams
bleached all-purpose flour	¾ cup (lightly spooned into the cup and leveled off) plus 2½ tablespoons	3.9 ounces	110 grams
granulated sugar, for coating the dough balls	½ cup	3.5 ounces	100 grams

PREHEAT THE OVEN Twenty minutes or longer before baking, set an oven rack in the middle of the oven and preheat the oven to 325°F/160°C.

TOAST AND BREAK THE WALNUTS Spread the walnuts evenly on a baking sheet and bake for about 10 minutes to enhance their flavor. Stir once or twice to ensure even toasting and avoid overbrowning. Turn the walnuts onto a clean dish towel and roll and rub them around to loosen the skins. Coarsely break the nuts into a bowl, scraping off and discarding as much of the skins as possible. Discard the skins and cool the walnuts completely.

MAKE THE DOUGH Cut the butter into 1 inch cubes, wrap in plastic wrap, and refrigerate until ready to use.

In a food processor, process the walnuts, the ⅓ cup granulated sugar, the powdered sugar, and cocoa until the walnuts are finely ground.

Add the butter and pulse it in until the cocoa mixture is absorbed by the butter.

Add the flour and pulse it in until there are a lot of little moist, crumbly pieces and no dry flour particles remain.

Empty the dough into a plastic bag and press it from the outside of the bag just until it holds together. Remove the dough from the plastic bag and place it on a very large sheet of plastic wrap. Using the plastic wrap, knead the dough only a few times until it becomes one smooth piece. Divide the dough into thirds, about 5 ounces/143 grams each. Wrap 2 of the pieces in plastic wrap and refrigerate them while rolling the first piece.

ROLL THE DOUGH INTO BALLS In a small bowl or large custard cup, place the granulated sugar for coating the dough balls. Have ready a flat-bottomed glass tumbler, its bottom lightly coated with nonstick cooking spray.

Measure out 12 scant tablespoons of dough (about 0.4 ounce/12 grams each). Roll each piece of dough between the palms of your hands into a 1 inch ball. Set the dough balls a minimum of 2 inches apart on a cookie sheet.

Coat the bottom of the glass tumbler with sugar by pressing it into the sugar. Use the tumbler to flatten each dough ball to about 1½ inches in diameter. Recoat the tumbler with sugar before flattening the next dough ball.

BAKE THE COOKIES Bake for 10 minutes. For even baking, rotate the cookie sheet halfway around. Continue baking for 10 to 15 minutes, or until the cookies are firm enough to lift from the sheet but still soft when pressed lightly on top. (Do not overbake or the cookies may develop a burned flavor.)

COOL THE COOKIES Set the cookie sheet on a wire rack and let the cookies cool for a couple of minutes so that they will be firm enough to transfer to a wire rack to finish cooling. Use a pancake turner to lift the cookies onto another wire rack. Cool completely.

While each batch of cookies is baking, shape the dough for the next batch.

STORE Airtight: room temperature, 3 weeks; frozen, 6 months.

THE DUTCH PECAN SANDIES

OVEN TEMPERATURE 325°F/160°C

BAKING TIME 20 to 22 minutes for each of two batches

*T*hese flavorful and fragile cookies (pictured on page 323) are downright dangerous: the perfect balance of sugar, spice, and salt that makes you take just one more and then another and another. I met master baker Kierin Baldwin on my first visit to The Dutch in Soho, New York City, when I asked to meet the baker who made the heavenly brioche buns for the restaurant's fried oyster sliders. It turns out Kierin is even better known for her fabulous pies and cookie selection.

SPECIAL EQUIPMENT Two 15 by 12 inch cookie sheets, nonstick or lined with parchment | A 12 by 8 inch or larger flat baking sheet or thin cutting board that can fit in the freezer | A 2 inch plain round cookie cutter, lightly coated inside with nonstick cooking spray

COOKIE DOUGH

MAKES 22.6 OUNCES/642 GRAMS

	VOLUME	WEIGHT	
unsalted butter	16 tablespoons (2 sticks)	8 ounces	227 grams
granulated sugar	3 tablespoons	1.3 ounces	37 grams
turbinado sugar, preferably Sugar in the Raw	2½ tablespoons	1 ounce	30 grams
dark brown sugar	2½ tablespoons, firmly packed	1.3 ounces	37 grams
vanilla powder (or pure vanilla extract)	⅛ teaspoon plus ¹⁄₁₆ teaspoon (or ½ tablespoon/7.5 ml)	.	.
fine sea salt	½ teaspoon plus ⅛ teaspoon	.	3.7 grams
pecan halves	1½ cups	5.3 ounces	150 grams
unbleached all-purpose flour, preferably Gold Medal or Heckers	1½ cups (lightly spooned into the cup and leveled off) plus 3 tablespoons	7.3 ounces	206 grams
whole wheat flour	2½ tablespoons	0.8 ounce	22 grams
ground cinnamon	½ teaspoon plus ⅛ teaspoon	.	1.4 grams

CLARIFY AND BROWN THE BUTTER (BEURRE NOISETTE) Have ready a fine-mesh or cheesecloth-lined strainer suspended over a 2 cup glass measure with a spout.

In a medium heavy saucepan over very low heat, melt the butter. Raise the heat to low and cook, uncovered, watching carefully to prevent burning. Move away any foam on the surface to check the progress. As soon as the milk solids become a deep brown, immediately pour the butter through the strainer into the glass measure, scraping the solids into the strainer.

Measure or weigh ¾ cup plus 1 tablespoon/195 ml/5.7 ounces/161 grams of browned butter. Let it cool until solid, or refrigerate it for 1 to 1½ hours until set but still soft. (If it becomes too hard, let it soften until malleable.) Refrigerate or freeze the milk solids for a future use (see page 514).

PREHEAT THE OVEN Twenty minutes or longer before baking, set an oven rack in the middle of the oven and preheat the oven to 325°F/160°C.

MAKE THE DOUGH In the bowl of a stand mixer fitted with the flat beater, mix the granulated sugar, turbinado sugar, brown sugar, vanilla, and salt on low speed until combined. Add the browned butter and beat, starting on low speed and gradually raising the speed to medium. Continue beating on medium speed for 1 minute. The mixture will become light and like a buttercream in consistency.

In a food processor, pulse the pecans, all-purpose flour, whole wheat flour, and cinnamon until the pecans are coarsely chopped. Add this mixture to the mixer bowl. Beat on low speed for 10 to 15 seconds, or until the dough is well blended and comes away from the sides of the bowl.

CHILL THE DOUGH Scrape the mixture onto a large sheet of plastic wrap. Use the wrap to press down on the dough, kneading it lightly just until smooth.

Divide the dough in half, 11.3 ounces/321 grams each. Wrap each piece loosely in plastic wrap and press to form flat discs. Refrigerate 1 disc while you make the first batch.

ROLL THE DOUGH AND CUT THE COOKIES Roll the dough disc between two large sheets of plastic wrap into a ⅜ inch thick disc, 7½ inches in diameter or larger. Slide the baking sheet under the bottom piece of plastic wrap. Cut out as many 2 inch cookies as possible, but do not remove them from the rest of the dough.

CHILL THE DOUGH Cover the dough with plastic wrap and freeze for about 10 minutes, or until rigid.

Cinnamon Sugar Topping

	VOLUME	WEIGHT	
granulated sugar	1½ tablespoons	0.7 ounce	19 grams
ground cinnamon	¾ teaspoon	.	1.6 grams
turbinado sugar, preferably Sugar in the Raw	1 tablespoon	0.5 ounce	13 grams

MAKE THE TOPPING In a large custard cup or small bowl with a flat bottom, whisk the granulated sugar and cinnamon until uniform in consistency.

Place the turbinado sugar in a small custard cup.

SET THE DOUGH DISCS ON THE COOKIE SHEET Use a small offset spatula or your fingers to peel away the dough surrounding the cut cookies and set it on another sheet of plastic wrap. Cover these dough scraps and let them soften.

Coat both sides of each cookie in the cinnamon sugar mixture. Occasionally stir the sugar and cinnamon. Set the cookies a minimum of ½ inch apart on a cookie sheet. Cover the cookies with plastic wrap and refrigerate while rolling out the remaining dough.

Knead together the dough scraps and reroll them. Cut as many cookies as possible and repeat chilling, coating, and setting a maximum of 16 cookies on the cookie sheet. Sprinkle the cookies lightly using half of the turbinado sugar. Knead any remaining dough into the second batch.

BAKE THE COOKIES Bake for 10 minutes. For even baking, rotate the cookie sheet halfway around. Continue baking for 10 to 12 minutes, or until the cookies turn a golden brown and are firm when pressed very lightly with a fingertip.

COOL THE COOKIES Set the cookie sheet on a wire rack. Let the cookies cool completely. The cookies will be very fragile after baking but will firm up by the following day.

Repeat rolling, cutting, and chilling with the second batch of dough. For the last piece of dough, set it in the cookie cutter and press it down with the handle of a wooden spoon to form an even disc. Use your finger to push it out of the cookie cutter.

STORE Airtight: room temperature, 3 weeks; frozen, 3 months.

THE ISCHLER

OVEN TEMPERATURE 350°F/175°C

BAKING TIME 6 to 10 minutes for each of four batches

𝒯his Austrian cookie ranks as one of the finest of all time. It was created in the wonderful Zauner Bakery in the spa town of Bad Ischl, which was said to be the favorite vacation spot for Emperor Franz Joseph. The classic method is to sandwich the fragile, thin almond cookies with apricot lekvar or preserves and then to dip the cookies halfway into melted chocolate. Because I am one-quarter Austro-Hungarian (my great grandfather fought in Franz Joseph's army), I feel I am qualified to adapt the recipe slightly by spreading the melted chocolate onto the entire inside of the cookies so that I have the glorious taste of apricot and chocolate with every bite.

SPECIAL EQUIPMENT Two 15 by 12 inch cookie sheets, nonstick or lined with parchment | A 2¼ inch scalloped or plain round or heart-shape cookie cutter

COOKIE DOUGH

MAKES 27.6 OUNCES/782 GRAMS

	VOLUME	WEIGHT	
unsalted butter, cold	16 tablespoons (2 sticks)	8 ounces	227 grams
powdered sugar	1 cup (lightly spooned into the cup and leveled off) plus 2 tablespoons	4.7 ounces	132 grams
sliced almonds, preferably unblanched (see Notes, page 361)	2 cups	7 ounces	200 grams
about ½ large egg, lightly beaten	1 tablespoon plus 1 teaspoon (20 ml)	0.7 ounce	21 grams
pure vanilla extract	1 teaspoon (5 ml)	.	.
bleached all-purpose flour	1¾ cups (lightly spooned into the cup and leveled off) plus 1 tablespoon	7.8 ounces	220 grams
fine sea salt	¼ teaspoon	.	1.5 grams

MAKE THE DOUGH FOOD PROCESSOR METHOD Cut the butter into ½ inch cubes and let the cubes soften slightly while measuring out the remaining ingredients. The butter should be cool but soft enough to press flat (60° to 70°F/15° to 21°C).

Process the powdered sugar and almonds until the almonds are very fine. Add the butter and process until smooth and creamy. Add the egg and vanilla and process until incorporated, scraping down the sides of the bowl as needed. In a medium bowl, whisk together the flour and salt. Add it to the processor and pulse just until incorporated. The mixture will be in moist and crumbly particles and hold together if pinched.

STAND MIXER METHOD Soften the butter to 65° to 75°F/19° to 23°C.

Using a nut grater, grate the almonds until very fine.

In the bowl of a stand mixer fitted with the flat beater, cream the almonds, powdered sugar, and butter, starting on low speed and gradually increasing the speed to medium, until fluffy. Scrape down the sides of the bowl. Add the egg and vanilla and beat until blended.

In a medium bowl, whisk together the flour and salt.

On low speed, gradually add the flour mixture to the butter mixture. Mix until incorporated and the dough just begins to come away from the sides of the bowl.

CHILL THE DOUGH Scrape the mixture into a plastic bag and, using your knuckles and the heels of your hands, press it together. Transfer the dough to a large sheet of plastic wrap and use the wrap to press down on the dough, kneading it until it is smooth.

Divide the dough into quarters, about 6.9 ounces/195 grams each. Wrap each piece loosely with plastic wrap and press to flatten into discs. Rewrap tightly and place in a gallon-size reclosable freezer bag. Refrigerate for a minimum of 2 hours or up to 2 days to firm and give the dough a chance to absorb the moisture evenly, which will make rolling easier.

PREHEAT THE OVEN Twenty minutes or longer before baking, set an oven rack in the middle of the oven and preheat the oven to 350°F/175°C.

ROLL AND CUT THE COOKIES Remove a dough disc from the refrigerator and set it on a lightly floured surface. Lightly flour the dough and cover it with plastic wrap. Let the dough soften for about 10 minutes, or until it is malleable enough to roll. Roll the dough ⅛ inch thick, moving it from time to time and adding more flour if necessary to keep it from sticking. (See Notes, page 361.)

Cut out twenty 2¼ inch cookies. Set them a minimum of ½ inch apart on a cookie sheet. Set aside any scraps, covered with plastic wrap, to knead together with the scraps from the next three batches.

BAKE THE COOKIES Bake for 4 minutes. For even baking, rotate the cookie sheet halfway around. Continue baking for 2 to 6 minutes, or just until they begin to brown at the edges.

COOL THE COOKIES Set the cookie sheet on a wire rack and let the cookies cool for about 1 minute so that they will be firm enough to transfer to a wire rack to finish cooling. Use a pancake turner to lift the cookies onto another wire rack. Cool completely.

While each batch of cookies is baking, remove the next dough disc to soften before rolling and then roll the dough for the next batch. After the last batch is cut, if desired, knead together all of the scraps and repeat chilling, rerolling, and cutting.

SUPER FIRM CHOCOLATE GANACHE FILLING

MAKES 1⅓ CUPS/10 OUNCES/285 GRAMS

	VOLUME	WEIGHT	
bittersweet chocolate, 60% to 62% cacao, chopped	.	8 ounces	227 grams
heavy cream, hot	¼ cup (59 ml)	2 ounces	58 grams

MAKE THE GANACHE FILLING In a microwavable bowl, stirring with a silicone spatula every 15 seconds (or in the top of a double boiler set over hot, not simmering, water, stirring often—do not let the bottom of the container touch the water), heat the chocolate until almost completely melted.

Remove the chocolate from the heat source and stir until fully melted.

Pour the cream on top of the chocolate and stir until smooth. The mixture should drop thickly from the spatula. Set it aside in a warm place. If the ganache thickens before all of it is used, it can be restored in the microwave with 3 second bursts or in a double boiler set over hot or simmering water.

APRICOT LEKVAR FILLING

MAKES 2¾ CUPS/651 ML/29.6 OUNCES/840 GRAMS

	VOLUME	WEIGHT	
dried apricots	2⅔ cups	1 pound	454 grams
water	2 cups (473 ml)	16.7 ounces	473 grams
granulated sugar	1 cup plus 2 tablespoons	8 ounces	225 grams
lemon zest, finely grated	2 teaspoons, loosely packed	.	4 grams
apricot or peach brandy	1 teaspoon (5 ml)	.	.

MAKE THE LEKVAR FILLING In a medium saucepan with a tight-fitting lid, combine the dried apricots and water and let them sit for 2 hours to soften.

Bring the water to a boil, cover the pan tightly, and simmer for 20 to 30 minutes on the lowest possible heat until the apricots are very soft when pierced with a skewer. If the water evaporates, add a little extra.

In a food processor, process the apricots and any remaining liquid, the sugar, lemon zest, and brandy until smooth.

Scrape the apricot mixture back into the saucepan and simmer, stirring constantly to prevent scorching, for 10 to 15 minutes, or until deep orange in color and very thick. When lifted, a tablespoon of the mixture will take about 3 seconds to fall from the spoon.

Transfer the lekvar to a bowl and let it cool completely. You will need only about ⅔ cup/ 158 ml/7.1 ounces/202 grams, but it keeps just about indefinitely refrigerated. Making a smaller amount risks scorching the lekvar. Lekvar made from dried apricots is the most delicious and concentrated, but the apricot glaze that follows makes a viable alternative.

FILL THE COOKIES Using a small offset spatula or butter knife, spread the bottoms of half of the cookies, up to ⅛ inch from the edge, with a very thin layer of the apricot filling (about ¾ teaspoon/3.7 ml). Spread the bottoms of the remaining cookies with a slightly thicker layer of the ganache (about ½ tablespoon/6 grams). Set the chocolate coated cookies, coated side down, on the apricot coated cookies. Let them sit for a minimum of 30 minutes for the ganache to set completely.

STORE Airtight: room temperature, 5 days; frozen, 6 months.

Alternative: APRICOT GLAZE

MAKES ABOUT ⅔ CUP/158 ML/8.9 OUNCES/253 GRAMS

	VOLUME	WEIGHT	
apricot preserves	1⅓ cups	14.5 ounces	412 grams

MAKE THE GLAZE Have ready a strainer suspended over a 2 cup microwavable measure with a spout that has been lightly coated with nonstick cooking spray.

In a microwavable container, or in a small saucepan on the cooktop, bring the preserves to a boil. Press them through the strainer into the measure. There will be about 2 tablespoons plus 2 teaspoons of residue to discard and there should be ¾ cup plus 2 tablespoons/207 ml/11.7 ounces/333 grams of strained apricot.

In the microwave, reduce the apricot to about ⅔ cup/158 ml/8.9 ounces/253 grams. It should be very thick but still fluid. (The apricot preserves are applied piping hot so that they are still spreadable in a very thin layer, but when cooled become deliciously intense and sticky.) Set the measure in a pan surrounded by hot water to keep the apricot glaze fluid, or return it to the microwave if it becomes too thick to spread. If necessary, stir in a little water. Spread the apricot glaze on the cookies while it is hot.

NOTES In perfecting the recipe, I discovered that a small decrease in the proportion of butter and almonds to flour and the addition of a very small amount of egg make the dough hold together more easily when rolling and also produce a slightly firmer cookie that is tender but not too fragile. Placing plastic wrap on top of the dough when rolling helps greatly to create smooth dough with no cracks.

Unblanched almonds provide a true almond flavor to the cookie. If you prefer to use blanched almonds, it is a good idea to toast them lightly to bring out the flavor. Be sure to use sliced almonds because they are much easier to grind to a fine consistency.

If you prefer to have a thicker cookie, it's fine to roll the dough ¼ inch thick. Because this will result in only half the number of sandwich cookies, you may opt to double the recipe for the dough.

LEMON JAMMIES

OVEN TEMPERATURE 350°F/175°C

BAKING TIME 10 to 12 minutes for each of four batches

𝓕or the lemon lover, delicate sandwich cookies that can either contain a gilding of jam or be made extra lemony with lemon buttercream or lemon curd, as pictured.

SPECIAL EQUIPMENT Two 15 by 12 inch cookie sheets, nonstick or lined with parchment | A 2¼ inch scalloped or plain round cookie cutter | A ¾ inch round cutter or a large pastry tube

COOKIE DOUGH

MAKES 23.7 OUNCES/672 GRAMS

	VOLUME	WEIGHT	
lemon zest, finely grated	2 tablespoons, loosely packed	.	12 grams
superfine sugar	⅔ cup	4.7 ounces	133 grams
fine sea salt	¼ teaspoon	.	1.5 grams
unsalted butter, cold	13 tablespoons (1½ sticks plus 1 tablespoon)	6.5 ounces	184 grams
1 large egg, lightly beaten	3 tablespoons plus ½ teaspoon (47 ml)	1.8 ounces	50 grams
pure vanilla extract	1 teaspoon (5 ml)	.	.
bleached all-purpose flour	2⅔ cups (lightly spooned into the cup and leveled off)	11.3 ounces	320 grams
Lemon Neoclassic Buttercream (page 365), jam, jelly, or lemon curd; for filling the cookies	½ cup	4 ounces	113 grams

MAKE THE DOUGH FOOD PROCESSOR METHOD Process the lemon zest with the sugar and salt until the zest is very fine.

Cut the butter into several pieces and add it with the motor running. Process until smooth and creamy. Add the egg and vanilla and process until incorporated, scraping down the sides of the bowl as needed. Add the flour and pulse in just until incorporated. The mixture will hold together if pinched.

STAND MIXER METHOD Soften the butter to 65° to 75°F/19° to 23°C. Chop the lemon zest until very fine.

In the bowl of a stand mixer fitted with the flat beater, cream the sugar and butter on medium speed until fluffy. Add the lemon zest, egg, and vanilla and beat until blended. Scrape down the sides of the bowl.

In a small bowl, whisk together the flour and salt.

On low speed, gradually add the flour mixture to the butter mixture. Mix until incorporated and the dough just begins to come away from the sides of the bowl.

CHILL THE DOUGH Scrape the mixture onto a large sheet of plastic wrap and use the wrap to press down on the dough, kneading it until it is smooth.

Divide the dough into thirds, about 7.9 ounces/224 grams each. Wrap each piece loosely with plastic wrap and press to flatten into discs. Rewrap tightly and place in a gallon-size reclosable freezer bag. Refrigerate for 2 hours or up to 2 days to firm and give the dough a chance to absorb the moisture evenly, which will make rolling easier.

PREHEAT THE OVEN Twenty minutes or longer before baking, set an oven rack in the middle of the oven and preheat the oven to 350°F/175°C.

ROLL AND CUT THE COOKIES Remove a dough disc from the refrigerator and set it on a lightly floured surface. Lightly flour the dough and cover it with plastic wrap. Let the dough soften for about 10 minutes, or until it is malleable enough to roll. Roll the dough ⅛ inch thick, moving it from time to time and adding more flour if necessary to keep it from sticking.

Cut out sixteen 2¼ inch cookies. Mark the centers of half the cookies with a needle or the tip of a knife. Use the ¾ inch round cutter or pastry tube to cut out the centers from the marked cookies. (If using a plastic cutter, or parchment-lined cookie sheet, it's best to do this after placing the cookies on a cookie sheet.) Set the cookies a minimum of ½ inch apart on the cookie sheet.

BAKE THE COOKIES Bake the cookies for 5 minutes. For even baking, rotate the cookie sheet halfway around. Continue baking for 5 to 7 minutes, or just until they begin to brown lightly.

COOL THE COOKIES Set the cookie sheet on a wire rack and use a pancake turner to lift the cookies onto another wire rack. Cool completely.

While each batch of cookies is baking, roll the dough for the next batch. After the last batch is cut, knead together all the scraps and reroll them, chilling them first if necessary.

FILL THE COOKIES Using a small offset spatula or butter knife, spread the bottoms of the cookie halves without the cutouts with heaping ½ teaspoons of lemon buttercream or your favorite jam, jelly, or curd, and set the second set of cookies with the cutouts on top, bottom sides down, to create the sandwiches.

STORE Airtight: room temperature, 1 day with buttercream (3 weeks with lemon curd, jam, or jelly); frozen, 6 months.

Lemon Neoclassic Buttercream

MAKES 1 CUP/ABOUT 8 OUNCES/226 GRAMS

	VOLUME	WEIGHT	
about 2 large egg yolks	1½ tablespoons (22 ml)	1 ounce	28 grams
superfine sugar	3 tablespoons	1.3 ounces	37 grams
corn syrup	2 tablespoons (30 ml)	1.4 ounces	41 grams
unsalted butter (65° to 75°F/ 19° to 23°C)	8 tablespoons (1 stick)	4 ounces	113 grams
lemon zest, finely grated	1 tablespoon, loosely packed	.	6 grams
lemon juice, freshly squeezed	2 tablespoons (30 ml)	1.1 ounces	32 grams
pure vanilla extract	½ teaspoon (2.5 ml)	.	.

BEAT THE EGG YOLKS In a medium bowl, with a handheld mixer, beat the egg yolks on high speed until light in color.

MIX THE LIQUID INGREDIENTS Have ready a 1 cup glass measure with a spout, lightly coated with nonstick cooking spray.

In a small saucepan, preferably nonstick, using a silicone spatula, stir together the sugar and corn syrup until all of the sugar is moistened. Heat over medium-high, stirring constantly, until the sugar dissolves and the syrup begins to bubble around the edges. Stop stirring completely and continue cooking for a few minutes until the syrup comes to a rolling boil. (The entire surface will be covered with large bubbles. At this point, the temperature of the syrup on an instant-read thermometer, if using, should read 238°F/114°C.) Immediately transfer the syrup to the glass measure to stop the cooking.

MAKE THE BUTTERCREAM Beat the sugar syrup into the egg yolks in a steady stream. Do not let the syrup fall on the beaters or they will spin it onto the sides of the bowl. Continue beating on high speed for 5 minutes. Let it cool completely. To speed cooling, place the buttercream in an ice water bath (see page 538) or in the refrigerator and stir occasionally.

COMPLETE THE BUTTERCREAM When the outside of the bowl feels cool, beat in the butter by the tablespoon on medium-high speed. The buttercream will not thicken until almost all of the butter has been added. Add the lemon zest, lemon juice, and vanilla and beat on low speed until incorporated. Raise the speed to high and beat until smooth and creamy. The buttercream may separate at first, but it will come together on beating.

Place the buttercream in an airtight container. Use it at once or set it aside for up to 4 hours. If keeping it longer than 4 hours, refrigerate it. Bring it to room temperature before using, to prevent curdling, and rebeat to restore the texture.

COCONUT CRISPS

MAKES TWENTY-TWO 2¼ INCH COOKIES

OVEN TEMPERATURE
375°F/190°C

BAKING TIME
10 to 14 minutes for each of two batches

*W*hat started off as an idea for a pie crust turned out to make a terrifically addictive cookie (pictured on page 323). Baked in small rounds, the dough becomes extra crispy and flavorful. At first bite the flavor is rather subtle but it then magically evolves into a lingering coconut flavor.

SPECIAL EQUIPMENT Two 15 by 12 inch cookie sheets, no preparation needed or lined with parchment | A 2¼ inch scalloped or plain round cookie cutter

COOKIE DOUGH

MAKES 13.4 OUNCES/380 GRAMS

	VOLUME	WEIGHT	
unsalted butter, cold	8 tablespoons (1 stick)	4 ounces	113 grams
bleached all-purpose flour	1¼ cups (lightly spooned into the cup and leveled off)	5.3 ounces	150 grams
sugar	¼ cup	1.8 ounces	50 grams
flaked unsweetened coconut	¼ cup	1 ounce	30 grams
fine sea salt	⅛ teaspoon	.	0.7 gram
1 large egg	3 tablespoons plus ½ teaspoon (47 ml)	1.8 ounces	50 grams

MAKE THE DOUGH Cut the butter into ½ inch cubes and refrigerate it until ready to use.

In a food processor, process the flour, sugar, coconut, and salt until the coconut is finely ground. Add the cold butter cubes and pulse until the butter is no larger than small peas. Add the egg and pulse just until incorporated, about 8 times. The dough will be in crumbly pieces.

Empty the dough into a plastic bag and press it from the outside of the bag just until it holds together. Remove the dough from the plastic bag and place it on a very large piece of plastic wrap. Using the plastic wrap, knead the dough only a few times until it becomes one smooth piece. There should be no visible pieces of butter. (Visible pieces of butter in the dough will melt and form holes during baking. If there are visible pieces of butter, continue kneading the dough or use the heel of your hand to press them in a forward motion to spread them into the dough.)

CHILL THE DOUGH Divide the dough in half, about 6.7 ounces/190 grams each. Wrap each piece loosely with plastic wrap and press to flatten into 5 by ½ inch thick discs. Rewrap them tightly and refrigerate for 30 minutes, or until firm enough to roll. The dough can be refrigerated for up to 3 days or frozen for up to 6 months.

PREHEAT THE OVEN Thirty minutes or longer before baking, set an oven rack in the middle of the oven and preheat the oven to 375°F/190°C.

ROLL THE DOUGH Set a dough disc between two lightly floured large sheets of plastic wrap. If the dough has been chilled for more than 30 minutes, let it sit for about 5 to 10 minutes, until it is malleable enough to roll. Roll it evenly into a ¼ inch thick disc. While rolling the dough, sprinkle the dough with a little more flour on each side as needed and, if it softens significantly, slip it onto a baking sheet and refrigerate it until firm. From time to time, flip the dough with the plastic wrap, and lift off and flatten out the plastic wrap as necessary to make sure it does not wrinkle into the dough.

Cut out a total of eleven or twelve 2¼ inch cookies and set the cookies about ½ inch apart on a cookie sheet. Knead together the scraps and reroll them, chilling them first if necessary.

BAKE THE COOKIES Bake the cookies for 5 minutes. For even baking, rotate the cookie sheet halfway around. Continue baking for 5 to 9 minutes, or until pale gold and brown around the edges.

COOL THE COOKIES Set the cookie sheet on a wire rack and use a pancake turner to lift the cookies onto another wire rack. Cool completely.

While the first batch of cookies is baking, roll out the dough for the second batch.

STORE Airtight: room temperature, 3 weeks.

New Spin on Rollie Pollies

OVEN TEMPERATURE
425°F/220°C

BAKING TIME
8 to 13 minutes for each of two batches

*Y*ou will never discard leftover scraps of pie or pastry dough after you try these cookies. Not only are dough scraps great to have in the freezer for "windfall pies"—little pies that can be made after harvesting a serendipitous discovery of a small amount of berries or other fruit—but when sweetened and flavored, the scraps transform into buttery delicious, crisp cookies. My new spin on these cookies is to flatten them into ovals, which not only makes them larger, it also gives them a more artistic design.

SPECIAL EQUIPMENT Two 15 by 12 inch cookie sheets, no preparation needed or lined with parchment

Flaky Pie or Pastry Dough

	VOLUME	WEIGHT	
dough scraps	.	8 ounces	227 grams
superfine sugar (see Note, page 370)	2 tablespoons plus 1 teaspoon	1 ounce	30 grams
ground cinnamon	¼ teaspoon	.	0.5 gram
turbinado sugar, preferably Sugar in the Raw	.	.	.

PREHEAT THE OVEN Thirty minutes or longer before baking, set an oven rack in the middle of the oven and preheat the oven to 425°F/220°C.

PREPARE THE DOUGH Cut the scraps of dough into similar lengths and lay them on a sheet of plastic wrap, overlapping them slightly. Sprinkle the dough lightly with flour and cover with a second sheet of plastic wrap. Roll lightly to make the dough adhere. Then lift away the top sheet of plastic wrap and use the bottom sheet to help fold the dough into thirds, like a business letter. Wrap the dough well in plastic wrap and refrigerate it while preparing the sugar mixture.

Highlights for Success

If you are using milder cinnamon or you prefer a stronger cinnamon flavor, increase the cinnamon to ½ teaspoon.

Refrigerating the dough before cutting it makes it firm enough to cut evenly. It also causes the sugar to dissolve slightly, helping the layers of dough to adhere to one another.

MAKE THE FILLING In a small bowl, stir together the superfine sugar and cinnamon until evenly mixed.

ROLL THE DOUGH Divide the dough into 2 equal pieces. Roll each piece of dough into a narrow 12 by 6 inch rectangle, ⅛ inch thick. Discard the top sheet of plastic wrap and sprinkle the dough evenly with the sugar mixture. Use the bottom sheet of plastic wrap to lift the dough along the long side, and tightly roll up the dough into a cylinder about 1 inch in diameter. Wrap each cylinder with the bottom sheet of plastic wrap and refrigerate for 1 to 8 hours.

Remove and discard the plastic wrap from 1 cylinder. With a sharp knife, cut the cylinder on a diagonal into 1 inch thick slices. Any gaps will seal on rolling. Roll out each slice into a 2 inch long by 1½ inch wide oval to resemble a rose. For a glimmer of sparkle, lightly sprinkle the tops with the turbinado sugar. Place the cookies on a cookie sheet at least 1 inch apart.

BAKE THE COOKIES Bake for 6 to 9 minutes, or until the bottoms are browned. Flip each cookie over, rotate the cookie sheet, and continue baking for 2 to 4 minutes, or until the other side browns.

COOL THE COOKIES Set the cookie sheet on a wire rack and use a pancake turner to lift the cookies onto another wire rack. Cool completely.

While the first batch of cookies is baking, shape the dough for the second batch.

STORE Airtight: room temperature, 3 weeks; frozen, 6 months.

NOTE If superfine sugar is unavailable, granulated sugar can be processed to a fine texture in a food processor.

GIANT JAM COOKIE

OVEN TEMPERATURE 350°F/175°C

BAKING TIME 30 to 35 minutes

$\mathcal{M}$y longtime friend Jeanne Bauer came back from a trip to Seattle having discovered a version of this extraordinary cookie. This is the perfect celebration cookie for someone special who prefers cookies to cakes! Sugar cookie dough sandwiches scarlet raspberry jam that peeks through little cut-outs in whatever shape suits the sentiment or occasion. Be warned: The jam cookie is one of those things that looks simple and elegant, but it takes the skill of a craftsperson to achieve.

SPECIAL EQUIPMENT One 13 to 14 inch round pizza pan, or baking pan, lined with parchment | A flat baking sheet or 13 inch or larger cardboard round | An expandable flan ring or 12 inch cardboard template | A small decorative cookie cutter | Two flat baking sheets, lightly coated with nonstick cooking spray

COOKIE DOUGH

MAKES ABOUT 2⅔ CUPS/28 OUNCES/810 GRAMS

	VOLUME	WEIGHT	
unsalted butter, cold	16 tablespoons (2 sticks)	8 ounces	227 grams
bleached all-purpose flour	3⅓ cups (lightly spooned into the cup and leveled off)	14.1 ounces	400 grams
fine sea salt	¼ teaspoon	.	1.5 grams
turbinado sugar, preferably Sugar in the Raw	½ cup	3.5 ounces	100 grams
2 large eggs	⅓ cup plus 1 tablespoon (94 ml)	3.5 ounces	100 grams

MAKE THE DOUGH FOOD PROCESSOR METHOD Cut the butter into ½ inch cubes and refrigerate until ready to use.

In a medium bowl, whisk together the flour and salt.

In a food processor, process the sugar until fine. Add the cold butter cubes and pulse until the sugar disappears. Add the flour mixture and pulse until the butter is no larger than small peas. In a small bowl, lightly whisk the eggs. Add them to the mixture and pulse just until incorporated, about 8 times. The dough will be in crumbly pieces.

Empty the dough into a plastic bag and press it from the outside of the bag just until it holds together. Remove the dough from the plastic bag and place it on a very large sheet of plastic wrap. Using the plastic wrap, knead the dough only a few times until it becomes one smooth piece. There should be no visible pieces of butter. (Visible pieces of butter in the dough will melt and form holes during baking. If there are visible pieces of butter, continue kneading the dough or use the heel of your hand to press them in a forward motion to spread them into the dough.)

HAND METHOD In a medium bowl, stir together the flour, sugar (use superfine or fine granulated), and salt. With a pastry cutter or two knives, cut in the cold butter until the mixture resembles coarse meal.

In a small bowl, lightly beat the eggs. Mix them into the flour mixture until the dough comes together and can be formed into a large ball. Knead the dough lightly to make it smooth and malleable.

CHILL THE DOUGH Divide the dough into 2 equal pieces, 14.3 ounces/405 grams each. Wrap each piece loosely with plastic wrap and press to flatten into 6 inch discs. Rewrap them tightly and refrigerate for 30 minutes, or until firm enough to roll.

The dough can be refrigerated for up to 3 days or frozen for up to 6 months.

ROLL THE DOUGH Remove a dough disc from the refrigerator. Set the dough between large sheets of lightly floured plastic wrap. If the dough has been chilled for more than 30 minutes, let it sit for about 5 to 10 minutes, or until it is malleable enough to roll.

Roll the dough between the two pieces of plastic wrap to a little larger than 12 inches in diameter and ⅛ inch thick. Remove the top piece of plastic wrap. Use the bottom piece to lift the dough onto the flat baking sheet or cardboard round. Lay the parchment-lined pizza pan on top and invert the dough onto it. Remove the plastic wrap. Use the expandable flan ring, or a pizza wheel or small sharp knife with the cardboard template as a guide, to cut a 12 inch disc. If using the pizza wheel or knife, take care not to cut through the parchment. Cover the dough with the plastic wrap and refrigerate it for at least 30 minutes or freeze it for 5 to 10 minutes so that it is firm.

Repeat with the remaining dough, but instead of inverting it, slip it, still on the bottom piece of plastic wrap, onto a flat sheet pan. Trim it to 12 inches and freeze it for at least 10 minutes. Use a long sharp knife to score 12 wedges, being careful not to cut all the way through the dough. (To mark even wedges, first make 2 score lines dividing the dough into quarters, and then score each quarter into thirds.)

Any leftover dough scraps can be rerolled and formed into smaller cookies.

Use a small decorative cookie cutter to cut out a shape from every other wedge, this time going all the way through the dough. Cover the dough with plastic wrap and freeze it for 10 minutes, or until the decorative cutouts are firm enough to be lifted out neatly. Remove the dough from the freezer. Carefully use the cookie cutter to recut each shape on the same

cut marks. Lift out each cutout with the aid of a small metal spatula. Place these cutouts on a plastic wrap–lined sheet pan, cover them with plastic wrap, and keep them chilled. Use a wooden skewer, if necessary, to go around the cut-out openings so that they are cleanly and precisely cut.

Place the dough disc with the cutout openings in the freezer for at least 15 minutes, or until frozen solid and rigid.

RASPBERRY JAM GLAZE

	VOLUME	WEIGHT	
seedless raspberry jam	1 cup plus 2 tablespoons	12.6 ounces	357 grams

MAKE THE GLAZE In a 2 cup microwavable measure with a spout, lightly coated with non-stick cooking spray, or in a medium saucepan, preferably nonstick, on the cooktop, cook the jam until it is reduced to 1 cup/237 ml/11.2 ounces/317 grams. Cover tightly and let it come to room temperature. It should be thick but spreadable. If necessary, stir in a little Chambord raspberry liqueur or water.

COMPOSE THE COOKIE Remove the plastic wrap from the dough disc on the pizza pan and spread the raspberry glaze evenly over it up to within ½ inch from the edge. Lightly brush a little water onto this ½ inch border.

Remove the second dough disc from the freezer. Set one of the prepared flat baking sheets on top and invert it. Peel off the plastic wrap and reinvert the dough onto the second prepared flat baking sheet. Quickly, before it softens, slide the rigid dough evenly on top of the glazed dough so that the edges meet. Brush each cut-out piece of dough with a little water and place it on a dough wedge without a cutout.

Use a fork to press the two layers of the edge together, making a radiating design in the pastry. Use a wooden skewer to make many little holes, avoiding the cutout designs. Refrigerate, covered with plastic wrap, for at least 15 minutes or up to 24 hours before baking.

PREHEAT THE OVEN Twenty minutes or longer before baking, set an oven rack in the middle of the oven and preheat the oven to 350°F/175°C.

BAKE THE COOKIE Bake for 15 minutes. For even baking, rotate the pan halfway around. Continue baking for 15 to 20 minutes, or until pale golden and lightly browned at the edges. The glaze visible through the cutouts will be bubbling.

COOL THE COOKIE Set the pan on a wire rack and let it cool for at least 30 minutes, or until room temperature, before serving. Slip a large pancake turner under the cookie to dislodge it and slide it onto a large flat plate or cutting board. Cut through the score lines to the bottom of the cookie. If desired, dust with powdered sugar.

STORE Airtight: room temperature, 10 days; refrigerated, 3 weeks; frozen, 6 months.

COOKIE STRUDEL

MAKES TWO 11½ BY 2½ INCH STRUDELS; 10 TO 12 SERVINGS

OVEN TEMPERATURE
350°F/175°C

BAKING TIME
40 to 45 minutes

$\mathcal{T}$he tender dough used for this strudel reminds me of another of my favorite cookies: Rugelach (page 379). Actually, the dough is quite similar, only instead of cream cheese, it contains sour cream, and instead of being shaped into individual spirals, it is shaped into long, slim rolls. The incredible sour cream dough is easy to work with, but it bakes up fragile and flaky. It is not strong enough to use for a fruit filling, but is perfect for the rugelachlike filling of currants, nuts, and apricot preserves.

I discovered this very special heirloom recipe years ago when I stayed at the historic Mercersburg Inn in Mercersburg, Pennsylvania. Sandy Filkowski, the innkeeper, had to get permission from her mother, Dorothy Thompson, who created this recipe many years ago and who has never before divulged it. It is a perfect treat for an afternoon tea or after dinner dessert to serve with coffee.

PLAN AHEAD The strudel is best made a minimum of 6 hours ahead.

SPECIAL EQUIPMENT One 15 to 12 inch cookie sheet, lined with parchment or aluminum foil

COOKIE DOUGH
MAKES 12.5 OUNCES/354 GRAMS

	VOLUME	WEIGHT	
bleached all-purpose flour	1 cup (lightly spooned into the cup and leveled off) plus 1 tablespoon	4.5 ounces	128 grams
fine sea salt	⅛ teaspoon plus ¹⁄₁₆ teaspoon	.	1.1 grams
unsalted butter (70° to 75°F/ 21° to 23°C)	8 tablespoons (1 stick)	4 ounces	113 grams
sour cream	½ cup	4.3 ounces	121 grams

MAKE THE DOUGH In a medium bowl, whisk together the flour and salt. Add the butter and sour cream and mash and stir with a wooden spoon until the mixture forms a ball.

CHILL THE DOUGH Divide the dough in half, about 6.2 ounces/177 grams each, and scrape each piece onto a sheet of plastic wrap. Using the plastic wrap, knead each half of the dough several times until it becomes one smooth piece. There should be no visible pieces of butter. Press and form each piece into a 4 by 4 inch square. Refrigerate for a minimum of 2 hours or up to overnight.

FILLING

	VOLUME	WEIGHT	
pecans or walnuts, coarsely chopped	½ cup	2 ounces	57 grams
dried currants	¼ cup plus 2 tablespoons	2 ounces	56 grams
ground cinnamon	⅛ teaspoon	.	.
apricot preserves	½ cup plus 2 tablespoons	7 ounces	200 grams

MAKE THE FILLING In a medium bowl, with a fork, stir together the pecans, currants, and cinnamon until well mixed.

ROLL THE STRUDEL On a floured pastry cloth with a floured rolling pin, or between floured sheets of plastic wrap, roll the first piece of dough into an 11 by 9 inch rectangle. Turn the dough two or three times and flour it lightly as necessary to be sure it does not stick.

Spread half of the apricot preserves (¼ cup plus 1 tablespoon/3.5 ounces/100 grams) evenly over the dough, leaving a margin of about ½ inch all around. Sprinkle half of the filling mixture evenly over the apricot.

Using the pastry cloth or plastic wrap to lift the dough along the long side, roll up the dough, brushing off the excess flour as you go. Flip the roll onto the lined cookie sheet, seam side down. Tuck the ends under ½ inch. The strudel will be 10 by 2 inches.

Repeat with the remaining dough and filling. Place the second strudel next to the first, leaving at least 1 inch between them. With a small sharp knife, cut 3 or 4 small horizontal steam vents into the top of each strudel. Bake at once, or cover the strudels with plastic wrap and refrigerate for up to 24 hours before baking.

PREHEAT THE OVEN Twenty minutes or longer before baking, set an oven rack at the highest level and preheat the oven to 350°F/175°C.

Topping

	VOLUME	WEIGHT	
sugar	½ tablespoon	.	6 grams
ground cinnamon	¼ teaspoon	.	.
milk	1 tablespoon (15 ml)	0.5 ounce	15 grams

MAKE THE TOPPING In a small bowl, stir together the sugar and cinnamon.

BAKE THE STRUDEL Bake for 20 minutes. After the strudel has baked for 20 minutes, with a pastry brush, brush each roll with milk and sprinkle the rolls evenly with the cinnamon sugar topping. For even baking, rotate the cookie sheet halfway around. Continue baking for 20 to 25 minutes, or until lightly browned.

COOL THE STRUDEL Set the cookie sheet on a wire rack. Cool completely.

The inside of the pastry has the best texture if allowed to sit for at least 6 hours before serving.

To serve, use a serrated knife to cut ½ inch diagonal slices. For a crisper texture, place the slices, cut side down, on an aluminum foil–lined cookie sheet and bake at 350°F/175°C for 10 minutes before serving.

STORE Airtight: room temperature, 5 days; refrigerated, 8 days; frozen, 3 months.

RUGELACH

OVEN TEMPERATURE
350°F/175°C

BAKING TIME
15 to 20 minutes

*I*f there were just one sweet treat in the world, would that it were rugelach. The comfortingly soft yet crisp and flaky cinnamon-imbued dough—with the sticky tang of caramelized apricot, juicy plump chewiness of raisins, and earthy crunch of walnuts, all rolled into each and every bite—is utterly irresistible.

SPECIAL EQUIPMENT Two 15 by 12 inch cookie sheets, lined with aluminum foil | Two wire racks, lightly coated with nonstick cooking spray

COOKIE DOUGH

MAKES 13 OUNCES/370 GRAMS

	VOLUME	WEIGHT	
bleached all-purpose flour	1 cup (lightly spooned into the cup and leveled off) plus 1 tablespoon	4.5 ounces	128 grams
fine sea salt	⅛ teaspoon	.	0.7 gram
cream cheese (65° to 75°F/ 19° to 23°C)	½ cup minus 1 tablespoon	4 ounces	113 grams
unsalted butter (65° to 75°F/ 19° to 23°C)	8 tablespoons (1 stick)	4 ounces	113 grams
granulated sugar	2 tablespoons	0.9 ounce	25 grams
pure vanilla extract	½ teaspoon (2.5 ml)	.	.

MAKE THE DOUGH In a small bowl, whisk together the flour and salt.

HANDHELD MIXER METHOD In a mixing bowl, on medium speed, beat the cream cheese and butter until blended. Beat in the sugar and vanilla. On low speed, beat in the flour mixture just until incorporated, no more than 30 seconds.

Rugelach and Hamantaschen (page 384)

FOOD PROCESSOR METHOD Have the cream cheese and butter chilled. Cut the butter into ½ inch cubes. In a food processor, place the cream cheese. With the motor running, add the butter and process until smooth and creamy, scraping down the sides of the bowl once or twice. Add the sugar and vanilla and process for a few seconds to incorporate them. Add the flour mixture and pulse in just until the dough starts to clump together.

CHILL THE DOUGH Scrape the dough onto a piece of plastic wrap and press it together to form a ball. Divide the dough in half, about 6.5 ounces/185 grams each. Wrap each piece loosely in plastic wrap and press to form flat discs. Rewrap tightly and refrigerate for a minimum of 1 hour or up to 3 days (or freeze for up to 6 months).

FILLING

	VOLUME	WEIGHT	
granulated sugar	3 tablespoons	1.3 ounces	37 grams
light brown Muscovado sugar, or dark brown sugar	2 tablespoons, firmly packed	1 ounce	27 grams
ground cinnamon	¼ teaspoon	.	0.5 gram
golden raisins (see Note)	¼ cup plus 2 tablespoons	1.9 ounces	54 grams
walnuts, coarsely chopped	½ cup	1.8 ounces	50 grams
Apricot Lekvar Filling (page 360) or apricot preserves	¼ cup (59 ml)	2.7 ounces	76 grams

MAKE THE FILLING In a medium bowl, with your fingers, mix the granulated sugar, brown sugar, and cinnamon until evenly combined. Divide the mixture equally between two small bowls. Combine the golden raisins and the chopped walnuts and divide them equally between two additional small bowls.

NOTE If the raisins are not soft, soak them in ½ cup/118 ml boiling water for 30 minutes to 1 hour and then drain them well.

ROLL THE DOUGH Remove a piece of the dough from the refrigerator and let it sit on the counter for about 5 to 10 minutes, or until it is malleable enough to roll.

Using a floured rolling pin, on a floured mat or lightly floured surface, roll out the dough into about a 9 inch circle, ⅛ inch thick, rotating it often and adding flour as necessary to be sure it is not sticking. If the dough becomes too soft or sticky at any time, briefly refrigerate it until it is firm enough to roll.

ADD THE FILLING Mark the center of the dough with the tip of a knife. Using the back of a tablespoon or small offset spatula, spread the dough evenly with 2 tablespoons/30 ml of the apricot lekvar, avoiding about 1 inch in the center because the preserves will push forward when the triangles of dough are rolled up. (If using the preserves, stir them with a fork to break up any large pieces, but do not heat the preserves or beat them because they will thin out.)

Sprinkle half of the sugar mixture over the lekvar. Sprinkle evenly with half of the raisin and walnut mixture. Press the filling gently but firmly over the dough. Slip a large spatula under the dough disc to loosen it from the work surface. Using a pizza wheel or long sharp knife, cut the dough into 12 triangles. (Cut the dough first into quarters, and then cut each quarter into thirds.)

SHAPE THE RUGELACH Use a thin knife or spatula, if necessary, to loosen the triangles from the work surface. Starting at the wide end, roll up the triangle and bend the ends around to form a slight crescent shape, turning them toward the point. Place the rugelach, point underneath, about 1½ inches apart on a prepared cookie sheet.

TOPPING

	VOLUME	WEIGHT	
granulated sugar	1 tablespoon	0.5 ounce	13 grams
ground cinnamon	½ teaspoon	.	1.1 grams
milk	1 tablespoon (15 ml)	0.5 ounce	15 grams

MAKE THE TOPPING In a small bowl, stir together the sugar and cinnamon for the topping. Divide the mixture equally between two small bowls.

APPLY THE TOPPING Lift each rugelach with your fingers and, with a pastry brush, brush it with the milk. Holding the rugelach over a medium bowl, use a sugar dredger or your fingers to sprinkle the rugelach evenly with the cinnamon sugar, letting the excess fall into the bowl. Set it back on the cookie sheet.

Refrigerate the rugelach, covered with plastic wrap, for at least 30 minutes or up to over-night, or until firm. Repeat with the second disc of dough.

PREHEAT THE OVEN Twenty minutes or longer before baking, set oven racks in the upper and lower thirds of the oven and preheat the oven to 350°F/175°C.

BAKE THE RUGELACH Bake for 10 minutes. For even baking, rotate the cookie sheets half-way around and reverse their positions from top to bottom. Continue baking for 5 to 10 minutes, or until lightly browned.

COOL THE RUGELACH Set the cookie sheets on uncoated wire racks or on a heatproof surface and let the rugelach cool for a few minutes to firm slightly. During baking, a little of the apricot always melts out onto the foil. It is therefore necessary to remove the rugelach from the foil before the apricot hardens. Use a small pancake turner to transfer the rugelach to the prepared wire racks to cool completely. The apricot filling that leaks onto the foil liner can be peeled off and makes for a delicious baker's treat!

STORE Airtight: room temperature, 5 days; frozen, 3 months.

Variations: SCHNECKEN

Roll each dough disc into an 8 inch square instead of a round, sprinkle with the filling, roll it jelly roll style, and slice into ½ inch thick slices. Brush the top of each slice lightly with the milk, sprinkle with the cinnamon sugar, and set, sugared side up, about 1½ inches apart on the prepared cookie sheet.

For the following two variations, eliminate the cinnamon and the brown sugar and use a total of 5 tablespoons/2.2 ounces/62 grams superfine sugar for the filling.

CHOCOLATE RASPBERRY RUGELACH

Replace the apricot with seedless raspberry jam, replace the walnuts with almonds, and replace the raisins with 6 tablespoons/2.8 ounces/80 grams Valrhona chocolate pearls or mini chocolate chips.

CRAN-RASPBERRY RUGELACH

Replace the apricot with seedless raspberry jam, replace the walnuts with almonds, and replace the raisins with dried cranberries.

Hamantaschen

OVEN TEMPERATURE
350°F/175°C

BAKING TIME
15 to 20 minutes

I love poppy seeds, but I never enjoyed bakery hamantaschen because I didn't like the sturdy sweet dough. I therefore decided to create the hamantaschen of my dreams with dough that is tender, slightly flaky, very buttery, and vanilla imbued (pictured on page 380). Elliott and I like the crunch of poppy seeds, so I do not cook the seeds into a smooth paste, but I do offer directions for those who prefer it. Solo makes a good quality poppy seed filling; if you substitute it, be sure to add the lemon zest and apricot lekvar or preserves.

SPECIAL EQUIPMENT One 15 by 12 inch cookie sheet, lined with parchment | A 3 inch scalloped or plain round cookie cutter

Sweet Cookie Crust (Pâte Sucrée)

MAKES ABOUT 1⅓ CUPS/14.8 OUNCES/420 GRAMS

	VOLUME	WEIGHT	
unsalted butter, cold	8 tablespoons (1 stick)	4 ounces	113 grams
bleached all-purpose flour	1⅔ cups (lightly spooned into the cup and leveled off)	7 ounces	200 grams
fine sea salt	⅛ teaspoon	.	0.7 gram
turbinado sugar, preferably Sugar in the Raw, or granulated sugar	¼ cup	1.8 ounces	50 grams
1 large egg yolk	1 tablespoon plus ½ teaspoon (17 ml)	0.7 ounce	19 grams
heavy cream	3 tablespoons (44 ml)	1.5 ounces	43 grams
pure vanilla extract	1 teaspoon (5 ml)	.	.

MAKE THE COOKIE DOUGH Cut the butter into ½ inch cubes and refrigerate until ready to use.

In a medium bowl, whisk together the flour and salt.

In a food processor, process the sugar until fine. Add the cold butter cubes and pulse until the sugar disappears. Add the flour mixture and pulse until the butter is no larger than small peas.

In a small bowl, stir together the egg yolk, cream, and vanilla. Add it to the mixture and pulse just until incorporated, about 8 times. The dough will be in crumbly pieces.

Empty the dough into a plastic bag and press it from the outside of the bag just until it holds together. Remove the dough from the plastic bag and place it on a very large sheet of plastic wrap. Using the plastic wrap, knead the dough only a few times until it becomes one smooth piece. There should be no visible pieces of butter. (Visible pieces of butter in the dough will melt and form holes during baking. If there are visible pieces of butter, continue kneading the dough or use the heel of your hand to press them in a forward motion to spread them into the dough.) Press the dough together to form a ball.

CHILL THE DOUGH Divide the dough in half, about 7.4 ounces/210 grams each. Wrap each piece loosely with plastic wrap and press to flatten it into a disc. Rewrap tightly and refrigerate for a minimum of 30 minutes, or until firm enough to roll. It can be refrigerated for up to 3 days or frozen for up to 6 months.

POPPY SEED FILLING

MAKES 1 CUP/10.2 OUNCES/290 GRAMS

	VOLUME	WEIGHT	
poppy seeds (see Notes, page 387)	¾ cup	4 ounces	113 grams
milk	⅓ cup (79 ml)	2.9 ounces	81 grams
granulated sugar	¼ cup	1.8 ounces	50 grams
honey	1 tablespoon plus 1 teaspoon (20 ml)	1 ounce	28 grams
lemon zest, finely grated	2 teaspoons, loosely packed	.	4 grams
Apricot Lekvar Filling (page 360), or preserves (see Notes, page 387)	2 tablespoons (30 ml), *divided*	1.3 ounces	38 grams

MAKE THE FILLING In a poppy seed grinder, spice mill, or blender, grind the poppy seeds. They will fluff up to equal about 1 cup.

In a small saucepan, heat the milk. Add the poppy seeds, stirring for a few seconds until the milk is absorbed. Remove the pan from the heat and stir in the sugar, honey, lemon zest, and 1 tablespoon/15 ml/0.6 ounce/19 grams of the apricot lekvar until incorporated. Cool the filling to room temperature. Place the remaining apricot lekvar in a small bowl, cover tightly with plastic wrap, and reserve for glazing.

EGG GLAZE

	VOLUME	WEIGHT	
2 large egg yolks	2 tablespoons plus 1 teaspoon (35 ml)	1.3 ounces	37 grams
milk	2 teaspoons (10 ml)	.	10 grams

MAKE THE EGG GLAZE In a small bowl, whisk together the egg yolks and milk. Strain the mixture into another small bowl, pushing it through with the back of a spoon or letting it sit for a few minutes to flow through the strainer. Discard the thicker part that does not pass through the strainer.

ROLL THE DOUGH AND SHAPE THE HAMANTASCHEN Remove a disc of dough from the refrigerator. If the dough has been chilled for more than 30 minutes, let it sit for about 5 to 10 minutes, or until it is malleable enough to roll.

Using a floured rolling pin, on a floured pastry mat or counter, roll out the dough into a rectangle, ⅛ inch thick, rotating the dough often and adding flour as necessary to be sure it is not sticking. Cut out 3 inch discs of dough. Use a thin knife or spatula, if necessary, to loosen the discs from the surface. Place them on the prepared cookie sheet. Gather up the scraps and knead them together lightly. Shape the dough into a flat patty, wrap it in plastic wrap, and refrigerate it until firm enough to reroll.

Repeat with the remaining disc of dough. Gather up the scraps and add them to the scraps in the refrigerator. Once all the hamantaschen have been shaped, the dough scraps can be used to make more, but reroll the scraps only once.

COMPOSE THE HAMANTASCHEN One at a time, brush the outer ½ inch of each dough disc with a thin coating of egg glaze. It is not necessary to brush the center. Place 2 teaspoons/0.4 ounce/12 grams poppy seed filling mounded in the center. Firmly pinch the dough together in three equally spaced places to form the three-corner hat effect. (Alternatively, water will also work well to seal the dough.) For a lovely color and slight shine, brush the outside of the dough lightly with the egg glaze.

Arrange the hamantaschen about 1½ inches apart on the prepared cookie sheet. Refrigerate, covered with plastic wrap, for at least 30 minutes or up to overnight, or until firm.

PREHEAT THE OVEN Twenty minutes or longer before baking, set an oven rack in the middle of the oven and preheat the oven to 350°F/175°C.

BAKE THE HAMANTASCHEN Bake for 8 minutes. For even baking, rotate the cookie sheet halfway around. Continue baking for 7 to 12 minutes, or until lightly browned.

Poppy seeds have a high oil content and are therefore prone to rancidity, especially if purchased already ground. When poppy seeds start to become rancid, they taste very bitter. Store both whole and ground poppy seeds in the freezer. If you are purchasing ground poppy seeds, and don't have a scale, measure out ¾ cup.

The best way to grind poppy seeds is in a specially designed poppy seed grinder. A spice mill or blender will work, but not quite as well—a food processor not at all.

COOL AND GLAZE THE HAMANTASCHEN Set the cookie sheet on a wire rack. If any of the sides of the dough has collapsed, use two metal spatulas to lift in any filling that may have leaked out and re-form the shape of the hamantaschen. Use a pancake turner to transfer the hamantaschen to another wire rack to cool completely. When cool, brush the poppy seed filling with the remaining 1 tablespoon of apricot lekvar or sieved apricot preserves (see Notes). If necessary, stir in a little apricot brandy or hot water to make it more liquid.

STORE Airtight: room temperature, 5 days; frozen, 3 months.

NOTES I find that whole poppy seeds have a bitter quality when used in this quantity, which is why they need to be ground. Because I like a slight crunch, I heat the poppy seeds only for a short time. For a smoother poppy seed paste, in a poppy seed grinder, spice mill, or blender, grind ½ cup plus 1 tablespoon/ 3 ounces/84 grams poppy seeds. (There will be about ¾ cup.) Place the ground poppy seeds in a small saucepan. In place of the milk, add ¼ cup plus 2 tablespoons/89 ml/ 3.1 ounces/89 grams hot water to the poppy seeds. Cook over low heat, stirring often, for about 3 to 6 minutes. The poppy seeds will gradually absorb the water, swelling and becoming more pastelike. Add water, by the tablespoon, as needed, to keep the paste from scorching. When the poppy seed paste has the consistency of peanut butter, remove it from the heat and add the sugar, honey, and lemon zest. Cool completely. (There will be a little less than ¾ cup; use 1½ teaspoons per cookie.)

Poppy seed paste can be stored in an airtight container in the freezer for several months.

If using apricot preserves instead of lekvar, place about ¼ cup/59 ml/2.7 ounces/78 grams apricot preserves in a microwavable container and bring it to a boil in the microwave. Alternatively, place it in a small saucepan and bring it to a boil over medium-low heat on a cooktop, stirring constantly. Using the back of a spoon, push it through a fine-mesh strainer into a small bowl, and discard the small amount of pulp.

Variations: Replace the poppy seed filling with 1 cup/237 ml/8.2 ounces/232 grams of apricot or prune lekvar (pages 360 or 107).

MINI GÂTEAUX BRETONS

MAKES THIRTY-EIGHT 1⅜ INCH COOKIES

OVEN TEMPERATURE 325°F/160°C

BAKING TIME 14 to 16 minutes

*T*his classic French cake from Brittany makes the most buttery cookies I know. They will keep for as long as a week at room temperature, making them perfect for holiday gift giving.

SPECIAL EQUIPMENT 38 mini brioche pans, 1 inch at the bottom, 1¾ inches at the top (1 tablespoon capacity), uncoated (if you do not have enough brioche pans, bake in batches) | A baking sheet | A long, thin sewing needle for unmolding

COOKIE DOUGH

MAKES 13.4 OUNCES/380 GRAMS

	VOLUME	WEIGHT	
blanched sliced almonds	¼ cup	0.9 ounce	25 grams
superfine sugar (see Notes, page 390)	¼ cup plus 2 tablespoons, *divided*	2.6 ounces	75 grams
fine sea salt (see Notes, page 390)	⅛ teaspoon	.	0.7 gram
unsalted butter, preferably high fat (or high-quality unsalted butter), 65° to 75°F/19° to 23°C (see Notes, page 390)	9 tablespoons (1 stick plus 1 tablespoon) (or 1¼ sticks)	4.5 ounces (or 5 ounces)	128 grams (or 142 grams)
2 large egg yolks, at room temperature	2 tablespoons plus 1 teaspoon (35 ml)	1.3 ounces	37 grams
kirsch, dark rum, or water	½ tablespoon (7.5 ml)	.	.
pure vanilla extract	¾ teaspoon (3.7 ml)	.	.
bleached all-purpose flour	1 cup (lightly spooned into the cup and leveled off) plus ½ tablespoon	4.4 ounces	125 grams

PREHEAT THE OVEN Twenty minutes or longer before baking, set an oven rack in the middle of the oven and preheat the oven to 325°F/160°C.

TOAST THE ALMONDS Spread the almonds evenly on a baking sheet and bake for about 10 minutes, or until pale gold. Stir once or twice to ensure even toasting and avoid over-browning. Cool completely.

In a food processor, process the almonds with 2 tablespoons/0.9 ounce/25 grams of the sugar and the salt until fairly fine but not powder fine. Alternatively, use a nut grater to grate the almonds finely, and then combine with the 2 tablespoons sugar and the salt.

MIX THE DOUGH In the bowl of a stand mixer fitted with the flat beater, mix together the remaining sugar and the butter on low speed for about 1 minute, or until smooth and creamy. Scrape down the sides of the bowl.

On low speed, beat in the egg yolks, 1 at a time, beating for about 20 seconds between each addition. Scrape down the sides of the bowl. Add the almond mixture, liquor or water, and vanilla and mix on low speed until the almond mixture is moistened. Beat for about 20 seconds until evenly incorporated.

Add the flour in four parts, turning off the mixer between additions, and beating on the lowest speed for about 15 seconds between each addition. Detach the beater and, with a silicone spatula, finish mixing any flour that may remain, reaching to the bottom of the bowl.

Scrape the dough onto a piece of plastic wrap. Wrap tightly and refrigerate the dough for 30 minutes, or until firm.

FILL THE BRIOCHE PANS Scoop out rounded teaspoons of the dough (0.3 ounce/10 grams). Roll each piece of dough between the floured palms of your hands into a 1 inch ball and set it into a brioche pan. (Be sure to flour your hands or the gâteaux will stick to the molds when baked.) Press the dough balls into the pans. They will come almost to the top of each pan. If the dough is sticky, refrigerate the dough until firmer. Use your pinky finger to press the dough into the fluted edges. Set the dough-lined brioche pans at least ½ inch apart on the baking sheet.

BAKE THE GÂTEAUX Bake for 14 to 16 minutes, or until deep golden brown. (An instant-read thermometer should read about 205°F/96°C.)

COOL AND UNMOLD THE GÂTEAUX Set the baking sheet on a wire rack to cool for 10 minutes. Use the needle to slip between one of the edges of the pan and the gâteaux to loosen it and invert it onto another wire rack. Cool completely.

STORE Airtight: room temperature, 5 days; refrigerated, 10 days; frozen, 3 months.

NOTES Golden baker's sugar from India Tree (see page 511) imparts an especially lovely flavor to this cookie.

Vermont salted butter, which is very lightly salted, has just the right amount of salt for this recipe (other salted butters usually contain more salt). If using it, use only $\frac{1}{16}$ teaspoon salt. Butter with 80 percent fat contains about 1 tablespoon more water than the 86 percent, which will result in a slightly moister crumb. If this is your preference and you want to use the higher 86 percent butter, you can add the water to the batter when adding the almonds.

Chocolate Sweetheart Madeleines

MAKES 100 MINI MADELEINES OR 25 LARGE MADELEINES

OVEN TEMPERATURE
350°F/175°C

BAKING TIME
10 to 12 minutes for mini madeleines; 14 to 15 minutes for large madeleines

I've usually found madeleines to be dry if not enjoyed immediately after baking. To ensure against dryness, I based these madeleines on one of my ultra-moist and chocolaty chocolate cakes, The Chocolate Domingo. When I attended the Pastry Chef Conference at the Culinary Institute of America in Greystone, California, each of the attendees was asked to make a recipe. My offering was these mini madeleines. Chef Robert Ellinger, owner of Baked to Perfection in Port Washington, New York, and founder of the Guild of Baking and Pastry Arts, gave me a much cherished compliment— he said that from then on, these were the chocolate madeleines he would make in his bakery.

SPECIAL EQUIPMENT Mini madeleine molds (1½ teaspoons capacity) or large madeleine molds (2 tablespoons capacity), preferably silicone, lightly coated with baking spray with flour (see Notes, page 393. If silicone, set them on wire racks and then on baking sheets) | A small pastry bag fitted with a ⅜ or ½ inch round pastry tube or a quart-size reclosable freezer bag with a ½ inch semicircle cut from one corner | An artist's brush

Ganache Glaze

MAKES ½ CUP/118 ML/4.3 OUNCES/123 GRAMS

	VOLUME	WEIGHT	
bittersweet chocolate, 60% to 62% cacao, chopped	.	1.5 ounces	42 grams
heavy cream	¼ cup plus 2 tablespoons (89 ml)	3.1 ounces	87 grams

MAKE THE GANACHE GLAZE In a small food processor, process the chocolate until very fine (see Notes, page 393).

In a 1 cup microwavable measure with a spout (or in a small saucepan over medium heat, stirring often), scald the cream (heat it to the boiling point; small bubbles will form around the periphery).

With the motor of the food processor running, pour the cream through the feed tube in a steady stream. Process for a few seconds until smooth. Scrape the ganache into a glass bowl, cover it with plastic wrap, and set it in a warm place.

BATTER

MAKES 14.1 OUNCES/400 GRAMS

	VOLUME	WEIGHT	
unsweetened (alkalized) cocoa powder	¼ cup plus 2 teaspoons (sifted before measuring)	0.7 ounce	21 grams
sour cream	⅓ cup	2.9 ounces	81 grams
1 large egg, at room temperature	3 tablespoons plus ½ teaspoon (47 ml)	1.8 ounces	50 grams
pure vanilla extract	¾ teaspoon (3.7 ml)	.	.
bleached cake flour	¾ cup (sifted into the cup and leveled off) plus ½ tablespoon	2.7 ounces	78 grams
superfine sugar	½ cup	3.5 ounces	100 grams
baking powder	⅜ teaspoon	.	1.7 grams
baking soda	⅛ teaspoon	.	0.7 gram
fine sea salt	¼ teaspoon	.	1.5 grams
unsalted butter (65° to 75°F/ 19° to 23°C)	7 tablespoons (¾ stick plus 1 tablespoon)	3.5 ounces	100 grams

PREHEAT THE OVEN Twenty minutes or longer before baking, set oven racks in the upper and lower thirds of the oven and preheat the oven to 350°F/175°C.

MIX THE COCOA AND LIQUID INGREDIENTS In a medium bowl, whisk the cocoa, sour cream, egg, and vanilla just until the consistency of slightly lumpy muffin batter.

MAKE THE BATTER In the bowl of a stand mixer fitted with the flat beater, mix the flour, sugar, baking powder, baking soda, and salt on low speed for 30 seconds. Add the butter and half of the cocoa mixture. Mix on low speed until the flour mixture is moistened. Raise the speed to medium and beat for 1½ minutes. Scrape down the sides of the bowl.

With the mixer off between additions, add the remaining cocoa mixture in two parts, starting on medium-low speed and gradually raising the speed to medium. Beat on medium speed for 30 seconds after each addition to incorporate the ingredients and strengthen the structure. Scrape down the sides of the bowl.

If you do not have enough molds to bake all of the madeleines soon after making the batter, chill the extra batter in the refrigerator.

PIPE THE BATTER INTO THE MOLDS Fill the pastry bag or freezer bag about three-quarters full with the batter. Pipe the batter into the molds' cavities, filling them about half full (4 grams in each mini mold cavity, or 16 grams in each large mold cavity).

BAKE THE MADELEINES Bake for 10 to 12 minutes (14 to 15 for large ones), or until the madeleines spring back when pressed lightly in the centers.

COOL THE MADELEINES Set the baking sheets on wire racks and let the madeleines cool in the molds for 5 minutes. If using silicone molds, simply use your finger to push each madeleine up and out of the mold from underneath. If using metal molds, use a toothpick or pin to carefully dislodge the madeleines from the molds. Invert the madeleines onto a flat baking sheet lined with plastic wrap that has been lightly coated with nonstick cooking spray.

GLAZE THE MADELEINES If necessary, reheat the ganache glaze with 3 second bursts in the microwave or in a hot water bath. With the artist's brush, coat the tops of the madeleines with the glaze, brushing lengthwise along the grooves. As the glaze sets, it will darken and some of it will be absorbed. Brush with a second, lighter coat of glaze to make it even and shiny.

STORE Airtight: room temperature, 3 days; refrigerated, 5 days; frozen, 2 months.

NOTES After coating the molds with baking spray with flour, use a pastry brush to brush out any excess spray to prevent air bubbles from forming in the fluted tops of the madeleines.

If you don't have a small food processor, chop the chocolate with a large chef's knife and then transfer it to a glass bowl. Pour the hot cream over the chocolate and stir until melted and smooth.

WOODY'S BLACK AND WHITE BROWNIES

OVEN TEMPERATURE 325°F/160°C

BAKING TIME 25 to 35 minutes

*A*t Christmastime, Woody always looked forward to his mother's tradition of making bourbon brownies, covered with white icing and topped with melted dark chocolate. He adapted her recipe components with favorites of mine, including my Barcelona Brownies from *Rose's Heavenly Cakes*. The resulting Black and White Brownies are a miracle of textures, varying from chewy to creamy to melt in the mouth. They are the perfect expression of chocolate. The brownies themselves are also excellent without the toppings.

SPECIAL EQUIPMENT One 8 by 2 inch square baking pan, wrapped with a cake strip, coated with shortening, lined with two pieces of crisscrossed parchment or heavy-duty aluminum foil (bottom and sides), extending a few inches past the edge of the pan, attached to each other by a thin coating of shortening, then lightly coated with baking spray with flour

BROWNIE BATTER

	VOLUME	WEIGHT	
pecan halves	1 cup plus 2 tablespoons	4 ounces	113 grams
unsalted butter	14 tablespoons (1¾ sticks)	7 ounces	200 grams
bittersweet chocolate, 60% to 62% cacao, chopped	.	3 ounces	85 grams
unsweetened (alkalized) cocoa powder	⅔ cup (sifted before measuring)	1.8 ounces	50 grams
sugar	1 cup	7 ounces	200 grams
3 large eggs, at room temperature	½ cup plus 1½ tablespoons (140 ml)	5.3 ounces	150 grams
pure vanilla extract	2 teaspoons (10 ml)	.	.
cream cheese (65° to 70°F/ 19° to 21°C), cut into pieces	⅓ cup	3 ounces	85 grams
all-purpose flour, either bleached or unbleached	½ cup plus 2 tablespoons (lightly spooned into the cup)	2.7 ounces	76 grams
fine sea salt	a pinch	.	.

PREHEAT THE OVEN Twenty minutes or longer before baking, set an oven rack in the middle of the oven and preheat the oven to 325°F/160°C (300°F/150°C if using a Pyrex or dark pan).

BREAK AND TOAST THE PECANS Break the pecans into medium pieces. Spread them evenly on a baking sheet and bake for about 10 minutes to enhance their flavor. Stir once or twice to ensure even toasting and avoid overbrowning. Cool completely.

MELT THE BUTTER AND CHOCOLATE In a double boiler over hot, not simmering, water (do not let the bottom of the container touch the water), melt the butter and chocolate, stirring often. Scrape the melted chocolate mixture into the bowl of a stand mixer or large mixing bowl.

MAKE THE BATTER STAND MIXER METHOD In the bowl of a stand mixer fitted with the flat beater, beat the cocoa and sugar into the melted chocolate mixture on medium speed until incorporated. Scrape down the sides of the bowl. Beat in the eggs and vanilla for about 30 seconds. The mixture will become thick and glossy. Beat in the cream cheese until only small bits remain. Add the flour and salt and mix on low speed just until the flour is moistened, about 10 seconds. Add the pecans and mix for 3 seconds.

HAND METHOD In the bowl containing the melted chocolate mixture, whisk in the cocoa and then the sugar until incorporated. Whisk in the eggs and vanilla until the mixture becomes thick and glossy. With a blending fork or wooden spoon, stir in the cream cheese until only small bits remain. Add the flour and salt and stir just until the flour is moistened. Stir in the pecans.

FILL THE PAN Scrape the batter into the prepared pan and smooth the surface evenly with an offset spatula.

BAKE THE BROWNIE Bake for 25 to 35 minutes, or until the batter has set only to 1 inch from the edge and a toothpick inserted 1 inch from the edge comes out clean. (An instant-read thermometer inserted into the center should read about 190°F/88°C.)

COOL THE BROWNIE Let the brownie cool in the pan on a wire rack until completely cool to the touch, about 2 hours. To speed cooling, the pan can be set in the refrigerator. Run a small metal spatula between the pan and the parchment to ensure that no batter has leaked through and stuck to the sides. Gently grasp the ends of the parchment and lift it up a little to make sure the brownie will release from the pan. If desired, lift the brownie out of the pan, use a long serrated knife to level the top, then return the brownie to the pan.

WHITE CHOCOLATE BUTTERCREAM

MAKES ABOUT 2 CUPS/13.2 OUNCES/375 GRAMS

WHITE CHOCOLATE CUSTARD BASE

MAKES ABOUT 1¼ CUPS/10.8 OUNCES/306 GRAMS

	VOLUME	WEIGHT	
white chocolate containing cocoa butter, chopped	.	5.3 ounces	150 grams
unsalted butter (65° to 75°F/ 19° to 23°C)	5½ tablespoons (½ stick plus 1½ tablespoons)	2.7 ounces	78 grams
2 large eggs, at room temperature	⅓ cup plus 1 tablespoon (94 ml)	3.5 ounces	100 grams

MAKE THE WHITE CHOCOLATE CUSTARD BASE Have ready a fine-mesh strainer suspended over a medium bowl.

In a double boiler over barely simmering water (do not let the bottom of the container touch the water), melt the white chocolate and butter, stirring often until smooth and creamy. Whisk the eggs lightly to break them up and then whisk them into the melted chocolate until incorporated. With a silicone spatula, continue stirring, being sure to scrape the mixture from the bottom of the container so that it doesn't risk overcooking. Stir until an instant-read thermometer reads 160°F/71°C. The mixture will have thickened slightly. Pour it at once into the strainer and press it through.

Cover it tightly and refrigerate for about 1 hour, stirring every 15 minutes, until cool to the touch. (An instant-read thermometer should read 65° to 70°F/19° to 21°C.) To speed cooling, place the bowl in an ice water bath (see page 538), stirring often.

COMPLETED WHITE CHOCOLATE BUTTERCREAM

	VOLUME	WEIGHT	
unsalted butter (65° to 75°F/ 19° to 23°C)	5 tablespoons (½ stick plus 1 tablespoon)	2.5 ounces	71 grams
White Chocolate Custard Base (page 397)	1¼ cups	10.8 ounces	306 grams
pure vanilla extract	1 teaspoon (5 ml)	.	.

COMPLETE THE BUTTERCREAM In the bowl of a stand mixer fitted with the whisk beater, beat the butter on medium-low speed until creamy, about 30 seconds.

Gradually beat the white chocolate custard base into the butter, scraping down the sides of the bowl as needed. Raise the speed to medium-high and beat for 2 minutes. The color will lighten and stiff peaks will form when the beater is raised. Cover and set aside for 1½ to 2 hours, or until the mixture is slightly thickened and spongy. It should be no warmer than 70°F/21°C. If necessary, place the bowl in an ice water bath for a few minutes, stirring constantly. Beat on medium-high speed until smooth, light, and creamy, about 30 seconds. Add the vanilla and beat just until incorporated.

The volume of the buttercream will vary depending on the temperature of the ingredients and the shape of the mixer bowl.

FROST THE BROWNIE Scrape the white chocolate buttercream onto the brownie and, using a small offset spatula, evenly frost it with about 1½ cups/9.7 ounces/275 grams of the white chocolate buttercream. (Refrigerate or freeze the leftover buttercream for future use.) Refrigerate the frosted brownie for a minimum of 1 hour to firm the buttercream before applying the ganache glaze.

DARK CHOCOLATE GANACHE GLAZE

MAKES ¾ CUP PLUS 2 TABLESPOONS/8.4 OUNCES/238 GRAMS

	VOLUME	WEIGHT	
bittersweet chocolate, 60% to 62% cacao, chopped	.	4.6 ounces	130 grams
heavy cream	½ cup (118 ml)	4.1 ounces	116 grams
bourbon, preferably Maker's Mark (or pure vanilla extract)	1 tablespoon (15 ml) (or 1 teaspoon/5 ml)	0.5 ounce	15 grams

MAKE THE DARK CHOCOLATE GANACHE GLAZE Have ready a fine-mesh strainer suspended over a 2 cup glass measure with a spout.

In a food processor, process the chocolate until very fine. Transfer it to a small heatproof glass bowl.

In a 1 cup or larger microwavable measure with a spout (or in a small saucepan over medium heat, stirring often), scald the cream (heat it to the boiling point; small bubbles will form around the periphery) and pour it over the chocolate. Cover the bowl for 5 minutes to let the chocolate melt. Using a silicone spatula, gently stir together the chocolate and cream until smooth. Stir in the bourbon until smooth. Press the mixture through the strainer and cool it to warm room temperature so that it is still fluid but not warm to the touch (75° to 82°F/24° to 28°C). (This takes only about 10 minutes, so set it in a warm spot to keep it pourable. If it becomes too firm, reheat it in the microwave with 3 second bursts, or in the top of a double boiler.)

GLAZE THE BROWNIE Starting at the center, with the measuring cup's spout just above the buttercream, slowly pour the ganache glaze, moving the cup as needed to coat all the buttercream. With the small offset spatula, smooth the glaze evenly on top. Refrigerate for a minimum of 1 hour to set the glaze.

UNMOLD AND CUT THE BROWNIES Grasp two of the opposite overhanging edges of the parchment and lift out the brownie. Set it on a countertop. If desired, for perfectly squared off corners, use a serrated knife to trim the sides of the brownie. Use a thin bladed knife, run under warm water and wiped dry between each cut, to cut the brownie into squares. To retain the pristine white of the buttercream, cut straight down and then pull the knife straight out. If desired, cut each square in half diagonally to make triangles.

STORE Airtight: room temperature, 1 day; refrigerated, 2 weeks; frozen, 6 months.

Luxury Chocolate Buttercrunch Toffee

MAKES 1¾ POUNDS/800 GRAMS; 20 SERVINGS

OVEN TEMPERATURE
350°F/175°C

BAKING TIME
7 to 9 minutes

*M*y Mahogany Buttercrunch Toffee is perhaps the favorite recipe in *Rose's Christmas Cookies*. But this version is even more balanced and delicious—using Muscovado brown sugar and sandwiching the toffee between two coats of chocolate. The acidity in the brown sugar reacts with the baking soda to separate the toffee into layers, giving the toffee a less sticky and finer texture.

SPECIAL EQUIPMENT One 17¼ by 12¼ by 1 inch half sheet pan, lined with a nonstick liner such as a Silpat, or a nonstick or buttered cookie sheet, set near the cooktop

Toffee

	VOLUME	WEIGHT	
bittersweet chocolate, 53% to 70% cacao (see Note, page 403)	*divided*	6 to 12 ounces	170 to 340 grams
sliced almonds, preferably blanched	1¾ cups, *divided*	6.2 ounces	175 grams
light brown Muscovado sugar, or dark brown sugar	1¼ cups, firmly packed	9.5 ounces	270 grams
corn syrup	¼ cup (59 ml)	2.9 ounces	82 grams
unsalted butter (65° to 75°F/ 19° to 23°C)	8 tablespoons (1 stick)	4 ounces	113 grams
water	2 tablespoons (30 ml)	1 ounce	30 grams
pure vanilla extract	1 teaspoon (5 ml)	.	.
baking soda	½ teaspoon	.	2.7 grams

Luxury Chocolate Buttercrunch Toffee, Pecan Praline Scheherazades (page 404), and Bourbon Pecan Butter Balls (page 406)

CHOP THE CHOCOLATE Finely process or chop the chocolate and divide it equally between a small bowl and either a microwavable bowl or the top of a double boiler.

PREHEAT THE OVEN Twenty minutes or longer before baking, set an oven rack in the middle of the oven and preheat the oven to 350°F/175°C.

TOAST AND GRIND THE ALMONDS Spread the almonds evenly on a baking sheet and bake for about 7 minutes, or until pale gold. Stir once or twice to ensure even toasting and avoid overbrowning. Cool completely. In a food processor, process until medium-fine. Divide the ground almonds equally between two small bowls.

MAKE THE TOFFEE In a heavy medium saucepan, preferably nonstick, using a wooden spatula or spoon, stir together the brown sugar, corn syrup, butter, and water. (Avoid using a silicone spatula because the long stirring time over heat can deform the spatula's handle.) Over medium heat, bring the mixture to a boil, stirring constantly. Continue boiling, stirring often, until an instant-read thermometer reaches 285°F/140°C. Immediately remove the saucepan from the heat because the temperature will continue to rise. The correct temperature is critical to achieving a smooth, not crumbly, texture. When the temperature reaches 290°F/143°C, stir in the vanilla and baking soda.

COAT THE TOP OF THE TOFFEE Pour the toffee mixture evenly into a 10 by 7 inch oval onto the prepared half sheet pan or cookie sheet, using the wooden spatula or a silicone spatula to scrape out only the toffee that is in a liquid state. Immediately scatter half of the chopped chocolate over the hot toffee. After about 5 minutes, the chocolate will be soft enough to spread with a long metal offset spatula in an even layer over the surface of the toffee. Sprinkle half of the chopped almonds evenly over the chocolate and use a small offset spatula to press them into the chocolate. Refrigerate for about 40 minutes to 1 hour, or until cool and the chocolate is set, with the surface temperature about 65°F/19°C. The almonds should barely move when pressed gently.

Carefully lift the toffee from the Silpat and flip it over.

MELT THE REMAINING CHOCOLATE In the small microwavable bowl, stirring with a silicone spatula every 15 seconds (or in the top of a double boiler set over hot, not simmering, water, stirring often—do not let the bottom of the container touch the water), heat the remaining chocolate until almost melted.

Remove the chocolate from the heat source and stir until fully melted.

COAT THE BOTTOM OF THE TOFFEE Pour the chocolate onto the toffee and use the long offset spatula to spread it evenly over the surface. If the chocolate hardens, wave a hair dryer over the surface to soften it so that the almonds will stick. Immediately sprinkle the remaining chopped almonds evenly over the chocolate, using a small offset spatula to press them into the chocolate.

Highlights for Success

The higher the temperature of the finished toffee mixture, the crunchier the texture, but too high and it will taste burned and have a crumbly texture. The purpose of the corn syrup is to minimize the possibility of a crumbly texture. An accurate instant-read thermometer is essential for this recipe (see page 539).

Refrigerate the toffee again for about 30 minutes, or until cool and the chocolate has set firmly, about 62°F/17°C. Break the toffee into irregular pieces.

STORE Airtight: room temperature, 1 month. (After 1 month it is still delicious, but the sugar may start to crystallize.)

NOTE The percentage of cacao in the chocolate coating and the amount of chocolate used will determine not only the degree of bitterness in the chocolate, but will also have an impact on the contrast and balance of flavor between the toffee and the chocolate.

Pecan Praline Scheherazades

OVEN TEMPERATURE
325°F/160°C

BAKING TIME
7 to 10 minutes

*S*cheherazade's was the first story I remember from childhood. I adored the tale of the beautiful and clever woman who saved her own life by intriguing her murderous husband with a thousand and one unfinished stories so compelling that he kept her alive to hear the next one and then the next. These candies (pictured on page 401), like Scheherazade's stories, are so delicious one can never have enough of them. They are even wonderful frozen. The golden syrup and crème fraîche lend a lilting flavor and slight tang to balance the delicious butterscotch-y sweetness.

SPECIAL EQUIPMENT A medium heavy saucepan, preferably with a pour lip (minimum 1 quart) | A nonstick liner such as a Silpat, or a sheet of nonstick aluminum foil or foil lightly coated with nonstick cooking spray

Pecan Praline Mixture

	VOLUME	WEIGHT	
pecan halves	½ cup	1.8 ounces	50 grams
crème fraîche or heavy cream	¼ cup plus 2 tablespoons (89 ml)	3.1 ounces	87 grams
unsalted butter (65° to 75°F/ 19° to 23°C)	1½ tablespoons	0.7 ounce	21 grams
golden syrup or corn syrup	¼ cup plus 2 tablespoons (89 ml)	4.5 ounces	127 grams
light brown Muscovado sugar, or dark brown sugar	⅓ cup (firmly packed)	2.5 ounces	72 grams
granulated sugar	2 tablespoons plus 2 teaspoons	1.2 ounces	33 grams
fine sea salt	¼ teaspoon	.	1.5 grams
pure vanilla extract	⅜ teaspoon (1.8 ml)	.	.
fleur de sel (optional)	⅛ to ¼ teaspoon	.	.

Highlights for Success

PREHEAT THE OVEN Twenty minutes or longer before baking, set an oven rack in the middle of the oven and preheat the oven to 325°F/160°C.

CUT AND TOAST THE PECANS Cut the pecans into medium-small pieces and place them in a coarse-mesh strainer. Shake the strainer to remove the nut dust. Spread the pecan pieces evenly on a baking sheet and bake for about 7 minutes to enhance their flavor. Stir once or twice to ensure even toasting and avoid overbrowning. Empty the pecans into a medium glass bowl.

COOK THE PRALINES In the saucepan, stir together the crème fraîche, butter, golden syrup, brown sugar, granulated sugar, and salt until the sugars are moistened. Bring the mixture to a boil over medium heat, stirring constantly with a silicone spatula. Reduce the heat to medium-low and continue boiling for 7 to 10 minutes, stirring constantly but gently, until an instant-read thermometer reads 260°F/127°C or a few degrees lower because the temperature will continue to rise.

Remove the saucepan from the heat and, as soon as the mixture reaches temperature, immediately pour it over the pecans in the bowl. Using the silicone spatula, fold the pecans into the caramel and let the mixture cool to 175°F/79°C, about 8 to 15 minutes. Stir in the vanilla.

SHAPE THE PRALINES Set the Silpat or nonstick aluminum foil on the counter. Use tablespoons, lightly coated with nonstick cooking spray, to drop 1 tablespoon rounds of the mixture (about 0.7 ounce/20 grams each) onto the Silpat or foil. Use a small offset spatula or the back of the spoon to even and shape the pralines into 2 inch rounds. If the mixture becomes too stiff, soften it in the microwave with 5 second bursts.

While the pralines are still warm, sprinkle them with a touch of fleur de sel.

COOL THE PRALINES Let the pralines cool completely. Wrap each one in a small piece of plastic wrap.

STORE Wrapped airtight: room temperature, 1 month (low humidity); refrigerated, 6 months; frozen, 9 months.

Variation: YUM ROLLS

These came about because my husband, Elliott, wanted to avoid having sticky fingers. The balls are pop-in-the-mouth size. When the praline mixture is no longer hot but still warm enough to shape, roll heaping teaspoons between the palms of your hands to form 1 inch round balls (about 0.3 ounce/10 grams each). Let the praline balls cool to room temperature. Wrap each one in a small piece of plastic wrap.

BOURBON PECAN BUTTER BALLS

*T*his variation on a southern classic is lighter and less sweet than tradition usually dictates. These bourbon balls (pictured on page 401) are most delicious when allowed to mellow for at least a day. If you love the flavor of bourbon as much as I do, but find it too harsh to drink straight, these are for you.

PLAN AHEAD For the best flavor, make the balls a minimum of 1 day ahead.

CHOCOLATE DOUGH

MAKES ABOUT 31.7 OUNCES/900 GRAMS

	VOLUME	WEIGHT	
1 recipe Double Chocolate Oriolos (page 351) or one and one-half 9 ounce packages of chocolate wafers	.	13.5 ounces	383 grams
unsalted butter, cold	4 tablespoons (½ stick)	2 ounces	56 grams
pecan halves	1½ cups	5.3 ounces	150 grams
powdered sugar	1¼ cups (lightly spooned into the cup and leveled off)	5 ounces	144 grams
unsweetened (alkalized) cocoa powder	½ cup plus 2 tablespoons (sifted before measuring)	1.7 ounces	47 grams
corn syrup	¼ cup (59 ml)	2.9 ounces	82 grams
bourbon, preferably Maker's Mark (see Notes, page 407)	3 to 5 tablespoons (44 to 74 ml), *divided*	1.5 to 2.6 ounces	42 to 70 grams
granulated sugar, for coating the dough balls (see Notes, page 407)	¾ cup	5.3 ounces	150 grams

MAKE THE COOKIE CRUMBS Use a food processor or blender (in several batches) to pulverize the cookies into fine crumbs. Empty them into a large bowl.

MAKE THE DOUGH Cut the butter into 4 pieces.

FOOD PROCESSOR METHOD Process the pecans with the powdered sugar and cocoa until finely ground. Add the butter and corn syrup and process until combined. Add this mixture to the cookie crumbs and, with your fingers or a wooden spoon, mix until uniform in consistency.

HIGHLIGHTS FOR SUCCESS

Homemade chocolate wafers result in moister, softer, and more delicious bourbon balls.

HAND METHOD Soften the butter to 65° to 75°F/19° to 23°C. Use a nut grater to grate the pecans. Sift the powdered sugar and cocoa into the bowl with the cookie crumbs. Add the butter, pecans, and corn syrup. With a wooden spoon, stir until uniform in consistency.

MIX IN THE BOURBON Add 3 tablespoons/44 ml of the bourbon to the cookie crumb mixture. With a wooden spoon, stir the mixture until it is uniform in consistency and begins to clean the bowl. Add a teaspoon at a time of the remaining bourbon if the mixture is too dry to hold together. Let the mixture sit for 30 minutes to absorb evenly. Add more bourbon if necessary.

ROLL THE BOURBON BALLS AND COAT WITH SUGAR Use 1 level tablespoon (0.7 ounce/20 grams) of the mixture and press and roll each one between the palms of your hands to shape it into a 1¼ inch ball. If the mixture becomes dry, add more bourbon.

Place the granulated sugar in a small bowl. Add 1 ball at a time and roll it around in the sugar. The coating is most attractive when dipped 3 times. Redip after the sugar starts to disappear. Place the balls in a paper towel or crumpled parchment–lined airtight container.

STORE Airtight: room temperature, 6 weeks; frozen, 6 months.

NOTES Bourbon gives the best flavor; however, most whiskeys can be substituted. A mixture of ¼ cup/59 ml/2 ounces/59 grams water and 1 tablespoon/15 ml pure vanilla extract can also be substituted.

Granulated sugar is recommended for coating the balls. Superfine sugar will coat the balls with a whiter appearance.

Brandy Snap Cannoli

MAKES TWELVE TO FOURTEEN 4 TO 4½ INCH COOKIES

OVEN TEMPERATURE
350°F/175°C for the brandy snaps; 300°F/150°C for the pistachios

BAKING TIME
7 to 10 minutes for the brandy snaps; 7 minutes for the pistachios

annoli reign supreme among Italian pastries. I have adapted this recipe from one given to me many years ago by Sanford D'Amato of Sanford Restaurant in Milwaukee, Wisconsin. Sanford has elevated cannoli to a new level of refinement. I much prefer the buttery and brandied caramel flavor and delicate chewy-crisp texture of a brandy snap shell to the traditional fried pastry shell. The mascarpone pastry cream filling is also lighter than the traditional ricotta filling, and the dried currants and dried cherries that replace the usual citron or candied fruit add a welcomed tartness. The burnt orange color of the brandy snap shell and the bright green pistachios that garnish the piped cream filling peeking out from the edges make these cannoli as elegant visually as they are refined in flavor and texture.

PLAN AHEAD The cannoli shells, the pastry cream, and the pistachio garnish can be prepared 3 days ahead. The shells should not be filled more than 2 hours ahead of serving to maintain crispness.

SPECIAL EQUIPMENT Two 15 by 12 inch cookie sheets, nonstick or lightly coated with non-stick cooking spray (avoid insulated or cushioned sheets) | One ¾ inch diameter dowel or cannoli mold, lightly coated with nonstick cooking spray | A large pastry bag or gallon-size reclosable freezer bag, fitted with a ⅝ inch star pastry tube

BRANDY SNAP BATTER

	VOLUME	WEIGHT	
unsalted butter	5 tablespoons plus 1 teaspoon	2.6 ounces	75 grams
golden syrup or corn syrup	⅓ cup (79 ml)	4 ounces	113 grams
light brown Muscovado sugar, or dark brown sugar	2 tablespoons, firmly packed	1 ounce	28 grams
ground ginger	¾ teaspoon	.	0.7 gram
salt	a pinch	.	.
bleached all-purpose flour	½ cup (lightly spooned into the cup and leveled off) plus 1½ tablespoons	2.5 ounces	72 grams
brandy	2 teaspoons (10 ml)	.	.

PREHEAT THE OVEN Twenty minutes or longer before baking, set oven racks in the upper and lower thirds of the oven and preheat the oven to 350°F/175°C.

MAKE THE BATTER In a 2 cup microwavable measure with a spout, lightly coated with nonstick cooking spray (or in a small heavy saucepan over medium heat, stirring often), combine the butter, golden syrup, brown sugar, ginger, and salt and bring the mixture to a boil, watching it carefully so that it does not bubble over.

Remove the container from the heat source and whisk in the flour and brandy. If using a saucepan, transfer the batter to a heated 2 cup glass measure with a spout.

Pour the batter onto the cookie sheets to form 2 to 2¼ inch rounds, spacing them 3 inches apart because the batter will spread to about 4 to 4½ inches. (If the batter begins to thicken, heat it in a microwave for a few seconds or place the glass measure in a pan of hot water. A thinner batter makes lacier cookies.)

BAKE THE COOKIES Bake for 4 minutes. For even baking, rotate the cookie sheets halfway around and reverse their position from top to bottom. Continue baking for 3 to 6 minutes, or until the cookies are a deep golden brown and filled with holes.

SHAPE AND COOL THE COOKIES Set the cookie sheets on wire racks and let the cookies cool on the sheets for about 1 minute or until they can be lifted without wrinkling but are still flexible. Use a pancake turner to lift each cookie from the sheets, shaping it before removing the next one so that they stay warm and flexible.

Roll each cookie loosely around the dowel, with the smooth bottom side against the dowel, so that its edges just overlap enough to seal. The wrapped cookie shell should be no more

In order to maintain a round tubular shape and crisp texture, it is necessary to avoid making the brandy snaps in humid weather.

The color of the baked cookies needs to be a deep golden brown. A darker brown cookie will become too fragile for filling and serving.

than 1 inch in diameter. Leave the dowel in the cookie and press down firmly on the seam against the dowel for a few seconds.

As soon as it is rolled, place each cookie, seam side down, on another wire rack to cool. If the cookies become too rigid to roll, return them briefly to the oven. If a cookie begins to sag while cooling, reshape it to a cylindrical shape. Alternatively, if you have more than one dowel, leave the dowels in the cookies until they harden enough to keep their shape.

The cookies can be stored in an airtight container at room temperature for up to 1 week.

NOTE If increasing the recipe, use a proportionally larger microwavable measure or saucepan. To keep the batter fluid for subsequent batches, set the container with the remaining batter in a pan of hot water and cover the top of the container with plastic wrap.

CANNOLI FILLING

MAKES 2½ CUPS/23 OUNCES/650 GRAMS

PASTRY CREAM

MAKES ½ CUP PLUS 2 TABLESPOONS/5.9 OUNCES/166 GRAMS

	VOLUME	WEIGHT	
½ large egg	1½ tablespoons (23 ml)	0.9 ounce	25 grams
cornstarch	2¼ teaspoons	.	7 grams
half-and-half	½ cup (118 ml), *divided*	4.3 ounces	121 grams
granulated sugar	2 tablespoons	0.9 ounce	25 grams
vanilla bean, split lengthwise (or pure vanilla extract)	½ inch piece (or ¼ teaspoon/1.2 ml)	.	.
fine sea salt	a pinch	.	.
unsalted butter	1 teaspoon	.	.

MAKE THE PASTRY CREAM Have ready a fine-mesh strainer suspended over a small bowl.

In a small bowl, whisk together the egg and cornstarch. Gradually add 2 tablespoons/30 ml/1.1 ounces/30 grams of the half-and-half, whisking until the mixture is smooth and the cornstarch is dissolved.

In a medium saucepan, place the sugar and vanilla bean pod. Use your fingers to scrape and rub the seeds into the sugar. Stir in the remaining half-and-half and the salt. Over medium heat, bring the mixture to a full boil, stirring constantly. Whisk 2 tablespoons of this hot mixture into the egg mixture. Pass the egg mixture through the strainer into the small bowl.

Bring the half-and-half mixture back to a boil over medium heat. Remove the vanilla pod (rinse and dry it for future use). Quickly add all of the egg mixture, whisking rapidly. Continue whisking rapidly for about 20 to 30 seconds, being sure to go into the bottom edge of the pan. The mixture will become very thick. Remove the mixture from the heat and whisk in the butter. (If not using the vanilla bean, whisk in the vanilla extract.) Immediately pour the mixture into a bowl and place a piece of plastic wrap lightly coated with nonstick cooking spray directly on the surface of the cream to keep a skin from forming. Let the mixture cool to room temperature, about 45 minutes, then refrigerate until cold.

COMPLETED CANNOLI FILLING

	VOLUME	WEIGHT	
Pastry Cream (see page 411)	½ cup	4.7 ounces	133 grams
mascarpone, preferably imported, or whipped cream cheese	¾ cup plus 2 tablespoons	8 ounces	227 grams
heavy cream, cold	½ cup (118 ml)	4.1 ounces	116 grams
blanched unsalted pistachios	¼ cup plus 2 tablespoons	2 ounces	58 grams
dried cherries	¼ cup	1 ounce	28 grams
dried currants	¼ cup	1 ounce	28 grams
bourbon, preferably Maker's Mark	¼ cup (59 ml)	2 ounces	56 grams
granulated sugar	2 tablespoons	0.9 ounce	25 grams
orange zest, finely grated	2 tablespoons, loosely packed	.	12 grams
Grand Marnier	1 tablespoon (15 ml)	0.5 ounce	14 grams
powdered sugar, for dusting the cannoli shells	.	.	.

PREHEAT THE OVEN Twenty minutes or longer or longer before baking, set an oven rack in the middle of the oven and preheat the oven to 300°F/150°C.

MAKE THE FILLING Remove the pastry cream and mascarpone from the refrigerator to soften slightly (no more than 30 minutes).

Into a medium bowl, pour the heavy cream and refrigerate for at least 10 minutes. (Chill a handheld mixer's beaters alongside the bowl.)

Spread the pistachios on a baking sheet and bake for about 7 minutes, or until they barely begin to color to enhance their flavor. Stir once or twice to ensure even toasting and avoid overbrowning. Cool completely and chop coarsely.

With sharp kitchen scissors, cut the dried cherries into ¼ inch pieces.

In a small saucepan, preferably nonstick, place the cherries, currants, bourbon, granulated sugar, and orange zest and, stirring often with a silicone spatula, bring them to a boil. Simmer the mixture for 3 to 4 minutes, scraping the liquid onto the fruits, until almost all of the liquid has evaporated. Transfer the mixture to a small bowl and let it cool completely.

With a handheld mixer, starting on low speed and gradually raising the speed to medium-high as it thickens, whip the cream just until soft peaks form when the beater is raised.

In a medium bowl, place the mascarpone and fold in the dried fruits. Fold in the pastry cream and the Grand Marnier. Gently fold in the whipped cream just until evenly blended.

FILL THE CANNOLI Up to 2 hours before serving, place the filling in the prepared pastry bag and pipe the mixture into the brandy snap shells. To make a decorative star finish, as you reach the end, gradually ease the pressure as you pull the tube away. Pipe another star into the opposite end. Sprinkle the ends with the chopped pistachios and dust the shells lightly with the powdered sugar.

STORE Room temperature, 2 hours. (The completed cannoli filling can be refrigerated for 24 hours.)

DATTELKONFEKT
(DATE CONFECTIONS)

MAKES FORTY-EIGHT 2 INCH COOKIES

OVEN TEMPERATURE
350°F/175°C

BAKING TIME
10 to 15 minutes for each of four batches

I fell in love with this confection in 2010 when Naomi Lewin, a host on WQXR radio in New York City, made these for me when she interviewed me for a Christmas show she called Nutcracker Sweets. And how deliciously sweet these are! Essentially, they are chopped date and almond meringues. The nuts add crunch, the dates contribute a marvelously moist and chewy interior, and the whole is encased in a thin, crisp meringue shell. This is a family heirloom from Naomi's *Oma* ("grandmother") Hanna Gaaertner, who emigrated from Germany.

SPECIAL EQUIPMENT Two 15 by 12 inch cookie sheets (lined with parchment if not using the back-oblaten) | Optional: a small pastry bag (or disposable pastry bag or quart-size reclosable freezer bag with a ½ inch semicircle cut from the tip or one corner)

DATE NUT MERINGUE
MAKES 25.4 OUNCES/720 GRAMS

	VOLUME	WEIGHT	
sliced almonds, preferably unblanched	2½ cups	8.8 ounces	250 grams
pitted dates, about 36	2 cups	8.8 ounces	250 grams
3 large egg whites, at room temperature	¼ cup plus 2 tablespoons (89 ml)	3.2 ounces	90 grams
sugar	1 cup	7 ounces	200 grams
pure vanilla extract	1 teaspoon (5 ml)	.	.
50 mm/2 inch round back-oblaten (see Note, page 416; optional)	48 rounds	.	.

PREHEAT THE OVEN Twenty minutes or longer before baking, set an oven rack in the middle of the oven and preheat the oven to 350°F/175°C.

CHOP THE ALMONDS AND THE DATES In a food processor, process the almonds until fine but not beginning to become pasty. Empty them into a medium bowl.

Process the dates until chopped and beginning to clump together. (Alternatively, use a knife that has been lightly coated with nonstick cooking spray.) Return the almonds to the food processor and process them together with the dates just until the dates are evenly dispersed and separate.

BEAT THE EGG WHITES INTO A MERINGUE In the bowl of a stand mixer fitted with the whisk beater, beat the egg whites on medium-low speed until soft peaks form when the beater is raised. Raise the speed to medium-high and gradually beat in the sugar. Continue beating for 5 minutes. The meringue will be very glossy but will not hold a peak when the beater is raised.

ADD THE ALMOND AND DATE MIXTURE TO THE MERINGUE Add the vanilla and the almond and date mixture to the meringue and beat on low speed just until incorporated.

PIPE OR SPREAD THE DATE NUT MERINGUE Scoop about one-quarter of the meringue into the pastry bag, if using. If using the back-oblaten, holding one back-oblaten in your hand, pipe a mound of the batter, about 1 inch high (0.5 ounce/15 grams), onto it. Leave a ⅛ inch exposed edge of the back-oblaten because the batter will expand sideways. Set the cookie on a cookie sheet. Alternatively, use a small metal spatula to spread the mixture onto the back-oblaten. Smooth the top of the meringue mound with a fingertip first dipped lightly in water. Pipe or spread 11 more meringue mounds.

(If not using the back-oblaten, pipe 2 inch wide mounds onto the prepared cookie sheets, leaving a minimum of 1 inch in between each. If making some cookies with back-oblaten and some without, bake each type on separate cookie sheets because the back-oblaten cookies take longer to bake.)

BAKE THE COOKIES Bake 10 to 15 minutes, or until set and the tops are lightly browned. (When pressed very lightly with a fingertip there will be very little give.)

COOL THE COOKIES Set the cookie sheet on a wire rack and let the cookies cool on the cookie sheet until room temperature.

While each batch of cookies is baking, pipe the meringue mixture for the next batch.

STORE Airtight: room temperature, 2 weeks; frozen, 2 months.

NOTE Back-oblaten are thin edible wafers made with flour and are used in Germany as the base for confections to prevent sticking. They are available on the Internet. Alternatively, you can use sheets of parchment to line the cookie sheets.

Back-oblaten rectangle sheets can be cut easily into circles with small sharp scissors for the traditional appearance of these cookies. Alternatively, the back-oblaten can be cut in 2 by 2 inch squares and the batter mounded and sides squared off with a wet spatula.

MERINGUE BIRCH TWIGS

OVEN TEMPERATURE
225°F/105°C

BAKING TIME
3 hours plus 20 minutes

I think of these marvelous meringue cookies as "Jolly Good Fallowes" because the person who created the recipe is Gary Fallowes, my dear friend and partner for his NewMetro Design Rose Collection of home baking and cooking tools. Every Christmas he sends a surprise package of something special he has baked. The year he sent these amazing meringues I asked him for the recipe for this book. They are the lightest and least sweet meringues I've ever encountered. If baked until tan in color, they will have a slightly toasty taste that accentuates their subtle raspberry flavoring. Set in a crystal vase or tall glass, they make a spectacular presentation.

SPECIAL EQUIPMENT Two 17¼ by 12¼ by 1 inch half sheet pans, lined with nonstick liners such as Silpats or parchment | A large disposable pastry bag fitted with a ¼ inch round decorating tip (number 12) | An artist's brush | A disposable pastry bag for the chocolate drizzle

MERINGUE

	VOLUME	WEIGHT	
3 large egg whites, at room temperature	¼ cup plus 2 tablespoons (89 ml)	3.2 ounces	90 grams
cream of tartar	⅜ teaspoon	.	1.2 grams
superfine sugar	½ cup	3.5 ounces	100 grams
pure vanilla extract	¼ teaspoon (1.2 ml)	.	.
fine-quality raspberry flavoring, or flavor of your choice (see Note, page 418)	⅛ teaspoon	.	.
bittersweet chocolate, 60% to 70% cacao, chopped	.	3 ounces	85 grams

PREHEAT THE OVEN Twenty minutes or longer before baking, set oven racks in the upper and lower thirds of the oven and preheat the oven to 225°F/105°C.

BEAT THE EGG WHITES INTO A STIFF MERINGUE In the bowl of a stand mixer fitted with the whisk beater, beat the egg whites and cream of tartar on medium-low speed until foamy. Gradually raise the speed to medium-high and beat until soft peaks form when the beater is raised. Gradually beat in the sugar, 1 tablespoon at a time, until stiff peaks form when the beater is raised slowly. Scrape down the sides of the bowl. Add the vanilla and flavoring and continue beating for 30 seconds. Scrape down the sides of the bowl. Continue beating for 1 minute. The meringue should be stiff and glossy.

PIPE THE MERINGUE TWIGS Fill the pastry bag fitted with the tip with the meringue. Pipe a small dot of meringue in each corner of the pan underneath the parchment to secure the paper. Pipe either 15 inch long twigs (the length of the pans) or 12 inch long twigs (the width of the pans) in rows about ⅜ inch apart. Use a wet artist's brush to tamp down the peak that forms when lifting the tip away.

BAKE THE MERINGUE TWIGS Bake for 1 hour and 20 minutes without opening the oven door. Turn off the oven and let the twigs dry for 2 hours (1 hour if the oven has a pilot light).

COOL THE MERINGUE TWIGS Set the sheet pans on wire racks or on a heat resistant surface. Cool completely.

DRIZZLE THE MERINGUE TWIGS WITH MELTED CHOCOLATE In a small microwavable bowl, stirring with a silicone spatula every 15 seconds (or in the top of a double boiler set over hot, not simmering, water, stirring often—do not let the bottom of the container touch the water), heat the chocolate until almost completely melted.

Remove the chocolate from the heat source and stir until fully melted.

Pour the chocolate into the second pastry bag. Cut a very small semicircle into the tip of the bag and drizzle the melted chocolate back and forth over the rows of meringue twigs. Let the chocolate set before carefully loosening and removing the twigs from the liner with a small offset spatula.

STORE Airtight: room temperature (low humidity), 3 months.

NOTE Intense and pure flavorings are available from Mandy Aftel of Aftel Perfumes, and from La Cuisine (see page 527).

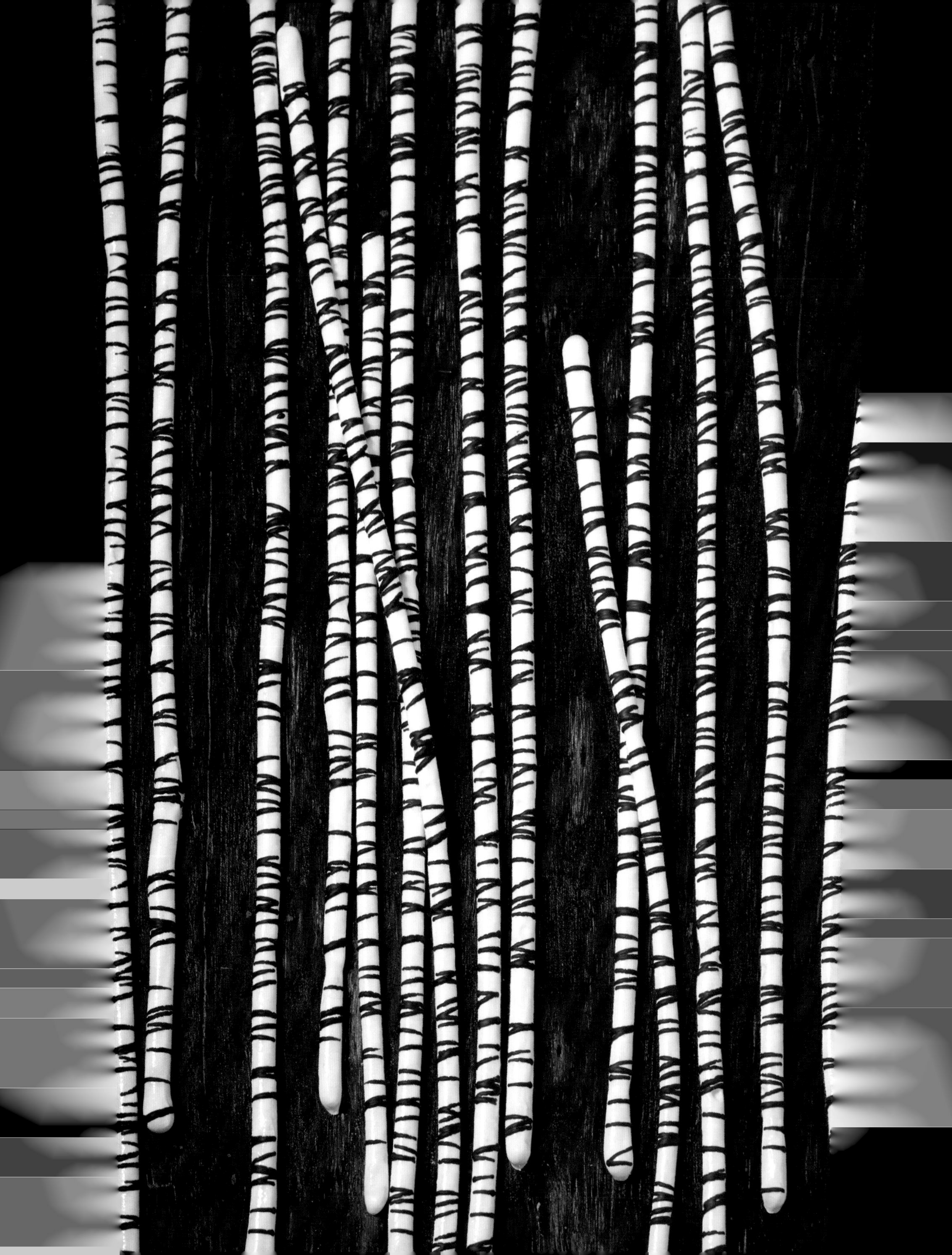

Praline Pecan Meringue Ice Cream Sandwiches

MAKES FORTY 2½ INCH COOKIES (20 SANDWICHES)

OVEN TEMPERATURE 350°F/175°C

BAKING TIME 10 to 15 minutes for each of two batches

*T*his is a greatly treasured recipe. It was given to me many years ago by chef Vinnie Scotto, who was one of the most gifted and generous people I have ever known. I first met him when he was chef at Fresco by Scotto in New York City. I followed him to Scopa, and then to Gonzo, which was his first restaurant. Gonzo was a family affair, with Vinnie's sister Donna serving as maître d' and his father as accountant. Tragically, Vinnie died in his early thirties. Two decades later, Donna reconnected with me through LinkedIn and sent me this recipe. I cannot express the joy of rediscovery I felt—it was like having a little of Vinnie returned to me. When I tried the recipe, to my great delight, it was exactly as I remembered. This meringue cookie is light, slightly chewy, and exceptionally flavorful due to the use of brown sugar and the addition of pecans. I have never tasted anything like it before or since. My favorite ice creams for this cookie sandwich are coffee or vanilla. The mellow chocolate piping sauce that I created specially for this cookie elevates it to an elegant dinner dessert.

SPECIAL EQUIPMENT Four 15 by 12 inch cookie sheets, lined with parchment | A 2 inch ice cream scoop or ¼ cup measure

Praline Pecan Meringue Cookies

	VOLUME	WEIGHT	
pecan halves	3 cups, *divided*	10.6 ounces	300 grams
4 large egg whites, at room temperature	½ cup (118 ml)	4.2 ounces	120 grams
light brown Muscovado sugar, or dark brown sugar	1¼ cups plus 2 tablespoons, firmly packed	10.6 ounces	300 grams

PREHEAT THE OVEN Twenty minutes or longer before baking, set oven racks in the upper and lower thirds of the oven and preheat the oven to 350°F/175°C.

TOAST AND PREPARE THE PECANS Spread the pecans evenly on a baking sheet, set the pan on the upper rack, and bake for about 5 minutes, or just until light brown, to enhance their flavor. Stir once or twice to ensure even toasting and avoid overbrowning. Cool completely.

Praline Pecan Meringue Ice Cream Sandwiches and Fudgy Chocolate
Ice Cream Sandwiches (page 424)

Divide the pecans into two equal parts. Leave one part whole and chop the other part into medium-fine pieces.

MAKE THE MERINGUE In the bowl of a stand mixer fitted with the whisk beater, beat the egg whites and brown sugar on medium speed until well mixed, about 1 minute. Scrape down the sides of the bowl. Raise the speed to medium-high and beat for about 5 minutes, or until very thick and light in color. Add the whole and chopped pecans and, using a silicone spatula, fold them into the meringue.

SHAPE THE COOKIES Use a tablespoon to drop 10 dollops of the pecan meringue (0.6 ounces/17 grams each) onto each of two prepared cookie sheets, at least 1½ inches apart. Using a small offset spatula, shape the dollops into ½ inch high by 2¼ inch wide discs. They will spread to about 2½ inches but will not widen on baking. Stir the mixture from time to time to ensure that each spoonful includes some of the pecans. If necessary, use a metal spatula to coax the meringue into a more even disc.

BAKE THE COOKIES Bake for 10 to 15 minutes. The meringues will crack slightly in an attractive manner. Check for doneness. A metal cake tester inserted into one of the cracks will come out sticky and the cookies will give slightly to pressure. (An instant-read thermometer should read about 190°F/88°C.) If more baking is required, rotate the cookie sheets halfway around, reverse their positions from top to bottom, and continue baking for a few more minutes.

While the first batch of meringues is baking, shape the second batch of meringues.

COOL THE COOKIES Set the cookie sheets on wire racks and let the meringues cool completely on the sheets. They will firm on sitting and become easy to lift off the parchment using a small pancake turner. Sandwich them with ice cream or store the unfilled meringues airtight for up to 2 months.

ICE CREAM FILLING

	VOLUME	WEIGHT	
ice cream of your choice, softened	about 1½ quarts	.	.

SANDWICH THE COOKIES WITH ICE CREAM Assemble only half of the ice cream sandwiches at a time to keep the ice cream from melting. Refrigerate the ice cream for 20 minutes before sandwiching the cookies to soften it slightly. Set sheet pans or cookie sheets in the freezer to chill.

Set 10 of the cookies, bottom sides up, on one of the chilled sheet pans. Set scoops of ice cream, about ¼ cup in size, on top of each cookie. Place a second cookie, bottom side down, on top. When the ice cream is soft enough to press down easily, evenly press the top of each cookie until the ice cream comes almost to the edge. The ice cream should be about ½ inch thick.

Cover the sandwiches with a sheet of plastic wrap and set them in the freezer until firm. Then wrap each sandwich separately in plastic wrap and store in an airtight container in the freezer. Repeat with the remaining cookies.

STORE Airtight: frozen, 2 months.

Optional: ROSE BLEND GANACHE PIPING GLAZE

MAKES A FULL ½ CUP/5 OUNCES/143 GRAMS

	VOLUME	WEIGHT	
white chocolate containing cocoa butter, chopped	.	2.3 ounces	66 grams
dark chocolate, 60% to 62% cacao, chopped	.	1.2 ounces	33 grams
heavy cream, hot	¼ cup (59 ml)	2 ounces	58 grams

MAKE THE GANACHE PIPING GLAZE Have ready a fine-mesh strainer suspended over a small bowl.

In a small microwavable bowl, stirring with a silicone spatula every 15 seconds (or in the top of a double boiler set over hot, not simmering, water, stirring often—do not let the bottom of the container touch the water), heat the white chocolate and dark chocolate until almost completely melted.

Remove the chocolates from the heat source and stir until fully melted.

Pour the hot cream on top of the chocolates and stir until smooth. Press the mixture through the strainer. Let the glaze cool, stirring very gently to avoid creating air bubbles, every 15 minutes until a small amount of the glaze dropped from the spatula mounds a bit before smoothly disappearing. (An instant-read thermometer should read about 75°F/23°C.) Use the glaze at once, or cover, set aside, and reheat it in the microwave with 3 second bursts, or in a hot water bath.

Scrape the glaze into a disposable pastry bag. Cut a very small semicircle into the tip of the bag and drizzle the glaze over the ice cream sandwiches.

Return the ice cream sandwiches to the freezer for a few minutes until the piping glaze is firm, and then wrap each sandwich separately.

The piping glaze can be stored for 2 weeks refrigerated or 3 months frozen.

Variation: PRALINE PECAN MERINGUE COOKIES

The praline pecan meringue is delicious to eat as a puffy cookie. Make the batter as directed on page 420 and simply drop the tablespoon dollops onto the cookie sheets without spreading them or reshaping them. Bake for 12 to 17 minutes and cool as directed.

FUDGY CHOCOLATE
ICE CREAM SANDWICHES

OVEN TEMPERATURE 350°F/175°C

BAKING TIME 8 to 10 minutes for each of four batches

*T*his is a fabulously delicious chocolate cookie that is fudgy when frozen. The edges of the cookies are crisp, which provides a charming contrast to the chewy interior of the cookie and the creamy ice cream filling. My favorite ice cream for filling the cookie sandwich is cherry vanilla, but, of course, chocolate goes with many other flavors, even more chocolate (as pictured on page 421)! The optional chocolate sauce is the dipping sauce version of my ganache piping glaze (see page 423).

PLAN AHEAD The dough requires 3 hours to freeze before baking or it can be frozen for 3 months. The optional chocolate dipping sauce needs to be made at least 2 hours ahead, but can be made several hours ahead and reheated.

SPECIAL EQUIPMENT Two 15 by 12 inch cookie sheets, nonstick or lined with parchment | Two 12 by 1⅝ inch (measured from the inside) cardboard tubes from paper towel rolls, cut into halves (or PVC plastic piping cut into four 6 inch lengths) | A sharp knife with a 1½ to 2 inch wide blade | A 2 inch ice cream scoop or ¼ cup measure

COOKIE DOUGH

MAKES 21.2 OUNCES/600 GRAMS

	VOLUME		WEIGHT	
bittersweet chocolate, 60% to 62% cacao, chopped	.		1.5 ounces	42 grams
bleached all-purpose flour	1 cup (lightly spooned into the cup and leveled off) plus 3 tablespoons	5 ounces		142 grams
unsweetened (alkalized) cocoa powder	½ cup (sifted before measuring)	1.3 ounces		37 grams
baking soda	½ teaspoon	.		2.7 grams
fine sea salt	⅛ teaspoon	.		0.7 gram
1 large egg, lightly beaten	3 tablespoons plus ½ teaspoon (47 ml)	1.8 ounces		50 grams
heavy cream	3 tablespoons (44 ml)	1.5 ounces		43 grams

	VOLUME	WEIGHT	
light corn syrup	2 teaspoons (10 ml)	0.5 ounce	14 grams
pure vanilla extract	1 teaspoon (5 ml)	.	.
superfine sugar	¾ cup	5.3 ounces	150 grams
unsalted butter (65° to 75°F/ 19° to 23°C)	10 tablespoons (1¼ sticks)	5 ounces	142 grams

MELT THE CHOCOLATE In a small microwavable bowl, stirring with a silicone spatula every 15 seconds (or in the top of a double boiler set over hot, not simmering, water, stirring often—do not let the bottom of the container touch the water), heat the chocolate until almost completely melted.

Remove the chocolate from the heat source and stir until fully melted. Let it cool until it is no longer warm to the touch but is still fluid, about 10 minutes.

MIX THE DRY INGREDIENTS In a small bowl, whisk together the flour, cocoa, baking soda, and salt. Sift them onto a sheet of parchment.

MIX THE LIQUID INGREDIENTS In a small bowl, whisk the egg, cream, corn syrup, and vanilla just until lightly combined.

MAKE THE DOUGH In the bowl of a stand mixer fitted with the flat beater, beat the sugar and butter on medium speed until well mixed, about 1 minute. Scrape down the sides of the bowl. Gradually beat in the egg mixture. It should take about 15 seconds. Scrape in the chocolate and beat until thoroughly incorporated, about 1 minute. Scrape down the sides of the bowl. Detach the flat beater and add the flour mixture. Stir until moistened. Reattach the flat beater and beat on low speed until incorporated, about 15 seconds. The dough will be like a fluffy but thick butter cake batter.

Scrape the dough onto a piece of plastic wrap. Use the plastic wrap to flatten it into a 6 by 5 inch rectangle and refrigerate it for at least 1½ hours until firm enough to shape. (An instant-read thermometer should read below 63°F/17°C.)

SHAPE THE DOUGH LOGS Divide the rectangle of dough into quarters, about 5.3 ounces/ 150 grams each. Work with 1 piece at a time and refrigerate the rest.

Set the dough on a piece of plastic wrap and wrap the plastic wrap around the entire piece of dough. Roll the dough into a log about 1½ inches in diameter and about 5½ inches long. Slide the log into one of the cardboard tubes and set it upright in the freezer. Repeat with the remaining dough logs. Freeze the dough logs for at least 2 hours, or until an instant-read thermometer reads below 32°F/0°C to firm it for even cutting. (If not using the cardboard tubes, lay the dough logs on their sides but turn them a few times to keep them round.) The dough cuts most easily when not frozen solid, so it helps to let it soften slightly before slicing.

The unbaked dough can be frozen for up to 3 months.

PREHEAT THE OVEN Twenty minutes or longer before baking, set an oven rack in the middle of the oven and preheat the oven to 350°F/175°C.

CUT THE DOUGH INTO COOKIES It is best to bake one cookie sheet at a time to ensure that the cookies can be removed from the sheet as soon after baking as possible so that they stay soft. Remove a frozen dough log from the freezer and cut 12 slices ⅜ inch thick. Set the slices 2 inches apart on a cookie sheet and bake at once.

BAKE THE COOKIES Bake for 4 minutes. For even baking, rotate the cookie sheet halfway around. Continue baking for 4 to 6 minutes, or just until set but still soft to the touch.

COOL THE COOKIES Set the cookie sheet on a wire rack and let the cookies cool for about 1 minute, or just until they can be lifted with a pancake turner to a wire rack to continue cooling. (Do not leave them on the cookie sheet because they will continue to bake and become brittle.) They will bend slightly but become flat when set on the wire rack to cool. As soon as the cookies are cool, sandwich them with the ice cream or store them airtight.

While each batch of cookies is baking, shape the dough for the next batch.

The cookies can be stored in an airtight container for 1 week at room temperature, 2 weeks refrigerated, or 1 month frozen.

Ice Cream Filling

	VOLUME	WEIGHT	
ice cream of your choice, softened	about 1½ quarts	.	.

SANDWICH THE COOKIES WITH ICE CREAM Assemble only half of the ice cream sandwiches at a time to keep the ice cream from melting. Refrigerate the ice cream for 20 minutes before sandwiching the cookies to soften it slightly. Set sheet pans or cookie sheets in the freezer to chill.

Set 12 of the cookies, bottom sides up, on one of the chilled sheet pans. Set scoops of ice cream, about ¼ cup in size, on top of each cookie. Place a second cookie, bottom side down, on top. When the ice cream is soft enough to press down easily, evenly press the top of each cookie until the ice cream comes almost to the edge. The ice cream should be about ½ inch thick.

Cover the sandwiches with a sheet of plastic wrap and set them in the freezer until firm. Then wrap each sandwich separately in plastic wrap and store in an airtight container in the freezer. Repeat with the remaining cookies.

STORE Airtight: frozen, 1 month.

Optional: Custom Rose Blend Ganache Dipping Sauce

MAKES 2 CUPS PLUS 2 TABLESPOONS/20 OUNCES/564 GRAMS

	VOLUME	WEIGHT	
white chocolate containing cocoa butter, chopped	.	8.2 ounces	232 grams
dark chocolate, 60% to 62% cacao, chopped	.	4.1 ounces	116 grams
heavy cream	1 cup (237 ml)	8.2 ounces	232 grams

MAKE THE GANACHE DIPPING SAUCE Have ready a fine-mesh strainer suspended over a medium glass bowl.

In a food processor, process the white chocolate and dark chocolate until very fine.

In a 1 cup microwavable measure with a spout (or in a small saucepan over medium heat, stirring often), scald the cream (heat it to the boiling point; small bubbles will form around the periphery).

With the motor of the food processor running, pour the cream through the feed tube in a steady stream. Process for a few seconds until smooth. Press the ganache through the strainer and let it sit for about 2 hours, or until it puddles thickly and then disappears when dropped from a spatula. Cover it after the first hour to prevent evaporation.

Reheat the sauce in a double boiler set over hot, not simmering, water (or very carefully in a microwave with 3 second bursts, stirring gently to ensure that it doesn't overheat or incorporate any air). The best consistency is at 72° to 75°F/22° to 24°C.

Serve as a dipping sauce or spoon on top of each sandwich cookie.

The sauce can be stored for 2 weeks refrigerated or 3 months frozen.

BREADS AND YEAST PASTRIES

*B*ecause bread is my greatest baking passion, inevitably, since writing *The Bread Bible*, I have discovered many new breads and some tweaks that benefit other popular ones. The bread chapter in this book, however, is limited to those that work as breakfast breads, such as Crumpets; as dessert breads, such as the Sugar Rose Brioche; or as part of a cheese course, such as the 100% Whole Wheat Walnut Loaf. I have also included my final and ultimate rendition of one of my favorite yeast pastries—Caramel Buns—and a strong new contender for the title, Kouigns Amann. I also discovered how much more moist and flavorful a bread, such as the Swedish Apricot Walnut Bread, is when a small amount of old sourdough starter is added. Because not everyone is committed to maintaining a starter, I experimented with substituting a biga (see page 430), which is simply a mixture of flour, water, a tiny amount of yeast, and salt that is allowed to sit for a minimum of 6 hours or up to 3 days to develop acidity and flavor. To my delight, it worked just as well as the sourdough starter.

I am also offering my three best preserves that money can't buy, as a baker's "dividend" to accompany the crumpets, brioche, White Chocolate Club Med Bread, whole wheat bread, or any bread of your choice. They are the only preserves I make rather than purchase because I enjoy the jam-making process and because the homemade versions are a world apart from any commercial ones I've ever tasted.

Timing

The function of a pre-ferment, or dough starter, is to add flavor, texture, and shelf life to bread. A pre-ferment consists of flour, water, yeast, and sometimes salt, in varying proportions. A small amount is mixed before the rest of the dough to start the fermentation process. A biga, an Italian pre-ferment, is close to the consistency of bread dough (from 50 to 78.7 percent water, or hydration). It is usually mixed at least 6 to 24 hours ahead and used within 3 days. Because of its stiff consistency, it is the strongest (in terms of gluten) of the pre-ferments and is particularly useful for strengthening the network of gluten in breads with a high water content. (*Biga* is the Italian word for a two-wheel chariot. It seems reasonable that it should be used to describe this pre-ferment for bread baking because it is a vehicle that adds great impact in terms of flavor and strength to bread dough.)

If a biga overmatures and deflates, the bread will have smaller holes. If the biga is refrigerated for much past 3 days, it will become too acidic, weakening the gluten and adding a very sour flavor. It can, however, be frozen for up to 3 months. It will lose some yeast activity, but will still contribute complexity to the flavor of the bread. What I most love about a biga is the flexibility it gives you when it comes to timing. It takes only a few minutes to mix, and then, anytime within the next 3 days, all you add is the rest of the flour, a little yeast, and the salt, and you're well on your way to fantastic bread! My biga is fairly soft, so it integrates easily into the rest of the dough.

Ideally, a biga needs to be made several days ahead, but it shortens the fermentation time of the dough. Some of the bread recipes in this book use a sponge starter alone to achieve similar results. A sponge starter has a higher percentage of water and yeast and needs to sit only from 1 to 4 hours because a liquid consistency starter ferments more quickly. If it sits for the maximum time, it will develop more flavor and speed the rising of the mixed dough. If time does not allow for a 4 hour fermentation, it is also fine to refrigerate the sponge overnight after the first hour. If using a bread machine, let the sponge come to room temperature before mixing. If using an electric stand mixer, the friction of the dough hook will heat the dough, making it unnecessary to bring the sponge to room temperature first. I have also found that the sponge starter can sit at 60°F/16°C for as long as 12 hours with no adverse results.

Also, to help fit bread making into your schedule, most doughs, after sitting at room temperature for 30 minutes, can be refrigerated overnight and allowed to continue rising, if necessary, the next day. If the dough is to have two rises, then it can be refrigerated after the first rise.

Some Special Tips

- I prefer to add the water to the bread machine container or mixer bowl before the flour because, when I set the container on the scale and then add the water, it is easy to pour in a little too much and equally easy to remove it, whereas if the flour is already in the bowl, the water will start to mix with the flour and it will be harder to remove.

- If making a recipe using a sponge starter, such as the White Chocolate Club Med Bread, and it suits your schedule best to let it rise overnight, you can let the sponge sit at 60°F/16°C, or refrigerate it, for up to 12 hours.

- Bread rises best in a moist environment, 75° to 85°F/24° to 29°C (see bread proofer, page 539). To make your own bread proofer, place a container or cup filled with hot water in a plastic box or a microwave oven. Change the water every 30 minutes. You can also use a conventional oven without a pilot light but with the light turned on to provide heat.

- The range of time for bread rising is not only related to the temperature of the rising environment, but also to how often bread is made in your kitchen. Because I have been baking bread often for more than a decade, my bread dough rises faster due to all of the friendly flora in the air.

- Stretching the dough gently between risings helps to develop elasticity, resulting in a good rise and shape to the finished loaf. When the recipe says to give the dough "a four-sided stretch and fold," set the dough on a lightly floured counter and pat it into a rough square. One at a time, gently pull out and stretch each of the four edges and then fold them into the center. Press the center of the dough so that the dough sticks together, turn it over, round the dough by tucking the corners under, and return it to the rising container, smooth side up.

- When dough is retarded overnight (set in the refrigerator overnight before baking), it will develop more flavor but will be slightly lower in height after baking.

- If dough is shaped when cold, the components will not be evenly distributed, so the resulting crumb may have bubbles and the texture may be uneven. If the dough has been refrigerated, remove it to room temperature 30 minutes to 1 hour before shaping. (Brioche, however, is such a soft, moist dough that it is best rolled when cold, because it will require less flour to keep it from sticking.)

- Always place the dough, smooth (skin) side down, on a very lightly floured counter to begin shaping. Too much flour causes the dough to slip. You want the dough to grab slightly onto the counter as you push against it to tighten the outer "skin," which will help to support and maintain the shape of the loaf.

- Let bread cool completely before cutting because the baking process continues while the bread is still hot.

Storing Yeast Breads and Pastries

Most breads and pastries are best eaten the day they are baked or up to 2 days later. When you want to maintain a crisp crust, store bread or pastries uncovered or in a brown paper bag. Once a bread has been cut, it is important to keep the cut edge from drying. Cover it with plastic wrap or stand it on the cut end.

Most breads and pastries freeze well. It works well to slice them, wrap the slices well in plastic freezer wrap such as Freeze-Tite, and then place them in a reclosable freezer bag. If freezing the loaf whole, underbake it slightly (until an instant-read thermometer reads 180° to 190°F/82° to 88°C). Defrost the loaf at room temperature for several hours, then finish baking for 10 to 15 minutes at the same temperature at which it was originally baked.

Troubleshooting Bread

PROBLEM: Bread does not rise enough.
SOLUTION: Use fresh yeast. Do not overproof. Soft, rich doughs, such as brioche, however, should be allowed a full proof so that they do not pull in at the sides when baked.

PROBLEM: The bread bursts and cracks.
SOLUTION: The dough is underproofed—let it rise until when pressed gently with a fingertip, it fills in slowly.

PROBLEM: The bread has too tight a grain.
SOLUTION: Use more liquid and/or avoid adding too much flour when handling the dough. (Dough sticks less to wet hands.) Use the bench scraper as an extension of your hand to lift and move the dough.

GOLDEN RULES OF BREAD BAKING

Weigh or measure ingredients carefully for consistent flavor and texture.

Use the ingredients specified in the recipe. For more details, see the Ingredients chapter (page 509).

FLOUR Use the flour specified in the recipe or one of similar protein content.

Whole wheat flour must be freshly ground or stored for up to 3 months at cool room temperature. Because whole wheat flour includes the germ of the wheat kernel, which is high in oil and prone to rancidity, it will develop an off taste if stored longer. Alternatively, it can be stored in the freezer for several years. If freshly ground, it should be used within 3 to 4 days or after 3 weeks, due to enzyme activity in between that time period that would make it less stable.

White wheat unbleached flour, unless frozen, has an expiration date of about 1 year and will lose strength if it ages beyond it.

WATER It is usually best to use room temperature tap water. However, the minerals in very hard water, or the lack of minerals in very soft water, may noticeably affect the taste and texture of bread. Very hard water will toughen the dough and slow down fermentation, and very soft water will soften the dough and make it sticky. If your water quality is suspect, use bottled water. You don't want one too high in minerals, nor do you want distilled water, which has none at all.

MILK When adding milk to bread dough, **I prefer to use dry milk powder.** King Arthur's Baker's Special Dry Milk is ideal for the highest rise and best flavor (see page 515).

YEAST Use instant yeast for the most reliable results. Stored airtight in the freezer, it will stay fresh and alive for as long as 2 years, or even longer. Add the instant yeast to the flour in the recipe and avoid either ice water or water hotter than 110°F/43°C.

Mix the yeast into the flour before adding salt. If salt comes into direct contact with yeast, it will kill the yeast.

BUTTER Use a high quality unsalted butter with standard fat content unless high butterfat is called for in the recipe or if making clarified butter.

Cut dough with a sharp knife or scissors. Avoid tearing it because it will weaken the dough. For the best shape, after cutting dough, let it rest, covered, for 20 minutes before shaping.

Shape the dough well. A taut outer "skin" will result in the highest rise. For the best shape, use the pan size indicated in the recipe.

Use a baking stone in the oven for the highest rise. Alternatively, set the oven temperature 25° to 50°F/ 15° to 30°C higher than the temperature indicated in the recipe and then lower it after the first 10 minutes of baking, once the oven has had a chance to regain the drop in temperature resulting from opening the door.

Preheat the oven for a minimum of 20 minutes before baking up to 350°F/175°C, 30 minutes if higher, or 45 minutes if using a baking stone.

Cut bread with an electric knife, serrated knife, or a meat slicer to avoid compressing and crushing the crumb.

CRUMPETS

GRIDDLE TEMPERATURE
350°F/175°C (or 375°F/190°C if nonstick)

COOKING TIME
8 to 10 minutes

I have revisited the crumpet recipe from *The Bread Bible* many times since the book was published because I wanted to create more of the holey texture characteristic of a commercial crumpet. I found that I could add significantly more liquid to achieve this goal. So this is my recipe for "as good as it gets crumpets."

PLAN AHEAD If you are planning to enjoy the crumpets for an early brunch, make the batter and griddle them the day before.

SPECIAL EQUIPMENT One griddle, preferably electric and nonstick, or a large sauté pan | Three 3¾ by ¾ inch high pastry rings (see Note, page 434)

CRUMPET BATTER

	VOLUME	WEIGHT	
Gold Medal bread flour (or half other brand bread flour, half unbleached all-purpose flour), see page 511	1 cup (lightly spooned into the cup and leveled off), plus 3 tablespoons	5.5 ounces	155 grams
instant yeast	¾ teaspoon	.	2.4 grams
sugar	½ teaspoon	.	.
cream of tartar	¼ teaspoon	.	0.8 gram
fine sea salt	½ plus ⅛ teaspoon	.	3.7 grams
water, lukewarm (110° to 115°F/ 43° to 46°C)	¾ cup plus ½ tablespoon (185 ml)	6.5 ounces	185 grams
milk	3 tablespoons (44 ml)	1.6 ounces	45 grams
baking soda	¼ teaspoon	.	1.4 grams

MAKE THE CRUMPET BATTER In the bowl of a stand mixer fitted with the flat beater, mix the flour, yeast, sugar, and cream of tartar on low speed for 30 seconds. Add the salt and beat for a few seconds. Add the lukewarm water and, gradually raising the speed to medium, beat for about 5 minutes, or until completely smooth.

LET THE BATTER RISE Set the bowl in a warm place (ideally 75° to 85°F/24° to 29°C) until the batter more than doubles and just begins to fall, 1 to 1½ hours. (See page 539 for recommended rising environments.)

In a small saucepan, warm the milk to lukewarm (110° to 115°F/43° to 46°C). Stir in the baking soda until dissolved. Then gently stir the mixture into the batter. Return the bowl to the warm place for 30 minutes.

PREHEAT THE GRIDDLE OR SAUTÉ PAN If using an electric griddle, preheat it to 350°F/175°C (or 375°F/190°C if nonstick). If using a sauté pan, heat it on medium-low heat for about 3 minutes, or until hot enough to sizzle a drop of water, or an infrared thermometer reads no higher than 400° to 425°F/200° to 220°C (depending on the type of pan used). Set the three rings on the griddle and coat the inside of each ring with nonstick cooking spray.

FRY THE CRUMPETS Gently fold into the batter any liquid that may have separated on standing. Spoon or pour the batter into the first ring to fill it two-thirds full. It should begin to form bubbles immediately. If the bubbles do not burst to form holes in the next few minutes, add a little more lukewarm water, a tablespoon at a time, to the batter in the bowl. As soon as the top surface of the crumpets dulls and is set, about 5 to 7 minutes, use tongs to lift off the rings and a pancake turner to lift up the crumpets. If they are golden brown underneath, flip them over and fry for about 3 minutes, or until pale golden.

COOL THE CRUMPETS Remove the crumpets from the griddle and set them on a wire rack. Repeat with the remaining batter, coating the rings again with nonstick cooking spray for each batch.

TOAST THE CRUMPETS Toast the crumpets until they are warmed through and the outsides are crisp. Serve with butter and jam.

STORE In a brown paper bag: room temperature, 1 day; airtight: frozen, 3 months (thaw before toasting).

NOTE Disposable pastry rings can be made easily from heavy-duty aluminum foil, or reusable rings can be cut from aluminum flashing (available at most hardware and home improvement stores). FOR EACH ALUMINUM FOIL RING: Mark and cut a 14 by 4 inch strip. Mark the foil along its length at ⅞ inch. Fold the foil along the markings. Continue folding the foil 2 more times to form a 14 by 1 inch strip with 4 layers of foil. FOR EACH ALUMINUM FLASHING RING: Mark and then use metal shears or sharp utility scissors to cut a 14 by 1 inch strip. FOR BOTH TYPES OF RINGS: Wrap each ring around a 4 inch diameter can. Use two small paper clips to secure the overlapping ends to form a ring. Remove the ring from the can and adjust it to be as round as possible.

Cadillac Café Milk Chocolate Bread Pudding

SERVES 9

OVEN TEMPERATURE
350°F/175°C

BAKING TIME
15 to 17 minutes for the baguette slices; 45 to 55 minutes for the bread pudding

When I first met my friend Wendy Shear, she was a screenwriter living in Los Angeles. Wendy is a person to whom no one can say no. It was still beyond expectation, however, that she succeeded in coaxing the Cadillac Café to share this signature recipe for the first time. It is an easy to prepare, sublimely light, and milk chocolaty bread pudding. The exposed tops of the baked baguette slices become crisp on baking and add a delightful crunch. One would never guess how simple it is to create the beautiful arrangement of the bread.

SPECIAL EQUIPMENT One 17¼ by 12¼ by 1 inch half sheet pan | Nine 3 by 1¾ inch (5 ounce capacity) soufflé molds or ramekins, lightly coated with nonstick cooking spray | Nine small bowls | One 18 by 12 by 2 inch sheet pan or roasting pan for a water bath

Baguette Slices

	VOLUME	WEIGHT	
1 baguette, 14 inches long, 1 to 2 days old	.	8 to 10 ounces	226 to 283 grams
clarified butter, see page 514 (or unsalted butter)	6 tablespoons (85 ml) (8 tablespoons; 1 stick)	2.6 ounces (4 ounces)	73 grams (113 grams)

PREHEAT THE OVEN Twenty minutes or longer before baking, set an oven rack in the middle of the oven and preheat the oven to 350°F/175°C.

TOAST THE BREAD Use a serrated knife to slice the bread into ¼ inch slices. There will be about 5½ cups. In a small saucepan, melt the clarified butter.

Arrange the bread slices on the half sheet pan and brush each side with the melted butter. Bake for 7 minutes. For even baking, rotate the sheet pan halfway around. (There is no need to turn over the slices.) Continue baking for about 8 minutes, or until crisp.

COOL THE BREAD Remove the pan to a wire rack. The butter will form foam, which mostly will be absorbed by the slices within several minutes. Rearrange the slices into 9 groups with some of the smaller slices in each group. (There will be 8 to 9 slices per group.)

MILK CHOCOLATE CUSTARD

MAKES 6 CUPS/52.9 OUNCES/1,500 GRAMS

	VOLUME	WEIGHT	
8 (to 12) large egg yolks	½ cup plus 4 teaspoons (138 ml)	5.2 ounces	149 grams
2 large eggs	⅓ cup plus 1 tablespoon (94 ml)	3.5 ounces	100 grams
sugar	½ cup	3.5 ounces	100 grams
pure vanilla extract	1 tablespoon (15 ml)	.	.
fine sea salt	a pinch	.	.
heavy cream	3 cups (710 ml)	24.5 ounces	696 grams
milk	1 cup (237 ml)	8.5 ounces	242 grams
milk chocolate, 35% to 41% cacao, preferably Guittard or Valrhona, chopped	.	8 ounces	227 grams
bourbon, preferably Maker's Mark (optional)	about ¼ cup (59 ml) or to taste	2 ounces	56 grams

MAKE THE CHOCOLATE CUSTARD In a medium bowl, whisk together the egg yolks, eggs, sugar, vanilla, and salt until thoroughly blended.

In a medium heavy saucepan over medium heat, stirring often, warm the cream and milk. Gradually whisk this mixture into the egg mixture.

In a small microwavable bowl, stirring with a silicone spatula every 15 seconds (or in the top of a double boiler set over hot, not simmering, water, stirring often—do not let the bottom of the container touch the water), heat the chocolate until almost completely melted. Remove the chocolate from the heat source and continue stirring until fully melted. Gradually whisk the melted chocolate into the cream mixture until uniform in consistency.

ASSEMBLE THE BREAD PUDDING Pour ⅔ cup/158 ml/5.8 ounces/165 grams of the custard into each of five of the small bowls. Layer a group of 9 slices into each bowl, cut side down, and move them around to coat them with the custard. Repeat with the remaining bowls and slices. After all nine of the bowls are filled, let the slices absorb the custard mixture for 15 minutes more. Then turn the slices over to let the slices absorb more of the custard on the other side for another 15 minutes.

Overlap 4 of the soaked bread slices around the inner edge of one of the soufflé molds. Continue with the remaining 5 slices from the bowl to form rings, working toward the center. If necessary, bend the slices and allow them to crack to fit well. Use the smaller slices for the center. The completed rings will form the shape of a rose.

Pour the remaining custard over the bread slices. The custard will come almost to the top of the mold. Cover the mold with plastic wrap to keep the slices from moving. Repeat with the other soufflé molds. When all are completed, let the molds sit for 10 minutes before baking. Remove the plastic wrap. If necessary, reposition any bread slices to retain the shape of a rose.

BAKE THE BREAD PUDDING Place the soufflé molds in the sheet pan and pour hot water into the pan to come halfway up the sides of the molds. Bake for 45 to 55 minutes, or until a thin-bladed knife inserted near the center comes out clean. (An instant-read thermometer should read 170° to 180°F/77° to 82°C.)

COOL THE BREAD PUDDING Use sturdy tongs to remove the soufflé molds from the water bath and set them on a wire rack to cool completely, about 1½ hours. (If not adding the bourbon, it's fine to let them cool until warm and then serve immediately.)

After the bread pudding has cooled completely, the soufflé molds can be wrapped airtight and refrigerated for up to 5 days before reheating.

PREHEAT THE OVEN Twenty minutes or longer before baking, set an oven rack in the middle of the oven and preheat the oven to 350°F/175°C.

REHEAT AND SERVE THE BREAD PUDDING If desired, with a thin skewer, poke several holes in between the bread slices in each mold. Drizzle each mold with about 1 teaspoon/5 ml of bourbon. Loosely cover the tops with aluminum foil and set the molds on the baking sheet. Heat for about 10 to 15 minutes, or until thoroughly warm.

STORE Airtight: refrigerated, 5 days.

Variation: SLICED BREAD PUDDING

The bread pudding can be baked in a 9 by 2 inch round cake pan and served as slices.

Toast and cool the bread slices, but do not arrange them in groups.

Make the chocolate custard (see page 436).

ASSEMBLE THE BREAD PUDDING Pour half of the custard into the pan. Arrange the bread slices, standing upright, in slightly overlapping rows in the prepared pan. The arranged slices will fill the pan only about two-thirds full. Pour the remaining chocolate custard evenly over the bread slices. It will come almost to the top of the pan and as the bread absorbs the custard, the bread will expand and fill the pan more. Evenly space the rows of slices to fill the pan. Cover the pan lightly with plastic wrap, which will help to keep the slices from floating. Let it stand for 45 minutes while the bread absorbs more of the chocolate custard. If any of the bread slices rise up and float in the mixture during this time, reposition them so that more of the custard can be absorbed.

BAKE THE BREAD PUDDING Place the cake pan in the roasting pan and pour hot water into the roasting pan to come halfway up the sides. Bake for 45 to 55 minutes, or until a thin-bladed knife inserted near the center comes out clean. (An instant-read thermometer should read 170° to 180°F/77° to 82°C.)

COOL AND UNMOLD THE BREAD PUDDING Remove the pan from the water bath and set it on a wire rack to cool completely, about 2 hours.

Run a small metal spatula between the sides of the pan and the bread pudding, pressing firmly against the pan with the spatula. Place a flat plate, covered with plastic wrap that has been lightly coated with nonstick cooking spray, on top of the pan and invert it. Reinvert the pan onto a cutting board. If the bread pudding does not release, use a small torch or wipe the sides and bottom of the pan with a dish towel that has been run under hot water and wrung out.

After the bread pudding has cooled completely, it can be wrapped airtight and refrigerated for up to 5 days before composing and reheating. The bread pudding can be sliced when it is cold, but should be allowed to warm up to room temperature before reheating.

PREHEAT THE OVEN Twenty minutes or longer before baking, set an oven rack in the middle of the oven and preheat the oven to 350°F/175°C.

PORTION THE BREAD PUDDING Slice the bread pudding into 8 to 10 portions. Cut each portion into 3 slices and arrange them on the baking sheet. If desired, drizzle each serving with about 1 teaspoon/5 ml of bourbon. Loosely cover the slices with aluminum foil and heat for about 10 minutes, or until thoroughly warm.

With a pancake turner, lift the slices and arrange them decoratively on serving plates. Grate bittersweet chocolate lavishly on top.

Rum Raisin French Toast Royale

OVEN TEMPERATURE
350°F/175°C

BAKING TIME
45 to 55 minutes

*C*innamon raisin bread is so delicious, lightly toasted and buttered, I could eat it for dessert. The secret to keeping the spirals from separating is to add the raisins to the dough. Made into French toast and flambéed, it serves as an impressive celebration brunch.

PLAN AHEAD Make the bread at least 1 day ahead for making the French toast.

SPECIAL EQUIPMENT One 8½ by 4½ inch (6 cups) loaf pan, coated with nonstick cooking spray | A baking stone or baking sheet

Dough Starter (Sponge)

	VOLUME	WEIGHT	
water, at room temperature (70° to 80°F/21° to 27°C)	1 cup (237 ml)	8.4 ounces	237 grams
honey	1 tablespoon plus ½ teaspoon (17 ml)	0.8 ounce	24 grams
unbleached all-purpose flour	1½ cups (lightly spooned into the cup and leveled off) plus 2½ tablespoons	7 ounces	200 grams
instant yeast	½ teaspoon	.	1.6 grams

MAKE THE DOUGH STARTER (SPONGE) In a medium bowl, or in the bowl of a stand mixer fitted with the whisk beater, place the water, honey, flour, and yeast. Whisk by hand or beat on medium speed for about 2 minutes until very smooth to incorporate air. The dough starter will be the consistency of a thick batter.

If using the Bread Machine Method, scrape the starter into the container. If using the Stand Mixer Method, scrape down the sides of the bowl. Cover with plastic wrap and set the starter aside while you make the flour mixture.

Dough

	VOLUME	WEIGHT	
unbleached all-purpose flour	1½ cups (lightly spooned into the cup and leveled off) minus 1 tablespoon	6.1 ounces	172 grams
nonfat dry milk, preferably King Arthur's Baker's Special (see Note, page 443)	2 tablespoons	0.8 ounce	23 grams
instant yeast	½ teaspoon	.	1.6 grams
unsalted butter, must be very soft (75° to 90°F/23° to 32°C)	5 tablespoons (½ stick plus 1 tablespoon)	2.5 ounces	71 grams
fine sea salt	1¼ teaspoons	.	7.5 grams
raisins	½ cup plus 1½ tablespoons	3 ounces	85 grams

COMBINE THE FLOUR MIXTURE In a medium bowl, whisk together the flour, dry milk, and yeast. Sprinkle the flour mixture over the dough starter, forming a blanket of flour, and cover it tightly with plastic wrap. Let it ferment for 1 up to 4 hours at room temperature, or 1 hour at room temperature and up to 24 hours refrigerated. During this time, the dough starter will bubble through the flour blanket in places.

MAKE THE DOUGH BREAD MACHINE METHOD Add the butter to the container. Program the machine to mix for 3 minutes and set it to go through the 3 minutes of mixing. Let the dough rest (autolyse) for 20 minutes.

Program the machine to knead for 10 minutes. Add the salt and set it to go through the knead cycle, which will include 3 minutes of mixing and 7 minutes of kneading. Add the raisins after 4 minutes of kneading.

STAND MIXER METHOD Attach the dough hook. Add the butter and mix on low speed for 1 minute, or until the flour is moistened to form a rough dough. Scrape down the sides of the bowl for any bits of dough. Cover the top of the bowl with plastic wrap and let the dough rest for 20 minutes. Sprinkle on the salt and knead the dough on medium speed for 7 to 10 minutes. It will not come away from the bowl until toward the last minute or so of kneading. The dough will be smooth and shiny and stick to your fingers. With a spatula that has been lightly coated with nonstick cooking spray, scrape down any dough clinging to the sides of the bowl.

Cover the bowl with plastic wrap and let the dough relax for 10 minutes. Add the raisins and, on low speed, mix for about 2 minutes to incorporate them as evenly as possible.

For both methods, do not worry about how well the raisins distribute because when the dough is deflated and folded after the first rise, the raisins will continue to distribute more evenly. The dough should be slightly sticky. If it is very sticky, knead in a little flour. If it is not at all sticky, knead in a little water.

LET THE DOUGH RISE Using a spatula or dough scraper that has been lightly coated with nonstick cooking spray, scrape the dough into a 2 quart/2 liter dough rising container or bowl that has been lightly coated with nonstick cooking spray. Push down the dough and lightly coat the surface with nonstick cooking spray. (The dough should weigh about 28.6 ounces/810 grams.) Cover the container with a lid or plastic wrap. With a piece of tape, mark the side of the container at approximately where double the height of the dough should be after rising. Let the dough rise in a warm place (ideally at 75° to 85°F/24° to 29°C) until it reaches the mark, 1 to 1½ hours. (See page 539 for recommended rising environments.)

DEFLATE AND CHILL THE DOUGH Using a spatula or dough scraper that has been lightly coated with cooking spray, turn the dough onto a floured counter and gently press down on it to form a rectangle. It will be full of air and resilient. Try to maintain as many of the air bubbles as possible. Give the dough a business letter turn (fold it into thirds), brushing off any excess flour, and again press down on it or roll it out into a rectangle. Rotate it 90 degrees so that the closed end is facing to your left. Give it a second business letter turn and round the corners.

Set the dough back in the container. Lightly coat the top, cover, and refrigerate for 30 minutes to 1 hour to firm the dough for rolling.

Cinnamon Sugar Spiral Filling

	VOLUME	WEIGHT	
granulated sugar	2 tablespoons	0.9 ounce	25 grams
light brown Muscovado sugar, or dark brown sugar	1 tablespoon, firmly packed	0.5 ounce	14 grams
ground cinnamon	½ tablespoon	.	3.3 grams
about ¾ large egg, lightly beaten and strained	2 tablespoons (30 ml)	1.1 ounces	32 grams

MAKE THE CINNAMON SUGAR SPIRAL FILLING In a small bowl, stir together the granulated sugar, brown sugar, and cinnamon. Rub out any lumps with your fingers.

SHAPE THE DOUGH, FILL, AND LET IT RISE Turn the dough onto a lightly floured counter and press down on it with floured hands to form a rectangle. Roll the dough into a 14 by 7½ inch rectangle, flouring the counter and the rolling pin if necessary to keep it from sticking. It will be about ¼ inch thick. Make the upper third slightly thicker, not too much or the spiral will be off center, and make the last 2 inches thinner because it will wind up on the bottom. Also, roll it thinner for about ¾ inch along the longer sides because they will be tucked under after shaping to keep the filling from leaking and sticking to the pan.

Brush the dough with the egg, leaving a ¾ inch margin all around. Sprinkle the sugar mixture evenly over the dough, avoiding the ¾ inch margin. Starting from the top, roll the dough tightly as you would a jelly roll. While rolling, brush the top of the dough with the egg, up to ¾ inch from each end. Squeeze the dough gently all along the length of the cylinder with each roll so that it will adhere well to the filling, until 2 inches from the end. When you come to the end, make a seam by tightly pinching all along the edges of the dough to seal in the filling. Push in any dough on the sides that may have worked its way out and pinch the sides of the dough tightly together to seal. Tuck them under, and set the shaped dough in the prepared loaf pan, pushing it down firmly. It will be ½ inch from the top.

Cover the pan loosely with plastic wrap that has been lightly coated with nonstick cooking spray. Let the bread rise in a warm place (ideally 75° to 85°F/24° to 29°C) for 1 hour and 15 minutes to 2 hours. The highest point should be 1½ inches above the sides of the pan and when pressed lightly with a fingertip, the dough should keep the impression.

PREHEAT THE OVEN Forty-five minutes or longer before baking, set an oven rack in the lower third of the oven and place the baking stone or baking sheet on it. Place a cast iron pan, lined with aluminum foil to prevent rusting, or a sheet pan on the floor of the oven. Preheat the oven to 350°F/175°C.

BAKE THE BREAD Mist the dough with water. Quickly but gently set the pan on the hot baking stone or sheet pan and toss a handful (about ½ cup) of ice cubes into the pan on the oven floor. Immediately shut the door and bake for 25 minutes. For even baking, rotate the pan halfway around.

Continue baking for 20 to 30 minutes, or until medium golden brown on top and a skewer inserted into the center comes out clean. (An instant-read thermometer inserted into the center should read 195° to 211°F/90° to 99°C.)

COOL THE BREAD Remove the bread from the oven, unmold it from the pan, and transfer it to a wire rack to cool completely, top side up, at least 2 hours.

STORE If eating the bread plain or as toast: room temperature, 2 days; airtight: frozen, 3 months.

NOTE 2 tablespoons is the volume for 0.8 ounce/23 grams of King Arthur's Baker's Special Dry Milk. If using another brand of "instant" dry milk, use the same weight, which will be double the volume (¼ cup).

French Toast

	VOLUME	WEIGHT	
cinnamon raisin bread, preferably 2 or 3 days old	partial loaf	8 ounces	227 grams
4 large eggs	¾ cup plus 2 teaspoons (187 ml)	7 ounces	200 grams
heavy cream	½ cup (118 ml)	4.1 ounces	116 grams
milk	2 tablespoons (30 ml)	1 ounce	30 grams
granulated sugar	2 tablespoons	0.9 ounce	25 grams
light rum	2 tablespoons (30 ml), *divided*	1 ounce	28 grams
pure vanilla extract	½ teaspoon (2.5 ml)	.	.
nutmeg, freshly grated	¼ teaspoon	.	.
unsalted butter, frozen	1 tablespoon	0.5 ounce	14 grams
Décor: powdered sugar and/or pure maple syrup	.	.	.

SLICE THE BREAD Use a serrated knife to cut four 1 inch thick slices. If the dough was baked the same day, let the slices sit on wire racks for a few hours to dry so that they will absorb more of the custard.

MIX THE CUSTARD AND SOAK THE BREAD In a medium bowl, lightly whisk together the eggs, cream, milk, sugar, 1 tablespoon/15 ml of the rum, the vanilla, and nutmeg just to blend them.

Pour the custard into a pan large enough to hold the bread in a single layer and place the slices of bread in the pan. Let the bread soak up the custard for a minute or so and then turn over each slice so the second side can absorb all of the remaining custard. It helps to use two pancake turners. Move the bread slices around to be sure they pick up all of the custard. Cover the pan tightly with plastic wrap and refrigerate it until ready to fry the bread in the morning.

HEAT THE SERVING PLATES AND PREHEAT THE GRIDDLE If using an electric griddle, preheat it to 375°F/190°C (or 400°F/200°C if nonstick). If using a sauté pan, heat it on medium-low heat for about 3 minutes, or until hot enough to sizzle a drop of water, or an infrared thermometer reads no higher than 400° to 425°F/200° to 220°C (depending on the type of pan used).

Impale the frozen butter on a fork or hold it carefully on either side and run it quickly along the surface of the hot griddle or pan to film it lightly with butter.

Place heatproof dinner plates in the oven and turn the heat to low.

FRY THE FRENCH TOAST Fry the French toast for 2 to 3 minutes on each side, or until golden brown and an instant-read thermometer inserted into the centers reads about 170°F/77°C. If any of the custard remains in the pan, spoon it on top of the bread as it fries.

SERVE THE FRENCH TOAST Cut the bread slices diagonally in half and arrange them on the heated plates. If desired, flambé the remaining rum as follows: Dim the lights in order to see when the rum flames and pour the remaining 1 tablespoon of the rum into a large metal ladle. Hold it over the flame of a gas burner or candle until heated. Then tilt the ladle slightly and the rum will ignite. Pour the flaming rum over the French toast. Sprinkle lightly with powdered sugar and pass the maple syrup.

White Chocolate Club Med Bread, Sour Cherry and Currant Jam (page 505),
True Orange Marmalade (page 503), and Concord Grape Jelly (page 507)

WHITE CHOCOLATE
CLUB MED BREAD

OVEN TEMPERATURE
350°F/175°C

BAKING TIME
40 to 50 minutes

*M*y darling cousin Elizabeth Granatelli brought me the idea for this recipe after a visit to Club Med, where guests are presented with a loaf of it at the end of each stay. I adapted a version using my Soft White Sandwich Loaf recipe from *The Bread Bible* as the base. Adding little cubes of white chocolate to the dough results in small lacy holes lined with a sweet coating of the chocolate. This bread proved to be quite a challenge because the white chocolate close to the surface of the bread became very dark brown. After seven tries, just as I was about to give up, I thought of a great technique: I held out about one-third of the dough before adding the chocolate to the rest, and then wrapped the dough without the chocolate around the shaped loaf. I'm so glad I persisted—this is fantastic bread, incredibly soft and flavorful. It is especially delicious lightly toasted and spread with butter and strawberry jam. It makes a great and unusual breakfast or tea bread.

SPECIAL EQUIPMENT One 9 by 5 inch (8 cups) loaf pan, lightly coated with nonstick cooking spray | A baking stone or baking sheet

MAKE THE CINNAMON RAISIN BREAD Make the recipe on page 440, but replace the raisins with 4 ounces/114 grams of high-quality white chocolate, chopped into ¼ to ½ inch pieces (¾ cup), which are added after rolling out the dough. (Do not make the cinnamon sugar spiral filling.)

SHAPE THE DOUGH, FILL, AND LET IT RISE Turn the dough onto a lightly floured counter and press down on it with floured hands to form a rectangle. Roll the dough into a 12 by 6 inch rectangle, flouring the counter and the rolling pin if necessary to keep it from sticking. With a sharp knife, cut off a 4½ by 6 inch strip (8.5 ounces/242 grams) from one end. Wrap this dough lightly in plastic wrap and refrigerate while shaping the larger piece.

Roll the larger piece of dough to lengthen it to about 12 inches. Strew the white chocolate evenly on top of the dough. Roll up the dough to encase the chocolate and then knead it to incorporate the chocolate evenly. Sprinkle lightly with flour if it is very sticky. Set it aside, covered with plastic wrap, for 20 minutes.

Lightly flour the counter and roll the dough containing the chocolate into a 9 by 8 inch rectangle. Shape the dough into a log, starting from the top and rolling down to the bottom. When you reach the bottom edge of the dough, pinch it firmly against the outside of the dough to make a tight seam. Set the shaped loaf, seam side down, on the counter.

Roll the smaller piece of dough into a 9 by 8½ inch rectangle. It will be about ⅛ inch thick. Lightly spritz or brush water on top. Set the shaped loaf, horizontally and centered near the bottom of the dough rectangle, seam side down. Wrap the dough rectangle snuggly around the shaped loaf so that the two edges meet, and pinch them together all along the bottom edge. Set it seam side down on the counter and pinch together the sides of the dough to enclose the loaf. Tuck the sides under and set the shaped dough in the prepared loaf pan, pushing it down firmly. It will be about 1 inch from the top.

Cover the pan loosely with plastic wrap that has been lightly coated with nonstick cooking spray. Let the bread rise in a warm place (ideally 75° to 85°F/24° to 29°C) for 1 hour and 15 minutes to 2 hours. The highest point should be 1 inch above the sides of the pan and when pressed lightly with a fingertip, the dough should keep the impression. (See page 539 for recommended rising environments.)

PREHEAT THE OVEN Forty-five minutes or longer before baking, set an oven rack in the lower third of the oven and place the baking stone or baking sheet on it. Place a cast iron skillet, lined with aluminum foil to prevent rusting, or a sheet pan on the floor of the oven. Preheat the oven to 350°F/175°C.

BAKE THE BREAD Mist the dough with water. Quickly but gently set the pan on the hot baking stone or baking sheet and toss a handful (about ½ cup) of ice cubes into the pan on the oven floor. Immediately shut the door and bake for 25 minutes. For even baking, rotate the pan halfway around.

Continue baking for 15 to 25 minutes, or until medium golden brown and a skewer inserted into the center comes out clean. (An instant-read thermometer inserted into the center should read 195° to 211°F/90° to 99°C.)

COOL THE BREAD Remove the bread from the oven, unmold it from the pan, and transfer it to a wire rack to cool completely, top side up, at least 2 hours.

STORE Room temperature, 2 days; airtight: frozen, 3 months.

GOLDEN ORANGE PANETTONE WITH CHOCOLATE SAUCE

MAKES ONE 5½ BY 6½ INCH HIGH LOAF (5½ BY 6 INCH IF BAKED IN A PAPER LINER);
FOURTEEN TO SIXTEEN ½ TO ¾ INCH SLICES

OVEN TEMPERATURE 325°F/160°C

BAKING TIME 60 to 70 minutes

*S*everal years ago, I chose to make my best panettone recipe, originally created for *The Bread Bible*, for a demonstration at the Food Arts Pastry Conference at the CIA Greystone, organized by *Food Arts* and *Food & Wine* magazines founders Michael and Ariane Batterberry. The next morning, a charming chef from Istanbul, Yusuf Yaran, came up to me and whispered in my ear, "I couldn't stop thinking about you since yesterday!" My eyes widened with alarm until he whispered further, "Your panettone!"

I gave one of the panettone from the demo to the Batterberrys, and it was Ariane who suggested a variation of chocolate and orange.

This is an easy bread to make, and the actual work time involved is not long; however, the production time is lengthy so it does require significant advance planning. Sliced, toasted, and laced with chocolate glaze, the panettone is a divine holiday dessert.

PLAN AHEAD Make the biga 3 days ahead, make the dough at least 1 day or up to 2 days ahead, and bake the panettone at least 8 hours ahead.

SPECIAL EQUIPMENT A heavy-duty stand mixer with whisk and flat beaters | A 6 by 4 inch paper panettone mold, or a 6 by 6 inch round metal coffee can or soufflé dish, coated with shortening and bottom and sides lined with parchment | A baking stone or baking sheet

BIGA *(see Notes, page 453)*

MAKES ALMOST ⅓ CUP/2.7 OUNCES/78 GRAMS

	VOLUME	WEIGHT	
Gold Medal bread flour (or half other brand bread flour, half unbleached all-purpose flour), see page 511	¼ cup (lightly spooned into the cup and leveled off) plus 2 tablespoons	1.7 ounces	49 grams
instant yeast	1/16 teaspoon	.	0.2 gram
water, at room temperature (70° to 80°F/21° to 27°C)	2 tablespoons (30 ml)	1 ounce	30 grams

The addition of a biga or sourdough starter offers acidity, which strengthens the dough, gives it depth of flavor, and keeps it moist for up to 5 days. Golden refiner's syrup also adds both flavor and moisture-keeping qualities.

Baking at a lower temperature keeps the rich bread from overbrowning, at the same time producing a slightly thicker crust, which makes it unnecessary to hang the bread upside down as is required in many traditional recipes.

I no longer use the traditional Fiori di Sicilia, a citrus and vanilla flavoring in many panettone recipes, because I find it leaves an unpleasantly bitter aftertaste.

MAKE THE BIGA In a small bowl, whisk together the flour and yeast. With a silicone spatula or wooden spoon, stir in the water. Continue stirring for 3 to 5 minutes, or until very smooth. The biga should be tacky enough to cling slightly to your fingers.

Cover the bowl tightly with plastic wrap that has been lightly coated with nonstick cooking spray (or place it in a 1 cup food storage container that has been lightly coated with nonstick cooking spray and cover it with a lid). Set it aside until almost doubled in volume and filled with bubbles. At warm room temperature (80°F/27°C), this will take about 6 hours. Stir it down. Refrigerate it for 3 days before making the dough.

DRIED FRUIT FILLING

	VOLUME	WEIGHT	
candied orange peel, fine quality (see Notes, page 453)	1 cup	4.2 ounces	120 grams
golden raisins	¼ cup	1.3 ounces	36 grams
Triple Sec or water	2 tablespoons (30 ml)	1 ounce	30 grams
pure vanilla extract	1 teaspoon (5 ml)	.	.
pure orange oil, preferably Boyajian (or orange zest)	¼ teaspoon/1.2 ml (or 1 tablespoon, loosely packed)	.	(6 grams)

MAKE THE FILLING Cut the candied orange peel into ¼ inch cubes and place the cubes in an airtight container. (If they seem dry, add them to the raisins for soaking.)

Have ready a small strainer suspended over a ramekin or custard cup.

In a 1½ cup or larger jar, combine the raisins, Triple Sec, vanilla, and orange oil. Cover tightly and shake to coat well with the liquid. Set the jar aside for a minimum of 2 hours or preferably overnight. Turn it occasionally to redistribute the liquid. Empty the raisins and soaking liquid into the strainer and press the raisins to release most of the liquid, about 1 tablespoon/15 ml. Set the strainer with the raisins on a small plate and cover the ramekin with the reserved liquid tightly to prevent evaporation.

DOUGH STARTER (SPONGE)

	VOLUME	WEIGHT	
water, at room temperature (70° to 80°F/21° to 27°C)	½ cup (118 ml)	4.2 ounces	118 grams
Biga (see page 449)	about ⅓ cup	2.7 ounces	78 grams
Gold Medal bread flour (or half other brand bread flour, half unbleached all-purpose flour), see page 511	¾ cup (lightly spooned into the cup and leveled off), plus ½ tablespoon	3.5 ounces	100 grams
2 large egg yolks	2 tablespoons plus 1 teaspoon (35 ml)	1.3 ounces	37 grams
golden syrup or corn syrup	1 tablespoon (15 ml)	0.7 ounce	21 grams
instant yeast	¾ teaspoon	.	2.4 grams

MAKE THE DOUGH STARTER (SPONGE) Into the bowl of a stand mixer fitted with the whisk beater, pour the water. Use sharp scissors, dipped in water if it is sticky, to cut the biga into many small pieces, letting them drop into the water. Add the flour, egg yolks, golden syrup, and yeast, and beat on medium speed until very smooth, about 2 minutes. The dough starter will be the consistency of a very thick batter. Remove the whisk beater, scrape down the sides, and cover the bowl.

DOUGH

	VOLUME	WEIGHT	
Gold Medal bread flour (or half other brand bread flour, half unbleached all-purpose flour), see page 511	1 cup (lightly spooned into the cup and leveled off) plus 3 tablespoons	5.5 ounces	156 grams
nonfat dry milk, preferably King Arthur's Baker's Special (see Notes, page 453)	1½ tablespoons	0.5 ounce	14 grams
instant yeast	¾ teaspoon	.	2.4 grams
salt	½ teaspoon plus ¹⁄₁₆ teaspoon	.	3.4 grams
3 (to 4) large egg yolks, cold	3½ tablespoons (52 ml)	2 ounces	56 grams
golden syrup or corn syrup	2 tablespoons (30 ml)	1.5 ounces	42 grams
reserved liquid (from the dried fruit filling)	about 1 tablespoon (15 ml)	.	.
unsalted butter, must be very soft (75° to 90°F/23° to 32°C), see Notes, page 453	10 tablespoons (1 stick plus 2 tablespoons)	5 ounces	142 grams

COMBINE THE FLOUR MIXTURE In a small bowl, whisk together the flour, dry milk, and yeast. Then whisk in the salt. Sprinkle the flour mixture over the dough starter, forming a blanket of flour, and cover it tightly with plastic wrap. Let it ferment for 1½ to 2 hours at room temperature, or 1 hour at room temperature and up to 24 hours refrigerated. During this time, the dough starter will bubble through the flour blanket in places.

MIX THE DOUGH Attach the flat beater. Add the egg yolks, golden syrup, and reserved liquid from the soaked raisins, and on low speed beat for about 1 minute, or until the flour is moistened. Raise the speed to medium and beat for about 5 minutes, or until the dough is smooth and shiny but very soft and sticky. It will not pull away from the bowl completely.

Add the butter by the tablespoon, waiting until the butter is almost completely absorbed before adding the next tablespoon. Continue beating until all of the butter is incorporated. The dough will be very soft and elastic and will almost completely pull away from the bowl. Scrape down the sides of the bowl, cover the bowl with plastic wrap or a dish towel, and let the dough rest for 10 minutes.

Scrape the dough onto a very well floured counter and pat or roll it into a rectangle (the exact size is unimportant). Sprinkle on the orange peel and raisins, draw up the sides of the dough to enclose the filling, and knead the dough briefly until incorporated, adding as little flour as possible to keep it from sticking. Do not be concerned if the orange peel and raisins are not evenly distributed because the "turns" after rising will accomplish this. (The dough should weigh about 33.3 ounces/945 grams.)

FIRST RISE Transfer the dough into a 3 quart/3 liter rising container or bowl that has been lightly coated with nonstick cooking spray. Lightly coat the surface of the dough with nonstick cooking spray. Cover the container with a lid or plastic wrap. With a piece of tape, mark the side of the container at approximately where double the height of the dough should be after rising. Let the dough rise in a warm place (ideally 75° to 85°F/24° to 29°C) until it reaches the mark, 1½ to 2 hours. (See page 539 for recommended rising environments.)

Refrigerate the dough for 1 hour to firm it, which will prevent the butter from separating. Gently deflate the dough by stirring it with a silicone scraper and return it to the refrigerator for another hour so that it will be less sticky to handle.

REDISTRIBUTE THE YEAST AND SECOND RISE Turn the dough onto a lightly floured counter and press or roll it into a rectangle, lightly flouring the top of the dough if needed. Give the dough a business letter turn (fold it into thirds), brushing off any excess flour, and again press or roll it into a rectangle. Rotate it 90 degrees (one-quarter turn) so that the closed end is facing to your left. Give it a second business letter turn and round the corners. Coat a gallon-size reclosable freezer bag with nonstick cooking spray and set the dough inside. Close the bag without pressing out all the air.

Refrigerate it for 6 hours or up to 2 days to let the dough ripen and harden. After the first hour and again after the second hour, with your hand flat against the outside of the bag, press down the dough.

SHAPE THE DOUGH AND LET IT RISE Remove the dough from the refrigerator. Cut open the bag and peel it away from the dough. With cupped hands, gently shape the dough into a ball.

Try to keep as much air as possible in the dough. Set it into the paper panettone mold or prepared coffee can. It will be about 2½ inches high. Cover it loosely with plastic wrap that has been lightly coated with nonstick cooking spray. Let the dough rise in a warm place (ideally 75° to 85°F/24° to 29°C) for 2 to 3 hours, or until the dough almost doubles and comes to the top of the paper, about 4 inches high. (The dough is slow to rise because it was shaped cold from the refrigerator and it takes at least an hour to come to room temperature.)

PREHEAT THE OVEN Forty-five minutes or longer before baking, set an oven rack at the lowest level and place a baking stone or baking sheet on it. Place a cast iron skillet, lined with aluminum foil to prevent rusting, or a sheet pan on the floor of the oven. Preheat the oven to 325°F/160°C.

BAKE THE PANETTONE Use sharp scissors dipped in water to snip a 1 inch deep cross into the top of the dough. Quickly but gently set the pan on the hot baking stone or baking sheet and toss ½ cup of ice cubes into the pan on the oven floor. Immediately shut the door and bake for 30 minutes. Tent the panettone with foil to prevent overbrowning. Continue baking for 30 to 40 minutes, or until a skewer inserted into the center comes out clean. (An instant-read thermometer inserted into the center should read 184° to 195°F/84° to 90°C.)

COOL THE PANETTONE Remove the panettone from the oven, still in its mold or pan, to a wire rack to cool for 30 minutes. If using the paper mold, let it cool completely. If using a coffee can or soufflé dish, unmold the panettone and finish cooling it on a soft pillow (cover the pillow with a piece of plastic wrap to keep it clean) placed on the counter. When cooled completely, wrap the panettone airtight in plastic wrap or aluminum foil and then place it in a reclosable gallon freezer bag. For the best flavor, let it mellow for at least 8 hours at room temperature.

To serve, remove the paper and cut the loaf lengthwise in half. Slice each half in long ½ to ¾ inch thick slices.

MAKE THE CHOCOLATE DRIZZLE GLAZE Make the recipe on page 95. Pour the glaze into a disposable pastry bag or a quart-size reclosable freezer bag with a very small semicircle cut from the tip or one corner and close it securely.

Transfer the panettone slices onto serving plates and drizzle lines of chocolate back and forth over the tops.

STORE Room temperature, 2 days; airtight: frozen, 3 months.

NOTES If you have a liquid sourdough starter, simply stir in enough flour to make it into a soft dough consistency and use it in place of the biga.

Pastry Chef Central (see page 527) carries an excellent-quality candied orange peel from France.

1½ tablespoons is the volume for 0.5 ounce/14 grams of King Arthur's Baker's Special Dry Milk. If using another brand of "instant" dry milk, use the same weight, which will be double the volume (3 tablespoons).

If desired, melting and browning about one-fifth of the butter (2 tablespoons/30 ml) offers an extra rich, delicious flavor.

Babka

OVEN TEMPERATURE
350°F/175°C

BAKING TIME
45 to 55 minutes

$\mathcal{W}$hen I was growing up in New York City, we lived twenty-two blocks from Lichtman's Bakery, which was famous for its babka. Many a Sunday my dad would drive over to pick one up for breakfast. I've tried for years to produce the babka of my memory and finally discovered that the secrets to achieving a beautiful spiral of filling that does not burst through the top or separate into wide gaps inside are to make a very sticky dough and to add egg white to the filling, which expands along with the dough during baking. The dough is softer and less rich than brioche because it has about half the butter, one-third the egg, and double the water.

SPECIAL EQUIPMENT One 12 to 15 cup Nordic Ware Classic Anniversary Bundt Pan or a one-piece metal fluted tube pan, lightly coated with nonstick cooking spray

Dough Starter (Sponge)

	VOLUME	WEIGHT	
water, at room temperature (70° to 80°F/21° to 27°C)	½ cup (118 ml)	4.2 ounces	118 grams
Gold Medal bread flour (or half other brand bread flour, half unbleached all-purpose flour), see page 511	½ cup (lightly spooned into the cup and leveled off)	2.3 ounces	65 grams
nonfat dry milk, preferably King Arthur's Baker's Special (see Note, page 458)	2 tablespoons	.	23 grams
instant yeast	½ tablespoon	.	4.8 grams

MAKE THE DOUGH STARTER (SPONGE) In the bowl of a stand mixer fitted with the whisk beater, place the water, flour, dry milk, and yeast. Beat on medium speed for about 2 minutes until very smooth to incorporate air. The dough starter will be the consistency of a thick batter. Scrape down the sides of the bowl, remove the beater, and set aside the dough starter, covered with plastic wrap.

DOUGH

	VOLUME	WEIGHT	
Gold Medal bread flour (or half other brand bread flour, half unbleached all-purpose flour), see page 511	2¾ cups (lightly spooned into the cup and leveled off)	12.6 ounces	356 grams
sugar	¼ cup plus 2 tablespoons	2.6 ounces	75 grams
instant yeast	½ tablespoon	.	4.8 grams
fine sea salt	1 teaspoon	.	6 grams
unsalted butter, must be very soft (75° to 90°F/23° to 32°C)	8 tablespoons (1 stick)	4 ounces	113 grams
2 large eggs, cold	⅓ cup plus 1 tablespoon (94 ml)	3.5 ounces	100 grams
water, at room temperature (70° to 80°F/21° to 27°C)	¼ cup (59 ml)	2.1 ounces	59 grams
pure vanilla extract	1 teaspoon (5 ml)	.	.

COMBINE THE FLOUR MIXTURE In a medium bowl, whisk together the flour, sugar, and yeast. Then whisk in the salt. Sprinkle the flour mixture over the dough starter, forming a blanket of flour, and cover it tightly with plastic wrap. Let it ferment for 1 to 4 hours at room temperature, or 1 hour at room temperature and up to 24 hours refrigerated. During this time, the dough starter will bubble through the flour blanket in places.

MIX THE DOUGH Attach the dough hook. Add the butter, eggs, water, and vanilla, and beat on low speed for about 1 minute, or until the flour is moistened. Raise the speed to medium and knead for about 7 minutes, or until the dough is shiny and very elastic. It will not clean the sides of the bowl, but it will start forming long strands around the dough hook. The dough will be very sticky.

LET THE DOUGH RISE Using a spatula or dough scraper that has been lightly coated with nonstick cooking spray, scrape the dough into a 2 quart/2 liter dough rising container or bowl that has been lightly coated with nonstick cooking spray. It will be very soft and elastic and will stick to your fingers unmercifully. Do not be tempted to add more flour at this point; the dough will firm considerably after rising and chilling. Push down the dough and lightly coat the surface with nonstick cooking spray. (The dough should weigh about 2 pounds/910 grams; it will increase slightly in weight after rolling and folding it.) Cover the container with a lid or plastic wrap. With a piece of tape, mark the side of the container at approximately where double the height of the dough should be after rising. Let the dough rise in a warm place (ideally at 75° to 85°F/24° to 29°C) until it reaches the mark, about 1 to 1½ hours. (See page 539 for recommended rising environments.)

DEFLATE AND CHILL THE DOUGH Flour the counter and your hands because the dough will still be very sticky. Using a spatula or dough scraper that has been lightly coated with cooking spray, remove the dough to the counter, and deflate it gently with your fingertips.

Round the dough by gently stretching it out in a few places and folding it in to the center. The dough will be very soft.

Set the dough back in the container. Lightly coat the surface with nonstick cooking spray, cover, and refrigerate it for a minimum of 1 hour or up to overnight. (If overnight, deflate it gently after the first hour or two. Let it sit at room temperature for 30 minutes before shaping.)

ALMOND FILLING

	VOLUME	WEIGHT	
blanched sliced almonds	¼ cup plus 2 tablespoons	1.3 ounces	37 grams
light brown Muscovado sugar, or dark brown sugar	½ cup, firmly packed	3.8 ounces	108 grams
unsalted butter (65° to 75°F/ 19° to 23°C)	2 tablespoons	1 ounce	28 grams
golden syrup or corn syrup	1 tablespoon (15 ml)	0.7 ounce	21 grams
ground cinnamon	1 teaspoon	.	2.2 grams
almond paste	¼ cup	2.5 ounces	70 grams
1 large egg white, at room temperature	2 tablespoons (30 ml)	1 ounce	30 grams

MAKE THE FILLING In a small food processor, process the almonds until fine. Add the brown sugar, butter, golden syrup, and cinnamon. Pinch off pieces of the almond paste and place them on top. Process until uniformly combined, scraping down the sides of the bowl as necessary. Add the egg white and pulse until combined.

SHAPE THE DOUGH, FILL, AND LET IT RISE Turn the dough onto a well-floured counter and press down on it with floured hands to form a rectangle. Roll the dough into a 16 by 14 inch wide rectangle, flouring the counter and the rolling pin if necessary to keep the dough from sticking. It will be about ¼ inch thick. Brush off any excess flour from the top.

Using an offset spatula, gently spread the almond filling on the dough, leaving a ½ inch margin at the top and a 1 inch margin at the bottom. Spread the filling slightly thicker for the middle third of the dough because some of the filling will move toward the bottom while rolling.

Starting from the top, use your fingers and a long plastic ruler to roll up the dough and to help support the dough as you roll it. (Slip the edge of the ruler slightly under the dough and use it to lift up and roll the dough.) With each roll, dust any flour from the surface of the dough, and press firmly all along the dough roll to keep it from separating. To keep the rolled dough even and prevent it from becoming thicker in the middle, use your hands to ease the dough gently toward the ends. Work carefully without rushing. When you reach the bottom edge of the dough, pinch it firmly against the outside of the dough to make a tight seam. Pinch the ends of the dough firmly together and brush off any excess flour. The dough roll will be between 18 and 20 inches long and quite floppy.

Carefully lift the dough, supporting it as well as possible, and coil it into the prepared pan, overlapping it by about 2 inches. Place it with the seam side up because this will become the bottom of the babka when unmolded. Press it down firmly into the pan. It will come up to 2½ inches from the top of a 15 cup pan (2 inches in a 12 cup pan).

Cover the pan loosely with plastic wrap, lightly coated with nonstick cooking spray. Let the dough rise in a warm place (ideally 75° to 85°F/24° to 29°C) for 45 minutes to 1½ hours, or until the highest point is ½ inch from the top of the pan (level with the top in a 12 cup pan).

PREHEAT THE OVEN Twenty minutes or longer before baking, set an oven rack in the lower third of the oven and set a cast iron pan, lined with aluminum foil to prevent rusting, or a sheet pan on the floor of the oven. Preheat the oven to 350°F/175°C.

BAKE THE BABKA Quickly but gently set the pan on the rack and toss a handful (about ½ cup) of ice cubes into the pan on the oven floor. Immediately shut the door and bake for 30 minutes. For even baking, rotate the pan halfway around. Cover the top loosely with foil if it is already golden brown.

Continue baking for 15 to 25 minutes, or until golden brown. (An instant-read thermometer inserted between the tube and the sides should read 200° to 212°F/93° to 100°C.)

BUTTER GLAZE

	VOLUME	WEIGHT	
unsalted butter	3 tablespoons	1.5 ounces	42 grams

MAKE THE GLAZE In a small saucepan over medium heat (or in a 1 cup microwavable measure with a spout), melt the butter.

UNMOLD AND COOL THE BABKA Lay a sheet of parchment on the counter and place a wire rack on top. Remove the babka from the oven and unmold it onto the wire rack. If necessary, use a wooden skewer to dislodge the bread. Brush the melted butter onto the crust to soften it. Let the babka cool until warm, about 2½ hours. The top crust may have a dark line where the two ends of the dough overlapped in the pan.

STORE Room temperature, 2 days; frozen, 3 months.

NOTE 2 tablespoons is the volume for 0.8 ounce/23 grams of King Arthur's Baker's Special Dry Milk. If using another brand of "instant" dry milk, use the same weight, which will be double the volume (¼ cup).

Variation: CHOCOLATE ALMOND SCHMEAR FILLING

For people who enjoy a chocolate babka, this is my favorite chocolate schmear filling, which I created for the kugelhopf in *The Bread Bible*.

	VOLUME	WEIGHT	
bittersweet chocolate, 55% to 62% cacao, chopped	.	3 ounces	85 grams
cake crumbs, fresh or stale	1 cup, loosely packed	4 ounces	113 grams
unsalted butter (65° to 75°F/ 19° to 23°C)	4 tablespoons (½ stick)	2 ounces	56 grams
golden syrup or corn syrup	1 tablespoon (15 ml)	0.7 ounce	21 grams
1 large egg, at room temperature	3 tablespoons plus ½ teaspoon (47 ml)	1.8 ounces	50 grams
almond paste	2½ tablespoons	1.5 ounces	42 grams

MELT THE CHOCOLATE In a small microwavable bowl, stirring with a silicone spatula every 15 seconds (or in the top of a double boiler set over hot, not simmering, water, stirring often—do not let the bottom of the container touch the water), heat the chocolate until almost completely melted.

Remove the chocolate from the heat source and stir until fully melted. Let it cool until it is no longer warm to the touch but is still fluid.

In a food processor, place the cake crumbs, butter, golden syrup, and egg. Pinch off pieces of the almond paste and place them on top. Process until uniformly combined, scraping down the sides of the bowl as necessary. Add the melted chocolate and process for another few seconds until uniformly blended. Scrape the mixture into a small bowl. Cover and let it sit until spreadable, about 1 hour.

Spread the filling onto the dough in the same way as the almond filling (see page 457).

Variation: APRICOT AND CREAM CHEESE SCHMEAR FILLING

This tangy, creamy filling was adapted from the *Standard Baking Co. Pastries* cookbook by Alison Pray and Tara Smith.

APRICOT FILLING

	VOLUME	WEIGHT	
dried apricots	1½ cups	9 ounces	255 grams
lemon juice, freshly squeezed and strained (about 3 large lemons)	½ cup (118 ml)	4.4 ounces	126 grams
orange juice, freshly squeezed and strained (about 2 large oranges)	½ cup (118 ml)	4.3 ounces	121 grams
sugar	2 tablespoons	0.9 ounce	25 grams

MAKE THE APRICOT FILLING In a medium heavy saucepan, combine the dried apricots, lemon juice, orange juice, and sugar. Over medium-low heat, simmer the mixture until the apricots are very soft when pierced with a skewer and the lemon and orange juices are reduced by half, 20 to 25 minutes. (To confirm that the juices are reduced, start by weighing the pan and the combined ingredients. Set a heat pad on the scale, set the pan with the mixture on top, and tare out the weight. When the juices look like they have been reduced by half, return the pan to the scale. The weight will be −4.3 ounces/−122 grams.) In a small food processor, puree the apricot mixture until it has a jamlike consistency. Scrape it into a small glass bowl and cover it with plastic wrap until ready to use.

CREAM CHEESE FILLING

	VOLUME	WEIGHT	
1 large egg white, at room temperature, lightly beaten	2 tablespoons (30 ml), *divided*	1 ounce	30 grams
pure vanilla extract	½ teaspoon (2.5 ml)	.	.
pure almond extract	½ teaspoon (2.5 ml)	.	.
orange zest, freshly grated	¼ teaspoon	.	0.5 gram
fine sea salt	a pinch	.	.
cream cheese (65° to 75°F/19° to 23°C)	¾ cup plus 2 tablespoons	8 ounces	227 grams
sugar	2 tablespoons	0.9 ounce	25 grams

MAKE THE CREAM CHEESE FILLING In a small bowl, whisk 1 tablespoon/15 ml/0.5 ounce/ 15 grams of the egg white, the vanilla, almond extract, orange zest, and salt until evenly combined. Reserve the remaining egg white, covered. In a medium bowl, with a handheld mixer, beat the cream cheese and sugar until combined. Add the egg mixture and beat until evenly incorporated.

SPREAD THE FILLINGS Brush the dough with the reserved egg white, leaving a ½ inch border on all sides. Using a small offset spatula, spread the apricot filling evenly over the egg white wash. Spread the cream cheese filling evenly over the apricot filling.

Classic Brioche

*B*rioche is the queen of all breads. Golden, soft, and buttery, it can be made into a simple loaf, filled and coiled into buns, or braided into elaborate shapes. It serves in this book as the base for three marvelous breads: Monkey Dunkey Bread (page 465), Caramel Buns (page 470), and the Sugar Rose Brioche (page 476).

PLAN AHEAD Make the dough 1 day ahead.

Dough Starter (Sponge)

	VOLUME	WEIGHT	
water, at room temperature (70° to 80°F/21° to 27°C)	2 tablespoons (30 ml)	1 ounce	30 grams
sugar	1 tablespoon	0.5 ounce	13 grams
Gold Medal bread flour (or half other brand bread flour, half unbleached all-purpose flour), see page 511	½ cup (lightly spooned into the cup and leveled off) plus 1 tablespoon	2.5 ounces	71 grams
instant yeast	¼ teaspoon	.	0.8 gram
1 large egg, at room temperature	3 tablespoons plus ½ teaspoon (47 ml)	1.8 ounces	50 grams

MAKE THE DOUGH STARTER (SPONGE) In a small bowl, or in the bowl of a stand mixer fitted with the whisk beater, place the water, sugar, flour, yeast, and egg. Whisk by hand or beat on medium speed for about 2 minutes until very smooth to incorporate air. The dough starter will be the consistency of a very thick batter. If whisking by hand, at first the dough starter may collect inside the whisk, but just shake it out and keep whisking. If it is too thick to whisk, it means it has too much flour and it will be necessary to add a little of the egg normally added when mixing the dough. Scrape down the sides of the bowl.

If using the Bread Machine Method, scrape the starter into the container of the bread machine. If using the Stand Mixer Method, scrape down the sides of the bowl and remove the whisk beater. Set the dough starter aside, covered with plastic wrap, while you make the flour mixture.

DOUGH

	VOLUME	WEIGHT	
Gold Medal bread flour (or half other brand bread flour, half unbleached all-purpose flour), see page 511	1 cup (lightly spooned into the cup and leveled off) plus 3 tablespoons	5.5 ounces	156 grams
sugar	2 tablespoons	0.9 ounce	25 grams
instant yeast	1¼ teaspoons	.	4 grams
fine sea salt	½ teaspoon	.	3 grams
2 large eggs, cold	⅓ cup plus 1 tablespoon (94 ml)	3.5 ounces	100 grams
unsalted butter, must be very soft (75° to 90°F/23° to 32°C)	8 tablespoons (1 stick)	4 ounces	113 grams

COMBINE THE FLOUR MIXTURE In a small bowl, whisk together the flour, sugar, and yeast. Then whisk in the salt. Sprinkle the flour mixture over the dough starter, forming a blanket of flour, and cover it tightly with plastic wrap. Let it ferment for 1½ to 2 hours at room temperature, or 1 hour at room temperature and up to 24 hours refrigerated. During this time the dough starter will bubble through the flour blanket in places.

MAKE THE DOUGH Bread Machine Method Program the machine to mix for 3 minutes and knead for 15 minutes. Add the eggs and mix the dough for 3 minutes. Then let it proceed to the knead cycle for 8 to 12 minutes, or until the dough is smooth, shiny, and elastic. If necessary, carefully reach in with a plastic spatula and scrape any flour or dough that collects in the corners of the container. Add the butter all at once and continue the kneading cycle until the butter is incorporated, about 3 minutes, scraping down the sides if necessary.

LET THE DOUGH RISE For the first rise, turn off the machine and let the dough rise (with the lid closed) for 1½ to 2 hours, or until approximately doubled.

CHILL THE DOUGH Remove the container from the bread machine, cover it with plastic wrap, and refrigerate it for 1 hour.

Return the container to the bread machine (the plastic wrap can be left in place) and deflate the dough by pressing the Mix button or starting the dough cycle and mixing for about 30 seconds. Return the container to the refrigerator for another hour so that it will be less sticky to handle.

Stand Mixer Method Attach the dough hook. Add the eggs to the dough starter and beat on low speed for about 1 minute, or until the flour is moistened. Raise the speed to medium and beat for 2 minutes. Using a silicone spatula lightly coated with nonstick cooking spray, scrape down the sides of the bowl. Continue beating for about 5 minutes, or until

Highlights for Success

the dough is smooth and shiny but very soft and sticky. It will mass around the dough hook, but it will not pull away from the bowl completely. Add the butter by the tablespoon, waiting until the butter is almost completely absorbed before adding the next tablespoon. Continue beating until all of the butter is incorporated.

LET THE DOUGH RISE Using a spatula or dough scraper that has been lightly coated with nonstick cooking spray, scrape the dough into a 2 quart/2 liter dough rising container or bowl that has been lightly coated with nonstick cooking spray. The dough will be very soft and elastic and will stick to your fingers unmercifully. Do not be tempted to add more flour at this point because the dough will firm considerably after chilling. Lightly coat the surface with nonstick cooking spray and push down the dough. Cover the container with a lid or plastic wrap. With a piece of tape, mark on the side of the container at approximately where double the height of the dough should be after rising. Let the dough rise in a warm place (ideally at 75° to 85°F/24° to 29°C) until it reaches the mark, 1½ to 2 hours. (See page 539 for recommended rising environments.)

CHILL THE DOUGH Refrigerate the dough for 1 hour to firm; this will prevent the butter from separating. Gently deflate the dough by stirring it with a silicone spatula. Return it to the refrigerator for another hour so that it will be less sticky to handle.

For both methods, turn the dough onto a well-floured surface and press down or roll it into a rectangle, flouring the surface and dough as needed to keep the dough from sticking. The exact size of the rectangle is not important. Give the dough a business letter turn (fold it into thirds), brushing off any excess flour, and again press down on it or roll it out into a rectangle. Rotate it 90 degrees so that the closed end is facing to your left. Give it a second business letter turn and round the corners. Dust it lightly on all sides with flour. Wrap it loosely but securely in plastic wrap and then place it in a gallon-size reclosable freezer bag and refrigerate for 6 hours or up to 2 days to let the dough ripen (develop flavor) and firm.

SHAPE THE DOUGH Remove the dough from the refrigerator and gently press down the dough to deflate it. Press and roll the dough into a rectangle and shape it as specified in the recipe.

NOTE Gold Medal bread flour (or the combination of half higher protein bread flour and half unbleached all-purpose flour) yields the most feathery texture and highest rise (about 1 inch higher than using all unbleached all-purpose flour).

Variation: Classic Brioche Loaf

OVEN TEMPERATURE 350°F/175°C

BAKING TIME 30 to 40 minutes

SPECIAL EQUIPMENT One 8½ by 4½ inch (6 cups) loaf pan, lightly coated with nonstick cooking spray, oil, or butter

Press or roll the dough into a rectangle 7½ inches wide and about 5 inches long. Roll it from the top in three turns, being sure to brush off any excess flour, pressing with your thumbs to seal the dough. Place it, seam side down, in the prepared pan, pressing it down firmly. Cover it with plastic wrap lightly coated with nonstick cooking spray, and allow it to rise at room temperature until the top of the dough reaches the top of the pan, 1½ to 2 hours.

Egg Glaze

	VOLUME	WEIGHT	
1 large egg yolk	1 tablespoon plus ½ teaspoon (17 ml)	0.7 ounce	19 grams
heavy cream	1 teaspoon (5 ml)	.	.

MAKE THE EGG GLAZE In a small bowl, whisk together the egg yolk and cream. Cover tightly with plastic wrap to prevent evaporation.

PREHEAT THE OVEN Twenty minutes or more before baking, set an oven rack at the lowest level of the oven and preheat the oven to 350°F/175°C.

GLAZE, SLASH, AND BAKE THE BRIOCHE Brush the top of the dough with the egg glaze. With a sharp knife or straight-edge razor blade, make a ¼ to ½ inch deep, lengthwise slash in the dough, starting about 1 inch from either end of the pan. Set the pan in the oven. Bake for 35 to 40 minutes, or until golden brown and an instant-read thermometer reads 190°F/88°C.

UNMOLD AND COOL THE BRIOCHE Unmold the brioche onto a wire rack. Allow it to cool until it is barely warm, at least 2 hours.

STORE Room temperature, 2 days; airtight: frozen, 2 months.

Monkey Dunkey Bread

OVEN TEMPERATURE 350°F/175°C

BAKING TIME 30 to 40 minutes

The name "monkey bread" is believed to have derived from the casual way in which the balls of dough are piled into the pan before baking. Because each ball of dough is dunked into a butter sugar mixture before placing it in the pan, I have always thought of it as monkey dunkey bread. And because I love the combination of the soft and buttery brioche dough with slightly melted dark chocolate, I came up with the idea of stuffing each ball with chocolate. This is the most marvelous combination of textures: The brown sugar butter caramelizes onto the bottom and sides of the buns and forms a crunchy sugar coating on top, complemented by the slightly chewy soft caramel and the downy soft interior surrounding the delicious surprise of bittersweet chocolate in the center. These are breathtakingly fabulous. If you believe in gilding the lily, the addition of ganache drizzle glaze (see page 95) will do the trick, plus it hints at the presence of more chocolate on the inside.

PLAN AHEAD Make the brioche dough 1 day ahead.

SPECIAL EQUIPMENT One 10 inch (16 cups) two-piece metal tube pan, lightly coated with nonstick cooking spray (see Note, page 466) | A foil-lined baking sheet

Dough

	VOLUME	WEIGHT	
Classic Brioche Dough (page 461)	.	**19 ounces**	540 grams
chocolate pearls or bittersweet mini chips, 55% to 62% cacao	about 1 cup	6.5 ounces	183 grams

Dunking Sauce

	VOLUME	WEIGHT	
unsalted butter	10 tablespoons (1 stick plus 2 tablespoons)	5 ounces	142 grams
corn syrup	1 tablespoon (15 ml)	0.7 ounce	20 grams
light brown Muscovado sugar, or dark brown sugar	½ cup, firmly packed	3.8 ounces	108 grams

MAKE THE DUNKING SAUCE In a medium microwavable bowl (or in a saucepan over medium heat), melt the butter with the corn syrup and brown sugar, stirring once or twice (or constantly, if over direct heat) until the mixture comes to a boil. (An instant-read thermometer should read about 200°F/93°C.) Set it aside to cool just until warm, about 1 hour, and then set it in a warm place.

ROLL AND FILL THE DOUGH Turn the dough out onto a lightly floured counter and divide it in half. Cover one half and refrigerate it. Roll the other half into a 4 by 4 inch square. Use a sharp knife to cut it into 1 by 1 inch squares (0.6 ounce/17 grams) to make 16 pieces. Roll the dough into balls, flouring your fingers lightly if necessary. Keep the dough covered as much as possible so that it doesn't dry.

With a small rolling pin or wooden dowel, roll each ball into a 2 inch disc. Use your fingers to press the edges gently to make them thinner. Set about 1 teaspoon of the chocolate pearls or chips on the center. Bring up the dough to encase the chocolate and pinch the top firmly to seal the dough. Place the dough, pinched side down, on the counter, and with a cupped hand placed over it, roll it into a smooth ball. Place it on a baking sheet. Cover the balls as they are shaped with plastic wrap that has been lightly coated with nonstick cooking spray, and roll the rest of the dough. Set the dough balls in the refrigerator. Repeat rolling, filling, and shaping with the second piece of dough. When rolling the dough balls, it is best to work quickly so that the dough does not start to rise.

COMPOSE THE BREAD Whisk the dunking sauce to a uniform consistency. Starting with the refrigerated balls, gently dunk them 1 at a time into the dunking sauce, coating all sides. Set the coated balls in the prepared pan, pinched side down and slightly apart, because they will expand during rising. (A flat whisk, fork, or small slotted spoon works well for dunking the balls and placing them in the pan, but you can also use your fingers.) Stir the dunking sauce often to keep it from separating. When completed, the dough balls will fill the pan about one-third full. Drizzle any remaining dunking sauce over the balls.

Cover the pan with plastic wrap that has been lightly coated with nonstick cooking spray. Let the dough balls rise in a warm place (ideally at 75° to 85°F/24° to 29°C) for 50 minutes to 1½ hours until they expand and when pressed lightly with a fingertip, the depression fills in very slowly. The buns will expand sideways rather than in height. (See page 539 for recommended rising environments.)

PREHEAT THE OVEN Twenty minutes or longer before baking, set an oven rack at the lowest level and set the prepared baking sheet on it. Preheat the oven to 350°F/175°C.

BAKE THE BREAD Set the pan on the hot baking sheet. Bake for 30 to 40 minutes, or until the bread is golden and a skewer inserted into the center comes out clean. (An instant-read thermometer inserted into the dough part of one of the balls, between the outside and the center tube of the pan, should read about 190°F/88°C.) The balls will have risen to fill the pan about half full.

MAKE THE GLAZE While the buns are baking, make the caramel drizzle glaze (alternatively, the glaze can be made up to 3 days ahead).

NOTE Some 10 inch tube pans will measure only 12 cups, which is fine. The buns will rise to fill this smaller pan about three-quarters full.

CARAMEL DRIZZLE GLAZE

MAKES A FULL ½ CUP/133 ML/6 OUNCES/170 GRAMS

	VOLUME	WEIGHT	
sugar	½ cup	3.5 ounces	100 grams
corn syrup	½ tablespoon (7.5 ml)	.	10 grams
water	2 tablespoons (30 ml)	1 ounce	30 grams
heavy cream, hot (see Variation, page 469)	¼ cup (59 ml)	2 ounces	58 grams
unsalted butter (65° to 75°F/19° to 23°C)	1 tablespoon	0.5 ounce	14 grams
pure vanilla extract	½ teaspoon (2.5 ml)	.	.

MAKE THE CARAMEL DRIZZLE GLAZE Have ready a 1 cup heatproof glass measure with a spout, lightly coated with nonstick cooking spray.

In a medium heavy saucepan, preferably nonstick, stir together the sugar, corn syrup, and water until all of the sugar is moistened. Heat, stirring constantly, until the sugar dissolves and the syrup is bubbling. Stop stirring completely and let the mixture boil undisturbed until it turns a deep amber (360°F/180°C, or a few degrees lower because the temperature will continue to rise).

Remove the mixture from the heat and as soon as it reaches temperature, slowly and carefully pour the hot cream into the caramel. It will bubble up furiously. Use a silicone spatula or wooden spoon to stir the mixture gently, scraping the thicker part that settles on the bottom. Return the pan to very low heat, continuing to stir gently for 1 minute, until the mixture is uniform in color and the caramel is fully dissolved.

Remove it from the heat and gently stir in the butter until incorporated. The mixture will be a little streaky but will become uniform in color once cooled and stirred. Pour the caramel into the prepared glass measure and let it cool for 3 minutes. Gently stir in the vanilla and let the caramel cool until no longer warm to the touch, stirring gently three or four times.

The glaze keeps covered for up to 3 days at room temperature and for at least 3 months refrigerated.

UNMOLD AND GLAZE THE MONKEY BREAD If the caramel drizzle glaze was made in advance, reheat it until warm to the touch. (To reheat, if the glaze is in a heatproof glass container at room temperature, microwave it for 1 minute, stirring twice. Alternatively, place the container in a pan of simmering water and heat, stirring occasionally, until warm, about 7 minutes.)

Remove the pan from the oven and let the bread cool on a wire rack for 10 minutes. Place the pan on top of a canister that is smaller than the opening at the bottom of the pan's outer rim. Push the sides down firmly and evenly. Slip a metal spatula between the bread and the bottom of the pan and gently loosen the bread from the pan. Use two large pancake turners, slipped between the bottom of the bread and the pan, to lift the bread onto a serving plate.

The glaze can be decoratively laced onto the monkey bread from a glass measure with a spout, but for the greatest precision, pour the glaze into a pastry bag fitted with a ⅛ inch round decorating tip (number 4) or into a quart-size reclosable freezer bag with a very small semicircle cut from one corner.

Pour or pipe the glaze to create a decorative lacing effect. Serve immediately or while still warm (it will stay warm for about an hour). Encourage people (by example) to use their fingers to break off the warm buns.

The monkey bread may be eaten at once or reheated in a preheated 350°F/175°C oven for 15 minutes, loosely wrapped in aluminum foil, or in the microwave for 30 seconds with a heatproof glass of boiling water alongside (10 seconds for a cluster of 3 buns).

STORE Loosely covered to keep the caramel from softening: room temperature, 2 days; frozen, 2 months.

Variation: Bourbon Butterscotch Caramel

For a mellow butterscotch quality, substitute 2 tablespoons/30 ml of bourbon for an equal amount of the cream. Add it with the vanilla.

CARAMEL BUNS

OVEN TEMPERATURE
375°F/190°C (350°F/175°C if using dark pans)

BAKING TIME
18 to 22 minutes

*T*hese are my ultimate sticky buns. The key to perfection is baking them in a ring so that they bake evenly. Baking the buns in separate containers, as I've done in the past, may give them a perfect shape, but also makes them denser and slightly chewier. I prefer this new ring method, setting a Ball jar filled with boiling water in the center to create steam, which makes the buns puffier and softer. Also, instead of baking the buns on top of the caramel, I now add the caramel after baking, which results in equal amounts for each. I've doubled the caramel, adding a small amount first to attach the pecans and then more to cascade down the sides. Once the brioche dough is made, it takes about three hours to make the caramel buns. It is so worth it.

PLAN AHEAD Make the brioche dough 1 day ahead.

SPECIAL EQUIPMENT Two 9 by 2 inch round cake pans, lined with sheets of aluminum foil large enough to wrap down the outsides of the pans (the excess foil will serve as handles for lifting out the buns after baking), lightly coated with nonstick cooking spray | Two 2 cup Ball jars, or ramekins with 3 inch diameter bases

DOUGH

	VOLUME	WEIGHT	
Classic Brioche Dough (page 461)	.	19 ounces	540 grams

CARAMEL BUN FILLING

	VOLUME	WEIGHT	
raisins	½ cup	2.5 ounces	72 grams
dark rum	2 tablespoons (30 ml)	1 ounce	28 grams
boiling water	¼ cup (59 ml)	2.1 ounces	59 grams
pecan halves	¼ cup	0.9 ounce	25 grams
light brown Muscovado sugar, or dark brown sugar	¼ cup, firmly packed	1.9 ounces	54 grams
granulated sugar	1 tablespoon	0.5 ounce	13 grams
ground cinnamon (see Note, page 473)	1½ to 2 teaspoons	.	3.3 to 4.4 grams
about ½ egg, lightly beaten	1 tablespoon (15 ml)	.	.

PREHEAT THE OVEN Twenty minutes or longer before baking, set an oven rack in the middle level of the oven and preheat the oven to 375°F/190°C.

MAKE THE CARAMEL BUN FILLING In a small heatproof bowl, place the raisins and rum. Add the boiling water, cover, and let stand for at least 1 hour so the raisins can become plump with the rum. When ready to fill the dough, place the raisins in a strainer suspended over a small bowl. Lightly press them to remove excess liquid and reserve the liquid for the glaze.

BREAK AND TOAST THE PECANS Break the pecans into medium pieces into a strainer. Shake the strainer to remove the nut dust. Spread the pecan pieces evenly on a baking sheet and bake for about 5 minutes to enhance their flavor. Stir once or twice to ensure even toasting and avoid overbrowning. Cool completely. (The whole pecans for the topping [see page 474] can be toasted on a separate sheet at the same time.)

In a medium bowl, combine the chopped pecans, brown sugar, granulated sugar, and cinnamon. With your fingertips, break up any sugar lumps.

ROLL AND FILL THE DOUGH Have ready a small bowl with the lightly beaten egg.

Turn the dough onto a lightly floured counter. Roll the dough into a 13 to 14 inch wide by 12 inch long rectangle, moving the dough and flouring it as necessary to keep it from sticking. Brush off any excess flour from the top.

Brush the dough, right up to the edges, with the egg. Sprinkle the dough evenly with the sugar mixture and the raisins.

Starting from the top, use your fingers and a long plastic ruler to roll up the dough and to help support the dough as you roll it. (Slip the edge of the ruler slightly under the dough and use it to lift up and roll the dough.) With each roll, dust any flour from the surface of the dough, and press firmly all along the dough roll to keep it from separating. Push together the ends of the roll so that they are the same thickness as the middle and the roll is 12 inches long. Lightly sift flour evenly over the entire roll (not the cut edges).

CUT THE DOUGH AND LET IT RISE Dental floss works best to slice the dough, but a sharp serrated knife also works well. To use the dental floss, slide a 9 inch long piece under the dough, cross the two ends over each other, and pull firmly to slice evenly through the dough. Slice the roll into 4 equal pieces and then slice each piece into thirds (each piece will be about 1 inch thick) to make 12 buns.

To make the caramel buns freshly baked for brunch the following day, as soon as they are shaped and placed in the pans, refrigerate them for up to 14 hours. They will take about 2½ hours to rise before baking. To speed rising to about 1½ hours, place them in a proof box with hot water. (See page 539 for recommended rising environments.)

Set the Ball jars in the centers of the cake pans. There is no need to coat them because the dough does not stick to the glass. Set the buns in the pans, evenly spaced about ¾ inch apart, with the seams facing sideways. Lightly press in any raisins that have popped up. There is no need to press the buns down because they will rise sideways, but very little if at all in height. They start off 1¼ inches from the tops of the pans and will be about the same height after rising. Cover the pans with plastic wrap that has been lightly coated with nonstick cooking spray. Let the buns rise in a warm place (ideally 75° to 85°F/24° to 29°C) for 1 to 1½ hours, or until the sides touch.

PREHEAT THE OVEN Thirty minutes or longer before baking, set an oven rack at the lowest level. Preheat the oven to 375°F/190°C (350°F/175°C if using dark pans).

BAKE THE BUNS Fill the Ball jars about half full with boiling water. Place the pans on the oven rack and bake for 10 to 12 minutes, or until the buns are beginning to brown. Remove the Ball jars and cover the pans loosely with aluminum foil.

Continue baking for 8 to 10 minutes, or until a skewer inserted into the centers comes out clean. (An instant-read thermometer inserted into the centers should read 180° to 210°F/82° to 99°C.)

While the buns are baking, make the glaze.

NOTE If using a very strong specialty cinnamon, use only ½ tablespoon.

Arranging the buns in the pan.

Caramel Bun Glaze

	VOLUME	WEIGHT	
reserved raisin-soaking liquid (from page 472)	.	.	.
unsalted butter	1 tablespoon	0.5 ounce	14 grams

MAKE THE CARAMEL BUN GLAZE In a small saucepan over high heat, stirring constantly to prevent scorching (or in a 1 cup microwavable measure with a spout, lightly coated with nonstick cooking spray), boil the raisin-soaking syrup until it is reduced to 1½ to 2 tablespoons/22.5 to 30 ml. In the microwave it will take about 3 minutes, but watch carefully toward the end to prevent scorching. Add the butter and stir until melted.

GLAZE AND COAT THE BUNS WITH CARAMEL Remove the pans from the oven and set them on wire racks. Brush the buns evenly with the glaze. Unfold the aluminum foil ends from the outsides of the pans and use the ends to lift the buns out of the pans. Use a small pancake turner to slip under each bun to dislodge it from the foil and lift it, carefully separating it from the adjoining buns. Set each bun slightly apart from the other. The buns can be coated with caramel while they are still hot or at room temperature.

Soft Sticky Caramel

MAKES 1 CUP/237 ML/10.6 OUNCES/300 GRAMS

	VOLUME	WEIGHT	
granulated sugar	1 cup	7 ounces	200 grams
corn syrup	1 tablespoon (15 ml)	0.7 ounce	20 grams
water	¼ cup (59 ml)	2.1 ounces	59 grams
heavy cream, hot	6 tablespoons (89 ml)	3.1 ounces	87 grams
unsalted butter (65° to 75°F/ 19° to 23°C)	2 tablespoons	1 ounce	28 grams
pure vanilla extract	2 teaspoons (10 ml)	.	.
pecan halves, lightly toasted	48 (about ¾ cup)	2.6 ounces	75 grams

MAKE THE SOFT STICKY CARAMEL Have ready a 2 cup microwavable measure with a spout, lightly coated with nonstick cooking spray.

In a heavy 6 cup saucepan, preferably nonstick, stir together the sugar, corn syrup, and water until all of the sugar is moistened. Heat, stirring constantly, until the sugar dissolves and the syrup is bubbling. Stop stirring completely and let it boil undisturbed until it turns a deep amber (360°F/180°C, or a few degrees below because the temperature will continue to rise).

Highlights for Success

Leaving flour on the outside of the dough helps in detaching the buns after baking and seals in the crust, keeping the buns fresher.

Remove it from the heat, and as soon as it reaches temperature, slowly and carefully pour the hot cream into the caramel. It will bubble up furiously. Use a silicone spatula or wooden spoon to stir the mixture gently, scraping the thicker part that settles on the bottom. Return it to a very low heat, continuing to stir gently for 1 minute, until the mixture is uniform in color and the caramel fully dissolved.

Remove it from the heat and gently stir in the butter until incorporated. The mixture will be a little streaky but will become uniform once cooled and stirred.

Pour the caramel into the prepared glass measure and let it cool for 3 minutes. Gently stir in the vanilla and let it cool to room temperature, stirring it gently once or twice.

COMPLETE THE CARAMEL BUNS Pour some of the caramel evenly over the buns and set 4 pecans on top of each. Pour the rest of the caramel over the pecan topped buns, letting it run over the sides. If the caramel hardens, microwave it in 6 second bursts until pourable.

STORE Loosely covered to keep the caramel from softening: room temperature, 2 days; airtight: frozen, 2 months. The buns may be eaten at once or reheated in a preheated 350°F/175°C oven for 15 minutes, loosely wrapped in foil, or in a microwave for 30 seconds with a heatproof glass of boiling water alongside to keep them soft (10 seconds for individual buns).

SUGAR ROSE BRIOCHE

OVEN TEMPERATURE
325°F/160°C

BAKING TIME
About 1 hour and 20 minutes

*T*his is a stunning new spin on brioche shaping. The technique was introduced to me via The Fresh Loaf, a web forum for amateur bread bakers. The original recipe was for a bread from the Caucasus with a savory filling, but as you can see, the technique works for shaping any kind of bread. Cinnamon sugar makes a beautiful design inside the brioche and is perfect for breakfast or a holiday brunch.

PLAN AHEAD Make the brioche dough 1 day ahead.

SPECIAL EQUIPMENT One 10 by 2½ to 3 inch high springform pan, well coated with nonstick cooking spray | A slightly larger silicone pan or 2 cake strips | A baking sheet

DOUGH

	VOLUME	WEIGHT	
Classic Brioche Dough (page 461)	a double recipe	38 ounces	1,080 grams

FILLING

	VOLUME	WEIGHT	
1 large egg, at room temperature	3 tablespoons plus ½ teaspoon (47 ml)	1.8 ounces	50 grams
fine sea salt	a pinch	.	.
superfine sugar	⅓ cup	2.3 ounces	67 grams
ground cinnamon (see Note, page 480)	4 to 6 teaspoons	0.3 to 0.5 ounce	9 to 13 grams

ROLL AND FILL THE DOUGH In a small bowl, whisk the egg and salt and strain the mixture into another small bowl. Push it through with the back of a spoon or let it sit for several minutes to flow through the strainer. There will be about 2 tablespoons/30 ml/ 1.2 ounces/33 grams. Discard the thicker part that does not pass through the strainer.

HIGHLIGHTS FOR SUCCESS

Coiling the dough with most of the cut sides up keeps the cinnamon filling from being in contact with the bottom of the pan and sticking or burning.

Using a fine-mesh strainer, sift the sugar and cinnamon into a small bowl and whisk to combine them evenly.

Turn the dough onto a well-floured counter and flour the top. With your fingertips, press down the dough to flatten it evenly. With a rolling pin, roll the dough into a 20 to 22 inch circle, moving the dough and flouring it as necessary to keep it from sticking. Brush off any excess flour.

Brush the entire surface of the dough with the beaten egg, using as little as possible to create an even coating. (Too much egg wash will dissolve the sugar, making the dough more difficult to shape.) Sift and smooth the cinnamon sugar as evenly as possible over the dough.

Starting from the top, use your fingers and a long plastic ruler to roll up the dough and to help support the dough as you roll it. (Slip the edge of the ruler slightly under the dough and use it to lift up and roll the dough.) With each roll, dust any flour from the surface of the dough, and press firmly all along the dough roll to keep it from separating. Work carefully without rushing. When you reach the bottom edge of the dough, pinch it firmly against the outside of the dough to make a tight seam. Pinch the ends of the dough firmly together, and arrange the roll so that most of the seam is facing up.

CUT THE DOUGH Use a long sharp chef's knife to cut the dough roll cleanly lengthwise into equal halves, cutting along the seam as much as possible. Use sharp shears to finish cutting through the bottom parts of the slash where the dough tends to stick together.

TWINE THE 2 DOUGH STRANDS Keeping the cut sides up, starting in the middle, cross the 2 long pieces of dough over each other to form an X. Always keeping the cut sides facing up, lift up the bottom two ends of the dough and cross the upper one under the lower one. Continue twisting the strands in this way until you reach the ends of the dough and then pinch them together. Repeat with the other two ends of the dough to form a spiral.

SHAPE THE BREAD AND LET IT RISE Unlock the springform pan and slide the pan bottom under the dough, starting with one end at the center. Without lifting the dough spiral from the surface, coil it tightly around itself, always being sure to keep the cut sides facing up. The center will protrude upward to form a whorl resembling a rose. Tuck the remaining end underneath the coil.

Reattach the sides of the pan. The dough will not fill the pan until after rising, when it will have spread to touch the sides. Set the pan in the silicone pan or encircle the pan with 2 cake strips. Cover it loosely with plastic wrap that has been lightly coated with nonstick cooking spray. Let the dough rise in a warm place (ideally at 75° to 85°F/24° to 29°C) for 40 minutes to 1½ hours, or until doubled. The dough will touch the sides of the pan and the center will rise about ½ inch above it. (See page 539 for recommended rising environments.)

PREHEAT THE OVEN Twenty minutes or longer before baking, set an oven rack at the lowest level of the oven and preheat the oven to 325°F/160°C.

LEFT TO RIGHT: Rolling up the dough. The pinched seams. Cutting the dough.

LEFT TO RIGHT: Forming an X with the dough strands. Twining the dough strands. Coiling the bread.

BAKE THE BREAD Set the pan on the baking sheet. Bake for 20 minutes. For even baking, rotate the pan halfway around and tent it loosely with a large piece of aluminum foil.

Continue baking for about 1 hour, or until golden. (An instant-read thermometer inserted into the center should read 200° to 205°F/93° to 96°C.) The bread will have risen well above the sides of the pan.

UNMOLD AND COOL THE BREAD Run a small metal spatula between the sides of the pan and the bread, pressing firmly against the pan. Release the sides of the pan. Use two large pancake turners, slipped between the bottom of the bread and the pan, to lift the bread onto a wire rack. Let it cool just until warm or room temperature.

STORE Room temperature, 2 days; frozen, 2 months. If you want to freeze slices, freeze them first before stacking them and placing them in reclosable freezer bags so that they do not stick together.

NOTE If using a very strong specialty cinnamon, use only 4 teaspoons.

KOUIGNS AMANN

OVEN TEMPERATURE
400°F/200°C

BAKING TIME
20 to 27 minutes

I've long considered the sticky bun to be my number one pastry in the world, but that was until my friend Marko Gnann, a world traveler and inveterate sweet tooth, told me about kouign amann (pronounced keh-WEEN-ah-mahn)—a butter and sugar rich yeast pastry from Brittany. (It is actually very similar to a croissant, but with less butter and a lot more sugar.) Shortly after hearing about it, Woody and I happened upon one of the best of its kind at Maison Georges Larnicol, on Boulevard Saint-Germain in Paris, where they were called kougnettes. On researching the pastry, I discovered that most bakers consider it best in a commercial setting, with sheeters to roll the dough quickly and evenly, but I was determined to try to replicate it. After the first attempt, a disaster of sticky pastry that leaked tons of butter on baking, I came close to giving up. The second try was good but not laminated enough, so the texture was more cakelike than pastry and didn't seem quite worth the effort. I put it aside for several months but eventually started thinking about it again, and new ideas came to mind: using a stronger, higher protein flour; giving the dough fewer turns ("folds"); and adding the sugar only to the final turn. With these new inspirations, the formerly undoable became easily manageable and on the third try produced what Woody and I now consider to be our top favorite pastry. The Beta Bakers, who tested many of the recipes in this book, were in complete agreement. The interior (pictured on the cover) is made up of soft and open-crumbed layers of dough that capture pockets of sugar syrup, all encased in a crisp shell of golden brown caramel bliss.

PLAN AHEAD The dough takes about 6 hours from start to finish, including baking. The actual hands-on time is very short, because the dough does most of the work, but it is necessary to follow the time schedule strictly.

SPECIAL EQUIPMENT Eight 4 by ¾ inch pastry rings (see Note, page 487) | A 17¼ by 12¼ by 1 inch half sheet pan covered with aluminum foil, dull side up

PASTRY DOUGH

	VOLUME	WEIGHT	
bread flour, preferably King Arthur	3 cups (lightly spooned into the cup and leveled off) minus 1½ tablespoons	13.8 ounces	390 grams
instant yeast	2 teaspoons	.	6.4 grams
fine sea salt	1¾ teaspoons	.	10.5 grams
water, cool room temperature	1 cup (237 ml)	8.4 ounces	237 grams
unsalted butter, melted and cooled	2 tablespoons	1 ounce	28 grams
unsalted butter, preferably high butterfat (see page 514), 60° to 70°F/16° to 21°C	16 tablespoons (2 sticks)	8 ounces	227 grams
sugar, preferably superfine	1 cup	7 ounces	200 grams

MAKE THE DOUGH In the bowl of a stand mixer, with a hand whisk, mix together the flour, yeast, and then the salt. Add the water and the melted butter. Attach the dough hook and, starting on low speed, mix until the flour mixture is moistened, scraping down the sides of the bowl as necessary. Continuing on low speed, beat for 4 minutes. The dough will be silky smooth and have cleaned the sides of the bowl, but it will stick to the bottom and be very soft and slightly sticky to the touch. Cover the bowl and let it rest at room temperature for 30 minutes. Meanwhile, prepare the butter square.

MAKE THE BUTTER SQUARE Place the softened butter on a large sheet of plastic wrap and wrap it loosely. If the butter is cold, pound it lightly with a rolling pin to flatten and soften it. Then knead it together using the plastic wrap and your knuckles to avoid touching the butter directly. Shape the butter into a 5 inch square (it will be about ¾ inch high). At this point, the butter should be firm but workable—68° to 70°F/20° to 21°C. Use it at once or set it in a cool area. The butter should be the same consistency as the dough when they are rolled together or it will break through the dough and not distribute evenly.

MAKE THE DOUGH PACKAGE Roll out the dough on a well-floured surface to an 8 inch square. Place the plastic wrapped butter square diagonally in the center of the dough square and lightly mark the dough at the edges of the butter with the dull side of a clean ruler or a knife. Remove the butter and roll each marked corner of the dough into a flap. The dough will be slightly elastic. Unwrap and place the butter on the dough. Wrap the butter by stretching the flaps slightly to reach across the butter square. Brush off any flour on the first three flaps before stretching over the fourth flap to wrap the butter square securely. It will form a 5¾ inch square dough package. Pinch together the seams to seal it well.

MAKE THE FIRST TURN On the well-floured surface, keeping the dough seam side up and lightly floured, gently roll the dough package into a 13 by 7 inch rectangle. It will be about ¼ inch thick. Roll into the corners and use a bench scraper or a ruler to maintain an even rectangle. If the dough blisters, gently press the blister down. If the butter breaks through,

dust the area lightly with a little flour before brushing off all excess flour from the surface of the dough. Fold the dough into thirds as you would fold a business letter. This is the first turn.

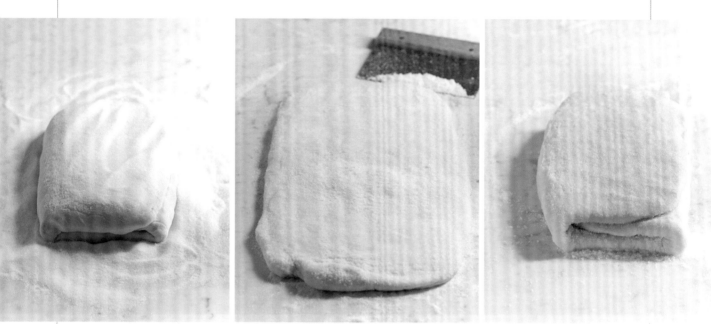

LEFT TO RIGHT: The third turn: sprinkling the dough with sugar. Rolling the sugared dough. Folding the sugared dough into thirds.

LEFT TO RIGHT: Dough rolled out to a 16 by 8 inch rectangle. Bringing up the corners. Pressing the corners into the dough.

Wrap the dough package with plastic wrap and refrigerate it for 1 hour. (The dough should weigh about 2 pounds 7 ounces/1,120 grams.)

MAKE THE SECOND TURN Before each turn, move the dough so that the closed end is facing to the left. Repeat the same process of rolling and folding as for the first turn, but every once in a while, flip over the dough to keep the seams aligned. (The upper part tends to roll more than the bottom.) Cover the dough with plastic wrap and refrigerate for another hour.

MAKE THE THIRD TURN Clean the work surface and sprinkle with about half of the sugar in a rectangle the width of the dough. Set the dough on top and sprinkle most of the remaining sugar on top of it. Roll the dough again into a 14 by 8 inch rectangle, flipping it over from time to time. Scrape sugar from the work surface and sprinkle it and some of the remaining sugar on top of the dough until all but 2 to 3 tablespoons of the sugar have been rolled into the dough. With a bench scraper, form the dough into an even rectangle.

Fold the dough into thirds, wrap it with plastic wrap, and freeze for 30 minutes. Then refrigerate it for 30 minutes. Spread the remaining sugar on the work surface in a rectangle, which will be used for rolling the dough and shaping.

PREPARE THE RINGS AND PAN Set the pastry rings on the prepared sheet pan and lightly coat the insides and bottom with nonstick cooking spray.

ROLL AND SHAPE THE DOUGH Set the dough on top of the sugar on the work surface. Roll it from the center to the edges, then as necessary to form a 16 by 8 inch rectangle. It will

LEFT TO RIGHT: Bringing up the corners a second time. Pressing the dough together. Placing each kouign in a pastry ring.

The dough for kouigns amann is very similar to Danish dough but with sugar rolled into the final turn. Because sugar increases browning, the milk and egg used in Danish dough are replaced with water here in order to prevent excessive browning or burning.

High fat butter and high protein bread flour are ideal to keep the butter layers from breaking through the dough. The consistency of the dough and butter must be the same to distribute the butter evenly throughout the dough, so maintaining the correct temperature of the butter is critical.

Because the sugar compromises the structure of the dough, only three turns are given before shaping in order to maintain the most layered texture.

After shaping, the dough should not be kept at a temperature warmer than 80°F/27°C. Baking it at 400°F/200°C keeps as little butter as possible from leaking out of the dough.

be about ⅜ inch thick. Cut the dough into 8 equal pieces. Each will be about a 4 inch square (average weight should be 4.9 ounces/140 grams). The dough will now be somewhat sticky as the sugar becomes syrupy. Roll 1 of the squares into a 5½ to 6 inch square. Bring up the four corners to the center and press down firmly over the top of the dough. Cup the dough square into the palm of your hand to support it and keep the four corners together. Repeat folding, bringing up the corners to the center a second time. This will be more difficult because the dough is now thicker, but simply press it down in the center (if necessary, dip your fingertip in sugar) and push it together as well as possible. Set the dough in a prepared pastry ring on the sheet pan. Repeat with the other dough squares. Each one will open up slightly and take its own shape, which is part of its charm.

Cover the shaped dough with an 18 by 12 by 2 inch sheet pan, or loosely with plastic wrap that has been lightly coated with nonstick cooking spray, and let it sit in a warm place (ideally at 75° to 80°F/24° to 27°C, but no higher than 80°F/27°C) for 30 minutes, or until the dough has risen about 1½ times and most of the dough touches the sides of the rings. (See page 539 for recommended rising environments.)

Once the dough is shaped, the baking time can be delayed for up to 2 hours by lightly covering the kouigns with plastic wrap and refrigerating them. The rising time, once the kouigns are removed from the refrigerator, will take about 45 minutes to an hour, but the baking time will be the same and the results comparable. (Refrigerating the kouigns for longer than 2 hours prevents the dough from rising.)

PREHEAT THE OVEN Thirty minutes or longer before baking, set an oven rack at the lowest level. Preheat the oven to 400°F/200°C.

BAKE THE KOUIGNS Bake for 12 minutes. For even baking, rotate the pan halfway around. Continue baking for 8 to 15 minutes, or until the pastries are caramelized and the edges are deeply browned. (An instant-read thermometer should read a minimum of 212° to 215°F/100° to 102°C.)

COOL THE KOUIGNS Set the pan on a wire rack. Use tongs to lift off the pastry rings and a pancake turner to lift each kouign onto another wire rack that has been lightly coated with nonstick cooking spray and set over paper towels to catch any leaking butter. (About 2 tablespoons of butter will have leaked from the kouigns onto the aluminum foil.) If any of the kouigns cannot be removed from the rings, return them to the oven for a few minutes to soften the caramel. Let the kouigns cool for about 10 minutes. The texture is softest and the kouigns most delicious when eaten just baked and while still warm.

STORE In a paper bag: room temperature, 2 days. To reheat: 8 to 10 seconds in a microwave or 3 to 5 minutes in a preheated 350°F/175°C oven.

NOTE Disposable pastry rings can be made easily from heavy-duty aluminum foil, or reusable rings can be cut from aluminum flashing (available at most hardware and home improvement stores).

FOR EACH ALUMINUM FOIL RING: Cut a 14 by 4 inch strip. Mark the foil along its length at ⅞ inch. Fold the foil lengthwise along the markings. Fold the foil lengthwise two more times to form a 14 by 1 inch strip with 4 layers of foil.

FOR EACH ALUMINUM FLASHING RING: Use metal shears or sharp utility scissors to cut a 14 by 1 inch strip.

FOR BOTH TYPES OF RINGS: Wrap each ring around a 4 inch diameter can. Use 2 small paper clips to secure the overlapping ends to form a ring. Remove the ring from the can and adjust it to be as round as possible.

Variation: SOUFFLÉED FRENCH TOAST

Stale (2 days or older) kouigns amman make fabulous souffléed French toast. For every 2 kouigns amman (8.5 ounces/240 grams), make the following custard mixture.

	VOLUME	WEIGHT	
3 large eggs	½ cup plus 1½ tablespoons (140 ml)	5.3 ounces	150 grams
heavy cream	⅓ cup (79 ml)	2.7 ounces	77 grams
milk	2 tablespoons (30 ml)	1 ounce	30 grams
pure vanilla extract	1 teaspoon (5 ml)	.	.

MAKE THE CUSTARD Split the kouigns in half lengthwise. In an ovenproof baking dish just large enough to hold the kouigns in a single layer, whisk together the eggs, cream, milk, and vanilla. Place each kouign half, cut side down, in the custard. Cover tightly with plastic wrap and refrigerate for 8 hours or overnight.

PREHEAT THE OVEN Twenty minutes or longer before baking, set the oven rack in the middle of the oven and preheat the oven to 350°F/175°C.

BAKE THE FRENCH TOAST Cover the baking dish loosely with aluminum foil. Bake for 10 minutes. Remove the foil and continue baking for 5 to 10 minutes, or until an instant-read thermometer inserted into the center of one of the kouigns reads 160°F/71°C.

SWEDISH APRICOT WALNUT BREAD

MAKES ONE 11 BY 4 BY 2½ INCH HIGH LOAF

OVEN TEMPERATURE
325°F/160°C for the walnuts; 450°F/230°C, then 400°F/200°C for the bread

BAKING TIME
7 minutes for the walnuts; 35 to 45 minutes for the bread

I discovered this exceptional bread called *speja* (which translates as "scout" or "spy") from an award winning Swedish book by baker Johan Sörberg when I visited his bakery, Riddarbageriet, in Stockholm. I bought the book but, of course, it was in Swedish. Happily, one of the commenters on my blog offered to translate it for me. The original recipe involved making a sourdough starter, but because I didn't want anyone to miss out on this special bread, I adapted it using a simple biga, which also gives it amazing depth of flavor.

PLAN AHEAD Make the biga a minimum of 1 day or preferably 3 days ahead. (The longer amount of storage offers more flavor.)

SPECIAL EQUIPMENT A baking sheet lined with a 14 by 8 inch sheet of parchment | A baking stone or baking sheet

BIGA

MAKES 9 TABLESPOONS/4.8 OUNCES/137 GRAMS

	VOLUME	WEIGHT	
Gold Medal bread flour (or half other brand bread flour, half unbleached all-purpose flour), see page 511	¼ cup (lightly spooned into the cup and leveled off) plus 1 tablespoon	1.4 ounces	40 grams
pumpernickel flour (coarse rye)	⅓ cup (lightly spooned into the cup and leveled off)	1.4 ounces	40 grams
instant yeast	¹⁄₁₆ teaspoon	.	0.2 gram
fine sea salt	⅛ teaspoon	.	0.8 gram
water, at room temperature (70° to 80°F/21° to 27°C)	¼ cup (59 ml)	2.1 ounces	59 grams

MAKE THE BIGA In a small bowl, whisk together the bread flour, pumpernickel flour, and yeast. Whisk in the salt. With a silicone spatula or wooden spoon, stir in the water. Continue stirring for 3 to 5 minutes, or until very stiff and smooth. The biga should be tacky enough to cling slightly to your fingers.

Cover the bowl tightly with plastic wrap that has been lightly coated with nonstick cooking spray (or place it in a 2 cup food storage container that has been lightly coated with nonstick cooking spray and cover with a lid). Set it aside until almost doubled to 1 cup in volume and filled with bubbles. At warm room temperature (80°F/27°C), this will take about 6 hours. Stir it down. Use it at once, or for the best flavor, refrigerate it for up to 3 days before making the dough.

DOUGH

	VOLUME	WEIGHT	
walnut halves	½ cup	1.8 ounces	50 grams
water, at room temperature (70° to 80°F/21° to 27°C)	½ cup (118 ml)	4.2 ounces	118 grams
Biga (see page 488)	9 tablespoons	4.8 ounces	137 grams
Gold Medal bread flour (or half other brand bread flour, half unbleached all-purpose flour), see page 511	1¼ cups (lightly spooned into the cup and leveled off)	5.6 ounces	160 grams
instant yeast	¾ teaspoon minus ⅟₁₆ teaspoon	.	2.2 grams
fine sea salt	¾ teaspoon	.	4.5 grams
golden raisins	full ½ cup	2.8 ounces	79 grams
5 to 6 dried apricots		1.8 ounces	50 grams

PREHEAT THE OVEN Twenty minutes or longer before baking, set an oven rack in the middle level of the oven and preheat the oven to 325°F/160°C.

TOAST AND BREAK THE WALNUTS Spread the walnuts evenly on a baking sheet and bake for 7 minutes to enhance their flavor. Stir once or twice to ensure even toasting and avoid overbrowning. Turn the walnuts onto a clean dish towel and roll and rub them around to loosen the skins. Coarsely break the nuts into a bowl, scraping off and discarding as much of the skins as possible. Cool completely.

MAKE THE DOUGH BREAD MACHINE METHOD Into the container of the bread machine, pour the water. Use sharp scissors, dipped in water if it is sticky, to cut the biga into many small pieces, letting them drop into the water. Add the flour and yeast. Program the machine to mix for 3 minutes and set it to go through the 3 minutes of mixing. Let the dough rest (autolyse) for 20 minutes.

Program the machine to knead for 10 minutes. Add the salt and set the machine to go through the knead cycle, which will include 3 minutes of mixing and 7 minutes of kneading.

Let the dough rest for 20 minutes. Add the raisins and walnuts and reset the machine to mix for 3 minutes.

STAND MIXER METHOD Into the bowl of a stand mixer fitted with the dough hook, pour the water. Use sharp scissors, dipped in water if it is sticky, to cut the biga into many small pieces, letting them drop into the water. Add the flour and yeast, and mix on low speed for about 1 minute, or until the flour is moistened enough to form a rough dough. Scrape down any bits of dough from the sides of the bowl. Sprinkle on the salt and knead the dough on medium speed for about 7 minutes. The dough should be very elastic and smooth, and sticky enough to cling to your fingers. Cover the top of the bowl with plastic wrap and let the dough rest for 20 minutes. Add the raisins and walnuts and knead on low speed for about 1 minute, or until evenly incorporated.

LET THE DOUGH RISE TWICE Using a spatula or dough scraper that has been lightly coated with nonstick cooking spray, scrape the dough into a 2 quart/2 liter dough rising container or bowl that has been lightly coated with nonstick cooking spray. Push down the dough and lightly coat the surface with nonstick cooking spray. (The dough should weigh about 18 ounces/510 grams.) Cover the container with a lid or plastic wrap. With a piece of tape, mark the side of the container at approximately where double the height of the dough should be after rising. Let the dough rise in a warm place (ideally at 75° to 85°F/24° to 29°C) until it reaches the mark, 1 to 1½ hours. (See page 539 for recommended rising environments.)

Using a spatula or dough scraper that has been lightly coated with nonstick cooking spray, turn the dough onto a lightly floured counter and gently press down on the dough to form a rectangle. Give it a four-sided stretch and fold (gently stretch out one side at a time and fold it into the center). Round the corners and set it back into the container.

Again, lightly coat the surface of the dough with nonstick cooking spray, cover with plastic wrap, and mark where double the height should now be after rising. (The dough will fill the container fuller than before because it is puffier with air.) Let it rise until it reaches the mark, about 45 minutes to 1 hour. If time allows, for extra flavor, give the bread the second rise overnight in the refrigerator instead.

Turn the dough onto a lightly floured counter and press the dough down to flatten it slightly. The dough will still be sticky, but use only as much flour as absolutely necessary. Cover the dough and let it rest for 20 minutes before shaping (1 hour if it has been refrigerated).

SHAPE THE DOUGH AND LET IT RISE Gently flatten the dough into a 7 by 5 inch rectangle, with the longer side facing you. Fold down the two upper corners about 3 inches to form a triangle and press down the dough. Set the apricots in a staggered row lengthwise across the dough, under the triangle. Starting from the top, roll the dough to encase the apricots. When you reach the bottom edge of the dough, pinch it firmly against the outside of the dough to make a tight seam. The torpedo-shaped dough should be about 10 by 3 by 2 inches high. Set it on the prepared baking sheet.

Cover the dough loosely with plastic wrap that has been lightly coated with cooking spray. Let the dough rise in a warm place (ideally at 75° to 85°F/24° to 29°C) for about 45 minutes to 1 hour, until about 11 by 3½ by 2⅛ inches high, and when pressed gently with a fingertip, the depression fills in very slowly.

PREHEAT THE OVEN Forty-five minutes or longer before baking, set an oven rack at the lowest level and place the baking stone or baking sheet on it. Place a cast iron pan, lined with aluminum foil to prevent rusting, or a sheet pan on the floor of the oven. Preheat the oven to 450°F/230°C.

SLASH AND BAKE THE BREAD With a straight-edge razor blade or sharp knife, make three ½ inch deep by 2½ inch long diagonal slashes in the top of the dough. Start the first slash about 1 inch from the top end of the dough and start each of the following 2 slashes about 1 inch before the end of the preceding one.

Mist the dough with water. Quickly but gently set the baking sheet on the hot stone or baking sheet and toss a handful (about ½ cup) of ice cubes into the pan on the oven floor. Immediately shut the door and bake for 5 minutes. Lower the heat to 400°F/200°C and continue baking for 15 minutes. For even baking, rotate the pan halfway around.

Continue baking for 15 to 20 minutes, or until the bread is golden brown and a skewer inserted into the center comes out almost clean. (An instant-read thermometer inserted into the center should read about 205°F/96°C.)

COOL THE BREAD Remove the bread from the oven and transfer it from the baking sheet onto a wire rack to cool completely, top-side up, at least 2 hours.

STORE Room temperature, 2 days; airtight: frozen, 3 months.

CRANBERRY CHRISTMAS BREAD

MAKES ONE 12 BY 6 BY 2¾ INCH HIGH LOAF

OVEN TEMPERATURE
325°F/160°C for the walnuts; 400°F/200°C, then 350°F/175°C for the bread

BAKING TIME
7 minutes for the walnuts; 50 to 60 minutes for the bread

I published this bread first in *The Bread Bible*, but then found that adding a simple dough starter (biga) gave it extra flavor, softer texture, and a longer shelf life. This bread is perfect with cheese and so beautiful that it is especially appropriate for the holidays.

PLAN AHEAD Make the biga a minimum of 1 day or preferably 3 days ahead.

SPECIAL EQUIPMENT A 10 inch or longer baking sheet, preferably insulated, or a double layer of two baking sheets, lined with a 14 by 8 inch sheet of parchment

BIGA

MAKES ABOUT 1 CUP/8.3 OUNCES/236 GRAMS

	VOLUME	WEIGHT	
Gold Medal bread flour (or half other brand bread flour, half unbleached all-purpose flour), see page 511	1 cup (lightly spooned into the cup and leveled off) plus 2 teaspoons	4.8 ounces	136 grams
instant yeast	¹⁄₁₆ teaspoon	.	0.2 gram
fine sea salt	¼ teaspoon	.	1.5 grams
water, at room temperature (70° to 80°F/21° to 27°C)	½ cup minus 1 tablespoon (100 ml)	3.5 ounces	100 grams

MAKE THE BIGA In a small bowl, whisk together the flour and yeast. Whisk in the salt. With a silicone spatula or wooden spoon, stir in the water. Continue stirring for 3 to 5 minutes, or until very stiff and smooth. The biga should be tacky enough to cling slightly to your fingers.

Cover the bowl tightly with plastic wrap that has been lightly coated with nonstick cooking spray (or place it in a 2 cup food storage container that has been lightly coated with nonstick cooking spray and cover with a lid). Set it aside until almost doubled to 1⅔ cups in volume and filled with bubbles. At warm room temperature (80°F/27°C), this will take about 6 hours. Stir it down. Use it at once, or for best flavor refrigerate it for up to 3 days before making the dough.

CRANBERRIES

	VOLUME	WEIGHT	
dried cranberries	1 cup	5 ounces	144 grams
hot water	½ cup (118 ml)	4.2 ounces	118 grams

SOAK THE CRANBERRIES In a small bowl, place the dried cranberries and water. Cover with plastic wrap and let the cranberries soak until they are softened and plump, stirring once, 30 minutes. Empty the cranberries into a strainer set over a small bowl. Press the cranberries gently to release any excess liquid and pour the liquid into a 1 cup glass measure. (There should be 6 tablespoons/89 ml.) Add enough water to come to the ¾ cup minus 1 tablespoon level/163 ml/5.7 ounces/163 grams, and set it aside, covered with plastic wrap, to use for making the dough. If planning to mix the dough the following day, cover the cranberries and the cranberry water with plastic wrap and refrigerate them overnight.

DOUGH

	VOLUME	WEIGHT	
walnut halves	2 cups, *divided*	7 ounces	200 grams
whole wheat flour (see Note, page 497)	¼ cup (lightly spooned into the cup and leveled off) plus 2 tablespoons	1.8 ounces	50 grams
Gold Medal bread flour (or half other brand bread flour, half unbleached all-purpose flour), see page 511	1¾ cups (lightly spooned into the cup and leveled off)	8 ounces	227 grams
nondiastatic malt powder, or barley malt syrup, or sugar	1 tablespoon	.	9.3 grams, or 21 grams, or 13 grams
instant yeast	1 to 1⅛ teaspoons (see Note, page 495)	.	3.2 to 3.6 grams
fine sea salt	1⅛ teaspoons	.	6.7 grams
reserved cranberry water (70° to 80°F/21° to 27°C)	¾ cup minus 1 tablespoon (163 ml)	5.7 ounces	163 grams
Biga (see page 493)	about 1 cup	8.3 ounces	236 grams
canola or safflower oil	1 tablespoon (15 ml)	0.5 ounce	13 grams
flour for kneading	⅓ cup (lightly spooned into the cup and leveled off)	1.5 ounces	43 grams

PREHEAT THE OVEN Twenty minutes or longer before baking, set an oven rack in the middle level of the oven and preheat the oven to 325°F/160°C.

PREPARE THE WALNUTS AND FLOUR MIXTURE Spread the walnuts evenly on a baking sheet and bake for 7 minutes to enhance their flavor. Stir once or twice to ensure even toasting and avoid overbrowning. Turn the walnuts onto a clean dish towel and roll and rub them around to loosen the skins. Coarsely break the nuts into a bowl, scraping off and discarding as much of the skins as possible. Cool completely. Set 1½ cups of the walnuts aside.

Place the remaining ½ cup of walnuts in a food processor along with the whole wheat flour and process for about 1 minute, or until finely ground. Pulse in the bread flour, malt, and yeast. (Note: If planning to give the dough the second rise overnight, use only 1 teaspoon/3.2 grams yeast; otherwise use 1⅛ teaspoons/3.6 grams.) Then pulse in the salt. Set the flour mixture aside.

MAKE THE DOUGH BREAD MACHINE METHOD Into the container of the bread machine, pour the cranberry water. Use sharp scissors, dipped in water if it is sticky, to cut the biga into many small pieces, letting them drop into the water. Add the flour mixture. Program the machine to mix for 3 minutes and set it to go through the 3 minutes of mixing. Let the dough rest (autolyse) for 20 minutes.

Program the machine to knead for 10 minutes. Add the oil and reserved broken walnuts and set the machine to go through the knead cycle, which will include 3 minutes of mixing and 7 minutes of kneading. Let the dough rest for 20 minutes.

STAND MIXER METHOD Into the bowl of a stand mixer fitted with the dough hook, pour the cranberry water. Use sharp scissors, dipped in water if it is sticky, to cut the biga into many small pieces, letting them drop into the water. Add the flour mixture and mix on low speed for about 1 minute, or until the flour is moistened, to form a soft, rough dough. Scrape down any bits of dough on the sides of the bowl. Cover the top of the bowl with plastic wrap and let the dough rest for 20 minutes. Add the oil and reserved broken walnuts and knead on medium speed for 7 minutes. The dough should be smooth and elastic. After the first 3 minutes, if the dough still appears sticky and does not begin to pull away from the sides of the bowl, add a little of the flour for kneading, 1 tablespoon at a time.

ADD THE CRANBERRIES Sprinkle the counter with some of the flour for kneading and roll the dough into about a 14 by 10 inch rectangle. Sprinkle the cranberries evenly over the dough and, starting from one of the short ends, roll up the dough as you would a jelly roll.

Form the dough into a ball and knead it lightly. After the cranberries are added, the dough will become sticky and will need a little more of the extra flour.

LET THE DOUGH RISE TWICE Place the dough in a 2 quart/2 liter dough rising container or bowl that has been lightly coated with cooking spray. Push down the dough and lightly coat the surface with nonstick cooking spray. (The dough should weigh about 2 pounds 6 ounces/1,075 grams after adding the cranberries and 2 pounds 7.4 ounces/1,114 grams after adding the extra flour.) Cover the container with a lid or plastic wrap. With a piece of tape, mark on the side of the container approximately where double the height should be after rising. Let the dough rise in a warm place (ideally at 75° to 85°F/24° to 29°C) until it reaches the mark, about 1½ to 2 hours. (See page 539 for recommended rising environments.)

Using a spatula or dough scraper that has been lightly coated with cooking spray, remove the dough to a floured counter and gently press down on it to form a rectangle. Give it a four-sided stretch and fold (gently stretch out one side at a time and fold it into the center). Round the corners and set it back in the container.

Again, lightly coat the surface of the dough with nonstick cooking spray, cover with plastic wrap, and mark where double the height should now be after rising. (The dough will fill the container fuller than before because it is puffier with air.) Let the dough rise until it reaches the mark, about 1 to 1½ hours. Alternatively, place the dough in a sprayed gallon-size reclosable freezer bag and refrigerate it overnight. Deflate it once or twice after the first hour and then the second hour to prevent overproofing. Remove it to room temperature for 1 hour before shaping.

SHAPE THE DOUGH AND LET IT RISE Turn the dough onto a lightly floured counter. Gently flatten the dough into a 7 by 5 inch rectangle, with the longer side facing you. Fold down the two upper corners about 3 inches to form a triangle and press down the dough. Starting from the top, roll the dough. When you reach the bottom edge of the dough, pinch it firmly against the outside of the dough to make a tight seam. The torpedo-shaped dough should be about 10 by 3½ by 2½ inches high. Set it on the prepared baking sheet.

Cover the dough loosely with plastic wrap that has been lightly coated with cooking spray. Let the dough rise in a warm place (ideally at 75° to 85°F/24° to 29°C) for about 45 minutes to 1 hour, or until about 12 by 4½ by 2¾ inches high and when pressed gently with a fingertip, the depression fills in very slowly.

PREHEAT THE OVEN Thirty minutes or longer before baking, set an oven rack at the lowest level and place a cast iron skillet, lined with aluminum foil to prevent rusting, or a sheet pan on the floor of the oven. Preheat the oven to 400°F/200°C.

SLASH AND BAKE THE BREAD For an attractive contrast, dust the dough evenly with flour before slashing (rye flour has a particularly good taste). Alternatively, if the dough is sticky, let it sit, uncovered, for 5 minutes to dry slightly. With a straight-edge razor blade or sharp knife, make ¼ to ½ inch deep parallel crosswise slashes in the top of the dough about 1½ inches apart.

If not dusting the dough with flour, mist the dough with water. Quickly but gently set the baking sheet on the oven rack and toss a handful (about ½ cup) of ice cubes into the pan on the oven floor. Immediately shut the door and bake for 5 minutes. Lower the heat to 350°F/175°C and continue baking for 25 minutes. For even baking, rotate the bread halfway around.

Highlights for Success

Soaking the cranberries not only softens them but also produces a naturally sweetened liquid that permeates the bread and turns the crust a magnificent golden brown.

The walnuts are toasted very lightly to keep them from turning blue in the crumb. Because some of the nuts will work their way to the top of the crust and continue to brown, it is best to toast them only lightly.

This bread takes longer to rise because of the extra weight of the whole wheat flour, cranberries, and nuts. Extra risings make the grain more even and lighter.

A softer dough results in a lighter texture ideal for this bread. Do not work in too much flour.

If using malt syrup instead of malt powder, it will produce a browner crumb instead of the rosy hue. Because the long baking required for this large loaf and the sugar contained in the cranberry soaking water conspire to create a very brown crust, this bread should not be baked on a baking stone.

Continue baking for 20 to 30 minutes, or until the crust is golden and a skewer inserted into the center comes out clean. (An instant-read thermometer inserted into the center should read about 205°F/96°C.)

COOL THE BREAD Remove the bread from the oven and transfer it from the baking sheet to a wire rack to cool completely, top side up, at least 2 hours.

STORE Room temperature, 2 days; airtight: frozen, 3 months.

NOTE If purchasing whole wheat flour, be sure to use it within 3 months or freeze it (it will keep for at least a year in the freezer). If grinding your own wheat berries, use the flour within 3 days or wait for 3 weeks, due to certain enzymes that would render it undesirable for bread baking during this time period; after this time it should be used within 3 months or frozen.

100% WHOLE WHEAT WALNUT LOAF

MAKES ONE 9½ BY 5 BY 4⅛ INCH HIGH LOAF

OVEN TEMPERATURE
325°F/160°C for the walnuts; 450°F/230°C, then 400°F/200°C for the bread

BAKING TIME
7 minutes for the walnuts; 45 to 55 minutes for the bread

*T*his is my best whole wheat bread. It is healthful, wheaty, full of flavor, and has a great texture. It is also an excellent bread when made without the walnuts. The walnut oil, however, produces a more mellow flavor and a slightly higher rise. Sliced thin, this bread is an ideal accompaniment to cheese, especially to blue cheese.

PLAN AHEAD Make the dough starter 1 to 4 hours ahead of mixing the dough.

SPECIAL EQUIPMENT One 9 by 5 inch (8 cups) loaf pan, lightly coated with nonstick cooking spray | A baking stone or baking sheet

DOUGH STARTER (SPONGE)

	VOLUME	WEIGHT	
water, at room temperature (70° to 80°F/21° to 27°C)	1¾ cups plus 1 tablespoon (429 ml)	15.1 ounces	429 grams
honey	1 tablespoon plus 1 teaspoon (20 ml)	1 ounce	28 grams
whole wheat flour (see Notes, page 502)	2 cups (lightly spooned into the cup and leveled off)	9.2 ounces	260 grams
instant yeast	½ teaspoon	.	1.6 grams

MAKE THE DOUGH STARTER (SPONGE) In a large bowl, or in the bowl of a stand mixer fitted with the whisk beater, place the water, honey, flour, and yeast. Whisk until very smooth to incorporate air, about 3 minutes. The dough starter will be the consistency of a thin batter. Scrape down the sides of the bowl.

If using the Bread Machine Method, scrape the starter into the container of the bread machine. If using the Stand Mixer Method, scrape down the sides of the bowl. Set the starter aside, covered with plastic wrap, while you make the flour mixture.

DOUGH

	VOLUME	WEIGHT	
whole wheat flour (see Notes, page 502)	1½ cups (lightly spooned into the cup and leveled off) plus 1 tablespoon	7.3 ounces	206 grams
vital wheat gluten (see Notes, page 502)	2 tablespoons plus 2 teaspoons	0.8 ounce	24 grams
instant yeast	½ teaspoon	0.8 ounce	1.6 grams
walnut halves	1⅔ cups	5.9 ounces	166 grams
walnut, canola, or safflower oil, at room temperature	⅓ cup (79 ml)	2.5 ounces	72 grams
fine sea salt	1¾ teaspoons	.	10.5 grams

COMBINE THE FLOUR MIXTURE In a medium bowl, whisk together the flour, vital wheat gluten, and yeast. Sprinkle the flour mixture over the dough starter, forming a blanket of flour, and cover it tightly with plastic wrap. Let it ferment for at least 1 and up to 4 hours at room temperature. After 1 hour there will be hairline cracks in the flour blanket. On longer standing, the starter will bubble through the flour blanket in several places.

PREHEAT THE OVEN Twenty minutes or longer before baking, set an oven rack in the middle of the oven and preheat the oven to 325°F/160°C.

TOAST AND BREAK THE WALNUTS Spread the walnuts evenly on a baking sheet and bake for 7 minutes to enhance their flavor. Stir once or twice to ensure even toasting and avoid overbrowning. Turn the walnuts onto a clean dish towel and roll and rub them around to loosen the skins. Coarsely break the nuts into a bowl, scraping off and discarding as much of the skins as possible. Cool completely.

MAKE THE DOUGH Bread Machine Method Program the machine to mix for 3 minutes and set it to go through the 3 minutes of mixing. Let the dough rest (autolyse) for 20 minutes.

Program the machine to knead for 10 minutes. Add the oil and set the machine to go through the knead cycle, which will include 3 minutes of mixing and 7 minutes of kneading. After the first 3 minutes of mixing, add the salt. After the first 3 minutes of kneading, add the walnuts. The dough will not be elastic at this point and will not form a ball. It should be sticky enough to cling to your fingers. If it is not at all sticky, spray it with a little water and knead it in.

STAND MIXER METHOD Attach the dough hook. Mix the dough for about 1 minute until the flour is moistened to form a rough dough. Scrape down any bits of dough on the sides of the bowl. Cover the top of the bowl with plastic wrap and let the dough rest for 20 minutes. Add the oil and mix the dough on low speed for 7 minutes, adding the salt after the oil is mixed in. Add the walnuts and continue kneading for 3 minutes. The dough will not be elastic at this point and will not form a ball. It should be sticky enough to cling to your fingers. If it is not at all sticky, spray it with a little water and knead that in.

LET THE DOUGH RISE TWICE Using a spatula or dough scraper that has been lightly coated with nonstick cooking spray, scrape the dough into a 3 quart/3 liter dough rising container or bowl that has been lightly coated with nonstick cooking spray. Push down the dough and lightly coat the surface with nonstick cooking spray. (The dough should weigh about 2 pounds 9 ounces/1,173 grams.) Cover the container with a lid or plastic wrap. With a piece of tape, mark the side of the container approximately where 1½ times the height should be after rising. Let the dough rise in a warm place (ideally at 75° to 85°F/24° to 29°C) until it reaches the mark, 40 minutes to 1 hour. (See page 539 for recommended rising environments.)

Using a spatula or dough scraper that has been lightly coated with nonstick cooking spray, remove the dough to a floured counter and flour the top. Gently press it down to form a rectangle. It will now be quite elastic. Give it a four-sided stretch and fold (gently stretch out one side at a time and fold it into the center). Round the corners and return it to the container.

Again, lightly coat the surface of the dough with nonstick cooking spray, cover with plastic wrap, and mark where 1½ times should now be after rising. (The dough will fill the container fuller than before because it is puffier with air.) Let it rise until it reaches the mark, 45 minutes to 1 hour (or refrigerate it overnight and remove it to room temperature for 1 hour before proceeding).

SHAPE THE DOUGH AND LET IT RISE Turn the dough onto a lightly floured counter and, with your fingertips, dimple the dough to get rid of air bubbles. Gently flatten the dough into an 8 inch wide rectangle. It will still be slightly sticky, but use only as much flour as absolutely necessary. Shape the dough into a loaf, starting from the top and rolling down to the bottom. With each roll, push the dough away from you with your thumbs to tighten the roll. When you reach the bottom edge of the dough, pinch it firmly against the outside of the dough to make a tight seam. Set the shaped dough in the prepared loaf pan, pushing it down firmly. It will fill the pan to the top. Cover it loosely with plastic wrap that has been lightly coated with nonstick cooking spray and let it rise in a warm place (ideally at 75° to 85°F/24° to 29°C) for 45 minutes to 1 hour. The highest point should be 1½ inches above the top of the pan and when pressed gently with a fingertip, the depression fills in very slowly.

PREHEAT THE OVEN Forty-five minutes or longer before baking, set an oven rack at the lowest level and set the baking stone or baking sheet on it. Place a cast iron skillet, lined with aluminum foil to prevent rusting, or a sheet pan on the floor of the oven. Preheat the oven to 450°F/230°C.

BAKE THE BREAD Quickly but gently set the pan on the baking stone or baking sheet and toss a handful (about ½ cup) of ice cubes into the pan on the oven floor. Immediately shut the door. Lower the temperature to 400°F/200°C and bake for 25 minutes. For even baking, rotate the pan halfway around. Continue baking for 20 to 30 minutes, or until the bread is medium brown and a skewer inserted into the center comes out clean. (An instant-read thermometer inserted into the center should read 200° to 205°F/93° to 96°C.)

COOL THE BREAD Remove the bread from the oven, unmold it from the pan, and transfer it to a wire rack to cool completely, top side up, at least 2 hours.

STORE Room temperature, 2 days; airtight: frozen, 3 months.

NOTES If purchasing whole wheat flour, be sure to use it within 3 months or freeze it (it will keep for at least a year in the freezer). If grinding your own wheat berries, use the flour within 3 days or wait for 3 weeks due to certain enzymes that would render it undesirable for bread baking during this time period; after this time it should be used within 3 months or frozen.

The vital wheat gluten strengthens the structure of the dough and makes the baked bread less dense.

Variation: BASIC WHOLE WHEAT LOAF

The whole wheat bread can be made without the walnuts or walnut oil. The shaped dough will fill the pan to about ½ inch from the top and should rise to 1¼ inches above the sides of the pan before baking.

TRUE ORANGE MARMALADE

MAKES ABOUT 8 CUPS (8 OR 9 HALF-PINT JARS)

A world away from commercial marmalade in fresh, bright clarity of flavor, this conserve (pictured on page 446) is a pleasure to make because the entire house is filled with the perfume of oranges. It is not all that time-consuming either. The most labor-intensive part is slicing the fruit, which takes about an hour.

Seville oranges from California are available for only a short period of time, from January through March. They are very high in acidity, which aids in gelling, and have the most intensely true orange flavor.

PLAN AHEAD The orange and lemon slices must soak for a combined 48 hours before you proceed with the marmalade.

SPECIAL EQUIPMENT Eight or nine half-pint canning jars (see Notes, page 504) | A canning pot or large pot with a rack (see Notes, page 504)

	VOLUME	WEIGHT	
5 (to 8) Seville oranges, depending on size	·	21 ounces	595 grams
½ navel orange	·	3.5 ounces	100 grams
½ lemon	·	1.2 ounces	35 grams
water	6½ cups (1,538 ml)	3 pounds 6 ounces	1,538 grams
sugar	about 8 cups	about 3 pounds 8 ounces	about 1,600 grams
lemon juice, freshly squeezed	1 tablespoon (15 ml)	0.6 ounce	16 grams

PREPARE THE FRUIT Wash the oranges and lemon with dish detergent and a scrubbing pad. Slice the Seville oranges, navel orange, and lemon as thinly as possible, removing and reserving all of the seeds. You should have about ¼ cup of seeds. Place them in a small bowl and add about 6 tablespoons/89 ml of water. Cover the bowl and set it aside.

Place the orange and lemon slices in a large nonreactive pot, at least 5 quart/5 liter capacity. Add the water, cover, and let it sit for 24 hours.

COOK THE MARMALADE Place the pot over medium heat and bring the fruit to a boil. Let it boil, uncovered, for 30 minutes. Remove it from the heat, cover, and let it sit for another 24 hours.

Measure the fruit and liquid. You should have about 8 cups. Add an equal volume of sugar. (If there is less fruit mixture, add less sugar.)

Bring the mixture to a boil over medium heat and cook, uncovered, stirring often, until thickened, about 35 minutes. (An instant-read thermometer should read 221° to 225°F/ 105° to 107°C.) To test the thickness of the mixture without a thermometer, pour a teaspoon of the mixture onto a small plate and place it in the freezer for 2 minutes. It should wrinkle slightly when gently pushed with a fingertip. It will thicken considerably upon cooling. With a small spoon, lift out any seeds you may have missed that rise to the surface.

PREPARE THE JARS While the mixture is boiling, sterilize the canning jars by filling them with boiling water. Also pour boiling water over the inside of the lids.

MAKE THE PECTIN In a microwave or in a small saucepan over low heat, warm the seeds to melt the liquid, which will have hardened to a gel. Place the mixture in a strainer suspended over a small bowl and let it drain. This jellied liquid is natural pectin. When the fruit mixture is cooked, add this pectin and the lemon juice to it and boil for another 10 minutes, stirring often. Set the rack in the bottom of the canning pot. Bring enough water to a boil to cover the jars by 1 inch.

CAN THE MARMALADE Pour the hot marmalade into the sterilized jars, leaving ⅜ inch headspace. Screw on the caps and place the jars on the rack in the water bath. Cover, return the water to a boil, and then boil the jars for 10 minutes. Remove the jars and let them cool before checking the seal. (When you press on the center of the lid, it will feel totally firm and unyielding.)

STORE In a dark area: cool room temperature, at least 2 years.

NOTES Half-pint jars can hold only 7 fluid ounces because of the ⅜ inch headspace required on top.

Jars in the water bath must be sitting on a rack to let the water flow all around them, and the water must be high enough to cover them by 1 inch. They must be upright to expel any air inside the jars, producing a vacuum that seals the jar. You may also invert the jars onto a folded towel until cool instead of boiling the jars. (The air trapped in the headspace will travel upward through the hot preserves and be sterilized.)

HIGHLIGHTS FOR SUCCESS

To slice the oranges and lemon, use a very sharp knife. Cut a thin slice from each end of the oranges and lemon and cut these discs of peel into thin julienne pieces. Cut each orange and the lemon in half from cut end to cut end. Place the orange and lemon halves cut side down and slice the short way (starting from a cut end).

Once the mixture has reached the correct thickness and gelling point, turn the heat off immediately or overgelling may occur and it will be necessary to add water and reheat, and the resulting preserves will not be as smooth as they could be.

A nonreactive pan must be used due to the high acidity of the fruit.

Sour Cherry and Currant Jam

MAKES ABOUT 4 CUPS (4 HALF-PINT JARS)

Cherries are unusually low in pectin, the naturally occurring substance that thickens fruit into a jamlike consistency. Because of this, it is necessary to add extra pectin, and extra sugar as well, for cherry jam to set. I tried for more than twenty years to make a cherry jam without adding the tons of sugar required by the added pectin. Because currants are so high in natural pectin, which does not require extra sugar, and because they blend so well with the cherries in my "Churrant" Pie (page 204), I decided to employ them for this jam, and the results were everything I had hoped for. The tart sour cherries are the star here. The currants mainly provide the consistency, enhancing without interfering with the cherry flavor.

This garnet jam (pictured on page 446) is equally good spread on pumpernickel bread as on my white chocolate bread (page 447). It also makes a deliciously sweet-tart sauce for duck or pork, especially if you add a little chicken stock and cream. Frozen currants and cherries work perfectly. Thaw them completely before proceeding.

SPECIAL EQUIPMENT A jelly bag and stand or large strainer lined with several layers of cheesecloth, dipped in water and wrung well, set over a bowl | Four half-pint canning jars (see Notes, page 506) | A canning pot or large pot with a rack (see Notes, page 506)

	VOLUME	WEIGHT	
pitted sour cherries	4 cups	23 ounces	652 grams
sugar	2⅔ cups	18.8 ounces	532 grams
fresh red currants, rinsed, drained, and stemmed	4 cups	21.6 ounces	612 grams
water	½ cup (118 ml)	4.2 ounces	118 grams

MAKE THE JAM In a large nonreactive saucepan, preferably nonstick, combine the cherries and sugar.

In a small nonreactive saucepan, place the well-drained currants and the water. With a potato masher or fork, crush the currants slightly. Bring the mixture to a boil and simmer for 10 minutes.

Spoon the currant mixture into the jelly bag and let it drip through. Squeeze the bag or cloth. You should have at least ⅔ cup/158 ml of juice. If you have less, chances are the liquid evaporated during simmering, so add enough water to make up the difference.

Highlights for Success

PREPARE THE JARS Sterilize the canning jars by filling them with boiling water. Also pour boiling water over the inside of the lids. Set the rack in the bottom of the canning pot and bring enough water to a boil to cover the jars by 1 inch.

Add the currant juice to the cherry mixture and bring it to a boil, stirring constantly. Boil rapidly, stirring often, until it reaches the gelling point, about 8 minutes. Watch carefully, adjusting the heat, because the mixture tends to bubble up and over. (An instant-read thermometer should read 225°F/107°C.)

To test the thickness of the mixture without a thermometer, remove the pan from the heat and dip a large clean metal spoon into it. Let the liquid fall back into the pan. The last 2 drops should merge and sheet off the spoon. (Or place a tablespoon of the liquid on a chilled plate and freeze it for 2 minutes, or until cold. It should wrinkle when pushed gently with a fingertip.)

CAN THE JAM Pour the hot jam into the sterilized jars, leaving ⅜ inch headspace. Do not scrape the pan or it may cause lumping. Screw on the caps and place the jars on the rack in the water bath. Cover, return the water to a boil, and then boil the jars for 10 minutes. Remove the jars and let them cool on a folded towel before checking the seal. (When you press on the center of the lid, it will feel totally firm and unyielding.)

The juices will be very liquid until cool. During cooling, the cherries will float to the top. They can be distributed evenly by inverting the jars every 30 minutes until barely warm—about 2½ hours. At this point the liquid will suddenly gel. It will continue to thicken during the next 2 days of storage and should not be moved during this time.

If, after that time, it has not thickened sufficiently, it can be emptied into a pan and cooked for a few minutes more to the proper gelling point.

STORE In a dark area: cool room temperature, at least 2 years.

NOTES Half-pint jars can hold only 7 fluid ounces because of the ⅜ inch headspace required on top.

Jars in the water bath must be sitting on a rack to let the water flow all around them and the water must be high enough to cover them by 1 inch. They must be upright to expel any air inside the jars, producing a vacuum, which seals the jar. Alternatively, you may invert the jars onto a folded towel until cool instead of boiling them. The air trapped in the headspace will travel upward through the hot preserves and be sterilized.

Concord Grape Jelly

*T*his is the grape used for Concord grape wine and, of course, commercial grape jelly, the classic companion to peanut butter in sandwiches. The back roads around Hope, New Jersey, where my husband, Elliott, and I live, are filled with Concord grape vines and the winy, juicy grapes make wonderful jelly (pictured on page 446). I was inspired to turn these grapes into jelly by my friend Diane Kniss, who lives in Woodstock, New York, and makes tons of jars every fall to offer as much appreciated Christmas presents. The flavor of homemade grape jelly is incomparable.

SPECIAL EQUIPMENT Four half-pint canning jars (see Notes, page 508) | A canning pot or large pot with a rack (see Notes, page 508)

	VOLUME	WEIGHT	
Concord grapes (4 pounds to allow for bad grapes and stems)	9⅓ cups	3 pounds 8 ounces	1,588 grams
water	1 cup (237 ml)	8.4 ounces	237 grams
sugar	3 cups	21.2 ounces	600 grams

MAKE THE JELLY Wash the grapes, drain, and stem them, discarding any bad grapes. Weigh or measure the amount of grapes needed.

PREPARE THE JARS Sterilize the canning jars by filling them with boiling water. Also pour boiling water over the inside of the lids. Set the rack in the bottom of the canning pot and bring enough water to a boil to cover the jars by 1 inch.

In a large saucepan, place the well-drained grapes and the water. With a potato masher or large fork, crush the grapes slightly. Bring the mixture to a boil, stirring often. Reduce the heat, cover, and simmer the grapes for 5 to 10 minutes, or until they have collapsed completely.

Strain the mixture through a fine-mesh strainer and discard the pits and skins. You should have 3½ cups/828 ml of pulp (29.5 ounces/836 grams).

Empty the pulp into a clean saucepan and stir in the sugar. Over medium heat, stirring constantly, bring the mixture to a boil.

Boil, stirring occasionally, for about 15 minutes. As the conserve begins to thicken, lower the heat to a simmer to avoid scorching and stir constantly until it reaches the gelling

Highlights for Success

Fifty-eight ounces of unblemished grapes, stemmed, yield 56 ounces. Grapes can be frozen in quart canning jars for future use.

A large unlined copper pot is traditional for jam or jelly making because the faster the grapes or berries and syrup cook, the better the flavor and gelling. Be sure to use a pot with a large diameter to speed evaporation of the syrup.

Once the mixture has reached the correct thickness and gelling point, turn off the heat immediately or overgelling may occur and it will be necessary to add water, strain, and reheat, and the resulting jelly will not be as smooth as it could be.

point. (An instant-read thermometer should read 221° to 225°F/105° to 107°C.)

To test the thickness of the mixture without a thermometer, remove the pan from the heat and dip a large clean metal spoon into it. Let the liquid fall back into the pan. The last 2 drops should merge and sheet off the spoon. (Or place a tablespoon of the liquid on a chilled plate and freeze it for 2 minutes, or until cold. It should wrinkle when pushed gently with a fingertip.)

CAN THE JELLY Pour the hot jelly into the sterilized jars, leaving ⅜ inch headspace. Do not scrape the pan or it may cause lumping. (If lumping occurs, straining will not help because it causes the jelly to thin.) Screw on the caps and place the jars on the rack in the water bath. Cover, return the water to a boil, and boil the jars for 10 minutes. Remove the jars and let them cool on a folded towel before checking the seal. (When you press on the center of the lid, it will feel totally firm and unyielding.)

Concord grapes vary in acidity from year to year, which affects thickening. The jelly takes 2 days in the jar to thicken completely and should not be moved during this time. If, after that time, it has not thickened sufficiently, it can be emptied into a pan and cooked for a few minutes more to the proper gelling point.

STORE In a dark area: cool room temperature, at least 2 years.

NOTES Half-pint jars can hold only 7 fluid ounces because of the ⅜ inch headspace required on top.

Jars in the water bath must be sitting on a rack to let the water flow all around them and the water must be high enough to cover them by 1 inch. They must be upright to expel any air inside the jars, producing a vacuum, which seals the jar. Alternatively, you may invert the jars onto a folded towel until cool instead of boiling them. The air trapped in the headspace will travel upward through the hot preserves and be sterilized.

INGREDIENTS AND BASIC RECIPES

When it comes to baking, the type and quality of ingredients used play a critical role. The kind of flour, for example, will have a direct effect on the texture of the baked goods. The brand of chocolate and cacao content will affect both the texture and the flavor. I therefore offer this focused section that includes information about those ingredients that are vital to the success of the recipe and those that are my personal preferences. Further understanding and details are offered on my blog, www.realbakingwithrose.com. Enter the word "ingredients" in the search box.

For all recipes in this book, weights are given in both the metric and avoirdupois (ounces/ pounds) systems. Grams generally have been rounded off to the nearest whole number without decimal points, the ounces to the nearest decimal point. Either system works, but do not expect the mathematics to correlate exactly. I prefer weighing to measuring for its superior speed and precision, but if you choose measuring, it's important to have the right techniques.

(*Ingredient Sources are listed on page 527*)

FLOUR

Flour is the single most important ingredient in baking. The type of flour used, particularly its protein content and whether it is bleached or unbleached, is critical to the outcome. There are five main types of flour I use in this book: bleached cake flour, bleached and unbleached all-purpose flour, pastry flour, and bread flour.

Bleaching flour is a chemical process that accelerates the natural processes of aging. One of the effects is the oxidation of carotenoid pigments in the flour, which turns the flour from ivory to white. More significant, however, are the resulting alteration of the protein molecules, which effectively denatures their gluten-forming capability, and the roughening of the surface of the starch granules. Both of these changes promote gelatinization of the starch during baking (the absorption of water and setting of the starch granules due to heating). This is important because the ability of the flour to gelatinize is critical to the ultimate texture of baked goods.

Low protein flour produces more tenderness, such as in cakes; higher protein results in a firmer and more chewy texture, as in bread. The protein content of bleached all-purpose flour can vary from brand to brand and even harvest to harvest, from 8 to 14 grams of protein per cup, averaging 11 grams. Store flour tightly covered and away from heat so that it doesn't absorb moisture or dry out. Well-stored bleached flour will keep for several years. Unbleached flour has a one year shelf life at room temperature and several years if frozen. Whole wheat flour must be freshly ground as needed or stored in the freezer after 3 months at cool room temperature. Because whole wheat flour includes the germ of the wheat kernel, which is high in oil and prone to rancidity, it will develop an off taste if stored longer. If freshly ground, it should be used within 3 or 4 days or after 3 weeks, due to enzyme activity in between that time period that makes it less stable.

APPROXIMATE PERCENTAGE OF PROTEIN CONTAINED IN COMMONLY AVAILABLE FLOURS

SWANS DOWN OR SOFTASILK CAKE FLOUR	8 percent
KING ARTHUR QUEEN GUINEVERE CAKE FLOUR	8 percent
WHITE LILY BLEACHED ALL-PURPOSE FLOUR	9 percent
KING ARTHUR PASTRY FLOUR	9.2 percent
WONDRA FLOUR	9.8 percent
GOLD MEDAL OR PILLSBURY BLEACHED ALL-PURPOSE FLOUR	about 11 percent (regional brands may be significantly lower); unbleached is slightly higher
KING ARTHUR UNBLEACHED ALL-PURPOSE FLOUR	11.7 percent
HECKERS FLOUR	12 percent
GOLD MEDAL BREAD FLOUR	12.3 percent
KING ARTHUR BREAD FLOUR	12.7 percent

FLOUR FOR CAKES

The two flours that I use most often for cakes are bleached cake flour and bleached all-purpose flour.

Where indicated in the recipe, bleached cake and bleached all-purpose flour can be used interchangeably as long as the weight is the same. If you are measuring by volume, refer to Ingredient Equivalences and Substitutions (page 526). Cake flour results in a more tender crumb that is ideal for most cakes. If you desire extra tenderness and have only bleached all-purpose flour on hand, you will need to use the suggested amount of potato starch or cornstarch in place of some of the all-purpose flour. However, in some instances, I like the higher protein of all-purpose flour so that the cake has enough structure and slices without falling apart.

If you are using a national brand of bleached all-purpose flour, the volume given in a recipe will be less than that of cake flour for the same weight. If, however, you are using regional brands, especially from the South, such as White Lily, the protein will be very similar to cake flour and you can use the same volume.

For home bakers in the United Kingdom and other places where bleached flour is not readily available, blogger Kate Coldrick has come up with a technique that uses a microwave to treat commonly available flour so that it performs as successfully as bleached flour. I wrote about it in *Rose's Heavenly Cakes* and have also posted the instructions on my website, www.realbakingwithrose.com.

For many sponge cakes, I use Wondra flour, created by General Mills Gold Medal. It is produced by a patented process called agglomeration, which enables the flour particles to dissolve instantly in liquid, yielding a tender crumb. It works well for angel food cakes and for sponge cakes such as génoise and biscuit (except for chocolate ones, which acquire a less desirable flavor).

Measure Wondra flour either by sprinkling it directly out of the canister (which is a bit slow) or by spooning it lightly into the measuring cup and leveling it off. The weight is the same with both methods.

Flour for Pies, Tarts, and Pastries

The flours I use for pies and pastry are pastry flour or bleached all-purpose flour. Pastry flour, as the name implies, contains the ideal protein content to produce a good balance of flakiness and tenderness.

Flour for Cookies

I use bleached all-purpose flour for cookies. Unbleached all-purpose or bread flour, which have more protein, result in cookies that are darker in color. Because gluten absorbs more of the liquid components, the cookies also turn out less puffy and flatter.

Flour for Bread

Bread flour and unbleached all-purpose flour have higher protein contents than bleached all-purpose flour, and as such are better for making many types of bread. The gluten-forming proteins in flour connect when liquid is added to form gluten, which creates the structure and shape of the bread, and also its chewy texture. Higher protein also results in more browning.

Gold Medal bread flour and Heckers flour have about 12 percent protein, which offers the lightest crumb and the ideal structure. Most other bread flours are higher in protein, so to approximate the right amount, use half bread flour and half unbleached all-purpose flour.

Sugar

The types of sugar I have used for these recipes are superfine or fine granulated sugar, powdered sugar, turbinado sugar, and light or dark brown sugar. My preference is cane sugar.

Refined superfine granulated sugar results in the finest texture and most neutral flavor in many baked goods such as cakes and cookies, adding a sweetness that balances and accentuates the other ingredients. Fine granulated cane sugar can be substituted for superfine sugar; you can also process fine granulated sugar in a food processor when superfine is desired. In most cookies, for example, superfine sugar will give a finer crumb with less cracking.

Powdered sugar contains about 3 percent cornstarch to prevent lumping. (India Tree's Powdered Cane Sugar is the finest and smoothest I have found.)

In some recipes I specify turbinado, or raw, sugar, which has large crystals and a slightly higher amount of molasses, for the extra flavor it offers. The amount of molasses varies between different brands. My preference is Sugar in the Raw.

When it comes to light brown and dark brown sugars, I adore the flavor of Muscovado from the tropical island of Mauritius off the coast of Africa in the Indian Ocean. The special robust and complex flavor of the sugar is derived from sugar cane grown in volcanic ash. Billington's is one brand; it is imported from England and available in fine groceries, gourmet and health food stores, and from India Tree. Its light brown and dark brown sugars contain the same amount of molasses as the more commonly available light and dark brown sugars, but the quality is superior.

If replacing light brown Muscovado sugar with more commonly available brown sugar, it is best to use an equal weight of dark brown. (The volume will be slightly less but not significantly, so you can use

How to Measure Ingredients

WEIGHING IS FASTER, EASIER, AND NEATER THAN MEASURING. But measuring by volume is fine as long as you do it carefully and accurately. The way I have presented the volume measures is the way in which I would measure them. Instead of writing 6 tablespoons sugar, I express it as ¼ cup plus 2 tablespoons because that is the more convenient approach. Also, the fewer measures used, the less room for error. Occasionally, for small amounts of dry ingredients such as ground cinnamon, which comes in bottles with small openings, I will call for 3 teaspoons instead of 1 tablespoon. But for sticky ingredients, I prefer giving the largest measuring spoon required because some of the ingredient always remains in the spoon, throwing off the final quantity if several spoonfuls are required.

FOR THOSE WHO MEASURE INSTEAD OF WEIGH, I use two methods for measuring flour, depending on which method correlates most closely to the desired weight. "Sifted into the cup" means that the flour is pushed through either a sifter or strainer into a measuring cup that is sitting on a counter or other flat surface. The cup is never touched or shaken. Only the handle is held when the excess is swept off with a long flat spatula or knife. Sifting yields the least amount of flour. "Lightly spooned into the cup and leveled off" refers to spooning flour into the measuring cup and then sweeping off the excess on the top. This yields more than sifting, but less than the "dip and sweep" method (dipping the cup into the bin to fill and then leveling off the top). Flours should be stirred lightly before measuring, except for Wondra flour, which doesn't tend to settle.

LIQUIDS ARE EXPRESSED IN MEASURING SPOONS, CUPS, AND MILLILITERS to avoid confusion between fluid ounces and weight ounces.

UNLIKE FLOUR, SUGAR IS MEASURED BY THE DIP AND SWEEP METHOD. This means that you dip the cup into the sugar bin to fill and then, without shaking or tapping it, sweep off the excess from the top.

ALL DRY INGREDIENTS SHOULD BE MEASURED IN A CUP DESIGNED FOR SOLIDS. Liquid ingredients, including golden and corn syrups, should be measured in a liquid measure with a spout. There is a difference in volume between liquid and solid measuring cups (see page 532).

the same volume indicated for the light brown Muscovado sugar.)

Equal volume of either type of brown sugar has the same sugar content as refined granulated white sugar, but brown sugar must be measured by packing it firmly into the cup (weighing is much easier). Dark brown sugar weighs the most because of its added molasses.

Store brown sugar in an airtight container, such as a canning jar, to keep it from losing moisture and solidifying. If the sugar should solidify, make a small shallow cup from a piece of aluminum foil and set it on top of the sugar in the container. Tear a paper towel in half, wet it, and squeeze out most of the water. Set the towel on top of the foil, not touching the sugar. Cover the container tightly and, within several hours, the sugar will have drawn the moisture from the paper towel and become soft and loose again. (This also works for granulated sugar.) If you run out of brown sugar and have white sugar and molasses on hand, it's easy to make your own (see Ingredient Equivalences and Substitutions, page 526).

Sugar Syrups

The syrups used in this book include store-bought sweeteners, such as golden syrup and molasses; simple syrups brushed onto cakes to add moisture and sometimes flavor; and concentrated sugar syrups, a key component in Italian meringue. When weighing or measuring syrup, use a container that has been coated with nonstick cooking spray so that it is easier to remove all of the syrup.

MOLASSES is refined from the concentrated juice of sugar cane and contains 24 percent water. I prefer Grandma's unsulfured mild flavor molasses for my recipes.

GOLDEN SYRUP (REFINER'S SYRUP) When, after many boilings, cane sugar syrup ceases to yield crystals, it is filtered and concentrated into this golden-colored syrup with lilting overtones of butterscotch and vanilla. It contains 15 to 18 percent water. Lyle's, a British company, packages it as Lyle's Golden Syrup. It can be used interchangeably with light corn syrup.

CORN SYRUP This syrup is primarily glucose with fructose added to prevent crystallization. It contains about 24 percent water, but it can be used interchangeably with golden syrup. I prefer light corn syrup to dark, which contains molasses.

Concentrated Sugar Syrups and Caramel

A supersaturated sugar solution begins with sugar partially dissolved in at least one-third its weight of cold water. It is stirred continuously until boiling, at which time all the sugar will dissolve. If sugar crystals remain on the sides of the pan, wash down the sides with a wet pastry brush. Once the sugar is dissolved, the solution is considered supersaturated and, to avoid crystallization, must not be stirred. As the water evaporates, the density of the solution increases and the temperature rises. As long as there is a lot of water in the syrup, the temperature does not rise much above the boiling point of the water. But once most of the water has boiled away, the temperature can then rise dramatically, passing through various stages and eventually rising to the temperature of pure melted sugar (320°F/160°C) when all the water is gone. Once the sugar has liquefied and all moisture is removed, the sugar then begins to caramelize, and its sweetening power decreases.

Supersaturated solutions are highly unstable, and recrystallization can occur from agitation (such as stirring) or even just upon standing if the solution was not properly heated in the first place (stirred constantly until it comes to a boil and then left undisturbed until it reaches temperature). The use of an "interfering agent" (so called because it interferes with crystallization), such as corn syrup, butter, cream of tartar, or citric acid, helps keep the solution stable by interfering with the formation of crystals (see Ruby Port Caramel, page 309). The addition of an acid such as a few teaspoons of lemon juice can sometimes restore recrystallized solutions to liquid consistency.

When heating sugar syrups and caramel, as the mixture approaches the desired finished temperature, be sure that the burner heat is no higher than medium-low. This helps to prevent the temperature of the syrup from rising after the syrup is removed from the heat. Depending on how quickly you work and how rapidly the temperature rises, you may prefer to remove the mixture from the heat at the moment it reaches temperature or a few seconds before.

Different temperatures, ranging from 350° to 380°F/177° to 193°C, are suitable for different types of caramel. When making a caramel sauce, for example, 380°F/193°C will offer a deep, intense flavor. Over 380°F/193°C and the caramel becomes unpleasantly bitter. I prefer dark amber for caramels, caramel sauce, and praline powder.

If you are not using a thermometer for caramel, use a clean clear or light-colored silicone spatula to determine the color. (Do not use the same spatula you used initially to stir the sugar because any granules of sugar remaining on the spatula will cause crystallization.)

A half cup of sugar makes ¼ cup/59 ml of liquid caramel (plus the residue that clings to the pot). Caramel is extremely difficult to make in humid weather because sugar is highly hygroscopic (meaning it attracts water). The moisture in the air will make the caramel sticky.

CARAMEL SAUCE

Caramel sauce is my favorite form of caramel. Its satiny smooth, sticky consistency makes it ideal to drizzle over cakes, tarts, and buns. Corn syrup is often added to caramel sauce; as an interfering agent, it helps prevent the caramel from crystallizing when stirred. (However, after the caramel is prepared, do not stir it too much, because it may eventually crystallize, especially on storage.) It also lowers the caramelization temperature. I adore the flavor of caramel, so I like to have as much depth of flavor in caramel sauce as possible without any burned taste. I like to bring the caramel up to 360°F/182°C for maximum flavor and for some applications as high as 380°F/193°C. The darker you make the caramel, the less sweet it will seem, but you risk burning it if you don't have an absolutely accurate thermometer.

When adding cream or butter, it's best to have the cream hot and the butter at room temperature to avoid splattering. Cold cream speeds the cooling and is practical if you are pressured for time, but it must be added very slowly.

DAIRY

BUTTER

It is best to choose grade AA or A butter for baking because it contains about 81 percent fat and 15.5 percent water. Lower grades often contain more water, which will have a detrimental effect in cake batter, will not work well at all in mousseline buttercreams, and will make a less tender pie crust and a puffier cookie.

I prefer unsalted butter because it makes it easier for the baker to control the amount of total salt in a recipe and because of its fresher flavor. I recommend a top-quality butter such as Organic Valley's cultured, Hotel Bar, or Land O'Lakes. It is best to weigh butter because a 4 ounce stick of butter when unwrapped often weighs only 3.86 ounces.

Organic Valley's European Style Cultured Butter is 84 percent butterfat; Vermont Butter & Cheese Creamery's Cultured Butter is 86 percent fat, the highest butterfat content of all American brands. These high fat butters stay pliant even when cold. They are ideal for making clarified butter, laminated pastries such as the Kouigns Amann (page 481), and buttercreams, but will throw off the balance of fat and liquid in a cake. Butter that is cultured has a higher acidity, which makes it softer, even when chilled.

When a recipe calls for softened butter, it means the butter should still feel cool but be easy to press down. This usually takes about 30 minutes at room temperature, but slicing it into smaller pieces speeds up the process.

Butter freezes well for several months with no perceptible difference in flavor or performance. Because butter is quick to absorb other aromas or odors, if freezing it, wrap it well in plastic wrap and place it in a plastic reclosable freezer bag.

CLARIFIED BUTTER AND BROWNED BUTTER (BEURRE NOISETTE)

Clarified butter is ideal for people who are lactose intolerant because it removes all the milk solids, leaving only the butter "oil." Several recipes in this book call for beurre noisette, or clarified butter that has browned to the color of *noisettes* (French for "hazelnuts"). Beurre noisette offers a richer, more delicious flavor than melted or clarified butter.

Clarified or browned butter will keep, covered, for months in the refrigerator, or just about indefinitely in the freezer because the milk solids have been removed. (It is the milk solids that cause butter to become rancid relatively quickly.) I always make extra clarified butter to have on hand. (The solids can be refrigerated for up to 3 weeks, or frozen for up to 6 months. They are excellent for adding flavor to bread and cookie doughs; a tablespoon or two can be mixed in when adding the flour.)

Once butter is either clarified or browned, you will have only 75 percent the volume or weight of the whole amount of butter you started with. For example, if you need 3 tablespoons of clarified or browned butter, start with 4 tablespoons of butter. If you are using a cheesecloth-lined strainer, start with about 1 tablespoon more than that because the cheesecloth will absorb some of the butter. Clarified butter weighs a little less than whole butter because whole butter still contains water and milk solids, which, for the same volume, weigh more than fat.

One cup of whole butter weighs 8 ounces/227 grams; 1 cup of clarified butter weighs 6.9 ounces/195 grams.

When butter is clarified, its water evaporates and most of the milk solids drop to the bottom. The milk solids cannot begin to brown until all of the water has evaporated. Butter that contains less water is ideal for clarifying because it sputters less. If the butter is frozen, allow it to defrost completely before clarifying in order to prevent burning.

TO CLARIFY BUTTER Melt the butter in a heavy saucepan over medium-low heat. When the butter looks clear, cook, watching carefully without stirring, until the solids begin to brown. Move aside any foam that forms in order to check the progress of the solids. (If necessary, skim off some of the foam and discard it.) When the bubbling noise diminishes, all of the water has evaporated, so the butter can burn easily. Strain the butter immediately through a fine-mesh strainer or cheesecloth-lined strainer. If time allows, instead of straining the butter, simply pour it into a container and allow it to set. The milk solids will settle to the bottom and can be removed easily by reheating the butter and pouring off the clear portion.

TO MAKE BEURRE NOISETTE After melting the butter as above, allow the solids to turn deep brown. As soon as they turn golden, stir constantly in order to disperse the flavor of the browned solids throughout the butter. Strain the butter immediately through a fine-mesh strainer or cheesecloth-lined strainer.

Milk

When milk is called for in a recipe, unless otherwise specified, use whole milk to obtain the ideal texture and flavor.

Dry Milk Powder

When bread recipes call for dry milk powder, my preference is King Arthur's Baker's Special Dry Milk. Compared with the results of using other brands of "instant" dry milk, its results are a smoother, more mellow flavor, a more tender texture, and a significantly higher rise.

Because the particles are so much finer than the more crystalline ones of instant dry milk, they pack down when being measured in a cup or spoon, so if replacing Baker's Special Dry Milk with instant dry milk, by volume you will need double the amount to arrive at the same weight.

Heavy Cream

Heavy cream, sometimes referred to as heavy whipping cream, contains 56.6 percent water and 36 to 40 percent fat (averaging 36 percent). Whipping cream has only 30 percent fat. The higher the butterfat and the colder the cream, the easier it is to whip and the more stable the whipped cream. My preference is Organic Valley or Stonyfield, both of which are 40 percent butterfat.

Though heavy cream will not whip after it has been frozen, frozen and thawed heavy cream can be used for making ganache. If the heavy cream available to you is difficult to beat and separates easily, you can increase the stability with cornstarch (see page 516), cream cheese, or gelatin. Commercial stabilizers, such as Cobasan, from Albert Uster Imports; Sanifax, from PatisFrance; and Whip It, from Dr. Oetker, are also available.

When whipped cream does not need to be made ahead or held at room temperature, it does not require stabilizers. All cream whips best if it is as cold as possible, so it helps to refrigerate the mixing bowl or mixer bowl and the mixer's beaters along with the cream (unnecessary if using the Rose MixerMate Bowl; see page 538). If you are whipping 1½ cups/ 355 ml or less of cream, a handheld mixer works better than a stand mixer.

CORNSTARCH-STABILIZED WHIPPED CREAM

MAKES 2 CUPS/8.6 OUNCES/244 GRAMS

	VOLUME	WEIGHT	
powdered sugar	1½ tablespoons	0.5 ounce	14 grams
cornstarch	1 teaspoon	.	.
heavy cream	1 cup (237 ml), *divided*	8.2 ounces	232 grams
pure vanilla extract	½ teaspoon (2.5 ml)	.	.

MAKE THE CORNSTARCH-STABILIZED WHIPPED CREAM In a small saucepan, combine the powdered sugar and cornstarch. Gradually stir in ¼ cup/59 ml of the cream. Bring the mixture to a boil to activate the cornstarch, stirring constantly, and simmer for a few seconds just until thickened. Scrape the mixture into a small bowl and allow it to cool just to room temperature. Stir in the vanilla.

In a chilled mixing bowl, beat the remaining cream just until traces of the beater marks begin to appear. Add the cooled cornstarch mixture in a steady stream, whipping constantly. Whip just until stiff peaks form when the beaters are raised.

LIGHTLY SWEETENED WHIPPED CREAM

MAKES 2 CUPS/8.6 OUNCES/244 GRAMS

	VOLUME	WEIGHT	
heavy cream, cold	1 cup (237 ml)	8.2 ounces	232 grams
superfine sugar	1 tablespoon	0.5 ounce	13 grams
pure vanilla extract	1 teaspoon (5 ml)	.	.

MAKE THE LIGHTLY SWEETENED WHIPPED CREAM In a mixing bowl combine the cream, sugar, and vanilla and refrigerate for at least 15 minutes. (Chill the handheld mixer's beaters alongside the bowl.) Whip the mixture, starting on low speed and gradually raising the speed to medium-high as it thickens, until it mounds softly when dropped from a spoon, or, if piping it, just until stiff peaks form when the beaters are raised.

SOUR CREAM

Sour cream contains 18 to 20 percent fat and is soured by the addition of lactic acid to light cream. In recipes, it can be replaced with whole milk yogurt, which has about 10 percent fat, without a significant difference in texture, but lower fat sour cream or yogurt will yield a less tender cake, and the cake or other baked item will be less delicious. Crème fraîche contains about 39 percent fat, so it is not interchangeable with sour cream except where specified.

CREAM CHEESE

Regular cream cheese contains 37.7 percent fat and 51 percent water. For my recipes, be sure to use a whole milk variety, preferably Philadelphia brand, and not a reduced fat or nonfat variety. Unopened, a package can be frozen for up to a year.

BEATING EGG WHITES FROM LEFT TO RIGHT: Soft peaks. Stiff peaks. Very stiff clumps.

EGGS

All of my recipes use USDA grade AA or A large eggs, which means that twelve eggs in the shell should weigh a minimum of 24 ounces/680 grams and a maximum of 30 ounces/850 grams. However, this does not mean that each egg is the same size. Also, the ratio of white to yolk in an egg can vary to such a degree that a recipe calling for 6 egg yolks may actually need as many as 9. It is therefore advisable to weigh or measure the yolks and whites. Since baked goods, especially cakes, are so dependent on eggs for their structure, I find it safer to weigh or measure even when I know I'm using large eggs. The weights given for eggs in the recipe ingredient charts are always without the shells. Values for recipes in this book are given for weight and volume, so it's fine to use any size eggs if you weigh or measure them. I recommend pasteurized eggs in the shell such as Safest Choice, especially for buttercreams.

Bring eggs to room temperature by placing the eggs, still in their unbroken shells, in hot water for 5 minutes.

When separating eggs, especially for whipping the whites, pour each white into a smaller bowl before adding it to the larger amount of whites. If even a trace of yolk or grease gets into the white, the white will be impossible to beat stiffly. If a small amount of yolk should get into the white, use the eggshell to fish it out. If the bowl in which you are beating the whites is not totally grease free, wet a paper towel, add a little vinegar to it, and wipe out the bowl. Then rinse the bowl and dry it well.

TO BEAT EGG WHITES In the bowl of a stand mixer fitted with the whisk beater, add the cream of tartar to the egg whites. Beat on medium-low speed until foamy. Gradually raise the speed to medium-high and beat until soft peaks form when the beater is raised. Gradually beat in the sugar and continue beating until stiff peaks form when the beater is raised slowly. For some recipes, such as The Renée Fleming Golden Chiffon (page 86), continue beating until very stiff clumps form when the beater is raised, about 2 minutes more.

STORING EGGS

Store eggs in a covered container, bottom (larger) sides up for maximum freshness. Egg whites keep in an airtight container in the refrigerator for up to 10 days. Unbroken yolks, covered with water or sprayed with nonstick cooking spray to prevent drying, will keep in an airtight container in the refrigerator for up to 3 days. Egg whites freeze perfectly and keep for at least 1 year. Store them in small containers because they should not be refrozen after thawing. It is also possible to freeze yolks. Stir in ½ teaspoon of sugar per yolk to keep them from becoming sticky after they are defrosted. (Remember to subtract this amount of sugar from any recipe in which you are using them.)

CREAM OF TARTAR

Also known as potassium acid tartrate, this by-product of wine making has an indefinite shelf life if not exposed to moisture or humidity. It can be used to stabilize beaten egg whites, as described on page xiv, and as an interfering agent in sugar syrups and caramel to inhibit crystallization. I also add a little to the water when baking a cake in a water bath to help prevent the aluminum pans from discoloring.

LEAVENING

BAKING POWDER

The words "double-acting" mean the baking powder will react, or liberate carbon dioxide, first from moisture during the mixing stage and then again when exposed to heat during the baking stage.

I use Rumford baking powder, an all-phosphate product containing calcium acid phosphate that is found in most supermarkets or health food stores. It lacks the bitter aftertaste associated with the aluminum in SAS (sodium aluminum sulfate) baking powders. (The advantage of SAS powders is that they release a little more carbon dioxide during the baking stage than during the mixing stage.) Argo baking powder is also an aluminum-free double-acting baking powder, containing sodium acid pyrophosphate, but reacts a little more in the baking stage than Rumford.

Because double-acting baking powder reacts in part when combined with moisture, it is important to store it in an airtight container to avoid humidity. It will also lose strength after about a year. Date the top or bottom of the can when you first buy it. To test if it is still active, sprinkle a little over hot water. If it fizzes actively, you can still use it.

BAKING SODA

Also known as sodium bicarbonate, baking soda works by reacting with an acidic ingredient in a recipe to release carbon dioxide. It has an indefinite shelf life if it is not exposed to moisture or humidity. If it clumps, it is hard to measure and must be sifted first.

YEAST

I prefer to use instant active dry yeast because of its reliability and because it can be added directly to flour without needing to be "proofed." This eliminates the possibility of killing the yeast by using water that is too hot. (Yeast will also die if subjected to ice-cold water.) It is fine to whisk the yeast into the flour before adding the water, but the yeast can also be soaked (hydrated) in warm water (at least four times its weight or three times its volume) for 10 minutes if you are in doubt as to whether it is still active. If the yeast has been frozen, allow it to come to room temperature before adding the water. Instant active dry yeast is nationally available in supermarkets under brand names such as Fleischmann's Bread Machine Yeast or RapidRise, Red Star's Quick Rise, Red Star's Instant Active Dry Yeast, SAF Instant, and SAF Gourmet Perfect Rise.

If unopened, instant yeast will keep at room temperature for up to 2 years. Once opened, it is best to store it in the freezer. If you buy it in bulk, remove a small amount for regular use and freeze both the larger and smaller amounts to ensure maximum shelf life, which is at least 1 year.

Instant active dry yeast has more live yeast cells than active dry yeast. One teaspoon/3.2 grams of instant active dry yeast is equal to 1¼ teaspoons/ 4 grams of active dry yeast.

Though it is advisable to soak (hydrate) active dry yeast, it is not necessary to "proof" it. Proofing is a good idea, however, as assurance that the yeast is still active. To proof it, add a small amount of sugar to the water so that the yeast will foam, demonstrating that it is alive and active.

CHOCOLATE

Most manufacturers now list the cacao content of chocolate on the wrapper.

The percentage of chocolate liquor, or cacao mass, listed on some bars as the percentage of cacao, which is how I refer to it, indicates the amount of cocoa solids and cocoa butter in the chocolate. Besides the cocoa solids and butter, the rest of the chocolate is mostly sugar. The percentage of cacao in the chocolate, however, does not necessarily indicate its degree of bitterness. Flavor also comes from the variety of beans used and the methods of production. The percentage of cacao in bittersweet, semisweet, or milk chocolate, though, does determine consistency of the chocolate. The higher the cacao percentage, the more cocoa solids and cocoa butter, which are solid at room temperature. Chocolate that has a higher percentage of cacao will make a cake crumb or frosting more firm as well as more chocolaty.

Baked goods have their best texture when the recommended cacao percentage in a recipe is followed. Ganache consistency, however, is easy to adjust, so if you find a chocolate you adore and the cacao percentage differs from that recommended in a recipe, simply alter the amount of cream as indicated in the chart of ganache proportions (see page 521).

SEMISWEET, BITTERSWEET, OR DARK CHOCOLATE

What I refer to as dark chocolate encompasses both semisweet and bittersweet. Most of the time, I use chocolate with a cacao percentage between 60 and 62 percent. I specify the percentage of cacao recommended; if the percentage is not indicated on the wrapper of a dark chocolate, it is most likely around 53 percent.

PURE CHOCOLATE

Pure chocolate, also referred to as bitter, baking, or unsweetened chocolate, contains only chocolate liquor, also called cacao (cocoa solids and cocoa butter), and flavorings. Depending on the variety of the cacao bean used, 50 to 58 percent (53 percent is the average) of the chocolate liquor is cocoa butter. Most of the remainder is cocoa solids. (This is the same amount present in chocolate nibs, the name for cacao beans after the pod is removed and before processing.) The chocolate liquor may contain flavorings such as vanilla or vanillin (synthesized vanilla). This is why Scharffen Berger, for example, labels its bitter chocolate as 99 percent cacao.

MILK CHOCOLATE

Milk chocolate contains chocolate liquor, milk solids, vanilla or vanillin, sugar, lecithin, and extra cocoa butter. High-quality milk chocolate usually contains between 34 and 45 percent and can even be as high as 53 percent cacao.

Milk chocolate does not have as long a shelf life as dark chocolate because the milk solids eventually become rancid (though more slowly than in white chocolate, due to the protective presence of cocoa solids in the milk chocolate). When melting milk chocolate, it is essential to stir often to prevent seeding (crystallization of the cocoa butter) due to the milk solids.

WHITE CHOCOLATE

Fine quality white chocolate contains cocoa butter (30 to 35 percent), milk solids, vanilla or vanillin, sugar, and lecithin. White chocolate can have no fat other than the residual butterfat from the milk solids and the cocoa butter that gives it its lovely deep ivory color and luxurious texture. Guittard produces an excellent white chocolate called Crème Française. Valrhona produces a white chocolate called Ivory and also one called Opalys, which is paler in color than the Ivory due to a higher percentage of milk solids. When added to my custom blend ganache, cake batters, and buttercreams, white chocolate adds extra melt-in-the-mouth quality and structure.

Melted white chocolate sets faster than dark chocolate, but it is softer at room temperature. Its shelf life is much shorter than that of dark chocolate because of the presence of milk solids and absence of cacao solids. When melting white chocolate, it is essential to stir often to prevent seeding due to the milk solids.

RECOMMENDED CHOCOLATES FOR BAKING

UNSWEETENED OR BITTER CHOCOLATE

Guittard Collection Etienne 100% Cacao Unsweetened Chocolate Gourmet Baking Bars

Scharffen Berger 99% cacao

Valrhona Cacao Pate Extra 100%

DARK CHOCOLATE

Amedei Toscano Black 63% cacao

Amedei Toscano Black 66% cacao

Felchlin Maracaibo 65% cacao

Felchlin Arriba 72% cacao

Guittard Collection Etienne 61% Cacao
Semisweet Chocolate Gourmet Baking Bars

Guittard Collection Etienne 64% Cacao
Semisweet Chocolate Gourmet Baking Bars

Guittard Collection Etienne 70% Cacao
Bittersweet Chocolate Gourmet Baking Bars

Lindt Excellence 70% cacao

Michel Cluizel 60% cacao (no lecithin)

Scharffen Berger Semisweet 62% cacao

Valrhona Le Noir Gastronomie (aka Extra Bitter
when sold in bulk) 61% cacao

Valrhona Manjari 64% cacao

Valrhona Palmira Fino Criollo 64% cacao

MILK CHOCOLATE

Felchlin Ambra Surfine 38% cacao

Felchlin Lait Accra 42% cacao

Guittard Collection Etienne Kokoleka Hawaiian
38% Cacao Milk Chocolate

Lindt 42% cacao

Michel Cluizel 45% cacao (no lecithin)

Scharffen Berger 41% cacao

Valrhona Le Lacté and Jivara Lactée 40% cacao

WHITE CHOCOLATE

Guittard Crème Française 31% cocoa butter,
35% milk solids, 33% sugar

Valrhona Opalys 33.6% cocoa butter, 33.6% milk
solids, 31.9% sugar

Valrhona Ivory 35% cocoa butter, 21.5% milk
solids, 41.6% sugar

CHOCOLATE CHIPS, BITS, AND PEARLS

The ubiquitous semisweet or bittersweet chocolate bits or chips usually contain 42.5 percent cacao unless otherwise stated and a total of 29 percent cocoa butter (see Chocosphere). Valrhona dark chocolate pearls can be used in place of chocolate bits or chips and are less sweet, containing 55 percent cacao and a total of 29 percent cocoa butter.

CHOCOLATE CURLS

HOW TO MAKE CHOCOLATE BLOCKS FOR CHOCOLATE CURLS In a small microwavable bowl, stirring with a silicone spatula every 15 seconds (or in the top of a double boiler set over hot, not simmering, water, stirring often—do not let the bottom of the container touch the water), heat the chocolate until almost completely melted.

Remove the chocolate from the heat source and, with a silicone spatula, stir until fully melted. Pour it into a silicone mold or flexible ice cube molds. A silicone financier or mini cake pan with bar-shaped molds works well, preferably one with 3 by 1 by 1¼ inch high (¼ cup/59 ml) cavities, each of which will hold 2.1 ounces/60 grams of melted chocolate. Allow the chocolate to set for several hours until completely firm before unmolding.

The chocolate needs to be moderately soft in order to curl without breaking or flattening. The small block of chocolate can be softened by placing it under a lamp or in a microwave using 3 second bursts. It usually takes a few tries to get the chocolate soft enough without oversoftening it, but once this point is reached, it will hold for at least 10 minutes, giving you enough time to make lots of beautiful curls.

I find the best utensil with which to make the curls is a sharp vegetable peeler. Hold it against the upper edge of the chocolate block and dig in the upper edge of the cutter, pulling it toward you. Increase pressure to form thicker, more open curls. Decrease pressure to make tighter curls. Until the chocolate is sufficiently warmed, it will splinter. When it becomes too warm, it will come off the block in strips that will not curl. But if the strips are not too soft, you can use your fingers to shape the curls. Keep your fingers cool by periodically dipping them into ice water and drying them well.

Ganache

Classic ganache is made with equal weights of chocolate and heavy cream or crème fraîche, which lends the ganache a slightly tangy quality. The resulting consistency is fine when using a low percentage chocolate, but if using a chocolate with 60 percent cacao or higher, I prefer to increase the amount of cream so that when the ganache sets, it doesn't pull away or separate from the cake or tart when it is served.

USE THE FOLLOWING PROPORTIONS FOR GANACHE, BASED ON 8 OUNCES/ 227 GRAMS CHOCOLATE:

FOR 60% TO 62% CACAO CHOCOLATE:
9 ounces/255 grams cream (about 1 cup plus 1½ tablespoons/259 ml)

FOR 63% TO 64% CACAO CHOCOLATE:
10 ounces/283 grams cream (about 1¼ cups/ 296 ml)

FOR 66% CACAO CHOCOLATE:
11 ounces/312 grams cream (about 1⅓ cups/ 316 ml)

FOR 70% CACAO CHOCOLATE:
12 ounces/340 grams cream (about 1½ cups/ 355 ml)

If you are adding butter, use high fat butter, preferably cultured, for the best flavor and texture. I like to add, in addition to the cream, up to one-third of the weight of the chocolate in butter and up to ½ teaspoon of liqueur per ounce of chocolate. So, for 6 ounces/170 grams chocolate, I add 1 to 2 ounces/ 28 to 56 grams (2 to 4 tablespoons) butter and 1 tablespoon/15 ml liqueur.

Ganache takes from 3 to 7 hours to cool, depending on the quantity and the temperature of the room. It should be left, uncovered, for about an hour to allow the heat to escape. Then it should be covered to prevent evaporation and left undisturbed to set. It is fine to stir gently two or three times during the first 30 minutes while the temperature is still above 85°F/29°C to equalize the temperature. (Rapid cooling would not give the cocoa butter a chance to form small stable crystals that melt gradually when eaten.) When the ganache is firm enough, press a piece of plastic wrap directly on the entire surface to keep the edges from drying.

If you need to use the ganache before it is thickened adequately, whisking it for a few seconds will do the trick but will also lighten the color. With the correct proportions, ganache will stay spreadable at room temperature for several days. Store it, covered, in a glass bowl or other glass container so that it does not pick up a metallic or other taste. It can be held at room temperature for up to 3 days. If you plan to store the ganache for longer, you can refrigerate it for up to 2 weeks or freeze it for up to 6 months after it has set. If frozen, remove it to the refrigerator overnight. Soften it by allowing it to sit at room temperature for several hours. If necessary, it can sit in an oven with no pilot light but with the oven light turned on and it will soften in about 2 hours. Alternatively, chunks of ganache can be scooped out with a large spoon and then softened in the microwave with 5 second bursts, stirring very gently to equalize the temperature, or in the top of a double boiler. Remove the ganache from the heat source when it is partially melted and stir very gently.

Cocoa Powder

Unsweetened cocoa powder is pulverized pure chocolate liquor with three-quarters of its cocoa butter removed. Most European cocoa powder is alkalized (Dutch processed), which means that the cocoa powder has been treated with a mild alkali to neutralize the acidity—this mellows its flavor and also makes it more soluble. The term "alkalized" may appear on the container, but a darker colored powder is a good indication that alkalization has taken place. Most alkalized cocoa contains 22 to 25 percent cocoa butter, while nonalkalized cocoa may contain only 10 to 21 percent cocoa butter. I prefer the flavor of alkalized cocoa, although the type of cocoa beans used and the degree of roasting also contribute to the flavor. Darker roasting produces a milder flavored cocoa powder. My favorite is Green & Black's, from England. It is sometimes available in specialty food stores in the United States. Second to that is Droste. I also like Pernigotti and Van Houten. Both contain 20 to 22 percent cocoa butter and are alkalized.

Cocoa powder offers a richer, stronger chocolate flavor to most baked goods than does bar chocolate, because fewer cocoa solids are necessary to achieve the same flavor intensity. It is usually desirable to dissolve cocoa powder in very hot water to unlock its full flavor. However, adding unsweetened chocolate to a cake or brownie batter, such as in The Chocolate FloRo Elegance (page 52) or Woody's Black and White Brownies (page 395), contributes a great melt-in-the-mouth quality because cocoa butter has a sharp melting point that is close to body temperature. This means that it is solid at room temperature but starts to melt as soon as it is in one's mouth and goes from the solid state to the melted state all at once.

It is not necessary to sift cocoa powder that will be dissolved in water. In recipes such as the Dark Chocolate Lacquer Glaze (page 296), it is advisable to process or sift the cocoa powder if it is lumpy so it will incorporate more evenly. Also, if measuring rather than weighing cocoa powder, you will get a more accurate and consistent measure if you sift it first and then spoon it lightly into the cup and level it off.

Storing Chocolate

The best way to store chocolate or cocoa is to keep it well wrapped in an airtight container at a temperature of 60° to 75°F/15° to 23°C, with less than 50 percent relative humidity. Chocolate is quick to absorb odors and must not be exposed to dampness. Under the proper conditions, dark chocolate should keep well for at least 2 years. Milk chocolate keeps, even under optimum conditions, for only a little over a year, and white chocolate for about a year.

Nuts and Seeds

Freshly shelled nuts have the best flavor, but shelled canned or bagged varieties are excellent and a lot more convenient. All nuts are prone to rancidity, but higher fat nuts such as walnuts, pecans, and macadamia nuts are more prone to spoilage than others. Always taste nuts before using them. Rancidity will ruin the flavor of a dessert, and it's often not possible to detect just by smelling. Nuts keep well for several years if stored airtight in the freezer. I use either plastic reclosable freezer bags, expelling all the excess air, or glass canning jars, filling the empty headspace with wadded up plastic wrap before freezing.

Hazelnuts (Filberts)

The skin on hazelnuts is very bitter and difficult to remove. An easy method was taught to me by the late Carl Sontheimer (founder of Cuisinart and father of the food processor). For up to 1 cup of nuts, pour 3 cups/700 ml of water into a large saucepan and bring it to a boil. Remove it from the heat and stir in ¼ cup of baking soda. Add the nuts and boil for 3 minutes. The water will turn a deep maroon from the pigment in the hazelnut skins. Test a nut by running it under cold water. The skin should slip off easily. If not, boil for a couple of minutes longer. Pour the nuts into a colander and rinse them under cold running water. Place several nuts in a bowl of cold water. Slide off the skins and place the nuts on a clean dish towel. As necessary, empty the bowl, refill with cold water, and add more nuts. Roll and rub them around to dry them.

TO TOAST HAZELNUTS Preheat the oven to 350°F/175°C. Set the hazelnuts on a baking sheet and bake for 20 minutes, or until lightly browned. Stir once or twice to ensure even toasting. Watch carefully so that they do not burn. They will turn a rich mahogany color.

Walnuts

Toasting walnuts (as described below) improves their flavor and has the added advantage of enabling you to remove most of the bitter skins easily—200 grams of walnuts have 9 grams of skins, or 4.5 percent!

Toasting Nuts

Lightly toasting nuts at 350°F/175°C for about 7 minutes greatly enhances their flavor. (At 375°F/190°C they will take about 5 minutes.) It is particularly desirable to toast walnuts because the skins are very bitter and toasting loosens most of them. Toast walnuts and pecans just to the point where their color is a shade darker than the freshly shelled nut. They should not be allowed to brown or they will become bitter.

Grinding Nuts

Frozen or refrigerated nuts must be brought to room temperature before grinding in order to keep them from exuding their oil. A tablespoon or two of cornstarch, flour, or powdered or granulated sugar—borrowed from the rest of the recipe—will help absorb oil and prevent ground nuts from clumping.

Poppy Seeds

These tiny gray-blue seeds are delicious when fresh, but they become bitter and rancid if held too long at room temperature. Store poppy seeds in the refrigerator or freeze them. They are more perishable when ground, so for the freshest flavor, grind them just before using. Penzeys Spices carries the "A-1" type called Holland Blue.

Salt

I use fine sea salt for baking because it is not iodized. Iodized salt can give an unpleasant taste to baked goods. Also, fine sea salt is easier to measure if you are measuring by volume and not weight, and it integrates more readily into batter than does a coarse salt. Salt is very difficult to measure accurately because it is extremely hygroscopic. It will readily grab water from the air, which will increase its weight slightly. In very humid conditions, it may be desirable to add a little extra salt; conversely, in very dry conditions, a little less.

Cinnamon

There are many varieties of cinnamon available. My favorite is Korintje because it is sweet and mellow (see Penzeys Spices). If choosing other types, such as Vietnamese, use only two-thirds the indicated amount, because the others are very intense, reminiscent of cinnamon Red Hots candies.

Oils for Baking

Canola and Safflower Oils

Flavorless vegetable oils that do not contain silicates, which prevent foaming, are the best choice for most baked goods made with oil.

Nonstick Cooking Spray

This product contains oil and lecithin. It is ideal for keeping cakes from sticking to the wire cooling rack, for spraying cookie sheets and bread pans, and for spraying rising containers for bread dough as well as the dough itself. I prefer Pam Original to other nonstick vegetable spray products because it has virtually no odor. The lecithin is a natural emulsifying agent derived from soybeans.

Baking Spray with Flour

Baker's Joy brand is an odor-free combination of flour and oil that is used for spraying onto baking pans to ensure a baked item's clean release. It is faster and neater than greasing and flouring. I prefer this brand because I have found other brands to impart an off taste and less reliable release.

Flavored Oils, Extracts, and Essences

Oils for Flavoring

The Boyajian line of citrus oils, which are extracted from the rind of the fresh fruit, includes orange, tangerine, lemon, and lime. The oils have a perfectly pure flavor without bitterness and are great for adding extra intensity to cakes and frostings. Perfumer Mandy Aftel also has a line of flavorful essences that includes coffee, bitter orange, blood orange, lemon, and vanilla. A few drops go a long way, so start with just a drop at a time. Store citrus oils in the refrigerator for up to 4 months; the other essences will keep indefinitely at room temperature.

Vanilla Extract

The most widely available top-quality vanillas are produced by Nielsen-Massey. I particularly like their Tahitian vanilla. My favorite vanilla extract is produced by Eurovanille and is imported by Crossings and usually carried by ChefShop.com. Other top-choice vanilla extracts are the Mexican vanilla carried by the Vanilla Queen, the New Zealand vanilla carried by Heilala, and the Hawaiian vanilla carried by the Hawaiian Vanilla Company. Use pure vanilla extract—vanilla "flavor," or imitation vanilla, is not an acceptable substitute. Vanilla extract should be dispensed judiciously; unlike the vanilla bean, vanilla extract will impart a bitter edge when used in excess. Nielsen-Massey, Heilala, and the Vanilla Queen make excellent vanilla bean pastes.

Store vanilla extract at room temperature in a cool, dark area away from direct heat. You can refrigerate it, but since flavoring material precipitates out when chilled, the bottle must be shaken before use. Stored at a cool temperature, vanilla extract will keep for years.

Vanilla Bean

The best vanilla beans come from Hawaii, Tahiti, Madagascar, Mexico, and New Zealand. Hawaiian and Tahitian beans, my personal favorites, are about twice the size of the others, with a floral quality so aromatic that I use one-half a bean in a recipe specifying one bean. To replace vanilla beans with extract, the rule of thumb is: a 2 inch piece of bean (or 1 inch piece if using Hawaiian or Tahitian) equals 1 teaspoon/5 ml of extract. Many types of vanilla beans are carried by Nielsen-Massey and the Vanilla Queen. They freeze well, keeping their moisture if wrapped airtight. Some chefs like to store their vanilla beans immersed in vanilla extract. This is more practical if you are using the vanilla for baking in quantity.

Fruits, Purees, and Preserves

Citrus Fruit

ZEST

Zest is the colored portion of the citrus peel or rind that is grated. The white portion, or pith, is bitter and should be avoided. Fruit should be zested before squeezing, which is why zest is sometimes listed in the ingredient lists slightly out of order from where it's added to the recipe. However, if you need only the juice but want to save the peels for another use, you can freeze the peels in a reclosable freezer bag and then zest them straight from the freezer when needed. Be sure to wash the fruit in liquid detergent and hot water and rinse it well or it will add a bitter taste to the recipe. If a recipe calls for finely grated zest, after grating it with a ZestN'est or Microplane grater, use a chef's knife to chop it to a fine consistency, or process it with some of the sugar in the recipe.

The reason I offer gram weights for zest, even though it is usually such a minute amount, is because it is so easy to set the ZestN'est on a scale, tare out the weight, and then zest the citrus fruit right into the container until the proper weight is reached, rather than trying to figure out how firmly to pack the zest into a measuring spoon.

APPROXIMATE YIELD OF JUICE AND ZEST FOR AN ORANGE AND LEMON

ONE ORANGE
Juice: ¼ to ½ cup (59 to 118 ml)
Zest: 2 to 3 tablespoons (12 to 18 grams)

ONE LEMON
Juice: 3 to 4 tablespoons (44 to 59 ml)
Zest: 1¼ to 2 teaspoons (2.5 to 4 grams)

Lemon Curd

Tiptree brand lemon curd, available in most supermarkets, is very close to and sometimes better than homemade because it is prepared by hand in small batches and made with lemons from Spain. It can be substituted for homemade lemon curd in any of the recipes in this book.

Bananas

As bananas ripen and develop black spots, their flavor becomes much sweeter, the peel thinner, and the pulp softer. It can take more than a week to reach this point. If you don't have time to wait for the bananas to ripen naturally, an alternative method of "ripening" is to freeze bananas in the peel overnight. They can be defrosted in less than 30 minutes in a room temperature water bath, then slit lengthwise and the pulp removed. Ripening bananas naturally, however, produces a sweeter flavor. Any extra banana pulp can be frozen for several months.

Coconut

Flaked unsweetened coconut is softer and fresher tasting than most commercially prepared coconut. It is available from specialty stores. Excellent-quality coconut in many textures and degrees of fineness is available in some Middle Eastern markets and Indian food stores such as Kalustyan's.

Purees

Perfect Purée of Napa Valley produces a wide variety of purees, including ginger, which can be frozen for as long as a year. Boiron purees are also top quality and are available through L'Épicerie.

Preserves

American Spoon makes excellent preserves, including their "Fruit Perfect" line, and fruit butters. Their strawberry and raspberry butters are fantastic additions to buttercreams.

Apricot and prune lekvar, a kind of very thick jam, are great to have on hand for cookies and fillings. They keep just about indefinitely in the refrigerator. Solo Foods' Apricot Filling and Prune Lekvar, available in most supermarkets, are good store-bought options; however, it is easy to make your own (see Prune Preserves and Caramel Cream Cake Roll, page 105, and The Ischler, page 356).

You can also use a good-quality apricot filling or preserves in place of lekvar. If using apricot preserves, you will need to strain and concentrate them slightly. In a small heavy saucepan, bring the contents of one 12 ounce/340 gram jar to a boil. Remove from the heat and strain it into a 2 cup or larger microwavable glass measure. You will have almost 1 cup/237 ml of preserves and about 2 teaspoons of residue to discard. Microwave the preserves on high for about 3 minutes, or until reduced to about ¾ cup/237 ml plus 2 tablespoons/207 ml. On cooling, the preserves will settle down to between ¾ cup to 13 tablespoons/ 177 to 192 ml. Stir before using, and if too thick to spread, add a little apricot brandy or water.

Golden Raisins

These are raisins that have been treated with sulphur dioxide, which prevents the raisins from darkening. Golden raisins are dried with artificial heat, which results in a moister, plumper product. They have a sweet but tangier flavor than dark raisins.

Flowers and Other Special Decorations

Fresh flowers and leaves offer beautiful and sometimes even flavorful additions to cakes, but be sure to choose only those flowers that have not been sprayed and are safe for human consumption. Not all flowers are edible and some are highly poisonous. Edible flowers include apple blossoms, borage flowers, citrus blossoms (orange and lemon), daylilies (not tiger lilies, which have spots), English daisies, hibiscus, hollyhocks, honeysuckle, lilacs, nasturtiums, pansies, petunias, roses, tulips, and violets. Rose geranium leaves and mint leaves also make lovely and aromatic garnishes, especially when sugared. You can also buy crystallized flowers. The most breathtaking ones are made by Sweetfields.

High Altitude

Altitude usually begins to affect baking at above 3,000 feet. Because each recipe is different, altitude guidelines can be given, but the proof truly is in the pudding. I recommend you consult *Chocolate Snowball: And Other Fabulous Pastries from Deer Valley Resort* by head baker Letty Halloran Flatt, who has been baking at high altitude for many years, and *Pie in the Sky* by baking authority Susan Purdy. You can also visit Susan's website, www.highaltitudebaking.com.

The USDA Lists the Following Recommendations for High-Altitude Adjustments

INGREDIENT ADJUSTMENT	3,000 FEET 914 METERS	5,000 FEET 1,524 METERS	7,000 FEET 2,134 METERS
decrease baking powder per teaspoon used	⅛ teaspoon	⅛ to ¼ teaspoon	¼ teaspoon
increase liquid per cup used	1 to 2 tablespoons (15 to 30 ml)	2 to 4 tablespoons (30 to 59 ml)	3 to 4 tablespoons (44 to 59 ml)

Ingredient Equivalences and Substitutions

Some Useful Substitutions for Emergencies

FOR	SUBSTITUTE
1 cup /7.6 ounces/217 grams light brown sugar	1 cup /7 ounces/200 grams granulated sugar plus ¼ cup/59 ml light molasses
1 cup /8.4 ounces/239 grams dark brown sugar	1 cup /7 ounces/200 grams granulated sugar plus ½ cup/118 ml light molasses
1 pound unsalted butter	1 pound lightly salted butter. Remove 1 teaspoon/6 grams salt from the recipe.
1 cup/237 ml whole milk	1 cup minus 1 tablespoon/222 ml half and half. Remove 1 tablespoon/0.5 ounce/14 grams of butter from the recipe and add 2 tablespoons/30 ml of water.
1 cup/237 ml half and half	¾ cup/177 ml whole milk plus ¼ cup/59 ml heavy cream or ½ cup/118 ml whole milk plus ½ cup/118 ml light cream
1 cup/3.5 ounces/100 grams sifted bleached cake flour	¾ cup/3 ounces/85 grams sifted bleached all-purpose flour plus 2 tablespoons/0.7 ounce/20 grams potato starch or cornstarch
1 cup/4 ounces/114 grams sifted bleached all-purpose flour	1 cup plus 2 tablespoons/4 ounces/114 grams sifted bleached cake flour or ¾ cup plus 1 tablespoon/4 ounces/114 grams Wondra flour (see page 511)
2 cups/8 ounces/228 grams sifted pastry flour	1⅓ cups/5.4 ounces/152 grams sifted bleached all-purpose flour plus ¾ cup/2.7 ounces/76 grams sifted bleached cake flour
1 teaspoon instant active dry yeast	1¼ teaspoons active dry yeast or 1½ teaspoons packed fresh yeast
1 packed tablespoon/0.75 ounce cake yeast	2 teaspoons/6.4 grams instant active dry yeast or 2½ teaspoons/8 grams active dry yeast
1 teaspoon/5 ml citrus oil	⅓ cup/1.1 ounces/32 grams zest, loosely packed
1 teaspoon/2 grams zest, loosely packed	$^{1}/_{16}$ teaspoon citrus oil

INGREDIENT SOURCES

AFTELIER PERFUMES (Chef's Essences)
www.aftelier.com 510-841-2111

ALBERT USTER IMPORTS (cobasan)
www.auiswiss.com 800-231-8154

AMERICAN ALMOND PRODUCTS
(praline paste, almond paste)
www.americanalmond.com

AMERICAN SPOON
(preserves, fruit butters, and syrups)
www.spoon.com 888-735-6700

BAKELS (rolled fondant)
www.bakels.com

BESSIE UNBLEACHED PASTRY FLOUR
(specialty flours)
www.thebirkettmills.com 315-536-3311

BOYAJIAN (citrus oils)
www.boyajianinc.com 800-965-0665

CHEFSHOP.COM
(vanilla and almond extracts; citrus oils)
www.chefshop.com 800-596-0885

THE CHEFS' WAREHOUSE (specialty baking ingredients)
www.chefswarehouse.com 718-842-8700

CHOCOSPHERE (chocolate)
www.chocosphere.com 877-992-4626

COCO SAVVY (crystallized flowers)
www.cocosavvy.com 619-985-7161

CROSSINGS (vanilla extract)
www.crossingsfinefoods.com 800-209-6141

EASY LEAF PRODUCTS (edible gold and silver leaf)
www.easyleaf.com 800-569-5323

EDIBLE GOLD
www.ediblegold.com 415-407-5097

FLAVORGANICS (peppermint and other organic extracts)
www.flavorganics.com 866-972-6879

GUITTARD (chocolate)
www.guittard.com 800-468-2462

HAWAIIAN VANILLA COMPANY
(vanilla extract, powder, and beans)
www.hawaiianvanilla.com 808-776-1771

HEILALA VANILLA (vanilla extract, powder, and beans)
www.heilalavanilla.com

INDIA TREE (Muscovado and powdered cane sugar)
www.indiatree.com 800-369-4848

KALUSTYAN'S (pistachios, dried fruit)
www.kalustyans.com 800-352-3451

KEENAN FARMS (pistachios)
www.keenanpistachio.com 559-945-1400

KING ARTHUR FLOUR (bread flour and dry milk powder)
www.kingarthurflour.com 800-827-6836

LA CUISINE (specialty flours, sugars, and flavorings)
www.lacuisineus.com 800-521-1176

LUCKS (food decorating supplies)
www.lucks.com 800-426-9778

MAISON GLASS (praline paste)
www.maisonglass.com 800-822-5564

NIELSEN-MASSEY (almond extract, vanilla extract, and vanilla bean paste)
www.nielsenmassey.com 800-525-7873

N.Y. CAKE (cake decorating and baking supplies)
www.nycake.com 800-942-2539

PARIS GOURMET (specialty foods)
www.parisgourmet.com, www.chocolatecrafter.com
800-727-8791

PASTRY CHEF CENTRAL
(candied orange peel and rolled fondant)
www.pastrychef.com 888-750-2433

PENZEYS SPICES (flavorings, spices, and herbs)
www.penzeys.com 800-741-7787

THE PEPPERMILL (kosher gourmet foods)
www.thepeppermillinc.com 866-871-4022

THE PERFECT PURÉE OF NAPA VALLEY (fruit purees)
www.perfectpuree.com 800-556-3707

PFEIL & HOLING (cake decorating supplies)
www.cakedeco.com 800-247-7955

SAFEST CHOICE (pasteurized eggs in the shell)
www.safeeggs.com 800-410-7619

SCHARFFEN BERGER (chocolate)
www.scharffenberger.com 866-608-6944

SWANS DOWN CAKE FLOUR
www.reilyproducts.com 800-535-1961

TAAM TOV FOODS (kosher chocolate)
718-788-8880 ext. 127

VALRHONA (chocolate)
www.valrhona-chocolate.com 888-682-5746

THE VANILLA COMPANY (vanilla extract and vanilla powder)
www.vanillaqueen.com 800-757-7511

VITAL CHOICE (organic nuts)
www.vitalchoice.com 800-608-4825

WILTON (cake decorating supplies and ideas)
www.wilton.com 800-794-5866

EQUIPMENT

$\mathcal{G}$ood-quality baking equipment is both attractive and functional. I like to keep my favorites, such as rolling pins, fluted tube pans, and decorative molds, on permanent display and close at hand. Because I so value well-designed tools, through the years I have always had an eye toward what I think would be the ideal pieces of equipment. This has led me to create my own line of bakeware under the name Rose Levy Bakeware. It is available from Amazon and LaPrima Shops. I have also partnered with NewMetro Design to create the Rose Line of bakeware.

Note that sources throughout this chapter are listed when distributors are exclusive or the item is hard to find, but this can change. Some places will special order or direct you to the distributor if they no longer carry a given item. And, of course, the Internet is an excellent way to search for just about anything.

There are more specific recommendations and descriptions further on in this chapter, but a quick overview of the basic equipment needed for baking in general is given opposite. It is important to set aside equipment that retains odors, such as plastic measuring spoons, silicone or rubber spatulas, cutting boards, and storage containers, to use only for baking because they can absorb odors from savory cooking. In addition, ingredients used in baking, especially butter and chocolate, pick up other aromas readily so be careful to isolate them.

(*Equipment Sources are listed on page 544*)

Essential Equipment for Baking

Scales for weighing ingredients

Measuring cups for liquids

Measuring cups for solids

Measuring spoons

Fine-mesh strainers and sifters

Fine grater

Spatulas: small metal spatulas (straight and offset) and silicone spatulas

Whisks

Heavy-duty stand mixer with BeaterBlade attachment or heavy-duty handheld mixer

Food processor

Bread machine, preferably Zojirushi (or heavy-duty stand mixer)

Ice cream scoop: 2 inch (for cupcake batter); 1½ inch (for cookie dough)

Rolling pin, preferably with sleeve

Pastry mat or cloth

Flour wand or dredger

Bench scraper

Pastry brush

Cookie cutters (plain and scalloped): 2 inch, 2¼ inch, and 3 inch

Disposable pastry bags

Oven thermometer

Instant-read thermometer

Pan liners: Silpat and parchment paper

Cake strips

Baking stone or unglazed quarry tiles

Spritzer for water (for baking bread)

Timer

Pot holders, preferably silicone

Wire racks (for cooling)

Torch or a blow dryer (for unmolding)

Ultra-Flex spatula (for serving)

Essential Pans and Baking Dishes

9 by 2 inch round (two)

9 by 3 inch springform or loose bottom

8 by 2 inch square

13 by 9 inch rectangle, preferably straight sided

10 cup fluted tube pan

10 inch (16 cup) two piece metal tube pan (however, some 10 inch pans will have wider center tubes and measure only 12 cups)

17¼ by 12¼ by 1 inch half sheet pans

Muffin pans (two 6 cup or one 12 cup, silicone or aluminum)

9 inch pie plate (4 cups)

9½ inch deep dish pie plate (6 cups)

9½ by 1 inch tart pan

10 to 12 inch round pizza pan

15 by 12 inch cookie sheet

8½ by 4½ inch loaf pan (6 cups)

9 by 5 inch loaf pan (8 cups)

Ovens

People are always asking me what my preference in ovens is, and it's hard to give a definitive answer because oven technology is constantly changing. For small apartments or second ovens, I recommend the Breville Smart Oven BOV800XL for its even baking. The smaller Breville Compact Smart Oven BOV650XL is not convection, but is also reported to be perfectly even. For larger ovens, consider the following common wisdom that I have noted over the years:

It is not safe to assume that the oven recommended by a friend will be exactly the same as one now being manufactured, even if it has the same model number.

When installing a new oven, make sure that the area where you place it is level or your cakes will not be. Because ovens can lose their calibration, check the oven if it takes more or less than the recommended time to bake a cake or other baked goods.

Manufacturers recommend lowering the temperature 25°F/15°C when using the convection setting. I find that with most countertop models (the Breville being an exception) it works to use the same temperature, up to 400°F/200°C, as a conventional oven.

Cakes and cookies generally bake most evenly as close to the center of the oven as possible. For cakes, this is usually accomplished by setting the oven rack in the lower third of the oven. One inch high sheet pans and cookies should bake on the rack in the middle position. Pies, tarts, and breads usually bake in the lower third of the oven. For proper air circulation, the sides of a pan should be no closer than 1 inch from the sides of the oven or from another pan.

When baking layer cakes, about three-quarters into the estimated baking time, turn the pans halfway around for even baking and, if baking on more than one rack, quickly reposition them top to bottom. Pies and tarts, cookies, and bread can be rotated halfway through the baking time. Sponge cakes should not be rotated or they will collapse.

Preheat the oven for a minimum of 20 minutes ahead of baking at 350°F/175°C, 30 minutes if baking at a higher temperature. If using a baking stone or baking sheet, preheat for a minimum of 45 minutes.

Baking Stones

The heat-retaining ability of baking stones or unglazed quarry tiles helps significantly to recover lost heat more quickly after the oven door has been opened. A stone also serves to provide more even baking for flaky pie crusts and breads. It pulls moisture from the bottom crust, which helps to prevent a soggy bottom crust for fruit pies and to ensure a crisper bottom crust for bread. The added benefit for bread is the initial heat boost, so vital for maximum oven spring. An oven stone is usually placed on the bottom rack or on the floor of the oven before the oven is preheated and the pan, or bread dough set on parchment, placed directly on the stone itself. It also serves to maintain even oven temperature for other baked items.

Processors and Mixers

Food Processors and Immersion Blenders

The Cuisinart and KitchenAid food processors set the standard. They are indispensable for grinding nuts and chocolate, grinding sugar to a superfine consistency, pureeing fruit, and all sorts of kitchen activities that prior to the processor took much longer to accomplish. I also like the Cuisinart Elite Collection 4 cup chopper/grinder for chopping small quantities of nuts or chocolate, and the tiny Cuisinart Mini-Mate Plus chopper/grinder for producing superfine citrus zest or dispersing vanilla bean seeds (just add a little sugar from the recipe).

Immersion blenders are also very handy, especially for small mixtures that don't work well in a large food processor or stand mixer. The KitchenAid immersion blender has many attachments and is an excellent product.

Heavy-Duty Stand Mixers

The ubiquitous KitchenAid is the mini version of the Hobart, a brand found in commercial kitchens all over the world. The 5 quart Artisan is KitchenAid's most popular model, so I used it to test all of the recipes in this book. The head tilts back to make scraping the bowl easy, and the mixer's adjustable beaters enable them to reach as close to the bottom of the bowl as possible for thorough and even mixing. If you plan to make large cakes, such as wedding cakes, or bread, however, KitchenAid's larger and more powerful 6 or 8 quart models or Cuisinart's 7 quart model will serve you better. An added feature on the larger KitchenAid mixer is a water jacket attachment to heat or chill the bowl while beating.

The 5 quart mixer can handle any mixture that does not exceed 4 quarts, for example, an 8 egg butter cake or 7 egg génoise. The 6 quart mixer can handle any mixture that does not exceed 5 quarts, such as a 9 egg butter cake or 11 egg génoise.

For smaller amounts of ingredients, such as cream for whipping, and for recipes that involve beating hot syrup into eggs or egg whites, a handheld mixer is more practical than a stand mixer. KitchenAid makes an excellent model. The Rose MixerMate Bowl is designed for handheld mixers and shaped to maximize contact with the beaters and the sides of the bowl without splatter. It is part of the Rose Line.

Heavy-duty stand mixers offer the choice of a flat "paddle" beater, a whisk beater, and often a dough hook. The flat beater is intended for general mixing; the whisk beater will whip as much air as possible into a mixture, such as when you beat egg whites or batter for sponge-type cakes; and the dough hook is for kneading bread. The Rose BeaterBlade for the KitchenAid is a flat beater with wings that scrape the sides and bottom of the bowl while it mixes. It virtually eliminates hand scraping and food buildup on the sides and bottom of the bowl. When using the BeaterBlade, or other beaters designed to scrape the bowl, for recipes where dry ingredients are being mixed into wet ingredients, you must install the mixer bowl's splash guard, lay a sheet of plastic wrap over the top of the bowl, or first hand-mix the dry ingredients to moisten them. Plastic wrap works better than a cloth towel draped over the bowl because any flour that leaps up will not cling to the plastic, and you can see what is happening to the mixture in the bowl. Even at the lowest speed, some of the dry ingredients can fly out of the bowl as the beater's scraping action churns the mixture upward.

If you are investing in a stand mixer, it pays to get an extra bowl and set of beaters for the many times egg whites need to be beaten after the rest of the ingredients have been mixed. Because the whites require a spotlessly clean bowl and beaters, a second set comes in very handy.

Always start mixing on low speed and gradually raise the speed to what is indicated in the recipe. If the volume of the ingredients is small in proportion to the mixer bowl, you will need to use higher speeds. The times listed in the recipes are for a stand mixer. The gradual increase in speed not only keeps the

ingredients from jumping out of the bowl but it is better for the gears of the mixer. The one exception to this practice is when beating hot syrup into stiffly beaten egg whites. Starting on low between each addition would overheat and deflate the whites.

KITCHENAID MIXING SPEEDS

LOW: number 2

MEDIUM-LOW: number 3

MEDIUM: number 4

MEDIUM-HIGH: numbers 6 to 8

HIGH: number 10

The Ankarsrum Assistent is the Rolls-Royce of mixers for bread dough. Its design is based on the spiral type mixers used in professional bread-baking kitchens, which are designed to mix dough with the least incorporation of air (referred to as oxygenating), which would decrease flavor. This beautifully designed 7.4 quart mixer can handle from one up to about eight loaves (1 to 12 pounds of dough using 4 to 23 cups of flour). The mixer comes with a sturdy stainless-steel bowl that rotates when the machine is turned on. It is equipped with a metal dough hook for larger amounts of dough, and a large plastic roller with grooves designed to simulate the action of fingers for kneading smaller amounts of dough. Both devices move back and forth as the bowl circles around. A detachable plastic scraper effectively scrapes the sides of the bowl as it mixes.

WEIGHING AND MEASURING DEVICES

SCALES

I much prefer weighing ingredients to measuring them for baking. It is faster, easier, and more reliable. It is ideal for determining quantities when reducing liquids, which is always difficult to do by eye alone.

Scales that have the ability to eliminate (tare) the weight of the bowl also make it possible to add the dry ingredients to the mixing bowl one after the other rather than having to use separate bowls for each.

Most bakers, including myself, prefer the metric system for its precision in weighing small quantities. There isn't any adjustment necessary if you have a metric scale and the recipes give metric amounts. If you do not have a scale with a digital readout, round off the grams to the nearest convenient number. The amount will still be quite accurate because, after all, 1 gram is only about 1/28 of an ounce.

Excellent quality electronic scales that can be switched back and forth from ounces to grams and pounds to kilograms are now widely available. With *The Cake Bible*, I became the first author of cookbooks geared toward the home baker and the professional to list weights for all ingredients. I have continued in each book to spearhead the movement toward weighing. My ultimate reward is the Rose Scale by Escali. It is a beautifully designed scale of the highest quality and durability. Its weighing range of up to 13 pounds/6 kilograms in increments of 0.1 ounce/1 gram is ideal for all the recipes in this book. For measuring minute amounts of ingredients, such as yeast or salt, I also recommend the Escali L600 "High Precision," with a weighing range of 0.1 gram to 600 grams.

Special Features

The Escali scales can be operated by A/C adaptor as well as by battery. When operated by battery, they have an automatic shutoff, but when using the optional adaptor (which works for both models listed), the scales stay on until they are turned off, which I prefer because the scales don't inconveniently time out when I am in the middle of weighing and get distracted for a few minutes. The scales are small and compact, not taking up much counter space.

The Rose Scale's adjustable-angle backlight display is easy to read even when using pans that are larger than the platform, which is easily removable. The display and the buttons are sealed to protect against accidental spills. There is also a tare button to remove the weight of the container and each ingredient after it is added. When pressed a second time, it gives you the total weight of everything that has been added.

Special Care for All Scales

Follow the manufacturers' directions for care, such as to avoid direct sunlight and uneven counters. Also do not weigh anything heavier than the maximum capacity of the scale because doing so will damage it and will not be covered by the warranty.

Liquid Measuring Cups

The most accurate and well-marked heatproof plastic and glass measuring cups I have found are made by POURfect and Anchor Hocking. A cup of water, read below the bottom of the meniscus (the curved upper surface), should weigh close to 8.4 ounces/237 grams. If using a metric cup, this is equal to 237 milliliters (as milliliters are based on the weight of water). The standard metric cup is 250 milliliters, about 1 tablespoon more than the standard U.S. cup.

The plastic POURfect beakers are designed to pour without dripping and are heat resistant. The glass cups by Anchor Hocking are ideal for pouring hot sugar syrups and caramel. I use my 1 cup measures the most, but 2 cup and 4 cup measures are also useful, especially for reducing liquids, which bubble up. When measuring sticky substances such as syrups and molasses, spray the cup (or measuring spoon, for smaller amounts) with nonstick cooking spray before using. This will help prevent the syrup from bubbling up and will make it easier to remove. A mini measure is accurate for measuring small amounts of liquid. It measures from 1 teaspoon/5 ml up to 6 teaspoons (2 tablespoons/30 ml).

Solid Measuring Cups

Solid measures must have unbroken smooth rims in order to make it possible to level off excess ingredients. POURfect makes beautifully accurate cups in a set of nine useful sizes: ⅛, ¼, ⅓, ½, ⅔, ¾, 1, 1½, and 2 cups.

Measuring Spoons

POURfect measuring spoons are my favorites because each one is perfectly accurate and they come in some unusual and practical sizes, starting with teaspoons—1/64, 1/32, 1/16, ⅛, ¼, ⅓, ½, ¾, 1, and 1½ (½ tablespoon)—and both 1 and 2 tablespoons.

The smallest ones correspond to a drop ($\frac{1}{64}$), a smidgen ($\frac{1}{32}$), a pinch ($\frac{1}{16}$), and a dash ($\frac{1}{8}$). They are also marked with milliliters (ml), making it possible for me to offer very precise ml values for small amounts of liquid called for throughout the book.

BAKING PANS

CAKE PANS

The cake pans I recommend are true to size, measured from the inside, both top and bottom, so if you buy or order them by mail, you know what you are getting. If, however, you go to a store and purchase brands other than those recommended, bring along a tape measure. Pans marked 9 inches may actually be larger or smaller at either the bottom or the top, or both, which will affect the volume and the way the cake bakes. Many 9 inch pans are actually only 8¾ to 8⅞ inches at the bottom, which results in a reduced capacity of about ⅓ cup. (This will still work for the recipes in this book, however.)

If you already have pans that are slightly too small, you can extend their capacity by coating the insides of the pan with shortening and lining the pan with a band of parchment that extends above the sides. Alternatively, fill the pans no higher than two-thirds full and bake any remaining batter as cupcakes. Otherwise, if the pan is too small, the batter will rise above the sides, causing it to overflow and collapse in the center. If the pan is too large, the exposed sides of the pan above the batter will reflect heat down into the cake batter, causing it to be pale, dry, and low in height.

Choose sturdy, heavy-gauge aluminum pans that are light in color with a dull finish. Dark pans will result in a very dark or burned crust. If you already have dark pans, when baking, reduce the oven temperature by 25°F/15°C. Different metals and pan coatings also affect the color of the cake's crust. Cast aluminum tube pans, for example, create a beautiful deep golden crust. Thinner aluminum pans will have a paler crust.

A nonstick finish is ideal for layer cake pans because it makes it possible to omit the parchment round (unless you are baking chocolate cakes, which don't release as well from the pan). I prefer a nonstick surface on the inside of fluted tube pans as well because the cakes unmold best, allowing the designs to make perfect impressions on the cake's surface.

There are only a few basic pans you will need to make most of the cakes in this book (see Essential Pans and Baking Dishes, page 529). Specialty pans, however, are fun and can create many beautiful and distinctive looking cakes. Where they are used in a recipe, whenever possible, I list a more commonly available alternative.

SILICONE PANS

Compared with metal or glass, silicone is still a relatively new technology in cake pans and kitchen equipment. It has some advantages but there are also instances where metal is the better choice. One of the problems about recommending silicone pans across the board is that not all silicone is created equal, and there is quite a variance in quality among products. Also, very few manufacturers produce a true-to-size 9 by 2 inch cake pan. Most are slightly larger. That being said, their slightly larger-than-standard size makes them ideal to use as containers in which to set loose-bottom or springform pans baked in a water bath because they keep the water from seeping in.

The main advantage of silicone pans is that when prepared properly (interior coated with baking spray with flour) and cooled completely, they will release the cake perfectly, with no crust stuck to the pan.

I find that silicone pans bake most evenly when set on wire racks, which allows for air circulation, and with the racks set on sheet pans for ease in transferring them in and out of the oven. Once baked, the cakes need to cool completely in the pans before unmolding. Unlike aluminum, deep fluted silicone tube pans do not conduct the heat well to the center of the cake and may require as long as 20 minutes of extra baking. They do not bake most cakes evenly, either in color or texture. Small silicone pans, such as those for cupcakes, however, are excellent for even baking. They need only slightly more time to bake and can be unmolded right away. Additional advantages are ease of unmolding, the pans don't dent, and they're easy to store. You can scrunch them up in a drawer or suitcase, and they always will pop back to their original shape. It is important to keep in mind, however, that although silicone can withstand temperatures of up to 500°F/260°C or even slightly higher, it cannot be subjected to direct heat from either a broiler or cooktop. The only other way in which it can be damaged is by cutting it.

LAYER CAKE PANS

In this book, the cake pans used most for butter layer cakes are 9 by 2 inches, in part because they are the most readily available, and also because one pan yields a single layer with enough height to be cut in half. I find that butter layer cakes baked in pans higher than 2 inches have a coarse texture.

For single layers, I created the recipe to mound slightly; for two layers, I created the recipe to be level in order for the cakes to stack easily. (This is a function of the amount of leavening: More leavening weakens the structure and produces flatter, less domed layers.)

My favorite manufacturers of sturdy straight-sided 2 inch high nonstick cake pans are Chicago Metallic and USA Pan's professional lines. They all measure a true 9 inches in diameter. The Chicago Metallic pans are dark gray in color, but they require the same baking temperature as lighter colored pans. I also like Fat Daddio's complete line and Parrish Magic Line's sturdy round, square, and rectangular pans, which have perfectly squared corners.

FLUTED TUBE PANS

Fluted tube pans are ideal for cakes that require no frosting or adornment beyond the exquisite design of the flutings. I like Nordic Ware for its huge variety of beautifully designed cast-aluminum fluted tube pans.

Some of my favorite Nordic Ware 10 cup fluted tube pans include the Bavaria, Elegant Heart, Rose Bundt, and, of course, the classic Anniversary Bundt, which works for 10 to 15 cups due to its narrow base and wider center tube. Any recipe that calls for a 10 cup fluted metal tube pan can also be baked in the standard 12 cup Bundt pan. If you have one of the older style tube pans that has a dark lining or dark exterior, be sure to lower the oven temperature by 25°F/15°C.

Kaiser makes a terrific 10 cup fluted commercial weight steel tube pan (8½ inch inside diameter) that is lined with silicone and is called La Forme Perfect Bundform. It has the conductivity of metal and the nonstick properties of silicone. Its silicone lining is just thick enough for perfect unmolding and easy cleanup without altering the baking time or height of the cake. (Note: Kaiser's website may refer to it as a 9 cup pan, but it is 10 cups.) The pan still must be sprayed with baking spray with flour in order to unmold perfectly.

STRAIGHT-SIDED TUBE PANS (AKA ANGEL FOOD PANS)

Be sure to purchase a two-piece tube pan for ease in unmolding. A standard pan holds 16 cups and is 10 inches by 4 inches; these pans are carried by Wilton and also distributed by Allied Metal Spinning. However, over the past few years, the standard-size angel food pan seems to have shrunk, and many other brands' pans hold only 14 cups. To measure the volume of your pan, line it with a clean plastic bag to prevent leaking and then fill it with water, cup by cup (see page 536). If your pan is smaller than 16 cups, you may want to decrease the recipe, or fill the pan almost to the top and bake the excess batter as cupcakes.

Angel food and chiffon cakes should be cooled upside down: The cakes will cling to the bottom of the pan and stretch downward to their full height. Once the cake is completely cool, it will be firm enough to prevent collapse of the delicate foam structure. For this reason, some pans have legs designed to support the pan when it is inverted, but they do not function very well because the cooling cake needs to be suspended a minimum of 4 inches above the counter or other surface to allow for the evaporation of steam. A large inverted funnel is ideal as a support. A slim, long-neck wine or glass soda bottle can also work well. Alternatively, if the opening of the pan is not large enough to fit over a bottle, you can raise a wire rack off the counter by setting it on three or four cans or drinking glasses, and then set the inverted pan on the rack to cool.

Sheet Pans

The standard half sheet pan is 17¼ by 12¼ by 1 inch (12 cups), measured from the inside top. My favorites are USA Pan nonstick and Lincoln Wear-Ever 13-gauge (#5314). It's fine to use one that is slightly larger or slightly smaller, but, if you are using it to bake a cake, the thickness of cake will vary accordingly.

Removable-Bottom and Springform Pans

Most springform or loose-bottom pans need to be protected from water seepage when set in a water bath (see page 538). I prefer Parrish Magic Line's sturdy, loose-bottom 3 inch high pans to a traditional springform. I like to use the removable bottom disks to transfer cake layers, and they are also available separately from the pan itself. Wilton makes a 9 by 3 inch springform perfect for the standard-size cheesecake. I love the model that has a glass bottom, which is ideal to use as the serving plate.

Muffin or Cupcake Pans

Traditionally, liners are used for muffins and cupcakes because they keep the small cakes fresher and make it easier to frost and transport them. The most elegant and beautiful disposable muffin cups come from Qualitá Paper Products. Small panettone paper pans, 2¾ by 2 inches (¾ cup plus 2 tablespoons/207 ml), are almost double the size of standard muffin cups. They are firm enough to stand alone (available from La Cuisine).

Silicone pans without liners give just the right support to produce cupcakes or muffins with the nicest domed shape. Individual silicone muffin molds called Sili-Cups are very pretty, but they are three-quarters the size of the cups in a standard muffin pan, so if a cupcake recipe makes 14 to 16 standard-size cupcakes, it will yield 19 to 21 cupcakes if using Sili-Cups. My favorite silicone pans have six cavities. Each cavity is the same capacity as that of the cups in a standard muffin pan: ½ cup/118 ml. As with other silicone pans, it is a good idea to set silicone muffin pans on wire racks and then set the racks on sheet pans or cookie sheets for support, so that air can circulate around them and ensure that they bake evenly—especially the middle row in the twelve cavity pan, which tends to bake more slowly.

A 2 inch ice cream scoop is great for dispensing cupcake or muffin batter quickly and neatly into the cups.

Pyrex Custard Cups and Ramekins

Similar sizes of custard cups and ramekins can be used interchangeably as long as their volumes are the same. The most commonly available Pyrex shallow custard cups, or dessert dishes, are 6 fluid ounces/177 ml (bottom 2¾ inches, top 3½ inches, 1⅞ inches high), and 10 fluid ounces/296 ml (bottom 3½ inches, top 4¼ inches, 1⅞ inches high). These are inter-changeable with Marianne or shortcake pans. You can also use 6 fluid ounce/177 ml ramekins or soufflé molds that are 3 by 2 inches.

Specialty Pans

UNUSUAL BABY PAN SHAPES

The "Rose's Marvelous Mini Cake Pan" has twelve bar-shaped cavities (3 by 1 by 1¼ inch high/¼ cup/59 ml). I use this pan for financiers and brownies so that each one has an identical size and perfect shape with a fine crust on all sides. I also use it as a mold for melted chocolate for making chocolate curls (see page 520).

Mini brioche pans from France are now available with nonstick coating. They are perfect for bite-size treats such as Mini Gâteaux Bretons (page 388) and Chocolate Ganache Tartlets (page 299). They measure 1 inch at the bottom and 1¾ inches at the top, with 1 tablespoon/15 ml capacity (see JB Prince).

For madeleines, silicone pans not only make unmolding easy, they also maintain the moisture of the madeleines better than metal pans.

HEART PANS

I love hearts, and Wilton makes the most beautifully shaped heart pans in varying sizes. The ones suggested for this book are 9 inches at their widest point by 8 inches in length (from the center of the bow to the point) by 2 inches high (8 cups).

How to Determine Pan Size

A round cake pan holds three-quarters of the volume of a square cake pan of the same size. To determine the volume of a square cake pan, multiply the volume of a round cake pan of the same diameter by 1.33. To determine the volume of an oddly shaped pan, use a measuring cup with a spout to pour water into the pan until it reaches the brim. I like to set a metal ruler on top of the pan so I know when the water is level with the top. If it's a two-piece pan, line it first with a clean plastic bag to keep the water from leaking out.

To determine the volume of a pan using a scale, set a sheet pan on top to contain any water that might spill, then set the pan to be measured on top. Tare out the weight of the pans. Fill the pan to be measured with water. One cup of water weighs 8.4 ounces/237 grams.

How to Prepare Cake Pans

BUTTER LAYER CAKE PANS Encircle the pan with a cake strip (see page 537). Coat the bottom of the pan with shortening. Top it with a parchment round and coat the entire interior of the pan with baking spray with flour. Wipe off the rim of the pan.

SPONGE CAKE PANS Coat the interior of the pan with baking spray with flour. Then set a parchment round in the bottom. (The round will stick to the cake, helping to remove the bottom crust, making it easier to brush the cake with syrup.) Wipe off the rim of the pan. There is no need to use a cake strip because sponge cakes do not tend to dome and also any dryness at the edges will be corrected when the cake is brushed with syrup.

FLUTED TUBE PANS Coat the interior of the pan evenly with baking spray with flour. Wipe off the rim of the pan. If the baking spray clumps, use an artist's paintbrush to even it out, which will prevent bubbles in the crust.

SHEET PANS Coat the interior of the pan with shortening or nonstick cooking spray and top with parchment. It helps to make a small snip into each corner to help the parchment ease around the curved edges. Have either the long sides or the short sides extend a few inches past the edges of the pan for easy removal of a cake. Coat the parchment with baking spray with flour and then wipe off the rim of the pan.

How Much to Fill Cake Pans

Most of my cakes call for 2 inch high pans. Unless otherwise specified in the recipe, *fill the pan no less than half full and no more than just under two-thirds.*

Here are some rules of thumb for odd-size pans: Classic génoise uses just under half the number of eggs as the cup capacity of the pan. Most butter cakes use just under one-quarter as many eggs as the cup capacity. For example, an 8⅔ cup capacity pan uses a 4 egg formula for classic génoise and a 2 egg formula for a butter cake (1 whole egg equals 2 egg yolks or 1½ egg whites).

Pie Plates

The terms pie "pan" and pie "plate" are used interchangeably by most people. The standard pie plate has a 4 cup capacity; the capacity of a deep dish pie plate is 6 cups.

I designed the Rose's Perfect Pie Plate to have a 4 cup capacity and to have deeply fluted scalloped edges, so that when dough is pressed into them, an attractive border automatically forms. The pie plate measures 11 inches going straight across, edge to edge, and 12 inches, including the rim, from the outside edge, down the inside, across the bottom, and up to the opposite outside edge.

Because the rim of the Perfect Pie Plate is wider than other pie plates', more dough will be needed and it will need to be rolled slightly larger. If you are using it for a single crust pie, make the amount of dough given for a deep dish 9½ inch pie; for a standard lattice pie, make the amount for a double crust pie; and for a double crust pie, make the amount for two deep dish 9½ inch pies. For a single crust or lattice pie, roll the dough for the bottom crust into a disc 14 inches in diameter and roll the dough for the strips to a 12 inch oval. (If making 12 strips you will need a minimum width of 9 inches; for 14 strips, a minimum width of 10½ inches.) For a double crust pie, roll the dough for the bottom crust to 12½ inches and the dough for the top crust to 13½ to 14 inches.

Fluted Tart Pans with Removable Bottoms

My favorite fluted two-piece tart pans are manufactured by Gobel and carried by JB Prince and La Cuisine. In addition to making it easier to unmold and serve a tart, the nonstick removable bottoms double as perfect transfer discs for moving cake layers. Wilton makes a heart-shape fluted two-piece nonstick tart pan that can be used interchangeably with a 9 inch round pan.

Cookie Sheets

The batch size of the cookie recipes in this book is formulated based on the standard 15 by 12 inch cookie sheet. A cookie sheet should not have a rim around the edge, so that air can circulate evenly around the cookies, but if a rimless cookie sheet is not available and you have a half sheet pan, simply invert it to make a rimless baking sheet. For cookies where I recommend an insulated or cushioned baking sheet or double pan to keep the bottoms from overbrowning, I value my T-fal AirBake insulated nonstick sheets.

Loaf Pans

The two sizes of loaf pans needed for some of the bread and cake recipes in this book are 8½ by 4½ inch (6 cup capacity) and 9 by 5 inch (8 cup capacity). Because the slope of a loaf pan's sides varies so much, the internal capacity of these pans can vary significantly. The less sharp the angle, the greater the capacity. It is best to measure the capacity of your loaf pan by pouring water into it from an accurate glass measure. USA Pan and Chicago Metallic make excellent heavyweight loaf pans with a nonstick interior that are 8½ by 4½ inches (6 cups). Silicone loaf pans are great, but choose ones that have support structures or stanchions on the sides so that they don't bulge outward during baking.

Miscellaneous Essentials

Cake Strips

When a layer cake bakes, the heat from the oven reaches the sides of the pan first and the center of the pan last. This causes the edges of the cake to rise and set before the center, which continues to rise, creating a dome in the center and dryness around the edges. Encircling a pan with cake strips slows down the baking at the sides of the pan so that the batter rises at the same rate as in the center, producing a more level cake that is more evenly moist throughout.

I used to make my own cake strips out of fabric that I moistened and fastened around the pan with a pin. Now, however, I've developed Rose's Heavenly Cake Strips, which are sold on Amazon and by LaPrima Shops. They are made of silicone and fit 9 and 10 inch round pans and 8 inch square pans (for smaller pans, use metal paper clamps or silicone bands to secure the excess length. There's no need to moisten or fasten them, and they are easy to clean in the dishwasher or with Soft Scrub. Silicone is the ideal substance for a cake strip because it is very slow to conduct heat. It also expands slightly during baking, making the strips easy to remove.

For larger or oddly shaped pans, you can make your own cake strips using a strip of aluminum foil long enough to encircle the pan with a little overlap. Wet some paper towels, fold them to the height of the pan, and lay them along the aluminum foil strip. Fold the foil over to encase the paper towels. Wrap the strip around the pan and secure it with a metal paper clip or clamp, or encircle the strip with a silicone band to hold it in place.

Foil Rings for Pies

The borders of pies and tarts are unprotected by the filling and tend to bake faster than the rest of the crust. It is, therefore, advisable to protect them right from the beginning of baking with an aluminum foil ring. Rings are available for purchase, but are not necessarily the right size for all pie plates. To make your own foil ring, tear off a piece of heavy-duty aluminum foil a few inches larger than the diameter of the pie plate or tart pan. As a guide, use a pot lid or cardboard circle and a pencil to mark a cutout in the center that will expose the pie's surface but not the decorative edge. With scissors, cut out the circle. Leaving at least a 3 inch border, cut around the outside to form a ring. Shape it so that it will curve over the rim of the pie crust. This ring can be rinsed and reused several times. It is best to set it over the pie at the start of baking to prevent overbrowning.

WIRE RACKS FOR COOLING

My favorite racks are Combrichon round wire racks from France. The wire is spaced closely together, offering good support for a cake or tart. To prevent cakes from sticking to the racks, I coat the racks lightly with nonstick cooking spray. I prefer stainless steel rectangular racks for sheet pans and cookie sheets.

BOWLS

An assortment of glass bowls, including Pyrex custard cups or dessert dishes, is ideal both for microwaving and storing. Glass bowls are microwavable, nonreactive, and don't retain odors. When calling for general sizes of bowls in the recipes, I use the following guidelines: A small bowl is about 4 cups (1 quart) capacity. A medium bowl is about 6 cups (1½ quarts) capacity. A large bowl is about 8 quarts capacity.

For melting chocolate, Rose's Silicone Baking Bowl, from Harold Import Co. (on Amazon), is perfect because it can be used both as a double boiler over a pan of hot water and in the microwave. It collapses into a flat disk for convenient storage.

POURfect makes plastic bowls designed for adding ingredients to a stand mixer bowl, even with the motor running, without danger of hitting the beater, spilling a single drop of liquid, or dropping a smidgen of flour. The bowls come in a wide range of sizes and are exceptionally light and easy to lift. They even have a small "rocker" below the teardrop-shape spout. It latches onto the bowl to keep it from slipping or falling into the mixer bowl.

The Rose MixerMate Bowl is designed for handheld mixers and shaped to maximize contact between the beaters and the sides of the bowl without splattering. It also works well for adding ingredients to a stand mixer.

SAUCEPANS, WATER BATHS, WARMING CONTAINERS, AND DEVICES

ROSE CARAMEL POT

I designed this 1 quart ceramic-lined saucepot as the best size, shape, and composition to use for caramel, crème anglaise, sugar syrups, and reducing liquids. The high sides prevent splashing and the ceramic lining ensures the maximum release of the liquid or sauce. It is suitable for use with all cooking surfaces, including induction.

ROSE DOUBLE BOILER

This 1¾ quart smooth, stainless steel, double-walled pot is the ideal double boiler because water can be poured between the walls of the pot, resulting in perfectly even and gentle heating for sauces, curds, and melting chocolate. It is suitable for use with all cooking surfaces, including induction.

WATER BATHS

ICE WATER BATH When a recipe says to cool the mixture to room temperature and you want to do this quickly, an ice water bath works well, providing the mixture is stirred constantly to equalize the temperature.

TO MAKE AN ICE WATER BATH Place about a quart of ice cubes in a large container and add enough cold water just to float them. Sprinkle a handful of coarse salt on top to lower the temperature (as if making ice cream). If the mixture to be cooled is in a glass bowl, which holds the temperature, and it should not be chilled beyond a specific point, as with mixtures containing gelatin, have ready some hot water in a large bowl to take the chill off the bowl when the mixture has reached the proper temperature. Setting the bowl briefly on a marble or granite countertop and then on a wire rack (for air circulation) will further draw out the heat.

HOT WATER BATH (BAIN-MARIE) AND DOUBLE BOILERS When using a hot water bath for baking custard-type cakes, such as cheesecakes, follow the recipe for preparing the pan and use very hot tap water (about 140°F/60°C). To prevent water marks from staining the water-bath pan, add 1 teaspoon of cream of tartar to the water.

If a cake is being baked in a pan with a removable bottom or a springform pan, instead of using aluminum foil to keep the pan water-tight, it works better to set the pan in a slightly larger silicone pan before placing it in the water bath.

There are many times when you need to heat something very gently over indirect rather than direct heat.

If you do not own a double boiler, or if the double boiler is too small, use a saucepan or pot slightly smaller in diameter than the mixing bowl. Fill the saucepan with a few inches of hot or simmering water and place the bowl on top of the saucepan. In most cases you will not want the bottom of the bowl to touch the water. Stir or fold the mixture continuously while heating.

WARMING CONTAINERS AND BREAD PROOFERS

Every dwelling has natural sources or areas for heating and cooling. An infrared thermometer makes it easy to determine yours. When letting yeasted dough rise, you will want a naturally warm spot. Above the refrigerator is one good option. I often use my microwave oven (not turned on) with a cup of very hot water in each of two corners to provide a nice warm temperature and humidity for raising dough. A large plastic box also works well. The electric proofer from Brød & Taylor is a controlled environment. It has a temperature range of 70° to 120°F/21° to 49°C. If an enclosed container is used, there is no need to cover the dough because it will not dry out.

BUTANE AND PROPANE TORCHES

Using a miniature torch is the professional way to heat the sides of a cake pan for perfect unmolding. Heating with a hair dryer also works, but it is slower. You can also use a torch to brown the edges of a meringue topping.

THERMOMETERS

INSTANT-READ THERMOMETERS Most instant-read thermometers are small enough to tuck into your pocket and they are virtually indispensable for making sugar syrups, caramel, and cream sauces; for melting chocolate; and for determining the temperature of baked goods. Two of the best are the Thermapen 5F thermometer, which has a range of −50° to 550°F/−46° to 288°C, and the CDN ProAccurate pocket thermometer, with a range of −40° to 450°F/−40° to 232°C. The Thermapen is more expensive, but it offers the quickest response.

POINT AND SHOOT THERMOMETERS Infrared thermometers, often referred to as "point and shoot," capture the invisible infrared energy naturally emitted from all objects. When aimed and the trigger is pulled, the thermometer instantly scans the surface temperature of an object from up to two feet away. This is a very useful tool for taking oven temperature and also the temperature of different areas in the refrigerator or room. The IR-Gun-S, by ThermoWorks, has a range of −76° to 1022°F/−60° to 550°C.

OVEN THERMOMETERS I use a laboratory cable thermometer from Omega (model number HH22). It is expensive, but it is far more accurate than most oven thermometers I have tested. It is designed for home use and can be used for two ovens at the same time. It is important for an oven thermometer to be read without your having to open the oven door because the temperature starts to drop immediately once the door is opened. For an oven with a window, the CDN model DOT2 and the Thermopen Chef-Alarm with oven clip and probe are also reliable.

Spatulas and Whisks

METAL SPATULAS

Small metal spatulas, both straight and offset, with narrow 4 inch blades are perhaps the most often used implements in my kitchen. They are perfect for leveling measuring spoons with dry ingredients, for spreading filling into pie and tart pans, for dislodging crust from the sides of a pan (if the pan is nonstick, a small plastic knife works better and won't damage the pan lining), for frosting the sides of a cake, and for making swirls in frosting. It is also helpful to have a long, narrow metal spatula for smoothing the top of a cake. Small and large offset spatulas are handy for spreading mixtures evenly in pans or for lifting very small cakes. A broad inflexible grill spatula or pancake turner is useful for lifting frosted cake layers or transferring cookies from the cookie sheet. For smoothing the sides of a cake, Parrish Magic Line makes a slim 6 by 3 inch stainless steel metal plate called the Icing Blade; a bench scraper also works well.

SILICONE SPATULAS

Flexible, high-heat spatulas made of silicone are efficient for scraping every last smidgen of batter from the bowl and for reaching down to the bottom of the bowl when folding mixtures together. I especially like clear or light-colored ones for making caramel, because the light color makes it possible to see the true color of the caramel and allows your eyes to be the thermometer. Since these spatulas retain odors, a separate set should be reserved for baking.

SLOTTED SKIMMER

A medium or large skimmer can double as a spatula and works even better to fold flour into batters because the small holes provide just the right resistance to blend in the flour with minimal deflating of the batter. For ease of use, bend back the handle slightly to decrease the angle.

WHISKS

I find three sizes of whisks particularly useful for baking: A small piano wire whisk, 10 inches long and 5 inches in circumference, with at least eight loops of fine wire, will reach into the corners of a saucepan, making it ideal for both preparing a smooth pastry cream and evenly mixing together dry ingredients. I recommend an enormous balloon whisk, 14½ inches in circumference, in place of a spatula for folding one mixture into another. Lastly, a whisk with a long handle is useful for stirring mixtures over hot water. Silicone-coated whisks, such as in my Rose Line, are well suited for use in pans with nonstick lining.

STRAINERS, SIFTERS, AND FOOD MILLS

STRAINERS

Stainless steel fine-mesh strainers are indispensable for a wide range of baking-related activities. You will need a small fine-mesh one for clarifying butter and a medium one for making Dark Chocolate Lacquer Glaze (page 296), sifting cocoa and flour, and evenly dusting powdered sugar or cocoa onto desserts (simply tap the side with a spoon or use the spoon to press the powdered sugar or cocoa through the mesh). A strainer is also needed for straining preserves, lemon curd, cream, and crème anglaise.

SIFTERS

The primary purpose of sifting is to separate and aerate flour particles, enabling them to mix more uniformly with the liquid in a recipe. However, sifting does not adequately mix dry ingredients. This is best accomplished in a mixer or by using a whisk. I prefer an electric sifter because it is so speedy. A mesh strainer with a tablespoon to press the flour through also works, but it is much slower.

FOOD MILLS

Lehman's Roma Food Mill is my preference for making fruit purees. Fitted with the optional berry screen, it pays for itself by extracting more puree than any other device. Unlike the average food mill, it does not allow even the tiniest raspberry seed to pass through.

LINERS, PARCHMENT, WRAPS, AND STORAGE CONTAINERS

REUSABLE LINERS

Reusable liners are one of my favorite products because absolutely nothing sticks to them, making them ideal for caramel and sticky candy such as toffee, meringues, and other delicate baked goods. Sometimes called super parchment or reusable parchment, they also make cleanup easy. Food service–quality Silpats, which are made from a combination of silicone and fiberglass, are not quite as nonstick as the Teflon-type of liners available for home use, but they are a lot more durable and are safe for temperatures up to 480°F/250°C (whereas Teflon-type liners are rated as safe only up to

425°F/220°C). Both types of liners are widely available at housewares and kitchen specialty stores. All nonstick liners can be reused countless times.

PARCHMENT

Parchment is available at cake decorating and baking supply stores and specialty stores in precut rounds, and in supermarkets, in rolls, for lining cake pans and baking sheets. Lining the bottoms of cake pans with parchment enables cakes to release perfectly when unmolding; if left uncoated, parchment helps to remove the bottom crust easily for sponge cakes that will be brushed with syrup. It also makes it easier to remove cookies, scones, or other items from a sheet pan or cookie sheet.

PLASTIC WRAP

Stretch-Tite is currently the best plastic wrap available. It clings tightly to the bowl or whatever else needs to be wrapped. It is not impermeable and therefore not suitable for freezing baked goods unless used in a couple layers, but the same manufacturer also produces a wrap designed for the freezer called Freeze-Tite. Not only is it significantly thicker, it is also wider (15 inches). The box features a sliding device that neatly cuts off a sheet of plastic wrap.

STORAGE BAGS

Choose heavy-duty plastic reclosable freezer bags for storing baked goods in the freezer. It is best to wrap the item first in freezer weight plastic wrap, place it in the bag, and expel as much air as possible before closing the bag. You can remove air by inserting a small drinking straw into the opening of the bag and sucking out the air.

GRATERS

ROSE ZESTN'EST

This ergonomically designed and self-contained device fits in the palm of your hand and makes it quick and easy to remove the maximum amount of citrus zest without removing the bitter pith. It also works well for grating chocolate. (It is the perfect implement for grating garlic quickly and neatly as well, and washes clean and odor free in a dishwasher.)

NUT GRATERS

If you are not using a food processor to grind nuts, a Mouli or Zyliss hand grater, with its finest drum, works well to grind nuts to an even and fine consistency.

ROSE JUICELAB CITRUS JUICER

This is the perfect juicer for squeezing juice from citrus fruit quickly and thoroughly. It has a cap for measuring from 1 teaspoon to 1 tablespoon and also works for storing the juice.

ROLLING PINS

Rolling pins are a very personal choice. I collect rolling pins and use them as wall decorations when I'm not using them to roll pastry. The ones I reach for most often are my 1¾ inch diameter, 20 inch long solid silicone or wood pins. I also find a small rolling pin very useful for smaller pieces of fondant and dough, especially the small rolling rods made by Fat Daddio's in both plastic and stainless steel, which are 7½ inches long by 1⅜ inch diameter.

Specially designed rubber bands that fit over the ends of a rolling pin and serve as spacers between the counter and rolling pin are great for ensuring an evenly rolled crust. (Note that stretching them to fit larger rolling pins will thin the bands, resulting in less space between the pin and the rolling surface.)

A knitted cotton rolling pin sleeve rubbed with flour works wonderfully to prevent sticking. (Most pastry sleeves that come with pastry cloths are too short for long rolling pins. Rolls of knitted cotton sleeving that can be cut to exact size are available at surgical supply stores.)

MAGIC DOUGH NON SLIP PASTRY MAT

This 18 by 24½ inch mat (the mat also comes in a smaller size) is the most nonstick surface I have found for rolling pastry, requiring only a light dusting of flour. Alternatively, a canvas pastry cloth rubbed with flour or large overlapping sheets of freezer weight plastic wrap work well.

Timers

Both CDN and ThermoWorks make attractive and good quality kitchen timers.

Cake Testers

The best wire cake testers have thin metal wires with loops at one end for hanging them and when used to test for doneness, make only a small hole in a cake. These can be found at Parrish Magic Line and Wilton. Wooden toothpicks are fine to use for some cakes as long as you remove the cake when just a few crumbs cling to them. I recommend them over the wire testers for a few recipes that require longer baking and where you do want the toothpick to come out clean to indicate doneness.

Brushes

Silicone brushes are useful for brushing syrup onto cakes. They are easier to clean than any other type of brush and are practically indestructible. Because the brushes retain odors, reserve a separate one for baking.

A small number 9 sable artist's paintbrush is the perfect implement for brushing glaze onto berries and for other decorative uses. The softest possible makeup brush, reserved only for this use, works well to restore the shine to Dark Chocolate Lacquer Glaze (page 296). A large soft silk brush is invaluable for brushing excess flour from dough.

Flour Wand or Dredger

This device is essentially a coiled oblong spring with a handle that, when expanded, picks up flour and, when waved over the dough or counter, dispenses a fine dusting of flour over it. Alternatively, a dredger (a container with holes in the top) works well for the same purpose.

Silicone Glove Pot Holders

Silicone gloves are preferred for removing baked goods safely from the oven and are especially effective when removing cakes from a water bath. Their ability to grip the sides of the pans makes them ideal for unmolding cakes from hot fluted tube pans.

Knives

LEVELING KNIVES

If you like to cut layer cakes in half horizontally (called torting), have a serrated blade longer than the diameter of the cake on hand. This is a difficult knife to find, but fortunately Parrish Magic Line carries one with a 14 inch deeply serrated blade. It also can be used to make wavy decorative lines on the surface of a frosted cake.

CAKE AND BREAD CUTTING KNIVES

A knife with deep serrations, such as a tomato knife or bread knife, does the best job of cutting a cake or loaf of bread without compressing it. For cheese-cakes, a piece of dental floss held taut cuts through the cake like a laser as long as there is no crust on the sides. Alternatively, use a sharp thin blade dipped in hot water and dried between each slice. Remove the slice by wiggling it slightly and pulling it out without lifting it upward.

BENCH SCRAPERS

Bench scrapers function as an extension of your hand. Metal bench scrapers are excellent for cleaning counters without scratching them. They are also great for gathering up dough, keeping the edges of dough even, and cutting dough. Plastic bench scrapers, which are flexible and have a rounded edge, are helpful for scraping a bowl or scooping up fillings.

Expandable Flan Rings

I use these metal rings, which expand from 7 to 14 inches in diameter, to cut perfectly even rounds of dough for pie and tart crusts.

Supports for Cakes and Tarts

CAKE TRANSFER DISKS

Nordic Ware makes a handy nonstick 10 inch round disk with a handle, called a cake lifter, which is designed to help transfer cakes and cake layers.

CARDBOARD ROUNDS

Cardboard rounds (also referred to as cake circles) are invaluable for supporting cake layers. They are available in large quantities from paper supply houses such as Qualitá Paper and in small packages from cake decorating and baking supply stores. My preference is to use slim gold or silver foil cake rounds, rather than corrugated rounds, because they require less decorative piping to hide the sides.

Equipment for Decorating

TURNTABLES

A turntable makes it easier to decorate all sides of a cake and to smooth the frosting evenly. For the average cake, an inexpensive plastic turntable such as a lazy Susan, sold in housewares stores and super-markets, works as well as a professional heavyweight footed variety. To bring the level up to the desired height, place the turntable on a large inverted cake pan. A turntable can be transformed into an elegant cake server by placing a large serving plate or piece of marble on top. Heavyweight turntables are available from cake decorating and baking supply stores. The most stable and smoothest turning model is from Fat Daddio's.

PASTRY TUBES AND TIPS

Small tubes, referred to as decorating tips, are used for small decorations. Larger tubes, referred to as pastry tubes, are used to pipe large festoons of whipped cream or to portion out batters or fillings. In the recipes, I have suggested the diameters of the tubes and numbers for the tips where you need to use them. I did not list numbers for the large tubes because they vary according to manufacturer. The numbers that are listed apply to Wilton, Ateco, and Parrish tips, available at cake decorating and baking supply stores. Be sure to choose seamless stainless steel tubes.

PASTRY BAGS AND PLASTIC RECLOSABLE FREEZER STORAGE BAGS

Pastry bags are useful not only for piping and decorating, but also for filling small cake pans and piping some cookie doughs. Silicone and disposable plastic pastry bags that can be cut to the desired size are available in cake decorating and baking supply stores, as are the more traditional nylon pastry bags. I also like to use heavy-duty reclosable quart- and gallon-size freezer bags, especially with children, because the bags are readily available and disposable, and the top of the bag seals shut so the filling can't work its way out of the bag should your grip be too relaxed.

If using a large pastry tube, simply cut off a small semicircle from one corner of the bag and insert the tube through the opening. When using a small decorating tip that might otherwise work its way back into the bag, insert the nozzle portion of a coupler first. Before filling, seal off the tube opening by twisting the bag directly above the tube and pushing it into the tube to keep the filling from leaking out. Set the bag over a wire bag holder, blender container, or large glass; fill the bag with the mixture; and close the bag securely.

An excellent alternative to using a pastry or other bag for piping caramel or chocolate glaze is a plastic squeeze bottle. An advantage is that the contents can be kept warm by placing the bottle in a hot water bath.

Equipment Sources

ANKARSRUM (the Assistent mixer)
www.ankarsrumoriginalusa.com 770-516-5000

BROADWAY PANHANDLER
(baking pans, gadgets, measuring and decorating tools)
www.broadwaypanhandler.com 866-266-5927

BRØD & TAYLOR (electric home proofer)
www.brodandtaylor.com 800-768-7064

CDN (thermometers and timers)
www.cdnw.com 800-338-5594

CHEF'SCHOICE (cutlery and sharpeners)
www.chefschoice.com 800-342-3255

CHICAGO METALLIC (cake, pie, and bread pans)
www.chicagometallicbakeware.com 800-272-0225

CUISINART (food processors and mixers)
www.cuisinart.com 800-726-0190

ESCALI (digital scales)
www.escali.com 800-467-6408

FAT DADDIO'S (baking pans and related equipment)
www.fatdaddios.com 866-418-9001

FANTE'S KITCHEN SHOP (baking pans, gadgets, and tools)
www.fantes.com 800-443-2683

JB PRINCE
(baking and pastry tools, including balloon whisks)
www.jbprince.com 800-473-0577

KALUSTYAN'S
(kitchen gadgets, including coconut graters)
www.kalustyans.com 800-352-3451

KITCHENAID
(heavy-duty stand mixers, food processors,
immersion blenders)
www.kitchenaid.com 800-541-6390

LA CUISINE (specialty bakeware, including
Combrichon round wire racks)
www.lacuisineus.com 800-521-1176

LAPRIMA SHOPS
(Rose's Perfect Pie Plate and Rose's Heavenly Cake Strips)
www.laprimashops.com

LEHMAN'S (Roma Food Mill)
www.lehmans.com 888-438-5346

MAGIC SLICE (Magic Dough pastry mat)
www.magicslice.com 630-543-0501

N.Y. CAKE
(cake and baking supplies, including silicone molds,
silicone and other spatulas)
www.nycake.com 800-942-2539

NEWMETRO DESIGN
(Rose Line, featuring BeaterBlade, MixerMate, ZestN'est)
www.newmetrodesign.com 800-624-1526

NORDIC WARE
(bakeware, including fluted and straight sided tube pans)
www.nordicware.com 877-466-7342

OMEGA (thermocouple oven thermometers and probes
such as model HH22)
www.omega.com 888-826-6342

PARRISH
(baking pans, including tube pans with removable
bottoms and springforms; Icing Blades; wire cake testers)
800-736-8443

PASTRY CHEF CENTRAL
(pastry, bread, and cake making equipment, including
molds, rings, pastry bags and tips)
www.pastrychef.com 888-750-2433

POURFECT (cup and spoon measures, mixing bowls)
www.pourfectbowl.com 480-699-6458

PYREX
(ovenproof glass measures, pie plates, mixing bowls)
www.pyrexware.com 800-999-3436

QUALITÁ PAPER PRODUCTS (disposable muffin cups
and other paper baking products)
www.qualitapaper.com 714-540-1077

ROSE LEVY BAKEWARE (custom bakeware, including
Rose's Heavenly Cake Strips, Rose Perfect Pie Plate)
www.realbakingwithrose.com

STRETCH-TITE (plastic food and freezer wrap)
www.stretchtite.com 800-343-6134

THERMOWORKS
(Thermapen, instant-read, and infrared thermometers)
www.thermoworks.com 800-393-6434

USA PAN (bread and baking pans)
www.usapans.com 724-457-4225

WILTON (cake decorating, baking pans, and other cake
baking supplies)
www.wilton.com 800-794-5866

Quick and Easy Recipes

Flourless and Mostly Flourless Recipes

Lactose Free Recipes

Main Component Recipes Using Only Egg Yolks

1 YOLK EQUALS 1 TABLESPOON PLUS ½ TEASPOON/17.2 ML/0.66 OUNCE/18.6 GRAMS

2 yolks/2 tablespoons plus 1 teaspoon/35 ml/ 1.3 ounces/37 grams

4 to 6 yolks/¼ cup plus 2 teaspoons/69 ml/ 2.6 ounces/74 grams

5 to 8 yolks/¼ cup plus 2 tablespoons/89 ml/ 3.3 ounces/93 grams

7 to 11 yolks/½ cup plus ½ teaspoon/121 ml/
4.6 ounces/130 grams

8 to 12 yolks/½ cup plus 4 teaspoons/138 ml/
5.2 ounces/149 grams

Main Component Recipes Using Only Egg Whites

**1 WHITE EQUALS 2 TABLESPOONS/30 ML/
1.1 OUNCES/30 GRAMS**

3 whites/¼ cup plus 2 tablespoons/89 ml/3.2 ounces/
90 grams

4 whites/½ cup/118 ml/4.2 ounces/120 grams

6 whites/¾ cup/177 ml/6.3 ounces/180 grams

16 whites/2 cups/473 ml/17 ounces/480 grams

Toppings and Fillings Using Only Egg Yolks

About 2 yolks/1½ tablespoons/22 ml/1 ounce/28 grams

2 yolks/2 tablespoons plus 1 teaspoon/35 ml/
1.3 ounces/37 grams

4 yolks/¼ cup plus 2 teaspoons/69 ml/2.6 ounces/
74 grams

8 to 12 yolks/½ cup plus 4 teaspoons/138 ml/
5.2 ounces/149 grams

10 to 14 yolks/¾ cup (177 ml)/6.5 ounces/186 grams

14 to 18 yolks/1 cup/237 ml/9.2 ounces/260 grams

Toppings and Fillings Using Only Egg Whites

1 white/2 tablespoons/30 ml/1 ounce/30 grams

2 whites/¼ cup/59 ml/2.1 ounces/60 grams

2½ whites/¼ cup plus 2 tablespoons/89 ml/
2.6 ounces/75 grams

4 whites/½ cup/118 ml/4.2 ounces/120 grams

INDEX